Complete
Accounting
for Cambridge IGCSE® & O Level

Second Edition

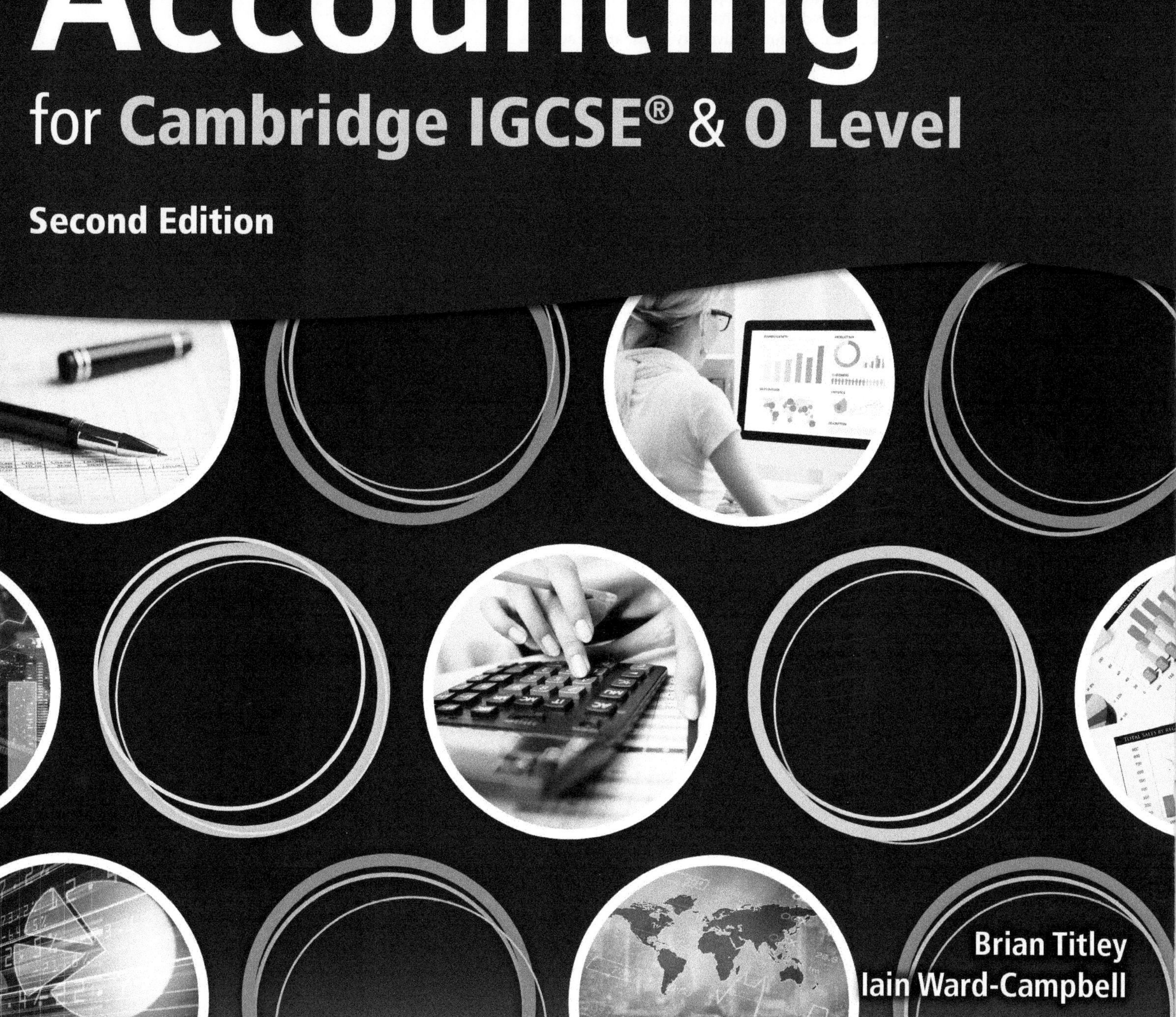

Brian Titley
Iain Ward-Campbell

Oxford excellence for Cambridge IGCSE® & O Level

OXFORD
UNIVERSITY PRESS

Great Clarendon Street, Oxford, OX2 6DP, United Kingdom

Oxford University Press is a department of the University of Oxford. It furthers the University's objective of excellence in research, scholarship, and education by publishing worldwide. Oxford is a registered trade mark of Oxford University Press in the UK and in certain other countries

© Brian Titley and Oxford University Press 2018

The moral rights of the authors have been asserted

First published in 2018

All rights reserved. No part of this publication may be reproduced, stored in a retrieval system, or transmitted, in any form or by any means, without the prior permission in writing of Oxford University Press, or as expressly permitted by law, by licence or under terms agreed with the appropriate reprographics rights organization. Enquiries concerning reproduction outside the scope of the above should be sent to the Rights Department, Oxford University Press, at the address above.

You must not circulate this work in any other form and you must impose this same condition on any acquirer

British Library Cataloguing in Publication Data
Data available

978 0 19 842523 6

10 9 8 7 6 5 4 3 2

Paper used in the production of this book is a natural, recyclable product made from wood grown in sustainable forests.
The manufacturing process conforms to the environmental regulations of the country of origin.

Printed in Great Britain by CPI Group (UK) Ltd., Croydon CR0 4YY

Acknowledgements
® IGCSE is the registered trademark of Cambridge International Examinations.

Cambridge International Examinations bears no responsibility for the example answers to test-style questions which are contained in this publication.

The publishers would like to thank the following for permissions to use their photographs:

Cover images: Shutterstock; **p3**: Steve Debenport/iStockphoto; **p3**: Sturti/iStockphoto; **p60**: Radius Images/Getty Images; **p60**: YinYang/iStockphoto; **p63**: Newscast/UIG/Getty Images; **p63**: Priyanka Sahi/The India Today Group/Getty Images; **p63**: Ulrich Baumgarten via Getty Images; **p193**: Christopher Furlong/Getty Images; **p193**: Jari Hindstroem/Shutterstock; **p327**: Peter Macdiarmid/Getty Images; **p350**: De Visu/Shutterstock; **p350**: Elena Elisseeva/Stutterstock; **p390**: Track5/iStockphoto; **p432**: Nataliya Hora/Shutterstock; **p432**: Dmitry Kalinovsky/Shutterstcok; **p453**: Marcin Balcerzak/Shutterstock; **p473**: Piotr Adamowicz/Shutterstock; **p480**: ASDF_MEDIA/Shutterstock; **p496**: Wragg/iStockphoto; **p496**: Konstantin Chagin/Shutterstock.

Artwork by Thomson Digital and OUP

Although we have made every effort to trace and contact all copyright holders before publication this has not been possible in all cases. If notified, the publisher will rectify any errors or omissions at the earliest opportunity.

Links to third party websites are provided by Oxford in good faith and for information only. Oxford disclaims any responsibility for the materials contained in any third party website referenced in this work.

1 The fundamentals of accounting

1.1	The purpose of accounting	1
1.2	The double-entry system of book-keeping	8
1.3	Business documents	30
1.4	Books of prime entry	44
1.5	The cash book	60
1.6	The general journal	99
1.7	The ledger	112
1.8	The trial balance	143
1.9	Adjustments to ledger accounts	156

2 Accounting procedures

2.1	Capital and revenue expenditure and receipts	191
2.2	Accounting for depreciation and disposal of non-current assets	209
2.3	Correction of errors	231
2.4	Control accounts	256

3 Final statements

3.1	Income statements	283
3.2	Statements of financial position	320

4 Preparation of financial statements

4.1	Sole traders	349
4.2	Partnerships	371
4.3	Clubs and societies	388
4.4	Incomplete records	401
4.5	Limited companies	417
4.6	Manufacturing accounts	432

5 Advanced principles

5.1	Financial relationships (ratio analysis)	442
5.2	Accounting principles	469

Support website: www.oxfordsecondary.com/9780198425236

Welcome to Complete Accounting for Cambridge O Level and IGCSE

Complete Accounting will build the skills and understanding you need for exams and future success

All businesses, whether large or small, must engage with accounting practices and principles if they are to function successfully. No matter what the aims of the business are, by employing good accounting practices businesses can keep accurate records of their profits and losses, make sensible decisions for the future and operate efficiently and professionally. Whether you want to one day become an accountant (either working for an accountancy firm or working in-house for a business), start your own business, or work for a major international company, the study of accounting will provide you with the knowledge, understanding and skills you will need to succeed.

By studying for the Cambridge O Level or IGCSE you will develop lifelong skills including:

- appreciation of the value and purpose of accounting for individuals, businesses, non-trading organisations and society as a whole
- knowledge and understanding of the basic principles, techniques. procedures and terminology which underpin successful accounting
- improved accuracy in numeracy, literacy, presentation and interpretation
- enhanced orderliness and logical thinking.

Complete Accounting will help you to build these skills quickly. It contains everything you need to master the content of the Cambridge O Level and IGCSE accounting syllabuses in an enjoyable and exciting way. It provides real insight into the way modern businesses and other organisations put accounting skills into practice and will give you the confidence you need in the recording, reporting, presenting and interpretation of financial information to build all the skills needed for success in your course.

The book is also an ideal resource for students working towards other introductory and professional accounting courses.

So, if you do plan to become an accountant one day then *Complete Accounting* provides the ideal foundation for your further studies and for a future career within the profession.

At the end of your course of studies for the Cambridge O Level or IGCSE, you will take two examination papers, which will assess your skills and understanding of the theory and concepts of accounting:

Cambridge O Level 'Accounting' & Cambridge IGCSE 'Accounting'

Paper 1	Multiple choice	35 multiple choice questions covering content from the whole syllabus	1 hour 15 minutes	30% of total marks
Paper 2	Structured questions	5 compulsory questions of 20 marks each covering content from across the syllabus.	1 hour 45 minutes	70% of total marks

The following key skills will be assessed in the examination papers. The importance given to each skill in each examination paper is also shown in the table:

Assessment objectives	Paper 1	Paper 2	Overall
Knowledge and understanding • demonstrate knowledge and understanding of facts, terms, principles, policies, procedures and techniques that are in the syllabus • demonstrate understanding of knowledge through numeracy, literacy, presentation and interpretation and apply this knowledge and understanding in various accounting situations and problems	80%	60%	65%
Analysis • select data which is relevant to identified needs of business • order, analyse and present information in an appropriate accounting form	20%	25%	25%
Evaluation • interpret and evaluate accounting information and draw reasoned conclusions		15%	10%

Complete Accounting will help you master these skills.

Best of luck with your studies!

Complete Accounting is supported by a website packed full of additional material specially written to support your learning. Everything in the book and on the website has been designed to help you prepare for your examinations and achieve your very best. You can access the website at www.oxfordsecondary.com/9780198425236

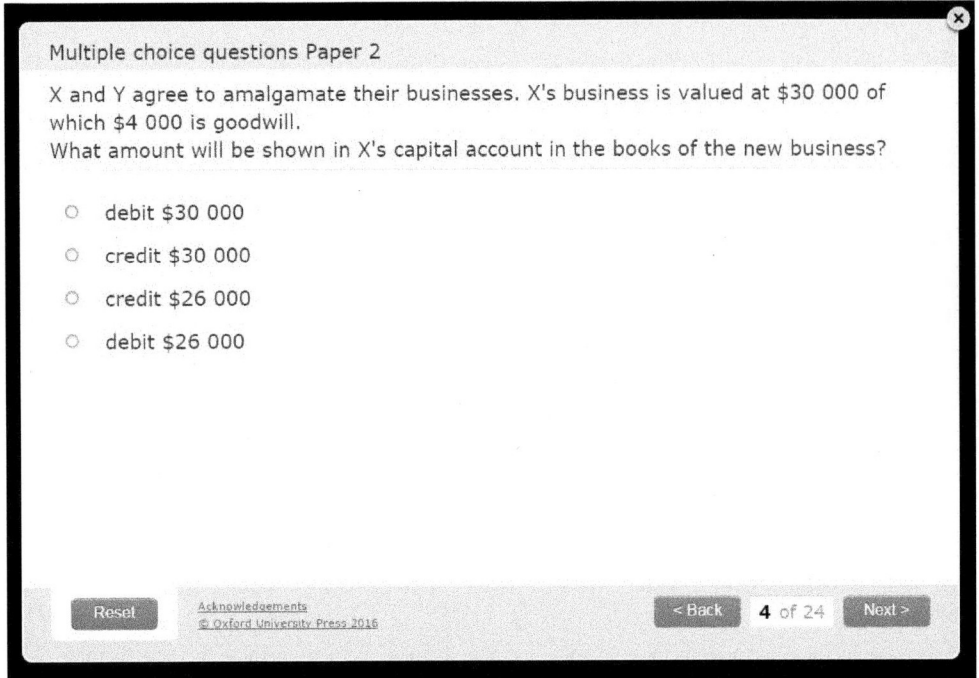

Glossary
A comprehensive revision tool that unpacks the vocabulary of the subject and carefully explains tricky terms.

Revision checklists
Check that you have covered all the essentials by printing out these handy summaries and ticking off those topics that you are confident about.

Sample accounting documents
A range of blank documents for you to practise your skills with – including invoices and credit notes, books of prime entry, ledger accounts and financial statements.

Interactive multiple choice tests
Quickly test your knowledge with interactive multiple choice questions – ideal for revision.

End of topic assessments
To complement each section of the book, you will find questions to help you put your learning into practice and prepare for assessment. These include multiple choice questions (written by the authors).

Answers
The website contains answers to all of the activities in the book, so that you can check your understanding as you progress through the course.

Syllabus overview	Units in Student Book
1 The fundamentals of accounting	
1.1 The purpose of accounting	1.1.1/1.1.2
• understand and explain the difference between book-keeping and accounting	1.1.2
• state the purposes of measuring business profit and loss	1.1.2
• explain the role of accounting in providing information for monitoring progress and decision-making.	1.1.2
1.2 The accounting equation	1.2.1
• explain the meaning of assets, liabilities and owner's equity	1.2.1
• explain and apply the accounting equation.	1.2.1
2 Sources and recording of data	
2.1 The double-entry system of book-keeping	
• outline the double entry system of book-keeping	1.2.2
• process accounting data using the double entry system	1.2.2
• prepare ledger accounts	1.7.1
• post transactions to the ledger accounts	1.7.2/1.7.3
• balance ledger accounts as required and make transfers to financial statements	1.7.5
• interpret ledger accounts and their balances	1.7.5
• recognise the division of the ledger into the sales ledger, the purchases ledger and the nominal (general) ledger	1.2.2/1.7.4
2.2 Business documents	1.3.1–1.3.3
• recognise and understand the following business documents: invoice, debit note, credit note, statement of account, cheque, receipt	
• complete pro-forma business documents	
• understand the use of business documents as sources of information: invoice, credit note, cheque counterfoil, paying-in slip, receipt, bank statement.	
2.3 Books of prime entry	1.4, 1.5.1–1.5.3, 1.5.5, 1.6.1
• explain the advantage of using various books of prime entry	1.4
• explain the use of and process accounting data in the books of prime entry: cash book, petty cash book, sales journal, purchases journal, sales returns journal, purchases returns journal and the general journal	1.4, 1.6.1 (general journal)
• post the ledger entries from the books of prime entry	1.4
• distinguish between and account for trade discount and cash discounts	1.4.6 (trade) 1.5.3 (cash)
• explain the dual function of the cash book as a book of prime entry and as a ledger account for bank and cash	1.5
• explain the use of and record payments and receipts made by bank transfers and other electronic means	1.5.1
• explain and apply the imprest system of petty cash.	1.5.5

3		Verification of accounting records	
	3.1	**The trial balance**	1.8
		• understand that a trial balance is a statement of ledger balances on a particular date	1.8.1
		• outline the uses and limitations of a trial balance	
		• prepare a trial balance from a given list of balances and amend a trial balance which contains errors	1.8.2–1.8.3
		• identify and explain those errors which do not affect the trial balance: commission, compensating, complete reversal, omission, original entry, principle.	1.8.3
	3.2	**Correction of errors**	2.3
		• correct errors by means of journal entries	2.3.1
		• explain the use of a suspense account as a temporary measure to balance the trial balance	2.3.1
		• correct errors by means of suspense accounts	
		• adjust a profit or loss for an accounting period after the correction of errors	2.3.3
		• understand the effect of correction of errors on a statement of financial position.	2.3.3
	3.3	**Bank reconciliation**	1.5.4
		• understand the use and purpose of a bank statement	1.5.4
		• update the cash book for bank charges, bank interest paid and received, correction of errors, credit transfers, direct debits, dividends, and standing orders	1.5.4
		• understand the purpose of and prepare a bank reconciliation statement to include bank errors, uncredited deposits and unpresented cheques.	1.5.4
	3.4	**Control accounts**	2.4
		• understand the purposes of purchases ledger and sales ledger control accounts	2.4.1
		• identify the books of prime entry as sources of information for the control account entries	2.4.1
		• prepare purchases ledger and sales ledger control accounts to include credit purchases and sales, receipts and payments, cash discounts, returns, irrecoverable debts, dishonoured cheques, interest on overdue accounts, contra entries, refunds, opening and closing balances (debit and credit within each account).	2.4.2 and 2.4.3
4		**Accounting procedures**	
	4.1	**Capital and revenue expenditure and receipts**	2.1
		• distinguish between and account for capital expenditure and revenue expenditure	2.1.2
		• distinguish between and account for capital receipts and revenue receipts	2.1.3
		• calculate and comment on the effect on profit of incorrect treatment	2.1.4

viii

		• calculate and comment on the effect on asset valuations of incorrect treatment.	2.1.4
	4.2	**Accounting for depreciation and disposal of non-current assets**	2.2
		• define depreciation	2.2.1
		• explain the reasons for accounting for depreciation	2.2.1
		• name and describe the straight-line, reducing balance and revaluation methods of depreciation	2.2.1
		• prepare ledger accounts and journal entries for the provision of depreciation	2.2.2
		• prepare ledger accounts and journal entries to record the sale of non-current assets, including the use of disposal accounts.	2.2.3
	4.3	**Other payables and other receivables**	1.9.1–1.9.5
		• recognise the importance of matching costs and revenues	1.9.1
		• prepare ledger accounts and journal entries to record accrued and prepaid expenses	1.9.2/3
		• prepare ledger accounts and journal entries to record accrued and prepaid incomes.	1.9.4/5
	4.4	**Irrecoverable debts and provision for doubtful assets**	1.9.6
		• understand the meaning of irrecoverable debts and recovery of debts written off	1.9.6
		• prepare ledger accounts and journal entries to record irrecoverable debts	1.9.6
		• prepare ledger accounts and journal entries to record recovery of debts written off	1.9.6
		• explain the reasons for maintaining a provision for doubtful debts	1.9.6
		• prepare ledger accounts and journal entries to record the creation of, and adjustments to, a provision for doubtful debts.	1.9.6
	4.5	**Valuation of inventory**	3.1.5, 5.1
		• understand the basis of the valuation of inventory at the lower of cost and net realisable value	
		• prepare simple inventory valuation statements	
		• recognise the importance of valuation of inventory and the effect of an incorrect valuation of inventory on gross profit, profit for the year, equity and asset valuation.	
5		**Preparation of financial statements**	
	5.1	**Sole traders**	3.1, 3.2, 4.1
		• explain the advantages and disadvantages of operating as a sole trader	
		• explain the importance of preparing income statements and statements of financial position	
		• explain the difference between a trading business and a service business	
		• prepare income statements for trading businesses and for service businesses	

	•	understand that statements of financial position record assets and liabilities on a specified date	
	•	recognise and define the content of a statement of financial position: non-current assets, intangible assets, current assets, current liabilities, non-current liabilities and capital	
	•	understand the inter-relationship of items in a statement of financial position	
	•	prepare statements of financial position for trading businesses and service businesses	
	•	make adjustments for provision for depreciation using the straight line, reducing balance and revaluation methods	
	•	make adjustments for accrued and prepaid expenses and accrued and prepaid income	
	•	make adjustments for irrecoverable debts and provisions for doubtful debts	
	•	make adjustments for goods taken by the owner for own use.	
5.2	**Partnerships**		4.2
	•	explain the advantages and disadvantages of forming a partnership	
	•	outline the importance and contents of a partnership agreement	
	•	explain the purpose of an appropriation account	
	•	prepare income statements, appropriation accounts and statements of financial position	
	•	record interest on partners' loans, interest on capital, interest on drawings, partners' salaries and the division of the balance of profit or loss	
	•	make adjustments to financial statements as detailed in 5.1 (sole traders)	
	•	explain the uses of and differences between capital and current accounts	
	•	draw up partners' capital and current accounts in ledger account form and as part of a statement of financial position.	
5.3	**Limited companies**		4.5
	•	explain the advantages and disadvantages of operating as a limited company	
	•	understand the meaning of the term limited liability	
	•	understand the meaning of the term equity	
	•	understand the capital structure of a limited company comprising preference share capital, ordinary share capital, general reserve and retained earnings	
	•	understand and distinguish between issued, called-up and paid-up share capital	
	•	understand and distinguish between share capital (preference shares and ordinary shares) and loan capital (debentures)	
	•	prepare income statements, statements of changes in equity and statements of financial position	

			make adjustments to financial statements as detailed in 5.1 (sole traders).	
	5.4	**Clubs and societies**		4.3
		•	distinguish between receipts and payments accounts and income and expenditure accounts	
		•	prepare receipts and payments accounts	
		•	prepare accounts for revenue-generating activities, e.g. refreshments, subscriptions	
		•	prepare income and expenditure accounts and statements of financial position	
		•	make adjustments to financial statements as detailed in 5.1 (sole traders)	
		•	define and calculate the accumulated fund.	
	5.5	**Manufacturing accounts**		4.6
		•	distinguish between direct and indirect costs	
		•	understand direct material, direct labour, prime cost and factory overheads	
		•	understand and make adjustments for work in progress	
		•	calculate factory cost of production	
		•	prepare manufacturing accounts, income statements and statements of financial position	
		•	make adjustments to financial statements as detailed in 5.1 (sole traders).	
	5.6	**Incomplete records**		4.4
		•	explain the disadvantages of not maintaining a full set of accounting records	
		•	prepare opening and closing statements of affairs	
		•	calculate profit or loss for the year from changes in capital over time	
		•	calculate sales, purchases, gross profit, trade receivables and trade payables and other figures from incomplete information	
		•	prepare income statements and statements of financial position from incomplete records	
		•	make adjustments to financial statements as detailed in 5.1 (sole traders)	
		•	apply the techniques of mark-up, margin and inventory turnover to arrive at missing figures.	
6	**Analysis and interpretation**			
	6.1	**Calculation and understanding of accounting ratios**		5.1.1./5.1.2/5.1.3
		•	Gross margin	
		•	Profit margin	
		•	Return on capital employed (ROCE)	
		•	Current ratio	
		•	Liquid (acid test) ratio	
		•	Rate of inventory turnover (times)	

		• Trade receivables turnover (days)	
		• Trade payables turnover (days)	
	6.2	**Interpretation of accounting ratios**	5.1.1./5.1.2/5.1.3
		• prepare and comment on simple statements showing comparison of results for different years	
		• make recommendations and suggestions for improving profitability and working capital	
		• understand the significance of the difference between the gross margin and the profit margin as an indicator of a business's efficiency	
		• explain the relationship of gross profit and profit for the year to the valuation of inventory, rate of inventory turnover, revenue, expenses, and equity.	
	6.3	**Inter-firm comparison**	5.1.2
		• understand the problems of inter-firm comparison	
		• apply accounting ratios to inter-firm comparison.	
	6.4	**Interested parties**	5.1.4
		• owners	
		• managers	
		• trade payables	
		• banks	
		• investors	
		• club members	
		• other interested parties such as governments, tax authorities, etc.	
	6.5	**Limitations of accounting statements**	5.1.4
		• historic cost	
		• difficulties of definition	
		• non-financial aspects.	
7	**Accounting principles and policies**		
	7.1	**Accounting principles**	5.2.1
		• matching	
		• business entity	
		• consistency	
		• duality	
		• going concern	
		• historic cost	
		• materiality	
		• money measurement	
		• prudence	
		• realisation	
	7.2	**Accounting policies**	5.2.2
		• comparability	
		• relevance	
		• reliability	
		• understandability	

Content at a glance

1.1	The purpose of accounting
1.2	The double-entry system of book-keeping
1.3	Business documents
1.4	Books of prime entry
1.5	The cash book
1.6	The general journal
1.7	The ledger
1.8	The trial balance
1.9	Adjustments to ledger accounts

Unit 1.1 The purpose of accounting

AIMS

By the end of this unit you should be able to

- understand and explain the difference between **book-keeping** and **accounting**
- state the purposes of measuring business **profit** and **loss**
- explain the role of accounting in providing information for monitoring progress and decision making

1.1.1 Starting and running a business

Good financial management is vital if a business is to survive and be successful

Each of us needs to be able to manage our finances. We need to know how much we expect to receive in wages for the work we do and from other sources of income, and how much we need to pay our bills and living expenses. If we get these wrong and are unable to pay our bills the consequences can be serious; we may face legal action from the people or organisations we owe money to and we may even lose our jobs and our homes.

The same is true for people who start up, own and run businesses. These are organisations that provide goods or services to other people and organisations. Regardless of how big or small a business is its owners will want to know:

- how much it is earning from the provision of its goods or services
- how much it is spending providing those goods or services
- how much it owns of value including its premises, equipment and bank deposits (the **assets** of a business)
- how much it owes to other people and organisations (the **liabilities** of the business)
- whether they are making the best use of the money they have invested in their business.

Without this information the business owners will not know if their business is earning enough money to cover its costs, when to pay its debts on time or how much their business may be worth. They will not have this information unless they keep detailed financial records about all the activities of their business.

Privately owned business organisations aim to make a profit

A business that is unable to earn enough money from its activities to cover its costs will make a **loss**. This means the owners will be losing money on the amount they have invested in their business. To stop the business losing money they must either take actions that will increase its income and reduce its costs or close it down.

This is because the main objective of people who own and run businesses is to make a **profit**. This means earning more money from the activities of their business than it costs to run.

For example, Jamil is an **entrepreneur**. This means he is a person with business know-how who is willing to risk time and money setting up and running a business organisation. If he is successful he will be rewarded with profit. If he is not successful his business will make a loss.

His new business earns **revenue** from the sale of goods to customers. However, his business must first buy these goods from other businesses. He also has to pay other organisations to supply services such as electricity, telephone services, insurance, cleaning and many more. These are the day-to-day running costs or **expenses** of a business.

▼ Profit is surplus income after all business costs incurred earning that income have been paid

At the end of his first year in business Jamil added up how much income it had earned over the year and how much it had cost to run his business in order to earn that income. This is shown as:

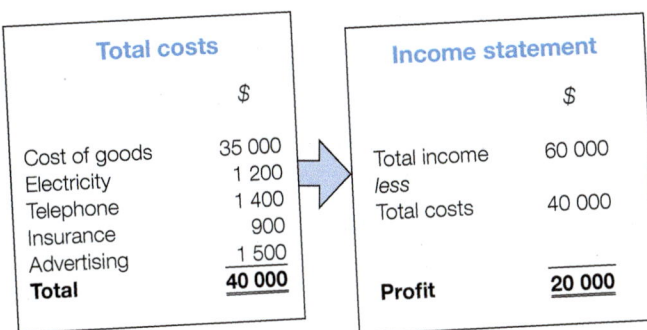

Total income		
		$
Revenue		60 000
Total		**60 000**

Total costs		
		$
Cost of goods		35 000
Electricity		1 200
Telephone		1 400
Insurance		900
Advertising		1 500
Total		**40 000**

Income statement		
		$
Total income		60 000
less		
Total costs		40 000
Profit		**20 000**

The difference between the total income of Jamil's business and its total costs was a healthy profit for the year of $20 000. Jamil was only able to calculate this because he had kept detailed records of all his business earnings and costs.

If, over the next year, the income from his business were to fall or its costs were to rise then his business may end up making a loss. However, with detailed information on his business income and costs and how these are changing over time he will be able take decisions that may prevent this from happening. For example, he might decide to buy and sell different products that customers are willing to pay a higher price for and change suppliers to those with lower prices to reduce his business costs.

Starting-up and running a business involves the exchange of goods, services and money with other people and organisations

Running a business involves the regular exchange of goods, services and money with many other people and organisations, including:

- **suppliers** who provide goods intended for resale to customers, or component parts and materials to make other goods
- **customers** who buy these goods
- **employees** who supply their labour to the business in return for wages or salaries
- suppliers of business services including electricity, telephone services, insurance and banking services, cleaning and maintenance and many others.

Every exchange is called a **business transaction** and the running of even the smallest business organisation can involve many hundreds or thousands of different business transactions each year. All of these must be accurately recorded if the owners of the business are to be able to manage its finances effectively and calculate the profit or loss from its activities.

▼ Business transactions

The purpose of accounting

ACTIVITY 1.1

Juanita has just finished her first three months in business, running a small shop that sells snacks and cold drinks to workers in nearby offices. She used her savings of $5 000 to set up her business in a small rented shop and to equip it with kitchenware and other equipment.

While Juanita is a good cook she is not very good at paperwork. At the end of her first three months she added up how much she had earned in sales revenue so far.

The total amount of cash she had received from customers was $2 400 while the total amount she had spent from cash on cooking ingredients and food and drinks to sell during the same period was $1 600. This meant she still had $800 in cash, more than enough she thought to keep her business running for the next three months and to return a small profit.

But Juanita had forgotten to take account of other goods and services supplied to her by other business organisations that she had yet to pay for. The amounts she owed were:

- $350 for three months of electricity
- $250 for three months of telephone services
- $1 000 for three months of unpaid rent

She was horrified to realise that she couldn't afford to pay all these debts. She also had no more savings she could draw from. Juanita therefore had no other option but to close her business and sell off the equipment she had purchased to pay off her debts.

1. How much capital did Juanita initially invest in her business?
2. How much did she spend on food, drinks and cooking ingredients to make goods for sale to her customers?
3. How much revenue did she earn from the sale of these goods?
4. What was the profit she earned from the sale of these goods?
5. Juanita also had expenses to pay. How much were her total expenses?
6. What was her profit or loss after deducting her total expenses?
7. Explain why Juanita was forced to close down her business.

 Answers to all activities can be found on the website.

1.1.2 The difference between book-keeping and accounting

Book-keeping is the process of recording business transactions

To calculate profit or loss a business must be able to add up and summarise the values of all its transactions on a regular basis. This means keeping detailed and up-to-date records on business transactions: the date each one occurred, items received or supplied, who they were received from or supplied to and their total prices. Doing this is called **book-keeping**.

Book-keeping records are entered into books called **books of prime entry** and **ledger accounts**. Together they will provide a complete record of every transaction a business has made and every $1 it has earned and every $1 it has spent or owes to other people and organisations. ➤ 1.2

Accounting involves the preparation of financial summaries and statements from book-keeping records

Book-keeping records in the books of a business will provide a long list of details about its many different transactions over a period of time but unless these details are added together and summarised it will very difficult to tell if the business has made a profit or loss from them.

It will also be difficult to know how each transaction affected the business. For example, have the debts of the business increased over time or decreased? Does the business own more or less assets than it did a year ago?

It is therefore sensible to group together similar types of transaction, such as all the transactions that involved purchasing goods from suppliers, all cash sales to customers, all equipment purchases, all cleaning and maintenance expenses, total wages and salaries paid to employees and much more.

Using book-keeping records to prepare financial summaries involves **accounting**. This refers to both the skill and processes necessary to calculate and report key measures of the financial health and performance of a business from its book-keeping records, notably:

(1) how much profit or loss it has made

(2) how much of value it owns (its assets) and how much it owes to other people and organisations (its liabilities).

▼ The book-keeping and accounting process

Recording transactions → Classifying and grouping transactions → Summarising financial information → Reporting and using financial information

The purpose of accounting is to measure the profit or loss and value of a business

The two most important financial summaries and reports produced by a business from its book-keeping records will be produced at the end of each accounting year. These are:

- The **income statement**: this summarises information about the income and different costs and expenses of the business, and therefore its profit or loss, over a 12-month period. ➤ 3.1

- The **statement of financial position**: this summarises financial information about the value of the business on the final day of an accounting year, notably how much of value the business owns and how much it owes to other people and organisations. ➤ 3.2

The **accounting year** of a business is the 12-month period covered by an income statement. Different businesses will have different accounting years. Some may produce an income statement at the end of every calendar year covering the period 1 January to 31 December.

However, most small businesses adopt accounting years beginning on the first day of the month in which they first started. So, for example, if a business began trading in June one year, its accounting year will run from the start of June each year to the end of May the following year.

Accurate financial summaries and statements will help the owners of a business to make decisions about its future

Jamil made a healthy profit of $20 000 from his business during its first year of trading. He withdrew $5 000 of this profit for his personal use and spent the remaining $15 000 on new equipment to expand his business. He was able to make these decisions and calculate their effect on his business because he had kept detailed financial records. From these he was also able to forecast how much additional revenue the new equipment may help him generate in future.

If he had not kept good book-keeping records he would be unaware of how much profit his business was making over time. Without this knowledge he may have taken some very unwise decisions. For example, what if he had decided to withdraw $30 000 from his business for his personal use or decided to spend $30 000 on new equipment to expand his business? His business had only generated $20 000 so either of these decisions would mean withdrawing an additional $10 000 in cash from the business bank account to pay for day-to-day running costs.

Alternatively, what if Jamil had borrowed $50 000 to buy new premises? Without financial records and summaries he would not know whether his business would be able to earn enough revenue to pay the extra expense of interest and eventually to repay the loans. It is also very unlikely that a bank would lend such a large sum of money to his business without evidence of its profit and ability to afford loan repayments.

Many different people and organisations connected with the business will also want information about its profitability

Financial statements are the most important documents a business can produce about its financial health and performance.

Many different groups of people will use them to make a judgment on the success or otherwise of the business and how its performance has changed over time. Here are some examples:

- Entrepreneurs who invest their time and money in starting and running businesses do so to make a profit. They will clearly want to know whether their aim is being met and by how much. That is, they will also want to know whether the profit from their business is more or less than they could have earned from other uses of their time and money. For example, could they have earned more from their money if they had saved it in a bank savings account instead?

- Suppliers who provide goods to the business on credit will want to know that it is capable of earning enough money to pay them on time and will continue to be successful so that it can make repeat purchases from them.

- A bank will want to know how much profit or loss a business is making before it decides whether or not to lend it money and on what terms. Business owners applying for a bank loan will need accounting information to demonstrate that their business will be able to meet future

▼ Good accounting information will help to inform many different business decisions

loan repayments. A bank will also want to know whether the business owns sufficient items of value, such as premises and equipment, that could be sold off to repay a loan if the business were to fail and cease trading.

- Employees of a business will be dependent on its continued success for their jobs and the payment of their wages and salaries. They too will also want to know whether it is profitable.

- The tax authorities of the government will want to check whether a business and its owners are paying the right amount of tax on their earnings or profits. ➤ 5.1

QUICK TEST

1. Why do the owners of a business need to keep proper financial records?
2. Explain **three** reasons why it is important to measure the profit or loss of a business.
3. A small business has received $45 000 in revenue from the sale of goods to its customers. The business was supplied these goods by another business at a cost of $20 000. The business owner also spent $8 000 on electricity, rent and other operating expenses during the same period in order to run his business and earn this revenue. How much profit did the business make?
4. Explain the difference between book-keeping and accounting.
5. Why would the owner of a business need accounting reports?

Unit 1.2 The double-entry system of book-keeping

AIMS

By the end of this unit you should be able to

- explain the meaning of **assets, liabilities** and **owner's equity**
- explain and apply the **accounting equation**
- outline the **double-entry system of book-keeping**
- process accounting data using the double-entry system
- recognise the divisions of the ledger into the **sales ledger**, the **purchases ledger** and the **nominal (general) ledger**

1.2.1 The accounting equation

A business needs money to invest in productive assets

To start up and run a business an entrepreneur will need money to obtain machinery, equipment, vehicles or simply to hold as cash to buy goods and to pay expenses. These are the productive resources or **assets** entrepreneurs will put to work in their businesses to make and sell goods or services to customers to earn income.

All businesses will need a combination of different assets:

- **Non-current assets** remain productive for several years and can be used over and over again in day-to-day operations to the benefit of the business. They include the business premises, machinery, equipment, furniture and vehicles.

- **Current assets** are used up quite quickly in business. They include inventories of goods for resale to customers and cash either held on the business premises or in the business bank account. Inventories of goods will be sold off for cash and cash itself will be used to invest in other assets or to pay for running expenses.

The **total assets** of a business will therefore include the cash, inventories, premises, machinery, vehicles, equipment and any other resources it owns that will enable it to earn an income. ▶ 3.2

To obtain assets entrepreneurs will have to use their own money or borrow money from other people and organisations, or use some combination of their own and borrowed funds:

- **Owner's capital** or **equity** is the money invested in business assets by the business owners from their own funds.

- **Liabilities** are financial obligations to repay money owed to other people and organisations. These include **non-current liabilities**, such as bank loans, which are amounts repayable in more than one year, and **current**

liabilities which will require repayment quickly, often within a few months in the accounting year, for example bank overdrafts and debts to suppliers for goods purchased from them on credit. ➤ **3.2**

For example, when Lavanda Harris set up her small business called Just Kidz to sell children's clothing, she used $3 000 of her own savings and borrowed a further $2 000 from a local bank. Her own capital and the bank loan provided her business with $5 000 cash (a current asset) from which she was able to buy some equipment (a non-current asset) and an inventory of clothes for resale (another current asset).

▼ Businesses invest money in productive assets

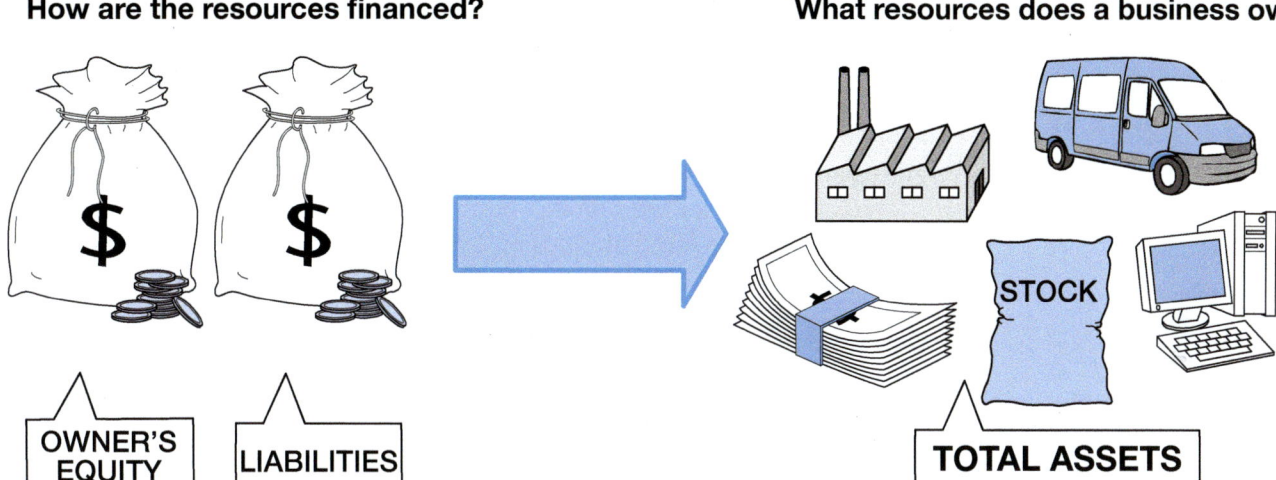

The accounting equation is the most important relationship in accounting

The total money invested in the total assets of a business will always be equal to the amount of capital owed by the business to its owners (the **owner's equity**) and the total of its **liabilities** to other people and organisations. That is:

> Total assets = Owner's equity + Total liabilities

This is a very simple but critically important relationship in business accounting. It tells us that the resources supplied by the business owners or from other sources will always be exactly equal to the resources of the business represented by its total assets.

The relationship is called the **accounting equation** and it is usually shortened and rewritten as follows:

> Assets = Equity + Liabilities

Or, by simply rearranging the accounting equation:

> Equity = Assets − Liabilities

The double-entry system of book-keeping

This tells us that the owner's equity invested in the business will always be equal to the value of business assets remaining after all business liabilities have been settled or paid off.

As we shall see, the accounting equation will always hold however much the business changes or grows over time. That is, the total assets of a business will always be equal to the sum of its owner's equity and total liabilities. This is the basis of all accounting.

The financial position of a business will change with each new transaction but the two sides of the accounting equation will always remain in balance

When Lavanda Harris started her 'Just Kidz' business venture with $3 000 of her own money she knew it was important to keep accurate records of every business transaction she made from day one. This was so she would know exactly how much it owned in assets and how much it owed in liabilities on any given day. The difference between her business assets and liabilities showed the value of her owner's equity. Lavanda recorded these details about the value of the assets, liabilities and equity of her business at the end of each day in a simple statement of the financial position of her business.

Transaction 1: the introduction of equity

Day one for Lavanda's business was 1 January last year. On this day Lavanda transferred $3 000 from her own savings into the bank account she had set up for Just Kidz at the local branch of a major bank.

The financial position of the business on this date shows Lavanda's savings of $3 000 entering the business as owner's equity. This **opening equity** of $3 000 was then available to her business to make purchases and to pay suppliers. The cash in the business bank account was a current asset of the business and exactly equal to owner's equity.

When capital is received:

| increase in owner's equity | increase in assets (cash in bank) |

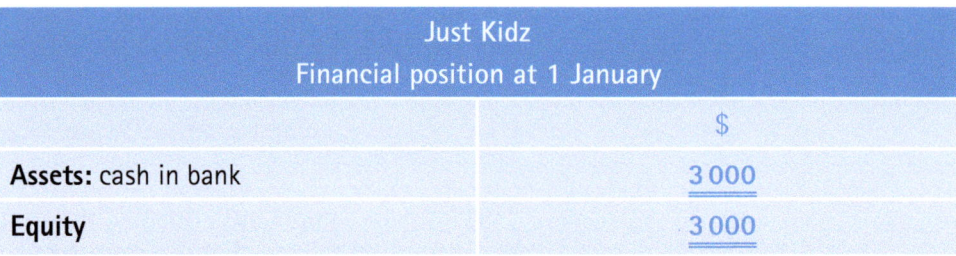

Just Kidz Financial position at 1 January	
	$
Assets: cash in bank	3 000
Equity	3 000

Transaction 2: the creation of a non-current liability (a bank loan)

To help start up her small business Lavanda applied for a bank loan for $2 000 and on 2 January this was agreed and the funds deposited into her business bank account. This transaction increased the total amount of cash in the bank account to $5 000 but created a non-current liability of $2 000 for the business to repay the loan.

To update the statement of the financial position of her business Lavanda listed the bank loan as a liability below the value of her business assets.

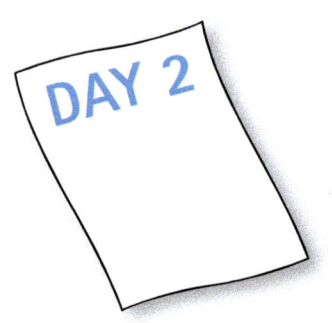

When a loan is deposited in the bank:

increase in assets (cash in bank) | increase in liabilities (bank loan)

Just Kidz Financial position at 2 January	
	$
Assets: cash in bank	5 000
less	
Liabilities: bank loan	2 000
Equity	3 000

You will notice that the value of the owner's equity invested in the business was unchanged at $3 000 but following the bank loan it could be calculated as the difference between total assets of $5 000 and total liabilities of $2 000.

Transaction 3: cash payment to acquire a non-current asset (equipment)

On 3 January Lavanda purchased computer equipment for her business so she could advertise and take orders using the Internet and also to keep computerised accounts. This meant the business had acquired a non-current asset because the equipment would be of use to the business over a number of years.

Lavanda withdrew $2 000 in cash from the business bank account to buy the computer equipment from a supplier.

The transaction therefore reduced the current asset of cash by $2 000 but created a new non-current asset for the business with a value of $2 000. As a result total assets were unchanged at $5 000 and remained equal to the total liabilities plus the owner's equity in the business.

When a non-current asset is bought for cash:

decrease in assets (cash in bank) | increase in assets (equipment)

Just Kidz Financial position at 3 January	
	$
Assets: equipment	2 000
cash in bank	3 000
	5 000
less	
Liabilities: bank loan	2 000
Equity	3 000

Transaction 4: the creation of a non-current liability to acquire a non-current asset (van)

On 4 January Lavanda bought a small van for her business for $6 000 so she would be able to make deliveries to local customers.

Lavanda bought the van on credit from a local supplier called Van Hire Ltd. Lavanda agreed to repay Van Hire Ltd. in 24 monthly instalments of $250 each. This created a non-current liability for Just Kidz.

The effect on the financial position of her business of acquiring the van, a non-current asset, was to increase the total assets of the business by $6 000 but increased its total liabilities by $6 000.

The two sides of the accounting equation were still in balance following the above transaction. That is, as at 4 January, total assets of $11 000 were equal to liabilities of $8 000 plus $3 000 of owner's equity.

The double-entry system of book-keeping

When a non-current asset is acquired on credit:

| increase in assets (delivery van) | increase in a liabilities (Van Hire Ltd.) |

Just Kidz Financial position at 4 January	
	$
Assets: delivery van	6 000
equipment	2 000
cash in bank	3 000
	11 000
less	
Liabilities: Van Hire Ltd.	6 000
bank loan	2 000
	8 000
Equity	3 000

Transaction 5: the purchase of a current asset (inventory) on credit

On 5 January, Lavanda purchased children's clothes for $4 000 from Clothing Importers Ltd. Lavanda had purchased the clothes with the purpose of selling them to customers to earn revenue.

Clothing Importers Ltd. agreed Lavanda could purchase the clothes on credit. This meant she did not have to pay for them immediately with cash but could pay for them later instead. In fact Lavanda was given up to 90 days to pay for her purchase in full. This created a current liability of $4 000 for Just Kidz called a **trade payable**: money owed to a supplier for the purchase of goods intended for resale.

Lavanda estimated it would take her around three months to sell off all the clothes she had purchased. Until then any unsold clothes would be a current asset for her business called **inventory**: goods held on the business premises or in storage awaiting sale to customers to earn revenue. ▶ 1.7

To update her statement of financial position on 5 January Lavanda therefore added inventory of $4 000 to her total assets and added trade payables of $4 000 to her total liabilities to record the amount she owed to Clothing Importers Ltd.

When a current asset is purchased on credit:

| increase in assets (inventory) | increase in liabilities (trade payables) |

Just Kidz Financial position at 5 January	
	$
Assets: delivery van	6 000
equipment	2 000
inventory	4 000
cash in bank	3 000
	15 000
less	
Liabilities: trade payable	4 000
Van Hire Ltd.	6 000
bank loan	2 000
	12 000
Equity	3 000

The fundamentals of accounting

The purchase of clothes on credit therefore increased total assets from $11 000 to $15 000 but at the expense of increasing total liabilities by $4 000 to $12 000. This meant the accounting equation was still in balance with $12 000 of liabilities and $3 000 of owner's equity invested in $15 000 of assets.

Transaction 6: the sale of a current asset (inventory) for immediate payment

Lavanda made her first sale on 6 January last year to her friends Anita and Ashok. They had two young children and liked the clothes Lavanda had bought from Clothing Importers Ltd.

As they were close friends Lavanda refused to charge them any more for the clothes than she had paid to Clothing Importers Ltd. for them.

In total Anita and Ashok selected clothes to the value of $600 and paid Lavanda in cash that she deposited into the business bank account later that same day. Inventory was therefore reduced by $600 to $3 400 but cash in bank increased by $600 to $3 600, leaving total assets and the overall financial position of Lavanda's business unchanged.

When goods are sold for immediate cash payment:

increase in assets (cash in bank)	decrease in assets (inventory)

Just Kidz Financial position at 6 January	
	$
Assets: delivery van	6 000
equipment	2 000
inventory	3 400
cash in bank	3 600
	15 000
less	
Liabilities: trade payable	4 000
Van Hire Ltd.	6 000
bank loan	2 000
	12 000
Equity	3 000

Transaction 7: the sale of a current asset (inventory) on credit terms and the creation of another current asset (a trade receivable)

On 7 January Lavanda received a request from the Fun Day Care Centre for Young Children to buy a selection of clothes from her inventory. Lavanda was keen to help the centre because its managers had said they were likely to place regular orders for clothes with Just Kidz. Lavanda therefore agreed that the centre could pay the cost price of $1 000 for its first order of children's clothes. In addition, she agreed the centre could take up to three months to make payment.

This was Lavanda's first big sale of goods on credit terms to a customer. The transaction reduced her inventory by $1 000 but created a new current asset to the same value called a **trade receivable**: money owed to the business by a customer who has been supplied goods on credit. A trade receivable is a current asset because the business will receive cash when the debt is paid off or settled by the credit customer, usually within a credit period of one to three months from the date of the sale. The total assets of Just Kidz were unchanged by the transaction.

The double-entry system of book-keeping

Fun Day Care Centre therefore became a trade receivable for Just Kidz when it was supplied children's clothes in return for agreeing to make payment of $1 000 within three months.

When goods are sold on credit terms:

| decrease in assets (inventory) | increase in assets (trade receivables) |

Just Kidz Financial position at 7 January	
	$
Assets: delivery van	6 000
equipment	2 000
inventory	2 400
trade receivable	1 000
cash in bank	3 600
	15 000
less	
Liabilities: trade payable	4 000
Van Hire Ltd.	6 000
bank loan	2 000
	12 000
Equity	3 000

Transaction 8: a reduction in a liability

A month later, on 8 February, Lavanda was required to make her first payment of $250 to Van Hire Ltd. for the supply of her delivery van. She did this by instructing her bank to transfer $250 from her business bank account to the bank account of Van Hire Ltd.

The transaction reduced her liability to Van Hire Ltd. by $250 (from $6 000 to $5 750) by reducing her cash in bank by $250 (from $3 600 to $3 350).

As a result, the value of the total assets of the business fell to $14 750. However, total liabilities were also reduced from $12 000 to $11 750. With owner's equity of $3 000 in the business unchanged the combined sum of equity and liabilities invested remained exactly equal to the revised value of its total assets.

Just Kidz Financial position at 8 February	
	$
Assets: delivery van	6 000
equipment	2 000
inventory	2 400
trade receivable	1 000
cash in bank	3 350
	14 750
less	
Liabilities: trade payable	4 000
Van Hire Ltd.	5 750
bank loan	2 000
	11 750
Equity	3 000

When a liability is paid with cash:

| decrease in current assets (cash in bank) | decrease in non-current liabilities (Van Hire Ltd.) |

14 The fundamentals of accounting

Transaction 9: the collection of a trade receivable

On 9 February last year Lavanda received early payment of $1 000 from the Fun Day Care Centre to clear its debt. Although the centre had another two months in which to make payment it had unexpectedly accumulated a cash surplus and decided to use it to settle its debt to Just Kidz for the clothes it had bought on credit on 7 January.

The centre had sent Lavanda a cheque for the sum of $1 000. Lavanda took this to her bank the very same day to deposit it into her business account. Once this was done her bank could use the cheque to collect payment from the bank holding the account of the Fun Day Care Centre. This is because a cheque is a written instruction to a bank to transfer money from the account of the person or organisation who has issued it to the account of the person or organisation named on the cheque to receive payment. ➤ 1.3

When a debt is collected:

| decrease in assets (trade receivables) | increase in assets (cash in bank) |

Just Kidz Financial position at 9 February	
	$
Assets: delivery van	6 000
equipment	2 000
inventory	2 400
trade receivable	0
cash in bank	4 350
	14 750
less	
Liabilities: trade payable	4 000
Van Hire Ltd	5 750
bank loan	2 000
	11 750
Equity	3 000

The cheque received by Lavanda from her customer reduced trade receivables by $1 000 to zero but cash in bank increased by $1 000. Total assets and the overall financial position of the business were unchanged by the transaction.

Every business transaction has two effects and will keep the two sides of the accounting equation in balance

Lavanda's statements of financial position demonstrate a number of important facts:

(1) Assets are listed in a statement of financial position in their order of permanence

This means assets are listed according to how long they last and remain in use in the business. So, the premises of the business will always be listed first followed by other non-current assets such as machinery, equipment and vehicles.

Current assets are used up quite quickly. They are listed after non-current assets and in the following order: inventory, trade receivables and then cash in bank. ➤ 3.1

The double-entry system of book-keeping · 15

(2) Each transaction has two effects

In some cases a transaction swapped one asset for another, with one increasing and the other decreasing by the same amount. For example when children's clothes were sold for cash, inventory was reduced but cash increased.

In other cases, a transaction caused an asset and a liability to increase or decrease by the same amount. For example, when Lavanda purchased goods on credit on 4 January both her assets and liabilities increased by $4 000.

(3) Regardless of the transaction, the total assets of the business always remain equal to the sum of its total liabilities and owner's equity

This means the two sides of the accounting equation always remained in balance:

$$\text{Assets} = \text{Equity} + \text{Liabilities}$$

In fact, however many more transactions Lavanda went on to make after 8 February last year and continues to make in the future, and however much the financial position of Just Kidz changed or changes as a result, the accounting equation will always stay the same: the total assets of the business will always be exactly equal to the total of the owner's equity and liabilities of the business.

ACTIVITY 1.3

1. Complete the following table.

	Current asset	Non-current asset	Current liability	Non-current liability
Buildings		✓		
Loan from a relative repayable within six months				
Cash on the business premises				
Money owed to suppliers				
Goods for sale held in storage				
Office furniture				
Bank loan repayable over 10 years				
Money owed by customers				
Cash in the business bank account				
Vehicles				
Machinery				

2. The following table shows details about the total assets, liabilities and equity of different businesses. For each one calculate the missing value using the accounting equation.

Business	Assets	Liabilities	Equity
A	$90 000	$40 000	
B	$2.25 million		$1 million
C		$235 000	$122 000
D	$250 000	$134 000	
E	$120 million		$65 million

3. Umar owns and runs a small business. The following information, in no particular order, was taken from his accounts on 31 March this year.

	$
Cash in bank	12 000
Equipment	23 000
Premises	145 000
Inventory	30 000
Trade payables	25 000
Delivery vehicles	14 000
Bank loan	60 000
Trade receivables	21 000
Fixtures and fittings	9 000

(a) What was the value of Umar's total assets at 31 March?

(b) What was the value of his total liabilities at 31 March?

(c) Use the accounting equation to calculate the value of Umar's equity as at 31 March.

(d) Prepare a simple statement of financial position for Umar's business as at 31 March.

1.2.2 Double-entry book-keeping

Book-keeping involves the recording of business transactions in journals and accounts

When Lavanda Harris started her Just Kidz business last year she recalculated its financial position after every transaction. However, as a business grows and the volume of its transactions increases it will become impossible to do this. Most business owners and managers will only calculate the total assets, liabilities and capital of their businesses at the end of each month or quarter. Some may even wait to do so until the end of each year they have been in business when they will prepare their formal statements of income and financial position. However often the owner or owners of a business choose to calculate its financial position, they will need to have kept accurate records of all its transactions over time to do so. ▶ 1.1

Records will be completed from a number of source documents issued or received by the business when transactions take place. For example, a business will issue a sales invoice to a customer when it sells goods on credit and a sales receipt when a payment for goods is received. Similarly, a business will receive a purchase invoice from a supplier when it buys goods on credit and will receive a receipt when it has settled its debt or purchased goods for cash. ▶ 1.3

Invoices, receipts, cheques and other documents provide the details and evidence necessary for a business to make book-keeping entries in its **books of prime entry**. These are the books in which transactions are first recorded in the date order they occurred.

A business will usually keep separate books for different types of transaction and usually write them up at the end of each day of trading. The books are:

- a **purchases journal** to record purchases on credit of goods intended for resale to customers
- a **purchases returns journal** to record any goods subsequently returned to their suppliers
- a **sales journal** to record goods sold to customers on credit terms
- a **sales returns journal** to record any goods subsequently returned by customers ➤ **1.4**
- a **cash book** to record all cash and bank account payments and receipts ➤ **1.5**
- a **general journal** to record transactions that are not entered into any of the other books of prime entry, for example, the purchase and sale of non-current assets on credit. ➤ **1.6**

We will look at these journals in more detail in Units 1.4–1.6.

The ledger contains all the accounts of a business

Periodically (usually at the end of each month) it is sensible for the business owners or managers to write up its accounts and produce the financial summaries they need to keep track of how much the business has earned over time, how much it has spent, what it owns and what it owes. This involves transferring or **posting** entries from its books of prime entry to business accounts kept in its **ledger.**

A business will usually open and maintain a separate account in its ledger for each type of asset it owns, each expense it incurs, each liability and source of income, as well as for each one of its suppliers of goods on credit and for each of its credit customers.

▼ The process of writing up the books in business

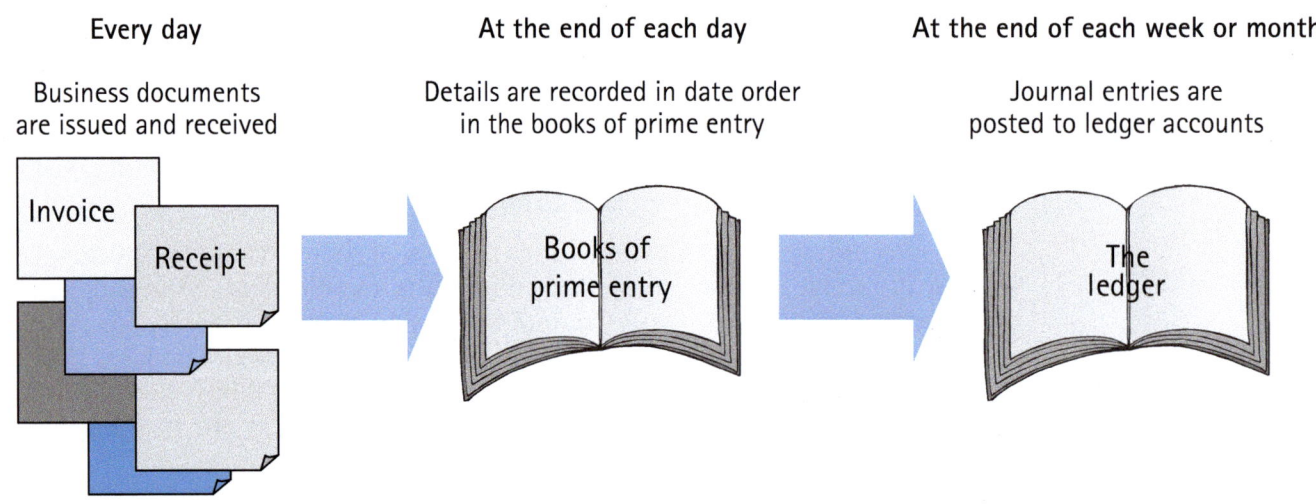

18   The fundamentals of accounting

Individual transactions listed in journals will then be posted (transferred) to their corresponding accounts. So, for example, rent paid for premises will be posted to the rent account, equipment purchases will be posted to the equipment account and purchases on credit from a supplier will be posted to a trade payable account in the name of that supplier.

Ledger accounts can be **personal**, **real** or **nominal**.

- **Personal accounts** are accounts for credit transactions with named suppliers and customers:
    - **Trade payables** are accounts with named suppliers who have supplied goods on credit terms. Trade payables are therefore amounts owed by the business to its suppliers that it will need to pay or settle reasonably quickly and no more than within the next 12 months or accounting year; ➤ 3.2
    - **Trade receivables** are accounts for named customers to whom the business has sold goods. Trade receivables are therefore amounts owed to the business by its credit customers that it expects to be paid reasonably quickly and certainly well within the next 12 month period or accounting year;

    Balances on personal accounts at the end of an accounting year will therefore represent the assets and liabilities of the business and will also be reported in its statement of financial position.

- **Real accounts** are used to record transactions involving equity, assets and liabilities. For example:
    - **the capital account** to record capital introduced to the business and withdrawn by the owner or owners. ➤ 1.6
    - **accounts for non-current assets** including the premises, machinery, vehicles and equipment owned by the business;
    - **cash and bank accounts** in the cash book to record all cash transactions; ➤ 3.2
    - **other payables** for items of value or amounts owed by the business to all other organisations or individuals. For example, other payables will include charges for electricity supplies and telephone services and all other services or items the business pays for in arrears after their use. Other payables will also include repayable loans and any money it has received from customers for items it has yet to deliver to them. ➤ 1.9
    - **other receivables** for items of value or amounts owed to the business by all other organisations and individuals, for example, for expenses the business has paid for in advance such as its annual insurance premiums or a loan it has made to an employee.

- **Nominal accounts** are used to record expenses including wages, electricity and rent, and incomes received from different sources including total sales revenue, interest on business savings and sales commission.

    Nominal accounts are opened at the start of an accounting year and then closed at the year end. The balance accumulated on each account for income earned or expense incurred is then transferred to the income statement to calculate profit or loss for that year. New nominal accounts will then be opened for transactions in the following accounting year.

Traditionally the ledger was a bound book with a different account written up on each page. These were replaced by ring binder folders into which individual sheets could be inserted for different accounts making it easier to add or remove accounts as necessary. Most modern businesses now write-up their ledgers using computerised accounting systems. ➤ **1.1**

The ledger is subdivided into the sales ledger, purchases ledger and general ledger

Moving to folders and computerised ledgers has made it easier to organise and group accounts according to whether they involve sales, purchases or expenses and other items.

It is usual for a business to subdivide its ledger into main three groups of accounts:

▼ Types of ledger

Sales ledger	Purchases ledger	General ledger
contains the personal accounts of customers (trade receivables)	contains the personal accounts of suppliers (trade payables)	contains all other payables and receivables; real accounts for assets, liabilities and equity; nominal accounts for income and expenses

- The **sales ledger** contains all the personal accounts of credit customers or **trade receivables**. From these the business can add up and track how much money it is owed by each of its credit customers and in total.

- It follows that the **purchases ledger** contains all the personal accounts of suppliers or **trade payables**. From these the business can add up and record how much it owes to its different suppliers and calculate its total liability to trade payables.

- All other accounts are kept in the **general ledger** (also sometimes called the **nominal ledger**). These will include all other payable and receivable accounts, real accounts for assets, liabilities and capital, and nominal accounts for income and expenses.

Transactions are recorded in ledger accounts as debits and credits

The system used to write up ledger accounts with transactions recorded in books of prime entry is known as the **double-entry system of book-keeping** – or **double-entry book-keeping**.

When Lavanda Harris began trading as Just Kidz, she discovered that each transaction had two effects. This meant that every transaction required two entries to be made in two different ledger accounts to record it.

For example, to start Just Kidz on 1 January last year Lavanda transferred $3 000 of her own savings into a bank account for the business. This transaction had the following impact on the financial position of her business:

The transaction: capital was received

| Impact 1: equity increased | Impact 2: assets (cash in bank) increased |

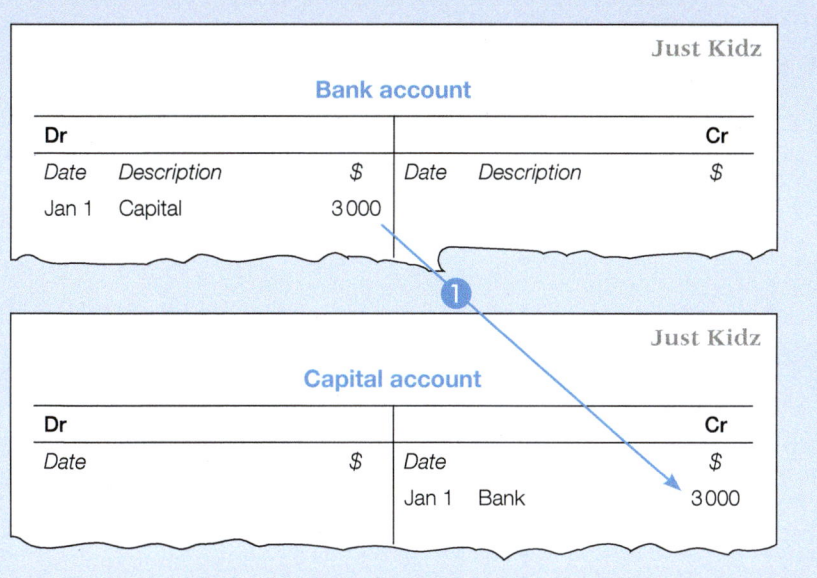

1.1 DOUBLE ENTRIES IN LEDGER ACCOUNTS FOR NEW CAPITAL AND THE CREATION OF AN ASSET

To record the transaction Lavanda opened two accounts in her ledger as follows:

- a capital account to record the opening equity of $3 000 invested in her business
- an asset account for the $3 000 of cash received in the business bank account.

The double entries for the transaction in these accounts are shown in illustration 1.1. For simplicity, only the first part of each page in these ledger accounts is shown.

Note the following important features of the ledger accounts in illustration 1.1:

- Each ledger account was divided into two sides with the name of the account at the top.
- The receipt of cash from the owner was entered to the left-hand side of the business bank account. This is the debit side of the account, shown as Dr. The debit records the fact that the cash paid into the bank account had been drawn from the capital provided by the business owners.
- The introduction of $3 000 of owner's equity to the business was entered to the right-hand side of the capital account. This is the credit side of the account, shown as Cr. The entry records equity capital being invested in business assets by its owners through the provision of cash to the business bank account. The credit to capital is the corresponding double entry for the debit to the bank account.
- Each entry includes a short description of the transaction showing the corresponding double-entry account, and the date the transaction occurred.

Let's consider another example. On 4 January Lavanda purchased a new van for $6 000 on credit terms from Van Hire Ltd. This transaction had the following impacts on the financial position of her business:

The double-entry system of book-keeping   21

The transaction: an asset was acquired on credit payment terms

| Impact 1: assets increased | Impact 2: liabilities increased |

Lavanda therefore had to open two further accounts in her ledger as follows:

- an asset account for motor vehicles to record the receipt of a van worth $6 000
- a liability (other payable) account to record the $6 000 owed to Van Hire Ltd.

These double entries are shown in illustration 1.2.

1.2 DOUBLE ENTRIES IN LEDGER ACCOUNTS FOR THE ACQUISITION OF AN ASSET ON CREDIT TERMS

Just Kidz

Motor vehicles (asset) account

Dr			Cr
Date	$	Date	$
Jan 4 Van Hire Ltd.	6 000		

Just Kidz

Van Hire Ltd. (other payable) account

Dr			Cr
Date	$	Date	$
		Jan 4 Motor vehicles	6 000

The double entries demonstrate the accounting equation:

- a debit entry for $6 000 to the motor vehicles account to record the increase in assets owned by the business
- a corresponding credit entry of $6 000 to a payable account to record the amount owed by the business to the supplier of the van, Van Hire Ltd.

However, it is also possible to increase one asset at the expense of another to leave the accounting equation in balance and the overall financial position of the business unchanged.

For example, last year on 7 January when Lavanda Harris sold children's clothes on credit to the Fun Day Care Centre her inventory was reduced by $1,000 but she created another asset, a trade receivable, of the same value. The transaction therefore had two effects on the financial position of her business:

The transaction: goods were sold on credit payment terms

| Impact 1: assets (inventory) decreased | Impact 2: assets (trade receivables) increased |

To record the transaction Lavanda had to open two more accounts in her ledger as follows:

- a sales account to record the sale of goods on credit for $1 000
- a trade receivables account for Fun Day Care Centre to record the amount it owed to her business.

The double entries for this transaction are shown in illustration 1.3.

22 The fundamentals of accounting

1.3 DOUBLE ENTRIES IN LEDGER ACCOUNTS FOR A SALE OF GOODS ON CREDIT

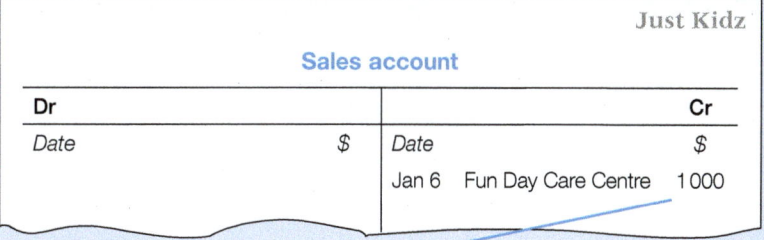

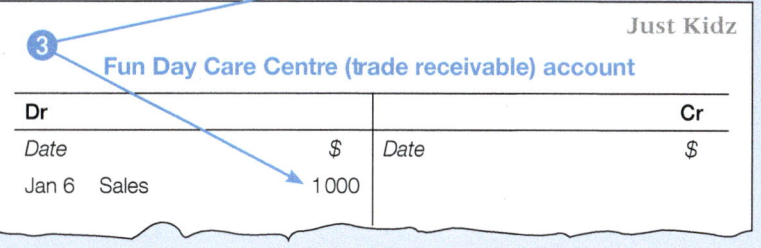

- The sale of clothes on credit terms to Fun Day Care Centre was recorded on the right-hand side or credit side of the sales account. The credit entry recorded the reduction in the value of her inventory of clothes – a current asset – by $1 000.

- The corresponding double entry was a debit to the trade receivable account Lavanda had opened for the Day Care Centre in her sales ledger. The debit entry to the account shows that the Day Care Centre owed Just Kidz money for the supply of goods on credit.

Applying the following rules for double-entry book-keeping will keep the accounting equation in balance

From the above examples we can bring together the combination of double entries that will be required in different ledger accounts when a transaction results in an increase in the assets of a business:

▼ Double entries for an increase in an asset

Asset account	Corresponding double-entry account		
	A liability account	Capital account	Another asset account
A debit entry Example: new equipment is purchased for $1 000	A credit entry The business receives a bank loan for $1 000 to buy the equipment	A credit entry *or* the owners provide $1 000 from their own savings to buy the equipment	A credit entry *or* $1 000 is paid out of the business bank account to buy the equipment

The double-entry system of book-keeping 23

Consequently, the following double-entry book-keeping rules will apply when a transaction results in a decrease in assets:

▼ Double entries for a decrease in an asset

Asset account	Corresponding double-entry account		
	Another asset account	Capital account	Another asset account
A credit entry Example: the business sells goods from its inventory for $800	A debit entry The goods are sold on credit to a customer, creating a trade receivable of $800	A debit entry *or* the goods are sold for cash and the owners use the $800 to buy personal items for themselves	A debit entry *or* the business owners deposit the cash payment of $800 received in the business bank account

Double-entry rules for changes to liabilities and capital are exactly the same. For example, an increase in a liability (a credit entry to a liability account) will require a corresponding increase (a debit entry) in an asset account, the owner's capital account or another liability account.

▼ Double entries for an increase in a liability

Liability account	Corresponding double-entry account		
	Any asset account	Capital account	Another liability account
A credit entry Example: the business takes out a loan of $2 000	A debit entry The business uses the loan to buy new computer equipment	A debit entry *or* the owners withdraw $2 000 from the business bank account for their own personal use	A debit entry *or* the loan is used to pay off a debt of $2 000 on a trade payable account with a supplier

▼ Double entries for a decrease in a liability

Liability account	Corresponding double-entry account		
	Any asset account	Capital account	Another liability account
A debit entry Example: the business settles a debt of $500 on a trade payable account with a supplier	A credit entry $500 is paid out of the business bank account to settle the debt	A credit entry *or* the owners provide an additional $500 from their own savings to settle the debt	A credit entry *or* the business takes out a loan of $500 to settle the debt

Similarly, if the owners increase the amount of equity invested in their business from their own funds (a credit to the capital account) there must be a corresponding increase (a debit entry) in an asset account and/or a reduction (a debit entry) in a liability account. This is because the increase in equity will be used to buy an asset and/or to pay off a liability.

This means that if the owners reduce the amount of equity they have invested in their business (a debit to the capital account), for example by withdrawing cash or goods for their own use, then there must be a corresponding decrease in cash in bank or inventory (a credit entry to an asset account) or an increase in the liabilities of the business (a credit entry to a liability account). ▶ 1.6

▶ Double entries for an increase in equity

Capital account	Corresponding double-entry account	
	Any asset account	Any liability account
A credit entry Example: the owners invest a further $10 000 of their own funds in their business	A debit entry Cash in bank is increased by $10 000	A debit entry *or* a bank loan of $10 000 is settled in full

▶ Double entries for a decrease in capital

Capital account	Corresponding double-entry account	
	Any asset account	Any liability account
A debit entry Example: the owners withdraw $5 000 from the business bank account for their own personal use	A credit entry Cash in bank is decreased by $5 000	A credit entry *or* a bank loan of $5 000 is taken out to provide the funds

ACTIVITY 1.4

David has started his own business selling gardening equipment and other supplies. During April, his first month in business, he undertook the following business transactions:

April:
1. He moved $2 000 of savings from his personal account to his business bank account.
2. He received a small business loan from his bank for $4 000.
4. He spent $600 on a personal computer and printer for his office.
7. He purchased office furniture for $500.
9. He purchased six lawn mowers to sell to customers. Full payment of $750 was not required for 90 days.
12. He purchased $300 worth of fertilisers, assorted garden chemicals and seeds for resale and stored them on the business premises.
17. Gardening tools that cost $420 were purchased for resale. Payment was not required for 60 days.
25. He sold two lawn mowers for $125 each and was paid in cash.
27. He bought shelving units for his storage room for $180.
30. He sold seeds and fertilisers worth $150 on credit.

All payments were made from his business bank account.

1. Prepare and update a statement of financial position for David's business after each transaction.
2. At the end of his first month in business:
   (a) How much capital of his own had David invested in his business?
   (b) How much were the total liabilities of his business?
   (c) What was the total value of all the assets of his business?
3. (a) Arrange the answers to question 2 (a–c) into the accounting equation.
   (b) Explain why the two sides of the equation are equal.

Let's look at one final example of double entries. Each month Lavanda spends $100 on petrol to fill up the tank of her delivery van. The cost of the petrol is a business expense. On 20 February last year Lavanda paid $100 in cash from her business bank account to her local garage for petrol she purchased that day. How do you think Lavanda recorded this transaction?

First, remember that every transaction has two effects or impacts. The cash purchase of petrol is no different and therefore affects two accounts in the general ledger:

- a nominal expense account for petrol received
- an asset account for bank transactions. ➤ **1.5**

Second, recall that expenses will be paid for from the income of the business. Expenses therefore reduce profits. This means that expenses should be recorded as debits in expense accounts. Debit entries will show that expense items have been received by the business. ➤ **1.7**

To record the petrol received Lavanda entered a debit of $100 to the ledger account for petrol expenses in her general ledger.

Then, to record the expense incurred she entered a credit for $100 to the ledger account for bank transactions. The credit entry showed cash being paid out of the account. This recorded the reduction in cash in bank – a current asset of the business – by $100. This expense also reduced the total assets of the business.

The transaction: the cash payment of an expense

Petrol expenses account	Bank account
A debit entry for $100 for petrol received	A credit entry for $100 for money paid out
Impact 1: expenses are increased	Impact 2: assets (cash in bank) are decreased

The double entries to these ledger accounts are shown in illustration 1.4.

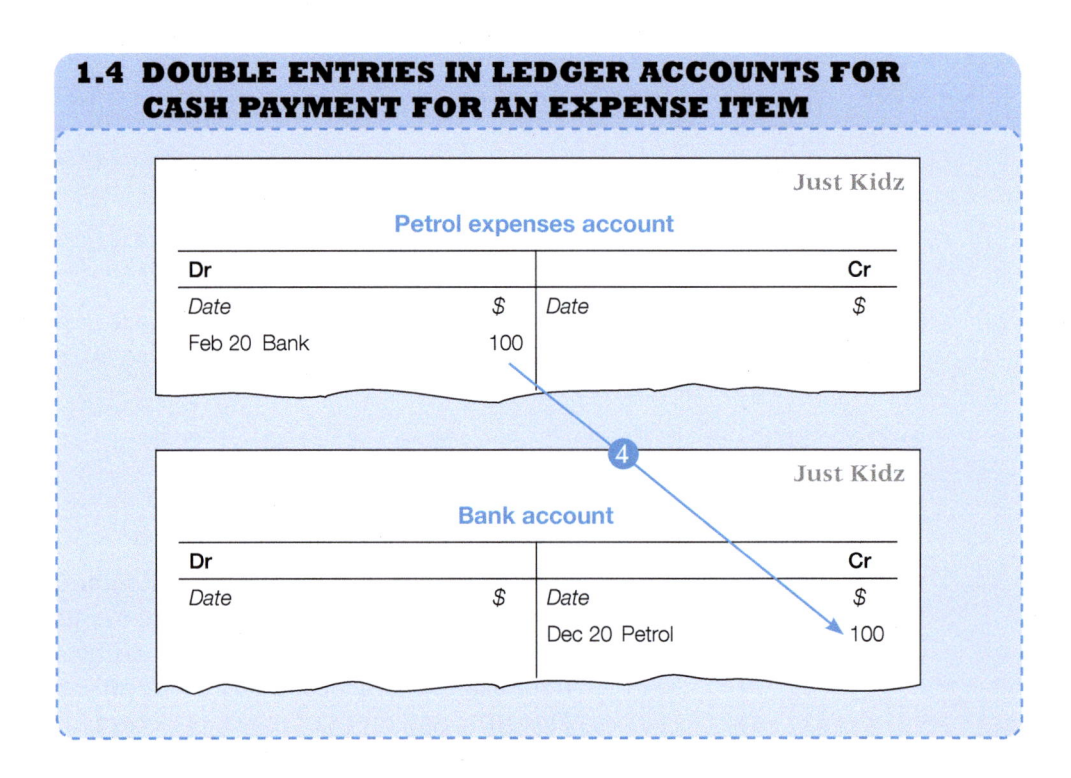

1.4 DOUBLE ENTRIES IN LEDGER ACCOUNTS FOR CASH PAYMENT FOR AN EXPENSE ITEM

Just Kidz

Petrol expenses account

Dr			Cr
Date	$	Date	$
Feb 20 Bank	100		

Just Kidz

Bank account

Dr			Cr
Date	$	Date	$
		Dec 20 Petrol	100

The fundamentals of accounting

Debit entries to ledger accounts are for money and items received; credit entries record money and items going out of the business

From all the above examples, we can now list some important features of ledger accounts:

- a ledger account has two sides ➤ **1.7**
- the left-hand side is used to record money and items of value coming *in* to the business. This side is the **debit side** denoted **Dr**
- the right-hand side is used to record money and items of value going *out* of the business. This side is the **credit side** denoted **Cr**.

We can now apply these rules to the different types of account in the ledger as follows:

Personal accounts	Real accounts	Nominal accounts
Debit amount owed by a customer	Debit what comes into the business	Debit expenses paid by the business
Credit amount owed to a supplier	Credit what goes out of the business	Credit income received by the business

Additionally,

- each entry to an account should include the date of the transaction, the name of the ledger account to which the corresponding double entry has been made and the amount involved.

We will look in more detail at the format and use of ledger accounts in Unit 1.7. We will also see many more examples of double entries in different ledger accounts throughout this book.

Total debits must always equal total credits in the ledger

If every transaction has two effects – one a debit for money or items received and the other a credit for money or items leaving the business – then the total of all debits in all ledger accounts must equal the total of all credits to all accounts in the same accounting year.

If total debits do not equal total credits it means an error must have been made in the recording of transactions, either in the books of prime entry or when they were posted to the ledger accounts as double entries. Or the error may have occurred when adding up total debits and credits in each account in the ledger at the end of the accounting year.

If there are errors then the profit or loss of the business will be wrong and misleading to users of financial statements. ➤ **5.1**

We also know that the accounting equation must always be in balance. If there are mistakes in the recording of transactions and the total assets do not equal total liabilities and capital then the financial position of the business will also be misleading.

Errors in accounting entries and calculations must be corrected before accurate statements of income and financial position can be prepared. ➤ **1.7**

ACTIVITY 1.5

From the jumble of business transactions (1–8) below find and match them with their corresponding double entry (A–H).

1 Cash in bank (an asset) is increased as cash received from a sale of goods is paid immediately into the bank account

G The inventory of goods (an asset) held by the business for resale to customers is increased

8 Cash in bank (an asset) is decreased following payment by cheque for the purchase of new computer equipment for the business

E Cash in bank (an asset) is reduced as a loan repayment is made

H Machinery (an asset) is increased

4 Trade payables (a liability) are increased as goods for resale are purchased on credit from AB Supplies Ltd.

B The inventory of goods (an asset) held by the business for resale to customers is reduced

7 Trade receivables (an asset) are reduced as payment is received from Salim Okar for goods he purchased from the business on credit two months ago

6 Cash in bank (an asset) is reduced as an electricity bill is paid

C Equipment (an asset) is increased

5 Trade receivables (an asset) are increased following a sale of goods on credit to George Falana

F Electricity expenses are increased

D Cash in bank (an asset) is increased as the payment of a debt is received in the bank account

2 Owner's equity is increased as the business owners invest an additional $30 000 of their own money in new machinery for their business

A The inventory of goods (an asset) held by the business for resale to customers is reduced

3 A commercial loan (a liability) is reduced as $500 of the loan is repaid following a transfer from the business bank account to the loan provider

QUICK TEST

1. What is owner's equity?
2. Which of the following are assets and which are liabilities of a business?
   (a) premises
   (b) a bank loan
   (c) a fork lift truck
   (d) money owed to a supplier
   (e) office furniture
   (f) computer equipment
   (g) inventory of goods for resale
   (h) money owed by a customer
   (i) savings in a bank deposit account
   (j) an inventory of stationery for office use
3. What is the accounting equation and why is it important?
4. On 30 April a business had total assets valued at $3 million and total liabilities of $1.25 million. How much equity did the owners have in their business?
5. On 31 January a business had the following assets, liabilities and capital:

   Machinery $110 000
   Cash in bank $4 000
   Outstanding bank loan $200 000
   Vehicles $30 000
   Inventory $26 000

   Equity $145 000
   Trade payables $55 000
   Trade receivables $30 000
   Premises $180 000
   Equipment $20 000

   Prepare a simple statement of the financial position of the business as at 31 January from this information.
6. What are the main subdivisions of the ledger and what type of accounts do each of the subdivisions contain?
7. What is double-entry book-keeping?
8. Complete the table to show the impact of the following transactions:

Transaction	Impact on assets	Impact on liabilities	Impact on capital
(a) The owner invests $16 000 of her own money in new equipment for her business	Increase		Increase
(b) $500 of goods are purchased on credit from a supplier			
(c) A cheque payment of $450 is made to buy a new computer for the office			
(d) The balance of $180 on a trade receivable is paid in full with cash by the credit customer			
(e) The business borrows $15 000 from a car finance company to buy a new van			
(f) The old van is sold off to a scrap merchant for $1 000 in cash			
(g) Immediate payment is received in cash from the sale of $225 worth of goods			

9. Which ledger account would you debit and which ledger account would you credit to record the double entries for each transaction in question 8?

Unit 1.3 Business documents

> **AIMS**
>
> By the end of this unit you should be able to
>
> ▸ recognise and understand the following business documents: invoice, debit note, credit note, statement of account, cheque, receipt
>
> ▸ complete proforma business documents
>
> ▸ understand the use of business documents as sources of information: invoice, credit note, cheque counterfoil, paying-in slip, receipt, bank statement

1.3.1 Recording financial transactions

Business documents are used to record sales, purchases and payments

Whenever a business exchanges goods and services with a customer or a supplier it is essential that it keeps detailed and accurate records. ➤ **1.1**

For example, when goods or services are sold on credit, the types of information a business will need to record include:

- customer details, including name and address
- type and amount of goods or services ordered or supplied
- price of individual items and total price including any discounts plus any **carriage outwards** or delivery charges to the customer's premises
- the total amount owed, when payment is due and how payment should be made.

When goods or services are purchased on credit a business will need to record:

- supplier details including name and account details
- type and amount of goods or services ordered or received
- price of individual items and total price including any discounts plus any **carriage inwards** or delivery charges to be paid to the supplier to transport the goods to the business premises
- the total amount owed to the supplier, when payment is due and how payment should be made.

Recording information about financial transactions requires a great deal of paperwork especially for purchases and sales on credit terms when goods or services are traded before payment for them is required. To make the recording of credit transactions less time consuming businesses have devised a number of different documents to use. Invoices, credit and debit notes, statements of accounts and receipts are just a few of the **business documents** used. These are the source documents for book-keeping records. Many business documents are now issued, completed and sent electronically via email to save time, paper and postage costs. The design of each type of document will differ from business to business but all will contain similar information.

ACTIVITY 1.6

This is the story of Malik Matheroo. He owns and runs a small vehicle repair, parts and garage business. Read the story and then answer the questions.

Malik phones Parts Supplies Ltd. to place an order for 17 oil filters at a total cost, including carriage, of $178.00.

The sales assistant at Parts Supplies Ltd. makes a written note of Malik's order but writes down 70 oil filters by mistake.

The next day 70 oil filters are delivered by van to Malik Motors.

"But I only ordered 17 filters!" Malik complains as the van driver tries to unload 70 boxes. The driver apologises and agrees to return the rest to Parts Supplies Ltd.

A week passes and Malik transfers $178.00 to the bank account of Parts Supplies Ltd. to pay for the supply and delivery of the 17 oil filters he ordered.

Two months pass and Parts Supplies Ltd. writes to Malik to demand full payment of $655 for the supply and delivery of 70 oil filters

Malik receives the demand and immediately phones Parts Supplies Ltd. He explains that he had only ordered 17 oil filters and the other 53 had been taken away by the van driver. However, neither Malik or Parts Supplies Ltd. has any record of the order or the delivery made.

In fact the van driver had lied. He did not return 53 oil filters to Parts Supplies Ltd. Instead he stole them and sold them for $50 to another garage.

"What a messy business" sighs Malik upon receiving an apology from Parts Supplies Ltd. "In future I think I'll buy my car parts from another supplier."

1. Give reasons why business organisations such as Malik Motors and Parts Supplies Ltd. should keep records of their financial transactions.

2. What information should Parts Supplies Ltd. record to make the process of selling its products easier, less wasteful and more secure?

Business documents

Activity 1.6 illustrates some of the reasons why accurate recording of transactions is vital in business. Businesses that fail to keep accurate records of all their transactions could not only lose money but may also lose their customers and eventually be forced to cease trading.

The types of documents that Malik Motors and Parts Supplies Ltd. should have used to make sure their transactions in the activity were carried out efficiently, and the order in which they should have used them, are shown in the diagram below. The types and order of the documents used are typical of many business transactions.

▼ Documents involved in a business transaction

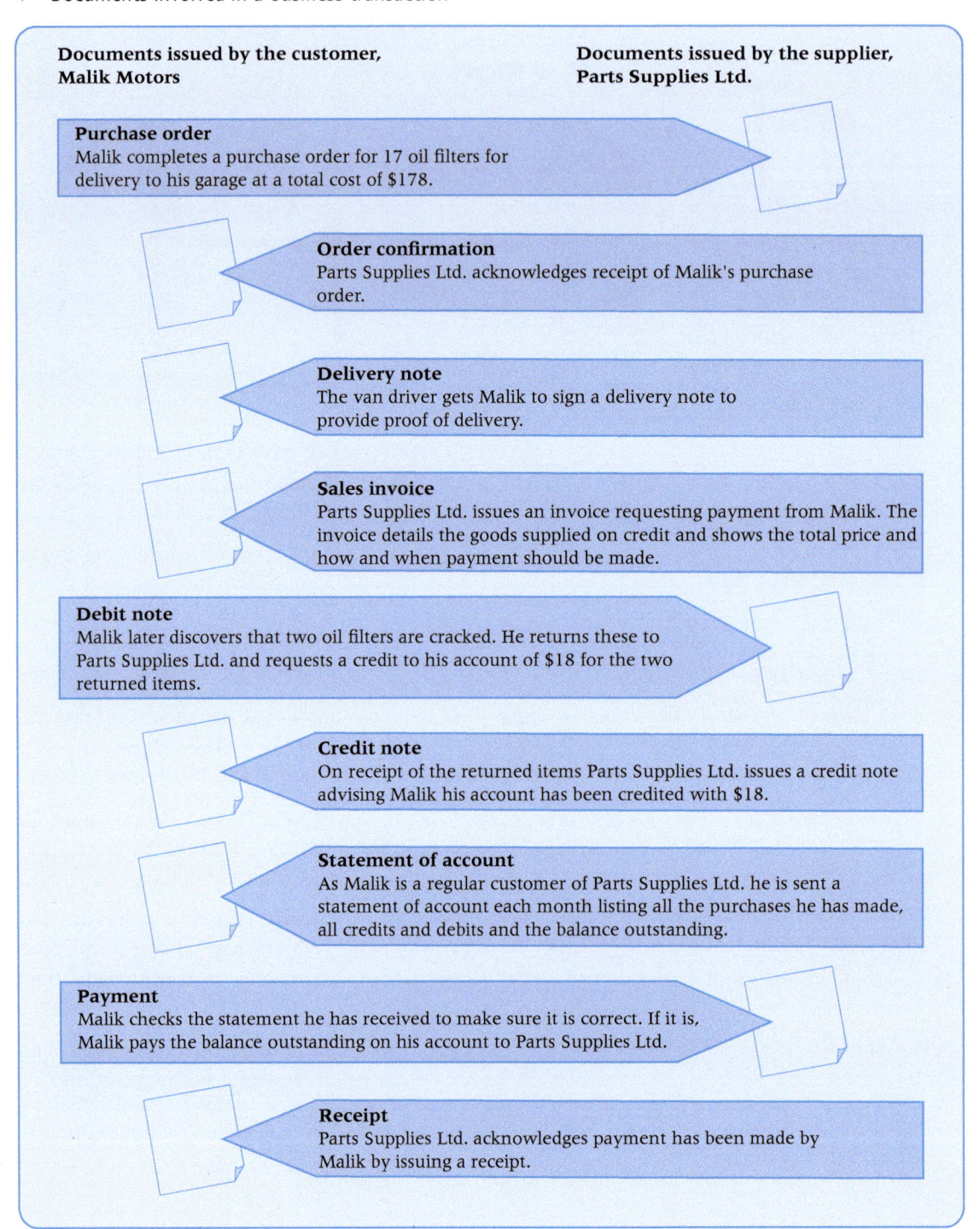

Documents issued by the customer, Malik Motors

Documents issued by the supplier, Parts Supplies Ltd.

Purchase order
Malik completes a purchase order for 17 oil filters for delivery to his garage at a total cost of $178.

Order confirmation
Parts Supplies Ltd. acknowledges receipt of Malik's purchase order.

Delivery note
The van driver gets Malik to sign a delivery note to provide proof of delivery.

Sales invoice
Parts Supplies Ltd. issues an invoice requesting payment from Malik. The invoice details the goods supplied on credit and shows the total price and how and when payment should be made.

Debit note
Malik later discovers that two oil filters are cracked. He returns these to Parts Supplies Ltd. and requests a credit to his account of $18 for the two returned items.

Credit note
On receipt of the returned items Parts Supplies Ltd. issues a credit note advising Malik his account has been credited with $18.

Statement of account
As Malik is a regular customer of Parts Supplies Ltd. he is sent a statement of account each month listing all the purchases he has made, all credits and debits and the balance outstanding.

Payment
Malik checks the statement he has received to make sure it is correct. If it is, Malik pays the balance outstanding on his account to Parts Supplies Ltd.

Receipt
Parts Supplies Ltd. acknowledges payment has been made by Malik by issuing a receipt.

1.3.2 Purchases and sales documents

An invoice records goods and services supplied on credit terms and is a request for payment

For many businesses most of their sales, especially to other businesses, are on credit terms. ➤ 1.2

When a business supplies a good or service to a customer and agrees to receive payment at a later date it will issue an **invoice** to record the sale on credit terms. One copy (the **purchase invoice**) is sent to the customer. A second copy (the **sales invoice**) is kept by the supplier.

The purpose of an invoice is to notify the customer of goods supplied on credit, their total price and when payment is due. It is a request for payment. Both the customer and supplier will record details from the invoice in their books of prime entry. ➤ 1.4

An invoice is one of the most important documents in business and will contain the following information:

- the name and address of the supplier
- the name and address of the customer
- the customer's account number
- a unique invoice number for ease of reference
- a full description of the items supplied
- the unit price of the individual items supplied
- the total price of the items, including any deductions for any trade discounts offered
- carriage charges, if any
- the date of the invoice, the total amount to pay to settle the invoice and when payment is due.

1.5 AN INVOICE

INVOICE

To: Malik Motors
7–9 Axelrod Avenue
Downtown DN1267

Parts Supplies Ltd.
Unit 19–22
Moleville Industrial Park
ADMINTON AD1980
Tel: 577 890 5432
www.partssupplies.com

Date	Order No.	Account No.	Invoice No.
19.9.201X	1853	702300	241

Qty	Description	Product code	Unit price	Total
17	Oil filters	34/OFW	$10.00	$170.00
			Sub-total	$170.00
			Less 10% trade discount	$17.00
			Goods total	$153.00
			Carriage	$25.00
			Total to pay	$178.00

Terms:
Payment due within 60 days
Cash discount of 2.5% for orders over $50 if payment received within 10 working days

E & OE

The invoice in illustration 1.5 was issued by Parts Supplies Ltd. to Malik Motors following the sale and delivery of oil filters on credit terms to the business.

You will notice that Parts Supplies Ltd. has reduced the total purchase price of the filters supplied to Malik Motors by 10%. This is a **trade discount** and the rate given often increases according to how much is purchased. It is used to encourage customers to buy in bulk.

Business documents 33

In addition, Parts Supplies Ltd. was willing to reduce the total price by a further 2.5% if Malik Motors paid the amount owed within 10 days of receiving the invoice. This is a **cash** (or settlement) **discount** and is offered to encourage credit customers (trade receivables) to settle their debts early. Unlike a trade discount a cash discount is not deducted from the total price shown on an invoice until payment is made and within the period stated. ➤ 1.5

Malik Motors buys many different types of goods and services from many different suppliers each year and receives a large number of invoices. Some invoices are for goods such as vehicle parts and tyres that are purchased for resale to customers. These are recorded as **purchases** in the purchases journal of the business. Other goods and services, such as office supplies, are bought by the business for use in its day-to-day operations. These are **expenses** and the amounts paid for them are recorded in the cash book of the business. ➤ 1.5

Every time Malik receives an invoice from a supplier, whether it is for a purchase of goods for resale or for expense items, it should be checked carefully before it is paid to make sure:

- it was not sent to his business by mistake
- the order reference quoted on it is the same as the purchase order
- the products listed match those received

ALLOWING FOR ERRORS AND OMISSIONS ON INVOICES

Invoices often have the letters E & OE printed on them. This stands for "Errors and omissions excepted" which means that if the supplier has made any mistakes or left anything off the invoice, the supplier has the right to correct the mistake later on and demand full payment.

ACTIVITY 1.7

You work in the accounts department of Computech Ltd., a major supplier of computer equipment and accessories. This purchase order has just been received from the head office of Bloomin' Marvellous Garden Centres. The goods will be delivered tomorrow and you have been asked to prepare an invoice (number 07/14567) to issue to the customer. The customer (account number 3170) qualifies for a trade discount and the delivery or carriage charge will be $25.00.

A blank invoice for you to complete is provided on the website.

Bloomin' Marvellous

Order No. 773
Date: 04.07.1X

Garden Centres plc
Cedar Gates Drive
Upper Shrubbery
Flowerton FT3984
Tel: 639 840 9843
www.bloominmarvellous.com

Supplier:
Computech Ltd.
Unit 19–22
Moleville Industrial Park
BYTEVILLE BV1980

Description	Qty	Reference	Unit price	Total price
Hi-Tek e24 monitors	5	HT/24/LED/27X3	$120.00	$600.00
Hi-Tek 1TB Ext. HDD	10	HT/1/EHDD/43P7	$84.00	$840.00
DVD-R x 10	20	DVDR/20D3	$5.00	$100.00

Delivery ASAP

Authorised by: *A. J. Bloomin*
for *Bloomin' Marvellous Garden Centres plc*

- the price given is the same as agreed or advertised
- all calculations are correct
- it contains any discounts agreed with the supplier.

Malik should only authorise payment to be made once he is satisfied an invoice is correct.

A debit note from a customer records money owed against an invoice by the supplier

When Malik took delivery of 17 oil filters from Parts Supplies Ltd. he did not notice that two of the filters were cracked. He only discovered this several days later when he opened the boxes they were in. He returned the two filters to Parts Supplies Ltd. along with a debit note requesting that his invoice be reduced by $18.00, the total price of the two filters less a trade discount of 10%.

1.6 A DEBIT NOTE

Debit note: D14
Parts Supplies Ltd.
Unit 19–22, Moleville Industrial Park,
Adminton AD1980

Date	Invoice No.	Customer Account No.
24.9.201X	241	702300

Malik Motors
7–9 Axelrod Avenue
Downtown DN1267

Tel : 675 899 5794
Cell : 7845 800 500
malikmot@gmail.net

The following goods have been returned – damaged in transit

	Unit price $	Total price $
2 oil filters	$10.00	$20.00
Less 10% trade discount		$2.00
Please issue a credit note for total amount:		$18.00

A **debit note** is a request from a customer to a supplier to reduce the total amount charged on an invoice. A customer will issue a debit note if:

- the supplier has made a mistake and has overcharged the customer
- goods were not received because they were lost or stolen in transit
- the customer has returned unsatisfactory or damaged goods.

The debit note sent by Malik Motors to Parts Supplies Ltd. is shown in illustration 1.6.

So that the supplier can identify the right invoice and amount to amend it is important for a debit note to contain the following information:

- the name and address of the supplier
- the name and address of the customer
- the customer's account number and the relevant invoice number
- the purpose of the debit note – for example, goods not received, returned or overcharged for
- details of the goods returned or overcharged for, including quantities and prices charged as well as any discounts
- how much in total the supplier owes the customer
- the date of issue.

Business documents

A debit note issued by a customer is not normally recorded by the customer or supplier in its books. This is because a debit note is simply a request from the customer to the supplier to reduce the total price of items recorded in the original invoice.

However, sometimes it is a supplier who issues a debit note to a customer. A supplier may do this if a previous invoice it issued contained errors or omissions, for example if it failed to include a delivery charge so the original amount charged to the customer was too low. Rather than issue a new invoice for the correct amount, the supplier can send the customer a debit note for the amount of the error.

A credit note from a supplier records an overcharged amount or overpayment on an invoice

Following the receipt of the debit note and returned parts from Malik Motors, Parts Supplies Ltd. sent a credit note to Malik to advise him that his trade receivable account had been credited with $18.00. The credit note is shown in illustration 1.7.

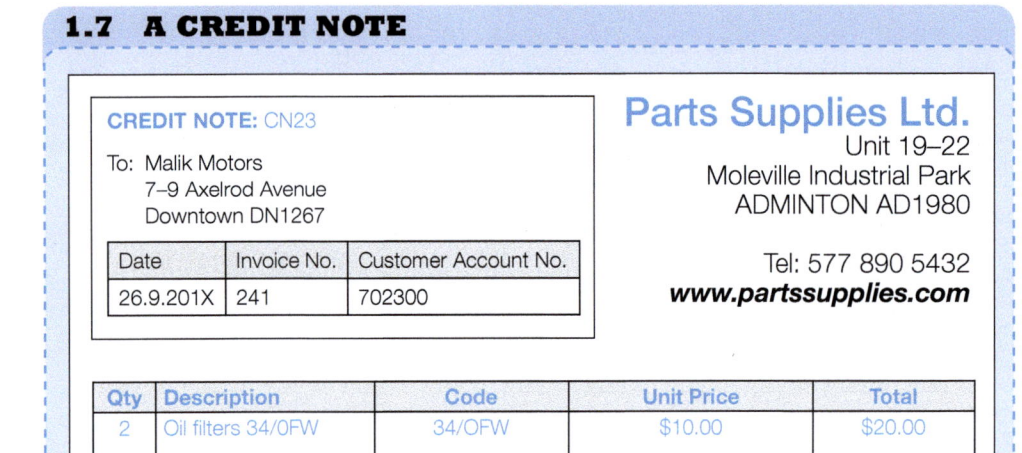

1.7 A CREDIT NOTE

CREDIT NOTE: CN23

To: Malik Motors
7–9 Axelrod Avenue
Downtown DN1267

Date	Invoice No.	Customer Account No.
26.9.201X	241	702300

Parts Supplies Ltd.
Unit 19–22
Moleville Industrial Park
ADMINTON AD1980

Tel: 577 890 5432
www.partssupplies.com

Qty	Description	Code	Unit Price	Total
2	Oil filters 34/0FW	34/0FW	$10.00	$20.00
			Sub-total	$20.00
			Less trade discount	$2.00
			Total credit	**$18.00**

Reason for credit:
Oil filters returned – damaged in transit

A credit note is issued by a supplier if the total price it has charged a customer on an invoice is more the amount that needs to be paid. This can happen because:

- the supplier made a mistake and overcharged the customer
- the customer did not receive goods because they were lost or stolen in transit
- the customer returned unsatisfactory or damaged goods.

The purpose of a **credit note** is to record an overcharged amount. It should contain the following information:

- the name and address of the supplier
- the name and address of the customer
- the relevant invoice number
- the customer's account number
- details of the goods returned or overcharged for, or any overpayment
- the date of issue.

If the customer has an account with the supplier then the amount recorded on the credit note will simply be credited to his or her account. Alternatively, a credit note can be used by the customer to pay for additional purchases up to the value stated on the credit note from the same supplier. A credit note allows a supplier to notify a customer of a credit to the customer's account without having to issue an amended invoice. This saves time and money.

To cancel an invoice in full, a credit note for the same amount as the invoice must be issued by the supplier. Once an invoice has been issued, received and recorded in the accounts of the supplier and customer, it can only be amended or cancelled through the issue of a credit note.

Credit notes are often printed in a different colour, usually red, to distinguish them from invoices. The supplier will record credit notes it has issued in its books as **sales returns**. A customer will record credit notes it has received for overcharged amounts on purchase invoices as **purchases returns**. ▶ 1.4

A statement of account is a summary of transactions between a supplier and its credit customer

At the end of each month, a supplier will usually issue a credit customer with a **statement of account**. A statement of account summarises all the customer's transactions with the supplier during the previous month.

1.8 A STATEMENT OF ACCOUNT

STATEMENT OF ACCOUNT

Parts Supplies Ltd.
Unit 19–22
Moleville Industrial Park
ADMINTON AD1980

Tel: 577 890 5432
www.partssupplies.com

Account: 702300
Name: Malik Motors
7–9 Axelrod Avenue
Downtown DN1267
Statement date: 30.9.201X

Date	Details	Debit	Credit	Balance
1.9	Balance brought down	$495.00		$495.00 Dr
8.9	Goods – invoice 239	$225.00		$720.00 Dr
11.9	Payment received		$495.00	$225.00 Dr
19.9	Goods – invoice 241	$178.00		$306.00 Dr
26.9	Returns CN23		$18.00	$403.00 Dr
29.9	Goods – invoice 243	$215.00		$600.00 Dr
	Balance now due			**$600.00 Dr**

Terms: Payment by 31.10.1X required
Dr = debit / CR = credit

Illustration 1.8 shows the statement of account issued by Parts Supplies Ltd. to Malik Motors at the end of September. The first entry records that Malik Motors owed the company $495 at the end of the month of August. This sum is the balance brought down on the account from the end of August and becomes the opening balance on the statement for September.

The statement of account shows that Malik paid off the balance outstanding on his account at the end of August on 11 September. The payment of $495 received by Parts Supplies Ltd. was recorded as a credit to Malik's account. A statement of account also acts as a receipt document confirming any payments made by the customer.

Business documents 37

During September Malik placed two further orders for car parts with Parts Supplies Ltd. In illustration 1.8, you can see entries for invoice 241 issued on 19 September for 17 oil filters and the subsequent credit note CN23 issued on the return of two filters that had been damaged in transit. At the end of September the balance on Malik's account was a debit balance of $600.

A statement of account is also a request to the customer for payment of the balance outstanding on the account. It shows how much the customer owed the supplier at the end of the previous month and this will be added to amounts owing on any new invoices issued during the month covered by the statement. From this total any credits from credit notes issued during the month will be deducted along with any payments received from the customer. This gives the total amount outstanding on the account due for payment.

It is more convenient for a customer to make one payment each month to pay off a debit balance on its account rather than having to make many different payments to settle each separate invoice from a supplier.

Before a supplier sends out a statement of account to a customer it should check it is accurate and contains all the following information:

- the name and address of the supplier
- the name and address of the customer
- the customer's account number
- the balance brought forward from the last account statement
- the month and date of the statement
- a record of all transactions made with the customer during the month, including all invoices and credit notes issued to the customer and any payments received
- the balance on the account after each transaction
- the closing balance owed by (or to) the customer at the end of the month after accounting for all transactions entered into the account.

A statement of account should always be checked against the customer's own book-keeping records to make sure they agree with the statement. However, there is no need for the customer or supplier to record the balance on a statement of account in its books: a statement is simply a useful record of the transactions between the two businesses that should already have been recorded individually in their books.

ACTIVITY 1.8

1. You work in the accounts department of Computech Ltd. TW Plastics plc has ordered some boxes of computer discs. Prepare an invoice in full for:

   ▸ 40 boxes of recordable discs at $5 per box (product code DVDR10X97)

   ▸ less a trade discount of 10%

   ▸ plus a delivery charge of $10.

   The invoice should be dated 3 April and numbered 37892.

2. Prepare a statement of account for TW Plastics plc using the following information for April. The company's account number is 654/0234 and the statement should be dated for the last working day of April.

   Date

   Apr 1   A debit balance of $2 300 brought forward from end March

   Apr 3   Invoice 37892

   Apr 4   Payment received for $2 300

   Apr 9   Credit note (CN156) issued for $300 for goods returned

   Apr 17 Invoice 37953 for 8 laptop computers – total to pay on invoice $4 200

   Apr 23 Invoice 37959 for 10 laserjet computer printers – total to pay $1 290.

   Don't forget to show the outstanding balance at the end of the month. Payment of this balance is due on 31 May 201X.

3. On receipt of the statement the finance director at TW Plastics plc telephones you to point out that invoice 37892 contained an error. Only 20 boxes of discs had been delivered. You check your own records and confirm the error. You must now issue TW Plastics plc a credit note (CN261) dated 1 May for the following:

   ▸ 20 boxes of recordable discs at $5 per box

   ▸ less a trade discount of 10%.

   Blank documents for you to complete are provided on the website.

1.3.3 Receipt documents

Receipts provide proof of purchase and payment

When you buy goods or services in a shop you will receive a receipt as proof of your purchase. Similarly, when an organisation makes payment for goods or services it purchased on credit, it will require proof from the supplier that payment has been made.

A number of documents are available to act as proof of payment. These are:

- sales receipts
- cheques
- statements of account
- bank account statements. ➤ 1.5

> **ACTIVITY 1.9**
>
> You work in the office at Malik Motors. You normally print out receipts for cash sales to customers from your computer. However, today (10 September) the computer has crashed.
>
> 1. Produce a handwritten receipt for Mr Chutani. He has just paid $150 in cash to have a new exhaust fitted to his car.
> 2. Explain the purpose of Malik Motors issuing the receipt to the business and to Mr Chutani.

A sales **receipt** is usually issued when payment for goods or services is immediate either in cash or by electronic bank transfer. ➤ 1.5

A sales receipt can take many forms but will usually include the following information:

- name and address of the seller or supplier that has made the sale
- the date the transaction took place
- a description of the goods or services supplied
- the price of each item
- the total price of all items including any discounts and sales or value added taxes
- the method of payment.

A receipt may be sent electronically by the supplier to a customer, printed out using a computer or electronic cash till or handwritten on a pre-printed form. Each receipt will be numbered for ease of reference.

A supplier will record each receipt it issues as a cash sale in its **cash book** while a customer issued with a receipt will also record the cash payment in its cash book. A cash book is used to record all cash flows into and out of a business. ➤ 1.5

Illustration 1.9 shows two examples. The first is an electronic till receipt issued to Malik by the local bookstore when he bought a book on classic cars and paid immediately with cash. The second is a handwritten receipt issued by a scrap merchant for the cash sale of scrap parts to Malik.

1.9 EXAMPLES OF SALES RECEIPTS FOR CASH PAYMENTS

```
        WELCOME TO
        BEST BOOKS LTD.

   Book              $25.00
   Balance due       $25.00
   CASH              $30.00
   CHANGE             $5.00

   THANK YOU FOR SHOPPING AT
        BEST BOOKS LTD.
```

```
        BROGAN SCRAP MERCHANTS
              Receipt         No. 5387
   Received from  Mr M Matheroo
   the sum of $  forty five dollars      $45—

   in payment for  Ford Fiesta headlamp units
                   and rear bumper
   Received by: J.W. Sharman   Date: 28. Sept 201X
                Sales Department
```

A cheque is a method of payment and also acts as a receipt

Invoices or balances on accounts may be paid by cheque. A **cheque** is a written order to a bank to pay the sum of money written on the cheque to the person or organisation named on that cheque. The person or organisation to whom the cheque is made payable is known as the **payee**. The sum of money stated on the cheque is then withdrawn from the bank account of the business that issued it and paid into (credited to) the bank account of the named payee.

All cheques pass through the bank clearing system that transfers funds between different banks. A cheque will only be cleared or authorised for payment once the bank holding the account from which the funds are to be withdrawn is satisfied that it has been completed correctly. It will make sure that the signature on it has not been forged and that the business has enough money in its account to pay the sum stated on the cheque.

The cheque below was issued by Malik Motors on 11 September to pay $495 to Parts Supplies Ltd. The receipt of the cheque by Parts Supplies Ltd. was recorded as a credit to the statement of account for September issued by Parts Supplies Ltd. to Malik Motors as shown in illustration 1.8.

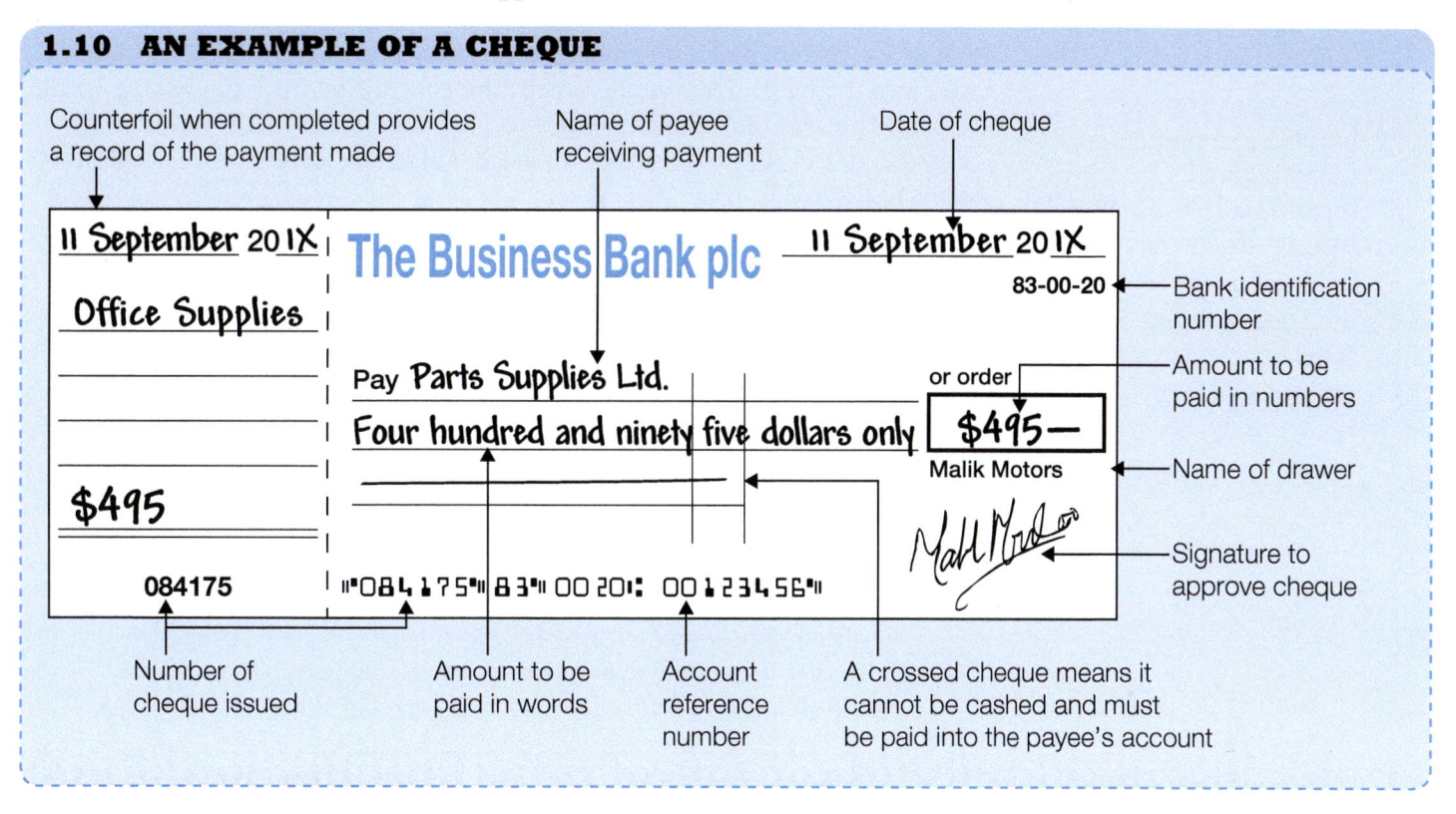

1.10 AN EXAMPLE OF A CHEQUE

Counterfoil when completed provides a record of the payment made

Name of payee receiving payment

Date of cheque

The Business Bank plc

11 September 20 1X
Office Supplies

$495

084175

Pay Parts Supplies Ltd.
Four hundred and ninety five dollars only

11 September 20 1X
83-00-20
or order
$495—
Malik Motors

"084175" 83" 00 20: 00123456"

- **Bank identification number**
- **Amount to be paid in numbers**
- **Name of drawer**
- **Signature to approve cheque**

Number of cheque issued | **Amount to be paid in words** | **Account reference number** | **A crossed cheque means it cannot be cashed and must be paid into the payee's account**

A cheque must contain enough information to enable a bank to transfer money easily and accurately between the bank account of the business and the account of the person or organisation it intends to pay, which may be held at a different bank. To do this pre-printed cheques with the following information are normally provided by banks to their account holders:

- the name of the bank account holder
- the name and address of the bank where the account is held
- the unique identification code or number of the bank branch
- the customer account number
- a cheque identification or serial number.

In addition, the person or organisation that completes a cheque must provide:

- the name of the payee
- the amount of money to be transferred to the payee
- the date the cheque was written
- a signature to authorise payment.

Business documents

A cheque is only valid if:

- it is written in ink or printed
- it is signed by the name of the account holder or, in the case of a business, by an authorised representative
- the amount in words is the same as the amount written in numbers
- the cheque is made payable to a named individual or organisation, or to "The Bearer" (the person holding the cheque)
- the cheque is dated and is not more than six months old.

It is usual to write or print out the sum to be paid in words as well as figures on a cheque to make sure the precise sum cannot be mistaken.

The account holder must also sign each cheque with his or her usual signature – one that is recognised by the bank as having the authority to authorise payment. In most large organisations, this will be the signature of the head of the finance or accounts department. Two signatories may even be required if the sum involved is very large.

The **cheque counterfoil** (as shown in illustration 1.10) can be kept by the customer's organisation to provide a record of the payment to enter into its cash book. ➤ 1.5

When a supplier receives a cheque, a **paying-in slip** is completed when it is paid into the bank. The supplier keeps the counterfoil from the paying-in slip to provide a record of the payment received and banked. This can then be recorded in the supplier's own cash book and in the statement of account it sends to the customer.

Therefore, when payment for goods or services is made by cheque there is no need for a receipt to be issued by the supplier. Confirmation that payment has been made by cheque is shown on the bank statement of both the customer who wrote the cheque and the bank statement of the supplier. A bank statement is simply a monthly statement of account issued by a bank to account holders recording all payments to and from their account.

ACTIVITY 1.10

1. You work in the accounts department of Computech Ltd. You have received the cheque below from a customer. Has it been completed correctly? Will you accept the cheque in payment for goods Computech has supplied? Explain your answers and mark any errors and omissions on the cheque.

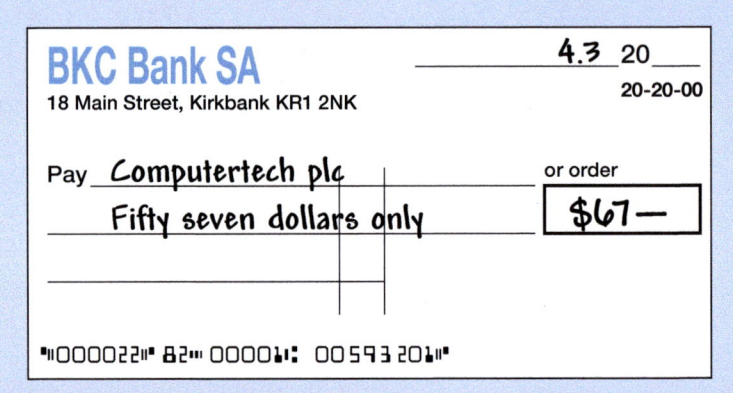

   ```
   BKC Bank SA                              4.3  20____
   18 Main Street, Kirkbank KR1 2NK              20-20-00

   Pay  Computertech plc              or order
        Fifty seven dollars only      $67—

   ⑈000022⑈ 82⑈ 00001⑈ 00593201⑈
   ```

2. Imagine you are the company signatory for cheques up to a value of $5 000. Write out three cheques for the following payments to suppliers of Computech Ltd.:

   $575.50 to Mesh Computers Ltd.

   $2 030 to TDK Corporation

   $1 550 to Airtel Ltd.

   Blank cheques are provided on the website.

QUICK TEST

1. Explain why suppliers issue invoices to customers for sales of goods or services on credit.
2. Give **four** important items of information an invoice should contain.
3. (a) Explain the difference between a trade discount and cash discount.
   (b) Give **two** reasons why a supplier may offer a credit customer a trade discount.
4. Explain **three** reasons why a customer might send a debit note to a supplier.
5. Under what circumstances would a supplier issue a credit note to a customer?
6. (a) What is a statement of account?
   (b) What explains the difference between the balance brought forward and the closing balance on a statement of account?
7. (a) What is a receipt?
   (b) Explain why suppliers issue receipts.
8. Is it necessary for a supplier to issue a receipt every time it receives a payment from a customer for goods or services supplied on credit? Explain.
9. (a) What is a cheque?
   (b) Give four important items of information it should contain.
10. Explain how a cheque can provide proof of payment.
11. Which source documents would a business issue to record the following transactions?
    - the sale of $500 of goods on credit to a regular customer
    - the return of some items from the same customer that had been delivered in error
    - the return of some damaged items to a supplier
    - the payment of a liability to a supplier by bank transfer.
12. Which source documents would a business expect to receive for the following transactions?
    - the purchase of $10 of goods with cash
    - the purchase of $350 of goods on credit from a regular supplier
    - the payment of the account balance outstanding with the same supplier.

Business documents

Unit 1.4 Books of prime entry

AIMS

By the end of this unit you should be able to

- explain the advantage of using various **books of prime entry**
- explain the use of and process accounting data in the books of prime entry – **cash book, petty cash book sales journal, purchases journal, sales returns journal, purchases returns journal** and **general journal**
- post the **ledger account** entries from the books of prime entry
- explain, calculate and account for trade discount (cash discount is dealt with in Unit 1.5).

1.4.1 What is a book of prime entry?

A journal is divided up into specialised books to make record keeping easier

Business documents, notably invoices, credit notes, receipts and cheque counterfoils, are the source documents for the book-keeping system of a business. ▶ **1.3**

As a business grows in size, the number and different types of transactions and the number of business documents it issues and receives will increase. Keeping these records simple and up to date can become quite difficult and time consuming. To keep the task manageable a business will use different **books of prime entry**. These are:

Books of prime entry	Types of transaction recorded
Purchases journal	Purchase invoices received for goods purchased on credit
Purchases return journal	Credit notes received for goods purchased on credit returned to suppliers
Sales journal	Sales invoices issued for goods sold on credit
Sales returns journal	Credit notes issued for goods sold on credit returned by customers
Cash book	Cash and bank receipts and payments
Petty cash book	Small, sundry cash payments
General journal	All other transactions that do not fit any other book of prime entry

Books of prime entry are also called books of original entry or day books. This is because transactions will initially be recorded in these books at the end of each day of trading and in the order they occur. Each book provides a list of transactions in date order and together they will provide a complete diary record of every business document issued or received by the business. This makes it easier to transfer these entries to different accounts in the ledger, usually at the end of each month, as shown in the following diagram:

▼ The book-keeping system in business

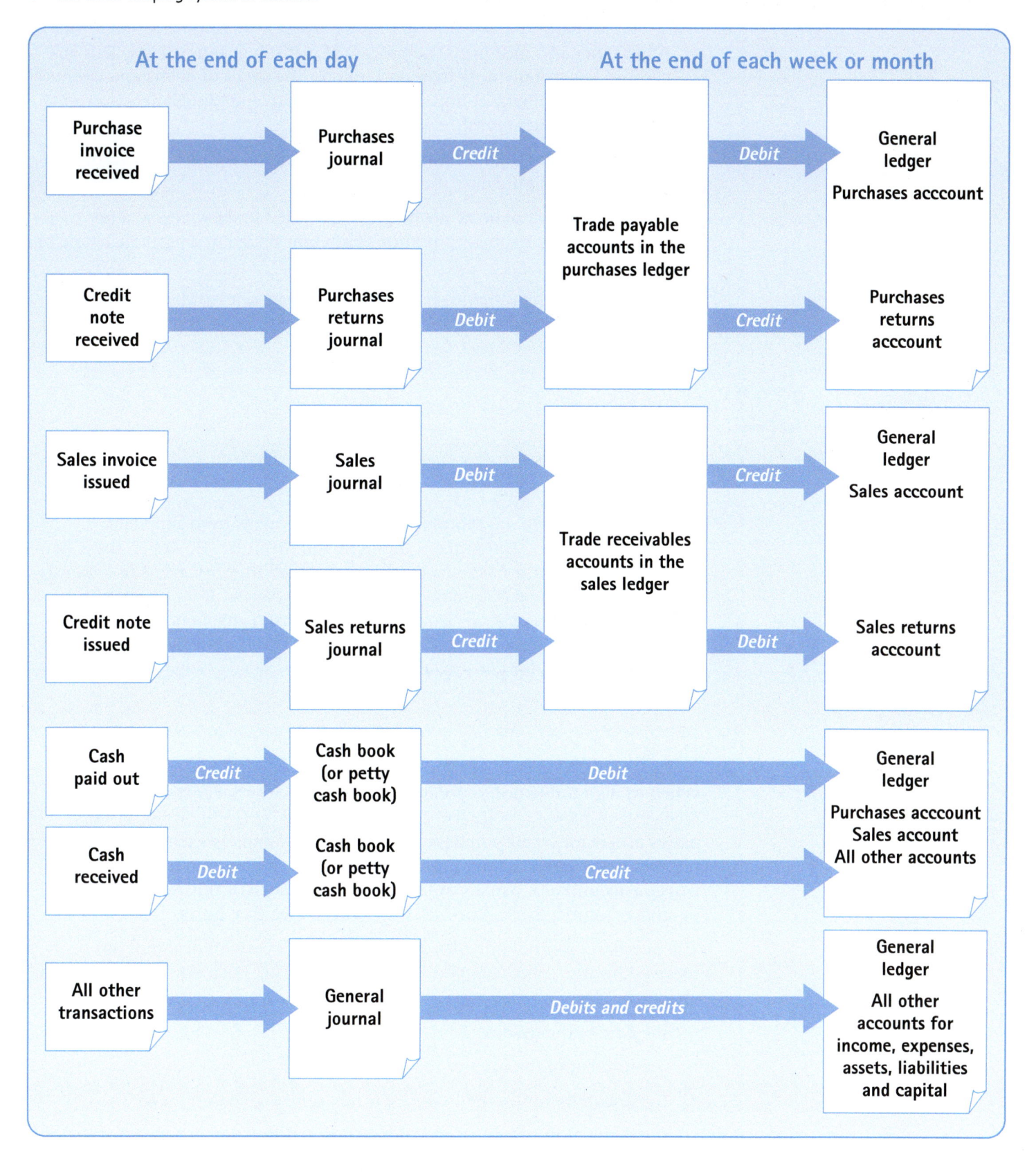

At the end of each day   **At the end of each week or month**

Source document	Book of prime entry		Ledger account (subsidiary)		General ledger account
Purchase invoice received	Purchases journal	Credit →	Trade payable accounts in the purchases ledger	Debit →	General ledger — Purchases account
Credit note received	Purchases returns journal	Debit →		Credit →	Purchases returns account
Sales invoice issued	Sales journal	Debit →	Trade receivables accounts in the sales ledger	Credit →	General ledger — Sales account
Credit note issued	Sales returns journal	Credit →		Debit →	Sales returns account
Cash paid out	Cash book (or petty cash book)	Credit		Debit →	General ledger — Purchases account, Sales account, All other accounts
Cash received	Cash book (or petty cash book)	Debit		Credit →	
All other transactions	General journal			Debits and credits →	General ledger — All other accounts for income, expenses, assets, liabilities and capital

Books of prime entry 45

Grouping together similar transactions into different books of prime entry has a number of advantages:

- It simplifies and speeds up the process of recording transactions. This is because it is usually only necessary to post the totals of debits and credits on each of the books of prime entry to the corresponding ledger accounts at the end of each month. ➤ 1.7

- It makes it easier to locate details about individual transactions according to their type and the date they occurred.

- It allows the task of book-keeping to be divided up between several different people in an organisation, each one skilled in a particular type of transaction.

This unit looks at the purchases, purchases returns, sales and sales returns journals. Units 1.5 and 1.6 in turn consider the cash book and the general journal.

1.4.2 The purchases journal

Purchases are goods bought from suppliers for the sole purpose of selling them on to customers

Like all businesses, Malik Motors buys all sorts of items from suppliers, including machinery, computer equipment and furniture. However, these items are not intended for resale to its customers. Instead they are assets or expense items used up in the day-to-day running of the business. It is important to separate these types of goods from those it buys from suppliers with the sole purpose of selling them at a profit to customers. This is done by recording only those goods it buys for resale as **purchases**.

Invoices received by a business for purchases on credit of goods for resale are recorded in its purchases journal

When Malik Motors orders goods for resale from a supplier the business receives a purchase invoice for the amount owed on credit. Malik Motors places orders for credit purchases from different suppliers each day and receives many purchase invoices. These invoices are entered into its **purchases journal**, usually at the end of each day. For this reason the purchases journal is also known as the **purchases day book**.

The purchases journal provides a diary record of every invoice that has been received from suppliers of goods intended for resale. Each entry will normally include:

- the date of the invoice
- the number of the invoice received
- the final amount on the invoice for the items purchased on credit
- the name of the supplier and the unique account number (A/C) of the trade payable account for that supplier in the purchases ledger of the business.

Illustration 1.11 shows the purchases journal kept by Malik Motors for the month of September. It records details from purchase invoices received from Parts Direct Ltd., Paint Your Wagon Ltd. and the Everymake Motor Spares Company for the supply of goods on credit to Malik Motors during that month.

1.11 AN EXAMPLE OF A PURCHASES JOURNAL

Purchases journal — Malik Motors

Date	Description	Invoice number	Amount $
Sep 8	Parts Direct Ltd. A/C 0346	239	360 ①
Sep 10	Paint Your Wagon Ltd. A/C 7881	5378	296 ②
Sep 19	Everymake Motor Spares Co A/C 9001	331	198 ③
Sep 25	Everymake Motor Spares Co A/C 9001	349	540 ④
Sep 30	Transfer to purchases account		$1 394 ⑤

Transferring entries from the purchases journal or any other book of prime entry to the ledger is called **posting**. The following transfers were made by Malik from his purchases journal above:

Trade payable accounts in the purchases ledger	Purchases account in the general ledger
① ② ③ ④	⑤
Each credit purchase is posted to the credit side (Cr) of the trade payable account of the relevant supplier in the purchases ledger.	The total for credit purchases for the month is posted to the debit side (Dr) of the purchases account in the general ledger.
Each entry records the amount owed or payable to that supplier.	The debit entry records the total value of goods received by the business. The debit is therefore the double entry for all the credit purchases posted to individual trade payable accounts.
Impact: liabilities (trade payables) are increased	Impact: assets (inventory) are increased

Illustration 1.12 shows the completed accounts for trade payables and purchases in the ledger of Malik Motors for September.

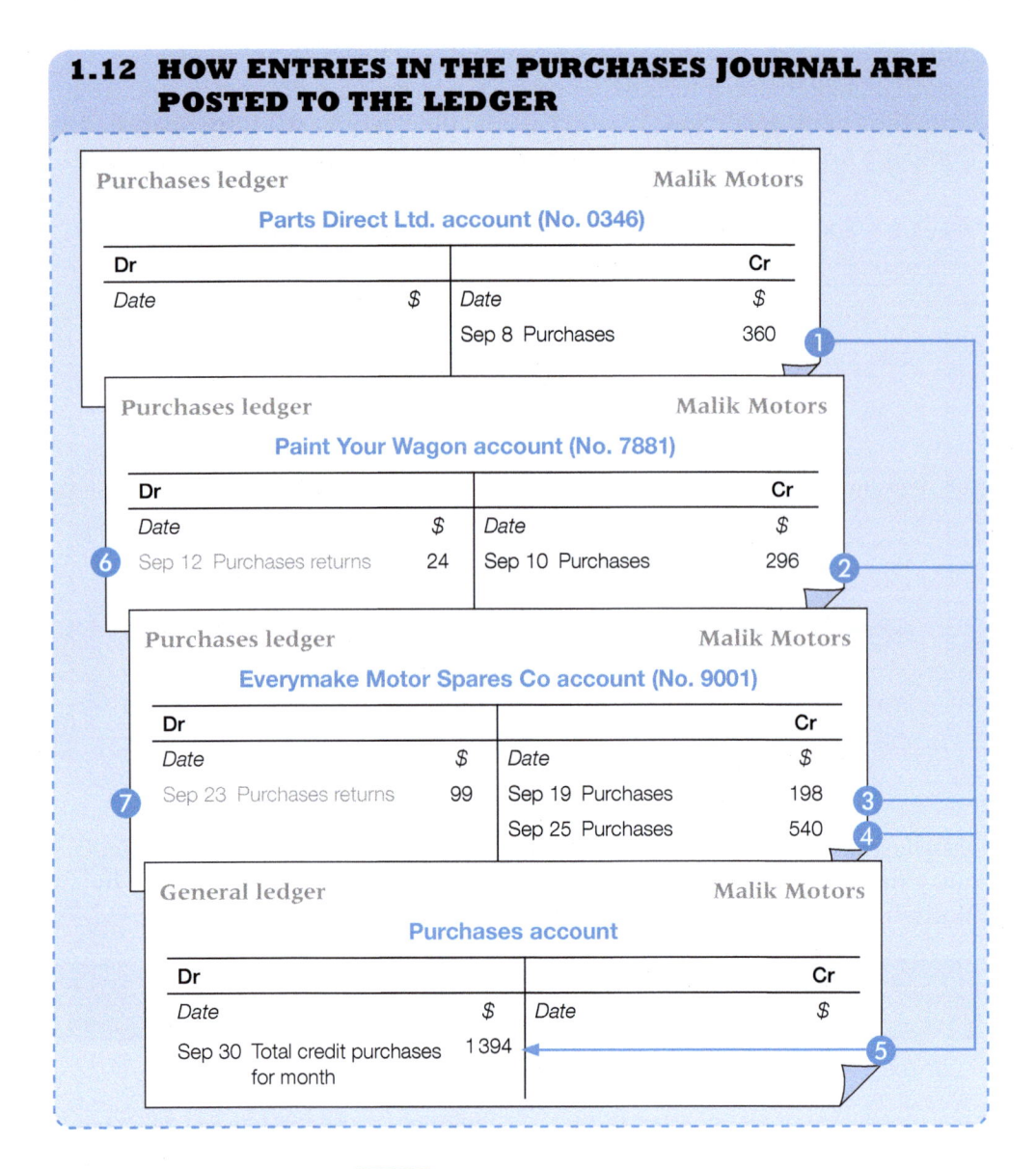

1.12 HOW ENTRIES IN THE PURCHASES JOURNAL ARE POSTED TO THE LEDGER

Purchases ledger — Malik Motors
Parts Direct Ltd. account (No. 0346)

Dr			Cr
Date	$	Date	$
		Sep 8 Purchases	360 ①

Purchases ledger — Malik Motors
Paint Your Wagon account (No. 7881)

Dr			Cr
Date	$	Date	$
⑥ Sep 12 Purchases returns	24	Sep 10 Purchases	296 ②

Purchases ledger — Malik Motors
Everymake Motor Spares Co account (No. 9001)

Dr			Cr
Date	$	Date	$
⑦ Sep 23 Purchases returns	99	Sep 19 Purchases	198 ③
		Sep 25 Purchases	540 ④

General ledger — Malik Motors
Purchases account

Dr			Cr
Date	$	Date	$
Sep 30 Total credit purchases for month	1394 ⑤		

Once completed the purchases ledger provides a record of all purchases on credit from each individual trade payable, the total amount owed to each one, and the total liability of the business to all its trade payables.

The purchases account in the general ledger records the increase in the inventory of goods held by the business as a result of its purchases on credit from its suppliers. ▶ 3.2

Illustration 1.12 also shows entries that have been made to trade payable accounts for purchases returns. These are explained in the next section.

1.4.3 The purchases returns journal

Credit notes received by a business are recorded in its purchases returns journal

Sometimes Malik finds it necessary to return goods purchased from a supplier. The supplier will then issue a credit note informing Malik that his account has been credited with the value of the returned items. ▶ 1.3

Malik records the credit notes he receives in his **purchases returns journal**. For each entry he records:

- the date the credit note was issued
- the number of the credit note received
- the total value of the credit note
- the name of the supplier and the unique account number of the trade payable account for that supplier in the purchases ledger.

The fundamentals of accounting

1.13 AN EXAMPLE OF A PURCHASES RETURNS JOURNAL

Purchases returns journal — Malik Motors

Date	Description	Credit note number	Amount $
Sep 12	Paint Your Wagon Ltd. A/C 7881	R675	24 ⑥
Sep 23	Everymake Motor Spares Co A/C 9001	CN457/9	99 ⑦
Sep 30	Transfer to purchases returns account		123

General ledger — Malik Motors

Purchases returns account

Dr			Cr
Date	$	Date	$
		Sep 30 Total purchases returns for month	123 ⑧

Illustration 1.13 shows the purchases returns journal of Malik Motors for the month of September. It records credit notes received from Paint Your Wagon Ltd. and Everymake Motors Spares Company on 12 and 23 September for wrongly supplied and damaged items returned to them by Malik.

Entries from the purchases returns journal were posted to ledger accounts as follows:

Trade payable accounts in the purchases ledger	Purchases returns account in the general ledger
⑥ ⑦	⑧
The value of each credit note received from a supplier for returned items is posted to the debit side (Dr) of the trade payable account of that supplier (see illustration 1.12).	The total value of items returned for the month (8) is posted to the credit side (Dr) of the purchases account in the general ledger (see illustration 1.13).
Each entry records a reduction in the amount owed or payable to that supplier.	The credit entry records the total value of goods returned to suppliers by the business. The credit is therefore the double entry for all the debits for returns posted to individual trade payable accounts.
Impact: liabilities (trade payables) are reduced	Impact: assets (inventory) are decreased

Books of prime entry

ACTIVITY 1.11

Date	Description	Supplier	Account	Document	Amount $
2	Purchase: 20 ltrs gloss paint	Paint It All plc	S1	Invoice 710	200
8	Purchase: plaster boards	Paint It All plc	S1	Invoice 777	150
16	Purchase: 40 bags of cement	Bricks'n'Fix Ltd.	S2	Invoice 203	400
19	Returns: 5 ltrs gloss paint	Paint It All plc	S1	Credit note	50
26	Purchase: 100 paving slabs	Bricks'n'Fix Ltd.	S2		700

Paul is a self-employed painter, decorator and builder. He likes to keep full accounting records for all the items he buys on credit. His transactions over the last month are listed in the table above.

1. Prepare a simple purchases journal and purchases returns journal and enter the transactions above into them.

2. Calculate and show the totals for purchases on credit and purchase returns at the end of the month.

3. How much in total did Paul owe at the end of the month to (a) Paint It All plc; (b) Bricks'n'Fix Ltd.?

4. Post the journal entries to the following accounts in Paul's ledger:
   - purchases ledger: trade payable account for Paint It All plc (account no. S1)
   - purchases ledger: trade payable account for Bricks'n'Fix Ltd. (account no. S2)
   - general ledger: purchases account
   - general ledger: purchases returns account.

5. Explain the advantages of maintaining journals for purchases and purchases returns.

1.4.4 The sales journal

Invoices issued by a business for credit sales to its customers are recorded in its sales journal

Like other businesses that keep full accounting records, Malik Motors enters all the sales on credit it makes to customers in its sales journal. The **sales journal** provides the business with a diary record of every sales invoice it has issued to its credit customers or trade receivables. ➤ 1.2

The sales journal is also referred to as the **sales day book**. This is because at the end of each day copies of all invoices issued during the day will usually be entered into the book. Each entry should include:

- the date of the credit sale
- the number of the invoice issued
- the final amount on the invoice for the items supplied on credit
- the name of the customer and the unique account number of the trade receivable account for that customer in the sales ledger of the business.

Illustration 1.14 shows the sales journal kept by Malik Motors for the month of September. It shows that sales of car parts and other goods were made on credit to a number of different customers.

These credit customers are trade receivables for Malik's business and each customer is identified in the books of the business by a unique account reference or number.

1.14 AN EXAMPLE OF A SALES JOURNAL

Sales journal — Malik Motors

Date	Description	Invoice number	Amount $	
Sep 4	Travelsafe Taxis Ltd. A/C 00045	MM152	108	⑨
Sep 7	Sundown Coach Tours A/C 00101	MM153	3 240	⑩
Sep 15	Travelsafe Taxis Ltd. A/C 00045	MM154	54	⑪
Sep 22	Horsepower Ltd. A/C 00112	MM155	900	⑫
Sep 30	Transfer to sales account		4 302	⑬

Entries from the sales journal were then posted to ledger accounts as follows:

Trade receivable accounts in the sales ledger	Sales account in the general ledger
⑨ ⑩ ⑪ ⑫	⑬
The value on each sales invoice issued to a supplier is posted to the debit side (Dr) of the trade receivable account of that customer.	The total value of credit sales for the month is posted to the credit side (Dr) of the sales account in the general ledger.
Each entry records an increase in the amount owed to the business by that customer.	The credit entry records the total value of goods supplied to credit customers by the business. The credit is therefore the double entry for all the debits to individual trade receivable accounts.
Impact: assets (trade receivables) are increased	Impact: assets (inventory) are decreased

Illustration 1.15 on the next page shows the completed accounts for trade receivables and sales in the ledger of Malik Motors for September.

Books of prime entry

1.15 HOW ENTRIES IN THE SALES JOURNAL ARE POSTED TO THE LEDGER

Sales ledger — Malik Motors

Travelsafe Taxis Ltd. account (No. 00045)

Dr			Cr
Date	$	Date	$
⑨ Sep 4 Sales	108	Sep 17 Sales returns	10 ⑭
⑪ Sep 15 Sales	54		

Sales ledger — Malik Motors

Sundown Coach Tours account (No. 00101)

Dr			Cr
Date	$	Date	$
⑩ Sep 7 Sales	3 240		

Sales ledger — Malik Motors

Horsepower Ltd. account (No. 00112)

Dr			Cr
Date	$	Date	$
⑫ Sep 22 Sales	900	Sep 25 Sales returns	180 ⑮

General ledger — Malik Motors

Sales account

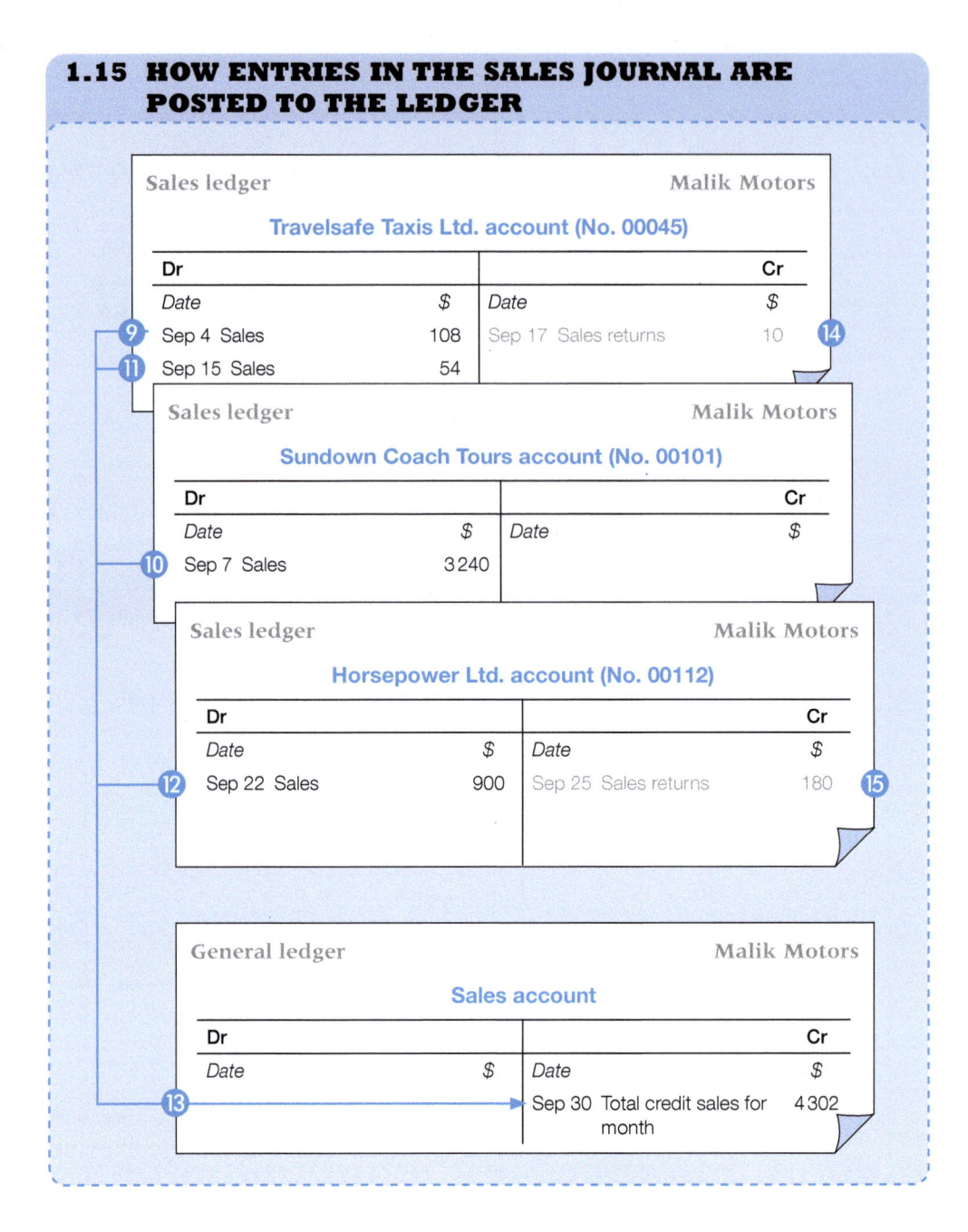

Dr			Cr
Date	$	Date	$
⑬		Sep 30 Total credit sales for month	4 302

Once completed the sales ledger provides a record of all sales on credit to each individual trade receivable. It shows the total amount owed by each one and the total asset value to the business to all its trade receivables. ➤ 3.2

The illustration also shows entries to trade receivable accounts for sales returns. These are explained in the next section.

1.4.5 The sales returns journal

Copies of credit notes issued by a supplier will be recorded in its sales returns journal

Credit customers will sometimes return goods to Malik Motors because:

- the wrong goods were delivered to them
- the goods they were supplied were damaged or faulty
- the goods were of poor quality.

When this happens the business will issue credit notes informing those customers that their accounts have been credited with the value of the returned items. ➤ 1.3

Malik Motors will also issue credit notes to those customers who have been mistakenly overcharged on an invoice. Like any other supplier, Malik Motors records the credit notes it issues at the end of each day in its **sales returns journal**.

Each entry to the sales journal will include:

- the date the credit note was issued
- the number of the credit note
- the total amount of the credit note
- the name of the customer and the unique account number of the trade receivable account of that customer in the sales ledger of the business.

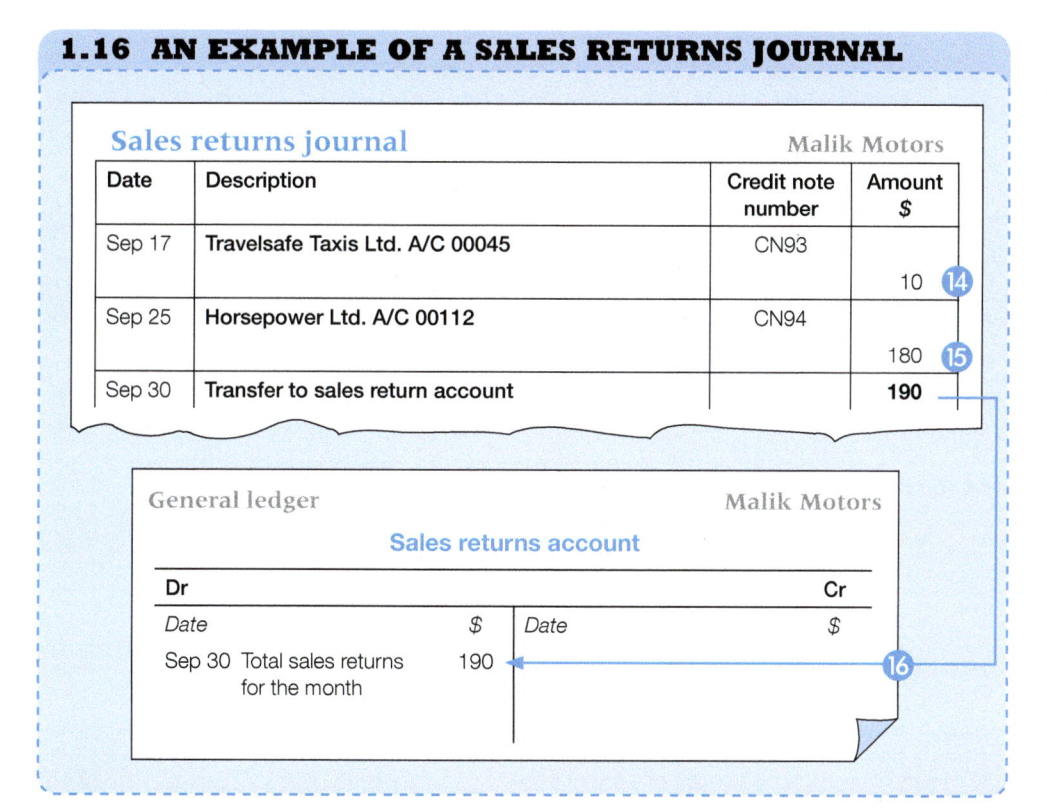

Illustration 1.16 shows an extract from the sales returns journal of Malik Motors for the month of September.

1.16 AN EXAMPLE OF A SALES RETURNS JOURNAL

Sales returns journal — Malik Motors

Date	Description	Credit note number	Amount $
Sep 17	Travelsafe Taxis Ltd. A/C 00045	CN93	10 ⑭
Sep 25	Horsepower Ltd. A/C 00112	CN94	180 ⑮
Sep 30	Transfer to sales return account		**190**

General ledger — Malik Motors

Sales returns account

Dr				Cr
Date		$	Date	$
Sep 30	Total sales returns for the month	190		⑯

Books of prime entry 53

Entries from the sales journal were posted to ledger accounts as follows:

Trade receivable accounts in the sales ledger	Sales returns account in the general ledger
⑭ ⑮	⑯
The value on each credit note issued to a customer is posted to the credit side (Cr) of the trade receivable account of that customer (see illustration 1.15).	The total value of sales returns for the month is posted to the debit side (Dr) of the sales returns account in the general ledger (see illustration 1.16).
Each entry records a reduction in the amount owed to the business by that customer.	The debit entry records the total value of goods returned to the business by credit customers. The debit is therefore the double entry for all the credits to individual trade receivable accounts.
Impact: assets (trade receivables) are decreased	Impact: assets (inventory) are increased

ACTIVITY 1.12

Date	Description	Customer	Account	Document	Amount $
4	Credit sale: Jumpers × 3	Snuggle Shop	C1	Invoice 27	150
9	Credit sale: Socks × 10 pairs	FootFall Ltd.	C2	Invoice 28	40
14	Credit sale: Baby clothes × 5	Just Kidz	C3	Invoice 29	80
15	Credit sale: Gloves × 5 pairs	Snuggle Shop	C1	Invoice 30	75
21	Returned items: Socks × 1 pair	FootFall Ltd.	C2	Credit note 2	4
27	Returned items: Jumper × 1	Snuggle Shop	C1	Credit note 3	50

Maria is the owner of a small business called Knit Quick, which makes and sells personalised knitted clothes to order. She likes to keep full accounting records for all the things she buys and sells on credit. Her sales transactions over the last month are listed in the table above.

1. Prepare a simple sales journal and sales returns journal and enter the transactions above into them.

2. Calculate the totals for credit sales and sales returns at the end of the month.

3. Post the journal entries to the following accounts in Maria's ledger for Knit Quick:
   - sales ledger: trade receivable account for Snuggle Shop (account no. C1)
   - sales ledger: trade receivable account for Footfall Ltd. (account no. C2)
   - sales ledger: trade receivable account for Just Kidz (account no. C3)
   - general ledger: sales account
   - general ledger: sales returns account.

4. What are the advantages of maintaining journals for sales and sales returns?

1.4.6 What is a trade discount?

Trade discounts reduce final sale prices but encourage customer loyalty and repeat sales

You will have noticed from the invoice displayed in the previous unit, and those recorded in the purchases and sales journals, that goods and services are often sold by suppliers to their customers at discounted prices. For example, Malik Motors received a 10% discount on the list price of parts it purchased from Parts Supplies Ltd. on 8 September. This reduced the **net price** charged on invoice 239 issued by Parts Supplies Ltd. to $360 from a total list price of $400 for the parts. The reduction is called a **trade discount**.

Malik Motors offers its credit customers a 10% trade discount on the list prices of goods and services it sells to them. For example, when Horsepower Ltd. purchased 10 car batteries on credit from Malik Motors on 22 September, Malik issued the company with an invoice for $900 which included a 10% discount on their usual retail price of $100 each.

Businesses will often reduce the prices at which they sell goods to their business customers. This is because another business does not want to pay the full retail price of any item it intends to sell on otherwise it will not be able earn a profit. Similarly, if the item will be used up in the running of the business it will want to keep its expenses as low as possible.

A trade discount is a fixed amount or percentage deducted from the catalogue, retail or list price of an item by a supplier when it is sold to another business. A trade discount is not normally offered to members of the public when they buy the same goods or services.

Like many other businesses, Malik Motors offers a trade discount to its business customers for the following reasons:

- to encourage its customers to place larger and repeat orders
- to persuade its customers to remain loyal to the business when placing future orders
- to encourage its customers to recommend the business to others
- to attract customers away from competing suppliers
- to increase sales.

Some large businesses may offer trade discounts of 20% or even more to their most important customers. However, because Malik Motors is a relatively small business it cannot afford to offer its business customers a trade discount of more than 10% on each item it sells. ➤ 5.1

For example, the business purchases car batteries for resale from Parts Direct Ltd. at a net price of $80 each. It then then adds a mark-up of $20 (or 25%) to this for profit. Malik Motors advertises batteries for sale to its customers at a retail price of $100 each. A trade discount of 20% – that is, $20 – on this price would wipe out any profit the business could make from their sale to customers.

So, instead Malik discounts his retail price to his customers by 10% to $90 leaving his business with a profit of $10 per battery sold.

Books of prime entry

▼ Calculating a trade discount

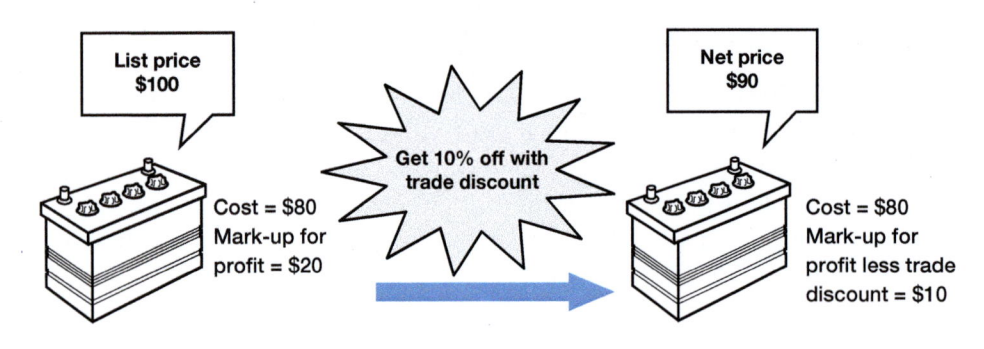

List price $100
Cost = $80
Mark-up for profit = $20

Get 10% off with trade discount

Net price $90
Cost = $80
Mark-up for profit less trade discount = $10

The trade discount offered by a supplier to a credit customer will vary according to:

- **the size of the customer order**: the bigger the order the bigger the discount that may be given because the more revenue and profit the supplier will earn from the order

- **the importance of the customer to the supplier**: large businesses that place regular orders with the supplier may be offered more generous discounts than smaller customers

- **how long the customer has been placing orders with the supplier**: new customers may receive lower discounts than customers who have had an account with the supplier for a long time

- **the profit made on each item sold**: the lower the amount of profit earned by a supplier on the sale of an item, the lower the trade discount it is likely to offer its customers. ➤ **5.1**

Trade discounts received by a business or allowed by the same business may be recorded in its purchases and sales journals for information. However, trade discounts received or allowed do not need to be posted to ledger accounts. This is because only the final price of items purchased or sold net of any trade discounts are recorded in the ledger.

ACTIVITY 1.13

Roy Aishani runs a small business. During August last year he issued the following invoices for credit sales:

Date	Description	Customer	Account	Invoice	Amount before trade discount $
Aug 5	120 boxes	A Deyhan	143	9/056	3 000
9	100 boxes	M Lauder	178	9/057	2 500
14	400 boxes	T Ebrahim	98	9/058	10 000
21	260 boxes	D Aaliyah	34	9/059	6 500

All the amounts shown were before Roy had deducted a trade discount of 5%.

1 Calculate the total net price to pay on each invoice (i.e. after the deduction of a 5% trade discount).

2 Write up Roy's sales journal with the following details from each invoice: customer name and account number; goods supplied; invoice number; total price before trade discount; the amount of the trade discount deducted; the total net price or amount receivable.

3 Calculate and show the total for credit sales at the end of the month to transfer to the sales account in the sales ledger.

During the same month Roy received the following invoices for his purchases on credit from suppliers:

Date	Description	Customer	Account	Invoice	Amount before trade discount $
Aug 1	500 boxes	Box Clever Ltd.	23	B17/1890	5 000
12	Bubble wrap x 1 000 metres	Wrapit Co SA	11	WX56/897	2 000
22	500 boxes	Box Clever Ltd.	23	B17/1967	5 000

All the amounts shown were before the deduction of 10% trade discount by his suppliers.

4 Calculate the total net price to pay on each invoice (i.e. after the deduction of a 10% trade discount).

5 Write up Roy's purchases journal with the following details from each invoice: supplier name and account number; goods supplied; invoice number; the total price before trade discount, the amount of the trade discount deducted; the total net price or amount payable.

6 Calculate and show the total for credit purchases at the end of the month to transfer to the sales account in the purchases ledger.

Books of prime entry

QUICK TEST

1. (a) What is a book of prime entry?; (b) List **six** books of prime entry.

2. Explain the advantages of having six books of prime entry.

3. Henna owns a hardware store. During the month of July last she received the following purchases invoices from suppliers:

Date		Invoice no.	Details
Jul	5	3780	Purchase invoice for $340 received from G Smith
	14	2167	Purchase invoice for $1,700 received from Boxhill Ltd.
	23	8761	Purchase invoice for $940 received from Camset Ltd.
	26	2314	Purchase invoice for $800 received from Boxhill Ltd.

Write up entries for the above transactions in the following:

(a) the purchases journal (remember to add up and show the total amount to be transferred to the purchases account at the end of the month); (b) the trade payable accounts in the purchases ledger.

4. Raakesh runs a small business supplying camera equipment. During last September he received the following credit notes from suppliers for goods purchased on credit that he had returned to them:

Date		Credit note no.	Details
Sep	4	C5689	Equipment with a value of $3 400 returned to Prism Ltd.
	9	CR453	Equipment with a value of $845 returned to Tripark Ltd.
	17	C5780	Equipment with a value of $560 returned to Prism Ltd.

Write up entries for the above transactions in the following:

(a) the purchases returns journal (remember to add up and show the total amount to be transferred to the purchases returns account at the end of the month); (b) the trade payable accounts in the purchases ledger.

5. Samuel runs an online business selling fishing equipment. During the month of April last he issued the following sales invoices to customers:

Date		Invoice no.	Details
Apr	3	145	Sales invoice for $420 issued to M Kolsi
	7	146	Sales invoice for $1 230 issued to W H Lawrence
	18	147	Sales invoice for $355 issued to K Moore
	27	148	Sales invoice for $225 issued to M Kolsi

Write up entries for the above transactions in the following:

(a) the sales journal (remember to add up and show the total amount to be transferred to the sales account at the end of the month); (b) the trade receivable accounts in the sales ledger.

6 Mario runs an online business selling fishing equipment. During the month of April last he issued the following sales invoices to customers:

Date	Invoice no.	Details
Sep 4	C5689	Equipment with a value of $3 400 returned to Prism Ltd.
9	CR453	Equipment with a value of $845 returned to Tripark Ltd.
17	C5780	Equipment with a value of $560 returned to Prism Ltd.

Write up entries for the above transactions in the following:

(a) the sales journal (remember to add up and show the total amount to be transferred to the sales returns account at the end of the month); (b) the trade receivable accounts in the sales ledger.

7 An item has a list price of $22.00. The supplier offers a credit customer a trade discount of 15%. What price will appear on the sales invoice issued to the customer to request payment?

8 Susan supplies packs of coffee to local bars and cafés. In her first month of trading in August last year she received or issued the following source documents for transactions:

Date	Source document	Details
Aug 9	Purchase invoice 2790	Received from Barista Ltd. for $1 400 less a 20% trade discount
11	Sales invoice 196	Issued to Café Mango for $2 000 less a 10% trade discount
15	Credit note C456	Received from Barista Ltd. for goods returned that had been invoiced for $400 less a 20% trade discount
21	Sales invoice 197	Issued to Café Mango for $1 800 less a 10% trade discount
17	Credit note CR23	Issued to Café Mango for goods returned that had been invoiced for $300 less a 10% trade discount
28	Purchase invoice 3078	Received from Barista Ltd. for $2 500 less a 20% trade discount

Use this information to write up the following books for Susan's business for the month of August:

(a) the relevant books of prime entry; (b) the trade payable account for Barista Ltd.; and (c) the trade receivable account for Café Mango.

Unit 1.5   The cash book

AIMS

By the end of this unit you should be able to

- explain the dual function of a **cash book** both as a book of prime entry and as a **ledger account for bank and cash**
- explain, calculate and account for **cash discount**
- understand the use and purpose of a **bank statement**
- update the cash book for bank charges, bank interest paid and received, correction of errors, credit transfers, direct debits, dividends and standing orders
- explain the use of and record payments and receipts made by bank transfers and other electronic means
- understand the purpose of and prepare a bank reconciliation statement to include bank errors, uncredited deposits and unpresented cheques
- explain and apply the **imprest system of petty cash**

1.5.1 Accounting for cash

Businesses hold cash in hand and in bank accounts to make payments and to receive monies

Businesses hold cash to make payments for the goods and services they buy. Most keep cash on their premises to make immediate cash purchases or to give change to customers who pay in cash. Cash held on the business premises is called **cash in hand**.

However, keeping too much cash on the premises can be risky. It can be stolen if the premises are broken into or even lost in a fire. Most businesses keep a much larger reserve of cash in a bank account. This is called **cash in bank** and is used to make and receive payments by cheques and electronic bank transfers. ▶ 1.3

Cash in hand and cash in bank are current assets because cash is used up quickly to pay for day-to-day business expenses. Any cash received will increase cash in hand or cash in bank. Any cash paid out will reduce cash in hand or cash in bank.

Every transaction of a business involving the exchange of cash should be recorded in its **cash book**. The cash book of a business is used to record all its cash receipts and payments, including bank deposits and withdrawals in the date order in which they occur.

▲ Cash in hand and cash bank are current assets used to make payments

The cash book is both a book of prime entry and also the ledger for cash and bank transactions

As so many business transactions involve the exchange of cash it saves time and effort to record them just once in a cash book. It is the book of prime entry for cash and bank transactions and also serves as the ledger accounts for cash and bank in the general ledger. ➤ 1.6

By completing its cash book a business is also completing its cash account and bank account. This helps a business in the following ways:

- All money paid out or received by a business can be recorded on the same page.

- It provides an up-to-date record of how much cash the business has available in hand or in bank to make payments.

- Any errors made recording cash transactions can be checked against total cash received or paid out and the balances for cash in hand and cash in bank.

Knowing how much cash is available is very important in business. A business may be very good at selling goods on credit at a profitable price but if it runs out of cash before its credit customers pay for their purchases the business will be unable to pay its running expenses. A business that runs out of cash and is unable to pay its debts will be **insolvent** and if it is unable to raise cash from other sources, such as a bank loan or the sale of some assets, it will be forced to stop trading. ➤ 5.1

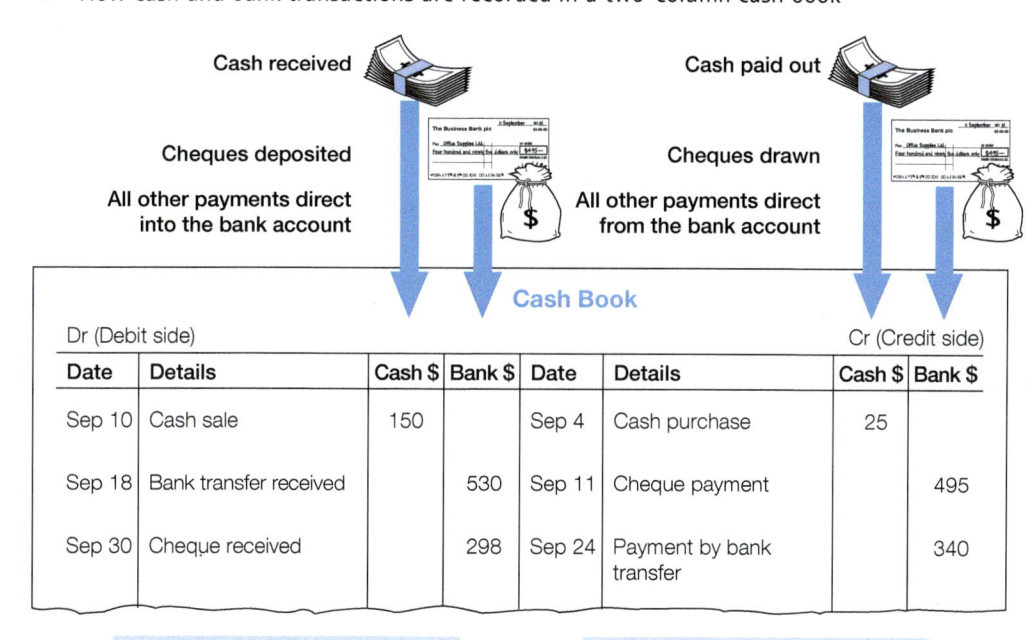

▼ How cash and bank transactions are recorded in a two-column cash book

Cash Book

Dr (Debit side)					Cr (Credit side)		
Date	Details	Cash $	Bank $	Date	Details	Cash $	Bank $
Sep 10	Cash sale	150		Sep 4	Cash purchase	25
Sep 18	Bank transfer received		530	Sep 11	Cheque payment		495
Sep 30	Cheque received		298	Sep 24	Payment by bank transfer		340

(Dr) Money received = increase in asset of cash

(Cr) Money paid out = decrease in asset of cash

A cash book has a debit side and a credit side, and each side has columns for cash in hand and for bank transactions

The diagram shows a simple extract from a cash book. Notice that the book is arranged like other ledger accounts in a "T" format. It has a debit side and a credit side but each side has two columns, one for cash transactions and the other for bank transactions. ➤ 1.2

The cash book   61

Entries to the debit side of the cash book record money received – an increase in the asset of cash held by the business:

- Cash received is entered in the cash column. For example, the cash book shows $150 of cash received by the business from a cash sale on 10 September.

- Any payments received and paid into the bank account, whether by cheque or bank transfer, are entered in the bank column. The cash book contains debit entries for a payment of $530 received by bank transfer on 18 September and a cheque for $298 received on 30 September.

Entries to the credit side of the cash book record money paid out – a reduction in the asset of cash held by the business:

- Cash paid out is entered in the cash column. For example, the cash book contains a credit entry for a payment of $25 from cash in hand on 4 September.

- Any payments made from the bank account by cheque or by bank transfer are entered into the bank column. In the simple cash book on page 68 there are credit entries for a cheque issued by the business on 11 September and a transfer of $340 from its bank account to the bank account of a supplier on 24 September.

Only a bank current account is used to make and receive payments

A business may have a number of bank accounts. However, only the bank current account of the business is used to make and receive regular payments from the trading activities of the business and should be recorded in its cash book.

A **bank current account** is an account that allows the account holder to make and receive payments using cheques and different forms of bank transfer.

Some banks charge account holders for using their current accounts, for example for each cash withdrawal and deposit and for each cheque or bank transfer received or made. Bank charges are an expense and will reduce the profit of the business.

In contrast, a **bank deposit account** is a bank account used to accept usually much larger and much less frequent deposits and withdrawals of cash than a current account. Bank deposit accounts are used for business savings and, unlike current accounts, will usually pay interest on the money held in them. Any interest paid on bank deposits or savings will increase the income of the business and, therefore, its profit for the year.

▼ How bank current accounts and deposit accounts compare

	Bank current account	Bank deposit account
Is the account used for day-to-day transactions?	Yes	No
Is it used for savings?	No	Yes
Does it pay interest?	No	Yes
Does it provide a cheque book to make payments from the account?	Yes	No
Can the account be overdrawn to borrow money from the bank on a short-term basis?	Yes	No
Are transactions recorded in the cash book?	Yes	No

Most business transactions today involve bank transfers to and from the bank current account of a business. To make a payment a business must instruct its bank to transfer money from its current account to the bank account of the payee – the named individual or organisation due to receive the payment. The business can do this by issuing a cheque or by asking its bank to set up a one-off or regular electronic bank transfer. The business can instruct its bank to do this over the telephone or by using banking facilities on the Internet.

Each instruction must include:

- the named holder of the bank account to receive payment
- the unique identification number of the bank account to receive payment
- the amount to be transferred to that bank account
- the date the transfer should take place.

Bank transfers are a fast and easy way of paying money owed to suppliers on a regular basis, for example to pay telephone and electricity charges each month or quarter or to settle accounts for goods bought on credit.

▼ Types of electronic bank transfer

Payment method	Bank instructions
Credit transfer	Pay a given amount of money to the bank account of a named individual or organisation on a specified date.
Standing order	Pay a fixed amount to the bank account of a named individual or organisation on the same day each month, quarter or year.
Direct debit	Pay regular but variable amounts to the bank account of a named individual or organisation. The amount and date of each payment will be as instructed by that individual or organisation. The main difference between a direct debit and a standing order is that the person or organisation being paid will specify the amounts to be paid and when each payment is required.
Bank debit card	This is a payment card used to make one-off, often small credit transfers without the need for prior instructions.

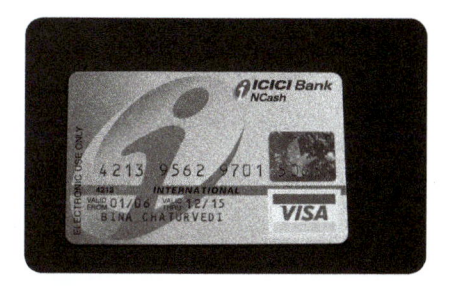

▲ Some bank debit cards

The cash book 63

The only time a transaction to or from the bank deposit account of a business will be recorded in its cash book is when:

- cash is withdrawn from cash in hand to pay into the deposit account or transferred from its current account to its deposit account
- money withdrawn from the bank deposit account is added to cash in hand or is transferred back to the bank current account.

1.5.2 Using and balancing off the cash book

In October, Malik Motors recorded the following transactions:

Date	Description	Amount $	Key
Oct 1	Balances brought down from the end of September: Cash in hand Cash in bank	180 342	A
3	Cash purchase for consignment of spark plugs	133	B1
4	Cash paid to window cleaner	17	B2
5	Cash sale	520	C1
6	Cash deposited in bank current account	200	C2
8	Cash sale deposited on the same day into bank current account	80	C3
10	Cash received from Travelsafe Taxis Ltd. to pay the balance on its account at the end September; deposited into bank current account on the same day	152	C4
12	Cash added to savings in bank deposit account	300	C5
15	Cash withdrawn from bank account	100	D
18	Cheque received from Van Hire Ltd. to settle outstanding debt	67	E1
18	Bank transfer from Sundown Coach Tours to pay off balance outstanding on its account at the end of September	3 159	E2
23	Bank loan received	2 200	F
24	Cheque (no. 10125) issued to AirTech SA for cleaning and maintenance of air conditioning units	235	G1
25	Credit transfer to Mekanic Ltd. for new hydraulic lifting equipment	5 430	G2
27	Standing order to telephone company to pay for quarterly line rental	69	G3
29	Direct debit to bank account of Parts Direct Ltd. to pay off balance outstanding on account	351	G3
29	Cash sale deposited later the same day into bank current account	200	G4

These transactions were entered in the cash book of Malik Motors as shown in illustration 1.17.

1.17 A CASH BOOK

Malik Motors

Cash Book

Dr							Cr
Date	Details	Cash $	Bank $	Date	Details	Cash $	Bank $
Oct 1	Balances b/d	180	342				
Oct 5	Sales	520		Oct 3	Purchases	133	
Oct 6	Cash		200	Oct 4	Cleaning	17	
Oct 8	Sales		80	Oct 6	Bank	200	
Oct 10	Travelsafe Taxis Ltd.		152	Oct 12	Savings	300	
Oct 15	Bank	100		Oct 15	Cash		100
Oct 18	Van Hire Ltd.		67	Oct 24	Equipment maintenance		250
Oct 18	Sundown Coach Tours		3159	Oct 25	Equipment		5430
Oct 23	Bank loan payable		2200	Oct 27	Telephone		69
Oct 29	Cash		200	Oct 29	Parts Direct Ltd.		351

We will now look in detail at how each of the transactions A to G was recorded in the cash book and the double entries they required in other ledger accounts.

A Cash in hand or in bank at the end of one month are the opening balances on the cash and bank accounts in the cash book at the start of the next month

At the end of last September Malik Motors held $180 of cash in hand and had $342 in cash in its bank current account. These were the opening balances on the cash account and bank account in its cash book for the month of October. The balances were entered to the debit side of the cash book on 1 October to show the money "received" or brought down in the book from the end of September. The entries were described as balances brought down or **balances b/d** in the cash book in illustration 1.17.

B Cash paid out for purchases of goods for resale or for expense items is a credit to cash

On 3 October Malik Motors used $133 from its cash in hand to pay for an urgent delivery of spark plugs. The transaction required the following double entries in the cash book and purchases account in the general ledger of the business. ▶ **1.7**

B1 For a cash purchase of goods for resale:

Purchases account	Cash account
Debit the account with the value of the goods received	Credit the account with cash paid out
Impact: inventory is increased	Impact: cash in hand is decreased

1.18 RECORDING A CASH PURCHASE OF GOODS FOR RESALE

Malik Motors

Cash Book

Dr							Cr
Date	Details	Cash $	Bank $	Date	Details	Cash $	Bank $
				Oct 3	Purchases	133	

(B1)

General ledger — Malik Motors

Purchases account

Dr				Cr
Date		$	Date	$
Oct 3 Cash		133		

On 4 October Malik Motors paid $17 from its cash in hand to the window cleaner for his services. The transaction required the following double entries in the cash book and the expense account for cleaning and maintenance in the general ledger. ➤ 1.7

(B2) For a cash expense:

Expense account	Cash account
Debit the account with the cash expense	Credit the account with cash paid out
Impact: expenses are increased	Impact: cash in hand is decreased

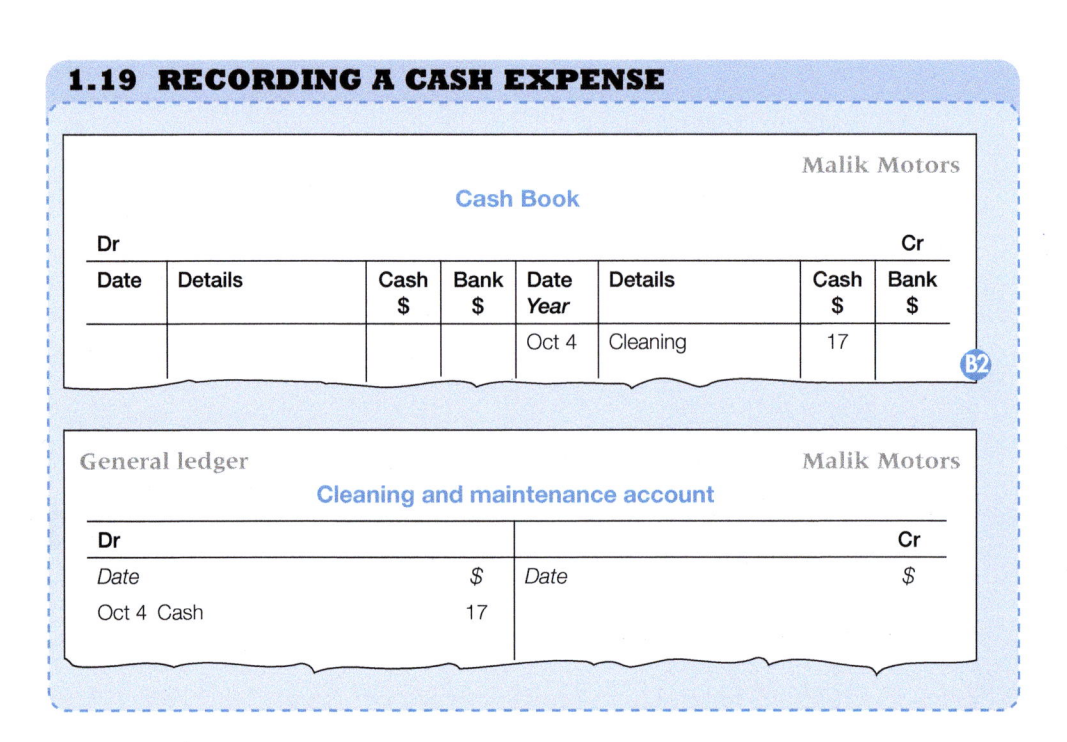

1.19 RECORDING A CASH EXPENSE

Malik Motors

Cash Book

Dr							Cr
Date	Details	Cash $	Bank $	Date *Year*	Details	Cash $	Bank $
				Oct 4	Cleaning	17	

(B2)

General ledger — Malik Motors

Cleaning and maintenance account

Dr				Cr
Date		$	Date	$
Oct 4 Cash		17		

The fundamentals of accounting

C **Cash received and deposited into the bank account requires a credit entry to cash and a debit entry to bank in the cash book**

Malik deposits most of the cash his business receives from cash sales into his bank current account. This is much safer than keeping a large amount of cash on the business premises. Movements of cash by the business to and from its bank current account require double entries to be made in the cash book.

For example, on 5 October the business received $520 from a cash sale. On 6 October $200 of the cash received was deposited into the business bank account. This meant $320 in cash was retained on the business premises.

The following double entries were therefore required to record these transactions in the ledger accounts of Malik Motors.

(C1) For a cash sale:

Cash account	Sales account
Debit the account with cash received from the cash sale	Credit the account with the cash sale of goods
Impact: cash in hand is increased	Impact: inventory is decreased

(C2) For cash received that is banked at a later date:

Bank account	Cash account
Debit the account with the cash deposit	Credit the account with the cash paid into the bank account
Impact: cash in bank is increased	Impact: cash in hand is reduced

1.20 RECORDING A CASH SALE RECEIVED AND THEN BANKED AT A LATER DATE

Malik Motors
Cash Book

	Date	Details	Cash $	Bank $	Date	Details	Cash $	Bank $
C1	Oct 5	Sales	520					
C2	Oct 6	Cash		200	Oct 6	Bank	200	

General ledger   Malik Motors
Sales account

Dr				Cr
Date		$	Date	$
			Oct 5 Cash	520

The cash book 67

The entry to the credit side shows cash of $200 leaving cash in hand to pay the bank account. The debit entry therefore records the bank receiving $200 from cash in hand.

The credit and debit entries for the cash deposited in the bank account are examples of **contra entries**. This is because the cash deposit involved a transfer from the cash account to the bank account and is therefore recorded on both sides of the cash book. ➤ **2.4**

On 8 October Malik Motors made a cash sale for $80 and banked the cash received later that same day. When this happens there is no need to record the receipt of the cash separately in the debit cash column. Instead it can be entered directly to the bank column on the debit side of the cash book as follows.

(C3) For cash received and banked the same day:

Bank account	Sales account
Debit the account with cash received	Credit the account with the cash sale of goods.
Impact: cash in bank is increased	Impact: inventory is decreased

1.21 RECORDING A CASH SALE RECEIVED AND BANKED ON THE SAME DAY

Malik Motors

Cash Book

Dr								Cr
Date	Details	Cash $	Bank $	Date	Details	Cash $	Bank $
Oct 8	Sales		80				

General ledger   Malik Motors

Sales account

Dr			Cr
Date	$	Date	$
		Oct 8 Cash	80

Similarly, when Malik Motors received $152 in cash from Travelsafe Taxis Ltd. on 10 October to pay off the balance on its trade receivable account at the end of September, the cash received was banked later that day. Only a single entry was required in the bank column on the debit side of the cash book to record the cash received.

68 The fundamentals of accounting

The double entry for the cash received was a credit entry to the trade receivable account of Travelsafe Taxis Ltd. in the sales ledger. The credit to its account reduced the amount owed by the taxi company to Malik Motors.

The transaction reduced the current asset of trade receivables of the business but increased its current asset of cash in bank instead. ➤ 1.2

(C4) For cash received from a trade receivable that is banked the same day:

Bank account	Trade receivable account
Debit the account with cash received	Credit the account with the cash received
Impact: cash in bank is increased	Impact: trade receivables are decreased

1.22 RECORDING CASH RECEIVED TO SETTLE A TRADE RECEIVABLE ACCOUNT

Malik Motors
Cash Book

Dr								Cr
Date	Details	Cash $	Bank $	Date	Details	Cash $	Bank $
Oct 10	Travelsafe Taxis Ltd.		152				

(C4)

Sales ledger — **Malik Motors**
Travelsafe Taxis Ltd. account (No. 00045)

Dr			Cr
Year	$	Year	$
Oct 1 Balance b/d	152	Oct 10 Bank	152

On 12 October Malik deposited $300 of surplus cash in hand into the bank deposit account for his business for safe keeping and to earn interest. This required a credit entry to the cash column to show cash paid out to the bank deposit account and a debit to the savings account to record the increase in the business asset.

(C5) For cash paid into a bank deposit or savings account:

Savings account	Cash (or bank) account
Debit the account with the cash deposited	Credit the account with cash withdrawn
Impact: asset is increased	Impact: cash in hand (or bank) is decreased

The cash book 69

1.23 RECORDING CASH PAID INTO THE BANK DEPOSIT ACCOUNT FOR BUSINESS SAVINGS

Malik Motors

Cash Book

Dr							Cr
Date	Details	Cash $	Bank $	Date	Details	Cash $	Bank $
				Oct 12	Savings	300	

C5

Malik Motors

General ledger

Savings account

Dr			Cr
Date	$	Date	$
Oct 12 Cash	300		

D Cash withdrawn from the bank account will require a debit to cash in hand and a credit to cash in bank in the cash book

When Malik runs short of cash in hand on the business premises he withdraws some cash from the business bank account. For example, on 15 October Malik withdrew $100 from cash in bank. This required him to make the following entries to the cash book for his business:

For cash withdrawn from the bank account:

Cash account	Bank account
Debit the account with the amount of cash received from the bank account	Credit the account with the amount of cash withdrawn
Impact: cash in hand is increased	Impact: cash in bank is decreased

1.24 RECORDING CASH WITHDRAWN FROM THE BANK ACCOUNT

Malik Motors

Cash Book

Dr							Cr
Date	Details	Cash $	Bank $	Date	Details	Cash $	Bank $
Oct 15	Bank	100		Oct 15	Cash		100

D

The credit entry shows cash of $100 being withdrawn from the bank account and being received as cash from the bank on the debit side. These entries are also examples of **contra entries**.

E **Payments received by cheque or bank transfer are recorded in the bank column on the debit side of the cash book**

On 18 October Malik Motors received a cheque issued by Van Hire Ltd. in payment for goods it had purchased on credit some months earlier. Malik took the cheque to the bank on the same day.

On the same day Malik also received notice from Sundown Coach Tours that the company had transferred $3 159 from its bank account into the bank account of Malik Motors to pay off the balance owing on its trade receivable account at the end of September. Although the outstanding debit balance on its account was $3 240 Sundown Coach Tours had deducted a cash discount of 2.5% from his balance – a sum of $81 – for early payment. ▶ **1.5.3**

The following double entries were required in the books of Malik Motors to record the receipt of the two payments from its credit customers:

(E1) For a cheque or **(E2)** bank transfer received from a trade receivable:

Bank account	Trade receivable account
Debit the account with the amount received or transferred into the account	Credit the account with the amount paid by the trade receivable
Impact: cash in bank is increased	Impact: trade receivables are decreased

1.25 RECORDING CHEQUES AND BANK TRANSFERS RECEIVED FROM TRADE RECEIVABLES

Malik Motors

Cash Book

	Dr					Cr		
	Date	Details	Cash $	Bank $	Date	Details	Cash $	Bank $
E1	Oct 18	Van Hire Ltd.		67				
E2	Oct 18	Sundown Coach Tours		3 159				

Sales ledger — **Malik Motors**

Van Hire Ltd. account (No. 0017)

Dr			Cr
Date	$	Date	$
Oct 1 Balance b/d	67	Oct 18 Bank	67

Sales ledger — **Malik Motors**

Sundown Coach Tours account (No. 00101)

Dr			Cr
Date	$	Date	$
Oct 1 Balance b/d	3 240	Oct 18 Bank	3 159
		Oct 18 Discount allowed	81
			3 240

> **F** A bank loan is a liability and will require separate ledger accounts for the loan received, subsequent loan repayments and loan interest charges

Malik Motors was successful in applying for a **commercial bank loan** for $2 200 from its bank to part-fund the purchase of some new equipment.

The loan amount was transferred into the bank account of Malik Motors on 23 October. The loan created a new liability for the business repayable over 22 months in equal monthly instalments of $100 per month.

To record the liability for the loan Malik opened a new ledger account. In addition to a credit entry for the loan received, monthly repayments were also recorded on the account. Each repayment was entered as a debit to reduce the credit balance for the loan outstanding at the end of each month.

In addition, the business also had to pay interest charges to the bank on the outstanding amount of the loan. The loan interest rate was fixed at 6% and interest charges for the first 12 months of the loan were $132 (6% of $2 200) or $11 per month ($132 ÷ 12 = $11). The loan interest charges were an additional expense of the business and so had to be recorded in a separate expense account.

Malik Motors received the bank loan on 23 October and made its first repayment with interest on 23 November. The following entries were made in the books of the business.

(F) For the bank loan received:

Bank account	Bank loan (payable) account
Debit the account with the amount of the loan received	Credit the account with the loan funds received
Impact: cash in bank is increased	Impact: liability is increased

For loan repayments:

Bank loan (payable) account	Bank account
Debit the account with the loan repayment	Credit the account with the loan repayment
Impact: liability is decreased	Impact: cash in bank is decreased

For loan interest charges:

Loan interest (expense account)	Bank account
Debit the account with the interest paid	Credit the account with the interest paid
Impact: expenses are increased	Impact: cash in bank is decreased

1.26 RECORDING A BANK LOAN RECEIVED, LOAN REPAYMENTS AND LOAN INTEREST CHARGES

Date	Details	Cash $	Bank $	Date	Details	Cash $	Bank $
F Oct 23	Bank loan		2 200				
				Nov 23	Bank loan		100
				Nov 23	Loan interest		11

General Ledger — Malik Motors
Bank loan (payable) account

Dr				Cr
Date		$	Date	$
Oct 31 Balance c/d		2 200	Oct 23 Bank	2 200
Nov 23 Bank		100	Nov 1 Balance b/d	2 200
Nov 30 Balance c/d		2 100		
		2 200		2 200

Loan amount outstanding at end of month after loan repayment

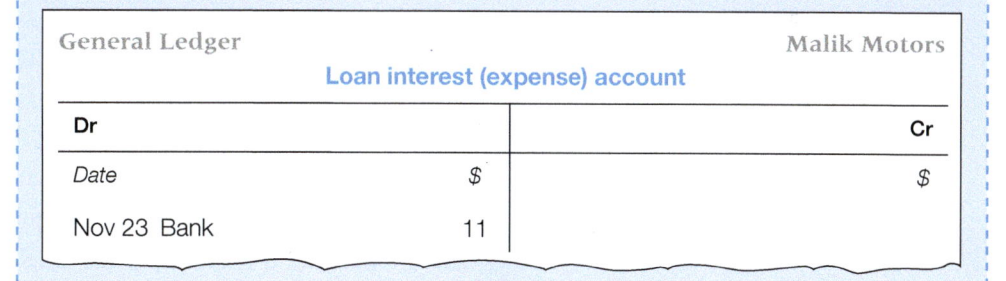

General Ledger — Malik Motors
Loan interest (expense) account

Dr			Cr
Date	$		$
Nov 23 Bank	11		

G **Payments made by cheque or bank transfer are recorded in the bank column on the credit side of the cash book**

On 24 October Malik Motors issued and sent a cheque for $235 to AirTech SA in payment for servicing the air conditioning system at the garage. The following double entries were required in the books of Malik Motors to record the payment:

(G1) **For a cheque drawn from the bank account to pay an expense:**

Equipment maintenance (expenses)	Bank account
Debit the account with the amount written on the cheque	Credit the account with the amount written on the cheque
Impact: expenses are increased	Impact: cash in bank is decreased

1.27 RECORDING A CHEQUE DRAWN FROM THE BANK ACCOUNT

Cash Book

Dr							Cr
Date	Details	Cash $	Bank $	Date	Details	Cash $	Bank $
				Oct 24	Equipment maintenance		235 (G1)

General ledger — Malik Motors

Equipment maintenance account

Dr			Cr
Date	$	Date	$
Oct 24 Bank	235		

During October Malik Motors also instructed its bank to make the following transfers from its current account.

(G2) On 25 October a one-off credit transfer was made to the bank account of Mekanic Ltd. in payment for supplying and installing a new hydraulic car lift at the garage. The cash book records the payment made as $5 430.

(G3) On 27 October a regular standing order for $69 was transferred to the bank account of the telephone company in payment for telephone services received over the previous three months. The same payment is made every three months in arrears by Malik Motors to the company.

(G3) On 29 October $351 was paid to the bank account of Parts Direct Ltd. by direct debit. The payment was in settlement of the balance outstanding on Malik Motor's account with the supplier as at the end of September. Malik Motors makes regular purchases of goods on credit from Parts Direct Ltd. and makes regular payments to the supplier each month but the amounts vary depending on the value of its purchases.

The transfers were entered into the books of Malik Motors as follows.

(G2) For a credit transfer from the bank current account for the purchase of an asset:

Equipment account	Bank account
Debit the account with the value of the asset purchased	Credit the account with the amount of cash transferred from the account
Impact: asset is increased	Impact: cash in bank is decreased

(G3) **For a standing order from the bank current account to pay a recurring expense:**

Expense account	Bank account
Debit the account with the amount paid to the supplier	Credit the account with the amount of cash transferred from the account
Impact: expenses are increased	Impact: cash in bank is decreased

(G4) **For a direct debit from the bank current account to pay a current liability:**

Trade payable account	Bank account
Debit the account with the amount transferred to the bank current account of the trade payable	Credit the account with the amount of cash transferred from the account
Impact: trade payables are decreased	Impact: cash in bank is decreased

1.28 RECORDING DIFFERENT BANK TRANSFERS FROM THE BANK CURRENT ACCOUNT

Malik Motors

Cash Book

Dr								Cr
Date	Details	Cash $	Bank $	Date	Details	Cash $	Bank $
				Oct 25	Equipment		5 430	(G2)
				Oct 27	Telephone		69	(G3)
				Oct 29	Parts Direct Ltd.		351	(G4)

General ledger — Malik Motors

Equipment account

Dr			Cr
Date	$	Date	$
Oct 25 Bank	5 430		

General ledger — Malik Motors

Telephone account

Dr			Cr
Date	$	Date	$
Oct 27 Bank	69		

Purchases ledger — Malik Motors

Parts Direct Ltd. account (No. 00346)

Dr			Cr
Date	$	Date	$
Oct 30 Bank	351		

The cash book

At the end of each month a business will balance off the cash and bank accounts in its cash book

At the end of the month Malik balanced off the cash and bank accounts in his cash book.

(1) He added up the total debits and total credits to the cash columns and found their difference. This can only ever be zero or a debit balance because the business cannot spend more cash than it keeps on its premises. A debit balance means the business has received more cash during the month than it has paid out.

If:	Balance on cash account is:	What does it mean?
total debits exceed total credits	debit balance (Dr)	The business has cash in hand on its premises
total debits equal total credits	zero	The business has run out of cash in hand on its premises

(2) He added up the total debits and total credits to the bank columns and found their difference. This can be a debit balance, zero or a credit balance.

If:	Balance on bank account is:	What does it mean?
total debits exceed total credits	debit balance (Dr)	The business has funds in its account: the bank account is a current asset
total debits equal total credits	zero	The business has spent all the funds in its account
total debits are less than total credits	credit balance (Cr)	The business has overdrawn its account: the bank account is a current liability

If the bank account in the cash book has a debit balance at the end of the month it means the business still has funds it can spend or draw from next month in its bank current account; it is a current asset of the business.

However, if the bank account has a credit balance it means the bank current account is **overdrawn**: the business has paid out more cash than it had available. It has had to borrow money from its bank. This means the bank account has become a current liability for the business because the overdrawn amount is repayable to the bank.

Illustration 1.17 on page 65 showed the cash book of Malik Motors from last October before it had been balanced off at the end of the month. Illustration 1.29 shows the same cash book but after it had been balanced off.

1.29 A BALANCED CASH BOOK

Malik Motors

Cash Book

Dr							Cr
Date	Details	Cash $	Bank $	Date	Details	Cash $	Bank $
Oct 1	Balances b/d	180	342				
Oct 5	Sales	520		Oct 3	Purchases	133	
Oct 6	Cash		200	Oct 4	Cleaning	17	
Oct 8	Sales		80	Oct 6	Bank	200	
Oct 10	Travelsafe Taxis Ltd.		152	Oct 12	Bank deposit	300	
Oct 15	Bank	100		Oct 15	Cash		100
Oct 18	Van Hire Ltd.		67	Oct 24	Equipment maintenance		235
Oct 18	Sundown Coach Tours		3 159	Oct 25	Equipment		5 430
Oct 23	Bank loan payable		2 200	Oct 27	Telephone		69
Oct 29	Cash		200	Oct 29	Parts Direct Ltd.		351
				Oct 31	Balances c/d ❶	150	215
		800	6 400		❷	800	6 400
Nov 1	Balances b/d	150	215				

❸

The total debits and credits in the cash and bank columns for the month were calculated as follows:

▼ Total debits and credits on the cash book in illustration 1.29

	DEBITS (cash received)		CREDITS (cash paid out)	
	Cash $	Bank $	Cash $	Bank $
Balances b/d on 1 October	180	342	–	–
Total cash paid out during October			650	6 185
Total cash received during October	620	6 073		
Totals for month	700	6 400	650	6 185
Balances c/d ❶ (differences between total debits and total credits)			150	215
Final totals ❷ including differences between total debits and credits	800	6 400	800	6 400
Balances b/d (1 November) ❸	150	215		

Malik balanced off his cash book at the end of last October as follows.

❶ He entered the debit balance of $150 for cash in hand to the credit column for cash transactions and the debit balance of $215 for cash in bank to the credit column for bank transactions. The entries were the balances to be

The cash book

carried down (balances c/d) to the next month. Entering the debit balances to the credit side of the cash and bank accounts meant the two sides of the two accounts were equal – or in balance.

2 He ruled off (drew a line under) the debit and credit columns to close them off to further entries and then entered their final totals in each one: $700 in the debit and credit columns for cash in hand and $6 400 in the debit and credit columns for cash in bank. He then underlined these totals with two lines to show the columns had been balanced off.

3 He brought down the "balances c/d" from the credit columns for cash and bank on 31 October to the debit columns for cash and bank on 1 November. The balances brought down (or balances b/d) were the opening balances on the cash and bank accounts for November. ➤ **1.7**

A business may borrow money from its bank by overdrawing its bank current account

At the end of October the bank account in the cash book of Malik Motors had a debit balance of $215. This meant the business had $215 in its account it could carry over to spend or draw from in November. But what if Malik Motors had overdrawn its bank account?

Imagine that Malik Motors had also made a bank transfer for $300 on 30 October to a supplier to purchase some car parts. To make the additional payment the business would have had to overdraw its bank account by $85 (that is, $215 less $300). The cash account, however, would have been unaffected. The cash book (with bank columns only) would have looked like this:

1.30 A BALANCED CASH BOOK WHEN THE BANK ACCOUNT IS OVERDRAWN

Malik Motors

Cash Book

Dr   Cr

Date	Details	Bank $	Date	Details	Bank $
Oct 1	Balances b/d	342			
Oct 5	Sales		Oct 3	Purchases	
Oct 6	Cash	200	Oct 4	Cleaning	
Oct 8	Sales	80	Oct 6	Bank	
Oct 10	Travelsafe Taxis Ltd.	152	Oct 12	Bank deposit	
Oct 15	Bank		Oct 15	Cash	100
Oct 18	Van Hire Ltd.	67	Oct 24	Equipment maintenance	235
Oct 18	Sundown Coach Tours	3 159	Oct 25	Equipment	5 430
Oct 23	Bank loan payable	2 200	Oct 27	Telephone	69
Oct 31	Balance c/d	85	Oct 29	Parts Direct Ltd.	351
			Oct 30	**Purchase of car parts**	**300**
		6 485			6 485
			Nov 1	Balances b/d	85

78 The fundamentals of accounting

The additional credit entry for $300 to the cash book in illustration 1.30 has increased total credits on the bank account from $6 185 to $6 485. With total debits unchanged at $6 400 the bank account now has a credit balance at the end of the month of $85 instead of a debit balance of $215.

A credit balance on the bank account means it is overdrawn and has become a current liability of the business because it must be repaid to the bank. The overdrawn amount is initially recorded as the balance carried down on the debit side of the account at the end of the month to make the two sides balance. It is then brought down to the credit side of the cash book at the start of the following month to record the liability on the account.

Overdrawing a bank account is a convenient way for a business to borrow money from its bank at short notice and for a short amount of time when more cash is being spent than received. This is called having a **bank overdraft**. However, the bank may charge the business a fee to have a pre-agreed bank overdraft facility and a high rate of interest on any amount overdrawn. The interest payable on the overdraft is a cost of finance for the business and will reduce its profit for the year. ➤ 3.1

ACTIVITY 1.14

The following transactions occurred in a small business during March.

Date	Description	$
Mar 3	Cash sales of goods paid direct into bank	325
5	Cheque payment made for purchase of new light fittings	148
6	Standing order payment for monthly insurance premium	65
7	Cash sales	390
9	Bank loan received	5 000
9	Bank loan arrangement fee paid by bank transfer	50
12	Cash sales	180
14	Cheque payment made to S Fernando	342
15	Direct debit to pay electricity charges	190
19	Standing order to pay rent	600
20	Cash payment to cleaner	75
21	Credit transfer to Fraser Construction Co Ltd.	5 300
26	Cash sales	660
28	Cash deposited in bank	800
30	Cash withdrawn from bank account for owner's personal use	500

The debit balances brought down on 1 March were $360 for cash in hand and $420 for cash in bank.

1 Write up the cash book for March and bring down the balances on 31 March.

2 What was the cash position of the business at the end of the month?

3 What advice, if any, would you give the business owner about managing cash in the business?

1.5.3 Allowing and receiving cash discounts

A three-column cash book can be used to keep a record of cash discounts

Businesses need cash to pay their day-to-day expenses. Many businesses encourage their trade receivables to pay the balances on their accounts quickly and will offer them a reduction in the amount payable if they do so. This reduction in the amount payable is called a **cash discount**. ➤ 1.3

A business may record two types of cash discount in its books:

- **Discount allowed**: a reduction in the total amount payable on a trade receivable account if the customer makes payment before the scheduled due date. A cash discount allowed by the business is a loss of income and therefore an expense to the business.

- **Discount received**: a reduction in the total amount the business must pay to a supplier to settle a trade payable account if it makes payment before the scheduled due date. A cash discount received by the business is therefore a saving or gain in income for the business on what it would have had to pay out to settle its account after the due date.

A note of any cash discounts allowed or received by a business can be kept in a **three-column cash book**. An extra column is added to the cash book on:

- the debit side to record discounts allowed (expense)
- the credit side to record discounts received (income).

However, the cash book is not the ledger account for cash discounts. At the end of each month the total of entries to the debit and credit columns for discounts will be posted to separate accounts for discounts allowed and discounts received in the general ledger.

A discount allowed encourages prompt payment by trade receivables but the loss of cash is an expense

Malik Motors allows its credit customers a 2.5% cash discount on the amount they owe if they settle their accounts in full within 30 days.

For example, when Sundown Coach Tours settled its account for September on 18 October the balance on its account was $3 240. However, the actual payment it made was $3 159 which included a cash discount of $81 – a reduction by 2.5% of $3 240 for early settlement. The cash discount enjoyed by Sundown Coach Tours was credited to its trade receivables account along with its payment of $3 159. Together these credits balanced off the $3 240 owing on the account.

If Sundown Coach Tours had settled its account at a later date, or if Malik Motors did not allow cash discounts, full payment of the account balance of $3 240 would have been required. The loss of $81 of income from the cash discount given to Sundown Coach Tours was an additional expense for Malik Motors.

12 × coach tyres at $300 each	Total price $3 600
(12 × $300 = $3 600)	
less 10% trade discount	Total net price $3 240
($3 600 × 10% = $360)	
less 2.5% cash discount	Total payable $3 159
($3 240 × 2.5% = $81)	

To record the payment received from Sundown Coach Tours and the expense of the cash discount the following double entries were required in the books of the business.

For the receipt of a trade receivable payment inclusive of a cash discount allowed:

Bank account	Trade receivable account
Debit the account with the payment received	Credit the account with the amount paid by the trade receivable
Impact: cash in bank is increased	Impact: trade receivable is decreased

Discounts allowed account	Trade receivable account
Debit the account with the amount of the cash discount.	Credit the account with the amount of the cash discount allowed
Impact: expenses are increased	Impact: trade receivable is decreased

1.31 RECORDING THE RECEIPT OF A TRADE RECEIVABLE PAYMENT INCLUSIVE OF A CASH DISCOUNT ALLOWED

Malik Motors

Cash Book

Dr									Cr
Date	Details	Discounts allowed $	Cash $	Bank $	Date	Details	Discounts received $	Cash $	Bank $
Oct 18	Sundown Coach Tours	81		3159					
Oct 31		81							

Sales ledger Malik Motors

Sundown Coach Tours (account No. 00101)

Dr				Cr
Date	$	Date		$
Oct 1 Balance b/d	3 240	Oct 18 Bank		3 159
		Oct 18 Discounts allowed		81
	3 240			3 240

General ledger Malik Motors

Discounts allowed account

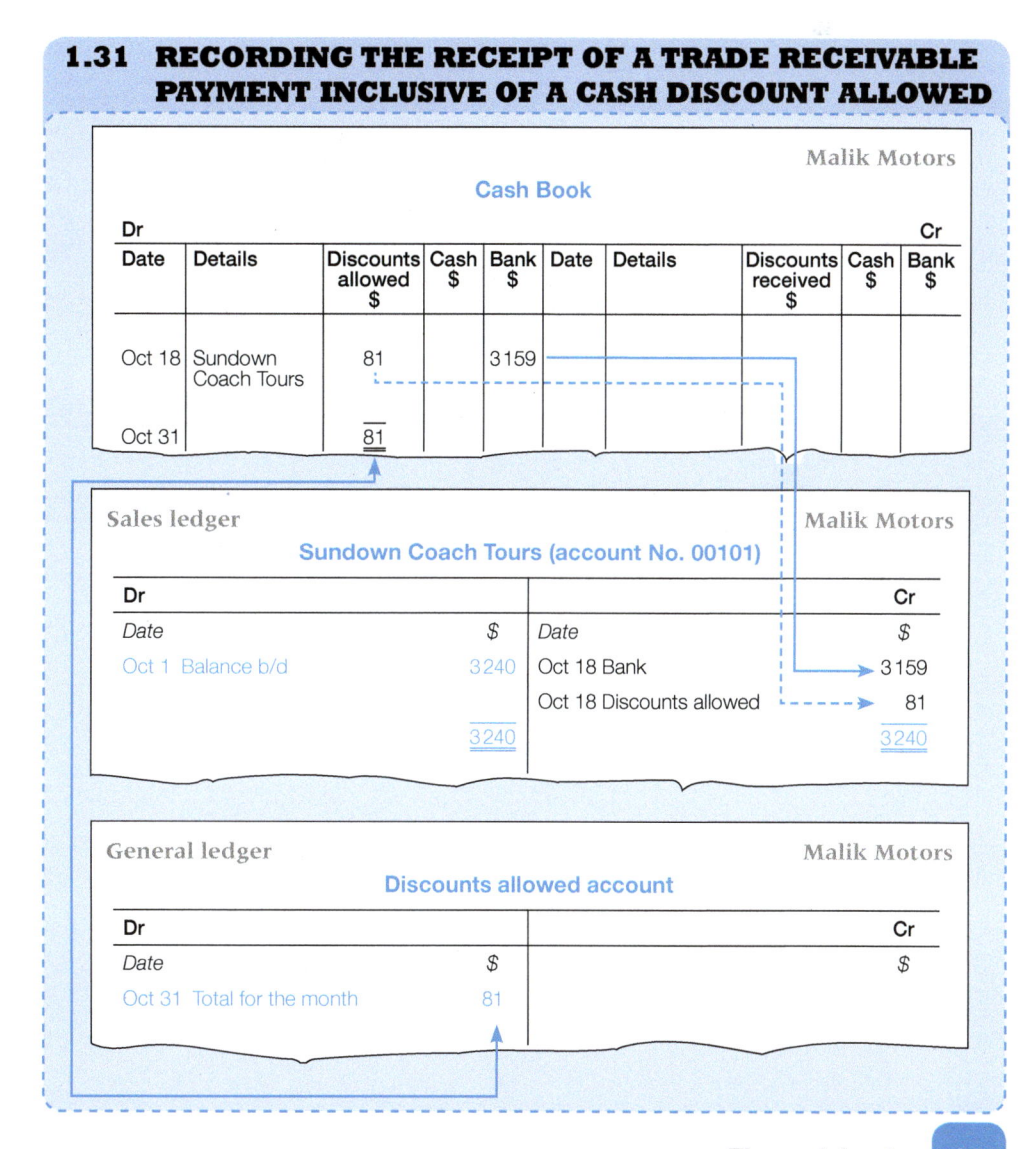

Dr			Cr
Date	$		$
Oct 31 Total for the month	81		

A discount received is treated as income received because it reduces cash paid out by the business

On 20 October Malik Motors settled its trade payable account with supplier Parts Direct Ltd. in full. The outstanding balance on the account was $360 but because Malik Motors made payment before the due date it was able to benefit from a cash discount of 2.5% – a discount on the total balance of $9. This meant Malik Motors only had to pay $351 to Parts Direct Ltd. to settle its account in full. Had the business settled its account after the due date it would have had to pay out $360 to do so.

A discount received is the equivalent of the business receiving additional income and must be recorded separately in an income account for discounts received in the ledger. The following double entries were made in the books of Malik Motors to record its payment to Parts Direct Ltd. and the cash discount it received.

For payment made to a trade payable inclusive of a cash discount received:

Trade payable account	Bank account
Debit the account with the amount paid to the trade payable	Credit the account with the amount paid to the trade payable
Impact: trade payable is decreased	Impact: cash in bank is decreased

Trade payable account	Discounts received account
Debit the account with the amount of the cash discount received	Credit the account with the amount of the discount received.
Impact: trade payable is decreased	Impact: income is increased

1.32 RECORDING A PAYMENT MADE TO A TRADE PAYABLE INCLUSIVE OF A CASH DISCOUNT RECEIVED

Malik Motors

Cash Book

Dr									Cr
Date	Details	Discounts allowed $	Cash $	Bank $	Date	Details	Discounts received $	Cash $	Bank $
					Oct 29	Parts Direct Ltd.	9		351
					Oct 31		9		

Purchases ledger — Malik Motors

Parts Direct Ltd. account (No. 00346)

Dr			Cr
Date	$	Date	$
Oct 29 Bank	351	Oct 1 Balance b/d	360
Oct 29 Discounts received	9		
	360		360

General ledger — Malik Motors

Discounts received account

Dr			Cr
	$		$
		Oct 31 Total for the month	9

1.5.4 Bank statements and the process of bank reconciliation

Banks produce regular bank statements of account for their current account holders

At the same time that a business will be recording all its bank transactions in the bank columns of its cash book, its bank will be recording the same transactions in a **bank statement** of account for the business.

A bank will issue a bank statement to each one of its current account holders at regular intervals, usually at the end of each month or when requested.

If the business keeps funds in its bank current account its cash book will record a debit balance on its bank account because it will be an asset or receivable account: the funds the business holds in its current account at the bank is owed by the bank to the business.

This means the opposite for the bank. The customer's account will be in credit because it is a liability or payable account: any money held in the account will be owed by the bank to its business customer.

If the bank statement issued to the business by its bank shows exactly the same bank transactions the business has recorded in its cash book over the same period then the credit balance on the statement will be identical to the debit balance on the bank account in the cash book.

▼ How transactions are recorded in the cash book versus the bank statement

	Bank account in the cash book of the business	Bank statement prepared by the bank for the business
Money paid into account	A debit entry	A credit entry
Money paid out from the account	A credit entry	A debit entry
There are funds in the account	A debit balance (an asset or receivable for the business)	A credit balance (a liability or payable for the bank)
The account is overdrawn	A credit balance (a liability or payable for the business)	A debit balance (an asset or receivable of the bank)

The reverse will be true if the business overdraws its current account at the bank: the customer's account will become a receivable or asset account for the bank because the customer will owe the bank the amount of money it has overdrawn. The debit balance on the statement should be identical to the credit balance on the bank account in the cash book of the business over the same period.

Often the transactions and balances recorded by a business in its cash book differ from those recorded by its bank in its bank statement.

It is important to identify the reasons for differences in the bank statement and cash book at the end of each month

Differences between bank statement and cash book records can occur for these reasons:

- **Errors and omissions**: a business may forget to record some bank transactions in its cash book or record some with errors. It may also not be aware of some transactions, such as transfers received, direct debit payments made or bank charges levied, until it receives its bank statement.

- **Timing differences that delay the recording of payments and receipts in the bank statement**: it can take time for banks to process cheques and different bank transfers. A business may record some of these transactions in its cash book before they have been processed and recorded in its bank statement.

Illustration 1.33 is the bank statement issued to Malik Motors by its bank at the end of last October. The first thing to notice is that it is presented using a running balance format: the debit or credit balance is recalculated and shown after every transaction. ➤ 1.7

Compare the bank statement with the balanced cash book of the business from illustration 1.29. It is shown below illustration 1.33 but this time with only the bank columns shown. You will immediately see that the bank statement records a credit balance of $300 on 31 October while Malik's cash book records a debit balance of $215. There are a number of differences between the two records that explain why and these have been highlighted. All other transactions in the two documents are otherwise identical.

1.33 AN EXAMPLE OF A BANK STATEMENT

BIG BANKING GROUP SA

Bank statement

Account no: 09901945
Account holder: Malik Motors
7–9 Axelrod Avenue
Downtown DN1267

Statement date: 31 October 201X

Date	Details	Debits $	Credits $	Balance $
Oct 1	Balances b/d		342	342 Cr
Oct 6	Cash deposit		200	542 Cr
Oct 8	Cash deposit		80	622 Cr
Oct 10	Cheque received from Travelsafe Taxis		152	774 Cr
Oct 15	Cash withdrawal	100		674 Cr
Oct 18	Cheque received from Van Hire Ltd.		67	741 Cr
Oct 18	Transfer received from Sundown Coach Tours		3 159	3 900 Cr
Oct 23	Bank loan funds transfer		2 200	6 100 Cr
① Oct 25	Credit transfer to Mekanic Ltd.	4 530		1 570 Cr
Oct 27	Standing order to Telephone Co	69		1501 Cr
② Oct 28	Direct debit to Segur Buildings Insurance Co	1600		99 Dr
Oct 29	Direct debit to Parts Direct Ltd.	351		450 Dr
③ Oct 30	Transfer received from Horsepower Ltd.		720	270 Cr
④ Oct 31	Dividend received from Speedcars SA		50	320 Cr
⑤ Oct 31	Bank charges	20		300 Cr

Dr = account is overdrawn

▼ Balanced cash book from illustration 1.29 with bank columns only

Malik Motors

Cash Book (bank account only)

Dr / Cr

Date	Details	Bank $	Date	Details	Bank $
Oct 1	Balance b/d	342			
Oct 6	Cash	200	Oct 15	Cash	100
Oct 8	Sales	80	Oct 24	Equipment maintenance	235 ⑦
Oct 10	Travelsafe Taxis	152	Oct 25	Equipment	5 430 ①
Oct 18	Van Hire Ltd.	67	Oct 27	Telephone	69
Oct 18	Sundown Coach Tours	3 159	Oct 29	Parts Direct Ltd.	351
Oct 23	Bank loan payable	2 200	Oct 31	Balance c/d	215
⑥ Oct 29	Sales	200			
		6 400			6 400
Nov 1	Balance b/d	215			

The cash book 85

Differences due to errors and omissions in the cash book

1 **A recording error in the cash book**: the credit transfer to Mekanic Ltd. for equipment purchased on 25 October was entered incorrectly in the cash book as $5 430. The bank statement shows the correct payment made was $4 530. The cash book overstated cash paid out from the bank account by $900. A debit for $900 should be added to the cash book to correct the error.

The following items were recorded in the bank statement but not in the cash book of the business.

2 **An unforeseen or overlooked payment**: a direct debit payment to the Segur Buildings Insurance Company on 20 October for $1 600 for a prepaid annual insurance premium was overlooked and not recorded in the cash book. ➤ **2.4**

3 **An unforeseen receipt**: a payment for $720 received by credit transfer on 30 October from Horsepower Ltd. was not recorded in the cash book.

4 **Dividends received**: on 31 October Malik Motors received $50 paid directly into its bank account by Speedcars SA. Malik Motors holds a small number of shares in the company and from time to time is paid a share of its profits. This is called a dividend. The business was unaware of the dividend it had received from Speedcars when it wrote up its cash book.

5 **Bank charges paid**: also on 31 October Malik Motors' bank deducted charges of $20 from the business current account. The fees were for the bank services the business had used during the month. The business was unaware of these charges at the time and did not record them in its cash book.

The cash book should be updated with these missing items.

Differences due to processing and other delays affecting payments and receipts

The following transactions were recorded in the cash book but did not appear in the bank statement because of timing differences.

6 **An uncredited deposit**: sometimes cash and cheques deposited at the bank will be recorded on the debit side of the cash book but will not appear as a credit in the bank statement. This is because it takes time for payments to be processed by banks and for money to be transferred between them.

Any deposits made towards the end of a month may not appear on the account holder's bank statement until the following month. This was the case when Malik deposited $200 of cash into the business bank account late on 29 October – a Friday and just before the weekend when the bank would have been closed. The cash book recorded the deposit but the bank statement for October did not.

7 **An unpresented cheque**: the cheque (no. 10125) for $235 issued by Malik Motors to AirTech SA for equipment maintenance on 24 October was recorded in the cash book but not the bank statement. This meant the money had not been debited from the current account of Malik Motors at the time the bank statement was prepared. Although AirTech SA had received the cheque it did not present it to its bank for payment until November.

A business must account for any differences between the balances on its bank statement and cash book so that its cash position at the end of the month is clear

It is important for a business to understand and account for any differences in its cash book and bank statement. This is so it can be sure of how much money it holds in its bank account at the end of each month – or by how much it has overdrawn its account. This requires carrying out a process called **bank reconciliation**. It involves two key stages:

(1) correcting any errors in the cash book and then updating it with any items that only appear in the bank statement

(2) preparing a bank reconciliation statement to account for the remaining difference in the balances on the bank statement and updated cash book due to timing differences recording receipts and payments.

Stage 1: Updating the cash book

The cash book should be updated at the end of the month as follows:

- Correct any errors in values recorded in the cash book (because item 1 in the cash book of Malik Motors was recorded in error as a credit entry for $5 430 rather than $4 530, the error had to be corrected by adding a debit entry for $900).

- Any debits in the bank statement that were not recorded in the cash book should be credited to the bank account in the cash book (items 2 and 5 in the bank statement for Malik Motors).

- Any credits in the bank statement that were not recorded in the cash book should be debited to the bank account in the cash book (items 3 and 4 in the bank statement for Malik Motors).

- Calculate revised totals for debits and credit entries in the bank columns and then balance off the cash book. The revised balance on the cash book at the end of the month will be the correct balance on the ledger account for cash in bank. However, this balance may still differ from the balance in the bank statement.

Illustration 1.34 shows the cash book of Malik Motors from last October after it had been updated. The updated items are shown are highlighted in bold.

1.34 A CASH BOOK UPDATED WITH ITEMS FROM THE BANK STATEMENT

Malik Motors

Cash Book (bank account only)

Dr   Cr

Date	Details	Bank $	Date	Details	Bank $
Oct 1	Balance b/d	342			
			Oct 15	Cash	100
Oct 6	Cash	200	Oct 24	Equipment maintenance	235
Oct 8	Sales	80	Oct 25	Equipment	5 430
Oct 10	Travelsafe Taxis	152	Oct 27	Telephone	69
Oct 18	Van Hire Ltd.	67	Oct 31	Parts Direct Ltd.	351
Oct 18	Sundown Coach Tours	3 159			
Oct 23	Bank loan payable	2 200			
Oct 29	Sales	200			
① Oct 31	Correction of error (Equipment)	900	Oct 31	Segur Buildings Insurance Co	1 600 ②
③ Oct 31	Horsepower Ltd.	720	Oct 31	Bank charges	20 ⑤
④ Oct 31	Dividend (Speedcars SA)	50	Oct 31	(Updated) Balance c/d	265
		8 070			8 070
Nov 1	(Updated) Balance b/d	265			

The debit balance on the updated bank account was $265. Although Malik was satisfied this was the correct balance on his cash book it was still less than the credit balance of $300 recorded in the bank statement. Malik had to prepare a bank reconciliation statement to account for the remaining difference.

Stage 2: Preparing a bank reconciliation statement

The second and final stage of bank reconciliation is to prepare a **bank reconciliation statement**. This is used to show why the balance on the updated cash book differs from the balance shown in the bank statement for the same month. The difference will be due to timing differences that delayed the recording of transactions in the bank statement after they had first been recorded in the cash book.

Two methods can be used to prepare a bank reconciliation statement:

Method 1: Start with the balance on the bank statement then:

- Add any debit entries in the cash book for uncredited deposits not included in the balance on the bank statement (item 6 in the cash book of Malik Motors).

- Deduct credit entries in the cash book for unpresented cheques (those that have not been paid into the bank account) that would have reduced the balance on the bank statement had they been included (item 7 in the cash book of Malik Motors). It is useful to list unpresented cheques with their numbers because it will help to identify them once they are finally presented and paid and appear in a future bank statement.

- Calculate the balance after all additions and deductions. This should be equal to the balance on the updated cash book. If it is not then something has been missed or an error made in the calculation.

Malik followed these steps to produce the bank reconciliation statement below for his business for the month of October. The bank reconciliation statement shows the difference between the balance of $300 on the bank statement and the balance of $265 on the updated cash book was due to an uncredited deposit of $200 and an unpresented cheque for $235 not appearing in the bank statement for that month.

1.35 A BANK RECONCILIATION STATEMENT PREPARED USING METHOD 1

Malik Motors

Bank Reconciliation Statement at 31 October 201X

	$
Balance on bank statement	300
⑥ Add: uncredited deposit	200
	500
⑦ Less: unpresented cheque (10125) – Air Tech Co	235
Balance on updated cash book	265

Alternatively, Malik could have produced a bank reconciliation statement in the following way.

Method 2: Start with the balance on the bank account in the cash book then:

- Deduct debit entries in the cash book for any uncredited deposits that did not appear in the bank statement (item 6 in the cash book of Malik Motors).

- Add credit entries in the cash book for any unpresented cheques that did not appear in the bank statement (item 7 in the cash book of Malik Motors).

- Calculate the balance after all additions and deductions. This should be equal to the balance on the bank statement.

Had Malik followed this alternative method the bank reconciliation statement for his business for last October would have looked as shown in illustration 1.36.

1.36 A BANK RECONCILIATION STATEMENT PREPARED USING METHOD 2

Malik Motors
Bank Reconciliation Statement at 31 October 201X

	$
Balance on updated cash book	265
⑥ *Less:* uncredited deposit	200
	65
⑦ *Add:* unpresented cheque (10125) – Air Tech Co	235
Balance on bank statement	300

1.5.5 The imprest system of petty cash

Petty cash is used to pay for small, everyday items

All organisations, whether large or small, will need to make many small purchases to support their business activities, from cleaning products to postage stamps and travel expenses. In most cases it would not be sensible to pay for these items by cheque or bank transfer so payment is usually made in cash.

For example, each week Malik Matheroo spends around $10 buying some tea and biscuits from a local supermarket for his employees to enjoy during their breaks. In addition, his business regularly needs soaps and detergents, kitchen towels and air fresheners. All these expenses will reduce profit.

The cost of each item may be quite small but over time these expenses can add up to a large amount of money. It is important to record and monitor these expenses. To do this Malik Motors uses a **petty cash book**.

A petty cash book is the book of prime entry for transactions using **petty cash**: the small amount of cash in hand a business will keep on its premises to pay for small everyday items. However, the petty cash book will also be the ledger account for cash in hand if all other, larger expenditures only involve bank transactions. This will mean the cash book of the business will only have bank columns to record debits and credits to cash in bank.

Petty cash vouchers are used to record small business expenditures

It is not practical for Malik to control every small item of business expenditure. Instead, postage stamps and other everyday items needed by the business can be bought when they are needed by Malik's employees. They will often use their own money which they can then claim back from the business. To do this they need to obtain a sales receipt as proof of their cash purchase and complete a **petty cash voucher**. For example, when Kailey the mechanic bought some degreaser using her own money she had to fill out a petty cash voucher to reclaim the expense from petty cash. The petty cash voucher she submitted is shown in illustration 1.37.

1.37 A PETTY CASH VOUCHER

PETTY CASH VOUCHER

Voucher No. **1**

DATE	ITEM	AMOUNT
3/11	Degreaser	$6	70
	TOTAL	$6	70

AUTHORISED BY _Jace Linard_ RECEIVED BY _Kailey Kattan_

A **petty cash voucher** is used to record the details of a small item of expenditure paid for from the petty cash of the business and should be signed by the employee making the claim. The petty cash voucher will then need to be checked against the sales receipt before payment can be authorised.

The design of petty cash vouchers can vary but all will need to include the same basic information, including space for signatures for the person authorising payment from petty cash and from the person receiving it.

Petty cash vouchers can be completed on a computer and then printed but will normally be completed by hand. You can buy pre-printed books of blank petty cash vouchers from suppliers of office stationery.

The petty cashier authorises the payment of petty cash from the imprest or cash float

Malik hasn't got the time to authorise and organise the repayment of petty cash vouchers to his employees. Last November he decided to set up an imprest system and delegated the task of managing petty cash to Jace Linard, one of his employees. This meant Jace became the **petty cashier** for the business responsible for managing petty cash and authorising the payment of petty cash vouchers up to a specified limit without the need to obtain Malik's approval.

Most businesses with employees operate an **imprest system**. It involves giving the petty cashier an agreed and fixed sum of petty cash at the start of each week or month called the **imprest** or **cash float** that will be sufficient to pay for all the small items of expenditure the business will need. Cash is drawn from the imprest every time a payment is made and recorded in the petty cash book.

At the end of each week or month – the **imprest period** – the float or imprest will be refilled to the agreed sum from cash in hand or withdrawn from the bank on the authorisation of the chief cashier, accountant or business manager. The reimbursement will be equal to the amount of petty cash spent during the previous imprest period. For example, if an imprest is set at $80 per week and by the end of the first week a total of $64 had been spent then $16 of petty cash would remain. At the start of the second week $64 will have to be added to petty cash to restore the imprest for that week back up to $80.

The cash book

In fact this is what happened at Malik Motors. Malik had set a imprest of $80 per week for the business. This meant no more than $80 of petty cash could be spent by his employees without his authorisation each week. By the end of the first week of operating the imprest system last November, petty cashier Jace had authorised petty cash vouchers to the value of $64. This meant the amount left in the imprest or float at the end of that week was $16. At the start of the second week Malik therefore supplied a further $64 in cash to Jace to restore the imprest back to $80.

▼ How an imprest system works

Week 1 (3–9 November)

3/11	Malik gives petty cashier Jace an $80 float Kailey claims $6.70 for degreaser Bartek buys $5 of postage stamps
4/11	Bartek claims $30 for petrol
5/11	Malik is paid $10.00 for tea and biscuits
6/11	Kailey claims $8.00 for a taxi fare
7/11	Kailey is paid $1.90 for newspapers
8/11	Bartek claims $2.40 for toilet gel
9/11	Petty cash paid out during week totals $64 ① Balance of cash in hand at end of week is $16

Week 2 (10–17 November)

10/11	Malik gives petty cashier Jace $64 in cash to restore the float to $80 ②

Each of the items authorised by Jace, the petty cashier, had to have a petty cash voucher like the one in illustration 1.37 completed by the person who made the expenditure.

It is the job of the petty cashier to record the petty cash vouchers in the petty cash book. Jace completed the petty cash book for week 1 as follows.

1.38 AN ANALYSED PETTY CASH BOOK

Malik Motors

Petty Cash Book

Dr											Cr
Date	Details	Total received $	Date	Details	Voucher no.	Total paid $	Cleaning $	Stationery and postage $	Petrol $	Travel $	Sundry expenses $
3/11	Cash	80.00	3/11	Degreaser	1	6.70	6.70				
			3/11	Postage	2	5.00		5.00			
			4/11	Petrol	3	30.00			30.00		
			5/11	Tea/biscuits	4	10.00					10.00
			6/11	Taxi fare	5	8.00				8.00	
			7/11	Newspapers	6	1.90					1.90
			8/11	Toilet gel	7	2.40	2.40				
						64.00	9.10	5.00	30.00	8.00	11.90
			9/11	Balance c/d		16.00 ①					
		80.00				80.00					
10/11	Balance b/d	16.00									
10/11 ②	Bank	$64.00									

Column totals are posted as debit entries to corresponding accounts in the general ledger

The first entry made in the petty cash book was a debit entry for the receipt of the cash float or imprest of $80. The cash for the imprest was withdrawn from the business bank account. The double entry for the receipt of petty cash was a credit to the bank ledger account for the sum withdrawn.

For cash withdrawn from the bank account for the imprest:

Petty cash account	Bank account
Debit the account with the amount of cash received	Credit the account with the amount of cash withdrawn
Impact: cash in hand is increased	Impact: cash in bank is decreased

Jace then entered the following details of each petty cash voucher paid out on the credit side of the petty cash book:

- date of payment
- details of each payment, for example taxi fare
- number of the approved petty cash voucher
- total amount approved on the voucher and paid out in total
- type of expense, recording the payment in the relevant expense column.

At the end of the week ending 9 November Jace balanced off the petty cash book as follows:

- ✓ He calculated and entered the total petty cash paid out during the week ($64).
- ✓ He deducted the total cash paid out ($64) from the imprest ($80) and recorded the balance carried down ($16) in the total paid column.
- ✓ He added together the total paid out to the balance carried down ($64 + $16) and checked that their sum was equal to the total debits in the total received column ($80). Remember that the amount of petty cash paid out and the amount remaining in hand must be equal to the imprest for each period.
- ✓ He entered the sum of total debits ($80) and total credits ($80) and then double underlined these totals to balance off and close the petty cash book at the end of the imprest period.
- ✓ At the start of the following imprest period on 10 November he brought down the balance of petty cash remaining ($16) at the end of the previous imprest period (ending 9 November) to the debit side of the petty cash book.
- ✓ He recorded a debit for cash of $64 received to restore the imprest to $80 for the imprest period starting 10 November.

Use of analysis columns can be added to a cash book to show how cash has been used

You will notice from illustration 1.38 a number of extra columns on the credit side of the petty cash book. These allowed the petty cashier Jace to record and analyse how the business was using its cash over time, including spending on regular items such as cleaning, travel and petrol. There is a final column to record all other small and irregular payments, or **sundry expenses**.

A cash book with additional columns added to monitor different uses of cash is called an **analysed cash book**. As well as recording each cash payment made in the total credit column, a second entry is made in one of the analysis columns.

Each analysis column will correspond to an account in the ledger so that entries can be easily transferred from the cash book to the relevant ledger at the end of each week or month. Any credit in the cash book is posted as a debit in the ledger. So, for example, the credit total of $9.10 for cleaning expenses recorded in the petty cash book of Malik Motors for the week ending 9 November was posted as a debit to the ledger account for cleaning expenses. Similarly, the credit total of $5 for stationery and postage expenses was posted to the debit side of the expenses account for stationery and postage on another page in the general ledger of the business. ➤ 1.7

At the end of each imprest period when the petty cash book is added up, the total amount of petty cash spent should be equal to the sum of the individual totals of all the analysis columns on the credit side.

As a business grows and the number and variety of transactions increase, owners and managers may need more financial information in order to manage the cash flow of their organisation effectively. Additional columns may be added to the petty cash book and also to the cash book for bank transactions.

For example, columns may be added to monitor how much cash the business is paying out for purchases, rent, advertising, insurance premiums and for personal drawings over time. Analysis columns may also be added to the debit side of the cash books to keep track of different sources of receipts including cash sales, proceeds from the sale of unwanted assets and interest on savings. Adding extra columns is especially easy when the books are maintained electronically.

ACTIVITY 1.15

Jace had to take some time off work so Malik asked you to be petty cashier at Malik Motors for the week beginning 10 November. During the week you recorded the following receipts and authorised the following payments from petty cash.

10/11	Balance on cash float brought down $16
10/11	$64 of cash received
11/11	$9.90 for stationery (petty cash voucher 8)
12/11	$10 for tea and biscuits (petty cash voucher 9)
13/11	$15.75 for computer disks (petty cash voucher 10)
14/11	$11.25 for a replacement key to be cut (petty cash voucher 11)
15/11	$7.50 for replacement lightbulbs (petty cash voucher 12)
16/11	$17 paid to window cleaner (petty cash voucher 13)

1. Copy the petty cash book in illustration 1.38 and add a further nine rows.

2. Complete the petty cash book for the period 10–16 November using the information above (the balance brought down and cash received on 10 November are already recorded in illustration 1.38).

3. Balance off all of the columns on the credit side of the petty cash book on 16 November by:
   (i) calculating and entering the total for each column;
   (ii) calculating and entering the debit balance for petty cash carried down at the end of the week and therefore the amount of cash required to restore the imprest to $80 on 17 November.

An imprest system is an effective way of controlling cash in an organisation and can be managed by a junior member of staff

Malik has noticed a number of benefits since he introduced an imprest system for petty cash in Malik Motors. These are the advantages:

- The job of managing petty cash can be given to a more junior member of staff, thereby freeing up the time of the business manager, accountant or finance director to concentrate on more important tasks. In a small business such as Malik Motors it is usually the owner who performs all these roles.

- The total amount of cash paid out can be controlled and checked easily and at any time. This is because the amount paid out each period can never be more than the total value of approved petty cash vouchers and their total cannot exceed the imprest set for each period.

- There is no need for a cash book or ledger account. Only a bank account is needed to record bank transactions because all cash expenses will be recorded in the petty cash book and only their totals need to be transferred to the relevent expense accounts in the general ledger at the end of each period.

These are the reasons why many organisations with employees find it useful and sensible to use an imprest system for petty cash.

QUICK TEST

1. Explain why a cash book is both a book of prime entry and a ledger account.
2. On which side of a cash book are (a) cash receipts recorded; (b) cash payments recorded?
3. What are the main purposes of (a) a bank current account; (b) a bank deposit account?
4. Total debits to the bank account in the cash book at the end of a month are $3 700. Total credits for the same month are $4 000. (a) What is the credit or debit balance on the account at the end of the month? (b) Is the account overdrawn or in surplus?
5. (a) What is a bank overdraft?; (b) How is an overdraft on the bank account recorded in (i) the cash book; (ii) the bank statement?
6. What is the purpose of a bank reconciliation statement?
7. Explain the difference between an unpresented cheque and a dishonoured cheque.
8. A business has a debit balance on its bank account in its cash book at the end of the month of $290. The following transactions were recorded in its cash book but not in its bank statement for the following reasons:
   - A cheque received for $50 has been refused.
   - A cheque it issued to a trade payable for $65 has yet to be presented for payment.

   What is the balance on its bank statement?

9 (a) What is an imprest?; (b) Explain the advantages of running an imprest system in a business.

10 Michael is a sole trader. On 1 January his business had cash in hand of $450 and cash in bank of $1 200. The following transactions took place during January:

Date	Details	Amount $
Jan 3	Cash sale of goods	90
9	Cheque received from trade receivable (B Menzies)	50
14	Cash purchase of office stationery	30
16	Bank transfer to trade payable (Samex Ltd.)	320
21	Direct debit payment to Electricity Company	160
25	Cash sale of goods	70
27	Cheque received from trade receivable (V Asheen)	270
31	Cash payment to cleaner	200
31	Bank charges on bank statement	20

All cheques received were banked on the same day they were received.

Write up the the two-column cash book of the business for January and show the balances on the cash account and bank account on 31 January.

11 Cara buys and sells musical instruments. On 1 July her business had cash in hand of $130 and cash in bank of $900. The following transactions took place during July.

Date	Details	Amount $
Jul 3	Cash sale	330
4	Cash deposited into bank account	300
10	Bank transfer to DJW Wholesalers	1 400
17	Cheque received from trade receivable (M Atkins)	550
21	Cash payment for vehicle repair	180
23	Rent paid by direct debit	500
25	Cash sale	120
25	Cheque issued to insurance company	90
31	Bank charges on bank statement	40

All cheques received were banked on the same day they were received.

Write up the two-column cash book of the business for July and show the balances on the cash account and bank account on 31 July.

12 Tanwir buys and sells jewellery. The balances below were taken from his books on 1 October:

Balances as at 1 October	$
Cash in bank	1 100
Cash in hand	390
Trade receivables:	
B Hill	1 500
Y Moulson	700
Trade payables:	
Unique Designs Ltd.	1 000
Fools Gold Ltd.	2 200

The following transactions then took place during October.

Date	Details	Amount
Oct 6	Cash sale	$1 250
9	Cheque received from B Hill in full settlement of his account balance	Balance on account less 5% cash discount
10	Bank transfer to Unique Designs Ltd. for full settlement of balance owing on account	Balance on account less 2.5% cash discount
14	Cheque received from Y Moulson in full settlement of her account balance	Balance on account less 3% cash discount
18	Cash sale	$670
21	Cash deposited in bank account	$1 700
27	Bank transfer to electricity supplier	$150
28	Bank transfer to Fools Gold Ltd. for full settlement of balance owing on account	Balance on account less 5% cash discount

All cheques received were banked the same day they were received

Write up the three-column cash book of the business for October. Show (a) the balances on the cash account and bank account on 31 October; (b) the totals for discounts allowed and received.

13 Hamood is a small trader. He buys and sells all his goods on credit. All payments made or received are by cheque or electronic bank transfer. The bank account in his cash book and the bank statement he has received from his bank for the month of June are shown below. There are differences between them and their balances do not agree.

Hamood's Cash Book (bank account only)

Dr			Cr		
Date		$	Date		$
Jun 1	Balance b/d	1 950	Jun 4	Carlson	500
Jun 6	Rogerson	650	Jun 17	Mehmet	770
Jun 19	Hamzah	300	Jun 29	Salim	330
			Jun 30	Balance c/d	1 300
		2 900			2 900

Bank Statement

Date	Details	Debit $	Credit $	Balance $
Jun 1	Balance b/f			1 950 Cr
Jun 4	Carlson	500		1 450 Cr
Jun 6	Rogerson		650	2 100 Cr
Jun 17	Mehmet	770		1 330 Cr
Jun 19	Hamzah		300	1 630 Cr
Jun 26	Dishonoured cheque – Rogerson	650		980 Cr
Jun 30	Bank charges	100		880 Cr

(a) Update Hamood's cash book and bring down the balance on 30 June.
(b) Prepare a bank reconciliation statement for Hamood as at 30 June.

14 Manisha's business uses a petty cash book with the following analysis columns:

- Stationery and postage
- Travel
- Cleaning
- Sundry expenses.

The imprest for each month is set at $250. On 1 March last year the balance on the petty cash book was $50 and the following petty cash transactions were made during the month:

Date	Details	Amount
Mar 1	Petty cashier receives cash to restore imprest	$200
4	Office stationery purchased	$45
7	Travel expenses	$12
9	Postage	$8
16	Travel expenses	$30
23	Cleaning products purchased	$15
27	Tea and biscuits purchased	$10
28	Payment to office cleaner	$60

Write up the petty cash book of Manisha's business for March. Balance off the petty cash book (including analysis columns) at the end of the month and restore the imprest on 1 April.

Unit 1.6 The general journal

AIMS

By the end of this unit you should be able to
- explain that the **general journal** is one of the books of prime entry
- explain the use of the journal
- enter those transactions, including correction of errors, that cannot be recorded in any special journal
- write relevant explanatory narrations for each entry

1.6.1 Uses of the general journal

Irregular transactions not recorded in any other book of original entry are recorded in the general journal

Transactions that cannot be recorded in any of the other books of prime entry are recorded in the **general journal** (or more, simply, the journal) before they are posted to ledger accounts. These transactions will involve one-off or irregular items such as:

- the initial introduction of capital to the business by its owner
- opening a journal for the first time for assets and liabilities
- the purchase and sale of non-current assets on credit terms
- the transfer of goods or assets in settlement of a debt
- the writing off of irrecoverable debts that cannot be collected ▶ 1.9
- depreciation of non-current assets ▶ 2.2
- the correction of errors ▶ 2.3
- transfers at the end of the accounting year to the income statement ▶ 3.1

For example, the extract from the general journal of Hana Chopra in illustration 1.39 on the next page records the one-off receipt of computer equipment from Sam Mishra in settlement of his business debt of $700. Instead of settling his account with cash, Sam Mishra wrote to Hana on 2 April last year offering her computer equipment from his shop worth $700 to settle his business debt. Hana was in need of a new computer system and so accepted Sam's offer on 8 April.

As Hana had accepted computer equipment worth $700 from Sam in full payment of his debt she had to credit his trade receivable account with $700 to settle his debt. Hana then had to record the receipt of $700 of computer equipment on the debit side of her ledger account for equipment to record the increase in the non-current assets of her business.

These double entries were initially recorded in Hana's general journal. This has a column for debits and a column for credits. Hana then posted the journal entries to her ledger accounts as shown in illustration 1.39.

1.39 RECORDING THE RECEIPT OF ASSETS IN FULL SETTLEMENT OF A TRADE RECEIVABLE ACCOUNT

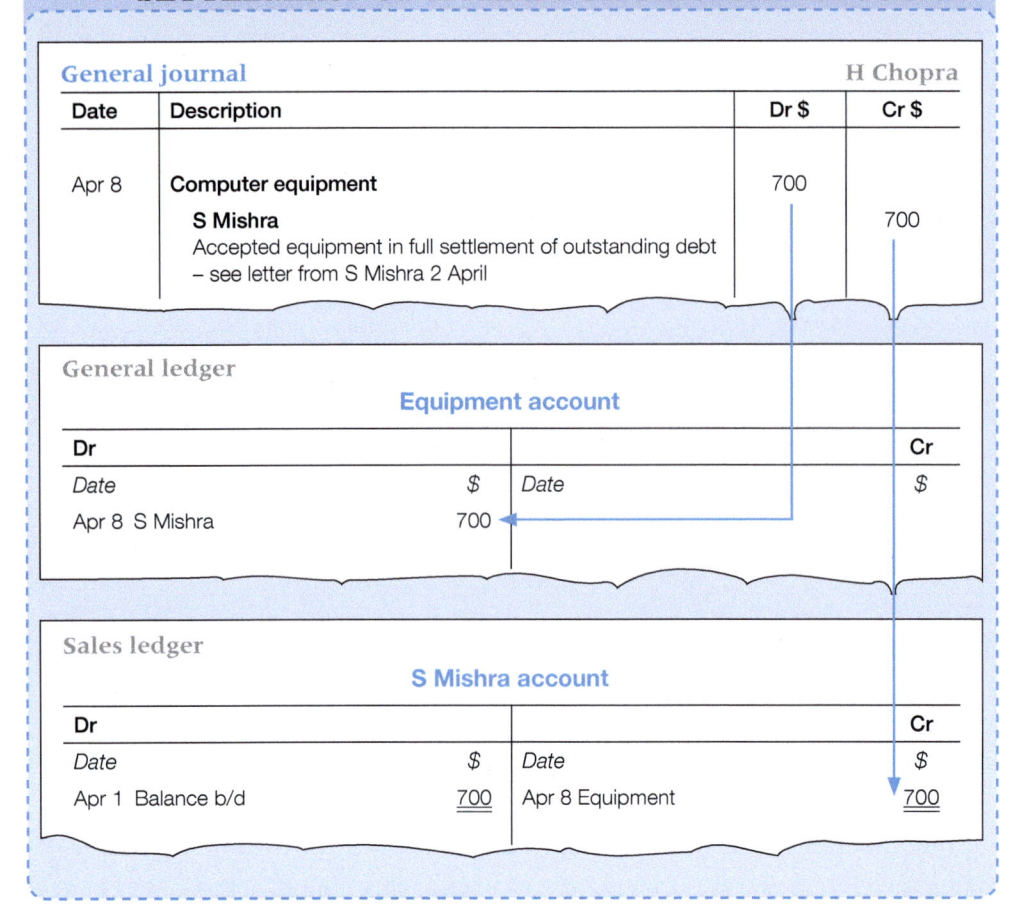

General journal — H Chopra

Date	Description	Dr $	Cr $
Apr 8	Computer equipment	700	
	S Mishra		700
	Accepted equipment in full settlement of outstanding debt – see letter from S Mishra 2 April		

General ledger

Equipment account

Dr					Cr
Date		$	Date		$
Apr 8 S Mishra		700			

Sales ledger

S Mishra account

Dr					Cr
Date		$	Date		$
Apr 1 Balance b/d		700	Apr 8 Equipment		700

Notice that the transaction was recorded in the general journal with the following details and in the following order:

1. the date it took place
2. the name of the account to be debited and the amount
3. the name of the account to be credited (always entered slightly to the right of **2**) and the amount
4. **narrative**: a brief description of the transaction and explanation of why it took place, including
5. a reference to the relevant source document for proof of the transaction. ➤ **1.3**

The same details will be recorded for every transaction entered into the general journal. The total amount debited should always be equal to the total amount credited to keep the accounting equation in balance. ➤ **1.2**

Entering details of double entries to the general journal makes their posting to ledger accounts easy. However, the general journal is not itself a double-entry account. Like the other books of prime entry it simply provides a record of transactions in their date order before they are posted to the relevant ledger accounts. ➤ **1.7**

The general journal is also used to record entries needed to correct errors

Errors will often be made recording transactions in journals or when posting journal entries to ledger accounts. For example, the wrong amounts may be entered or the right amounts entered but to the wrong accounts. It is also possible to enter amounts in the wrong columns, so a debit is recorded as a credit by mistake or a credit as a debit. ➤ **2.3**

For example, in illustration 1.40 Hana Chopra has used her journal to correct an error she had made some months earlier under-recording a cash sale in her cash book and sales account. Instead of recording $1 000 of goods sold and therefore cash received, she had by mistake only recorded $100. This meant her cash in hand, her total sales and also her profit for the year were all understated by $900.

The fundamentals of accounting

1.40 THE CORRECTION OF AN ERROR IN THE LEDGER USING THE JOURNAL

General journal — H Chopra

Date	Description	Dr $	Cr $
Oct 31	Cash	900	
	Sales		900
	Correction of error: cash sale for $1 000 entered in error as $100		

Cash Book

Dr								Cr
Date	Details	Cash $	Bank $	Date	Details	Cash $	Bank $
Oct 31	Balance c/d	5 500					
Oct 31	Sales	900					
		6 400					

Sales ledger

Sales account

Dr				Cr
Date		$	Date	$
			Oct 31 Balance c/d	117 000
			Oct 31 Cash	900
				117 900

To correct the error Hana made the following entries to her journal:

- a debit to the cash column in her cash book for $900 of cash received but not previously recorded
- a credit to sales for $900 of goods sold but not previously recorded.

She also added a narrative to explain the source of the error.

Hana then posted these entries to her cash book and ledger account for sales as shown.

Journal records reduce the risk of error and fraud

The general journal provides a full and permanent record of many different business transactions in the date order in which they occurred including narratives and references to their original source documents. It has the following advantages:

- Any errors discovered later on can be checked easily against source documents and it reduces the risk of making further errors when posting entries to the ledger accounts.
- It reduces the scope and risks of employees or other people and organisations making fraudulent (false) purchases or claims for money owed.
- It can be passed on to any qualified person or accountant to use to complete full and accurate ledger and final accounts for the business.

1.6.2 Opening entries

Opening entries in the general journal will be necessary when a business first starts up to record the capital introduced by the owner or owners

Most small businesses are set up and run by a single owner. These businesses are called **sole traders** or sole proprietorships and they are often financed from the personal savings of the owner.

1.41 RECORDING AN OPENING ENTRY FOR CAPITAL IN THE GENERAL JOURNAL

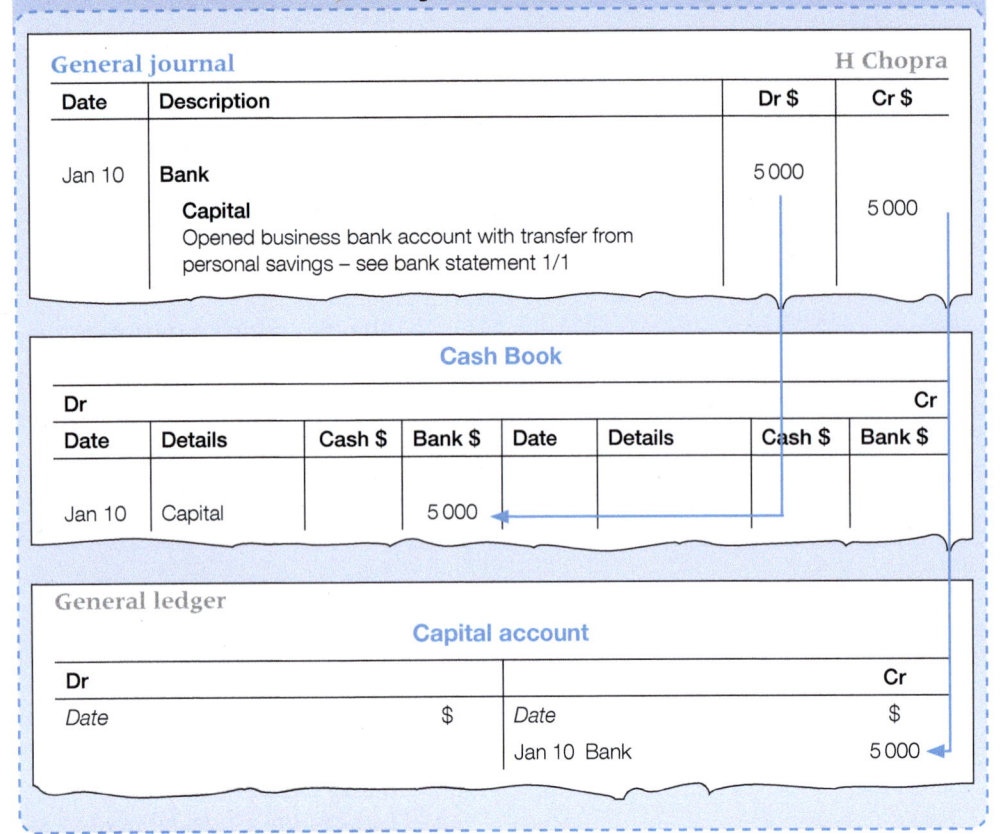

General journal — H Chopra

Date	Description	Dr $	Cr $
Jan 10	Bank	5 000	
	Capital		5 000
	Opened business bank account with transfer from personal savings – see bank statement 1/1		

Cash Book

Dr								Cr
Date	Details	Cash $	Bank $	Date	Details	Cash $	Bank $
Jan 10	Capital		5 000				

General ledger

Capital account

Dr			Cr
Date	$	Date	$
		Jan 10 Bank	5 000

For example, when Hana Chopra started her small business on 10 January last year she deposited $5 000 of her own money or **owner's equity** into the business bank account and immediately recorded the transfer in her general journal as follows:

- an opening debit entry for $5 000 to the bank account in the cash book to record cash received
- an opening credit entry to the capital account for $5 000 of equity owed to her by her business.

Hana also added a narrative to record the transfer of her personal savings to her business and a reference to the bank statement in which it appeared.

Hana transferred the journal entries as instructed to her cash book and ledger account for capital as shown in illustration 1.41.

Opening entries will also record the assets and liabilities of the business on start up or when ledger accounts are opened for the first time

As the name implies, an **opening entry** is a journal entry made when a business first starts to operate, for example to record opening equity, the first assets purchased or the first sale made. An opening entry to the journal is therefore the opening balance on a ledger account of the business at the start of trading. However, some businesses may have been trading for some time before they start to keep accounting records. They too will need opening entries for their assets, liabilities and capital to record in their ledger accounts once they set up their accounting systems.

For example, after years of trying, Hana finally persuaded her brother Manu to open and maintain proper books for the small business he had started over five years ago. This meant he had to identify and value all his business assets, liabilities and capital for the very first time. He did this and on 1 May last year he produced the information shown in illustration 1.42. Manu was able to calculate the value of his owner's equity as the difference between his business assets and liabilities as at 1 May using the accounting equation.

The fundamentals of accounting

Manu Chopra: balances as at 1 May

Assets at 1 May	$	Liabilities at 1 May	$
Premises	36 700	Trade payable – (E Gaddo)	8 800
Vehicles	5 450	Bank loan	17 000
Fixtures	1 200		
Inventory	390		
Cash in bank	3 250		
Cash in hand	760		
Total	47 750	Total	25 800

	$
Total assets	= 47 750
Total liabilities	= 25 800
Therefore:	
assets – liabilities	= 21 950
So, equity	= 21 950

Hana helped Manu enter these details to his general journal for the first time. The value of each opening asset was entered into the debit column and each opening liability was entered into the credit column. The amount of equity "owed" to Manu by his business was also entered into the credit column.

After he had made these opening entries to his general journal, Manu opened his ledger accounts, one for each asset and liability, and one for his owner's equity. Once these were prepared Manu was able to post the opening entries from his journal to his ledger accounts to be their opening balances. For example, illustration 1.43 below shows the opening entries posted by Manu to his vehicles account and trade payable account for supplier, E Gaddo.

1.42 RECORDING OPENING ENTRIES FOR ASSETS AND LIABILITIES IN THE GENERAL JOURNAL

General journal — Manu Chopra

Date	Description	Dr $	Cr $
May 1	Premises	36 700	
	Vehicles	5 450	
	Fixtures	1 200	
	Inventory	390	
	Cash in bank	3 250	
	Cash in hand	760	
	Trade payable (E Gaddo)		8 800
	Bank loan		17 000
	Equity		21 950
	Opening entries for assets, liabilities and equity at the date shown to open the books	47 750	47 750

ACTIVITY 1.16

Jake Dunn has never kept any books before. On 1 June he values his business assets and liabilities as follows:

Vehicle $6 000; equipment $14 500; inventory $740; bank $900; cash $360; B Hardy (trade payable) $2 600; H Golborne (trade payable) $5 700.

Show the opening entries to record these items in his general journal. Remember also to calculate and show the opening entry for equity.

1.43 OPENING ENTRIES FOR ASSETS AND LIABILITIES POSTED TO LEDGER ACCOUNTS

General ledger

Vehicles account

Dr			Cr	
Date		$	Date	$
May 1 Opening balance		5 450		

Sales ledger

E Gaddo account

Dr			Cr	
Date		$	Date	$
			May 1 Opening balance	8 800

The general journal

1.6.3 The purchase and sale of non-current assets

The purchase of new or replacement non-current assets will require entries in the general journal

When **non-current assets** such as premises, machinery and vehicles are acquired for the first time or if they are bought to replace old assets, they should be recorded in the general journal before they are posted to the ledger. This is because no other books of prime entry can be used for transactions involving non-current assets.

For example, Hana Chopra bought a second-hand delivery van for her small business on credit for $8 500 from Malik Motors on 17 January last year. The transaction meant she had acquired an asset for her business as well as a liability to pay Malik Motors at a later date the sum of $8 500 for the purchase of the van. She recorded the following entries, including a narrative, in her journal:

- a debit for $8 500 to the vehicles account to record the receipt of the van
- a credit of $8 500 to the other payable account for Malik Motors to record the business liability.

She then posted these entries to her ledger as shown in illustration 1.44.

1.44 RECORDING THE PURCHASE OF A NON-CURRENT ASSET IN THE GENERAL JOURNAL

General journal H Chopra

Date	Description	Dr $	Cr $
Jan 17	Vehicles	8 500	
	Malik Motors		8 500
	Purchase of delivery van on credit, see invoice MM891		

General ledger

Vehicles account

Dr				Cr
Date		$	Date	$
Jan 17 Malik Motors		8 500		

General ledger

Malik Motors account

Dr				Cr
Date		$	Date	$
			Jan 17 Vehicle	8 500

Non-current assets may be sold off by a business when they are no longer required or need to be replaced, or if the business needs to raise cash to pay off its debts

For example, when Hana Chopra sold off some old office furniture she no longer wanted for $430 to another local business owner, Aurelie Bachoo, she agreed to defer payment for 3 months. She recorded the sale of the furniture on credit to Aurelie in her general journal as follows:

- a debit entry for $430 to a non-trade (or other) receivable account for A Bachoo in the general ledger to record the sum owed
- a credit entry to the furniture account in the general ledger to record the decrease in her business assets by $430.

The journal entries and their transfers to the ledger are shown in illustration 1.45.

1.45 RECORDING THE SALE OF NON-CURRENT ASSETS IN THE GENERAL JOURNAL

General journal — H Chopra

Date	Description	Dr	Cr
Date		$	$
Apr 19	A Bachoo	430	
	Furniture		430
	Sale of unwanted display cabinets – see copy of handwritten sales receipt 137		

General ledger — A Bachoo account

Dr			Cr	
Date	$	Date		$
Apr 19 Furniture	430			

General ledger — Furniture account

Dr			Cr	
Date	$	Date		$
		Apr 19 A Bachoo		430

The transaction meant that Hana had reduced her non-current assets by $430 but increased her current assets of trade receivables by the same amount. Because increases in the value of assets are recorded in the ledger accounts as debits, any reductions in assets must be recorded as credits. To record the sale of any non-current assets by a business the following entries will always be required:

- a debit to cash or bank for the money received from the sale, or to a receivable account if the sale is on credit
- a credit to the account for the asset sold for the reduction in the assets.

ACTIVITY 1.17

Andrea Spyrou runs a small fitness studio. During the month of October she made the following transactions involving non-current assets.

12 Oct: Cash purchase of 20 weights for $400 (invoice 3/78)

16 Oct: Purchase of five training cycles on credit from Gym Supplies Ltd. for $2 500 (invoice GS75/1201)

21 Oct: Cash sale of one unwanted running machine for $300 (receipt 101).

Write up Andrea's general journal in date order with the name of the ledger accounts and double entries required for each transaction. Remember to include narratives.

1.6.4 Writing off irrecoverable debts

A business will need to record the loss of income from an irrecoverable debt that cannot be collected in its journal

Most businesses sell goods and services on credit to business customers but in some cases it can be difficult to recover the money owed. This is because the business customer is unable to pay its debt or has closed down. If this happens the debt is said to have turned bad and to be irrecoverable. That is, an **irrecoverable debt** is an amount owed to the business on a trade or other receivable account that cannot be collected or recovered. ➤ 1.9

An irrecoverable debt is a loss of income and therefore an expense to the business which will reduce its profit. To recognise the expense in its accounts the business must write off the irrecoverable debt. This involves closing the trade or other receivable account and transferring the balance written off to an irrecoverable debts account in the general ledger.

For example, Hana Chopra could not recover a debt of $75 from Joe Kramer. Hana had written a number of letters to Joe reminding him of his obligation to settle his debt but had found out he had been forced to close his business due to illness and had very little money left after his medical expenses. She decided to write off his irrecoverable debt on 30 April last year. This required her to make the following entries to her general journal:

- a debit entry for $75 to the expense account for irrecoverable debts for the debt written off
- a credit entry for $75 to the trade receivable account of J Kramer to clear the debt on the account.

Hana's journal entries and the transfers to her ledger are shown in illustration 1.46. Note that the narrative for the journal entries includes reference to the final demand notice Hana had sent to Joe Kramer on 28 April for repayment of his outstanding debt.

1.46 WRITING OFF AN IRRECOVERABLE DEBT

General journal H Chopra

Date		Dr	Cr
Apr 30	Irrecoverable debts	75	
	J Kramer		75
	Debt written off as irrecoverable. See final letter of 28 April, reference HC/JK3		

General ledger

Irrecoverable Debts account

Dr					Cr
Date		$	Date		$
Apr 30	J Kramer	75			

Sales ledger

J Kramer account

Dr					Cr
Date		$	Date		$
Apr 1	Balance b/d	75	Apr 30	Irrecoverable debts	75

ACTIVITY 1.18

On 30 October Andrea Spyrou decided to write off the outstanding debt on her trade receivable account for the Core Leisure Club Ltd. The company had closed down unexpectedly and owed Andrea $450 for a series of aerobics classes she had run at its club.

Add the appropriate entries to Andrea's general journal from activity 1.19 to show the debt written off, the ledger accounts to be debited and credited, and an informative narrative.

1.6.5 Transfers from ledger accounts to the income statement

The journal is also used to record transfers to the income statement at the end of an accounting year to calculate profit or loss for the year

At the end of an accounting year a number of accounts held by a business to record its income and costs will be closed and their balances transferred to an income statement to calculate profit for the year. The amounts transferred should first be recorded in the general journal of the business.

For example, Hana Chopra's accounting year runs from 1 January to 31 December each year. The following balances for income earned and costs incurred were taken from the accounts of her business at the end of last year:

Ledger account	Balances at 31 December ($)
Sales (revenue)	70 000 (Cr)
Purchases	32 000 (Dr)
Rent	3 600 (Dr)
Electricity	1 400 (Dr)
Telephone	800 (Dr)
General expenses	4 200 (Dr)

To close these accounts at the end of the year, Hana transferred their balances to the income statement for her business for that year. She entered the transfers in her general journal as follows:

1.47 JOURNAL ENTRIES FOR TRANSFERS TO THE INCOME STATEMENT AT THE YEAR END

General journal — H Chopra

Date	Details	Dr $	Cr $
Dec 31	Sales	70 000	
	Income statement		70 000
	Transfer of sales to income statement		
	Income statement	32 000	
	Purchases		32 000
	Transfer of purchases to income statement		
	Income statement	3 600	
	Rent		3 600
	Transfer of rent incurred to income statement		
	Income statement	1 400	
	Electricity		1 400
	Transfer of electricity expenses incurred to income statement		
	Telephone	800	
	Income statement		800
	Transfer of telephone expenses incurred to income statement		
	Income statement	4 200	
	General expenses		4 200
	Transfer of all other expenses incurred to income statement		

To close her sales account recording the revenue earned by her business during the year Hana recorded the following entries in her journal:

To transfer revenue earned to the income statement

Sales account	Income statement
Debit the account with the credit balance for revenue earned to balance off the account	Credit the statement with the debit from the account for total revenue earned
Impact: account is closed	Impact: profit for the year is increased

During the year Hana had sold all the goods she had purchased and recorded in her purchases account. That is, she had no unsold goods or inventory left over at the end of the year. To close her purchases and transfer the cost of the goods she had purchased to her income statement Hana therefore recorded the following entries in her journal:

To transfer the cost of purchases to the income statement

Income statement	Purchases account
Debit the statement with the credit to the account for the total cost of purchases	Credit the account with the debit balance for cost of purchases to balance off the account
Impact: profit for the year is decreased	Impact: account is closed

Similarly, to charge all the expenses her business had incurred during the year to her profit for the year Hana closed each expense account and transferred the amount incurred to her income statement as follows:

To transfer an expense incurred to the income statement

Income statement	Expense account
Debit the statement with the credit to the account for total expenses incurred	Credit the account with the debit balance for expenses incurred and balance off the account
Impact: profit for the year is decreased	Impact: account is closed

Once Hana had made these transfers from her accounts she was able to complete the simple income statement below for her business by deducting total debits from total credits to find her profit for the year:

▼ Simple income statement showing profit for the year

Hana Chopra
Summary income statement for year ended 31 December

	$	$
Total income (credits):		
Sales (revenue)		70 000
less		
Total costs (debits):		
Purchases	32 000	
Rent	3 600	
Electricity	200	
Telephone	4 200	
General expenses		42 000
Profit for the year		28 000

How to balance off and close a ledger account at the end of an accounting year is covered in more detail in Unit 1.7 and how to prepare a full income statement in Unit 3.1.

QUICK TEST

1. What is the general journal and what is it used for?
2. (a) Which of the following items would you record in the general journal?
   - A farm buys a combine harvester on credit from Agri-Supplies Ltd.
   - A new business owner deposits $12 000 of her savings to the business bank account.
   - A credit sale for $300 to C Perez has been recorded in error as $330.
   - An irrecoverable debt for $1 400 is written off.
   - A business owner withdraws $500 in cash from his business for his own use.

   (b) Which ledger account will you need to debit and which ledger account will you need to credit for each transaction?
3. (a) What is the narrative of a journal entry? (b) Explain why a narrative is necessary.
4. (a) What is an opening entry?; (b) When will a business need to record opening entries in the general journal?
5. Explain **three** advantages of keeping a general journal.

The general journal

6 Sanjay started up in business on 1 May last year. Prepare journal entries, including narratives, to record the following transactions during the month:

Date	Details	Amount $
May 1	Opening capital deposited in the business bank account	7 000
3	Cheque issued to purchase computer equipment	2 100
5	Cheque issued to purchase fixtures and fittings	1 600
6	Goods for resale purchased on credit from TXS Supplies Ltd.	5 000
12	Bank loan received	6 000
17	Bank transfer to purchase delivery van	6 000
21	Shop alarm system purchased on credit from Segura Ltd.	3 900

7 Babita runs a small shop. She had to close her business for the month of March last year to undertake repairs following a burst water pipe on her premises during February. During March, these transactions took place:

Date	Details	Amount $
Mar 2	Damaged inventory written off	1 200
5	Compensation received from the insurance company	5 000
8	Sold off water-damaged furniture and fittings for cash	160
13	Cheque issued to Brackett and Sons Ltd. for building works	2 500
18	Bought new furniture and fittings on credit from Outfitters SA	1 300
27	Wrote off irrecoverable debt on C Henning trade receivable account	450
28	Correction for sales in February of $200 recorded in error as $2 000	1 800

(a) Prepare journal entries, including narratives, to record the transactions.

(b) The bank account of Babita's business was overdrawn on 1 March by $400. Update the bank account in the cash book with relevant transactions from the above table and show the balance carried down on 31 March.

8 Karim buys and sells designer sunglasses. The statement of financial position of his business as at 1 September last year was as follows:

Karim

Statement of financial position as at 1 September

		$
Assets	Equipment	26 000
	Inventory	1 100
	Trade receivables	2 400
	Bank	4 000
		33 500
less		
Liabilities	Trade payables	3 500
Capital		30 000

The following transactions then took place during September:

Date	Details	Amount $
Sep 2	Bank loan received into the bank account	12 000
3	Cheque issued to pay for a new delivery van	12 000
8	Bank transfer to supplier Sunspot Ltd. to settle the account in full	3 500
12	Credit sale to T R Duncan	900
17	Purchased goods on credit from Spex Ltd.	5 000
26	Old delivery van sold for cash	3 000
30	Bank transfer to an employee to pay wages for the month	2 500

(a) Prepare journal entries including narratives for the transactions.

(b) Prepare an updated statement of the financial position of the business as at 30 September.

Unit 1.7 The ledger

AIMS

By the end of this unit you should be able to

- prepare **ledger accounts**
- post transactions to the ledger accounts
- balance ledger account as required and make transfers to financial statements
- interpret ledger accounts and their balances

1.7.1 Preparing ledger accounts

Ledger accounts should be prepared for sales, purchases and all other incomes, expenses, assets, liabilities and capital items that will appear in the general ledger

Once a business has prepared its various journals it is time to write up the ledger. A business will open and keep ledger accounts for every type of asset, liability, source of income and expense it has and also personal ledger accounts for each of its trade payables and trade receivables. The **ledger** is the "book" that contains all the different accounts of an organisation providing a permanent summary of all the transactions entered in journals. The cash book is also part of the ledger because it contains the ledger accounts for cash and bank transactions. ➤ 1.5

Entries in the various sales and purchases journals are simply lists of similar transactions in the order they occur. They do not group transactions by individual customer or supplier so that the amount owed by or to another person or organisation can be calculated at the end of day, month or year. ➤ 1.4

Similarly, transactions recorded in the general journal are listed in date order but are not grouped together according to what they were for, for example for rent paid or received.

The ledger is therefore arranged so that transactions can be grouped together according to customer, supplier and/or type of asset, liability, income or expense. Each page or section of the ledger will contain a different account which is written up with entries from the journal. This can be done at the end of each day, week or month but if it is left too long the task becomes a major one and more errors are likely to be made.

The process of transferring journal entries to the ledger is called **posting**. That is, each entry in a book of prime entry is posted to an account in the ledger. ➤ 1.4

Ledger accounts are usually arranged in a "T" shape to separate debits from credits

You may recall from Unit 1.2 that in their simplest form each ledger account is arranged into a "T" format, because the shape of each account is like a big letter "T". The title or name of the ledger account is shown on top of the "T" and debit (Dr) and credit (Cr) entries are made either side of it.

▼ Typical layout of a ledger account in a "T" format

		Name of account			
Dr					Cr
Date	Details	$	Date	Details	$

In double-entry book-keeping every transaction will affect two ledger accounts. For every entry to the debit side of an account there must be a corresponding credit entry to another account. Similarly, for every credit entry to an account there must be corresponding debit entry to another account. ▶ 1.2

It is important to determine whether an entry to a ledger account should be a debit or a credit. An easy way to decide and to remember is as follows:

- cash and anything else of value coming **in** to the business is a **debit**
- cash and anything else of value being taken **out** of the business is a **credit**.

For example, when a business owner starts up his or her own small business for the first time and invests $15 000 of his or her own equity the following double entries are made:

Bank account	Capital account
A *debit* entry for $15 000 deposited in the business bank account	A *credit* entry for $15 000 taken out of the owner's funds to invest as equity in the business

If the business now sells goods on credit for $400 to a customer the following double entries will be necessary.

Trade receivables account	Sales account
A *debit* entry of $400 for money owed by the credit customer that will eventually be paid *in* to the business	A *credit* entry for $400 of goods shipped *out* of the business to the customer

If the business buys some equipment from a supplier on credit for $6 000 the following double entries will be required:

Equipment account	Trade payable account
A *debit* entry for $6 000 of new equipment coming *in* to the business	A *credit* entry for $6 000 that will be paid *out* by the business in future to settle its debt to the supplier

1.7.2 Recording purchases in the ledger

Goods purchased by a business for resale will increase its inventory of goods

Purchases are goods bought for cash or on credit from suppliers that the business intends to sell to earn revenue. ➤ 1.4

Purchases of goods will increase the amount of **inventory** a business holds for the purpose of resale to customers. Inventory is a current asset to a business because it can be sold off to raise cash. It is important to keep a record of purchases to monitor how much the business has spent on goods, how much it owes to individual suppliers for goods they have supplied on credit and the sale of inventory.

To record purchases, a number of accounts must be opened in the ledger.

In the purchases ledger:	In the general ledger:
a **trade payable account** for each supplier to record purchases on credit from, and the amount owed to, each supplier	a **purchases account** to record all cash and credit purchases
	a **cash account** to record payments made for purchases in cash ➤ 1.5
	a **bank account** to record payments for purchases by cheque or bank transfer ➤ 1.5

In contrast, the purchase and cost of any other items used up in the day-to-day running of the business will be recorded as expenses in different expense accounts in the general ledger.

In this unit we will follow the example of Gemma Kardar, a small trader operating a mobile shop called Veg Out. Veg Out sells and delivers fresh fruit and vegetables direct to businesses and householders. She receives most of the produce she needs at regular intervals from two major fruit and vegetable suppliers, Agricol Ltd. and SD Fruits Ltd., but also makes occasional cash purchases from local farms.

The table below lists Gemma's purchases during the month of June last year.

▼ Veg Out purchase transactions (June)

Date	Cash transactions	Amount $	Key
June 5	Cash purchase of cucumbers from a local farmer	40	A1
11	Cash purchase of kiwi fruits from a local farmer	20	A1
17	Cash purchase of three bags of potatoes by cheque from a local farmer	30	A2
18	Return of one bag of potatoes purchased with cash to a local farmer	10	B
30	Bank transfer to Agricol Ltd.	75	E

Date	Credit transactions	Amount $	
June 2	Vegetables supplied on credit by Agricol Ltd.	100	C
16	Vegetables supplied on credit by SD Fruits Ltd.	100	C
25	Return of goods supplied on credit to Agricol Ltd.	25	D

A   **Purchases paid for immediately with cash or by cheque are recorded in the purchases account in the general ledger**

When Gemma Kardar purchased vegetables from local farmers on 5, 11 and 17 June last year she posted the following double entries to her ledger accounts for cash and purchases:

(A1) For cash only purchases:

Purchases account	Cash account
Debit the account at the end of the month with the balances for cash purchases on the cash account in the cash book	Credit the account with the cash paid out for each purchase
Impact: inventory is increased	Impact: cash in hand is decreased

(A2) For cash purchases by cheque or bank transfer:

Purchases account	Bank account
Debit the account at the end of the month with the balances for cash purchases on the bank account in the cash book	Credit the account with the cash paid out for each purchase
Impact: inventory is increased	Impact: cash in bank is decreased

The analysis for purchases in the cash book will provide a record of each individual cash or bank payment for purchased items. As such, only credit balances at the end of the month for total purchases on the cash and bank accounts in the cash book need to be posted to the debit side of the purchases account. The debit balance to the purchases account will record the goods that came *in* to the business during the month.

1.48 POSTING CASH PURCHASES TO THE PURCHASES ACCOUNT

Illustration 1.48 shows the ledger entries Gemma made but to keep things simple only the analysis column for purchases is shown on the credit side of her cash book. ▶ 1.5

G Kardar
Cash Book

Dr								Cr
Date	Details	Cash $	Bank $	Date	Analysis column for purchases	Cash $	Bank $
				Jun 5	Purchases	40	
				Jun 11	Purchases	20	
				Jun 23	Purchases		30
				Jun 30		60	30

General ledger   **A**   G Kardar
Purchases account

Dr				Cr
Date		$	Date	$
Jun 30	Cash	60		
Jun 30	Bank	30		

The ledger   **115**

B Purchases returns will reduce inventory

It is sometimes necessary for a business to return goods purchased to its supplier because they were supplied in error or faulty in some way. Goods bought for resale that are subsequently sent back to their suppliers are **purchases returns** or **returns outward**. ➤ 1.4

Goods returned to suppliers will reduce the amount of goods a business has to sell to its customers. A **purchases returns account** will need to be opened in the purchases ledger to record this movement of goods.

If the original purchase was paid for with cash, cheque or bank transfer then the refund for goods returned will increase the asset of cash in hand or in the bank. However, if the original purchase was on credit then the amount owed on the trade payable account for that supplier will be reduced.

On 18 June last year Gemma Kardar had to return one of three bags of potatoes she had purchased by cheque the previous day from a local farm at a total cost of $30. When Gemma had opened the bag she had found the potatoes were rotten and were not fit for resale. The farmer refunded her $10 in cash for the returned goods. Gemma therefore had to post entries for cash coming *in* to her business and goods going *out* as follows:

(B) For a cash purchase returned:

Cash account	Purchases returns account
Debit the cash account with each cash refund received	Credit the account at the end of the month with the balance(s) for purchases returned recorded in the cash and/or bank accounts in the cash book.
Impact: cash in hand is increased	Impact: inventory is decreased

1.49 POSTING CASH PURCHASES RETURNS

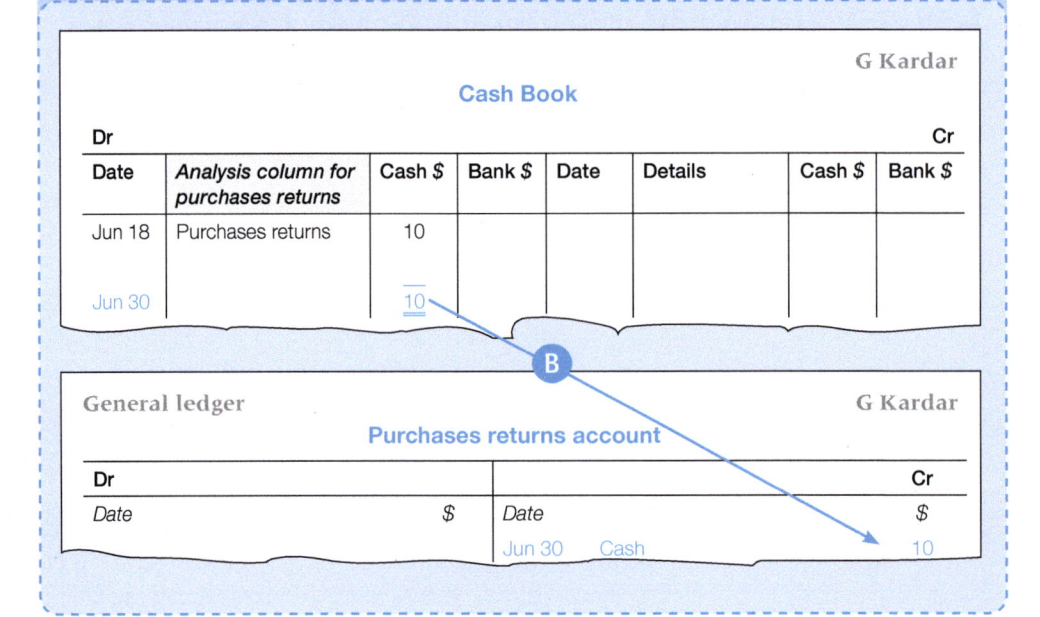

Cash Book — G Kardar

Dr								Cr
Date	Analysis column for purchases returns	Cash $	Bank $	Date	Details		Cash $	Bank $
Jun 18	Purchases returns	10						
Jun 30		10						

General ledger — G Kardar

Purchases returns account

Dr				Cr
Date	$	Date		$
		Jun 30	Cash	10

C–E **A credit purchase requires two sets of double entries to record the amount owed to the trade payable and when payment is made to settle the account**

The purchases ledger of a business contains the personal accounts of trade payables who have supplied it with goods for resale on credit payment terms. Purchases on credit from trade payables will increase the inventory of goods held by the business but will increase its current liabilities.

Agricol Ltd. and SD Fruits Ltd. make regular deliveries of fruit and vegetables to Gemma Kardar's Veg Out business. As they arrive Gemma records them in her purchases journal. From the table on page 114 listing her credit purchases from last June Gemma wrote up her purchases journal as follows:

▼ Veg Out purchases journal (June)

Purchases journal			G Kardar
Date	Description	Invoice number	Amount $
Jun 2	Agricol Ltd. Vegetables supplied	AG2899	100
Jun 16	SD Fruits Ltd. Fruit supplied	AG3304	100
Jun 30	Transfer to purchases account		200

At the end of the month Gemma posted the total for credit purchases on her purchases journal to the following ledger accounts:

(C) **For purchases on credit:**

Purchases account	Trade payable account(s)
Post total purchases from the purchases journal to the debit side of the account at the end of the month	For each supplier listed in the purchases journal, credit the supplier's trade payable account with purchases on credit from that supplier
Impact: inventory is increased	Impact: trade payables are increased

Gemma's updated accounts are shown in illustration 1.50 below. The total debit entry to her purchases account is the double entry for the individual credit entries she made to her trade payable accounts for Agricol Ltd. and SD Fruits Ltd.

It is good practice to post entries for credit purchases from the purchases journal to trade payable accounts as soon as possible so that each account is kept up to date with how much the business is owed. However, many businesses will wait to do so until the end of each month when they will also post the journal total to their purchases account. The single debit entry to the purchases account should always be exactly equal to the sum of the individual credit entries to trade payable accounts.

The ledger

1.50 POSTING CREDIT PURCHASES TO THE LEDGER

General ledger — G Kardar

Purchases account

Dr					Cr
Date		$	Date		$
Jun 30	Cash	60			
Jun 30	Bank	30			
Jun 30	Total from purchases journal	200			

(C)

Purchases ledger — G Kardar

Agricol Ltd. account

Dr					Cr
Date		$	Date		$
			Jun 2	Purchases	100

Purchases ledger — G Kardar

SD Fruits

Dr					Cr
Date		$	Date		$
			Jun 16	Purchases	100

However, on 25 June Gemma had to return a consignment of papayas costing $25 that had been delivered by mistake as part of her regular order by Agricol Ltd. In return Agricol Ltd. issued Veg Out a credit note for $25. Gemma initially recorded the goods returned in her purchases returns journal as follows:

▼ Veg Out purchases returns journal (June)

Purchases returns journal — G Kardar

Date	Description	Credit note number	Amount $
Jun 25	Agricol Ltd.	CN1437	25
	Fruit – delivery in error		
Jun 30	Transfer to purchases returns account		25

Purchases returns are posted to the ledger as follows:

(D) For credit purchases returned:

Trade payable account(s)	Purchases returns account
For each supplier listed in the purchases returns journal, debit the supplier's trade payable account with purchases returns to that supplier	Post total purchases returns from the purchases returns journal to the credit side of the account at the end of the month
Impact: trade payables are decreased	Impact: inventory is decreased

The single credit entry to the purchases returns account for total purchases returns is therefore the double entry for all the individual entries posted to the debit side of trade payable accounts.

The fundamentals of accounting

1.51 POSTING CREDIT PURCHASES RETURNS TO THE LEDGER

General ledger — G Kardar

Purchases returns account

Dr				Cr
Date	$	Date		$
		Jun 30	Cash	10
		Jun 30	Total from purchases returns journal	25

(D)

Purchases ledger — G Kardar

Agricol Ltd. account

Dr					Cr
Date		$	Date		$
Jun 30	Purchases returns	25	Jun 2	Purchases	100

Gemma has always settled her account with suppliers promptly and in full at the end of each month. Last June was no different when, on 30 June, she paid off the $100 she owed SD Fruits Ltd. for credit purchases she had made from the company on 16 June. However, the credit note for $25 issued by Agricol Ltd. on 25 June for goods returned had reduced the total amount Gemma owed to Agricol from $100 to $75. Gemma arranged for $75 to be transferred from her business bank account for Veg Out to the bank account of Agricol Ltd. on 30 June. Her ledger recorded the payment made as follows:

(E) For a payment of purchases on credit

Trade payable account	Cash (or bank) account
Debit the account of the supplier with the amount paid	Credit the cash (or bank) account with the amount paid out to the supplier in cash (or by cheque or bank transfer)
Impact: trade payable is decreased	Impact: cash in hand (or in bank) is decreased

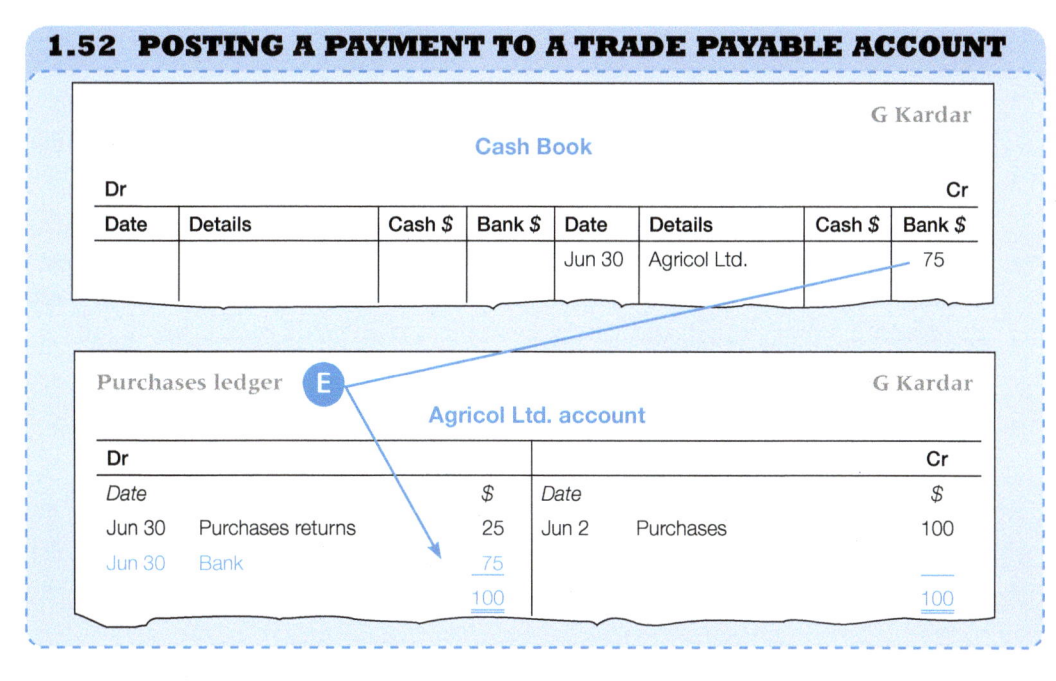

1.52 POSTING A PAYMENT TO A TRADE PAYABLE ACCOUNT

Cash Book — G Kardar

Dr							Cr
Date	Details	Cash $	Bank $	Date	Details	Cash $	Bank $
				Jun 30	Agricol Ltd.		75

Purchases ledger (E) — G Kardar

Agricol Ltd. account

Dr					Cr
Date		$	Date		$
Jun 30	Purchases returns	25	Jun 2	Purchases	100
Jun 30	Bank	75			
		100			100

Following her payment Gemma's trade payable account for Agricol Ltd. was "in balance" because both sides were equal to $100 at the end of the month. To show this the total of the debit entries and the total of credit entries to the account were underlined or ruled off with two lines. This also closed the account for June. As Gemma had paid off her liability to Agricol Ltd. in full there was no outstanding balance to carry down to 1 July.

The ledger 119

> **ACTIVITY 1.19**
>
> The purchases journal, purchases returns journal and cash book of V K Smith, a sole trader, for the month of September are shown below. Use the journal entries to complete the following accounts for the business for the month of September:
>
> - D Armero (trade payable) account
> - S Mbafeno (trade payable) account
> - purchases account
> - purchases returns account
>
> **Purchases journal**
>
> | Date | Description | Invoice number | Amount $ |
> |---|---|---|---|
> | Sep 8 | D Armero | A9/54 | 180 |
> | Sep 10 | S Mbafeno | M170 | 300 |
> | Sep 19 | S Mbafeno | M191 | 200 |
> | Sep 21 | D Armero | A9/324 | 135 |
>
> **Purchases returns journal**
>
> | Date | Description | Credit note | Amount $ |
> |---|---|---|---|
> | Sep 15 | D Armero | CD88 | 45 |
> | Sep 26 | S Mbafeno | RF16 | 40 |
>
> **Cash book**
>
> | Dr | | | | | | | Cr |
> |---|---|---|---|---|---|---|---|
> | Date | Details | Cash $ | Bank $ | Date | Details | Cash $ | Bank $ |
> | | | | | Sep 30 | D Armero | | 270 |
> | | | | | Sep 30 | S Mbafeno | | 460 |

1.7.3 Recording sales in the ledger

Sales earn revenue and reduce inventory

As only the cost of goods purchased by a business for resale are recorded as purchases in the accounts then it is only when these goods are sold that they are recorded as **sales**. ▶ 1.4

Sales earn **revenue** for a business and each additional sale will increase its revenue but reduce its inventory of goods for resale. It is important to keep a record of sales to monitor how much the business has earned from goods sold to customers, how much individual customers owe it for goods they have bought on credit and the movement of inventory.

To record sales the following accounts must be opened in the ledger:

In the sales ledger	In the general ledger
A **trade receivable account** for each customer to record sales of goods on credit to them and the amount they individually owe the business	A **sales account** to record credit sales
	A **cash account** to record payments received in cash ➤ 1.5
	A **bank account** to record payments received by cheque or bank transfer ➤ 1.5

Gemma Kardar sells and delivers fruit and vegetables for cash and on credit. Veg Out sales recorded for last June were as follows:

▼ Veg Out sales transactions (June)

Date	Cash transactions	Amount $	Key
Jun 6	Cash sale	35	F
Jun 8	Cash sale	45	F
Jun 15	Cash sale by cheque	60	F
Jun 16	Goods sold for cash returned by customer	15	G
Jun 30	Bank transfer received from Tariq Gill	50	J

Date	Credit transactions	Amount $	
Jun 7	Fruit and vegetables supplied to Tariq Gill	90	H
Jun 8	Return of goods supplied on credit to Tariq Gill	20	I
Jun 9	Return of goods supplied on credit to Tariq Gill	10	H
Jun 19	Fruits supplied on credit to Rupinder Bai	10	I

(F) Goods sold for cash or for payment by cheque are recorded in the sales account in the general ledger

The cash sales of Veg Out on 6, 8 and 15 June last year were posted to its ledger accounts by Gemma Kardar as follows:

(F) For cash sales:

Cash (or bank) account	Sales account
Debit the cash account with the cash received – or the bank account with each cheque or bank transfer amount received – from each sale	Credit the account at the end of the month with the balances for cash sales on the cash account and/or bank account in the cash book
Impact: cash in hand (or bank) is increased	Impact: inventory is decreased

The analysis column for sales in the cash book will record the amount of cash received in hand or direct to the bank account from each individual sale made. Only the debit balances at the end of the month for total sales on the cash and

The ledger 121

bank accounts in the cash book need to be posted to the credit side of the sales account. The credit to the sales account will also record the reduction in inventory during that month due to sales.

Illustration 1.53 shows the ledger entries Gemma made to her books. For simplicity only the analysis column for sales is shown on the debit side of her cash book.

1.53 POSTING CASH SALES TO THE LEDGER

Cash Book — G Kardar

Dr							Cr
Date	Analysis column for sales	Cash $	Bank $	Date	Details	Cash $	Bank $
Jun 6	Sales	35					
Jun 8	Sales	45					
Jun 16	Sales		60				
Jun 30		80	60				

General ledger — G Kardar
Sales account

Dr			Cr
Date	$	Date	$
		Jun 30 Cash	80
		Jun 30 Bank	60

G Sales returns will increase inventory

Goods returned by customers will increase the amount of goods held by the business as inventory even if they are returned to their original supplier because they were unwanted or faulty. A **sales returns account** will need to be opened in the sales ledger to record goods returned by customers.

If the original sale was paid for by cash, cheque or bank transfer then the customer will receive a refund for the return of those items in cash or by cheque or bank transfer. However, if goods purchased on credit are returned the business will issue a credit note to the customer and this will reduce the amount owed on the trade receivable account of that customer. ▶ 1.3

So when fruit and vegetables worth $15 originally sold for cash were returned by the customer to Gemma's mobile shop on 16 June she made the following entries to her ledger:

(G) For cash sales returned:

Sales returns account	Cash (or bank) account
Debit the account at the end of the month with the balances for cash sales returns on the cash account and/or bank account in the cash book	Credit the cash account with cash refunds paid out or credit the bank account with refunds paid via cheque or bank transfer to customers
Impact: inventory is increased	Impact: cash in hand (or bank) is decreased

1.54 POSTING CASH SALES RETURNS TO THE LEDGER

Cash Book — G Kardar

Dr							Cr
Date	Details	Cash $	Bank $	Date	Analysis column for sales returns	Cash $	Bank $
				Jun 16	Sales returns	15	
				Jun 30		15	

General ledger — G Kardar
Sales returns account

Dr			Cr	
Date		$	Date	$
Jun 30	Cash	15		

H – J A sale on credit requires two sets of double entries, one to record the amount owed by the trade receivable and when the account is settled

Tariq Gill is a credit customer of Veg Out. He runs a local restaurant. Gemma Kardar supplies the restaurant with fresh herbs, salad greens and fruit as required and on credit. Tariq has up to 60 days to pay off the balance on his trade receivable account with Veg Out at the end of each month.

Gemma made two sales and two deliveries of food produce to credit customers during June last year on the 7 and 19 June. She recorded them in her sales journal as follows:

▼ Veg Out sales journal (June)

Sales journal — G Kardar (Veg Out)

Date	Description	Invoice	Amount $
Jun 7	Tariq Gill Fruit and veg delivered	VO13	90
Jun 19	Rupinder Bai Fruit and veg delivered	VO14	80
Jun 30	Transfer to sales account		170

By the end of June, Gemma had supplied total goods on credit worth $170 to two credit customers – Tariq Gill and Rupinder Bai. She posted the total to the credit side of her ledger account for sales at the end of the month. This single credit entry was therefore the double entry for the individual debit entries she posted to the trade receivable accounts she maintained for her credit customers to record how much each one owed to her business:

(H) For sales on credit:

Trade receivable account(s)	Sales account
For each customer listed in the sales journal, debit the customer's trade receivable account with credit sales to that supplier	Post total sales from the sales journal to the credit side of the account at the end of the month
Impact: trade receivables are increased	Impact: inventory is decreased

The ledger

1.55 POSTING CREDIT SALES TO THE LEDGER

General ledger — G Kardar
Sales account

Dr						Cr
Date		$	Date			$
			Jun 30	Cash		80
			Jun 30	Bank		60
			Jun 30	Total from sales journal		170

(H)

Sales ledger — G Kardar
Tariq Gill account

Dr						Cr
Date			$	Date		$
Jun 7	Sales		90			

Sales ledger — G Kardar
Rupinder Bai account

Dr						Cr
Date			$	Date		$
Jun 19	Sales		80			

However, after taking his deliveries of fruit and vegetables, Tariq returned produce worth $20 on 8 June and $10 on 9 June to Veg Out. On both occasions Gemma issued a credit note to Tariq for the returned items and recorded them in her sales returns journal as follows:

▼ Veg Out sales returns journal (June)

Sales returns journal — G Kardar

Date	Description	Credit note number	Amount $
Jun 8	Tariq Gill Fruit – delivered in error	C2	$20
Jun 9	Tariq Gill Vegetables – unfit	C3	$10
Jun 30	Transfer to sales returns account		$30

Sales returns are posted to the ledger as follows:

(I) For credit sales returns:

Sales returns account	Trade receivable account(s)
Post the total sales returns to from all customers from the sales returns journal to the debit side of the account at the end of the month	For each customer listed in the sales returns journal, credit the customer's trade receivable account with sales returns to that customer
Impact: inventory is increased	Impact: trade receivables are decreased

The single debit to the sale returns account for total sales returns is therefore the double entry for all the individual credit entries to trade receivable accounts.

The fundamentals of accounting

1.56 POSTING SALES RETURNS TO THE LEDGER

General ledger — G Kardar

Sales returns account

Dr			Cr	
Date		$	Date	$
Jun 30	Cash	15		
Jun 30	Total from sales returns journal	30		

(I)

Sales ledger — G Kardar

Tariq Gill account

Dr			Cr		
Date		$	Date		$
Jun 7	Sales	90	Jun 8	Sales returns	20
			Jun 9	Sales returns	10

The return of $30 of produce by Tariq Gill to Veg Out during June reduced the amount owed on his trade receivable account from $90 to $60.

However, on 30 June Gemma had received a payment of $50 from Tariq by transfer from his business bank account. This required Gemma to make the following additional entries to her ledger:

(J) For payments received for sales on credit:

Cash (or bank) account	Trade receivable account
Debit the cash account with cash received or debit the bank account with the payment received by cheque or bank transfer	Credit the account with the payment received from the customer
Impact: cash in hand (or in bank) is increased	Impact: trade receivable is decreased

1.57 POSTING A PAYMENT RECEIVED FROM A TRADE RECEIVABLE

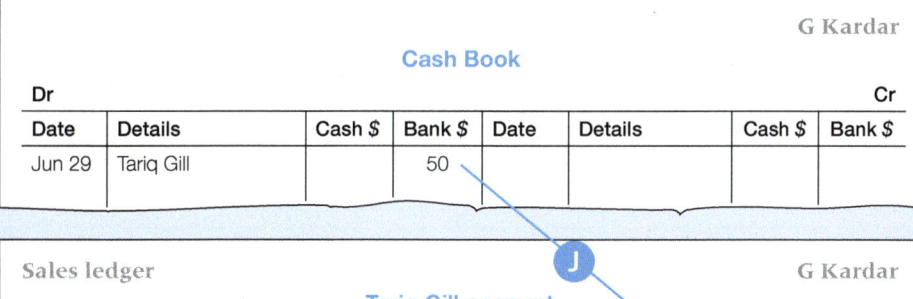

Cash Book — G Kardar

Dr				Cr			
Date	Details	Cash $	Bank $	Date	Details	Cash $	Bank $
Jun 29	Tariq Gill		50				

(J)

Sales ledger — G Kardar

Tariq Gill account

Dr			Cr		
Date		$	Date		$
Jun 7	Sales	90	Jun 8	Sales returns	20
			Jun 9	Sales returns	10
			Jun 30	Bank	50
			Jun 30	Balance c/d	10
		90			90
Jul 1	Balance b/d	10			

Following receipt of his payment for $50 Gemma was able to work out how much money Tariq Gill still owed her on his account. She did this by "balancing off" his trade receivable account at the end of the month as follows:

- The debit side of the account recorded total sales on credit to Tariq during June of $90.
- The credit side of the account recorded sales returns and payments from Tariq of $80 ($30 + $50).
- Total debits to the account therefore exceeded total credits by $10. That is, Tariq Gill's account had a debit balance of $10. This meant

The ledger 125

that Tariq still owed Gemma's business $10 at the end of June. This was entered as the balance carried down (c/d) on the credit side of his account.

- Entering the sum of $10 to the credit side of the account made the totals on the two sides of the account equal to $90. This meant the account was in balance. These totals were then underlined twice to show the account had been balanced off and closed for the month of June so no further entries could be made.

- The amount of $10 still owed by Tariq on his trade receivable account was then brought down (b/d) to the debit side of his account on 1 July. This showed the account had an opening debit balance at the start of July of $10.

ACTIVITY 1.20

The sales journal, sales returns journal and cash book of D Roth, for the month of October, are shown below. Use the journal entries to complete the following accounts for the business for the month of October:

- C Petersen (trade receivable) account
- S Jenkins (trade receivable) account
- sales account
- sales returns account

Sales journal

Date	Description	Invoice number	Amount $
Oct 5	C Petersen	10/109	450
Oct 12	S Jenkins	145-5082	200
Oct 17	S Jenkins	145-5150	150
Oct 22	C Petersen	10/187	675

Sales returns journal

Date	Description	Credit note	Amount $
Oct 15	C Petersen	C56/7	45
Oct 28	S Jenkins	CN155	25

Cash Book

Dr							Cr
Date	Details	Cash $	Bank $	Date		Cash $	Bank $
Oct 31	C Petersen		1 080				
Oct 31	S Jenkins		325				

126 The fundamentals of accounting

1.7.4 The general ledger

The general ledger contains all other ledger accounts for expenses, income, assets, liabilities and also for the personal drawings and capital of the business owners

The **general ledger** (or nominal ledger) is the ledger for all accounts other than those for trade payables and trade receivables. It contains the remaining double-entry accounts of a business for income, expenses, assets, liabilities and capital. Entries from the general journal will be posted to these accounts. ▶ 1.6

In the same way that an account is opened for each credit customer in the sales ledger and each supplier in the purchases ledger, an account will be opened in the general ledger for each type of asset, liability, source of income and expense. Each account will provide a record of increases and decreases over time in the value or amount of each one.

▼ Some examples of accounts in a general ledger

Income accounts	Expense accounts	Asset accounts	Liability accounts
Rent received	Rent	Cash	Bank loans payable
Commission received	Electricity	Bank	Interest payable
Interest received	Insurance	Inventory	Other payables
Discounts received	Telephone and internet	Other inventories	
Other income received	Stationery and postage	Fixtures and fittings	
	Wages and salaries	Equipment	
	Discounts allowed	Vehicles	
	Depreciation expense	Buildings	
	Vehicle expenses	Land	
	Advertising	Other receivables	
	Cleaning		
	Bad debts		
	Training		
	Sundry (or general) expenses		

In addition, the general ledger contains the accounts for the owner's equity invested in the business and any **drawings** made by the owner or owners from the business for their own use. These may include drawings of **goods for own use** taken from the inventory of goods for resale held by the business.

Every expense will require a double entry in an asset account or a liability account

Expenses are payments for items needed to run the business in order to earn revenue or to generate other incomes. Expenses buy in benefits such as premises, equipment, electricity and the efforts of employees that help a business sell its goods or services.

For every $1 spent on expenses, assets will decrease by $1 or liabilities will increase by $1. This is because expense items will usually be paid for with cash or bought from suppliers on credit for payment at a later date. Transactions involving expense items will require the following double entries in the ledger:

- a debit to an expense account to record the expense items coming *in* to the business
- a credit to the cash or bank account to record money paid *out* for the expense item, *or* a credit to an expenses payable account to record the liability to pay the supplier of the expense item in the future.

For example, the table below lists a number of expense transactions by a business during the month of January. On 3 January the business paid out $500 in cash to benefit from rented premises for a month. Because the payment of rent secured a benefit coming *in* to the business it is recorded as a debit to the rent expense account. The cash account in the cash book is credited with the payment to record money going *out* of the business and decreasing the value of its asset of cash.

▼ Some examples of business expenses

Transaction	Expense account	Entry required	Impact on assets or liabilities	Double entry required
January 3				
Paid $500 for rent for month by bank transfer	Rent	Debit rent account	Decrease in asset of cash in bank	Credit bank account
January 12				
Paid electricity bill of $120 with cash	Electricity	Debit electricity account	Decrease in asset of cash in hand	Credit cash account
January 17				
Purchased $200 of petrol on credit	Vehicle expenses	Debit vehicle expenses account	Increase in liability to supplier	Credit payable account for supplier of petrol
January 30				
Paid wages of $3 000 by cheque	Wages	Debit wages account	Decrease in asset of cash in bank	Credit bank account

Illustration 1.58 on the next page shows how the double entries above will be posted to accounts in the general ledger.

1.58 POSTING EXPENSES TO THE GENERAL LEDGER

Cash Book

Dr								Cr
Date	Details	Cash $	Bank $	Date	Details		Cash $	Bank $
Date				Date				
				Jan 3	Rent			500
				Jan 12	Electricity		120	
				Jan 30	Wages			3 000

Rent account

Dr					Cr
Date		$	Date		$
Jan 3	Bank	500			

Electricity account

Dr					Cr
Date		$	Date		$
Jan 12	Cash	120			

Vehicle expenses account

Dr					Cr
Date		$	Date		$
Jan 17	Petroleum Supplies Ltd.	200			

Petroleum Supplies Ltd. account

Dr					Cr
Date		$	Date		$
			Jan 17	Vehicle expense	200

Wages account

Dr					Cr
Date		$	Date		$
Jan 30	Bank	3 000			

Other income earned by a business will require a double entry in an asset account

In addition to revenue from sales a business may earn income in other ways, for example by renting out unused space in its premises to another business or from the interest it received on its savings in a bank deposit account. ➤ 1.5

A business may also earn commission from a supplier from the sale of its products. **Commission** will usually be paid as a percentage of the price of each product sold to encourage the business to sell more. For example, travel agencies will often earn commission from holiday companies for every holiday they sell.

Different accounts can be opened in the general ledger to record **incomes received** from different sources such as rent received, interest received and commission received.

The following double entries will be required to record an income received in the ledger:

- a debit to the cash or bank account to record the income received and paid in to the business.

- a credit to an income received account because that income will have been earned from providing another person or business with a benefit.

The ledger 129

For example, the table below shows income earned from different sources by a business during the month of January.

▼ Some examples of other business income received

Transaction	Income account	Entry required	Impact on assets or liabilities	Double entry required
Jan 7 Rent of $200 received in cash from sub-letting office on premises	Rent received	Credit rent received account	Increase in asset of cash in hand	Debit cash account
Jan 25 Commission of $500 received by bank transfer	Commission received	Credit commission received account	Increase in asset of cash in bank	Debit bank account

The double entries above will be posted as follows to the general ledger:

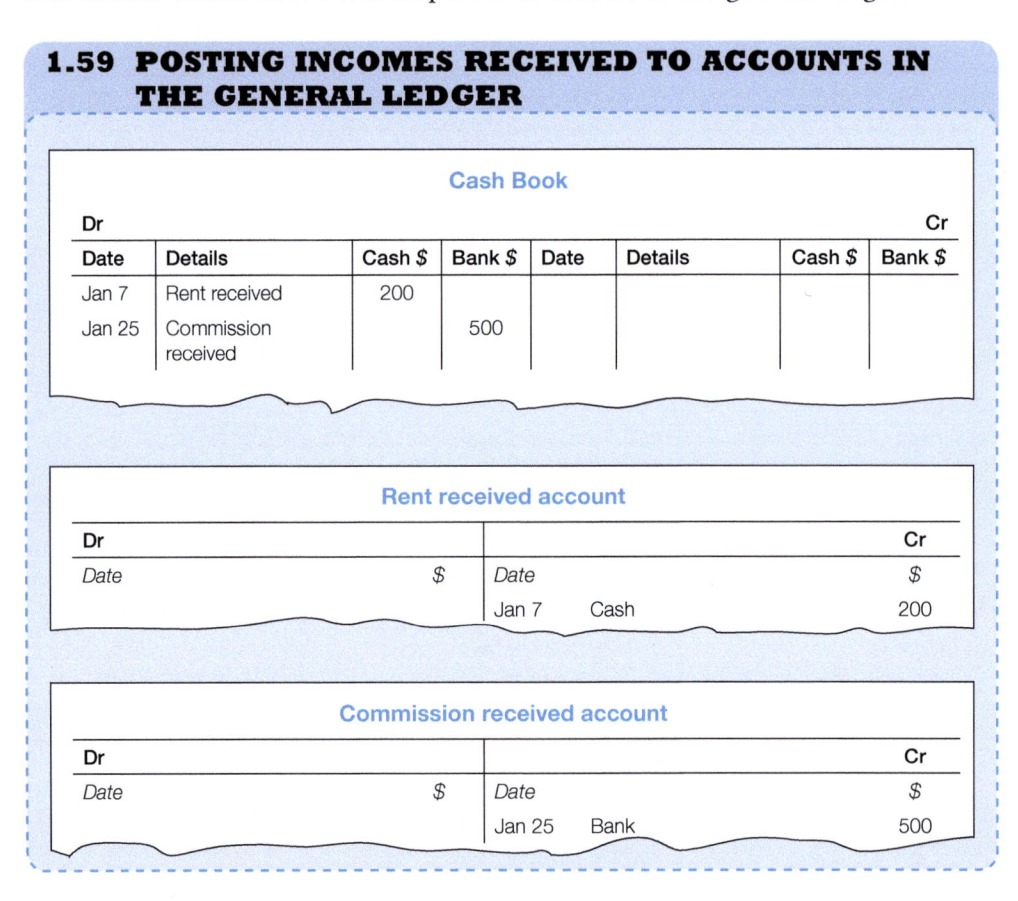

1.59 POSTING INCOMES RECEIVED TO ACCOUNTS IN THE GENERAL LEDGER

Cash Book

Dr								Cr
Date	Details	Cash $	Bank $	Date	Details	Cash $	Bank $
Jan 7	Rent received	200					
Jan 25	Commission received		500				

Rent received account

Dr			Cr
Date	$	Date	$
		Jan 7 Cash	200

Commission received account

Dr			Cr
Date	$	Date	$
		Jan 25 Bank	500

Personal drawings by business owners will reduce assets and therefore the owner's equity

Withdrawals of cash from the business by its owners for personal use are known as **drawings**.

A drawing will reduce the asset of cash available to the business. That cash cannot be used to pay expenses, buy assets or bring anything else of value *into*

The fundamentals of accounting

the business. The reduction in the asset of cash is therefore a reduction in the owner's equity. The following double entries will be required in the ledger to record drawings from cash:

For personal drawings from cash in hand or in bank:

Drawings account	Cash (or bank) account
Debit the account with the amount withdrawn by the owner(s) for own use	Credit the account with the amount withdrawn
Impact: drawings are increased	Impact: cash in hand (or bank) is decreased

For example, illustration 1.60 shows $1 000 of cash being withdrawn from the business on 11 September by the owner for his own use.

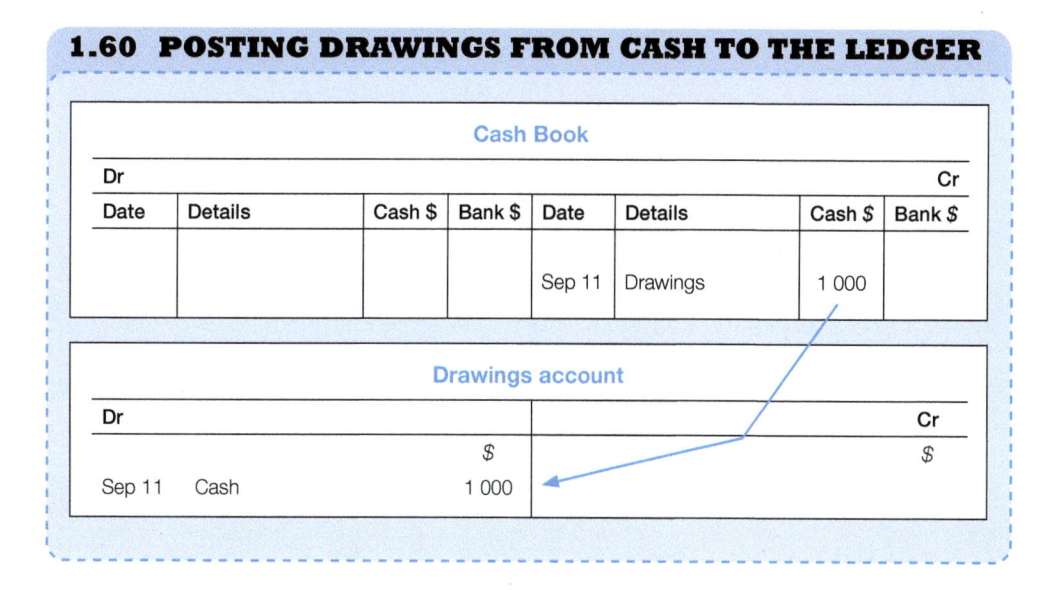

1.60 POSTING DRAWINGS FROM CASH TO THE LEDGER

Cash Book

Dr							Cr
Date	Details	Cash $	Bank $	Date	Details	Cash $	Bank $
				Sep 11	Drawings	1 000	

Drawings account

Dr			Cr
		$	$
Sep 11	Cash	1 000	

Drawings of goods for own use from inventory will reduce goods available to sell and the cost of purchases

It is also possible for business owners to take goods from their business for their own use.

Drawings of **goods for own use** will reduce the amount of inventory a business has. The goods taken will no longer be available to the business for sale to customers for revenue. The owners therefore "pay" for the goods they take through a reduction in the assets of their business and therefore the amount of owner's equity invested in it.

The transaction requires a credit to the purchases account to record the reduction in inventory and a debit to the drawings account to record the reduction in the owner's equity.

For drawings of goods for own use:

Drawings account	Purchases account
Debit the account with value of goods taken for own use	Credit the purchases account to reduce the goods available for sale
Impact: drawings are increased	Impact: inventory is decreased

For example, illustration 1.61 shows $30 of goods being withdrawn from the inventory of the business on 14 September for the owner's own use.

1.61 POSTING DRAWINGS FROM STOCK TO THE LEDGER

Purchases account

Dr				Cr
Date	$	Date		$
		Sep 14	Drawings	30

Drawings account

Dr				Cr
Date	$	Date		$
Sep 11 Cash	1 000			
Sep 14 Purchases	30			

ACTIVITY 1.21

Several transactions are listed below. The first column lists the ledger accounts into which a debit entry will be made for each transaction. The second column lists the ledger accounts into which corresponding credit entries must be made. Complete the table.

Transaction	Debit entry	Credit entry
Owner transfers money from business bank account to personal account for own use	Drawings account	
Employees are paid wages by cheque		Bank account
Insurance premium is paid by cash	Insurance account	
Credit purchase from QWS Ltd.	Purchases account	
Goods sold for cash are returned		Cash account
Equipment is purchased by cheque		Bank account
Commission on sales is received from a supplier by bank transfer	Bank account	
Surplus office supplies are sold off for cash		Office supplies account
Debt owed to the electricity company is settled with a bank transfer		Bank account
Goods purchased and paid for by cash are returned to the supplier	Cash account	

ACTIVITY 1.22

On 1 January Janick Pousson deposited $30 000 of his own money into a business bank account to start his own business selling designer shoes. He recorded the money leaving his personal account as a credit entry in the capital account and the money going into the business bank account as a debit. These double entries record the fact that the business owes him $30 000 of capital.

Capital account

Dr				Cr
Date	$	Date		$
		Jan 1	Bank	30 000

Cash Book (bank account only)

Dr			Cr
Date	$	Date	$
Jan 1 Capital	30 000		

During the month of January Janick also made the following business transactions.

Date	Transaction	Amount $
Jan 3	Paid monthly rent of retail premises by cheque	350
4	Bought shop fittings on credit from Retail Outfitters Ltd.	6 500
5	Purchased equipment (a cash till and safe) on credit from Seguro Ltd.	2 800
8	Purchased inventory of designer shoes for resale by cheque	15 000
9	Paid insurance premium by direct debit	200
13	Paid for advertising services by direct debit	1 600
15	Returned some of shoes purchased by cheque on 8 January to supplier	500
18	Withdrew cash from bank for petty cash imprest	300
21	Sold shoes for cash (banked the same day)	125
28	Sold shoes for cash (banked the same day)	210
29	Sold shoes and received payment by cheque	325
30	Shoes were returned by customer (refund by credit transfer)	125

Open the ledger accounts required to record the double entries for the above transactions. Make the double entries required in these accounts and including, where necessary, to the bank account above.

1.7.5 "Balancing off" accounts

Ledger accounts should be balanced off at the end of each month to compare total debits with total credits

We have already seen a number of accounts that have been balanced off. They included cash and bank accounts in the cash book of Malik Motors in Unit 1.5. Earlier in this unit we also saw how Gemma Kardar had balanced off a number of ledger accounts for her Veg Out business.

Balancing off a ledger account simply means adding up all the debit entries and all the credit entries on that account and finding the difference between them. The difference is the **balance on the account** at that time.

It is sensible to balance off all the ledger accounts at the end of each month to check for any errors, that they are up to date, and to keep track of:

- how much is owed on each trade and other payable account, and by the business in total liabilities
- how much is owed on each trade and other receivable account, and to the business in total receivables
- how much the business owns in total assets
- total income and expenses, to calculate profit or loss to date.

A business will also need to balance off all its accounts at the end of an accounting year to produce its statements of income and financial position. ➤ 3.1

Balancing off an account that has one entry is a simple matter. The balance at the end of the month is the same as the value of the entry made so there is no need to include totals.

For example, the capital account below has just one entry for $7 500 for opening capital that Gemma Kardar transferred from her own savings into the business bank account for her Veg Out business when she first started trading on 8 April last year.

1.62 A BALANCED-OFF LEDGER ACCOUNT WITH A SINGLE ENTRY

General ledger   G Kardar

Capital account

Dr				Cr
Date	$	Date		$
		Apr 8	Bank	7 500

As there were no further entries to the capital account during April the total on the account at the end of the month was a credit balance of $7 500. The account was balanced off simply by ruling off the credit balance with two lines.

Similarly, as Gemma did not make any further entries to the capital account during the month of May last year, the balance on the account at the end of

May was unchanged. In fact, the capital account would continue to have a credit balance of $7 500 at the end of each month until a new credit or debit entry is made to the account.

In contrast, the balancing off of an account with multiple entries involves more steps. For example, Gemma Kardar's equipment account from April last year has multiple entries to the debit side for equipment purchases she made during that month, some for cash and some on credit.

1.63 A BALANCED-OFF LEDGER ACCOUNT WITH A DEBIT BALANCE

General ledger   G Kardar

Equipment account

Dr					Cr
Date		$	Date		$
Apr 10	Bank	220	Apr 30	Balance c/d	1 700
Apr 15	Cash	75			
Apr 21	TJS Ltd.	490			
Apr 24	Hi-Tech Computers SA	760			
Apr 27	Bank	155			
		1 700			1 700
May 1:	Balance b/d	1 700			

The account shows that Gemma brought a total of $1 700 of equipment *in* to her business Veg Out during April last year. The balance on her equipment account at the end of that month was a debit balance of $1 700.

The entries in blue in the equipment account in illustration 1.63 show how Gemma balanced off the account at the end of April:

- First she entered $1 700 to the credit side to be the balance carried down from the end of the month ("balance c/d" for short). This meant the two sides of her account were now equal or balanced.

- She then added up the total debits and total credits on each side of the account and entered their values so they were level with each other on each side. To make it clear they were end of month totals or balances she ruled them off. The double lines below the column totals showed the account was in balance at the end of the month and closed to further entries.

- She opened the account for May with a debit entry of $1 700. This was the balance brought down from the end of April ("balance b/d" for short). The opening balance on the account for May was therefore the closing balance on the account at the end of April.

The ledger   135

In contrast, Gemma's sales account from her first month of trading in April last year had a credit balance of $450 at the end of that month. This showed total cash and credit sales of goods going *out* of the business during the month had been $450, and this is shown in illustration 1.64.

1.64 A BALANCED OFF LEDGER ACCOUNT WITH A CREDIT BALANCE

General ledger					G Kardar
		Sales account			
Dr					Cr
Date		$	Date		$
Apr 30	Balance c/d	450	Apr 30	Bank	80
			Apr 30	Cash	250
			Apr 30	Total from sales journal	250
		450			450
			May 1	Balance b/d	450

The entries in blue to the sales account in illustration 1.64 show how Gemma balanced off the account at the end of April:

- first she entered $450 to the debit side to be the balance carried down from the end of the month, or "balance c/d" for short. This meant the two sides of her account were now equal or balanced

- she added up the total debits and total credits on each side of the account and entered their values so they were level with each other on each side. To make it clear they were end of month totals or balances she ruled them off. The double lines below the column totals showed the account was in balance at the end of the month and closed to further entries

- she opened the account for May with a credit entry for $450. This was the balance brought down from the end of April or "balance b/d" for short. The opening balance on the account for May was therefore the closing balance on the account at the end of April.

But what if an account has debit and credit entries during the same period? For example, in September last year Gemma Kardar agreed to start selling goods on credit to Calum's Café and opened a trade receivable account in her sales ledger for her new customer. During that month she entered debits for all the individual sales on credit to Calum's Café and credits for sales returns and payments received from the business. These are shown in illustration 1.65.

1.65 BALANCING OFF A TRADE RECEIVABLE ACCOUNT WITH DEBIT AND CREDIT ENTRIES

Sales ledger   G Kardar

Calum's Cafe account

Dr					Cr
Date		$	Date		$
Sep 1	Sales	70	Sep 2	Sales returns	10
Sep 15	Sales	60	Sep 19	Bank	100
Sep 23	Sales	90	Sep 24	Sales returns	15
Sep 29	Sales	80	Sep 28	Bank	100
			Sep 30	Balance c/d ❸	❷ 75
		❶ 300		❺	300
❼ Oct 1	Balance b/d	75			

❻

Before balancing off, the total of debit entries on the trade receivable account for Calum's Café for the month was $300 and the total of credit entries was $225. The difference between them was a debit balance of $75. This showed Calum's Café owed Veg Out $75 on the account at the end of the month and would still owe the business this amount the next day at the start of the next month.

To balance off and close the account at the end of the month Gemma followed steps 1 to 7 below.

❶ Add up the total entries on each side of the account and find the difference between them by deducting (taking away) the lower total from the larger total. The account will have a **debit balance** if total debits exceed total credits or a **credit balance** if total credits exceed total debits.

❷ Enter the difference on the next line in the side of the account with the lower total. A debit balance will be entered on the credit side and a credit balance will be entered on the debit side.

❸ Write in the date – usually the last day of the month – and label the entry as balance carried down (balance c/d). This is the **closing balance** for the month.

❹ Add up the entries on both sides of the account again – they should now be equal.

❺ Enter the same total to both sides of the account so that they are level with each other and draw a line above and two lines under each total.

❻ Enter the same amount as the balance carried down to the opposite side of the account but below the underlined total.

❼ Write in the date for the first day of the next month and label the entry balance brought down (balance b/d). This is the **opening balance** for the new month.

The ledger

Following these steps meant that Gemma entered the closing balance of $75 to the credit side of the account so that the totals on both sides were equal to $300. She then closed the account by ruling off the totals with double lines. Then she entered the opening balance of $75 on the account for October to the debit side to show the amount still owed to her business by Calum's Café.

Following the same steps, Gemma also balanced off her trade receivable account for Tariq Gill at the end of last September as shown in illustration 1.66. However, Gemma only had to follow steps 1 and 5 to balance off and close the account at the end of September. This was because total debits and total credits to the account were already in balance because Tariq Gill had settled the full amount of $270 owing on his account that month. The balance to carry down at the end of the month was therefore zero.

1.66 BALANCING OFF A TRADE RECEIVABLE ACCOUNT

Sales ledger G Kardar

Tariq Gill account

Dr						Cr
Date		$	Date			$
Sep 1	Sales	110	Sep 15	Sales returns		15
Sep 14	Sales	85	Sep 30	Bank		270
Sep 26	Sales	90				
①		285	⑤		①	285

Gemma also followed the steps above to balance off her trade payable account at the end of last September for her supplier Agricol Ltd., as shown in illustration 1.67. This was to tell her how much she owed to her supplier at the end of the month.

Debit balance or credit balance?

In double-entry book-keeping:

- Cash and anything else of value coming *in* to a business is entered as a debit to a ledger account.
- Cash and anything of value going *out* of the business is entered as a credit to a ledger account.

This means that ledger accounts for items of value (assets) owned by a business or bought in to benefit the running of the business (expenses) will all have debit balances.

Ledger accounts that record money owed to others namely its liability accounts will all have credit balances.

A useful way to remember accounts that will have debit and credit balances at the end of each month and accounting year is:

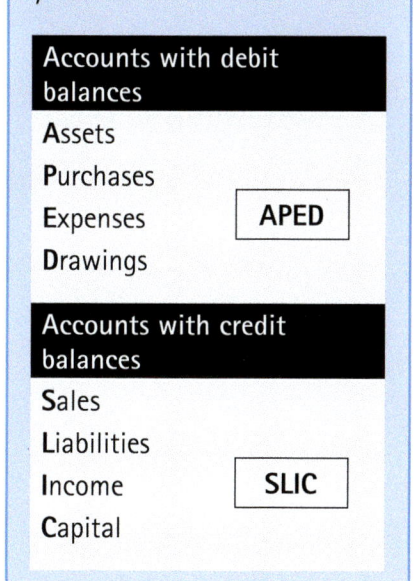

Accounts with debit balances
Assets
Purchases
Expenses   APED
Drawings

Accounts with credit balances
Sales
Liabilities
Income   SLIC
Capital

1.67 BALANCING OFF A TRADE PAYABLE ACCOUNT

Purchases ledger   G Kardar

Agricol Ltd. (trade payable) account

Dr Date		$	Cr Date		$
Sep 1	Purchases returns	12	Sep 1	Purchases	50
Sep 8	Purchases returns	15	Sep 8	Purchases	50
			Sep 17	Purchases	50
③ Sep 30	Balance c/d	② 173	Sep 24	Purchases	50
		200	⑤		200 ① ⑦
			Oct 1	Balance b/d	173 ⑥

Before balancing off, credits to the account for purchases from Agricol Ltd. added up to $200 while debits for purchases returns were just $27. This meant there was an outstanding credit balance on the account at the end of the month of $173. The credit to the trade payable account meant Gemma owed Agricol Ltd. $173 and this was the opening balance on the account for the month of October.

ACTIVITY 1.23

Balance off the following accounts at the end of January and bring down their balances on 1 February.

H Darsi account

Dr Date		$	Cr Date		$
Jan 3	Sales	350	Jan 6	Sales returns	350
Jan 10	Sales	670	Jan 21	Bank	210
Jan 18	Sales	210	Jan 29	Bank	500
Jan 25	Sales	435			

Xi Peng account

Dr Date		$	Cr Date		$
Jan 25	Cash	350	Jan 8	Purchases	75
Jan 25	Discounts received	15	Jan 11	Purchases	40
			Jan 23	Purchases	35
			Jan 29	Purchases	60

Now check your answer – sample answers to all activities are on the website.

The ledger

ACTIVITY 1.24

The following transactions were recorded in the cash book of Vikram Roberts for the month of November. Use this information to write up the ledger account for cash and to balance off the account on 30 November.

Nov	1	Cash in hand of $400 brought down from the end of the previous month
	2	Sold goods for $90 cash
	5	Cash purchase of $450 of goods for resale
	6	Sold goods for $55 cash
	11	Sold goods for $180 cash
	14	Received cash payment of $400 from B Assam to settle balance on account
	19	Customer returns goods bought for $32 cash. He is paid a refund for this.
	21	Paid electricity charges of $160 in cash
	29	Sold goods for $122 cash

QUICK TEST

1. List one type of ledger account you will find in (a) the sales ledger; (b) the purchases ledger and (c) the general ledger.

2. In which subdivision of the ledger would you find the following types of ledger accounts: income received, expenses, assets, liabilities and capital?

3. For each transaction in the table below identify (a) the two ledger accounts that will be affected; (b) what the impact will be on each account (an increase or decrease in value); and (c) which account you would credit and which account you would debit to record the impact.

   The first transaction has been completed to help you.

Transaction	Ledger account 1			Ledger account 2		
	Account	Impact	Dr or Cr	Account	Impact	Dr or Cr
Purchase of new equipment with cash	Equipment	Increase	Dr	Cash	Decrease	Cr
Received cheque payment from a trade receivable						
Goods for resale purchased for cash						
Credit transfer to pay off balance on trade payable account						
Owner withdraws cash for own use						
Vehicle purchased on credit from Vantastic Ltd.						
Electricity charges paid by cheque						

4. Balance off the ledger account below at the end of March.

   CXL Account

Dr					Cr
Date		$	Date		$
Mar 5	Sales	425	Mar 1	Balance b/d	100
Mar 19	Sales	300	Mar 10	Sales returns	425
Mar 30	Sales	340	Mar 28	Bank	500

5. Why is it useful for a business to balance off its ledger accounts periodically, for example, at the end of every month?

6. A trade receivable account has total debits of $11 000 and total credits of $9 000 at the end of a month of June. (a) What is the balance on the account?; (b) Is it a debit or credit balance?; (c) Suggest why knowing the balance on the account is useful.

7. A trade payable account has total debits of $7 000 and total credits of $5 700 at the end of a month. (a) What is the balance to be carried down on the account?; (b) Is it a debit or credit balance?; (c) Suggest why knowing the balance on the account is useful.

8. Explain why drawings are not recorded as a business expense.

9 Pauline started her business last May. She recorded the following transactions during her first month in business:

Date	Details	$
1	Pauline deposited her own money into a business bank account	6 500
2	Cheque issued to purchase equipment	1 200
4	Bank loan received by transfer from the bank	7 000
5	Delivery van purchased with a transfer from the business bank account	6 800
6	Goods for resale purchased on credit from Barrons Ltd.	1 500
10	Cash withdrawn for business use	150
11	Petrol for a van purchased with cash	60
14	Sale of goods on credit to D Ashcroft	780
17	Cash sale	170
19	Insurance premium paid in cash	25
21	Goods for resale purchased on credit from Barrons Ltd.	1 500
25	Cash sale	210
28	Pauline withdrew cash from business bank account for her own use	50
30	Cheque issued to Barrons Ltd. for payment on account	4 000

For each transaction (a) make entries to relevant books of prime entry; (b) post the entries to appropriate ledger accounts; and (c) balance off these accounts on 31 May.

10 The following balances were recorded for Sanaa's business on 1 June last year:

Balances as at 1 June	$
Cash in bank	5 700
Cash in hand	450
Bank loan	4 200
K Taggart (trade receivable)	2 800
Sullivan and Mills Co. Ltd. (trade payable)	4 500

The following transactions then took place during June.

Date	Details	Amount $
1	Paid balance on trade payable account in full by cheque	4 500
2	Cheque received from K Taggart	2 000
4	Bank transfer to purchase new fittings	560
5	Cash sale	270
6	Cash sale	110
10	Loan repayment by transfer from business bank account	200
11	Paid advertising expenses by cheque	430
14	Sanaa takes cash for her own use	40
17	Paid window cleaner in cash	30
19	Cash sale	240
21	Cheque payment to Car Jack Ltd. for vehicle repairs	880
25	Cash paid into business bank account	800
28	Credit purchase from Sullivan and Mills Co. Ltd.	2 300
30	Paid assistant's wages for the month by cheque	1 900

(a) Record double entries for the transactions in appropriate ledger accounts for Sanaa's business; and
(b) show the balances on these accounts at the end of the month.

Unit 1.8 The trial balance

AIMS

By the end of this unit you should be able to
- understand that the **trial balance** is a statement of ledger balances on a particular date
- outline the uses and limitations of a trial balance
- prepare a trial balance from a given list of balances and amend a trial balance that contains errors
- identify and explain those errors which do not affect the trial balance – **commission, compensating, complete reversal, omission, original entry, principle**

1.8.1 The purpose of a trial balance

A trial balance is a list of accounts and their balances in the ledger on a specific date

Preparation of a trial balance is a very important task. A **trial balance** is a list of the balances on the accounts in the ledger on a given date. Illustration 1.68 gives an example.

1.68 AN EXAMPLE OF A TRIAL BALANCE

Trial Balance At 31 March 2013	Dr $	Cr $
Capital		20 000
Cash	10 000	
Fixtures and equipment	95 000	
Sales		420 000
Purchases	250 000	
Rent	22 000	
Electricity	13 000	
General expenses	65 000	
Slater's Stationery Supplies		15 000
	455 000	455 000

A trial balance has a debit column and a credit column. After balancing off each ledger account each balance is entered into a trial balance according to whether it is a debit balance or a credit balance.

The debit and credit column entries in a trial balance are then added up. If they are equal then the trial balance is in balance. This will show that no errors have been made when adding up the double entries in the ledger accounts.

The trial balance 143

A trial balance should be drawn up at regular intervals to check that the books of the business balance and to prepare financial statements

A trial balance is not part of the double-entry system of book-keeping. It is simply a list of balances drawn up to check the arithmetical accuracy of all the double entries entered into the ledger. This list can be prepared at any time. Ideally the ledger accounts of a business should be balanced off and a trial balance prepared to check their accuracy at the end of each month. ➤ 1.7

It is also important for a business to draw up a trial balance at the end of each accounting year to help prepare its financial statements of income and financial position. ➤ 3.1

Preparing a trial balance has the following advantages in business:

- It provides a check on the accuracy of account balances in the ledger to ensure that entries have been made correctly.
- It helps to identify and avoid certain errors that can be made in the accounts.
- It makes preparation of financial summaries and statements much easier because they can be prepared from the balances in the trial balance rather than having to refer to every individual account.

1.8.2 Preparing a trial balance

A trial balance should balance: total debits must equal total credits

In double-entry book-keeping every transaction will require entries to two ledger accounts: a debit entry to one account and a corresponding credit entry to another. The sum of all debit entries to the ledger accounts of a business should always be equal to the sum of all credit entries in its accounts. Because of all the adding up this involves it is important to check whether the two are equal using a trial balance.

As each account in the ledger is balanced off, its balance is entered into the trial balance. If an account has more credits than debits over the same period the difference between them will be a credit balance and this will be entered in the credit column. For example, trade payable accounts will have credit balances at the end of an accounting year to show the amounts owed by the business to its suppliers of goods on credit. Accounts for sales, other payables and capital will also have credit balances.

In contrast, an account with more debits than credits will have a debit balance and this will be entered into the debit column of the trial balance. For example, trade receivable accounts will have debit balances at the end of an accounting year to show the amounts owed to the business by its credit customers. Accounts for purchases and expenses will also have debit balances since they reflect the costs of items the business has received over the year.

We will now look at the preparation of a more detailed trial balance using the accounts of Ben Ashoor in illustration 1.69. Ben has just started a small business with $17 450 of his own capital which he put into the business bank account he opened on 1 June. He is keen to keep accurate records and has just completed and balanced off his accounts at the end of his first month in business following the steps listed in Unit 1.7.

1.69 BEN ASHOOR'S ACCOUNTS AS AT 30 JUNE

Capital account

Dr					Cr
Date		$	Date		$
			Jun 1 Bank		17 450

Cash Book

Date	Details	Cash $	Bank $	Date	Details	Cash $	Bank $
Jun 1	Capital		17 450	Jun 12	General expenses		1 450
Jun 2	Sales	300		Jun 19	J Cappili		4 000
Jun 18	Sales	430		Jun 28	Office Supplies Ltd.	250	
Jun 26	C Parrish		750	Jun 30	Balance c/d	480	12 750
		730	18 200			730	18 200
Jul 1	Balance b/d	480	12 750				

General expenses account

Dr					Cr
Date		$	Date		$
Jun 12 Bank		1 450			

Keytech Ltd. (other payable) account

Dr					Cr
Date		$	Date		$
			Jun 1 Equipment		4 500

Equipment account

Dr					Cr
Date		$	Date		$
Jun 1 KeyTech Ltd.		4 500	Jun 30 Balance c/d		4 500
		4 500			4 500
July 1 Balance b/d		4 500			

The trial balance

J Cappili (trade payable) account

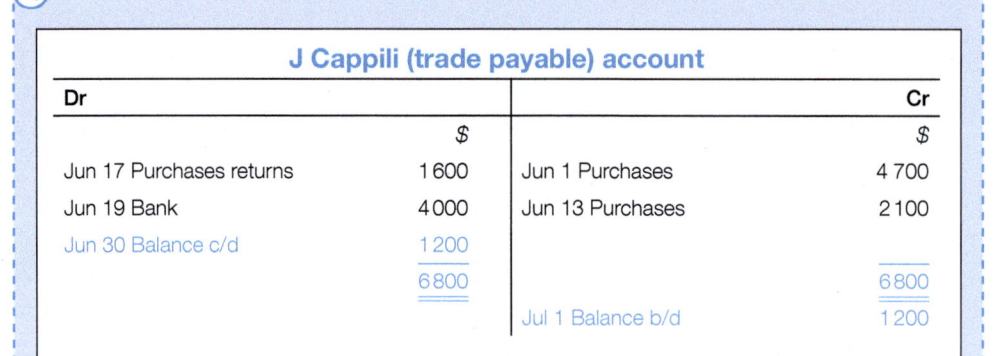

Dr			Cr
	$		$
Jun 17 Purchases returns	1 600	Jun 1 Purchases	4 700
Jun 19 Bank	4 000	Jun 13 Purchases	2 100
Jun 30 Balance c/d	1 200		
	6 800		6 800
		Jul 1 Balance b/d	1 200

Office Supplies Ltd. (trade payable) account

Dr			Cr
	$		$
Jun 7 Purchases returns	40	Jun 2 Purchases	350
Jun 28 Cash	250		
Jun 30 Balance c/d	60		
	350		350
		Jul 1 Balance b/d	60

Purchases account

Dr			Cr
	$		$
Jun 1 J Cappili	4 700	Jun 30 Balance c/d	7 150
Jun 2 Office Supplies Ltd.	350		
Jun 13 J Cappili	2 100		
	7 150		7 150
Jul 1 Balance b/d	7 150		

Purchases returns account

Dr			Cr
	$		$
Jun 30 Balance c/d	1 640	Jun 7 Office Supplies Ltd.	40
		Jun 17 J Cappili	1 600
	1 640		1 640
		Jul 1 Balance b/d	1 640

K Brown (trade receivable) account

Dr			Cr
	$		$
Jun 5 Sales	2 300	Jun 15 Sales returns	750
		Jun 30 Balance c/d	1 550
	2 300		2 300
Jul 1 Balance b/d	1 550		

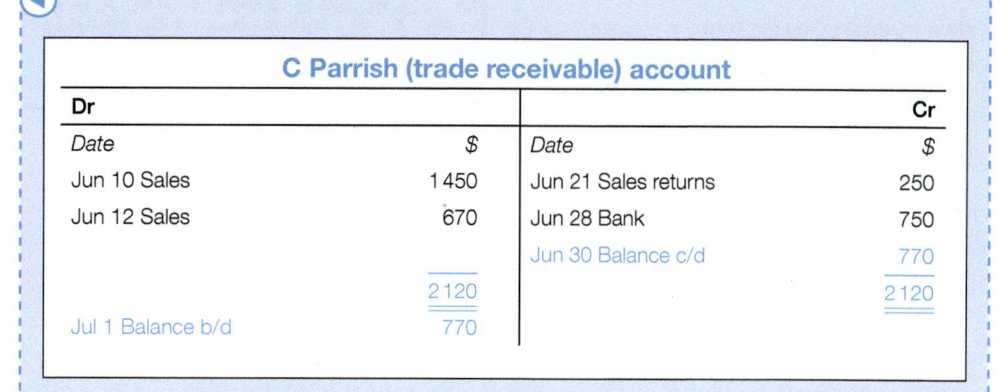

C Parrish (trade receivable) account

Dr			Cr
Date	$	Date	$
Jun 10 Sales	1 450	Jun 21 Sales returns	250
Jun 12 Sales	670	Jun 28 Bank	750
		Jun 30 Balance c/d	770
	2 120		2 120
Jul 1 Balance b/d	770		

Sales account

Dr			Cr
Date	$	Date	$
Jun 30 Balance c/d	5 150	Jun 2 Cash	300
		Jun 5 K Brown	2 300
		Jun 10 C Parrish	1 450
		Jun 12 C Parrish	670
		Jun 18 Cash	430
	5 150		5 150
		Jul 1 Balance c/d	5 150

Sales returns account

Dr			Cr
Date	$	Date	$
Jun 15 K Brown	750	30 Jun Balance c/d	1 350
Jun 21 C Parrish	600		
	1 350		1 350
Jul 1 Balance b/d	1 350		

After balancing off his accounts Ben entered their balances into a trial balance starting with the credit balance of $17 450 on his capital account as at 30 June.

He then entered the debit balances of $12 750 and $480 on the bank and cash accounts in his cash book as at 30 June into the debit column of his trial balance, and so on. ▶ **1.5**

Finally, Ben added up the balances in each column to check they were in balance. His completed trial balance is shown in illustration 1.70 on the next page.

ACTIVITY 1.25

A trial balance will be prepared from the ledger accounts. However, examination questions that require you to draw up a trial balance will normally just provide a list of account balances like the one below. These balances were taken from the accounts of Petra Anastasi at the end of her last accounting year, ending 31 December.

	$
Bank	2 150
Capital	35 000
Equipment	66 000
Trade payables	11 600
Drawings	13 950
Electricity	4 700
Insurance	2 000
Stationery and other expenses	7 900
Trade receivables	7 400
Cash	1 400
Sales	128 000
Purchases	72 000
Sales returns	12 500
Purchases returns	15 400

From the list:

1. Identify those accounts with (a) credit balances; (b) debit balances.

2. Prepare the trial balance for Petra as at 31 December.

1.70 BEN ASHOOR'S TRIAL BALANCE AT 30 JUNE

Ben Ashoor
Trial Balance At 30 June (Year 1)

	Dr $	Cr $
Capital		17 450
Bank	12 750	
Cash	480	
General expenses	1 450	
KeyTech Ltd.		4 500
Equipment	4 500	
J Cappili		1 200
Office Supplies Ltd.		60
Purchases	7 150	
Purchases returns		1 640
K Brown	1 550	
C Parrish	770	
Sales		5 150
Sales returns	1 350	
General expenses	**30 000**	**30 000**

When drawing up a trial balance it is useful to know which ledger accounts will have credit balances and which will have debit balances after they have been balanced off. Some of the most important ones are listed below.

Accounts that will have debit balances	Accounts that will have credit balances
Purchases	Sales
Sales returns	Incomes received
Expenses	Purchases returns
Equipment and other non-current assets	Trade payables
Inventory	Other payables
Trade receivables	Bank overdraft (if account is overdrawn)
Other receivables	Loans
Bank	Capital
Cash	
Drawings	

APED

That is, accounts for assets, purchases, expenses and drawings have debit balances

SLIC

That is, accounts for sales, liabilities, income and capital have credit balances

1.8.3 Sources of error and the trial balance

If a trial balance fails to balance the errors must be found and corrected

Look at the trial balance in illustration 1.71 below. Total debit entries are not equal to total credit entries. Not only have the column totals been added up incorrectly but the trial balance also contains other errors that will stop it from balancing.

1.71 A TRIAL BALANCE WITH ERRORS

Trial Balance At 31 December

	Dr $	Cr $
Sales		440 000
Sales returns	20 000	
Purchases	300 000	
Purchases returns		23 000
Operating expenses	92 000	
Equipment	70 000	
A K Mansilla		12 000
Stationery Supplies Ltd.		25 000
CJK Ltd.		22 000
Cash		6 000
Capital		35 000
	492 000	543 000

The errors in the trial balance are as follows:

① Entries in the sales ledger were incorrectly added up. The correct balance is $420 000.

② The entry for purchases is incorrect. The debit balance on the ledger is $340 000.

③ A K Mansilla is a trade receivable account (a debit balance) not a trade payable account (a credit balance).

④ Cash in hand of $6 000 has been entered wrongly as a credit balance (a liability) rather than as a debit balance (an asset).

⑤ A credit balance of $15 000 on the bank loan payable account is missing.

⑥ Column totals have been added up incorrectly.

1.72 THE CORRECTED TRIAL BALANCE FROM ILLUSTRATION 1.71

Corrected trial balance as at 31 December

	Dr $	Cr $	
Sales		~~440 000~~ 420 000	①
Sales returns	20 000		
Purchases	~~300 000~~ **340 000**		②
Purchases returns		23 000	
Operating expenses	92 000		
Equipment	70 000		
A K Mansilla	12 000	~~12 000~~	③
Stationery Supplies Ltd.		25 000	
CJK Ltd.		22 000	
Cash	6 000	~~6 000~~	④
Bank loan		15 000	⑤
Capital		35 000	
	~~492 000~~ 540 000	~~543 000~~ 540 000	⑥

These errors must be corrected if the trial balance is to balance. The corrected trial balance is shown in illustration 1.72. Each of the corrections is highlighted. Work through each of the corrections to make sure you understand them.

Errors in a trial balance can be the result of mistakes made recording transactions in journals and in the preparation and balancing off of ledger accounts. Mistakes may also be made in the drawing up and adding up of the trial balance itself. ▶ 1.6

▼ **Source of errors that will result in a trial balance failing to balance**

Errors in ledger accounts	Errors in preparing the trial balance
A ledger account has not been balanced off	The columns have been added up incorrectly
An error has been made adding up the entries in one of the ledger accounts	A debit has been entered that does not match the credit in one of the ledger accounts
A single entry for a transaction has been made without a corresponding double entry	A credit has been entered that does not match the debit in one of the ledger accounts
A transaction has been entered on the wrong side of the account	An account balance has been entered in the wrong column
	An account balance has been omitted

Always double check a trial balance: even if it balances there may still be errors

When a trial balance balances it simply means that the total of debit balances entered in the trial balance equals the total of credit balances entered. However, this is not proof that all the ledger accounts used to prepare the trial balance are correct.

For example, what if some transactions made by a business were never recorded in its books? Or if double entries were made correctly but on the wrong side of each account? These errors will not stop a trial balance from balancing but are still important to correct and record in the general journal to ensure that ledger accounts are accurate. ▶ **2.3**

A trial balance will still balance if the following types of error have been made.

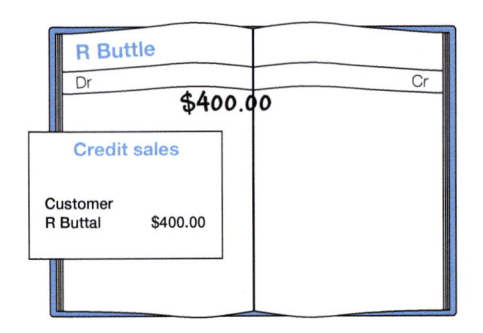

Error of commission

This type of error has occurred if double entries have been made correctly for a transaction but one of the entries has been made to the wrong account in the same ledger. For example, an error of commission will have been made if a credit sale to R Buttal has been entered as a debit to the trade receivable account of R Buttle. The total of all credit sales will be correct.

Compensating errors

Compensating errors involve two or more errors in the same account which cancel each other out so that the ledger accounts and the trial balance will still balance. For example, this would happen if a business failed to record a cash sale for $1 000 but during the same period also failed to record a cash purchase for $1 000. The two errors of omission in the sales and purchases accounts will cancel each other out as will the failure to record the same amount of cash received and cash paid out in the cash account.

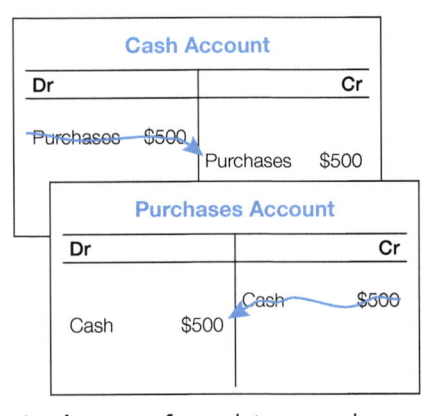

Error of complete reversal

Imagine a business purchases goods for resale and pays $500 in cash but debits the cash account by $500 and credits the purchases account with $500. The double entries balance but have been recorded on the wrong side of each account. The cash account should have been credited with the $500 paid out and the purchases account debited with the goods received.

▲ An error of commission

▲ An error of complete reversal

An error of complete reversal occurs when a debit entry is entered to the credit side of an account and the corresponding credit entry is entered to the debit side of the other account.

Error of omission

This describes a failure to record double entries for a transaction in the ledger accounts. Despite the error, because both the debit and credit entry for the transaction are missing from the books of the business the total of debit balances on its account will still equal the total of credit balances on its accounts if no other errors are present.

Error of original entry

This occurs when an incorrect value for a transaction is recorded in a source document or in a book of prime entry. The double entries posted to the ledger will record the same incorrect value. For example, if a business buys goods on credit from a supplier for $6 000 but records only $600 in the purchases journal then only $600 will be posted to the purchases account and trade payable account for the supplier. The accounts will balance but the business will have understated its purchases and trade payables by $5 400 each.

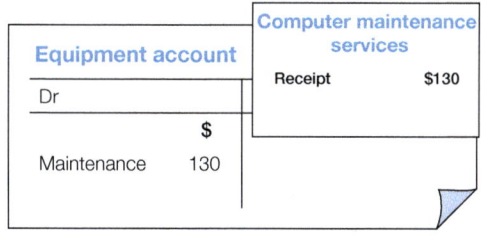

Error of principle

This occurs if a transaction has been recorded correctly – both the amount and on the right side of each account – but in the wrong type or class of account. For example, an error of principle will have been made if computer maintenance expenses were debited to the asset account for equipment.

▲ An error of principle

ACTIVITY 1.26

The following trial balance from the books of Arnold Been has been prepared in a hurry. A number of balances have been entered into the wrong columns.

Arnold Been
Trial Balance At 30 September

	Dr $	Cr $
Equipment	34 200	
Rent	2 400	
Bank	3 700	
Cash	2 175	
Repairs and maintenance	250	
General expenses	12 325	
Sales	100 000	
Purchases		57 000
Trade receivables		6 300
Trade payables	5 500	
Capital		14 500
Lighting and heating	1 550	
	161 200	77 800

In addition, the following errors in Arnold Been's accounting records were also discovered:

- $175 of cash paid for general expenses had not been recorded.

- $200 of expenses paid for the repair of a computer had been debited to the equipment account.

- A cash payment for $300 received was debited to the bank account instead of the cash account.

- The balance on trade receivables had been incorrectly entered as $6 300 and should have been recorded as $3 600.

- A cheque received in payment for cash sales of $1 000 was not recorded in the sales account and the bank account.

- The vehicles account had not been balanced off and was missing from the trial balance. As at 30 September the account had a debit balance of $2 800.

1. For each of the errors above identify the type of error that had been made.
2. Prepare a corrected trial balance for Arnold Been at 30 September.

Preparing and checking a trial balance: a checklist

✓ Draw up a template for a trial balance with three columns, the first column to list account names, the second to record debit balances and the final column to record credit balances. Add the title "Trial balance" along with the day and year on which it was prepared.

✓ Balance off the cash book and all the ledger accounts at the end of the month – or at the end of the accounting year. Enter the account names and their individual debit or credit balances into the appropriate columns of the trial balance.

Accounts with debit balances	Accounts with credit balances
Assets	**S**ales
Purchases	**L**iabilities
Expenses	**I**ncome
Drawings	**C**apital
APED	SLIC

✓ Add up the total of debit balances and total of credit balances. **The trial balance must balance.**

✓ If the two column totals are different then errors have been made and must be corrected. First check that the entries in each ledger account have been added up correctly. Then check that each ledger account balance has been entered correctly in the trial balance and in the right column.

✓ Now check the addition of the trial balance. Add up the balances in each column, first from top to bottom and then again from bottom to top to check your calculations thoroughly.

✓ If the two column totals are still not equal then investigate possible errors as follows:

▸ First try to find a single transaction equal to the difference and, if found, check that a double entry has been made for it in a ledger account.

▸ If not then try to find a transaction that is half the difference and check whether it has been entered twice by mistake on the same side of two double-entry accounts.

✓ If the source of the error has still not be found then you may need to check all the entries for every transaction in all the accounts since the date of the last trial balance. This is also useful to check that there are no additional errors in the accounts.

QUICK TEST

1. What is a trial balance?
2. Why do businesses prepare trial balances? Give **two** reasons.
3. What determines whether the balance on a ledger account is entered into the debit column or the credit column of a trial balance?
4. In which column of a trial balance should the balances of the following accounts be entered?:
   - cleaning expenses
   - sales returns
   - drawings
   - capital
   - motor vehicle expenses
   - insurance premiums
   - vehicles
   - computer maintenance
   - stock
   - a bank loan
   - purchases on credit from WSJ Ltd.
   - sales on credit to D Patel
5. Explain why a trial balance should balance.
6. At the end of its accounting year on 31 December the following list of balances was extracted from the books of a small business:

	$
Capital	40 000
Purchases	46 000
Sales	77 500
Cash in bank	2 300
Cash in hand	540
Trade payables	4 240
Trade receivables	3 600
Vehicles	16 000
General expenses	7 800
Rent	6 000
Electricity	1 500
Equipment	18 000
Drawings	12 000
Bank loan	8 000

Use the information to prepare a trial balance as at 31 December.

7. The following balances were taken from the books of a business on 31 July last year. Prepare a trial balance for the business as at 31 July.

	$
Sales	134 000
Sales returns	12 600
Purchases	67 000
Purchases returns	10 900
Bank overdraft	3 800
Cash	900
S Moran (trade receivable)	4 500
Chemex Ltd. (trade payable)	9 600
Equipment	25 000
Premises	75 000
Drawings	23 000
General expenses	16 300
Wages	32 000
Capital	108 000

8. Explain **three** reasons why a trial balance may not balance.

9. State the type of error that has been made in each of the following cases:
   - Sales to P Murray have been debited to B Murray's account.
   - Sales have been added up incorrectly and have been understated by $4 000 but purchases have been overstated by $4 000.
   - The return of some goods purchased on credit by Amina Kauser has been entered as a credit to the sales returns account and as a debit to Amina Kauser's account.
   - A new delivery vehicle purchased for $8 000 from Premier Motors Ltd. has been debited to the vehicle expenses account.
   - The payment of $500 for telephone charges has been recorded in the accounts as $5 000.

10. The following trial balance does not balance. In addition, when an invoice for goods purchased on credit was recorded it was entered in error as $1 500 instead of $15 000 and on the wrong side of the accounts. Make the necessary corrections to the draft trial balance below.

Draft Trial Balance at 30 September

	Dr $	Cr $
Machinery and equipment		125 000
Rent	11 000	
Cash	4 200	
General expenses	57 000	
Sales		270 000
Purchases	146 500	
Trade receivable	17 000	
Trade payable		30 500
Capital	86 000	
Drawings	25 800	
	347 500	425 500

Unit 1.9   Adjustments to ledger accounts

AIMS

By the end of this unit you should be able to

For other payables and receivables

- recognise the importance of matching costs and revenues
- prepare ledger accounts and journal entries to record **accrued and prepaid expenses**
- prepare ledger accounts and journal entries to record **accrued and prepaid incomes**

For irrecoverable debts and the provision for doubtful debts

- understand the meaning of irrecoverable debts and recovery of debts written off
- prepare ledger accounts and journal entries to record irrecoverable debts
- prepare ledger accounts and journal entries to record recovery of debts written off
- explain the reasons for maintaining a provision for doubtful debts
- prepare ledger accounts and journal entries to record creation of, and adjustments to, a provision for doubtful debts

1.9.1 Making adjustments to the accounts

To calculate profit a business must know how much income it has earned from its activities and how much those activities cost in the same accounting year

Privately owned businesses aim to make a profit from their activities. It is vital that each business is able to identify its:

- **total income**: sales revenues and any other incomes earned in the accounting year
- **total costs**: the costs of the goods or services it has sold and the expense items it has used up earning its total income that same year.

To calculate the profit or loss a business has earned over the course of an accounting year it is important that it matches only those total costs incurred during the year with the total income they helped to earn in the same period. This is called the **matching principle**.

The practical application of the matching principle in book-keeping means the ledger at the end of an accounting year must include:

- income earned during that year whether or not the business has received payment

- the costs of all goods or services sold and every expense item used up or incurred during the year to earn income, whether or not the business has made payment for them. ➤ **5.1**

Using this principle, the difference between the total income earned by a business during an accounting year and the total costs it has incurred earning that income in the same year is its **profit for the year** (or **loss for the year** if its total costs exceeded its total income). ➤ **3.1**

> Total income − total costs = profit (or loss) for the year
>
> *where:*
>
> Total income = revenue + all other incomes earned
>
> Total costs = cost of goods sold + all expenses incurred

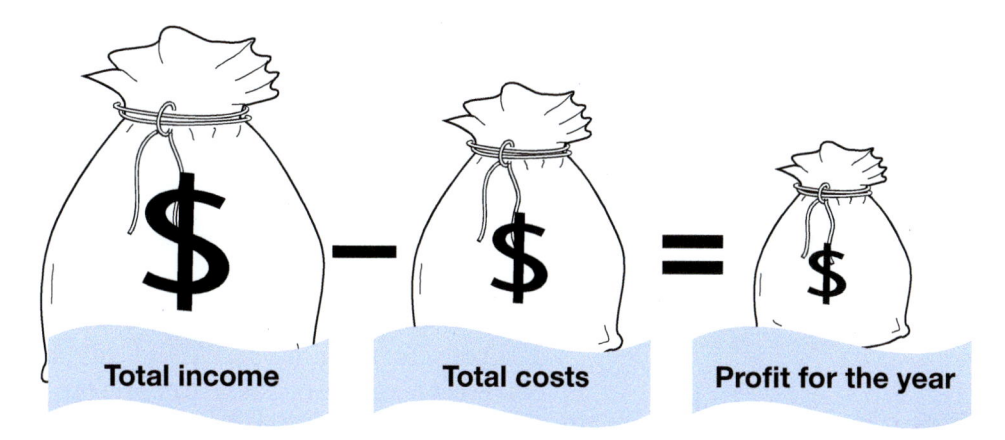

▲ A business will earn a profit if its total income is more than its total costs

End of year adjustments may be needed to ledger accounts for income and expenses before they can be balanced off and used to calculate profit for the year

At the end of its accounting year a business will balance off all the accounts in its ledger to draw up a trial balance and to calculate its profit or loss for the year. All incomes earned during the year should be credited to profit for the year and all costs incurred during the year should be charged to (deducted from) profit for the year. ➤ **1.7**

However, during the course of the year the business will only have recorded transactions in its journals and ledger accounts as it received or issued an invoice and received or paid out cash. This means the business will need to make a number of adjustments to its ledger accounts at the end of the accounting year to make sure they include the following:

- Any expense items already used up by the business which have yet to be invoiced or paid for – these are **accrued expenses**.

- Any incomes earned by the business from supplying goods or services to customers that it has yet to issue invoices for and collect payment – these are **accrued incomes**.

The business will also need to adjust its ledger balances at the end of the accounting year to exclude the following:

- Any expense items the business has paid for in advance but will not use until the next accounting year to earn income – these are **prepaid expenses**. They should only be charged to profit when they are used to the benefit of the business next year.

- Any incomes paid in advance by customers for goods or services that will not be supplied to them until the next accounting year – these are **prepaid incomes**. They should only be credited to profit when they are earned in the next year.

In addition, the business should include in its ledger and calculation of profit for the year:

- **Irrecoverable debts** that the business was unable to collect from its credit customers. The loss of income from irrecoverable debts will reduce profit for the year.

- **A provision for doubtful debts** that the business fears it may not be able to collect from its credit customers for goods or services supplied during the accounting year. The provision will also reduce profit for the year.

The following examples will illustrate why adjustments for the above items are necessary.

Kamal Baahar owns and runs Baahar Bakery. His accounting year runs from 1 January to 31 December. At the end of each accounting year he balances off all his ledger accounts so he can prepare his financial statements of income and financial position. Before he can do so he has to make some adjustments to a number of his accounts. He has to make sure they capture all income earned and all costs incurred earning that income during the year. Now imagine it is 31 December and Kamal is just about to balance off his ledger accounts.

Adjusting for an accrued expense

On 23 November Kamal's oven broke down and had to be repaired at a cost of $400. But, by the end of his accounting year Kamal had still not received an invoice from the oven repair company, or paid for the repair, so there was no record of it in his journal or ledger accounts. His business had however benefited from the repair since 23 November: without it his business could not have baked bread and earned revenue from sales. Kamal must include the cost of the repair in his expense account and in his calculation of profit for the year despite the fact that he will not have to pay for it until the following year. If Kamal did not include the expense incurred this year he would overstate his profit for the year by $400.

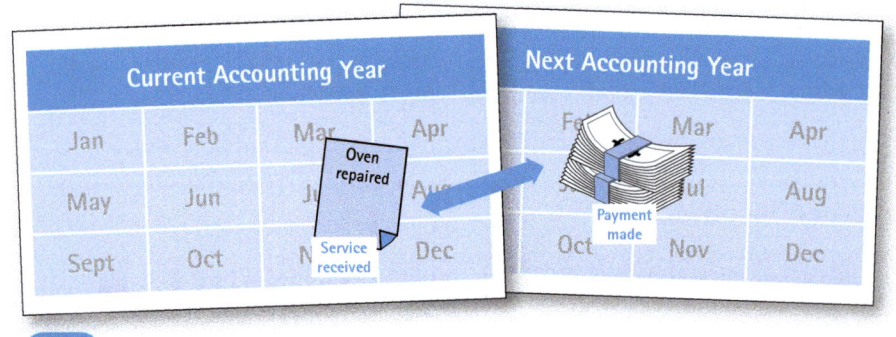

◀ An accrued expense has been used up or incurred in the current accounting year but will not be paid for until the following year. It should therefore be charged to profit for the current accounting year.

Adjusting for a prepaid expense

On 1 October Kamal had paid an insurance company in full a premium of $1 200 to provide insurance cover for his bakery over the next 12-month period to 30 September next year. However, at the end of the current accounting year his business had only benefited from three months (or $300) of the insurance cover. The remaining nine months of cover he paid for in advance would not benefit his business until next year. Kamal must therefore exclude the expense of the unused cover ($900) from his calculation of profit earned this year. Failure to do so would understate his profit by $900. Instead it should be charged to profit next year when the insurance cover will be used up to the benefit of his business.

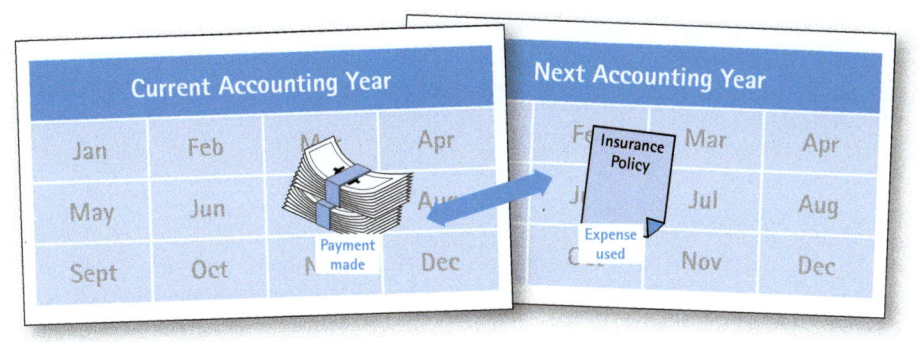

▲ A prepaid expense has been paid for in the current accounting year but will not be incurred until the following year. It should not be expensed to profit until next year.

Adjusting for an accrued income

In addition to the bread he makes on his premises Kamal sells cream cakes supplied by a major food products manufacturer called Cake-Bake Ltd. For every cake he sells Kamal receives a small percentage of the sale price from the company. This is called sales commission. As at 31 December Kamal was owed $200 in commission for cakes he had sold in his bakery between 1 October and 31 December but he will not receive payment from Cake-Bake Ltd. until the end of January next year. Rather than recording this income next year when the payment will be received Kamal should include the amount in his income account for sales commission this year – the year in which it was earned. He should also therefore include it in his calculation of profit for the year. Not to do so will understate his profit for the year by $200.

▲ An accrued income has been earned in the current accounting year but payment will not be received until the following year. It should therefore be included in profit for the current accounting year.

Adjusting for a prepaid income

Since 1 April Kamal has been renting out some space in his bakery premises to another business – a café that makes and sells sandwiches using bread from the bakery. The café pays Kamal a small rent of $150 per month every three months in advance. This also includes a contribution to the bakery's expenses for electricity and telecommunications.

▲ A prepaid income has been received in the current accounting year but will not be earned until the following year. It will contribute to profit next year and should not be included in profit for the current accounting year.

Adjustments to ledger accounts

On 28 December the café transferred $450 to the bakery's bank account for payment of rent in advance for the period from 1 January to 31 March next year. Although Kamal's bakery received $450 this year it will not earn this income until it supplies space in its premises, plus power and telecommunications to the café next year. This means Kamal should not include the prepaid income in his calculation of profit for the year. To do so would overstate his profit for the year by $450. Instead the income received should only contribute to the profit of the bakery once it has met its obligation to the café next year.

Adjusting for an irrecoverable debt

On 25 July D J Menzies, a major business customer of Baahar Bakery, closed down owing the bakery $580. As Kamal would be unable to collect this debt he had to write off the debt in his trade receivable account for D J Menzies. This meant his business had lost $580 of income from credit sales during the year. He should therefore record this loss of income in his account as an expense that will reduce his profit for the year by $580.

Making a provision for doubtful debts

Kamal sells many items from his bakery to business customers on credit. Every time bread and other products are supplied to credit customers the bakery incurs costs but earns income from their sale. This income will not actually be received until those customers settle their accounts in 30, 60 days' time or even 90 days' time in some cases.

As at 31 December most of Kamal's credit customers had paid off their accounts in full but some were not due to be settled until next year. The total owed on these remaining trade receivable accounts was $10 000. This was income the bakery had earned but had not received in the current accounting year. However, Kamal feared he may not be able to collect all of this income owed next year because some of his business customers may not pay up on time, in full and some may even close down before their payments are due. So, before he closed his accounts for the year and calculated profit Kamal included an additional expense for $500 just in case some of the income earned from credit sales was never received. This $500 addition to his business expenses for the year assumed he will be unable to collect 5% of the $10 000 of income his bakery was owed by his credit customers.

Profit or loss for the year is calculated in the income statement at the end of an accounting year

Once all necessary adjustments to ledger accounts have been made at the end of an accounting year, like those made by Kamal to the accounts for his bakery, their balances can be used to prepare the financial statements of the business. ▶ 1.2

Credit balances on accounts for sales and other incomes will be transferred to the income statement to calculate profit or loss for the year. The more income the business has earned during the year the more its profit (or the lower its loss) for that year is likely to be. ➤ 3.1

Debit balances for purchases of goods for resale and expense items will also be transferred to the income statement to calculate profit or loss for the year. The greater the total costs of goods sold and expense items incurred during the year the lower the profit (or the greater the loss) for the year is likely to be.

> **Income statement for the accounting year**
>
> Total credit balances for income earned
>
> less
>
> Total debit balances for costs of goods sold and expense items incurred
>
> =
>
> Profit (or loss) for the year

Balance transfers to the income statement at the end of an accounting year should be recorded in the general journal. ➤ 1.6

It is easy to see when the end of year balance on a ledger account has been transferred to the income statement to use in the calculation of profit or loss for that accounting year because it will include a debit or credit entry labelled "Income statement" equal to the final balance on the account. ➤ 3.1

ACTIVITY 1.27

Each of the following businesses has an accounting year that runs from 1 January to 31 December. For each of the following transactions suggest why adjustments to the accounts for the current year may be necessary:

1. On 17 September a hotel received an advanced payment of $250 from a customer to book a room for two nights from 20 March next year.

2. On 29 November a shop received decorating services from a supplier worth $1 300. The supplier has promised to issue the invoice for payment during January next year.

3. On 14 December a catering business paid $300 for a licence to erect a stall and sell food and drink at a major outdoor music festival that will take place in July next year.

1.9.2 Adjusting for accrued expenses

An accrued but unpaid expense should be charged to profit in the accounting year it was used to the benefit of the business

Expenses are recorded in the journals and ledger accounts when invoices are received for them and payments are made.

However, some expense items may be supplied to and used by a business well before it pays for them. These are **accrued expenses** because the expense items have been used to the benefit of the business. Any expenses that have not been invoiced or paid for by the end of the accounting year should be included in the ledger for that year so they can be charged to profit for the year.

Adjustments to ledger accounts | 161

We can look again at the Baahar Bakery owned and run by Kamal Bahaar. It has an accounting year that runs from 1 January to 31 December. On 23 November the oven broke down and had to be repaired at a cost of $400. By the end of his accounting year Kamal had still not received an invoice from the oven repair company or paid for the repair so there was no record of it in his journal or ledger accounts. However, as the repair had been carried out to the benefit of the business Kamal recorded the expense in the books of his bakery at the end of the accounting year as shown in illustration 1.73 below.

1.73 END OF ACCOUNTING YEAR ADJUSTMENT FOR AN ACCRUED EXPENSE

General Journal

Date	Description	Dr $	Cr $
Year 1 Dec 31	Repairs and maintenance expenses	400	
	Accrual (expenses payable)		400
	Repair on 23 November not yet invoiced		
	Income statement	400	
	Repairs and maintenance expenses		400
	Transfer balance to income statement		

General Ledger — Bahaar Bakery

Repairs and maintenance expenses account

Dr		$	Cr		$
Current year			*Current year*		
Dec 31	Balance c/d	400	Dec 31	Income statement	400
		400			400
			Next year		
			Jan 1	Balance b/d	400

The journal entries record:

- a debit for $400 for the expense incurred in the current accounting year so it could be charged to profit for the year
- a credit for $400 to accruals for the expense payable (a current liability) in the next accounting year
- the transfer of the debit balance on the expense account at the end of the accounting year to the income statement to include in the calculation of profit of loss for that year. ▶ 3.1

Kamal subsequently posted these entries to his ledger account for repairs and maintenance expenses as follows:

Account entry	What is it for?
A debit for $400 ❶	To recognise the expense incurred but not invoiced or paid for in the accounting year.
A credit for $400 ❷	To balance off the account at the end of the accounting year. The balance is transferred to the debit side of the income statement to include in the calculation of profit for the year.
A credit for $400 ❸	The balance brought down to the start of the next accounting year to record the unpaid expense (a current liability).

162 The fundamentals of accounting

Bahaar Bakery also pays electricity charges of $3 000 by direct debit every three months in arrears: a total of $12 000 for the year. Payments are normally transferred from the bank account of the Bakery to the electricity supply company on the 15th day of the month following the end of each quarter. Illustration 1.74 shows the electricity account of the bakery before it was balanced off at the end of the accounting year.

1.74 EXPENSE ACCOUNT BEFORE END OF YEAR ADJUSTMENTS AND BALANCING OFF

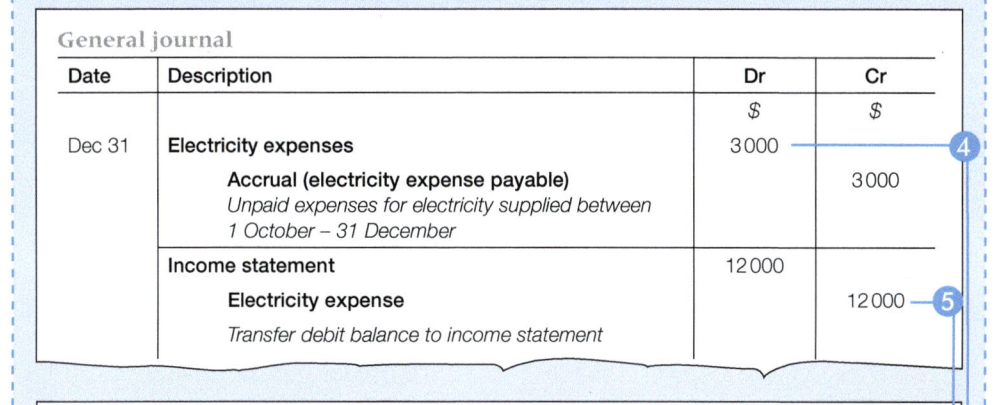

General ledger — Bahaar Bakery

Electricity expenses account

Dr				Cr
Current year		$	Current year	$
Apr 15	Bank	3 000		
Jul 15	Bank	3 000		
Oct 15	Bank	3 000		

The debit side of the account records total payments of $9 000 but the value of the electricity used during the year was $12 000. It is this amount that should be transferred to the income statement to calculate profit for the year.

However, charges due for electricity supplied to the bakery from 1 October to 31 December will not be invoiced and paid for until 15 January next year. Kamal therefore made the following entries to his journal at the end of the accounting year to record:

- a debit for $3 000 for the electricity expenses incurred but not yet paid so that it could be charged to profit for the year
- a credit for $3 000 to accruals for the electricity expenses payable (a current liability) in the next accounting year
- the transfer of the debit balance for $12 000 on the electricity account at the end of the current accounting year to the income statement to include in the calculation of profit for year. ➤ 4.1

Illustration 1.75 shows Kamal's electricity account from illustration 1.74 at the end of his accounting year after he had included entries for accrued expenses, transferred the balance for total expenses incurred to his income statement and, in doing so, closed the account.

1.75 END OF ACCOUNTING YEAR ADJUSTMENT FOR ACCRUED EXPENSES

General journal

Date	Description	Dr	Cr
		$	$
Dec 31	Electricity expenses	3 000	
	Accrual (electricity expense payable)		3 000
	Unpaid expenses for electricity supplied between 1 October – 31 December		
	Income statement	12 000	
	Electricity expense		12 000
	Transfer debit balance to income statement		

General ledger — Bahaar Bakery

Electricity expenses account

Dr					Cr
Current year		$	Current year		$
Apr 15	Bank	3 000	Dec 31	Income statement	12 000
Jul 15	Bank	3 000			
Oct 15	Bank	3 000			
Dec 31	Balance c/d	3 000			
		12 000			12 000
			Next year		
			Jan 1	Balance b/d	3 000

Adjustments to ledger accounts

Account entry	What is it for?
A debit for $3 000 ④	To recognise the expense incurred but not invoiced or paid for during the accounting year. It increases the balance on the account from $9 000 to $12 000.
A credit for $12 000 ⑤	To balance off the account at the end of the accounting year. The balance is transferred to the debit side of the income statement to include in the calculation of profit or loss for the next year.
A credit for $3 000 ⑥	The balance brought down to the start of the next accounting year to record the expenses payable (a current liability).

> **Making adjustments for accrued expenses: a checklist**
>
> ✓ It is important to match expenses incurred with the revenues and other incomes they help to earn in the same accounting year.
>
> ✓ An **accrued expense** is an expense that has been used up or incurred but has not yet been invoiced or paid for.
>
> ✓ Accrued expenses may include rents, electricity and telephone charges, and any wages and salaries paid in arrears.
>
> ✓ An accrued expense should be recognised in the accounts and charged to profit in the year it is incurred and before it is paid for. It is a current liability of the business until payment is made.
>
> ✓ Journal entries will record the adjustments needed for the expense incurred and payable at the end of an accounting year. For example, a business owes wages of $5 000 to its employees at the end of its current accounting year for their employment over the previous month. These will not be paid by the business until its next accounting year:
>
> General Journal
>
> | Date | Description | Dr $ | Cr $ | What are the entries for? |
> |---|---|---|---|---|
> | End of the accounting year | Wages account | 5 000 | | Wages incurred but not yet paid for at the end of the year |
> | | Accrual (liability) | | 5 000 | Wages payable in the next accounting year |
> | | Income statement | Balance | | To charge the debit balance for wages incurred to profit for the year |
> | | Wages account | | Balance | To transfer the debit balance for wages incurred to the income statement for the year |
>
> ✓ The expense incurred but unpaid during the current accounting year is debited to the expense account for the year. This increases the debit balance on the expense account charged to profit for the year.
>
> ✓ The debit entry is then carried down as an accrual to the credit side of the account to record the expense payable.
>
> ✓ Accrued expenses are recorded as other payables (a current liability) in a statement of financial position.

ACTIVITY 1.28

Lali Singh is about to balance off the ledger account below for telephone expenses for her accounting year ending 31 December. Her account records payments of $300 per month for Internet and telephone services every three months in arrears. Her next payment of $900 for the period 1 October–31 December is due on 5 February next year.

Make entries to Lali's general journal to record her accrued expenses, then balance off her expense account and bring down her accrual for expenses payable.

General journal

Date	Description	Dr $	Cr $

Lali Singh: telephone expenses account

Dr				Cr
Current year		$	Current year	$
May 2	Bank	900	Dec 31 Income statement	____
Aug 5	Bank	900		
Nov 3	Bank	900		
Dec 31	Balance c/d	____		____
			Next year	
			Jan 1 Balance b/d	____

1.9.3 Adjusting for prepaid expenses

Expenses that are prepaid in the current accounting year will not contribute to profit until the next accounting year when the expense will be used to the benefit of the business

Some expenses may be paid for by a business well in advance of those expense items being supplied and used in its day-to-day activities. These are **prepaid expenses**.

A prepaid expense will be recorded in the books of the business when it makes payment to the supplier of the expense item. However, any prepaid expense items that have not been used up by the business by the end of its accounting year should not be charged to its profit for that year. Instead that prepaid expense or **prepayment** is a current asset because it has paid for an expense item that will be used to benefit the business in the next accounting year.

Remember how Kamal Bahaar had paid $1 200 in advance for 12 months of insurance cover for his bakery on 1 October. His journal entries and ledger account for insurance expenses recorded the payment made as shown in illustration 1.76.

1.76 RECORDING A PAYMENT FOR EXPENSE ITEMS

Baahar Bakery

Cash Book

Dr							Cr
Date	Details	Cash $	Bank $	Date Year	Details	Cash $	Bank $
				Oct 1	Insurance expenses	1 200	

General Ledger   **Baahar Bakery**

Insurance expenses account

Dr		Cr	
Current year	$	Current year	$
Jan 1 Bank	320		
Apr 1 Bank	320		
Jul 1 Bank	320		
Oct 1 Bank	1 200		
	2 160		

The account also records previous payments for insurance cover during the year of $320 every three months. By the end of his current accounting year on 31 December he had recorded total payments on his insurance expense account of $2 160.

Despite paying $1 200 in advance for insurance cover on 1 October, by 31 December his bakery had only benefited from three months of that cover at a cost of $300. This expense should be charged to profit for the year. However, the remaining nine months of insurance cover worth $900 that Kamal had not used would not benefit his business until next year and should not be expensed to profit until then.

At the end of his current accounting year Kamal made the following entries to his journal as shown in illustration 1.77 to record:

- a credit for $900 to the insurance account for nine months of prepaid but unused insurance cover. This reduced total insurance expenses incurred during the year from $2 160 to $1 260

- a corresponding debit for the $900 of unused insurance cover. This prepaid expense will not be used or incurred until next year and until then it will be recorded as an expense receivable or current asset in the accounts

- a credit for $1 260 to transfer the total expenses incurred during the year on the account to the income statement to include in the calculation of profit for that year. ▶ 4.1

The fundamentals of accounting

1.77 END OF ACCOUNTING YEAR ADJUSTMENTS FOR PREPAID EXPENSES

Baahar Bakery

Cash Book

Dr				Cr			
Date	Details	Cash $	Bank $	Date	Details	Cash $	Bank $
				Oct 1	Insurance expenses		1 200

⑦

General Journal

Date	Description	Dr $	Cr $
Dec 31	**Prepayment (insurance expense receivable)**	900	
	Insurance expenses		900
	9 months of unused insurance paid in advance		
	Income statement	1 260	
	Insurance expenses		1 260
	Transfer of insurance expenses incurred to income statement		

⑨

⑧

General Ledger
Baahar Bakery

Insurance expenses account

Dr		$	Cr		$
Current year			*Current year*		
Jan 1	Bank	320	Dec 31	Income statement	1 260
Apr 1	Bank	320	Dec 31	Balance c/d	900
Jul 1	Bank	320			
Oct 1	Bank	1 200			
		2 160			2 160
Next year					
Jan 1	Balance b/d	900			

⑦

⑩

Once Kamal had posted the journal entries to the bakery's ledger account for insurance expenses and had balanced it off it recorded the following:

Account entry	What is it for?
⑦ A debit for $1 200	To record cash paid out of the bank account for 12 months of insurance cover
⑧ A credit for $1 260	To transfer the debit balance on the account at the year end for insurance expenses incurred during the year to the income statement to include in the calculation of profit or loss for the year
⑨ A credit for $900	To deduct nine months of unused insurance cover from the total of debit entries on the account. It reduces the debit balance to be expensed to the income statement from $2 160 of expenses paid to $1 260 for expenses incurred. It is described as a "prepayment c/d".
⑩ A debit for $900	To bring down the prepayment to the start of the next accounting year. Until the insurance cover is used up the prepayment is an expense receivable or current asset of the business.

Adjustments to ledger accounts **167**

Making adjustments for prepaid expenses: a checklist

✓ It is important to match expenses incurred with the revenues and other incomes they help to earn in the same accounting year.

✓ A **prepaid expense** is an expense paid for but not yet used up or incurred earning income.

✓ Expenses such as rent and insurance are often paid for in advance.

✓ A prepaid expense should not be charged to profit until it is used up or incurred. Until then the unused expense is a current asset of the business.

✓ Journal entries are required to record and adjust for a prepaid expense. For example, a business pays $6 000 for 12 months rent in advance. Four months of that rent (worth $2 000) is unused by the end of the accounting year:

General Journal

Date	Description	Dr $	Cr $	What are the entries for?
End of the accounting year	Prepayment (asset) Rent account	2 000	 2 000	The rental services receivable next year To deduct the unused rent at the year end from the total of debit entries on the account for rental payments made
	Income statement Rent account	Balance	 Balance	To charge the debit balance for rent expenses incurred to profit for the year To transfer the debit balance for rent expenses incurred to the income statement for the year

✓ An expense paid for but unused by the end of the accounting year is credited to the expense account. This reduces the debit balance of expenses charged to profit that year.

✓ The credit entry is then carried down as a prepayment to the debit side of the account to record the unused expense as an expense receivable in the next accounting year.

✓ Prepaid expenses are recorded as other receivables (a current asset) in a statement of financial position.

> **ACTIVITY 1.29**
>
> Ariel Robinson runs a small business. His current accounting year runs from 1 January to 31 December. During his current accounting year on 1 November he paid 12 months of rent for his premises in advance at a cost of $12 000. Payment was by bank transfer.
>
> Make entries to Ariel's cash book to record his payment of rent, then balance off his rent account at the end of the current accounting year and bring down the appropriate prepayment.
>
> Ariel Robinson
> **Cash Book**
>
> | Dr | | | | | | | | Cr |
> |---|---|---|---|---|---|---|---|---|
> | Date | Details | Cash $ | Bank $ | Date | Details | Cash $ | Bank $ |
> | | | | | | | | |
>
> **Ariel Robinson: rent expenses account**
>
> | Dr | | | | | Cr |
> |---|---|---|---|---|---|
> | Current year | | $ | Current year | | $ |
> | Jan 1 | Prepayment b/d | 11 520 | Dec 31 | Income statement | ---- |
> | Nov 1 | Bank | 12 000 | Dec 31 | Balance c/d | ---- |
> | Next year | | | | | |
> | Jan 1 | Balance b/d | ---- | | | |

1.9.4 Adjusting for an outstanding or accrued income

Income earned in an accounting year will contribute to profit in that year even if the payment of that income is not received until the following year

A business will earn most of its income in the form of revenue from the sale of goods or services to customers. However, a business may also earn some additional income in other ways including from renting out premises, commission on sales and interest on any business savings. ➤ **1.7**

It is important to record any income in the books of the business when it is earned so that it can be matched with the costs of the goods it sold or the expenses it incurred doing so.

Any income earned during an accounting year but not received by the end of that year is therefore an **accrued income** and should be included in the calculation of profit for the year. However, until payment of the accrued income is finally received from customers the amount owing or outstanding will be a current asset of the business.

Recall that Baahar Bakery earns income in the form of sales commission from Cake-Bake Ltd. from the sale of its cakes in the bakery. At the end of its current accounting year and before it had been written up in full and balanced off, the sales commission account in Bahaar Bakery's general ledger looked as shown in illustration 1.78.

1.78 INCOME ACCOUNT BEFORE END OF YEAR ADJUSTMENT AND BALANCING OFF

General Ledger — Bahaar Bakery

Sales commission account

Dr			Cr
Current year	$	Current year	$
		Apr 15 Bank	230
		July 16 Bank	180
		Oct 15 Bank	110

The sales commission account recorded payments received from Cake-Bake Ltd. during the current year equal to $520 ($230 + $180 + $110). However, at the end of the current accounting year on 31 December the Bahaar Bakery had earned $200 in sales commission from Cake-Bake Ltd. for the sale of its cakes in the bakery between 1 October and 31 December that year. Cake-Bake Ltd. will not however pay the bakery until January next year. Until then the accrued sales commission will be a current asset of the business.

Kamal therefore had to make the following adjustments to his books to record the accrued commission:

- a credit entry for commission of $200 earned but as yet unpaid in the current accounting year. This increased the credit balance on the account for income earned from $520 to $720

- a debit entry for the income receivable – a current asset worth $200 – because payment of the sale commission will not be received until the next accounting year

- the transfer of the credit balance for $720 on the sales commission account at the end of the current accounting year to the income statement to include profit for the year. ➤ 4.1

1.79 END OF ACCOUNTING YEAR ADJUSTMENTS FOR ACCRUED INCOME

General Journal

Date	Description	Dr $	Cr $
Dec 31	Accrual (sales commission receivable)	200	
	Sales commission		200 ⑪
	Income earned 1 October–31 December		
	Income statement		720
⑫	Sales commission	720	
	Transfer of commission earned to interest statement		

General Ledger — Baahar Bakery

Sales commission account

Dr				Cr
Current year	$	Current year		$
Dec 31 Income statement	720	Apr 15 Bank		230
		July 16 Bank		180
		Oct 15 Bank		110
		Dec 31 Balance c/d		200
	720			720
Next year				
⑬ Jan 1 Balance b/d	200			

The adjusted sales commission account therefore records the following:

Account entry	What is it for?
A credit for $200 ⑪	To recognise the income earned but not yet received by the end of the accounting year. It is described as an "accrual c/d" and it increases the total of income earned in the accounting year from **$520** to **$720**.
A debit for $720 ⑫	To balance off the account at the end of the accounting year. The balance is transferred to the credit side of the income statement to include in the calculation of profit or loss for the year.
A debit for $200 ⑬	The accrual brought down to the start of the next accounting year. Until the bakery receives the sales commission it is owed the accrual or income receivable will remain a current asset of the business.

Adjustments to ledger accounts

Making adjustments for accrued income: a checklist

✓ It is important to match income earned with the expenses incurred earning it in the same accounting year.

✓ An **accrued income** is an income that has not been received by the end of the accounting year in which it was earned.

✓ Accrued incomes may include rent from the sub-letting of premises, commission on the sales of another firm's products and interest on business savings paid in arrears.

✓ An accrued income should be recognised as earned income in the accounts and included in profit before it is received. Until then it will be a current asset of the business.

✓ Journal entries are required to adjust for an accrued income at the end of an accounting year. For example, a business sub-lets part of its premises to another business. At the end of its accounting year it is owed $900 in rent for the previous three months.

General Journal

Date	Description	Dr $	Cr $	What are the entries for?
End of the accounting year	Accrual (asset)	900		The rental income receivable in the next accounting year
	Rent received account		900	Rent earned but not yet received at the end of the year. This increases the credit balance on the account for rent income earned during the year.
	Rent received account	Balance		To transfer the credit balance for rent income earned to the income statement for the year
	Income statement		Balance	To include the credit balance for rent income earned in profit for the year

✓ An income earned but not received by the end of the accounting year is credited to the income account. This increases the credit balance on the income account transferred to the income statement to calculate profit for the year.

✓ The accrued income is then carried down to the debit side to record the income receivable in the next accounting year.

✓ Accrued income is recorded as other receivables (a current asset) in a statement of financial position.

ACTIVITY 1.30

Athil Barir is a self-employed teacher of accounts. He currently has a 12-month contract with a local college. The college year is divided into three terms and Athil is paid $6 000 per term. Athil receives payment a full month after each term completes. His next payment is due on 31 August.

It is now 31 July and the end of Athil's accounting year. Make appropriate entries to his general journal and ledger account below to record his accrued income and to balance off the account. Finally, bring down the accrual to open the income account for his next accounting year.

General journal

Date	Description	Dr $	Cr $

Athil Barir: teaching income account

Dr					Cr
Current year		$	Current year		$
Jul 31	Income statement	----	Jan 31	Bank	6000
			May 31	Bank	6000
			Jul 31	Balance c/d	----
Next year					
Aug 1	Balance b/d	----			

1.9.5 Adjusting for a prepaid income

A prepaid income received by a business will not contribute to profit until that income has been earned from the provision of goods or services to the customer

A prepaid expense by one business to a supplier of expense items will be a prepaid income to that supplier. A **prepaid income** is therefore a payment received before any goods or services have been supplied and invoiced to the customer.

Prepaid income is also sometimes known as deferred or **unearned income**. Until the business has met its obligation to supply items to a customer at a later date the amount of prepaid income it has received must treated as a current liability: if the business fails to deliver the items to the customer the prepaid income will have to be repaid.

Any income that has been received but not earned by the end of an accounting year should not be included in profit for that year.

1.80 INCOME ACCOUNT BEFORE END OF YEAR ADJUSTMENT AND BALANCING OFF

Baahar Bakery
Cash Book

Dr								Cr
Date	Details	Cash $	Bank $	Date	Details		Cash $	Bank $
Dec 28	Rent received		450					

General Ledger   **Baahar Bakery**
Rent received account

Dr				Cr
Current year	$	Current year		$
		Apr 1	Bank	450
		June 27	Bank	450
		Sept 29	Bank	450
		Dec 28	Bank	450
				1 800

Remember how since 1 April the Baahar Bakery, owned by Kamal Baahar, has been earning some additional income from rent paid to it by another business that runs a small café on the bakery premises. The café pays the bakery $450 every three months in advance. This included a payment to the bakery of $450 on 28 December for the period 1 January to 31 March next year. The rent received account of the bakery shown in illustration 1.80 records this and all the other payments of rent it received from the café during the current accounting year – a total of $1 800 rent received.

However, only $1 350 of the total rent received recorded in the ledger had been earned by the bakery by the end of its current accounting year. The prepayment of income received on 28 December was not an earned income but a current liability because the bakery had yet to supply the café with space in its premises, inclusive of power and telecommunications. Until the bakery does so between 1 January and 31 March next year it will not have settled its liability to the café and earned its prepayment.

Adjustments to ledger accounts **173**

So, although Kamal had recorded the cash payment received on 28 December in the books of his business he must exclude it from the calculation of his business profit for the current accounting year. To do this Kamal made the following entries to his books at the end of the year:

- a debit for $450 to the rent received account to remove this unearned income from the total of credits on the account of $1 800 for rent payments received

- a corresponding credit on the account for $450 of prepaid income that will be earned next year. Until then the prepayment received will be a current liability or income payable

- a debit for $1 350 to transfer the total income earned during the year on the account to the income statement to include in the calculation of profit for the year. ➤ 4.1

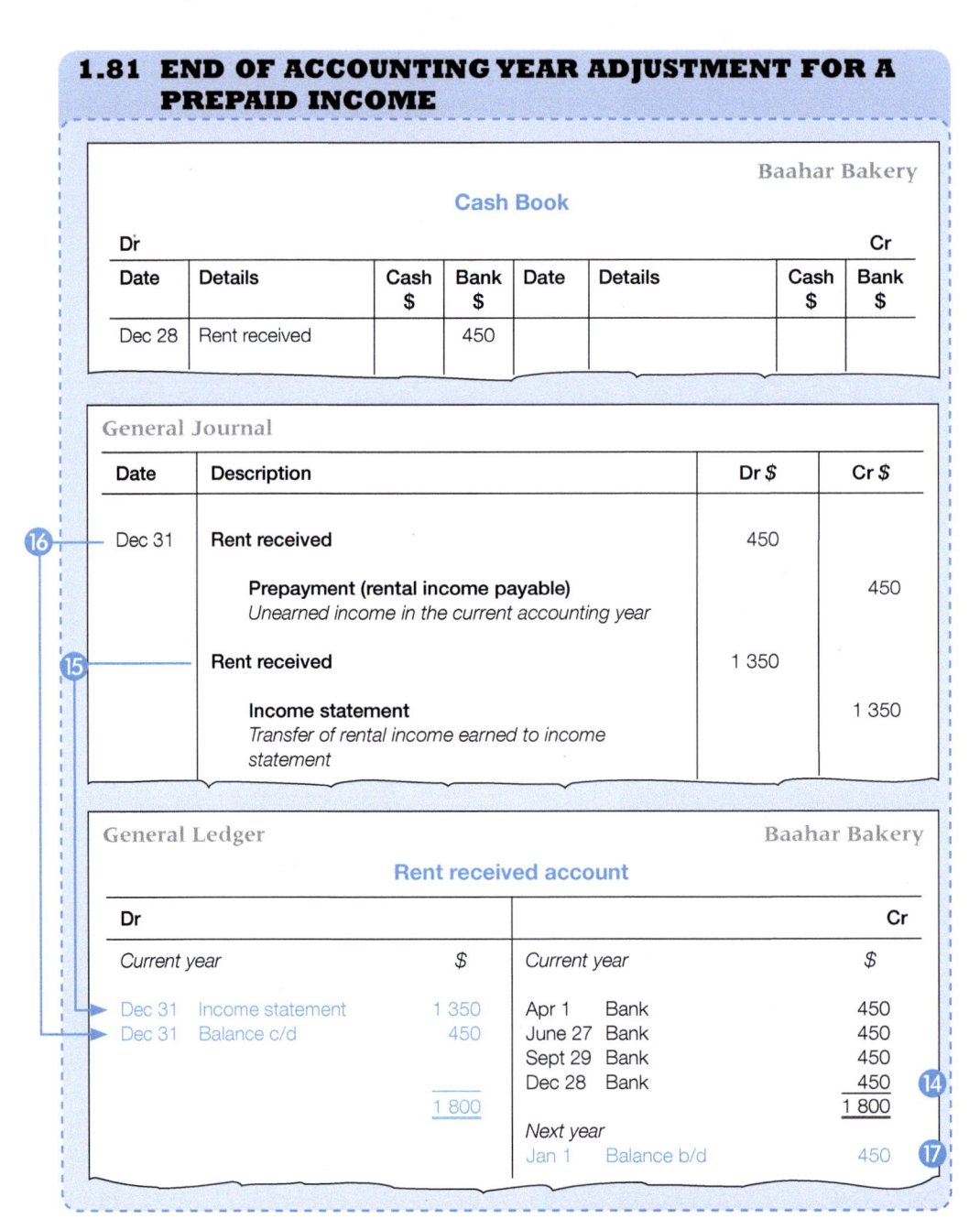

1.81 END OF ACCOUNTING YEAR ADJUSTMENT FOR A PREPAID INCOME

Baahar Bakery

Cash Book

Dr								Cr
Date	Details	Cash $	Bank $	Date	Details	Cash $	Bank $
Dec 28	Rent received		450				

General Journal

Date	Description	Dr $	Cr $
Dec 31	Rent received	450	
	Prepayment (rental income payable)		450
	Unearned income in the current accounting year		
	Rent received	1 350	
	Income statement		1 350
	Transfer of rental income earned to income statement		

General Ledger **Baahar Bakery**

Rent received account

Dr					Cr
Current year		$	*Current year*		$
Dec 31	Income statement	1 350	Apr 1	Bank	450
Dec 31	Balance c/d	450	June 27	Bank	450
			Sept 29	Bank	450
			Dec 28	Bank	450
		1 800			1 800
			Next year		
			Jan 1	Balance b/d	450

174 The fundamentals of accounting

Account entry	What is it for?
A credit for $450 ⑭	Cash received in the bank account for three months of rent paid in advance
A debit for $1 350 ⑮	To transfer the credit balance on the account at the year end for rental income earned during the year to the income statement to include in the calculation of profit or loss for the year
A debit for $450 ⑯	To deduct three months of unearned rental income from the total of credit entries on the account. It reduces the credit balance to be transferred to the income statement from $1 800 of rent received to $1 350 for rental income earned. It is described as a "prepayment c/d".
A credit for $450 ⑰	To bring down the prepayment to the start of the next accounting year. Until the bakery has supplied space in its premises the prepayment is an income payable or current liability.

Making adjustments for prepaid income: a checklist

✓ It is important to match income earned with the expenses incurred earning it in the same accounting year.

✓ A **prepaid income** is an income received that will not be earned until the following accounting year.

✓ Businesses that rent out properties or sell insurance will often receive prepayments from customers.

✓ A prepaid income should not be recorded in profit until it has been earned by the business from the supply of goods or services. Until then the prepaid income will be a current liability of the business.

✓ Journal entries are required to record and adjust for a prepaid income.

For example, an insurance company receives a prepayment of $1 200 from a customer for 12 months of insurance cover. At the end of its accounting year the insurance company had supplied only five months of cover worth $500 to the customer. The remaining seven months of cover worth $700 will be supplied to the customer in the next accounting year.

General Journal

Date	Description	Dr $	Cr $	What are the entries for?
End of the accounting year	Insurance received account	700		To deduct the unearned income at the year end from the total of debit entries on the account for payments received
	Prepayment (liability)		700	The unearned income – or liability to supply insurance in the next accounting year
	Insurance received account	Balance		To transfer the credit balance for income earned to the income statement for the year
	Income statement		Balance	To include the credit balance for income earned to profit for the year

Adjustments to ledger accounts

- ✓ An income received but unearned by the end of the accounting year is debited to the relevant income account. It reduces the credit balance to be transferred to the income statement to calculate profit for the year.

- ✓ The debit entry for the prepayment is then carried down to the credit side of the account to record the liability to supply goods or services in return in the next accounting year.

- ✓ Prepaid income is recorded as other payables (a current liability) in a statement of financial position.

ACTIVITY 1.31

A social club hires out its venue occasionally for parties and other events. On 27 March it received a payment of $500 to hire its venue over two days in the next August. The club's accounting year ends on 31 March.

Make entries to the club's general journal and income account below to record its prepaid income and to balance off the account at the end of its accounting year. Bring down any unearned income to open the account for the following accounting year.

General journal

Date	Description	Dr $	Cr $

Club Venue Hire – income received account

Dr		$			Cr $
Current year			Current year		
Mar 31	Income statement	----	Jun 5	Bank	250
Mar 31	Balance c/d	----	Oct 26	Bank	500
			Nov 14	Bank	250
			Jan 7	Bank	250
			Mar 27	Bank	500
			Next year		
			Apr 1	Balance b/d	----

176 The fundamentals of accounting

1.9.6 Adjusting for irrecoverable and doubtful debts

ACTIVITY 1.32

1. Read the article and explain why the profits of Santander Bank had fallen.

2. What do you think is meant by the following terms used in the article:

    "bad debts"

    "write offs for unrecoverable loans"?

Santander Bank profits hit by bad Spanish property loans

PROFITS AT the Spanish banking giant Santander have halved after it was forced to write off more bad debts. As a result, the eurozone's biggest bank said its profits in the first half of the year had halved to 1.7 billion euros ($2.6 billion).

In total Santander has written off 6 billion euros (just over $9 billion) in its accounts. Of this total, write offs for unrecoverable loans against Spanish properties were 2.8 billion euros.

The Spanish property market was the worst hit in Europe following the crash in property prices that started in 2008. Since then a rising number of homeowners and businesses have not been paying off their debts.

Irrecoverable debts that cannot be collected should be written off in the accounts and the loss of income charged to profit

In business it is sensible to allow for the possibility that some income earned but not received by the end of the accounting year may never be collected. ▶ 5.2

A **doubtful debt** is one that may not be paid. However, if it becomes clear that there is no chance of ever collecting the income owed, for example because the customer has closed down, then the amount owed will become a **an irrecoverable debt**.

If all reasonable steps have been taken to recover a debt but have failed to do so then the irrecoverable debt should be **written off** in the accounts. Doing so recognises the loss of income as a business expense so it can be charged to profit.

Recall how on 25 July D J Menzies, a major business customer of Baahar Bakery, closed down leaving a unpaid debt to the bakery of $580. This meant the bakery would never be able to collect $580 of income it had earned from credit sales to D J Menzies during the accounting year. To record this loss of income Kamal made the following entries to his books at the end of the year:

1.82 ADJUSTING FOR AN IRRECOVERABLE DEBT

General Journal

Date	Description	Dr $	Cr $
Dec 31	Bad debts (expense account)	580	
	D J Menzies (trade receivable)		580
	Uncollected debt from 25 July		

Sales Ledger   Baahar Bakery

D J Menzies account

Dr				Cr
Current year (1)	$	Current year (1)		$
Jul 1 Balance b/d	580	Dec 31 irrecoverable debts		580

General Ledger   Baahar Bakery

Irrecoverable debts account

Dr				Cr
Current year (1)	$	Current year (1)		$
Dec 31 D J Menzies	580	Dec 31 Income statement		580

Adjustments to ledger accounts 177

- a credit of $580 to the trade receivable account of D J Menzies to write off the debt in full and close the account
- a debit of $580 to the irrecoverable debts account to record the loss of income as an incurred expense
- a credit of $580 to the irrecoverable debts account at the end of the accounting year to transfer the debit balance to the income statement to charge the cost against profit for the year.

To write off an irrecoverable debt

Trade receivable account	Irrecoverable debts account
⑱ Bring down the balance owed on the account	Debit the loss of income ⑲
⑳ Credit the account with the balance written off to close the account	Credit the balance on the account and transfer it to the debit side of the income statement to charge it against profit for the year ㉑
Impact: trade receivables are decreased	Impact: expenses are increased

ACTIVITY 1.33

TVS Satellite Services started a business installing household satellite TV and telephone equipment on 1 April 2012. During its first year of trading it wrote off the following irrecoverable debts:

Receivable account	Amount written off
G Alvarez	$280
R J Delgado	$550
B Matthews	$430

Complete the general journal below with the entries required to write off the irrecoverable debts.

General journal

Date	Description	Dr $	Cr $
2013			
Mar 31	**Bad debts**	280	
	G Alvarez		280
	Debit balance on the trade receivable account written off		

Now post the journal entries to the trade receivable accounts and the irrecoverable debts account and balance them off. Remember to show the credit balance on the irrecoverable debts account transferred to the debit side of the income statement for the accounting year ended 31 March 2013.

G Alvarez account

Dr				Cr
2012		$		$
Oct 18	Sales	280		

R J Delgado account

Dr				Cr
2012		$		$
Dec 14	Sales	550		

B Matthews account

Dr				Cr
2013		$		$
Feb 6	Sales	430		

Irrecoverable Debts account

Dr			Cr
	$		$

Making adjustments to write off irrecoverable debts: a checklist

✓ An irrecoverable debt is a debt that cannot be collected.

✓ An irrecoverable debt is written off by crediting the trade receivable account with the amount owed and closing the account.

✓ A corresponding debit entry is made to record the loss of income as an expense (or cost) in the irrecoverable debts account. For example, the balance of $4 320 owing on a trade receivable account is written off by a business.

General journal

Date	Description	Dr $	Cr $	What are the entries for?
End of the accounting year	Irrecoverable debts expense	4 320		The loss of earned income – an expense incurred
	Trade receivable		4 320	To write off the balance owing on the account

✓ The balance on the irrecoverable debts account is transferred to the debit side of the income statement at the end of the accounting year. This will reduce profit for the year or increase loss.

A provision should be included in the accounts to cover the possibility that some debts may become irrevocable and may not be collected in the next accounting year

A **doubtful debt** is a debt on a receivable account that the business may not be able to collect. A doubtful debt will become an irrecoverable debt if it cannot be collected.

Adjustments to ledger accounts | 179

The possibility that some debts will not be collected should not be ignored by a business. It is important that its financial statements provide a true and fair view of its profit or loss for the year and overall financial position. It is sensible (or prudent) to include a **provision for doubtful debts** in the accounts at the end of a year. This will highlight any income earned from credit sales during that year that the business may not be able to collect from its trade receivables when their payments fall due next year.

A provision for doubtful debts assumes a certain proportion (amount) of the money owed to the business will not be collected. It has two effects on the business:

1 It creates an additional expense to be charged to profit for the year.
2 It reduces the asset of trade receivables – a current asset of the business.

A business can estimate the size of the provision it may need in a number of ways:

- by assessing the risk associated with each individual debt and making a provision for those with the highest risk of non payment
- by estimating the percentage of total debts that could become irrevocable based on past experience
- by adding up the value of all debts that are overdue or have been overdue the longest using an ageing schedule of trade receivables. ➤ 5.1

Based on his past experience Kamal Baahar always includes a provision for doubtful debts in the accounts of his bakery equal to 5% of the value of its trade receivables at the end of the accounting year. At 31 December in the current accounting year the value of the bakery's unsettled trade receivables is $10 000. This means Kamal will create a provision for doubtful debts in his books for $500 as follows:

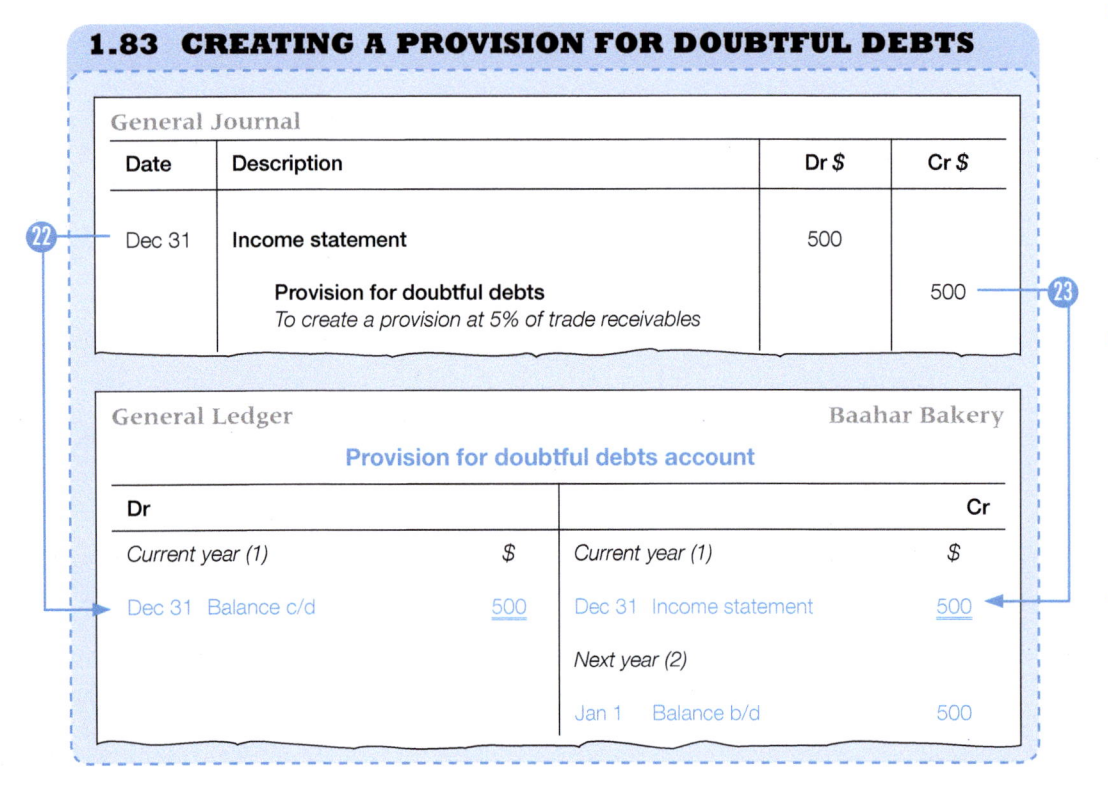

1.83 CREATING A PROVISION FOR DOUBTFUL DEBTS

General Journal

Date	Description	Dr $	Cr $
Dec 31	Income statement	500	
	Provision for doubtful debts		500
	To create a provision at 5% of trade receivables		

General Ledger   Baahar Bakery

Provision for doubtful debts account

Dr			Cr	
Current year (1)	$	Current year (1)		$
Dec 31 Balance c/d	500	Dec 31 Income statement		500
		Next year (2)		
		Jan 1 Balance b/d		500

- A credit of $500 to the ledger account for the **provision for doubtful debts**. The credit balance on the account records the provision as a reduction in the value of trade receivables – from $10 000 to $9 500.
- A debit of $500 to the income statement to expense the provision for doubtful debts to profit for the year. This reduces profit for the year by $500.
- A provision for doubtful debts reduces profit in the year it is created.

180   The fundamentals of accounting

To create a provision for doubtful debts

Income statement	Provision for doubtful debts account
Debit the statement with the provision for doubtful debts	Credit the account with the provision for doubtful debts
Impact: expenses are increased and profit for the year is reduced	Impact: trade receivables are decreased

Baahar Bakery
Extract from statement of financial position at 31 December (year 1)

	$
Trade receivables	10 000
less provision for doubtful debts	500
	9 500

The provision carried down on the provision for doubtful debts account reduces the value of trade receivables recorded in the statement of financial position, as this extract from the statement for Baahar Bakery shows. ▶ **3.2**

An increase in the provision for doubtful debts will further reduce the value of trade receivables and profit recorded in the financial statements of the business

It is sometimes necessary for a business to increase the provision it has made for doubtful debts in its accounts. This may become necessary if:

- the total of trade receivables at the end of the accounting year has risen

- worsening economic and business conditions are increasing financial problems among business customers and increasing risks of **default** (the non-payment of debts).

For example, imagine it is now a full year later and the end of another accounting year (2) for Baahar Bakery. At the end of last year (1) its trade receivables were $10 000 and Kamal created a provision for doubtful debts of 5% or $500 in the accounts. Kamal wishes to maintain the provision for doubtful debts at 5% but the trade receivables of his business are now $15 000. So, the provision needs to rise to $750 – an increase of $250 on the provision created last year. To record the increase in the books of the bakery Kamal makes the following entries:

- A credit of $250 to the ledger account for the provision for doubtful debts. The credit is added to the opening balance on the account so that the total provision or credit balance at the end of the year rises to $750. This credit balance reduces the expected value of trade receivables from $15 000 to $14 250.

- A debit of $250 to the income statement. This is to record as an expense the additional income Kamal expects he will be unable to collect from his trade receivables next year for credit sales his business has already incurred in the current accounting year. Income and profit for the year are reduced by $250.

Adjustments to ledger accounts

1.84 INCREASING A PROVISION FOR DOUBTFUL DEBTS

General Journal

Date	Description	Dr	Cr
Year 2		$	$
Dec 31	Income statement	250	
	Provision for doubtful debts		250
	To create a provision at 5% of trade receivables		

General Ledger — Baahar Bakery

Provision for doubtful debts account

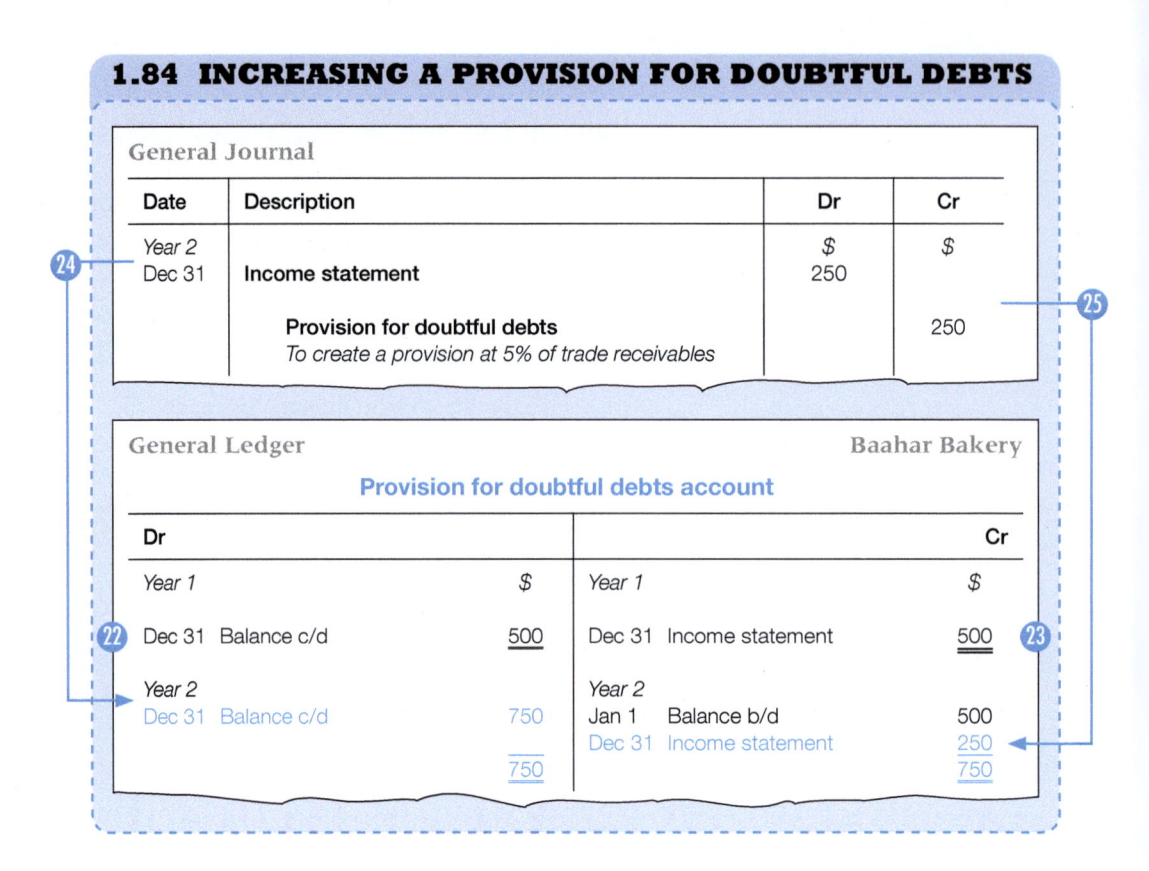

Dr			Cr
Year 1	$	Year 1	$
Dec 31 Balance c/d	500	Dec 31 Income statement	500
Year 2		Year 2	
Dec 31 Balance c/d	750	Jan 1 Balance b/d	500
		Dec 31 Income statement	250
	750		750

To increase a provision for doubtful debts

Provision for doubtful debts account	Income statement
Credit the account with the increase in the provision	Debit the statement with the increase in the provision
Impact: trade receivables are decreased by the total provision on the account	Impact: expenses are increased and profit for the year is reduced by the amount of the increase in the provision

The increase in the provision for doubtful debts reduces income and profit by the amount of the increase in the year it is recorded.

The total provision or credit balance carried down at the end of the accounting year (2) on the provision for doubtful debts account is used to adjust the value of trade receivables. This is recorded in the statement of financial position, as the extract opposite shows.

Baahar Bakery
Extract from statement of financial position as 31 December (year 2)

	$
Trade receivables	15 000
less provision for doubtful debts	750
	14 250

182 The fundamentals of accounting

A decrease in the provision for doubtful debts will increase the value of trade receivables and profit recorded in the financial statements of the business

It is also possible that over time a business will want to reduce the provision it has made in its accounts for doubtful debts. This may occur because:

- many of its debts have become irrevocable and had to be written off instead
- total trade receivables have decreased
- credit control by the business has improved and reduced non-repayment risks.

For example, imagine it is another year later and the end of a third accounting year for Baahar Bakery. Over the last year Kamal has improved credit control at his bakery by selling goods on credit only to the most reliable and financially secure business customers. Although his trade receivables have risen to $18 000 Kamal intends to reduce his provision for doubtful debts to just 3% of trade receivables, or $540. He must reduce the credit balance on the bakery's ledger account for the provision for doubtful debts from $750 to $540 – a reduction of $210. To do this he makes the following entries to his accounts:

1.85 REDUCING A PROVISION FOR DOUBTFUL DEBTS

General Journal

Date	Description	Dr	Cr
Year 3 Dec 31	**Provision for doubtful debts**	$ 210	$
	Income statement *To create a provision at 3% of trade receivables*		210

General Ledger Baahar Bakery

Provision for doubtful debts account

Dr			Cr	
Year 1		$	Year 1	$
Dec 31 Balance c/d		500	Dec 31 Income statement	500
Year 2			Year 2	
Dec 31 Balance c/d		750	Jan 1 Balance b/d	500
			Dec 31 Income statement	250
		750		750
Year 3			Year 3	
Dec 31 Income statement		210	Jan 1 Balance b/d	750
Dec 31 Balance c/d		540		
		750		750

- a debit of $210 to the ledger account for the provision for doubtful debts. The debit reduces the total provision on the account at the end of the accounting year to $540. The credit balance reduces the value of trade receivables from $18 000 to $17 460.

- a credit of $210 to the income statement. This records the additional income he expects to collect from trade receivables in the next accounting year for credit sales incurred and earned during the current year. Income and profit for the year is increased by the amount of the credit.

A reduction in a provision for doubtful debts increases income and profit in the year the reduction is made.

To decrease a provision for doubtful debts

Provision for doubtful debts account	Income statement
Debit the account with the decrease in the provision	Credit the statement with the decrease in the provision
Impact: trade receivables are decreased by the total provision on the account	Impact: income and profit for the year are increased by the amount of the reduction in the provision

㉖ ㉗

Trade receivables in the statement of financial position are adjusted by the credit balance carried down on the ledger account for the provision for doubtful debts.

Baahar Bakery
Extract from statement of financial position at 31 December (year 3)

	$
Trade receivables	18 000
less provision for doubtful debts	540
	17 460

Good credit control in business can reduce the risk of debts becoming irrecoverable

The only way a business can avoid irrecoverable debts is to stop supplying goods or services on credit. However, this is also likely to mean fewer customers, less revenue and lower profits.

Improving **credit control** can help a business reduce the risk of irrecoverable debts, reduce the provision it needs to make in its accounts and increase its cash flow from credit customers. Good credit control involves following a set of strict procedures including:

- **Credit checks** can be made to make sure a customer is financially secure and has a good history of paying off previous debts. A business can ask to see credit references from the customer's bank and one or more of its suppliers before a credit sale is agreed.

- A **credit limit** can be set for each credit customer so that these customers do not take on too much debt. The limit will usually be based on credit references and set low at first.

- An up-to-date **aged trade receivables schedule** can be kept which lists all the customers that owe the business money, how much each one owes and when the debts fall due so that they can be easily identified and payment reminders can be sent out if necessary. ➤ 5.1

- A business can offer **rewards** to encourage credit customers to settle their debts and on time, including increased credit limits and cash discounts for early repayments.

- Late payments can be discouraged by using **penalties**, for example by refusing to supply any more goods or services to the credit customer and charging interest on late payments.

- A business can threaten and, if necessary, take **legal action** to recover an irrecoverable debt. Legal action may result in the credit customer having to pay large legal costs. It is important that new and existing customers know what could happen if they do not pay their debts on time.

> ### Making adjustments for doubtful debts: a checklist
>
> ✓ A **provision for doubtful debts** assumes a certain proportion of the money owed to the business by its credit customers will not be collected.
>
> ✓ A provision will recognise doubtful debts as a reduction in the value of a current asset (trade receivables). The loss of value is charged to profit as an expense.
>
> ✓ To create a provision at the end of an accounting year a business will credit the account for the provision for doubtful debts and debit its income statement. For example, at the end of its accounting year the following business has trade receivables of $1 000 and creates a provision for doubtful debts of 2.5% of their value:
>
> General journal
>
> | Date | Description | Dr $ | Cr $ | What are the entries for? |
> |---|---|---|---|---|
> | End of the accounting year | Income statement | 25 | | To expense the potential loss of income to profit for the year |
> | | Provision for doubtful debts account | | 25 | A prudent reduction in the value of trade receivables |
>
> ✓ The value of trade receivables recorded in the statement of financial position is reduced by the full amount of the provision for doubtful debts (that is, by the credit balance on the account).
>
> ✓ To increase the provision, credit the ledger account and debit the income statement with an expense to record the additional income the business expects it will be unable to collect for credit sales it incurred during the year.
>
> ✓ To reduce the provision, debit the ledger account and credit the income statement to record the increase in income the business expects to collect from credit sales incurred during the year.

Some irrecoverable debts written off may be recovered at a later date

It is possible that an irrecoverable debt written off in a previous year is paid off or recovered in a later year. An **irrecoverable debt recovered** involves the receipt of a payment to settle a debt that has been previously written off in the accounts of a business.

For example, recall how on 25 July D J Menzies, a major business customer of Baahar Bakery, closed down leaving a debt of $580 to the bakery. As a result, Kamal Baahar wrote off the debt in full on the trade receivable account of DJ Menzies at the end of the accounting year.

Imagine now that it is six months later (in year 2) and on the 1 June the bakery receives a cheque for $580 from D J Menzies who has since re-opened his business. How should Kamal Baahar now account for this recovery of the debt in the books of his bakery?

When he wrote off the debt he closed the trade receivable account of DJ Menzies to any further entries and charged the irrecoverable debt as an expense to profit for the year. Kamal Baahar has two alternatives to account for the recovered debt:

Option 1 is to open an income account for irrecoverable debts recovered. The payment received is credited to the irrecoverable debts recovered account to record the income received.

Option 2 is, in addition to option 1, to re-open the trade receivable account of D J Menzies to reinstate the debt. The payment received is then credited to the account to settle the debt. This has the advantage of recording the full payment history of the customer on the same account.

The first option requires Kamal to make the following adjustments to its accounts:

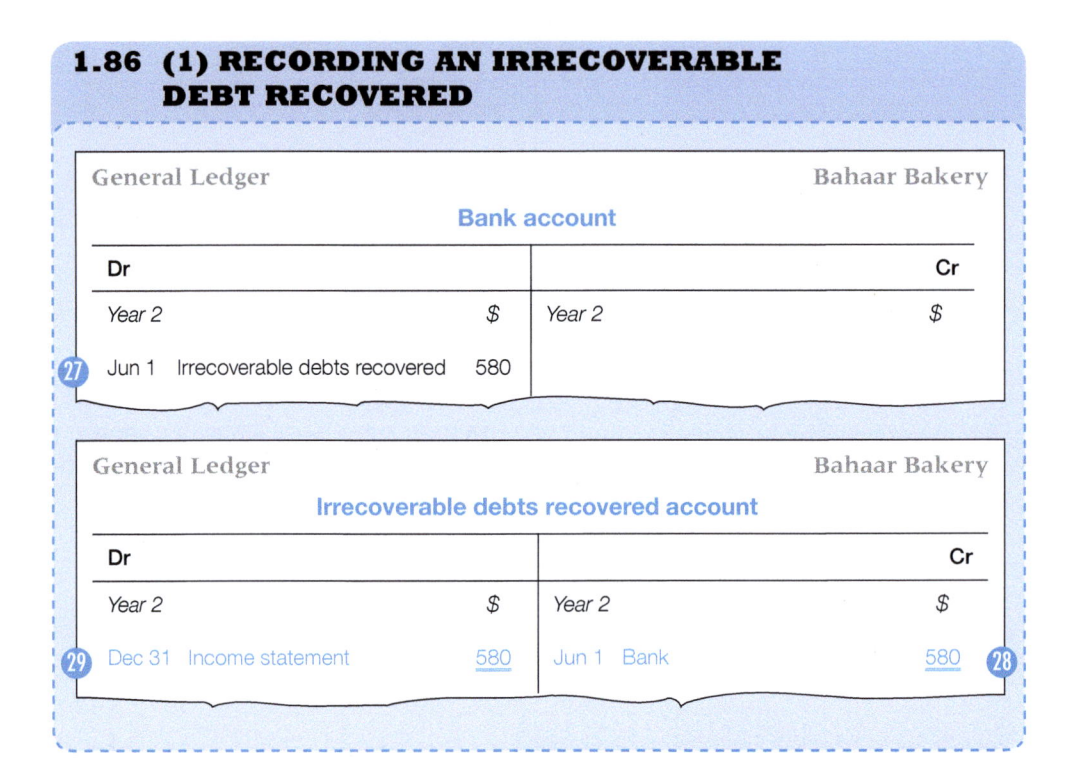

1.86 (1) RECORDING AN IRRECOVERABLE DEBT RECOVERED

General Ledger — Bahaar Bakery

Bank account

Dr					Cr
Year 2		$	Year 2		$
(27) Jun 1	Irrecoverable debts recovered	580			

General Ledger — Bahaar Bakery

Irrecoverable debts recovered account

Dr					Cr
Year 2		$	Year 2		$
(29) Dec 31	Income statement	580	Jun 1	Bank	580 (28)

(1) For an irrecoverable debt recovered

Bank account	Irrecoverable debts recovered account
(27) Debit the payment received	Credit the income received (28)
	Debit the balance on the account at the end of the accounting year and transfer it to the credit side of the income statement to include in profit (29)
Impact: cash in bank is increased	Impact: income and profit are increased

1.87 (2) RECORDING AN IRRECOVERABLE DEBT RECOVERED BY RE-OPENING THE RECEIVABLE ACCOUNT

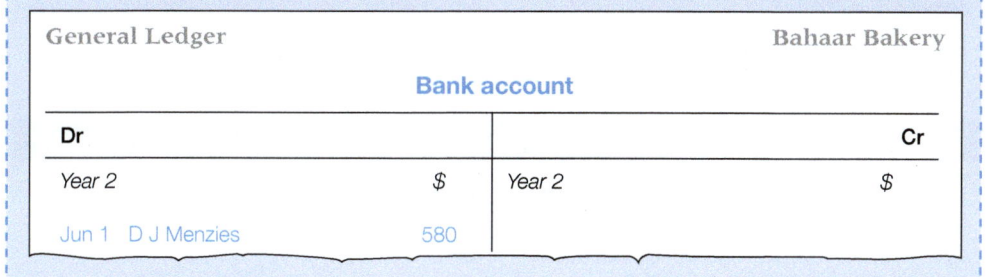

In the second option Kamal reinstates the debt on the trade receivable account of D J Menzies as shown in illustration 1.87.

General Ledger — Bahaar Bakery

Bank account

Dr					Cr
Year 2		$	Year 2		$
Jun 1	D J Menzies	580			

Sales Ledger — Bahaar Bakery

D J Menzies account

Dr					Cr	
Year 1			$	Year 1		$
(18) July 1	Balance b/d		580	Dec 31	Irrecoverable debts	580 (31)
Year 2				Year 2		
(32) Jun 1	Irrecoverable debts recovered		580	Jun 1	Bank	580

General Ledger — Bahaar Bakery

Irrecoverable debts recovered account

Dr					Cr
Year 2		$	Year 2		$
(33) Dec 31	Income statement	580	Jun 1	D J Menzies	580

(2) For an irrecoverable debt recovered

Bank account	Trade receivable account
Debit the account when the payment is received	Credit the account when the payment is received
Impact: cash in bank is increased	Impact: trade receivables are decreased

Trade receivable account	Irrecoverable debt recovered account
Debit the balance on the account and transfer it to the credit side of the irrecoverable debts recovered account	Credit the account with the balance from the trade receivable account to recognise the irrecoverable debt recovered as income is received
Impact: account is closed	Impact: income is increased

Irrecoverable debt recovered account	Income statement
At the end of the accounting year, debit the balance on the account and transfer it to the credit side of the income statement	At the end of the accounting year, credit the statement with the balance on the irrecoverable debts recovered account
Impact: account is closed	Impact: income and profit are increased

ACTIVITY 1.34

Rashid runs a small business. His accounting year runs from 1 June to the following 31 May.

He maintains a provision in his accounts for doubtful debts equal to 2% of trade receivables. On 31 May 2012 the total value of his trade receivables was $25 000. On 1 June 2012 he brought down a provision for doubtful debts of $500.

The following notable transactions took place during the year ended 31 May 2013:

- On 27 August goods to the value of $1 200 were sold on credit to Inessa.
- On 19 September a cheque for $1 000 was received from Inessa.
- On 16 January a payment of $400 was received from Nataliya by bank transfer to settle her debt that Rashid had written off in his accounts in 2011.
- On May 31 the balance outstanding on Inessa's account was written off as irrecoverable.

Also, as at 31 May 2013, Rashid calculates the value of his trade receivables as $20 000.

Use this information to write up and balance off the following accounts in Rashid's ledger for the accounting year ended 31 May 2013.

- Inessa Account
- Irrecoverable Debts Account
- Irrecoverable Debts Recovered Account
- Provision for Bad Debts Account

QUICK TEST

1. Explain the following terms:
   - prepaid expense
   - accrued expense
   - prepaid income
   - accrued income.

2. Explain why (a) prepaid expenses; and (b) accrued income are recorded as other receivables (current assets) in a statement of financial position.

3. Explain why (a) prepaid income; and (b) accrued expenses are recorded as other payables (current liabilities) in a statement of financial position.

4. What is the difference between an irrecoverable debt and a doubtful debt?

5. Explain why it is prudent to write off irrecoverable debts and to keep a provision for doubtful debts in the accounts of a business.

6. Explain **four** ways a business could reduce the risk of irrecoverable debts.

7. Saxon Ltd. sub-lets space in its premises to Petra from question 7. Its current accounting year also ends on 31 December.

   (a) Write up entries to the journal of Saxon Ltd.'s for the year to 31 December for (i) rent received from Petra; (ii) accrued income (the rental income owed by Petra) at 31 December; (iii) total rental income earned during the year to be transferred to Saxon Ltd.'s income statement and credited to its profit for the year.

   (b) Post the journal entries to the rent received account in Saxon Ltd.'s ledger. Balance off the account to show the accrued income to be carried down on 31 December and the income earned transferred to its income statement.

8. On 1 October last year Libby Clarke bought new camera equipment for her video business. On that day she paid a premium of $240 to Assurance Ltd. to provide insurance cover for the equipment until 30 September the following year. She made the following entries to her cash book to record the transaction:

   Libby Clarke
   Cash Book

Dr							Cr
Date	Details	Cash $	Bank $	Date Year	Details	Cash $	Bank $
				Oct 1	Equipment insurance		240

The accounting year of Libby's business ended 31 December.

   (a) Make entries in her journal to record (i) the prepaid insurance at the year end; (ii) the insurance expense incurred during the accounting year to be transferred to the income statement and charged to profit for that year.

   (b) Post all the journal and cash book entries (from 1 October to 31 December) to the ledger account for equipment insurance. Balance off the ledger account and show the prepaid expense to be carried down on 31 December.

9 (a) A business has trade receivables of $50,000. It maintains a provision for doubtful debts of 3%. How much should it enter into its accounts for the provision?; (b) At the end of the following accounting year trade receivables were $40 000. Describe the entries required in the ledger and the income statement to record the change in the provision necessary.

10 Stuart is a trader. It is 31 March and the end of his accounting year. Show the adjustments, if any, Stuart should make to his ledger accounts for each of the following:

(a) Mito is a trade receivable. He owes $500 for goods purchased on credit on 31 January. Payment is overdue by one month but Mito has promised to pay in full by the end of April.

(b) A debt of $800 has remained unpaid for two years. FJS Ltd. closed down early last year and Stuart is unable to trace the previous owners.

(c) Stuart maintains a provision of 4% for doubtful debts. Total trade receivables outstanding after allowing for Mito and FJS Ltd. are $14 000.

(d) A cheque for $250 has been received from a trade receivable, Tomiko, to settle in full a debt Stuart had written off on his trade receivable account two years ago.

The Unit 1 revision summary provides a quick guide to everything in this unit. Then, when you're ready, try the Unit 1 assessment activities.

The fundamentals of accounting

2 Accounting procedures

Content at a glance

2.1	Capital and revenue expenditure and receipts
2.2	Accounting for depreciation and disposal of non-current assets
2.3	Correction of errors
2.4	Control accounts

Unit 2.1 Capital and revenue expenditure and receipts

AIMS

By the end of this unit you should be able to

- distinguish between and account for **capital expenditure** and **revenue expenditure**
- distinguish between and account for **capital receipts** and **revenue receipts**
- calculate and comment on the effect on profit of incorrect treatment
- calculate and comment on the effect on asset valuations of incorrect treatment

2.1.1 Capital and revenue expenditures

Starting and running a business involves spending money on capital and revenue items

Last January Hedley Johnson started a new business, Hedjo Plastics, selling different types of plastic sheeting, pipes and mouldings for use in construction and home improvement projects.

Before his business could generate any revenue from the sale of these products, it had to spend money to acquire (buy) a range of different assets including premises, equipment, a delivery van, shelving and display units, office furniture and an inventory of plastic products to sell. Then, to run his business, Hedley had to pay for various expenses on a regular basis including electricity, insurance, advertising, office supplies and employee wages.

Whenever Hedley spent money from his business to obtain the various goods and services it required it incurred **expenditure**. To record the different expenditures in the books of his business Hedley classified them as follows:

- **capital expenditure**: money spent on non-current assets
- **revenue expenditure**: money spent on running expenses.

In accounting it is important to distinguish between different expenditures in this way. This is because capital expenditures will affect the financial position of the business while revenue expenditures will affect profit.

Capital expenditure is money spent to buy new or to improve existing machinery, equipment and other non-current assets

When Hedley Johnson started Hedjo Plastics he spent a significant amount of capital to buy premises, equipment, a delivery van and many other **non-current assets** that he would be able to use repeatedly over more than one accounting year to help his business earn revenue. ➤ 1.2

All of the money the business spent on acquiring these non-current assets involved **capital expenditure**.

Hedley also had to pay a number of other costs before his business could take ownership of them and start to use them. These included:

- legal fees to take ownership of the shop premises and delivery van
- the cost of painting the business name and logo on the delivery van
- delivery charges for the new equipment, shelving and display units
- the costs of constructing a new extension to the shop premises
- installation charges to fit the new equipment and units into the shop premises.

The money spent by the business on these items was also recorded as **capital expenditure**. Although many of the costs, such as delivery and installation charges, might appear to be routine expenses, without them the business would have been unable to benefit from the non-current assets it had

▲ The purchase and improvement of non-current assets involves capital expenditure

acquired. The payment of expenses associated with the purchase or improvement of non-current assets are included – or "capitalised" – in the total amount spent on the non-current assets.

In summary, **capital expenditures** are non-recurrent expenditures incurred by a business to:

- acquire non-current assets, including any associated legal and delivery costs
- improve or add to the value of existing non-current assets
- ensure that non-current assets are ready for use in the business, such as expenditure on the cost of installing new equipment.

As many non-current assets remain useful for several accounting years, capital expenditures on them will normally be financed from equity or from non-current liabilities such as long-term bank loans.

Revenue expenditure is money spent on the purchase of goods for resale or manufacture and day-to-day running expenses

In addition to the money Hedjo Plastics spent on non-current assets it also spent money on items that were used up in a relatively short period of time in the day-to-day operation of the business. These items included:

- the purchase of goods for resale
- the purchase of office stationery and other items, including delivery charges
- employee wages
- electricity for heating and lighting the premises and running equipment
- insurance of the business premises and vehicles
- the costs of cleaning, repairs and maintenance of the premises and equipment
- the costs of renovation and redecorating of the premises
- advertising, accounting and other professional services
- bank and loan interest charges

and many more.

▲ The purchase of goods for resale involves revenue expenditure

Money spent by a business on items that will be of benefit within the accounting year in which they were purchased is **revenue expenditure**. Some revenue expenditure will be incurred continually throughout the year, for example employee wages, energy costs and the cost of goods purchased for resale. Others may be less regular or involve one-off expenditures, for example payments for repairs and accountancy fees that provide a short-term benefit to the business.

It is because revenue expenditures involve regular spending that will benefit the business for less than one year that they will normally be financed from the recurrent revenue of the business or from current liabilities, notably trade payables and bank overdrafts. ▶ 1.2

ACTIVITY 2.1

In the first three months of trading Hedjo Plastics incurred the following expenditures:

Item	Amount $
Delivery vehicle	20 000
Painting of the business name and logo on the delivery vehicle	2 000
Vehicle insurance and fuel	2 500
Office stationery including paper and printing inks	1 600
Wages	6 000
Shop premises	80 000
Construction costs for an extension to the shop premises	15 000
Shelving and display units	4 000
Computer and other equipment	5 800
Advertising costs	1 300
Delivery charges for equipment, shelving and display units	750
Delivery charges for office supplies	50
Electricity	600
Business insurance premium	450
Purchases of plastic sheeting, pipes and mouldings for resale	14 400
Telephone and Internet	180
Legal fees to acquire the shop premises	2 700
Shop cleaning	150
Installation charges for equipment, shelving and display units	670
Delivery charges for plastic products	900
Accountant's fees	450

1 Draw a table like the one below and use it to identify from the list above those transactions that are capital expenditures and those that are revenue expenditures.

2 From the entries in your table calculate the total capital expenditure and total revenue expenditure of the business during its first three months of trading.

Capital expenditures	$	Revenue expenditures	$
Total capital expenditure		Total revenue expenditure	

194 Accounting procedures

It is important to distinguish between the costs of renovation, repair or maintenance of equipment and other non-current assets and the cost of making improvements to them. Money spent on making improvements to non-current assets, such as extending the business premises, will add value to those assets and their cost will be classed as capital expenditures.

In contrast, renovation works, repairs or maintenance designed to restore non-current assets to their original state or working order will not add additional value to those assets. Payments for these works involve one-off expense items or revenue expenditures.

2.1.2 Accounting for capital and revenue expenditures

Capital expenditures are recorded as debits to asset accounts and will increase the value of non-current assets in the statement of financial position of the business

On 2 January last year, Hedjo Plastics purchased a delivery van. It involved making two payments to the supplier of the van: one for the delivery van itself and the other to have the business name and logo painted on the sides of the van. Both payments involved capital expenditure.

To account for these capital expenditures, Hedley Johnson made the following entries to his business ledger:

Recording capital expenditure to acquire a non-current asset

Vehicles account	Bank account
A debit entry for $20 000 to the acquisition of the van	A credit entry for $20 000 to record money paid out
A debit entry for $2 000 to record the painting of the van	A credit entry for $2 000 to record money paid out
Impact: non-current assets are increased	Impact: cash in bank is decreased

The capital expenditure reduced the current asset of cash held in the business bank account but increased the value of the non-current assets of the business by $22 000. The increase in non-current assets was recorded in debit entries to the asset account for vehicles (see illustration 2.1).

Revenue expenditures are recorded as debits to expense accounts and will increase total expenses in the income statement

Activity 2.1 lists a number of revenue expenditures Hedjo Plastics had incurred during its first three months of trading last year. This included a payment of $600 on 31 March to the national power company for the supply of electricity over the previous three-month period from 1 January. Hedley Johnson recorded the revenue expenditure in his books as follows shown in illustration 2.2 and the table below.

2.1 DOUBLE ENTRIES IN LEDGER ACCOUNTS FOR CAPITAL EXPENDITURE TO ACQUIRE A NON-CURRENT ASSET

General Ledger — Hedjo Plastics

Vehicles account

Dr			Cr
Year 1	$	Year 1	$
Jan 2 Bank	20 000		
Jan 2 Bank	2 000		

General Ledger — Hedjo Plastics

Cash Book (bank account only)

Dr		Analysis column for vehicles only	Cr
Year 1	$	Year 1	$
		Jan 2 Vehicles	20 000
		Jan 2 Vehicles	2 000

2.2 DOUBLE ENTRIES IN LEDGER ACCOUNTS FOR REVENUE EXPENDITURES ON EXPENSE ITEMS

General Ledger — Hedjo Plastics

Electricity account

Dr			Cr
Year 1	$	Year 1	$
Mar 31 Bank	600		

General Ledger — Hedjo Plastics

Cash Book (bank account only)

Dr		Analysis column for vehicles only	Cr
Year 1	$	Year 1	$
		Mar 31 Electricity	600

Recording revenue expenditure incurred on expense items

Electricity account	Bank account
A debit entry to record electricity expenses	A credit entry to record cash paid out
Impact: expenses are increased	Impact: cash in bank is decreased

Revenue expenditure on expense items will increase total expenses and therefore reduce profit for the year recorded in the income statement at the end of the accounting year. ➤ 3.1

ACTIVITY 2.2

The table below is from activity 2.1. It reproduces the list of expenditures Hedjo Plastics incurred during its first three months of trading last year.

Complete the table to show the impact each expenditure will have on the profit or value of the non-current assets of the business. Remember this will depend on whether they were revenue or capital expenditures so refer back to your answers to activity 2.1 to help you. (Two have been completed for you.)

Item	Amount $	Impact on profit	Impact on non-current assets
Delivery vehicle	20 000	–	Increase by $20 000
Painting of the business name and logo on the delivery vehicle	2 000		
Vehicle insurance and fuel	2 500		
Office stationery including paper and printing inks	1 600		
Wages	6 000		
Shop premises	80 000		
Construction costs for an extension to the shop premises	15 000		
Shelving and display units	4 000		
Computer and other equipment	5 800		
Advertising costs	1 300		
Delivery charges for equipment, shelving and display units	750		
Delivery charges for office supplies	50		
Electricity	600	Decrease by $600	–
Business insurance premium	450		
Purchases of plastic sheeting, pipes and mouldings for resale	14 400		
Telephone and Internet	180		
Legal fees to acquire shop premises	2 700		
Shop cleaning	150		
Installation charges for equipment, shelving and display units	670		
Delivery charges for plastic products	900		
Accountant's fees	450		

Capital and revenue expenditure and receipts 197

The incorrect recording of a capital expenditure as a revenue expenditure will understate the profit for the year and financial position of the business

It is important to record capital expenditure accurately and in the correct ledger accounts. If this is not done then both the profit or loss of the business and the value of its assets will be incorrect.

For example, when Hedjo Plastics purchased a delivery van for $22 000 the business incurred capital expenditure. The additional expenditure increased the value of the non-current assets of the business and the benefit the van will have to the business.

However, had Hedley Johnson mistakenly recorded the payment of $22 000 as revenue expenditure in the account for vehicle expenses the error would have:

- understated the value of non-current assets of the business by $22 000
- overstated expenses by $22 000 and understated profit by $22 000.

Similar errors recording capital expenditures as revenue expenditures will have the same impact.

	Income statement	Statement of financial position
If a capital expenditure is recorded in error as a revenue expenditure:	expenses will be overstated	non-current assets will be understated
Impact:	profit will be understated	the financial position will appear less favourable

Business owners and other users of accounting information rely on measures of profit and financial position to make important decisions. Getting the figures wrong can have a major impact on their decisions, for example:

If profits are understated	If non-current assets are understated
• The owners may scale back their business in an attempt to reduce costs. • Banks may be unwilling to lend the business money and suppliers may be reluctant to sell it goods on credit. • It may look unattractive to other investors who may wish to invest in the business.	• Provisions for depreciation may be less than they should be. • The owners may sell off non-current assets or even the entire business too cheaply.

The incorrect recording of a revenue expenditure as a capital expenditure will overstate the profit for the year and financial position of the business

In the same way, it is important to record revenue expenditure accurately and in the correct accounts. For example, during the first three months of trading, Hedjo Plastics spent $2 500 on insurance and fuel for its delivery vehicle. Payment of these expenses incurred revenue expenditure because they will only benefit the business over a relatively short period.

If by mistake Hedley Johnson had recorded the revenue expenditure of $2 500 in the asset account for vehicles the error would have:

- overstated the value of non-current assets of the business by $2 500
- understated expenses by $2 500 and therefore overstated profit by $2 500.

Similar errors recording revenue expenditures as capital expenditures will have the same impact:

	Income statement	Statement of financial position
If a revenue expenditure is recorded in error as a capital expenditure:	expenses will be understated	non-current assets will be overstated
Impact:	profit will be overstated	the financial position will appear more favourable

Business owners and other users of accounting information rely on measures of profit and financial position to make important decisions. Getting the figures wrong can have a major impact on their decisions, for example:

If profits are overstated	If non-current assets are overstated
• It may persuade the owners to expand their business too quickly and take on more bank loans than a business can afford to pay from its revenues. • The owners may overdraw cash from the business bank account for their own use.	• It may give the impression the business is financially far stronger than it really is. • This in turn may persuade banks to lend it more money than it can really afford to repay.

ACTIVITY 2.3

Talia has drawn up financial statements for her business at the end of the accounting year that show a profit for the year of $60 000 and total non-current assets of $150 000.

However, you discover that she made several errors recording her expenditures during the year. The errors are listed in the table below.

Error	Impact of the error on profit for the year	Impact of the error on non-current assets
Capital expenditure of $6 000 for a new van was debited to the vehicle expenses account	Profit is understated by $6 000	Non-current assets are understated by $6 000
$500 of repairs to the roof were debited to the premises account		
Computer disks and inks costing $300 were debited to the asset account for computer equipment		
Installation costs of $2 000 for a new machine were debited to the repairs and maintenance account		
A new desktop computer costing $2 500 was debited to the expense account for office supplies		

Complete the table above to show the impact each error will have had on the calculation of profit for the year and the value of non-current assets in Talia's financial statements. (The first one has been completed for you.)

2.1.3 Types of receipt

A business receives funds from investments of owner's equity, the provision of loan capital or from the sale of non-current assets

When Hedley Johnson first started up Hedjo Plastics he invested his own personal savings in the business. This involved him transferring $100 000 from his personal bank account to the business current account. The money or capital received by the business was recorded in its books as a capital receipt.

Similarly, a few months later when Hedley arranged a bank loan for $50 000 for his business, repayable over 10 years, he recorded the receipt of the funds – or **loan capital** – in the business bank account as a capital receipt.

Capital is also received by a business when it sells off or "disposes" of non-current assets. For example, when Hedley sold off some spare land at the rear of his shop premises for $12 800 the money received from its sale was treated as a capital receipt.

In summary, **capital receipts** are non-recurrent receipts of money that will benefit the business for a long period of time (that is, more than one accounting year) including:

- owner's equity received from the owners of the business
- loan capital borrowed from banks and other lenders that is repayable over more than one accounting year
- the proceeds from the sale or "disposal" of non-current assets.

Capital receipts will normally be used to finance the capital expenditures of the business.

A business receives revenue when it sells goods or services to customers

Most receipts in business are **revenue receipts** from the sale of goods or services to customers on a daily basis.

In addition to sales revenue, a business may also receive money from:

- rental income
- sales commission
- interest on business savings
- dividends from investments in other businesses. ➤ 4.5

Any monies received from these sources will also be classified as **revenue receipts**.

Revenue receipts are recurring receipts that are available for meeting the day-to-day revenue expenditures of the business.

ACTIVITY 2.4

In the first three months of trading Hedjo Plastics received the following:

Item	Amount $
Introduction of owner's capital	100 000
10-year commercial bank loan	50 000
Sales	17 500
Interest on business savings	30
Payment from an advertising agency for use of space on the side wall of the shop	350
Rent for use of the garage owned by the shop	900
Sale of spare land at the rear of the shop	12 800
Commission on sales of plastic items from the manufacturer	790

1 Draw a table like the one below and use it to identify transactions in the list that are capital receipts and those that are revenue receipts.

2 From the entries in your table calculate the total capital receipts and total revenue receipts of the business during its first three months of trading.

Capital receipts	$	Revenue receipts	$
Total capital receipts		Total revenue receipts	

2.1.4 Accounting for capital and revenue receipts

Capital receipts will increase owner's equity or loan capital but will not increase the income or profit of the business

It is important to distinguish between capital and revenue receipts in accounting. This is because capital receipts will affect the financial position of the business while revenue receipts will affect its profitability.

For example, when Hedley Johnson introduced $100 000 of equity from his own savings to start up his business last January he recorded the following entries in the books of the business:

Recording a capital receipt for introduction of owner's equity

Bank account	Capital account
A debit entry for the money received from the owner	A credit entry for the capital "owed" to the owner
Impact: cash in bank is increased	Impact: owner's equity is increased

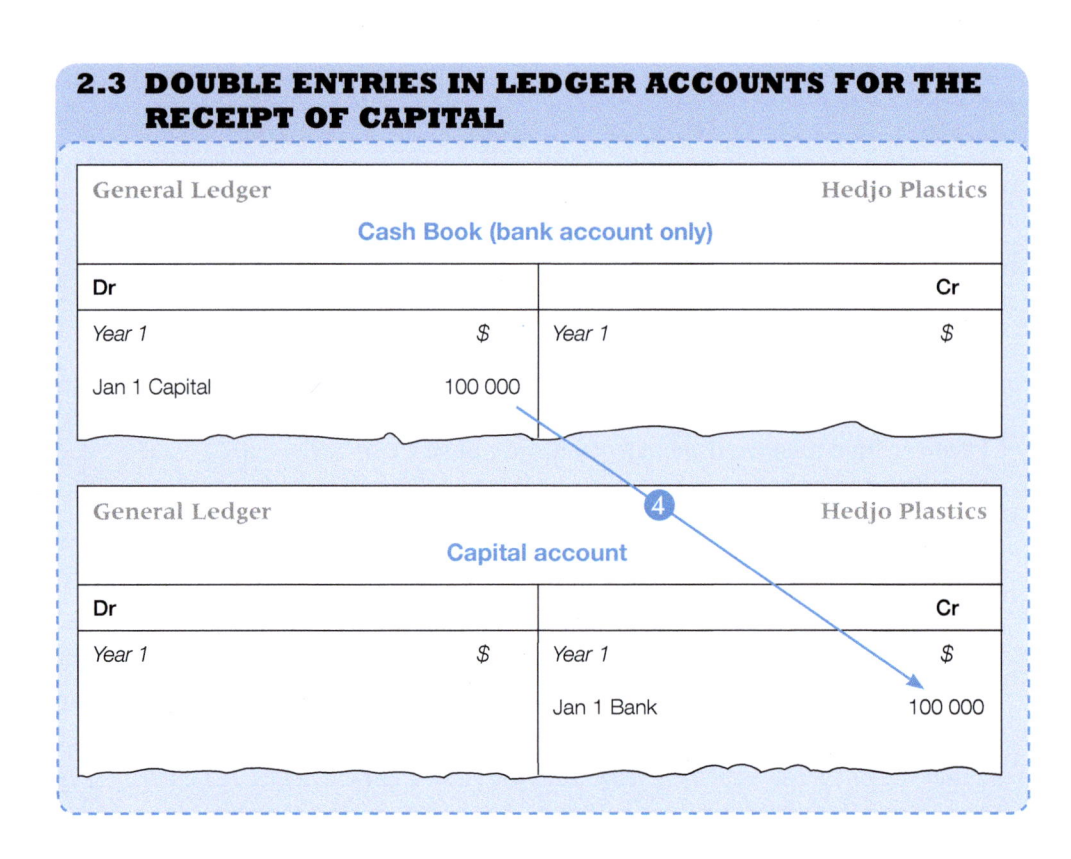

2.3 DOUBLE ENTRIES IN LEDGER ACCOUNTS FOR THE RECEIPT OF CAPITAL

General Ledger — Hedjo Plastics

Cash Book (bank account only)

Dr					Cr
Year 1		$	Year 1		$
Jan 1 Capital		100 000			

General Ledger — Hedjo Plastics

Capital account

Dr					Cr
Year 1		$	Year 1		$
			Jan 1 Bank		100 000

202 Accounting procedures

Similarly, when Hedjo Plastics received a 10-year bank loan for $50 000 a few months later, Hedley Johnson recorded the receipt of the loan capital as follows:

Recording a capital receipt for loan capital

Bank account	Bank loan account
A debit entry for loan capital received	A credit entry for the loan amount repayable to the bank
Impact: cash in bank is increased	Impact: non-current liabilities are increased

Capital receipts are for capital. They are not income and will not increase profit for the year. Capital receipts are recorded as credits to liability accounts in the ledger. This is because the owner's equity invested in the business belongs to the owner and loan capital is repayable to banks or other lenders.

The sum of owner's equity plus loan capital invested in a business is called its **capital employed**. ➤ 5.1

Revenue receipts increase the income and profit of the business

During its first three months of trading Hedjo Plastics earned $17 500 in revenue from the sale of goods. The business also received additional income of $2 070 in total from other sources including interest on business savings, sales commission and renting out garage and advertising space. All of the monies received were recorded in the books as revenue receipts.

Revenue receipts are recorded as credits to sales or income received accounts. Balances on these accounts will increase profit in the income statement of the business. ➤ 3.1

For example, at the end of its first three months of trading last year Hedjo Plastics received a payment of $900 for rent of its garage to another business organisation. Illustration 2.4 shows the double entries for the receipt recorded in the books of the business. No other entries to the cash book over the same period are shown.

Recording revenue receipts for cash sales

Bank account	Rent received account
A debit entry for the rental payment received	A credit entry for the rental of the space occupied
Impact: cash in bank is increased	Impact: revenue is increased

Capital and revenue expenditure and receipts

2.4 DOUBLE ENTRIES IN LEDGER ACCOUNTS FOR REVENUE RECEIPTS

General Ledger — Hedjo Plastics

Cash Book (bank account only)

Dr Analysis column for rent only			Cr
Year 1	$	Year 1	$
Mar 31 Rent received	900		

General Ledger — Hedjo Plastics

Rent received account

Dr			Cr
Year 1	$	Year 1	$
		Mar 31 Bank	900

ACTIVITY 2.5

The table below is from activity 2.4. It reproduces the list of receipts Hedjo Plastics incurred during its first three months of trading last year.

Complete the table to show the impact each receipt will have on the profit or the total capital employed in the business. Remember this will depend on whether they were revenue or capital receipts so refer back to your answers to activity 2.4 to help you. (The first one has been completed for you.)

Receipt	Amount $	Impact on profit	Impact on owner's equity or non-current liabilities
Introduction of owner's equity	100 000	–	Owner's equity is increased by $100 000
10-year commercial bank loan	50 000		
Sales	17 500		
Interest on business savings	30		
Payment from an advertising agency for use of space on the side wall of the shop	350		
Rent for use of the garage owned by the shop	900		
Sale of spare land at the rear of the shop	12 800		
Commission on sales of plastic items from the manufacturer	790		

The incorrect recording of a capital receipt as a revenue receipt will overstate revenue and profit for the year and understate capital

Capital receipts will increase the capital employed in the business either by increasing the owner's equity or loan capital invested in business assets. For example, if Hedley Johnson had mistakenly recorded the receipt of $50 000 of loan capital as income in his income statement, the error would have:

- overstated income and profit by $50 000
- understated loan capital (non-current liabilities) by $50 000.

With non-current liabilities understated the business may overlook the need to make regular repayments and may even take out further loans that it may not be able to afford.

	Income statement	Statement of financial position
If a capital receipt is recorded as in error as a revenue receipt:	• revenue and profit will be overstated	• capital employed (owner's equity or loan capital) in business assets will be understated

The incorrect recording of a revenue receipt as a capital receipt will understate revenue and profit for the year and overstate capital

Revenue receipts will increase the total income and profit of the business. If a revenue receipt is recorded as a capital receipt in error both revenue and profit will appear to be less than they should be and the capital employed in the business will be overstated.

For example, during its first three months of trading Hedjo Plastics received $900 from rent of its garage space to another organisation. If, instead of crediting the rent received account with the payment received, owner Hedley Johnson had credited it to the capital account, the error would have:

- understated profit by $900
- overstated owner's equity by $900.

With owner's capital overstated the owners may be tempted to increase their personal drawings from the business. This will reduce cash in the bank and may result in the business being unable to meet its future running expenses.

	Income statement	Statement of financial position
If a revenue receipt is recorded as in error as a capital receipt:	revenue and profit will be understated	capital employed (owner's equity or loan capital) in business assets will be overstated

ACTIVITY 2.6

Talia has drawn up financial statements for her business at the end of her accounting year. They show a profit for the year of $60 000, owner's equity of $90 000 and loan capital or non-current liabilities of $120 000. However, you discover that she made several errors recording her receipts during the year.

Error	Impact of the error on profit	Impact of the error on owner's equity or non-current liabilities
Interest on bank savings of $1 000 was credited by mistake to the loan account	Profit is understated by $1 000	Non-current liabilities are overstated by $1 000
A cash sale for $6 500 was credited to the capital account		
Proceeds of $800 from the sale of some surplus office furniture was credited to the sales account		
Annual interest of $1 400 received from the bank was credited to the bank loan account instead of the interest received account		

Complete the table to show the impact each error will have had on the calculation of profit for the year and the value of owner's equity or non-current liabilities in Talia's financial statements. (The impacts of the first error have been completed for you.)

QUICK TEST

1. Explain the following terms using examples:

   (a) capital expenditure;

   (b) revenue expenditure;

   (c) capital receipts;

   (d) revenue receipts.

2. Vijay owns a restaurant. Over the last month it spent and received the following amounts.

| | Expenditure || Receipt ||
	Capital	Revenue	Capital	Revenue
Sold off surplus furniture for $300				
Cash purchases of $1 460				
Arranged and received a bank loan for $2 000				
Purchased a new oven for $1700				
Bank charges were $25				
Paid $300 for the installation of the new oven				
Paid $500 in rent for the month				
Paid $3 500 in wages to restaurant staff				
Cash sales of $4 500				
Received $60 interest on business savings				
Purchased a supply of paper napkins for $45				
Vijay invested a further $1 000 from his personal savings				
Paid advertising costs of $175				

Identify the correct type of expenditure or receipt using a tick or cross in the appropriate column.

3. On 3 March Charlie Layiwola purchased a new machine for $15 000 and spent $2 000 on its installation. Six months later, on 10 September, he had to spend $1 500 on the repair of a broken drive belt and shaft, and $500 to replace the air filter.

   Write up the journal entries needed to record these transactions.

4. Megan owns a small flower shop. During the last month her business received the following amounts:

   ▸ $5 000 from her own savings to start her business

   ▸ a bank loan for $1 500

   ▸ cash sales of $750

   ▸ sales commission of $45

   ▸ $35 in cash from the sale of some old furniture from the shop

   ▸ interest of $5 on her business savings account.

   Calculate her total capital receipts and total revenue receipts during her first month of trading.

Capital and revenue expenditure and receipts

5   When Malik Matheroo bought a new hydraulic lift for his vehicle parts and repair business, Malik Motors, the following expenditures were incurred:

	Amount $
Hydraulic lift	3 300
Delivery charge	250
Safety clothing and goggles for the lift operator	245
Floor repairs and repainting of the lift area	630
Rewiring of the garage	1 200
Lift installation charge	980
Oils and lubricants for lift operation	125
Additional annual premium to insure the lift	220

Calculate the total capital expenditure and revenue expenditure of the business associated with the new equipment.

6   Santia runs a small business. During April she recorded the following transactions:

Date		Transaction	Amount $
Apr	4	Paid for a new computer and printer	3 000
	11	Paid to renew the insurance for her delivery vehicle	1 200
	23	Paid for replacement printer cartridges and paper	60
	30	Sold off surplus office furniture for cash	200

She recorded these in her journal as follows:

General Journal

Date	Description	Dr	Cr
Apr 4	Computer expenses	3 000	
	Bank		3 000
Apr 11	Vehicles	1 200	
	Bank		1 200
Apr 23	Computer equipment	60	
	Bank		60
Apr 30	Cash	200	
	Sales		200

(a) The debits for expenditures and credits for receipts are correct but the accounts are wrong. For each one explain why and identify what the correct account should be.

(b) Calculate the effect of each error on the profit and assets of her business.

(c) Write up the correct entries for the capital and revenue expenditures and receipts in Santia's journal.

(d) Explain why making errors in the calculation of profit or loss can cause serious problems for a business.

Unit 2.2 Accounting for depreciation and disposal of non-current assets

AIMS

By the end of this unit you should be able to

- define **depreciation**
- explain the reasons for accounting for depreciation
- name and describe the **straight-line, reducing balance** and **revaluation** methods of depreciation
- prepare ledger accounts and journal entries for the provision of depreciation
- prepare ledger accounts and journal entries to record the sale of non-current assets, including the use of disposal accounts

2.2.1 The depreciation of non-current assets

Non-current assets will lose value over time as they wear out or become out of date

The capital expenditure of a business in any given accounting year will not reduce profit for the year. This is because capital expenditure is incurred buying or acquiring non-current assets including premises, machinery, equipment and vehicles that will benefit the business over a number of years. Capital expenditure increases the value of non-current assets recorded in the statement of financial position of the business.

An important principle in accounting is that non-current assets should be valued in the accounts of a business at cost. The advantage of doing so is that their values can be easily checked against prices recorded on source documents. However, non-current assets will lose value over time as they are used repeatedly over more than one accounting year by a business to earn revenue:

- Many simply wear out through repeated use, for example the continual use of machines.
- Some non-current assets, such as oil wells, mines and quarries, will be depleted (used up) over time as their value is extracted from them.
- Technological change can result in some equipment, such as computers becoming out of date and unable to match the efficiency of more advanced equipment.
- Some non-current assets will no longer be suitable as a business expands or changes its activities. For example, as a business grows it may need to move into larger premises or invest in larger delivery vehicles.

- The working life or useful life of some non-current assets is determined by legal requirements. For example, vehicles and aircraft may have to be retired if they no longer meet strict safety requirements. In addition, some business premises are owned under leasehold arrangements. This means ownership of the premises is for an agreed number of years and will cease when the lease expires.

Depreciation is an estimate of the loss in value of a non-current asset over its useful life. Although there is no physical outflow of cash from the business due to depreciation, any loss of value in its non-current assets over time is nonetheless an expense for that business. At the end of each accounting year the business should charge any depreciation in the value of its non-current assets over the year to its profit.

This means the initial cost of a non-current asset will not be charged to profit in the accounting year it was acquired. Instead a business will spread the cost of its non-current asset over all the accounting years that will benefit from their use. That is, the business will expense part of the cost of each non-current asset to profit each year so that it is matched with the revenue each asset has helped to generate in each one of those years. This practice is an application of the matching (or accruals) principle of accounting and should continue until the asset is no longer usable, disposed of or replaced by the business. ➤ 5.2

The depreciation of non-current assets has two important effects on a business:

- It reduces the value of its non-current assets year on year.
- It reduces profit (or increases loss) each year.

Allowing for depreciation involves estimating the loss in value of a non-current asset over its useful or working life

On the day Hedley Johnson bought a delivery van for his business, Hedjo Plastics, he recorded it in his asset account for vehicles at cost. This included not just the cost of the van but also the cost of repainting the van with his business name and logo: a combined capital expenditure of $22 000. ➤ 2.1

2.5 OPENING ENTRIES TO THE LEDGER FOR THE COST OF ACQUIRING A NON-CURRENT ASSET

General Ledger   Hedjo Plastics

Vehicles account

Dr					Cr
Year 1		$	Year 1		$
Jan 2	Bank	20 000			
Jan 2	Bank	2 000			

However, Hedley knew his vehicle would wear out and lose value over time. He would therefore need to allow for depreciation in the value of the vehicle in his accounts each year. This required him to estimate the following:

(i) The useful life of the asset to his business. He decided this should be four years.

(ii) How much the asset may be worth at the end of its useful life when it would be disposed of. This end-of-life value or **residual value** may be an estimate of how much someone else may be willing to pay for the asset or simply its scrap value at this time. Hedley assumed the residual value of his van at the end of four years would be $8 000.

(iii) The annual loss in value of the asset over its useful life until its residual value is reached. There were alternative ways he could do this:

- **Straight-line method** – this charges the same fixed amount of depreciation to profit at the end of each accounting year over the useful life of the asset.

  If Hedley used this method he could calculate the annual deprecation charge for his van as follows:

  $$\text{Annual depreciation charge} = \frac{\text{cost of asset} - \text{residual value}}{\text{useful life of asset (years)}}$$

  So, the annual charge would be $= \frac{\$22\,000 - \$8\,000}{4} = \frac{\$14\,000}{4}$

  i.e. a fixed annual depreciation charge of $3 500 per year.

- **Reducing balance method** – this takes into consideration that some assets lose more value in their first few years than they do later on in their useful lives. The amount of depreciation charged each year to profit is reduced each year.

  To use this method Hedley will need to decide on a fixed annual rate of depreciation, such as 20% per year. This would be applied to the value of the van recorded in the statement of financial position at the start of each accounting year. So, the depreciation charge for the van at the end of the first year would be:

  Depreciation charge (end of year 1) = cost of asset × 20%
  = $22 000 × 0.20 = $4 400

  The depreciation charge of $4 400 will reduce the **net book value** of the van at the end of year 1 from $22 000 to $17 600. So, the depreciation charge for Hedley's van at the end of the second accounting year should be calculated as follows:

  Depreciation charge (end of year 2) = net book value of van × 20%
  = ($22 000 − $4 400) × 0.2
  = $17 600 × 0.2 = $3 520

  The depreciation charge of $3 520 for year 2 will further reduce the net book value of the van at the end of the year from $17 600 to $14 080.

  Hedley did not know which of these methods to use so to help him decide he applied both methods to his delivery van as follows:

Now:

Two years later:

In four years' time:

Accounting for depreciation and disposal of non-current assets

▼ Comparing alternative methods of estimating depreciation

	Straight-line method	Reducing balance method
Cost of the van at the start of year 1 ($):	22 000	22 000
Useful life of the van	4 years	4 years
How annual depreciation charge is calculated: (All charges will be rounded to the nearest dollar value)	Fixed annual charge = $\dfrac{\text{cost of van} - \text{residual value}}{4 \text{ years}}$	Annual charge = 20% of cost of van (year 1 only) and thereafter its net book value at the end of each year
End of year 1:		
Value of the van at the start of the year	22 000	22 000
Depreciation charge	3 500	4 400
Net book value	18 500	17 600
End of year 2:		
Value of the van at the start of the year	18 500	17 600
Depreciation charge	3 500	3 520
Net book value	15 000	14 080
End of year 3:		
Value of the van at the start of the year	15 000	14 080
Depreciation charge	3 500	2 816
Net book value	11 500	11 264
End of year 4:		
Value of the van at the start of the year	11 500	11 264
Depreciation charge	3 500	2 252
Net book value	8 000	9 012

The **net book value** of an asset at the end of any given accounting year is its cost price less the sum of all annual depreciation charges to date or **accumulated depreciation** over the period since its purchase or acquisition. ▶ 3.2

> Net book value of non-current asset = cost of asset − accumulated depreciation

From his calculations Hedley decided to use the straight-line method of estimating depreciation charges for the delivery vehicle. This was the simplest way to calculate the annual depreciation charge and the net book value of his non-current asset at the end of year. For the same reason it is the most popular method of depreciation used in business throughout the world. However, it is more usual for businesses to use the reducing balance method for depreciating their vehicles. This is because new vehicles tend to lose value more quickly during their first few years in use.

Different methods of depreciation are applied to different non-current assets

It is important for a business to choose a method of depreciation that is most appropriate to each of their different types of non-current asset.

For example, the reducing balance method is an accelerated method of depreciation that results in higher depreciation expenses in the earlier years of ownership of a non-current asset. It is often applied to cars and other motor vehicles because they lose value quickly.

Computer equipment is another example of a non-current asset that tends to be most useful when it is new because of the rapid pace in technological change. As such the reducing balance method may be combined with an assumption that the useful life of the equipment will perhaps be 2–3 years, to calculate annual depreciation charges.

▼ The reducing balance method of depreciation:

Advantages	Disadvantages
✔ Vehicles and some other equipment are most productive when they are new and generate less benefit to the business as they age. By charging more depreciation to profit early on, this method better matches costs with revenues.	✘ It is more complex than the straight-line method ✘ The negative impact of depreciation on profit is greatest in the first few years of use of the method

In contrast, non-current assets such as many buildings, aircraft, ships and machinery tend to remain useful for many more accounting years than cars and other vehicles and depreciate more slowly. For these assets applying simple straight-line depreciation to spread their cost evenly over their long useful lives is usually the most appropriate method to use. The construction, manufacture and acquisition of these non-current assets will often be financed from bank loans repayable in equal instalments over the same or similar lifetimes as the assets.

However, it also acceptable to use the straight-line method of depreciation for non-current assets such as computer equipment, cars and other motor vehicles. Many small businesses adopt this method because it is the simplest.

▼ The straight-line method of depreciation:

Advantages	Disadvantages
✔ It is a relatively simple method of depreciation	✘ An estimate of the useful life and residual value of the non-current asset is required ✘ It takes no account of the rate at which the asset will actually depreciate in value over time

---

Estimating the useful life of a non-current asset

The useful lives of non-current assets will vary depending on the type of asset, the pace of business and technological change, and in some cases what the assets are used for and how frequently. Some non-current assets will last much longer or hold their value better than others.

For example, premises may have useful lives lasting 50 years, or in some cases many more. On the other hand, computers may wear out or become out of date within two or three years.

For the purpose of estimating depreciation charges sensible judgments must be made about the useful lives of assets and also their residual values at the end of their lives. For example, any business that suggests its factory, shops or offices have a useful life of just two years and have a very low residual value may be accused of seriously overstating its annual depreciation expenses and therefore significantly understating its profit.

Land is in most cases the longest lived asset. As land is a limited resource with an indefinite life, and can be used for a range of different purposes throughout its life span, it is not a depreciable asset in accounting. This means no depreciation charges should be included in the accounts for land except where the use of the land will materially reduce or deplete its value to a business, for example due to mining, quarrying or pollution.

Some businesses own a large number of items that will be useful over more than one accounting year but which are individually too low in value to record and depreciate separately. For example, a construction business may own many different hand tools including saws, hammers and spanners while a restaurant will own many knives, forks, spoons, glasses and plates. Some of these items are likely to be replaced each year due to breakages or theft and it may be difficult to keep detailed records. It would be too time consuming to depreciate each item or group of similar items individually and possibly at different rates each year. In these cases the revaluation method of depreciation will be the most appropriate to use.

The **revaluation method of depreciation** involves re-estimating a "fair" value for the combined non-current assets at the end of each accounting year and then charging the fall in value to profit for the year.

For example, Hedley Johnson owns a large number of hand tools he needs to cut, shape and mould plastic items in his store. Their combined cost was $500 when Hedley first purchased them. However, during his first accounting year Hedley lost and broke a number of his hand tools and had to buy some replacements. At the end of the year Hedley then had to record a fair value for these assorted tools in his statement of financial position for his business. There were too many to value individually so he estimated and recorded a combined value for them as follows:

Date	Transaction	Amount $
Jan 3	Hand tools purchased recorded in cash book	500
Jul 15	*add* Additional tools purchased recorded in cash book	80
		580
Dec 31	*less* Revaluation of tools at year end	480
Dec 31	Annual depreciation charge for tools	100

The table shows that at the end of his first accounting year Hedley revalued his tools at $480 and charged depreciation of $100 against his profit for the year being the difference between their total cost and their revised value.

▼ The revaluation method of depreciation:

Advantages	Disadvantages
✔ It does not require an estimate of the useful life and residual value of the non-current asset	✘ The revaluation is based on individual opinion

> **ACTIVITY 2.7**
>
> Louise opened her steam cleaning business on 1 January two years ago. On this day she acquired the following assets. Their cost prices were as follows:
>
> | | $ |
> |---|---|
> | Machinery | 50 000 |
> | Furniture and fittings | 12 000 |
> | Premises | 115 000 |
>
> She has adopted the following accounting policies for annual depreciation charges:
>
> - Machinery has a useful life of 10 years and will be depreciated using the straight-line method. A scrap or residual value at the end of 10 years of $10 000 is assumed.
> - Furniture and fittings will be depreciated using the diminishing (reducing) balance method assuming an annual rate of depreciation of 20%.
> - Premises will be revalued. During the year these were extended at a total cost of $12 000. At the end of the first year of trading on 31 December the extended premises were revalued at $125 000. This was unchanged at the end of the second year.
>
> Calculate the depreciation charges for each type of non-current asset for each of the last two years ended 31 December and show their net book values on these dates.

It is sometimes necessary to increase the value of some non-current assets in the financial statements of the business

All non-current assets with the exception of land are depreciable assets and will lose value over time as they wear out or become outdated. However, some non-current assets may actually gain value over time simply because other people and organisations are willing and able to pay more for them than they originally cost. This is especially the case for land and property. Increasing demand for these non-current assets can significantly push up the prices at which they can be sold. When this happens it may be necessary to increase the values recorded for these non-current assets in the statement of financial position to describe their true value more accurately.

Land and property prices can also fall. For example, property prices fell dramatically in many countries following the global financial crisis in 2008 and in some areas have remained low since. When this happens it will be necessary to reduce their value in the accounts. This revaluation of non-current assets is however very different from the planned depreciation of an asset based on its age.

Businesses that own properties such as factory buildings, retail outlets, office blocks, hotels, golf courses and houses for rent, will often revalue them upwards and downwards over time in their financial statements as the market prices of land and different properties fluctuate.

Depreciation is an expense: it does not provide a cash reserve to fund the replacement of old non-current assets

It is a common misunderstanding that annual depreciation charges against profit for non-current assets are used to build up a cash reserve over time so that the business can buy replacements in the future. They do not. Depreciation charges are simply a book-keeping entry.

For example, when Hedley Johnson bought his delivery van for $22 000 it reduced the cash in his business by this amount but he did not charge it to profit that year. Instead he will charge part of its cost to his profit each year over the next four accounting years as he uses his vehicle to earn revenue. The profit recorded for each of those years will be lower as a result but the business will not have to pay out any more cash.

Accounting for depreciation and disposal of non-current assets

2.2.2 Recording depreciation in the journal and ledger accounts

Annual depreciation charges for the non-current asset will accumulate in the provision for depreciation account in the general ledger

Different non-current assets have different working lives and will be depreciated using different methods, so it is important for a business to record the following information about each type of non-current asset it uses:

Information required	Where the information is recorded
Cost of the non-current asset	Asset (at cost) account
Annual depreciation charges or expenses	Depreciation expense in income statement
Total of all annual depreciation charges to date	Provision for depreciation account
Net book value of the asset	Statement of financial position

Hedley Johnson maintains the following accounts for the non-current assets of his business Hedjo Plastics:

Debit the cost of the non-current asset to:	vehicles account	premises account	equipment account
Credit annual depreciation charges to:	provision for depreciation of vehicles account	provision for depreciation of premises account	provision for depreciation of equipment account

Recall that Hedley purchased a delivery vehicle at a cost of $22 000 when he started up in business on 1 January last year. He decided he would depreciate the vehicle in his accounts in equal instalments of $3 500 per year over four years.

At the end of his first accounting year ended 31 December last year Hedley had to update his accounts for vehicles as follows.

2.6 ACCOUNTING RECORDS FOR DEPRECIATION

❶ Balance off the **asset account** and take balance to the **statement of financial position**

General Ledger — Hedjo Plastics

Vehicles account

Dr		$			Cr $
Year 1			Year 1		
Jan 2	Bank	20 000	Dec 31	Balance c/d	22 000
Jan 2	Bank	2 000			
		22 000			22 000
Year 2					
Jan 1	Balance b/d	22 000			

216 Accounting procedures

2 Record the following double entries for the annual depreciation charge:
- Debit the **income statement** with the annual depreciation charge. This will increase expenses on the income statement and reduce profit for the year.
- Credit the **provision for depreciation account** with the annual depreciation charge.

General Journal — Hedjo Plastics

Date	Description	Dr	Cr
Year 1 Dec 31	Income statement	3 500	
	Provision for depreciation of vehicles *To charge annual provision to profit for the year*		3 500

General Ledger — Hedjo Plastics

Provision for depreciation of vehicles account

Dr					Cr
Year 1		$	Year 1		$
Dec 31	Balance c/d	3 500	Dec 31	Income statement	3 500
			Year 2		
			Jan 1	Balance b/d	3 500

3 Take the balance on the provision for depreciation account to the statement of financial position to record **accumulated depreciation**.

4 Calculate and record the **net book value** of the asset in the statement of financial position as follows:

Extract from statement of financial position at 31 December (year 1)

	Cost $	Accumulated depreciation $	Net book value $
Year 1			
Vehicles	22 000 **①**	3 500 **③**	**18 500** **④**

Now, using illustration 2.7, let's look at how Hedley will have to update the same accounts at the end of his second accounting year.

Accounting for depreciation and disposal of non-current assets

2.7 HOW DEPRECIATION ACCUMULATES IN THE ACCOUNTS

1 Balance off the asset account and take the balance to the statement of financial position. Unless any new assets have been acquired or old ones disposed of the balance will be the same as for the previous year.

General Ledger — Hedjo Plastics
Vehicles account

Dr					Cr
Year 1		$	Year 1		$
Jan 2	Bank	20 000	Dec 31	Balance c/d	22 000
Jan 2	Bank	2 000			
		22 000			22 000
Year 2			Year 2		
Jan 1	Balance b/d	22 000	Dec 31	Balance c/d	22 000
Year 3					
Jan 1	Balance b/d	22 000			

6 Record the double entries for the annual depreciation charge:
- Debit the income statement with the annual depreciation charge.
- Credit the provision for depreciation account with the annual depreciation charge. This is added to the balance on the account brought down from the end of the previous year so that depreciation charges steadily accumulate each year in the balance carried down.

General Journal — Hedjo Plastics

Date	Description	Dr	Cr
Year 2 Dec 31	Income statement	3 500	
	Provision for depreciation of vehicles		3 500
	To charge annual provision to profit for the year		

General Ledger — Hedjo Plastics
Provision for depreciation of vehicles account

Dr						Cr
Year 1		$	Year 1			$
Dec 31	Balance c/d	3 500	Dec 31	Income statement		3 500
Year 2			Year 2			
Dec 31	Balance c/d	7 000	Jan 1	Balance b/d		3 500
			Dec 31	Income statement		3 500
		7 000				7 000
			Year 3			
			Jan 1	Balance b/d		7 000

7 Transfer the balance on the provision for depreciation account to the statement of financial position to record accumulated depreciation.

8 Calculate and record the net book value of the asset in the statement of financial position as follows:

The entries made by Hedley to the books of his business for the straight-line depreciation of the delivery vehicle demonstrate the following key points:

- The value recorded in the non-current asset (at cost) account in the ledger does not change because depreciation is recorded separately.

- The annual depreciation charge recorded in the provision for depreciation account is always debited to the income statement. It ensures that part of the original cost of the asset is charged to profit each year over its useful life to match its contribution to revenue each year.

- Annual depreciation charges will accumulate in the balance carried down on the provision for depreciation account.

- The net book value of the non-current asset recorded in the statement of financial position will reduce each year by the increase in accumulated depreciation.

Accounting procedures

Extract from statement of financial position at 31 December (year 2)

	Cost $	Accumulated depreciation $	Net book value $
Year 2			
Vehicles	22 000 ⑤	7 000 ⑦	15 000 ⑧

ACTIVITY 2.8

1. You will recall that Hedjo Plastics owns a delivery vehicle that cost $22 000 which was acquired at the beginning of its first accounting year. The owner, Hedley Johnson, has decided to depreciate the asset in equal instalments of $3 500 over four years.

   (a) From illustration 2.7 write up the vehicles account and the provision for depreciation account in the books of Hedjo Plastics as they would appear at the end of its third accounting year.

   (b) Calculate the net book value of vehicles that will be recorded in the statement of financial position of Hedjo Plastics as at 31 December at the end of its third accounting year.

2. Anais Jeannot owns a hairstyling and beauty salon. On 1 April 2012 she purchased equipment costing $36 000 and decided that she would depreciate the equipment at the rate of 20% per year using the reducing balance method. Write up the following accounts in her ledger:

   (a) processing and steaming equipment account to show (i) the acquisition of the equipment; (ii) the balances carried down for the accounting years ended 31 March 2013 and 31 March 2014;

   (b) provision for depreciation account to show (i) the balances transferred to the income statement; and (ii) the balances carried down for the accounting years ended 31 March 2013 and 31 March 2014;

   (c) Calculate the net book value of Anais' equipment that she will record in her statements of financial position as at 31 March 2013 and 31 March 2014.

A separate account to record annual provisions for depreciation is not required if the revaluation method of depreciation is used

The business next door to Hedjo Plastics is a small coffee shop and café. It opened at the same time as Hedjo Plastics. On this day the owner invested $5 000 in cutlery, cups, mugs and other tableware for the business in addition to a further $12 000 in furniture, refrigeration equipment and coffee-making machines.

The owner decided to use the revaluation method to depreciate the cutlery and tableware of the business because they consisted of a large number of relatively low-value items of which some would be replaced each year due to damage or breakages. It would not be sensible to keep detailed records of the number and value of all these items.

The following information is available about the cutlery and tableware of the café from the cash book and general journal of the business for its first accounting year:

Date	Description	$
Jan 1	Cutlery and tableware purchased at cost	5 000 ⑨
Jul 12	*add* additional cutlery and tableware purchased at cost	1 600 ⑩
		6 600
Dec 31	*less* revaluation of cutlery and tableware at year end	6 000
Dec 31	Depreciation charge for the year	600 ⑪

The depreciation charge charged to the café's profit for its first accounting year was $600. The journal of the café and its asset account for cutlery and tableware were written up at the end of that year as shown in illustration 2.8.

2.8 ACCOUNTING ENTRIES WHEN THE REVALUATION METHOD OF DEPRECIATION IS USED

General Journal — The Café

Date	Description	Dr	Cr
Dec 31	Income statement	600	
	Cutlery and tableware		600
	To charge provision for depreciation to profit for the year		

General Ledger — The Café

Cutlery and tableware account

Dr		$			Cr	$
Year 1			Year 1			
Jan 1	Bank	5 000	Dec 31	Income statement		600 ⑪
Jul 12	Bank	1 600	Dec 31	Balance c/d		6 000
		6 600				6 600
Year 2						
Jan 1	Balance b/d	6 000				

⑨ ⑩ ⑫

The closing balance carried down on the account for the revalued asset is the **net book value** of the non-current asset. This is recorded in the statement of financial position.

When the revaluation method of depreciation is used there is no need to record annual depreciation charges in a separate account or to accumulate (add) those charges over time. This is because the non-current asset account will contain all the information needed to complete the financial statements at the end of an accounting year. This includes:

- The difference between total debits for non-current assets acquired and the balance carried down (the revalued non-current assets) is the depreciation charge for the year to be charged to profit for the year in the income statement.

- The balance carried down (the revalued non-current assets) is the net book value that will be recorded in the statement of financial position for the assets.

2.2.3 Accounting for the disposal of non-current assets

The sale or disposal of a non-current asset at the end of its useful life may result in a profit or loss when the proceeds of sale are compared to the net book value of the asset

When an asset reaches the end of its useful life it will be disposed of in one of the following ways:

- The non-current asset can be simply thrown or given away or sold off for scrap.
- It may be sold on to someone who can use the second-hand asset in his or her own business.
- It may be traded in for an allowance from the supplier against the cost of a replacement.

When a business disposes of a non-current asset it will need to:

- Remove any remaining details of the non-current asset from its accounting system.
- Compare any proceeds from its disposal against the net book value of the asset recorded in its statement of financial position. They will rarely be the same so it will be necessary to record either the profit or loss on the disposal.

For example, imagine four years have now passed and Hedley Johnson has just disposed of the delivery van of his business: he sold it for $6 500 on 19 February in his fourth accounting year.

Recall the following details about the van:

- It was acquired at the beginning of accounting year 1 at a cost of $22 000.
- It was assumed to have a useful life of four years and an estimated residual value at the end of its useful life of $8 000.
- It was depreciated using the straight-line method by $3 500 each year over four years.

Therefore, at the end of the fourth accounting year of the business ended 31 December:

- Accumulated depreciation of the van was $14 000 ($3 500 × 4 years).
- The net book value of the van in the accounts was $8 000 (cost price of $22 000 less $14 000 of accumulated depreciation).

To remove the van from his accounting system and record the profit or loss from its disposal Hedley will need to take the following steps:

⑬ First, open a **disposal account** for the vehicle. Then transfer the cost of the non-current asset from the ledger to the disposal account as follows:
  - debit the disposal account with the cost price of $22 000 paid for the van
  - credit the vehicles account with $22 000 to remove the non-current asset

⑭ Transfer the accumulated depreciation on the non-current asset to the disposal account:

ACTIVITY 2.9

In addition to the equipment Anais Jeannot acquired when she first started her hairstyling and beauty salon on 1 April 2012, she also purchased a large number of low-value items including scissors, clippers and straighteners. The total cost of all these items added up to $4 000 which she entered into a non-current asset account marked "Hair styling tools" in her business ledger.

Anais decided the best way to depreciate the value of the hair styling tools was to use the revaluation method. The following information was taken from her books:

- On 31 March 2013 she revalued the tools at $3 500.
- On 18 November 2013 she acquired additional tools costing $860 in total.
- On 31 March 2014 she revalued the tools at $3 800.

(a) Write up the journal entries required to record the annual depreciation charge for tools for the accounting years ended 31 March 2013 and 31 March 2014.

(b) Post the journal entries to the account for hair-styling tools in Anais' ledger.

(c) What net book values will Anais record for her hair styling tools in her statement of financial position as at 31 March 2013 and as at 31 March 2014?

- debit the balance of $14 000 for accumulated depreciation from the provision for depreciation of vehicles account and close the account
- credit $14 000 of accumulated depreciation to the vehicles disposal account.

The difference on the disposal account between the debit of $22 000 for the van at cost and the credit of $14 000 for accumulated depreciation is its net book value: $8 000.

⑮ To record the receipt of cash from disposal of the van in the cash book:
- debit the bank account in the cash book with $6 500 of cash received
- credit the disposal account for vehicles with $6 500 received in exchange for the van.

⑯ At the end of the accounting year calculate the profit or loss on the disposal of the van. The business will have made:
- a profit if the proceeds from the sale exceeded the net book value of the van
- a loss if the proceeds from the sale were less than the net book value of the van.

Hedley received $6 500 in cash from the sale of the delivery van, so he records a loss of $1 500 below the net book value of the van of $8 000.

⑰ Transfer the profit or loss on disposal to the income statement for Hedjo Plastics at the end of the accounting year:
- credit the disposal account for vehicles with the loss of $1 500, then balance off and close the account
- debit the income statement with the loss of $1 500.

Illustration 2.9 on the pages that follow shows how the full accounting records for the delivery van would look in the books of Hedjo Plastics after four years.

⑬ Open a disposal account and then make the following double entries to remove the non-current asset from the accounting system:

Disposal account for non-currrent asset	Non-current asset (at cost) account
Debit the account with the cost price of the asset	Credit the account with the cost price of the asset to close the account
Impact: the asset at cost is transferred to the account	Impact: the balance on the account is reduced to zero

2.9 (i) TO CLOSE AN ACCOUNT FOR A NON-CURRENT ASSET UPON DISPOSAL OF THAT ASSET

General Journal			Hedjo Plastics
Date	Description	Dr	Cr
Year 5 Feb 19	Vehicles disposal	22 000	
	Vehicles		22 000
	To transfer the cost of the van on disposal		

General Ledger — Hedjo Plastics

Vehicles account

Dr							Cr
Year 1			$	Year 1			$
Jan 2	Bank		20 000	Dec 31	Balance c/d		22 000
Jan 2	Bank		2 000				
			22 000				22 000
Year 2				Year 2			
Jan 1	Balance b/d		22 000	Dec 31	Balance c/d		22 000
Year 3				Year 3			
Jan 1	Balance b/d		22 000	Dec 31	Balance c/d		22 000
Year 4				Year 4			
Jan 1	Balance b/d		22 000	Dec 3	Balance c/d		22 000
Year 5				Year 5			
Jan 1	Balance b/d		22 000	Feb 19	Vehicles disposal		22 000

General Ledger — Hedjo Plastics

Vehicles disposal account

Dr					Cr
Year 5		$	Year 5		$
Feb 19	Vehicles	22 000			

Accounting for depreciation and disposal of non-current assets

14 Transfer the accumulated depreciation of the non-current asset to the disposal account for that asset. This will remove the depreciation from the accounting system.

Provision for the depreciation of non-currrent asset account	Disposal account for non-current asset
Debit the account with the balance for the accumulated depreciation on the non-current asset to close the account	Credit the account with the accumulated depreciation on the non-current asset
Impact: the balance on account is reduced to zero	Impact: the accumulated depreciation is transferred to the account

2.9 (ii) TO CLOSE THE PROVISION OF DEPRECIATION ACCOUNT FOR A NON-CURRENT ASSET UPON DISPOSAL

General Journal — Hedjo Plastics

Date	Description	Dr	Cr
Year 5 Feb 19	**Provision for depreciation of vehicles**	14 000	
	Vehicles disposal *To transfer total provision for the depreciation of the van on disposal*		14 000

General Ledger — Hedjo Plastics

Provision for depreciation of vehicles account

Dr				Cr	
Year 1 Dec 31	Balance c/d	$ 3 500	Year 1 Dec 31	Income statement	$ 3 500
Year 2 Dec 31	Balance c/d	7 000 / 7 000	Year 2 Jan 1 Dec 31	Balance b/d Income statement	3 500 / 3 500 / 7 000
Year 3 Dec 31	Balance c/d	10 500 / 10 500	Year 3 Jan 1 Dec 31	Balance b/d Income statement	7 000 / 3 500 / 10 500
Year 4 Dec 31	Balance c/d	14 000 / 14 000	Year 4 Jan 1 Dec 31	Balance b/d Income statement	10 500 / 3 500 / 14 000
Year 5 Feb 19	Vehicles disposal	14 000			

General Ledger — Hedjo Plastics

Vehicles disposal account

Dr			Cr		
Year 5		$	Year 4		$
Feb 19	Vehicles	22 000	Feb 19	Provision for depreciation of vehicles	14 000

224 Accounting procedures

The final stage involves recording the proceeds from the disposal of the asset and recording the profit or loss realised (achieved) on disposal.

⑮ To record the proceeds from disposal of the asset:

Bank account	Disposal account for non-current asset
Debit the account with the proceeds from the disposal of the asset (a capital receipt ➤ 2.1.4)	Credit the account with the proceeds from the disposal of the asset
Impact: cash in bank is increased	Impact: non-trading income is increased

2.9 (iii) DOUBLE ENTRIES FOR THE PROCEEDS FROM DISPOSAL OF A NON-CURRENT ASSET

General Journal — Hedjo Plastics

Date	Description	Dr	Cr
Year 5 Feb 19	**Bank**	6 500	
	Vehicles disposal		6 500
	Proceeds from the disposal of the delivery van		

General Ledger — Hedjo Plastics

Vehicles disposal account

Dr					Cr
Year 5		$	Year 5		$
Feb 19	Vehicles	22 000	Feb 19	Provision for depreciation of vehicles	14 000
			Feb 19	Bank	6 500

⑯ The balancing figure on the disposal account will be the profit or loss on disposal of the non-current asset. To calculate the profit or loss on disposal, compare total credits on the disposal with total debits. In the disposal account above total debits are $22 000 and total credits are $20 500. The account therefore has a credit balance of $1 500. This means the disposal resulted in a loss of $1 500.

⑰ To record a loss on disposal of a non-current asset in the income statement at the end of the accounting year:

Income statement	Disposal account for non-current asset
Debit the statement with the loss on disposal of the asset	Credit the account with the loss on disposal to balance off and close the account
Impact: profit for the year is reduced	Impact: the balance on the account is reduced to zero

Accounting for depreciation and disposal of non-current assets

2.9 (iv) RECORDING A LOSS ON THE DISPOSAL OF A NON-CURRENT ASSET AT THE END OF AN ACCOUNTING YEAR

General Journal — Hedjo Plastics

Date	Description	Dr	Cr
Year 5 Dec 31	Income statement	1 500	
	Vehicles disposal		1 500
	To transfer loss on the disposal of the delivery van		

General Ledger — Hedjo Plastics

Vehicles disposal account

Dr				Cr	
Year 5		$	Year 5		$
Feb 19	Vehicles	22 000	Feb 19	Provision for depreciation of vehicles	14 000
			Feb 19	Bank	6 500
			Dec 31	Income statement (loss on disposal)	1 500
		22 000			22 000

ACTIVITY 2.10

On 1 January 2009 Shakeel bought $8 000 of computer equipment to start his computer software design business. He adopted an accounting policy of depreciating the equipment in equal instalments of $1 500 per year over four years.

On 1 January 2013 the following balances were therefore brought down in the books of his business:

Computer equipment
(at cost) $8 000 Dr

Provision for
depreciation
of computer
equipment $6 000 Cr

On 15 July 2013 Shakeel sold off his old computer equipment and received a cheque for $1 400. No further depreciation on the equipment was provided for in the year of its disposal.

1. Make appropriate entries to the following records for the disposal of the equipment:

    (a) general journal;

    (b) computer equipment account;

    (c) provision for depreciation of computer equipment;

    (d) computer equipment disposal account.

Remember to balance off the ledger accounts following disposal and show the transfer of profit or loss from the disposal account to the income statement for the business for the accounting year ended 31 December 2013.

> **ACTIVITY 2.11**
>
> Yessica owns a small construction business. The accounting year of the business ends on 30 September.
>
> On 1 October 2013 the following balances were recorded in the general ledger of her business:
>
> Machinery (at cost) $45 000 Dr
>
> Provision for depreciation of machinery $39 000 Cr
>
> On 5 November 2013 Yessica sold off the machinery for scrap, receiving a cheque for $7 000. No further provision was made for depreciation of the machinery in the year of its disposal.
>
> 1 Make appropriate entries to the following records for the disposal of the equipment:
>
>   (a) general journal;
>   (b) machinery account;
>   (c) provision for the depreciation of machinery;
>   (d) machinery disposal account.
>
> Remember to balance off the ledger accounts following disposal. Also, show the profit or loss on the disposal account that Yessica will transfer to the income statement for her business for the accounting year ended 30 September 2014.

Now imagine that Hedley Johnson had instead managed to sell off his old delivery van for $8 900. This is above the net book value of the van and would mean he had made a profit from the sale of $900. The disposal account would therefore record a debit balance of $900 and the final entries to record the profit would need to be as follows:

Income statement	Disposal account for non-currrent asset
Credit the statement with the profit on disposal of the asset	Debit the account with the profit on disposal to balance off and close the account
Impact: profit for the year is increased	Impact: the balance on the account is reduced to zero

2.10 RECORDING A PROFIT ON THE DISPOSAL OF A NON-CURRENT ASSET AT THE END OF AN ACCOUNTING YEAR

General Journal   Hedjo Plastics

Date	Description	Dr	Cr
Year 6 Dec 31	Vehicles disposal	900	
	Income statement		900
	To transfer profit on the disposal of the delivery van		

General Ledger   Hedjo Plastics

Vehicles disposal account

Dr						Cr
Year 5		$		Year 5		$
Feb 19	Vehicles	22 000		Feb 19	Provision for depreciation of vehicles	14 000
Dec 31	Income statement (profit on disposal)	900		Feb 19	Bank	8 900
		22 900				22 900

Accounting for depreciation and disposal of non-current assets   **227**

QUICK TEST

1. (a) Explain the meaning and purpose of depreciation in accounting; (b) Describe, using examples, three reasons for the depreciation of non-current assets.
2. Explain the following methods of depreciation: (a) straight-line; (b) reducing balance; (c) revaluation.
3. For what types of non-current asset will use of the revaluation method of depreciation be most appropriate?
4. Explain the following terms:
   (a) accumulated depreciation;
   (b) net book value;
   (c) residual value;
   (d) useful life of an non-current asset.
5. List **three** ways a business might dispose of a non-current asset.
6. Explain why land is not a depreciable asset.
7. The extracts below are from the ledger of a small engineering business.

Machinery account

Dr					Cr
2012		$	2012		$
Jan 1	Bank	50 000	Dec 31	Balance c/d	50 000
2013			2013		
Dec 31	Balance c/d	50 000	Dec 31	Balance c/d	50 000

Provision for depreciation of machinery account

Dr					Cr
2012		$	2012		$
Dec 31	Balance c/d	5 000	Dec 31	Income statement	5 000
2013		$	2013		$
Dec 31	Balance c/d	10 000	Jan 1	Balance b/d	5 000
			Dec 31	Income statement	5 000
		10 000			10 000

(a) Explain why the balance on the asset account for machinery at cost is unchanged at the end of each accounting year.

(b) What method of depreciation has the business adopted for its machinery?

(c) What is the accumulated depreciation of the machinery at the end of the accounting year ended 31 December 2013?

(d) What net book value will be recorded for the machinery in the statement of financial position of the business at 31 December 2013?

8 Shafia owns and runs a small restaurant. On 1 July 2011 she issued cheques to purchase the following non-current assets:

	Cost price ($)	Depreciation method adopted
Equipment	14 000	Reducing balance at 25% per year
Furniture	5 000	Straight-line – equal instalments of $1 000 per year over 4 years
Tableware	4 000	Revaluation

The table also shows the depreciation methods Shafia adopted for each type of asset.

On 1 July 2012 tableware was revalued at $3 400. During the accounting year ended 30 June 2013, Shafia purchased additional tableware costing $800. At 30 June 2013 tableware was revalued at $3 600.

Using the above information:

(a) Calculate the annual depreciation charge for each type of non-current asset for the accounting years ended 30 June 2012 and 2013.

(b) Complete the following extract from Shafia's statement of financial position at 30 June 2014 to show how the net book value would be calculated and recorded for each type of asset:

Extract from statement of financial position at 30 June 2013			
Non-current assets	At cost	Accumulated depreciation	Net book value
Equipment			
Furniture			
Tableware			

9 The accounting year of Numa's business ends on 30 September. On 1 October 2010 she purchased the following non-current assets by bank transfer:

	Cost price ($)
Computer equipment	6 000
Office furniture	8 000

She adopted the following policies for the depreciation of the non-current assets of her business:

- Computer equipment will be depreciated using the reducing balance method at a rate of 50% per year.
- Office furniture will be depreciated using the straight-line method. It is expected to have a useful life of three years and residual value of $2 000.
- No further provision for depreciation of non-current assets is made in the year of their disposal.

On 18 November 2013 Numa sold her computer equipment for $1 400 and her office furniture for $1 100. Both sales were paid for by cheque.

Make the entries required to the following ledger accounts to record all the above transactions including disposal of the assets:

(a)	(b)
Computer equipment account	Office furniture account
Depreciation of computer equipment account	Depreciation of office furniture account
Disposal account for computer equipment	Disposal account for office furniture

Remember to balance off the asset and depreciation accounts at the end of the accounting years ended 30 September 2011, 2012 and 2013 and show the balances carried and brought down.

Also balance off the accounts following disposals and show the transfer of profit or loss that should be made from the disposal accounts to the income statement for the accounting year ended 30 September 2014.

Unit 2.3 Correction of errors

AIMS

By the end of this unit you should be able to

- correct errors by means of journal entries
- explain the use of the **suspense account** as a temporary measure to balance the trial balance
- correct errors by means of a suspense account
- adjust a profit or loss for an accounting period after the correction of errors
- understand the effect of correction of errors on a statement of financial position

2.3.1 Correcting errors that cause imbalance in a trial balance

When a trial balance does not balance a suspense account can be used as a temporary measure to make the two sides agree while the imbalance is investigated

Hedley Johnson owns and runs Hedjo Plastics. At the end of his first year in business Hedley produced a trial balance from his ledger accounts.

Producing a trial balance helped Hedley to:

- check the accuracy of account balances in the ledger for his business to ensure that all entries were made correctly
- identify and correct any errors that may have been made in the double-entry accounts in the ledger of the business
- prepare financial statements for his business to show profit and financial position. ➤ 1.8

It was immediately clear to Hedley that his trial balance did not balance. Total credits exceeded total debits by $500.

Hedjo Plastics

Draft Trial Balance For Year 1 at 31 December (Summary)

	Dr ($)	Cr ($)
Column totals	289 500	290 000
Suspense account	500	
	290 000	290 000

Correction of errors 231

Finding where errors were made can take time so rather than delay the preparation of draft financial statements from his trial balance Hedley included an extra debit balance in it for $500 to make the two sides equal. He labelled this the balance on the suspense account.

To do this he opened the following suspense account in the general ledger.

2.11 USING A SUSPENSE ACCOUNT TO CORRECT A TEMPORARY IMBALANCE IN A TRIAL BALANCE

General Ledger					Hedjo Plastics
		Suspense account			
Dr					Cr
Year 1		$	Year 1		$
Dec 31	Difference on the trial balance	500			

A **suspense account** is opened when the debit and credit balances in a trial balance disagree. The amount needed to make the two sides balance is entered to the suspense account:

- as a debit balance when total credit exceeds total debits in the trial balance, and

- as a credit balance when total debits exceed total credits in the trial balance.

A suspense account is normally used as a temporary account until the reasons for the discrepancies are investigated and corrected.

As errors are corrected the balance on the suspense account will be reduced. Once all the errors that have caused imbalance have been corrected the suspense account can be closed.

The balance on the suspense account is reduced as errors are found and corrected

Hedley Johnson's trial balance at the end of his first accounting year did not balance. All account balances were present and column totals were correct but total credits exceeded total debits by $500. He investigated the possible sources of this discrepancy and found the first error.

Error 1: Total credit purchases recorded in the purchases journal for May were $8 200 but Hedley had added them up incorrectly and posted only $8 000 to the purchases account. The debit balance on the purchases account was undercast (below) by $200.

To correct the error Hedley made the following entries to his accounts:

Account entry	What is it for?
Debit $200 to the purchases account	To correct the posting of an undercast total from the purchases journal. This increased the debit balance by $200.
① Credit $200 to the suspense account	To correct the posting of an undercast total from the purchases journal. This reduced the debit balance on the suspense account (and also therefore the imbalance on the trial balance) from $500 to $300.

2.12 CORRECTING UNDERCAST EXPENSES

General Journal — Hedjo Plastics

Date	Description	Dr ($)	Cr ($)
Year 1 Dec 31	Purchases	200	
	Suspense		200
	To correct the posting of undercast purchases		

Purchases Ledger — Hedjo Plastics

Purchases account

Dr			Cr		
Year 1		$	Year 1		$
Dec 31	Balance	70 000			
Dec 31	Suspense	200			
		70 200			

General Ledger — Hedjo Plastics

Suspense account

Dr			Cr		
Year 1		$	Year 1		$
Dec 31	Difference on the trial balance	500	Dec 31	Purchases	200

Illustration 2.12 shows that after correcting for undercast expenses there was still a debit balance of $300 on Hedley's suspense account. This was explained by two further errors he discovered:

Error 2: Discounts credited to trade receivable accounts had been entered correctly to the discounts allowed column in the cash book. However, the column total of $390 for the month of June had not been posted to the debit side of the discounts allowed account that month. ▶ 1.5

Correction of errors 233

To correct the error Hedley made the following entries to his accounts:

Account entry	What is it for?
Debit $390 to the discounts allowed account	To correct for the omitted entry. This increased the debit balance on the account by $390.
Credit $390 to the suspense account	To correct the omitted entry in the balance for discounts allowed transferred to the trial balance. This reduced the debit balance on the suspense account to zero but created a credit balance of $90 instead.

2.13 CORRECTING AN OMITTED ENTRY

General Journal — Hedjo Plastics

Date	Description	Dr ($)	Cr ($)
Year 1 Dec 31	**Discounts allowed**	390	
	Suspense		390
	To correct for the omission of discounts allowed during June from this ledger.		

General Ledger — Hedjo Plastics

Discounts allowed account

Dr				Cr
Year 1		$	Year 1	$
Dec 31	Balance	2 610		
Dec 31	Suspense	390		
		3 000		

General ledger — Hedjo Plastics

Suspense account

Dr					Cr
Year 1		$	Year 1		$
Dec 31	Difference on the trial balance	500	Dec 31	Purchases	200
			Dec 31	Discounts allowed	390

After correction of the second accounting error the balance on the suspense account became a credit balance of $90. This meant there was still an imbalance on the trial balance but now total debit balances exceeded total credit balances by $90. This remaining imbalance was explained by the following error:

Error 3: Sales commission of $540 received in September was correctly debited to the bank account in the cash book but was recorded as a credit for $450 by mistake when posted to the sales commission account. The balance at the end of the accounting year on the sales commission account was $90 less than it should have been.

To correct the error Hedley recorded the following entries to his accounts:

Account entry	What is it for?
Credit $90 to the sales commission account	To correct the misposting of sales commission received. This increased the credit balance on the account by $90.
Debit $90 to the suspense account	To correct the understatement of sales commission in the balance transferred to the trial balance. This reduced the credit balance of $90 on the suspense account to zero.

❸

2.14 CORRECTING THE MISPOSTING OF AN ENTRY TO THE LEDGER

General Journal — Hedjo Plastics

Date	Description	Dr ($)	Cr ($)
Year 1 Dec 31	**Suspense**	90	
	Sales commission		90
	To correct the misposting of sales commission received in September		

General Ledger — Hedjo Plastics

Sales commission account

Dr			Cr	
Year 1	$	Year 1		$
		Dec 31 Suspense		90
				4 500

General Ledger — Hedjo Plastics

Suspense account

Dr			Cr		
Year 1		$	Year 1		$
Dec 31	Difference on the trial balance	500	Dec 31	Purchases	200
Dec 31	Sales commission	90	Dec 31	Discounts allowed	390
		590			590

❸

Correction of the above errors reduced the balance on the suspense account to zero: debits to the suspense account were equal to credits to the account. This meant that Hedley had discovered and corrected all the errors in the books of his business that had caused the imbalance in his original trial balance. The totals on the two sides of his trial balance would now be in balance.

ACTIVITY 2.12

Sarah is a trader. Her financial year ends on 30 June. The trial balance she prepared on 30 June at the end of her most recent accounting year failed to balance. Total debits exceeded total credits by $2 500. To make the two sides agree she opened a suspense account with a credit balance of $2 500.

She then investigated and discovered the following sources of errors.

- The total of the purchases journal posted to the ledger had been overcast by $1 300.
- $600 of interest received on business savings had been entered to the bank account but had not been posted to the interest received account. The credit balance on the account was therefore $600 less than it should have been.
- The balance on the petty cash book, $120, had not been included in the trial balance.
- A payment of $80 for travel had been posted correctly to the bank account but misposted as $800 to the expense account for travel.

(a) Prepare the entries in Sarah's journal below to correct the above errors. (The first one has been completed for you.)

General Journal			
Date	Description	Dr ($)	Cr ($)
Jun 30	**Suspense**	1 300	
	Purchases		1 300

(b) Open the suspense account in Sarah's ledger with the credit balance of $2 500.

(c) Post the entries for correction of errors from Sarah's journal to her suspense account and balance off the account once all entries have been posted.

2.3.2 Correcting errors that are not revealed by a trial balance

Other accounting errors may be present in the books of a business even if debits equal credits in a trial balance

Just because the two sides of a trial balance agree does not mean there are no other errors in the books of the business. Many other errors may be present that will not be revealed by a trial balance and, as a result, they can often be more difficult to find.

We learnt in unit 1.8 that there are six types of error that will not be revealed by the trial balance because they affect both sides equally. These "double-sided" errors are:

▼ Errors that affect both sides of a trial balance

Type of error	Description of error
Error of commission	An entry is made on the correct side of an account for the correct amount but in the wrong account of the same class or type
Error of omission	The double entries for a transaction are not recorded in the ledger
Error of principle	An entry is made on the correct side of an account for the correct amount but in the wrong class or type of account
Error of original entry	The posting of an amount from a book of prime entry to the ledger results in both the debit and credit being equal but incorrect
Compensating error	When two or more errors for the same amount cancel each other out
Error of complete reversal	When a debit entry is recorded as a credit and the credit entry is recorded as a debit

When Hedley Johnson checked through the books of his business to find the errors that had caused his trial balance not to balance he uncovered a number of the above errors as follows:

An error of commission: a payment of $600 received on 3 March to settle the trade receivable account of A Murray was credited in error to the personal account of C Murray. The incorrect entries were as follows:

General Ledger					Hedjo Plastics
	Cash Book (bank account only)				
Dr					Cr
Year 1		$	Year 1		$
Mar 3 C Murray		600			

Sales Ledger					Hedjo Plastics
	C Murray account				
Dr					Cr
Year 1		$	Year 1		$
Mar 1 Balance b/d		1 100	Mar 3	Bank	600
			Mar 31	Balance c/d	500
		1 100			1 100

The error of commission reduced the balance owing on C Murray's account by $600 instead of clearing the balance on A Murray's account. There was a matching debit entry for the payment received in the bank account, so the two sides of the trial balance would still agree and not reveal the error.

Hedley made the following entries to the books of his business at the end of the accounting year to correct the error:

Account entry	What is it for?
Debit $600 to C Murray account	To remove the payment received from A Murray.
	This will increase the debit balance on the account by $600.
Credit $600 to A Murray account	To record the payment received from A Murray.
	This will reduce the debit balance on the account by $600.

④

2.15 CORRECTING AN ERROR OF COMMISSION

General Journal — Hedjo Plastics

Date	Description	Dr ($)	Cr ($)
Year 1 Dec 31	**C Murray**	600	
	A Murray		600
	To correct entry for payment from A Murray that was credited in error to the account of C Murray		

Sales Ledger — Hedjo Plastics

C Murray account

Dr		$			Cr $
Year 1			Year 1		
Mar 1	Balance	1 100	Mar 3	Bank	800
Dec 31	A Murray	600	Mar 31	Balance c/d	1 100
		1 700			1 700

④

Sales Ledger — Hedjo Plastics

A Murray account

Dr		$			Cr $
Year 1			Year 1		
			Dec 31	C Murray	600

An error of omission: when Hedley withdrew $3 000 from the business bank account on 18 November for his own personal use he failed to record any entries in the bank account or drawings account. As both the credit and debit entry for the transactions were missing from the ledger the error did not result in any imbalance in the trial balance.

To correct this oversight Hedley had to record the entries that he should have made when he originally withdrew $3 000:

Account entry	What is it for?
⑤ Debit $3 000 to the drawings account	To record drawings of $3 000.
	This will increase the debit balance on the account by $3 000.
Credit $3 000 to the bank account	To record the payment of drawings from the bank.
	This will reduce the balance of cash in bank by $3 000.

2.16 CORRECTING AN ERROR OF OMISSION

General Journal — Hedjo Plastics

Date	Description	Dr ($)	Cr ($)
Year 1 Dec 31	Drawings	3 000	
	Bank		3 000
	To correct the omission of entries for personal drawings on November 18		

General Ledger — Hedjo Plastics

Drawings account

Dr		$	Cr		$
Year 1			Year 1		
Dec 31	Balance	50 000			
Dec 31	Bank	3 000			
		53 000			

General Ledger — Hedjo Plastics

Cash Book (bank account only)

Dr		$	Cr		$
Year 1			Year 1		
Dec 31	Balance	23 400	Dec 31	Drawings	3 000
			Dec 31	Balance c/d	21 400
		23 400			23 400

Correction of errors **239**

An error of principle: on 24 August Hedley Johnson paid $250 by cheque to replace a broken window at the back of his shop premises. He recorded the transactions as follows:

General Ledger			Hedjo Plastics
Cash Book (bank account only)			
Dr			Cr
Year 1	$	Year 1	$
		Aug 24 Premises	250

General Ledger			Hedjo Plastics
Premises account			
Dr			Cr
Year 1	$	Year 1	$
Jan 1 Bank	82 700		
Feb 17 Bank	15 000		
Aug 24 Bank	250		

The repair was revenue expenditure of $250 and should have been recorded as a debit to an expense account for repairs. However, Hedley instead recorded it as capital expenditure resulting in a debit to the asset account for premises. ➤ **1.8**

Despite recording this entry in the wrong type or class of account, the trial balance did not reveal the error because there was a matching debit and credit entry for the transaction.

To correct the error Hedley had to make these additional entries to the books of his business:

Account entry	What is it for?
Credit $250 to the premises account	To remove the payment of repairs from the asset account.
	This will reduce the debit balance on the account by $250.
Debit $250 to the repairs account	To record the cost of repairs as an expense.
	This will increase the debit balance on the account by $250.

2.17 CORRECTING AN ERROR OF PRINCIPLE

General Journal — Hedjo Plastics

Date	Description	Dr ($)	Cr ($)
Year 1 Dec 31	**Repairs**	250	
	Premises		250
	To correct the entry for repairs debited in error to the premises account instead of to the repairs account		

Sales Ledger — Hedjo Plastics

Premises account

Dr					Cr
Year 1		$	Year 1		$
Jan 1	Bank	82 700	Dec 31	Repairs	250
Feb 17	Bank	15 000			
Aug 24	Bank	250			

General Ledger — Hedjo Plastics

Repairs account ⑥

Dr				Cr
Year 1		$	Year 1	$
Dec 31	Premises	250		

An error of original entry: on 30 April Hedley Johnson received an invoice from his supplier Mouldings Ltd. for $4 549 but when he recorded the invoice in the purchases journal he recorded the amount as $5 459 by mistake. When he later posted the transaction to his ledger he made the following entries:

Purchases Ledger — Hedjo Plastics

Mouldings Ltd account

Dr		Cr		
Year 1	$	Year 1		$
		Apr 30	Purchases	5 459

General Ledger — Hedjo Plastics

Purchases account

Dr			Cr
Year 1	$	Year 1	$
Apr 30 Mouldings Ltd	5 459		

Correction of errors   241

The error meant that the balances on both the trade payables account for Mouldings Ltd. and the purchases account were $910 more than they should have been ($5 459 *less* the correct invoice amount for $4 549). To correct the error both balances had to be reduced by $910.

Account entry	What is it for?
Debit $910 from the Mouldings Ltd. (trade payable) account	To correct overstated credit purchases on the account. This will reduce the credit balance on the account by $910.
Credit $910 to the purchases account	To correct the overstatement of credit purchases. This will reduce the debit balance on the account by $910.

2.18 CORRECTING AN ERROR OF ORIGINAL ENTRY

General Journal — Hedjo Plastics

Date	Description	Dr ($)	Cr ($)
Year 1 Dec 31	**Mouldings Ltd**	910	
	Purchases		910
	To correct over recording a purchase invoice received April 30		

Purchases Ledger — Hedjo Plastics

Mouldings Ltd account

Dr					Cr
Year 1		$	Year 1		$
Dec 31	Purchases	910	Apr 30	Purchases	5 459

General Ledger — Hedjo Plastics

Purchases account

Dr					Cr
Year 1		$	Year 1		$
Apr 30	Mouldings Ltd	5 459	Dec 31	Mouldings Ltd	910

A compensating error: Hedley found two unconnected errors which were for the same amount so they cancelled each other out:

- On 17 July he made entries for the payment of advertising costs of $330 as a debit of $30 to his account for advertising expenses and a credit to the bank account for $300 paid out. The debit balance on the advertising account was $300 less than it should have been.

- On 31 October he totalled the sales journal incorrectly. The correct total was $6 300 but he only posted $6 000 to the sales account. The credit balance on the sales account was undercast by $300.

Accounting procedures

The following entries were required to correct these recording errors:

Account entry	What is it for?
8 Debit $300 to the advertising account	To correct the understatement of advertising expenses.
	This will increase the debit balance on the account by $300.
Credit $300 to the sales account	To correct the undercasting of the sales journal.
	This will increase the credit balance on the account by $300.

2.19 CORRECTING A COMPENSATING ERROR

General Journal — Hedjo Plastics

Date	Description	Dr ($)	Cr ($)
Year 1 Dec 31	Advertising	300	
	Sales		300
	To correct the under recording of advertising expenses by $300 and the undercasting of the sales journal by $300		

General Ledger — Hedjo Plastics

Advertising account

Dr			$	Cr		$
Year 1				Year 1		
Jul 17	Bank		30			
Dec 31	Sales		300			

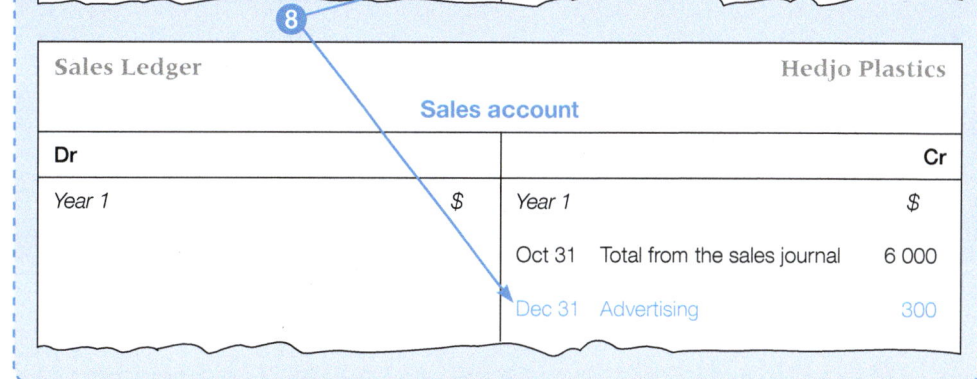

Sales Ledger — Hedjo Plastics

Sales account

Dr		$	Cr		$
Year 1			Year 1		
			Oct 31	Total from the sales journal	6 000
			Dec 31	Advertising	300

Correction of errors

Error of complete reversal: On 30 June Hedley Johnson had recorded the payment of $220 for electricity expenses as a debit to the bank account for the money paid out and as a credit to the electricity account for the electricity supplied.

As a result:

(i) the credit of $220 to the electricity account reduced the debit balance on the account by $220 instead of increasing it by $220;

(ii) the debit to the bank account increased cash in bank by $220 instead of reducing it by $220.

The trial balance did not reveal these errors because there were matching debit and credit entries.

General Ledger				Hedjo Plastics
Cash Book (bank account only)				
Dr				Cr
Year 1	$	Year 1		$
30 Jun Electricity	220			

General Ledger				Hedjo Plastics
Electricity account				
Dr				Cr
Year 1	$	Year 1		$
		30 Jun Bank		220

The following entries were necessary to correct for the error of complete reversal:

Account entry	What is it for?
Debit $440 to the electricity account	A debit entry for twice the amount of the error to: (i) offset the credit in error of $220 to the account; (ii) increase the debit balance on the account by $220.
Credit $440 to the bank account	A credit entry for twice the amount of the error to: (i) offset the debit in error of $220 to the account; (ii) increase the credit balance on the account by $220.

2.20 CORRECTING AN ERROR OF COMPLETE REVERSAL

General Journal			Hedjo Plastics
Date	Description	Dr	Cr
Year 1 Dec 31	**Electricity**	440	
	Bank		440
	To correct for recording of payment of electricity expenses of $220 on 30 June as a credit to expenses and a debit to the bank account for money received instead of a credit for money paid out		

General Ledger — Hedjo Plastics

Cash Book (bank account only)

Dr				Cr	
Year 1		$	Year 1		$
30 Jun	Electricity	220	Dec 31	Electricity	440

General Ledger — Hedjo Plastics

Electricity account

Dr				Cr	
Year 1		$	Year 1		$
Dec 31	Bank	440	30 Jun	Bank	220

Correction of errors 245

ACTIVITY 2.13

Oliver is a trader. His financial year ends on 30 September. Although the column totals agreed in the trial balance he prepared at the end of his most recent accounting year he discovered the following errors in his books.

Error	Description	Type of error?
a	A cash sale for $35 had been overlooked	
b	$3 000 of wages paid to employees had been credited to the wages account and debited to the bank account	
c	A payment of $2 700 for items purchased on credit from M Shah had been debited in error to the trade payable account for N Shah	
d	The sales journal and the ledger account for insurance were both undercast by $500	
e	Equipment installation charges of $1 400 had been debited to the repairs account	

1. Identify the type of accounting errors in the table above.
2. Write up the entries required in the journal below to correct the above errors. (The first one has been completed for you.)

General Journal			
Date	Description	Dr	Cr
Sept 30	Cash	35	
	Sales		35

2.3.3 Preparing draft and revised statements of profit or loss and financial position

The correction of errors will affect the calculation of profit or loss and/or the financial position of a business

Financial statements of income and financial position should be produced at the end of each accounting year. The preparation of a trial balance is the first step because it organises all the account balances from the ledger in once place and can be used to check for errors. ➤ 1.8

However, the investigation and correction of errors can take some time. Draft financial statements can be produced but will need to be revised once any accounting errors have been found and corrected.

Illustration 2.21 shows the trial balance Hedley Johnson produced for his business Hedjo Plastics at the end of its first accounting year. The trial balance did not balance so as a temporary measure Hedley opened the suspense account in illustration 2.11 (page 232) with a debit balance of $500 to make the two sides of his trial balance agree.

2.21 A TRIAL BALANCE INCLUDING A TEMPORARY BALANCE ON SUSPENSE ACCOUNT

Hedjo Plastics

Draft Trial Balance For Year 1 At 31 December

	Dr ($)	Cr ($)
Sales		117 000
Purchases	60 000	
Other income		9 500
Discounts allowed	2 610	
Expenses	32 040	
Total non-current assets at cost	97 950	
Trade receivables	23 500	
Cash in bank	23 400	
Trade payables		5 700
Bank loan		45 000
Capital		112 800
Drawings	50 000	
Suspense account	500	
	290 000	290 000

Note:
A provision for depreciation is to be created for $7 700

Using his trial balance Hedley produced the draft income statement shown in illustration 2.22, showing a draft profit for the year of $24 150 before the correction of accounting errors.

2.22 DRAFT INCOME STATEMENT SHOWING DRAFT PROFIT BEFORE CORRECTION OF ERRORS

Hedjo Plastics

Draft Income Statement For Year 1 Ended 31 December

	$	$
Total income:		
Sales	117 000	
Other income	9 500	
		126 500
less **Total costs:**		
Purchases	60 000	
Discounts allowed	2 610	
Expenses	32 040	
Depreciation charges	7 700	
		102 350
Draft profit for the year		24 150

Hedley also used his trial balance to produce the following draft statement of financial position for his business.

2.23 SUMMARISED STATEMENT OF FINANCIAL POSITION BEFORE CORRECTION OF ERRORS

Hedjo Plastics

Draft Statement Of Financial Position At 31 December (year 1)

	$	$
Total assets	137 150	
less		
Total liabilities	50 700	
		86 450
Capital	112 800	
add Draft profit for the year	24 150	
less Drawings	(50 000)	
		86 950
Suspense account (debit)		(500)
		86 450

The capital section of the draft statement of financial position includes the draft profit for the year of $24 150 from the draft income statement and, as a temporary measure, the debit balance of $500 from the suspense account to balance the accounting equation in the statement:

Capital = Assets − Liabilities

Because of the errors in Hedley's accounts, capital of $86 950 was not equal to the value of the assets of his business net of liabilities.

Revised financial statements should be prepared as soon as errors have been identified and corrected in the accounts

Sections 2.3.1 and 2.3.2 identified the errors in Hedley's accounts. They will have had the following impact on the draft profit and financial position of his business:

▼ Errors revealed by the trial balance

Error	Description	Impact on draft profit	Impact on draft financial position	Corrections required
1	Purchases journal was undercast by $200	• Costs understated by $200 • Profit overstated by $200	• Capital understated by $200	• Debit $200 to purchases account and credit suspense account • Deduct $200 from draft profit
2	$390 of discounts allowed were omitted	• Expenses understated by $390 • Profit overstated by $390	• Capital overstated by $390	• Debit $390 to discounts allowed account and credit suspense account • Deduct $390 from draft profit
3	Sales commission of $540 received was misposted as $450	• Income and profit both understated by $90	• Capital understated by $90	• Debit $90 to suspense account and credit sales commission account • Add $90 to draft profit

Correction of errors

▼ Errors **not** revealed by the trial balance

Error	Description	Impact on draft profit	Impact on draft financial position	Corrections required
4	Payment of $600 from A Murray was credited to C Murray.	• No impact	• No impact	• Debit $600 to C Murray account and credit A Murray
5	Drawings of $3 000 were not recorded	• No impact	• Cash in bank overstated by $3 000 • Drawings understated by $3 000	• Debit $3 000 to drawings account and credit $3 000 to bank account • Deduct $3 000 from total assets • Deduct $3 000 from capital
6	Repairs, $250, were debited to the premises account	• Expenses understated by $250 • Profit overstated by $250	• Non-current assets overstated by $250	• Debit $250 to repairs account and credit premises • Deduct $250 from draft profit • Deduct $250 from total assets
7	An invoice for $4 549 was recorded in the purchases journal as $5 459	• Cost of sales overstated by $910 • Profit understated by $910	• Trade payables overstated by $910	• Debit $910 to supplier's trade payable account and credit purchases • Add $910 to draft profit • Deduct $910 from total liabilities
8	Advertising expenses were understated by $300 Sales were undercast by $300	• Expenses understated by $300 • Revenue understated by $300 • Errors cancel so no overall impact on profit	• No impact	• Debit $300 to advertising account and credit sales account
9	Debit and credit entries for electricity expenses paid, $220, were reversed	• Expenses understated by $440 • Profit overstated by $440	• Cash in bank overstated by $440	• Debit $440 to electricity account and credit bank • Deduct $440 from draft profit • Deduct $440 from total assets

Following the discovery of these errors Hedley:

(i) prepared the journal entries necessary to correct them;

(ii) posted the entries to his ledger accounts to correct the errors;

(iii) produced the revised statement of profit for the year in illustration 2.24;

(iv) produced the revised statement of the financial position of his business in illustration 2.25.

The revised profit of the business after the correction of errors was therefore $23 870, being $280 less than Hedley had originally calculated in his draft statement in illustration 2.22.

His revised or corrected profit for the year was then taken down into his revised statement of financial position.

2.24 A STATEMENT OF REVISED PROFIT AFTER CORRECTION OF ERRORS

Hedjo Plastics

Statement Of Revised Profit For Year 1 Ended 31 December

	Increase in draft profit $	Decrease in draft profit $	Profit (or loss) for the year $
Draft profit for the year			24 150
Corrections			
1 Purchases		200	
2 Discounts allowed		390	
3 Sales commission	90		
6 Repairs		250	
7 Purchases	910		
8 Advertising		300	
Sales	300		
9 Electricity		440	
Totals	1 300	1 580	(280)
Revised profit for the year			23 870

ACTIVITY 2.14

Tulisa recently prepared a draft income statement for her business at the end of her accounting year. It recorded a draft profit of $9 000 for the year ending 31 March.

Tulisa then investigated and found the following errors in her accounts:

- Sales had been undercast by $7 000.
- She had failed to record an annual depreciation charge for equipment of $4 500.
- Interest of $1 500 received on her business savings had been entered as $150.
- A loan repayment for $600 had been debited to the bank account and credited to the loan account.
- The total of $2 180 of the discounts received column in the cash book for January had not been posted to the discounts received account. Individual entries for discounts received in trade payable accounts were, however, present and correct.

Prepare a revised statement of profit or loss for Tulisa's business.

2.25 SUMMARISED STATEMENT OF FINANCIAL POSITION AFTER CORRECTIONS OF ERRORS

Hedjo Plastics
Revised Statement Of Financial Position At 31 December (Year 1)

	$	$
Draft total assets	137 150	
5, 9 corrections to cash in bank	(3 440)	
6 correction to premises	(250)	
Revised total assets	**133 460**	
less Draft total liabilities	50 700	
7 correction to trade payables	(910)	
Revised total liabilities	**49 790**	
		83 670
Capital	112 800	
add Revised profit for the year	23 870	
less Drawings	(50 000)	
5 correction to drawings	(3 000)	
Revised capital		**83 670**

Correcting errors in the statement of financial position

Many more errors that we have considered in this section can affect a statement of financial position. For example, the following draft (summary) statement of financial position was produced by a small business from a trial balance that did not balance: total credits exceeded total credits by $10 000. A credit balance of $10 000 was therefore entered to the suspense account. This was added to capital in the statement to balance the accounting equation.

Draft Statement Of Financial Position At 30 September 201X

	$	$
Total assets	250 000	
less		
Total liabilities	135 000	
		115 000
Capital	90 000	
add Draft profit for the year	45 000	
less Drawings	(30 000)	
		105 000
Suspense account (credit)		10 000
		115 000

252 Accounting procedures

The following errors were then discovered and corrected in the books of the business:

Error	Description	Impact on draft financial position
A	An annual depreciation charge of $15 000 has not been included	Reduce non-current assets by $15 000; Reduce draft profit by $15 000
B	An irrecoverable debt for $8 500 was not written off	Reduce trade receivables (current assets) by $8 500; reduce draft profit by $8 500
C	Prepaid expenses of $3 000 were excluded	Increase prepaid expenses (current assets) by $3 000
D	Total trade payables were added up incorrectly and were understated by $1 000	Increase trade payables (current liabilities) by $1 000
E	New capital of $12 000 introduced was recorded in the bank account only	Increase capital by $12 000

Revised Statement Of Financial Position At 30 September 201X		
	$	$
Draft total assets	250 000	
A depreciation charge	(15 000)	
B irrecoverable debt written off	(8 500)	
C prepaid expenses	3 000	
Revised total assets	**229 500**	
less		
draft total liabilities	135 000	
D understatement on trade payables	1 000	
Revised total liabilities	**136 000**	
		93 500
Capital	90 000	
E introduction of new capital	12 000	
add revised profit for the year	21 500	
less drawings	(30 000)	
Revised capital		**93 500**

QUICK TEST

1. The following balances were taken from the books of Samuel at the end of his most recent accounting year ending 31 March.

Balances	$
Sales	65 000
Purchases	30 000
Total expenses	13 800
Non-current assets at cost	14 000
Cash in bank (Dr)	2 500
Bank loan	5 000
Capital	6 500
Drawings	12 000

   (a) Use the information to prepare a trial balance.

   (b) Open a suspense account and enter the difference on the trial balance required to make it balance.

   (c) Calculate draft profit for the year.

   The following errors explained the imbalance in the trial balance.

   (i) Sales had been overcast by $2 020.

   (ii) The payment of $460 for vehicle repairs (included in total expenses) had been entered correctly in the cash book but had been misposted to the debit side of the repairs account as $640.

   (iii) Drawings of $2 360 were recorded in the cash book but had not been recorded in the drawings account.

   There were no further errors in the accounting records of Samuel.

   (d) Prepare the journal entries required to correct each of the above errors.

   (e) Write up the suspense account with the corrections.

   (f) Prepare a statement of revised profit for the year ended 31 March.

2. Miranda prepared draft financial statements for her most recent accounting year ended 30 April and calculated a draft profit for the year of $14 670. She later discovered the following errors that had not been revealed by her trial balance.

   (i) Goods costing $2 000, purchased on credit from A Morston had not been entered in the accounting records.

   (ii) $650 of goods sold on credit to T Cley had been correctly entered in the sales account but had been entered into the account of C Trey.

   (iii) A vehicle expense, $500, had been posted to the vehicles account.

   (iv) A discount received from P Stanton for $190 had been entered in the discount allowed column in the cash book and credited to the account of P Stanton.

   (a) Name the each type of error in (i) to (iv) above.

(b) Prepare the journal entries required to correct each of the errors.

(c) Prepare a statement of revised profit for Miranda's accounting year.

3. The following balances were taken from the books of Elena at the end of her first year in business ending 30 September:

Balances	$
Sales	210 000
Purchases	120 000
Expenses	45 500
Non-current assets at cost	88 000
Trade receivables	23 800
Cash in bank (Cr)	3 400
Trade payables	19 800
Capital	76 000
Drawings	24 000

(a) Use the information to prepare a trial balance.

(b) Open a suspense account and enter the difference on the trial balance required to make it balance.

(c) Calculate the draft profit for the first year of Elena's business.

(d) Prepare in summary form a draft statement of the financial position of Elena's business at 30 September.

The following errors were subsequently discovered in the accounting records:

(i) Purchases had been undercast by $5 000.

(ii) The purchase of equipment, $2 200, by cheque was entered to the asset account for equipment at cost but was not recorded in the bank account in the cash book.

(iii) An irrecoverable debt for $2 000 had not been written off.

(iv) Prepaid expenses of $4 600 had been overlooked.

(v) An annual depreciation charge of $8 400 was overlooked.

(e) Write up the suspense account with corrections for errors (i) and (ii).

(f) Prepare a statement of revised profit for the year ended 31 September.

(g) Prepare a summarised statement of financial position at 30 September after correction of the above errors.

Unit 2.4 Control accounts

AIMS

By the end of this unit you should be able to

- understand the purposes of purchases ledger and sales ledger control accounts
- identify the books of prime entry as sources of information for the control account entries
- prepare purchases ledger and sales ledger control accounts to include **credit sales and purchases, receipts and payments, cash discounts, returns, irrecoverable debts, dishonoured cheques, interest on overdue accounts, contra entries, refunds, opening and closing balances** (debit and credit within each account)

2.4.1 Preparing control accounts

Control accounts are used to check the arithmetical accuracy of the sales ledger and purchases ledger

The ledger of a business is divided into three main parts: the purchases ledger, the sales ledger and the general ledger. ▶ 1.6

Personal accounts for suppliers who sell the business goods on credit terms (**trade payables**) will be kept in the purchases ledger. Personal accounts of customers who buy goods on credit from the business (**trade receivables**) will be kept in the sales ledger.

A small business may have relatively few accounts in its ledger and be able to prepare a trial balance and check for accounting errors quickly and easily. However, some businesses may have to maintain tens, hundreds or even thousands of different accounts in their ledgers. Checking the accuracy and totals of all these accounts can be a very time-consuming task. Businesses simplify and speed up this process using **control accounts**. These are used to provide an independent check on the arithmetical accuracy of entries posted to the sales and purchases ledgers. They are prepared on a monthly basis but they are not part of the double-entry accounting system:

- The **sales ledger control account** is used to check the accuracy of the totals for all the entries for transactions posted to trade receivable accounts in the sales ledger.
- The **purchase ledger control account** is used to check the accuracy of the totals for all the entries for transactions to trade payable accounts in the purchases ledger.

The balance on the sales ledger control account should equal the sum of balances on trade receivable accounts in the sales ledger

The following accounts were written up by Hedley Johnson in his sales ledger for the month of June during his first accounting year trading as Hedjo Plastics.

2.26 TRADE RECEIVABLE ACCOUNTS IN THE SALES LEDGER

Sales Ledger — Hedjo Plastics

A Murray account

Dr				Cr
Year 1		$	Year 1	$
Jun 1	Balance b/d	6 500	Jun 19 Sales returns	500
Jun 15	Sales	3 000	Jun 28 Bank	6 300
			Discounts allowed	200
			Balance c/d	2 500
		9 500		9 500

Sales Ledger — Hedjo Plastics

GK Designs account

Dr				Cr
Year 1		$	Year 1	$
Jun 1	Balance b/d	8 450	Jun 5 Sales returns	2 000
Jun 15	Sales	8 000	Jun 22 Bank	6 700
			Discounts allowed	250
			Balance c/d	7 500
		16 450		16 450

Sales Ledger — Hedjo Plastics

W Ramgoolan account

Dr				Cr
Year 1		$	Year 1	$
Jun 1	Balance b/d	550	Jun 30 Irrecoverable debts	550

Control accounts

The sum of the opening balances on the trade receivable accounts on 1 June was $15 500 and the sum of their closing balances carried down on 30 June was $10 000. The difference can be explained as follows:

Entries to trade receivable accounts:		$
Balances b/d on 1 June	6 500 + 8 450 =	15 500
add Total sales during June	3 000 + 8 000 =	11 000
less Total sales returns in June	500 + 2 000 =	2 500
less Total payments received in June	6 300 + 6 700 =	13 000
less Total discounts allowed in June	200 + 250 =	450
less Total irrecoverable debts written off in June	550 =	550
Balances c/d on 30 June	2 500 + 7 500 =	10 000

It is important to get the balance for total trade receivables right. It is the money owed to the business by its credit customers. It is a current asset and will be recorded in the statement of financial position at the end of an accounting year.

However, rather than adding up all the individual entries to his sales ledger to check the accuracy of the balance for total trade receivables Hedley decided instead to produce a sales ledger control account using the totals he had recorded in his books of prime entry during June. These are shown in illustration 2.27:

2.27 ENTRIES TO BOOKS OF PRIME ENTRY POSTED TO ACCOUNTS IN THE SALES LEDGER

Sales Journal Hedjo Plastics

Date	Description	Invoice number	Amount $
Jun 15	A Murray	HP67	3 000
Jun 28	G K Designs	HP68	8 000
Jun 29	A Murray	HP69	1 000
Jun 30	Transfer to sales account		12 000

Sales Returns Journal Hedjo Plastics

Date	Description	Credit Note	Amount $
Jun 5	GK Designs	CR12	2 000
Jun 19	A Murray	CR13	500
Jun 30	Transfer to sales returns account		2 500

Cash book Hedjo Plastics

Dr									Cr
Date	Details	Discounts Allowed $	Cash $	Bank $	Date	Details	Discounts Received $	Cash $	Bank $
Jun 22	G K Designs	250		6 700					
Jun 28	A Murray	200		6 300					
Jun 30		450		13 000					

General Journal Hedjo Plastics

Date	Description	Dr $	Cr $
Jun 30	Irrecoverable debts	550	
	W Ramgoolan		550
	Unpaid balance on account written off		

From the totals on his books of prime entry Hedley was able to prepare the following sales ledger control account:

2.28 AN EXAMPLE OF A SALES LEDGER CONTROL ACCOUNT

Sales Ledger Hedjo Plastics

Control account

Dr						Cr
Year 1		$	Year 1			$
Jun 1	Balance b/d	15 500	Jun 30	Sales returns		2 500
Jun 30	Sales	12 000		Bank		13 000
				Discounts allowed		450
				Irrecoverable debts		550
		27 500		Balance c/d		11 000
						27 500
Jul 1	Balance	11 000				

Control accounts

The table below summarises the totals entered to the purchases ledger control account above and the calculation of the balance carried down of $11 000 (the difference between total debits and total credits to the account):

Date		$
Jun 1	Balance b/d from sales ledger control account for May	15 500 Dr
Jun 30	*add* Total sales from the sales journal	12 000
	less Total sales returns from the sales returns journal	2 500
	less Total payments received from the cash book	13 000
	less Total cash discounts allowed from the cash book	450
	less Total irrecoverable debts written off from general journal	550
	Balance c/d on sales ledger control account	11 000 Dr

The balance carried down on the sales ledger control account should be exactly equal to the total of all the closing balances on the individual trade receivable accounts taken from the sales ledger for the same month. If they do not agree then errors must be present in those accounts.

It was immediately clear that the balance of $11 000 on the sales ledger control account at 30 June exceeded the total for $10 000 of balances Hedley Johnson had extracted from his sales ledger. This meant that Hedley had either:

- added up the balances on the accounts in his sales ledger incorrectly, and/or
- omitted or misposted entries to one or more of the trade receivable accounts.

The difference was due to an omitted entry to the account of A Murray for sales on credit of $1 000 on 29 June. Hedley had failed to post the initial entry he had made for this sale in his sales journal to A Murray's account in his sales ledger. This meant that:

- the amount owed by A Murray to his business was undercast by $1 000, and therefore
- total trade receivables recorded in the sales ledger were undercast by $1 000.

To correct the error Hedley had to post the sale to the debit side of A Murray's account and revise the balance carried down on the account.

A **sales ledger control account** provides a total trade receivables account which can be used to check the arithmetical accuracy of the sales ledger:

- if no errors have occurred, the balance on the sales ledger control account will be equal to the total of balances taken from trade receivable accounts in the sales ledger
- if errors have been made, the two balances will not agree. Errors will need to be identified and corrected.

▼ A sales ledger control account is prepared from the monthly totals on the following books of prime entry:

Type of entry	Book of prime entry
Credit sales	Sales journal ▶ 1.4
Sales returns	Sales returns journal ▶ 1.4
Payments received	Cash book ▶ 1.5
(Cash) Discounts allowed	Cash book ▶ 1.5
Irrecoverable debts written off	General journal ▶ 1.6

2.29 TRADE PAYABLE ACCOUNTS IN THE PURCHASES LEDGER

Purchases Ledger — Hedjo Plastics

Pipex Ltd account

Dr					Cr
Year 1		$	Year 1		$
June 4	Purchases returns	1 200	Jun 1	Balance b/d	7 000
June 26	Bank	5 300	Jul 12	Purchases	2 600
	Discounts received	100	June 21	Purchases	4 000
	Balance c/d	7 000			
		13 600			13 600

Purchases Ledger — Hedjo Plastics

Mouldings Ltd account

Dr					Cr
Year 1		$	Year 1		$
Jun 16	Purchases returns	600	Jun 1	Balance b/d	9 000
Jun 29	Bank	8 800	Jun 17	Purchases	7 300
	Discounts received	200			
	Balance c/d	6 700			
		16 300			16 300

Purchases Ledger — Hedjo Plastics

Plastico SA account

Dr					Cr
Year 1		$	Year 1		$
			Jun 1	Balance b/d	3 500

The balance on the purchases ledger control account should equal the total of balances on trade payable accounts in the purchases ledger

Illustration 2.29 shows the trade payable accounts written up by Hedley Johnson in his purchases ledger for the month of June during his first accounting year.

The balances brought down on the accounts on 1 June summed totalled to $19 500 ($7 000 + $9 000 + $3 500). This meant that at the start of the month Hedley owed a total of $19 500 to his suppliers of goods on credit.

From the balances at the end of June on the same accounts Hedley calculated that he owed a total of $13 700 to his suppliers of goods on credit. That is, he believed that the total trade payables of his business at the end of the month had reduced from $19 500 to $13 700.

Control accounts

Rather than add up all the individual entries to his trade payable accounts to check the accuracy of this amount, Hedley prepared a purchases ledger control account from totals recorded in his books of prime entry for June. These are shown in illustration 2.30.

2.30 ENTRIES TO BOOKS OF PRIME ENTRY POSTED TO ACCOUNTS IN THE PURCHASES LEDGER

Purchases Journal — Hedjo Plastics

Date	Description	Invoice number	Amount $
Jun 12	Pipex Ltd	P78/905	2 600
Jun 17	Mouldings Ltd	MD6/1003	7 300
Jun 21	Pipex Ltd	P78/987	4 000
Jun 30	Transfer to purchases account		13 900

Purchases Returns Journal — Hedjo Plastics

Date	Description	Invoice Note	Amount $
Jun 4	Pipex Ltd	C45/089	1 200
Jun 18	Mouldings Ltd	CX/1976	600
Jun 30	Transfer to purchases account		1 800

Cash book — Hedjo Plastics

Dr									Cr
Date	Details	Discounts Allowed $	Cash $	Bank $	Date	Details	Discounts Received $	Cash $	Bank $
					Jun 26	Pipex Ltd	100		5 300
					Jun 29	Mouldings Ltd	200		8 800
							300		14 100

From the totals on his books of prime entry Hedley was able to prepare the following purchases ledger control account:

2.31 AN EXAMPLE OF A PURCHASES LEDGER CONTROL ACCOUNT

Hedjo Plastics

Purchases ledger control account

Dr						Cr
Year 1		$		Year 1		$
Jun 30	Purchases returns	1 800		Jun 1	Balance b/d	19 500
	Bank	14 100		Jun 30	Purchases	13 900
	Discounts received	300				
	Balance c/d	17,200				
		33 400				33 400
					Balance b/d	17 200

The table below summarises the totals entered to the purchases ledger control account shown above and the calculation of the balance carried down of $17 200 (the difference between total debits and total credits to the account):

Date		$
Jun 1	Balance b/d from purchases ledger control account for May	19 500 Cr
Jun 30	*add* Total credit purchases from the purchases journal	13 900
	less Total purchases returns from the purchases returns journal	1 800
	less Total payments issued from the cash book	14 100
	less Total cash discounts received from the cash book	300
	Balance c/d on purchases ledger control account	17 200 Cr

The balance carried down on the purchases ledger control account should be equal to the total of all the balances on the individual trade payable accounts taken from the purchases ledger for the same month. If they do not agree then errors must be present in those accounts.

It was clear that the balance of $17 200 on the purchases ledger control account at 30 June exceeded the total for $13 700 of balances Hedley Johnson had extracted from his purchases ledger. This meant that Hedley had either:

- omitted or misposted entries to one or more of the accounts, and/or
- added up the balances on the accounts in his purchases ledger incorrectly.

When Hedley had added up the balances on his trade payable accounts on 30 June he had failed to include the balance on his account for Plastico Ltd., of $3 500. This explained the difference between the balance of $17 200 on his purchases ledger control account and the sum of $13 200 he had calculated in error for his total trade payables.

A **purchases ledger control account** provides a total trade payables account which can be used to check the arithmetical accuracy of the purchases ledger:

- if no errors have occurred, the balance on the sales ledger control account will be equal to the total of balances extracted from trade receivable accounts in the sales ledger

- if errors have been made, the two balances will not agree. Errors will need to be identified and corrected.

▼ A purchases ledger control account is prepared from the monthly totals on the following books of prime entry:

Type of entry	Book of prime entry
Credit purchases	Purchases journal ▶ 1.4
Purchases returns	Purchases returns journal ▶ 1.4
Payments issued	Cash book ▶ 1.5
Discounts received	Cash book ▶ 1.5

Preparing control accounts can help to identify accounting errors and prevent fraud

The preparation of control accounts by a business for its purchases and sales ledgers has a number of advantages:

- First, control accounts are used to check the arithmetical accuracy of the accounts they control in the sales and purchases ledger. Accounts will only need to be checked for errors when the total of closing balances extracted from a ledger differs from the closing balance on the control account for that ledger for the same month.

- Control accounts can be used to calculate the values of total trade receivables and total trade payables included in the trial balance and financial statements of the business at the end of an accounting year.

- Control accounts can also be used to identify and prevent any fraudulent (fake) entries being made to ledger accounts by a member of staff. This is because the balances on control accounts can reveal errors and discrepancies and can be prepared quickly and easily from totals from the books of prime entry by a senior manager or another accountant.

- If the trial balance does not balance, control accounts can be used to locate single-sided errors that may be present in ledger accounts. They will not, however, reveal any double-sided errors that will affect both sides of the trial balance. ▶ 2.3

> **ACTIVITY 2.15**
>
> Karina prepares control accounts for her purchases and sales ledgers at the end of each month. On 1 April last year the balances brought down on her control accounts were:
>
> | | $ |
> |---|---|
> | Purchases ledger control account | 25 600 (Cr) |
> | Sales ledger control account | 45 000 (Dr) |
>
> Totals from her journals for 1–30 April were:
>
> | | $ |
> |---|---|
> | Purchases journal | 34 000 |
> | Purchases returns journal | 8 700 |
> | Sales journal | 61 800 |
> | Sales returns journal | 11 500 |
>
> Totals taken from her cash book for 1–30 April were:
>
> | | $ |
> |---|---|
> | Payments received from trade receivables | 41 000 |
> | Discounts allowed | 1 050 |
> | Payments made to trade payables | 26 000 |
> | Discounts received | 2 400 |
>
> In addition, Karina's general journal recorded irrecoverable debts written off that month for $2 300.
>
> Using the above information prepare the following control accounts for Karina for the month of April last year:
>
> 1 Prepare the purchases ledger control account.
> 2 Prepare the sales ledger control account.
>
> Bring down the balances on the accounts on 1 May.

2.4.2 Making other entries to control accounts

Refunds to customers, interest charged on their overdue accounts, transfers and dishonoured cheques will also affect the total of trade receivables in the sales ledger

Less frequent transactions that will affect trade receivable accounts in the sales ledger are as follows:

▼ Other entries to trade receivable accounts in the sales ledger

Type of entry	Book of prime entry
Refund to a credit customer	Cash book
Interest charged on an overdue account	General journal
Inter-ledger transfer (or contra entry)	Purchases and sales journals
Dishonoured cheque	Cash book

A business will issue a **refund** to a credit customer who has overpaid a sales invoice or the balance on its trade receivable account. The refund paid will be entered to the accounts of the business as follows:

▼ To record a refund issued to a credit customer

Trade receivable account for the customer	Bank account (in the cash book)
Debit the amount of refund paid. This will cancel out the amount overpaid.	Credit the amount of refund paid
Impact: debit balance (asset) on the account is reduced	Impact: cash in bank is decreased

For example, on 13 July last year Hedley Johnson refunded an overpayment on the account of Fast Shop in his sales ledger. Instead of paying $440 to clear the balance on its account the owner of Fast Shop had paid Hedjo Plastics $550 by mistake. The account had a credit balance of $110. This meant Hedjo Plastics owed $110 to Fast Shop which it refunded at the end of the month.

2.32 RECORDING A REFUND PAID ON A TRADE RECEIVABLE ACCOUNT

Sales Ledger   Hedjo Plastics

Fast Shop account

Dr						Cr
Year 1		$	Year 1			$
Jul 1	Balance b/d	440	Jul 13	Bank		550
Jul 31	Bank	110				
		550				550

Another credit customer, Petra Smith, had not paid Hedjo Plastics the balance of $1 800 owing on her trade receivable account at the end of June last year within an agreed 30-day period. So, on 31 July Hedley Johnson added an **interest charge on the overdue account** of 5% or $90. This increased the debit balance on the account at the end of the month from $1 800 to $1 890.

▼ To record interest charges on an overdue trade receivable account

Trade receivable account for the customer	Interest charges received account
Debit interest charges	Credit interest charges
Impact: debit balance (asset) on the account is increased	Impact: income is increased

2.33 RECORDING INTEREST CHARGES ON AN OVERDUE TRADE RECEIVABLE ACCOUNT

Sales Ledger — Hedjo Plastics

Petra Smith account

Dr				Cr
Year 1		$	Year 1	$
Jun 1	Balance b/d	1 800		
Jul 1	Balance b/d	1 800		
Jul 31	Interest charges	90		
		1 890		

During July last year Hedjo Plastics also entered into the following transactions with one of its credit customers:

Date	Description	Amount $
Jul 4	Plastic sheeting sold on credit to Garden Care	750
Jul 22	Assorted plastic plant pots purchased on credit from Garden Care	100

This meant that Garden Care, a credit customer of Hedjo Plastics, had also become a supplier of goods on credit to the business. So, rather than the two businesses exchanging payments for the full amount of their purchases from each other Garden Care simply transferred the net amount of $650 due to Hedjo Plastics at the end of the month.

The remaining $100 to be paid on its trade receivable account in the sales ledger of Hedjo Plastics was offset by the pots it had sold the business for $100 on 22 July. The transaction required an **inter-ledger transfer** from the trade payable account for Garden Care in the purchases ledger to settle the balance of $100 on the trade receivable account for the same company in the sales ledger as follows:

▼ Recording contra entries in the journal

Hedjo Plastics

General Journal

Date	Description	Dr ($)	Cr ($)
Year 1 Jul 31	Garden Care (trade payable in purchases ledger)	100	
	Contra		100
	Contra entry offset against trade receivable for Garden Care		
	Contra	100	
	Garden Care (trade receivable in sales ledger)		100
	Contra entry offset against trade payable account for Garden Care		

Inter-ledger transfers are also known as offsetting or contra entries. They are made to the sales and purchases ledgers when a business transacts (deals) with another business organisation as both a supplier and a customer and then sets off the balances on its receivable and payable accounts for that organisation against each other to find the net amount or balance to be paid or received.

The following entries were posted to the ledger to record the above transactions with Garden Care:

▼ To record payments received and contra entries

Trade receivable account for Garden Care	Trade payable account for Garden Care
Debit sales on credit of $750	Credit purchases on credit of $100
① Credit the payment received for $650	
② Credit the net balance of $100 and transfer it to the debit side of the trade payable account for the same organisation in the purchases ledger	Debit the net balance of $100 from the trade payable account for the same organisation in the purchases ledger

268 Accounting procedures

2.34 RECORDING CONTRA ENTRIES IN THE SALES AND PURCHASE LEDGERS

Sales Ledger — Hedjo Plastics

Garden Care account

Dr				Cr
Year 1	$	Year 1		$
Jul 4 Sales	750	Jul 31 Bank		650
		Jul 31 Garden Care (purchases ledger)		100
	750			750

Purchases Ledger — Hedjo Plastics

Garden Care account

Dr				Cr
Year 1	$	Year 1		$
Jul 31 Garden Care (sales ledger)	100	Jul 22 Purchases		100

On 3 July last year Hedjo Plastics received a cheque payment for $600 from David Glenn, a credit customer of the business. When owner Hedley Johnson paid the cheque into the business bank account of Hedjo Plastics he made the following entries to the ledger:

▼ To record a payment received from a credit customer

Bank account (in the cash book)	Trade receivable account for the customer
Debit the payment of $600 received	Credit with the payment of $600 received
Impact: cash in bank is increased by $600	Impact: debit balance (asset) on the account is reduced by $600

However, Hedley Johnson later discovered that the bank used by David Glenn would not honour the cheque. This meant it would not pay out the amount on the cheque to Hedjo Plastics because David Glenn did not have enough funds in his business bank account. The cheque was a **dishonoured cheque** and Hedley had to make new entries to his business accounts to cancel out the receipt of the cheque in the ledger. ▶ 1.5

▼ To record a dishonoured cheque received from a credit customer

Trade receivable account for the customer	Bank account (in the cash book)
Debit amount, $600, of the dishonoured cheque	Credit amount, $600, of the dishonoured cheque
Impact: debit balance (asset) on account is increased by $600	Impact: cash in bank is decreased by $600

The entries to the ledger accounts are shown in illustration 2.35. Other entries to the bank account during the month are not shown.

Control accounts   269

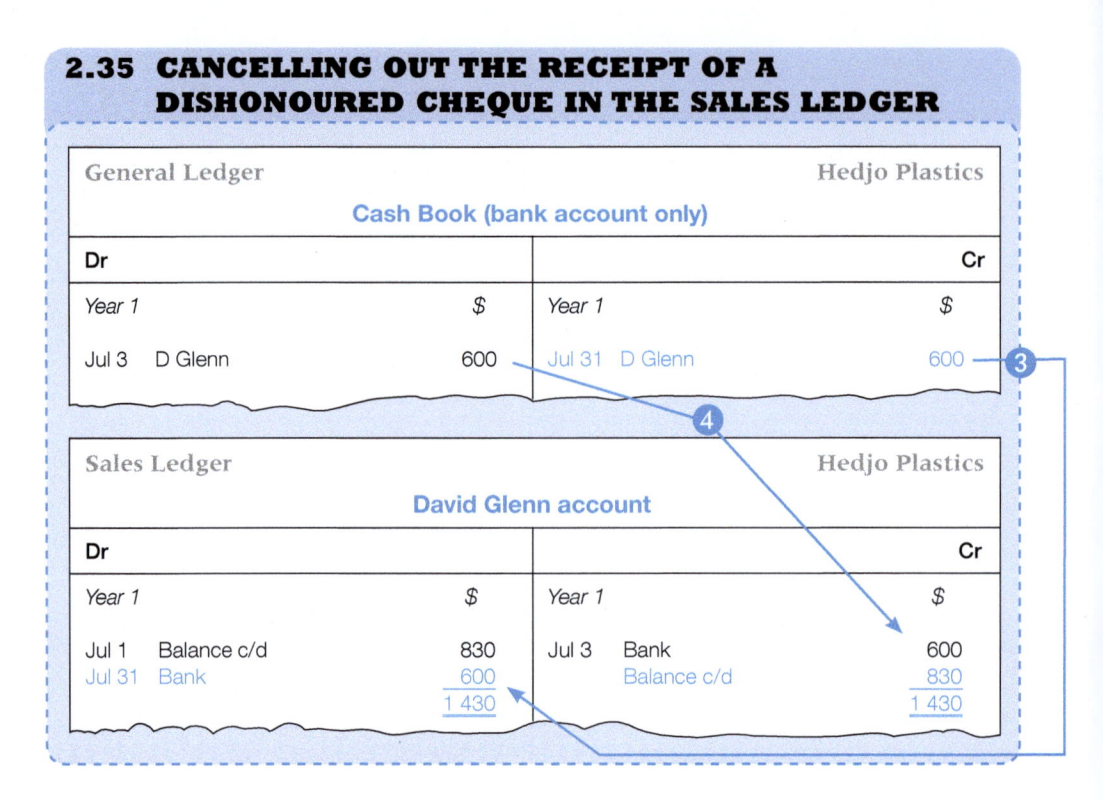

2.35 CANCELLING OUT THE RECEIPT OF A DISHONOURED CHEQUE IN THE SALES LEDGER

General Ledger — Hedjo Plastics

Cash Book (bank account only)

Dr					Cr
Year 1		$	Year 1		$
Jul 3	D Glenn	600	Jul 31	D Glenn	600

Sales Ledger — Hedjo Plastics

David Glenn account

Dr					Cr
Year 1		$	Year 1		$
Jul 1	Balance c/d	830	Jul 3	Bank	600
Jul 31	Bank	600		Balance c/d	830
		1 430			1 430

All the above transactions appeared in the sales ledger control account that Hedley Johnson prepared for Hedjo Plastics at the end of July last year from the following totals in his books of prime entry:

Date	Monthly totals for July (accounting year 1)	$
Jul 1	Balance b/d from sales ledger control account for June	11 000 Dr
Jul 31	add Total sales from the sales journal	13 500
	add Total refunds issued to trade receivables	110
	add Total interest charges on overdue trade receivable accounts	90
	add Total dishonoured cheques	600
	less Total sales returns from the sales returns journal	1 900
	less Total payments received from the cash book	9 570
	less Total discounts allowed from the cash book	370
	less Total irrecoverable debts written off	700
	less Total contra entries for transfers from trade payables	280
	Balance b/d from sales ledger control account	12 480 Dr

From the monthly totals from his books of prime entry for July last year Hedley prepared the following sales ledger control account:

2.36 AN EXAMPLE OF A SALES LEDGER CONTROL ACCOUNT WITH ADDITIONAL ENTRIES

Hedjo Plastics

Sales ledger control account

Dr					Cr
Year 1		$	Year 1		$
Jul 1	Balance b/d	11 000	Jul 30	Sales returns	1 900
Jul 31	Sales	13 500		Bank	9 570
	Bank (refunds issued)	110		Discounts allowed	370
	Interest charges	90		Irrecoverable debts	700
	Bank (dishonoured cheques)	600		Contra entries	280
				Balance c/d	12 480
		25 300			25 300
Aug 1	Balance b/d	12 480			

Refunds from suppliers, interest charged by suppliers on overdue accounts and inter-ledger transfers will also affect the total of trade payables in the purchases ledger

Less frequent transactions that will affect trade payable accounts in the purchases ledger are as follows:

▼ Other entries to trade payable accounts in the purchases ledger

Type of entry	Book of prime entry
Refund from a supplier	Cash book
Interest charged on an overdue account	General journal
Inter-ledger transfer (or contra entry)	Purchases and sales journals

If a business has overpaid a purchase invoice or overpaid the balance on its account with a supplier the supplier will issue a **refund** for the overpaid amount. The refund will be entered to the accounts of the business as follows:

▼ To record a refund received from a supplier

Bank account	Trade payable account for the supplier
Debit amount of refund received	Credit the amount of refund received. This will cancel out the overpayment
Impact: cash in bank is increased	Impact: credit balance (liability) on the account is increased

For example, on 24 July last year Hedley Johnson overpaid the balance on his account with Mouldings Ltd. by $900. Instead of paying $6 700 to clear the liability on the account he paid $7 600. The account had a debit balance of $900. This meant Mouldings Ltd. owed Hedjo Plastics $900. The company refunded the overpayment via bank transfer to the account of Hedjo Plastics on 31 July.

2.37 RECORDING A REFUND RECEIVED ON A TRADE PAYABLE ACCOUNT

Purchases Ledger — Hedjo Plastics

Mouldings Ltd account

Dr		$			Cr $
Year 1			Year 1		
Jul 24	Bank	7 600	Jul 1	Balance b/d	6 700
			Jul 31	Bank	900
		7 600			7 600

Also during July last year Hedley Johnson overlooked paying off the balance on his trade payable account for supplier Plastico SA. At the end of July the account was **overdue** by 31 days. As a result, the company added an interest charge of $175 to his account balance for late payment.

Hedley made the following entries to his accounts to record the interest charge on the overdue account:

▼ To record interest charged on an overdue trade payable account

Interest charges account	Trade payable account for the supplier
Debit the interest charged	Credit the interest charged
Impact: expenses are increased	Impact: credit balance (liability) on the account is increased

2.38 RECORDING INTEREST CHARGED ON AN OVERDUE TRADE PAYABLE ACCOUNT

Purchases Ledger — Hedjo Plastics

Plastico SA account

Dr		$			Cr $
Year 1			Year 1		
			Jun 1	Balance b/d	3 500
			Jul 1	Balance b/d	3 500
			Jul 31	Interest charges	175
					3 675

During July last year Hedjo Plastics also recorded the following transactions with one of its suppliers:

Date	Description	Amount $
Jul 6	Sealants purchased on credit from Seal-It Ltd.	$300
Jul 14	Plastic sheeting sold on credit to Seal-It Ltd.	$180

This meant that Seal-It Ltd., a supplier of Hedjo Plastics, had also become a credit customer of the business. So, rather than the two businesses exchanging payments for the full amount of their respective credit purchases from each other, Hedjo Plastics simply sent a cheque to Seal-It Ltd. for the net amount due of $120 at the end of the month.

This left a liability of $180 on the trade payable account of Seal-It Ltd. which was offset against the goods it had bought on credit from Hedjo Plastics. An **inter-ledger** transfer for $180, from the trade receivable account for Seal-It Ltd. in the sales ledger to its trade payable account in the purchases ledger, was required to settle the liability as follows:

Hedjo Plastics

General Journal

Date	Description	Dr	CR
Year 1 Jul 31	Seal-It Ltd (trade receivable in sales ledger)	180	
	Contra		180
	Contra entry offset against trade payable account for Seal-It Ltd		
	Contra	180	
	Seal-It Ltd (trade payable in sales ledger)		180
	Contra entry offset against trade payable account for Seal-It Ltd		

The following entries were posted to the ledger for the above transactions:

▼ To record payments issued and contra entries

Trade payable account for Seal-It Ltd.	Trade receivable account for Seal-It Ltd.
Credit purchases on credit of $300	Debit sales on credit of $180
Debit the payment made for $120 from the bank	
Debit the net balance of $180 and transfer it to the credit side of the trade receivable account for the same organisation in the sales ledger	Credit the net balance of $180 from the trade payable account for the same organisation in the purchases ledger

Control accounts

2.39 RECORDING CONTRA ENTRIES IN THE PURCHASES AND SALES LEDGERS

Purchases Ledger   *Hedjo Plastics*

Seal-It Ltd account

Dr					Cr
Year 1		$	Year 1		$
Jul 31	Bank	120	Jul 6	Purchases	300
Jul 31	Seal-It Ltd (sales ledger)	180			
		300			300

Sales Ledger   *Hedjo Plastics*

Seal-It Ltd account

Dr					Cr
Year 1		$	Year 1		$
Jul 14	Sales	180	Jul 31	Seal-It Ltd (purchases ledger)	180

All the above transactions appeared in the purchases ledger control account Hedley Johnson prepared for Hedjo Plastics at the end of July last year from the following totals in his books of prime entry:

Date		$
Jul 1	Balance b/d from purchases ledger control account for June	17 200 Cr
Jul 31	*add* Total purchases from the purchases journal	18 675
	add Total refunds received from trade payables	900
	add Total interest charges on overdue trade payable accounts	175
	less Total purchases returns from the purchases returns journal	3 100
	less Total payments issued from the cash book	18 000
	less Total discounts received from the cash book	370
	less Total contra entries for transfers from the sales ledger	280
	Balance c/d on purchases ledger control account	15 200 Cr

Notice that the total for contra entries made during the month is exactly the same as the total for contra entries included in the sales ledger control account for the month in illustration 2.36. This is because contra entries will affect the balances on trade receivables and on trade payables equally. They must be recorded in both the sales ledger control account (on the credit side) and the purchases ledger control account (on the debit side).

274   Accounting procedures

2.40 AN EXAMPLE OF A PURCHASES LEDGER CONTROL ACCOUNT WITH ADDITIONAL ENTRIES

Hedjo Plastics

Purchases ledger control account

Dr			Cr		
Year 1		$	Year 1		$
Jul 31	Purchases returns	3 100	Jul 1	Balance b/d	17 200
	Bank	14 700	Jul 31	Purchases	18 675
	Discounts received	370		Bank (refund received)	900
	Contra entries	280		Interest charges	175
	Balance c/d	15 200			
		36 950			36 950
			Aug 1	Balance b/d	15 200

ACTIVITY 2.16

The following information will be used to prepare the control accounts of a business for the month of September last year:

Monthly totals for September	Amount $	Book of prime entry
Credit sales	55 000	
Credit purchases	39 000	
Sales returns	10 000	
Dishonoured cheques	2 900	
Purchases returns	2 550	
Refunds received	1 200	
Refunds issued	2 700	
Discounts received	850	
Discounts allowed	1 500	
Contra entries	1 000	
Irrecoverable debts written off	3 500	
Interest charges on overdue trade receivables	400	
Interest charges on overdue trade payables	300	
Payments received from trade receivables	30 000	
Payments made to trade payables	35 000	

1. In the table, identify the books of prime entry from which the totals were obtained.
2. Prepare (a) the purchases ledger control account; and (b) the sales ledger control account, using the totals for the month in the table. The following opening balances brought down on 1 September in the control accounts should be as follows:

	$
Purchases ledger control account	22 000 (Cr)
Sales ledger control account	50 000 (Dr)

Control accounts 275

2.4.3 Opening and closing balances on control accounts

A purchases ledger control account can show both credit and debit balances if the business has prepaid or overpaid some suppliers or returned goods paid for

Trade payable accounts included in the purchases ledger account are current liability accounts: they record money owed by the business to suppliers of goods on credit. However, it is possible for a trade account to show a debit balance). This can happen if the business:

- prepays for goods ordered from the supplier
- overpays the amount owed
- returns goods purchased after it has paid for them.

It is usual to add up and record any debit balances on trade payable accounts separately from credit balances in a purchases ledger control account. This means a control account can show the debit balance and a credit balance at the same time.

▼ Balances on a purchases ledger control account

Debit balance	Total amount owed to the business by suppliers of goods on credit (trade payables)	Opening debit balance brought down is entered to the debit side Closing debit balance carried down is entered to the credit side to balance off the account
Credit balance	Total amount owed by the business to suppliers of goods on credit (trade payables)	Opening credit balance brought down is entered to the credit side Closing credit balance carried down is entered to the debit side to balance off the account

For example, in the month of August during its first accounting year Hedjo Plastics prepaid $2 100 to Plastico Ltd. for an order for some plastic sheeting. The business also overpaid the balance owing on its account with supplier Mouldings Ltd by $1 000. Together, there was a combined debit balance at the end of August of $3 100 to carry down on these trade payable accounts in the purchases ledger of Hedjo Plastics. This is shown as the **debit trade payable balances** in the following list of totals Hedley extracted from his books of prime entry for August:

Date	Monthly totals for August (accounting year 1)	$
Aug 1	Balance c/d from purchases ledger control account for July	15 200 Cr
Aug 31	Totals for the month:	
	Purchases from the purchases journal	16 700
	Refunds received from trade payables	0
	Interest charges on overdue trade payable accounts	0
	Purchases returns from the purchases returns journal	2 000
	Payments issued from the cash book	17 600
	Discounts received from the cash book	400
	Contra entries for transfers from the sales ledger	500
	Credit trade payable balances	3 100

From these totals Hedley prepared his purchases ledger control account for August by first listing those amounts he would enter to the debit side of the account and those he would enter to the credit side of the account as follows:

Date	Debits	$	Credits	$
Aug 1	Debit balance b/d	0	Credit balance b/d	15 200
Aug 31	Purchases returns	2 000	Purchases	16 700
	Payments issued	17 600	Refunds received	0
	Discounts received	400	Interest charges on overdue accounts	0
	Contra entries	500	Total debit trade payable balances	3 100
	Total debits	20 500	Total credits	35 000

2.41 A PURCHASES LEDGER CONTROL ACCOUNT WITH DEBIT AND CREDIT BALANCES

Hedjo Plastics

Purchases ledger control account

Dr						Cr
Year 1		$	Year 1			$
Aug 31	Purchases returns	2 000	Aug 1	Balance b/d		15 200
	Bank	17 600	Aug 31	Purchases		16 700
	Discounts received	400				
	Contra entries	500		Interest charges		0
	Balance c/d	14 500		Balance c/d		3 100
		27 000				35 000
Sep 1	Balance b/d	3 100	Sep 1	Balance b/d		14 500

The difference between total debits and total credits to the purchases ledger control account was a credit balance of $14 500 (total credits of $35 000 less total debits of $20 500).

The purchases ledger control account records two closing balances at 31 August:

- total debit trade payable balances of $3 100 for money owed to Hedley Johnson by his suppliers Plastico Ltd. and Mouldings Ltd. for prepayments and overpayments during the month;
- total credit trade payable balances of $14 500 for money owed by Hedley Johnson for credit purchases from all other suppliers of goods to his business.

A sales ledger control account can show both debit and credit balances if some credit customers have prepaid or overpaid their accounts or returned goods paid for

Trade receivable accounts in the sales ledger are current asset accounts: they record money owed to the business by credit customers. However, it is also possible for a trade receivable account to show a credit balance instead of a debit balance.

A credit balance on a trade receivable account records the money owed by the business to the credit customer. This may happen if the customer:

- prepays for goods ordered from the business
- overpays the amount it owes to the business
- returns goods purchased from the business after they have been paid for.

In each case the business will owe the customer a refund.

Credit balances on trade receivable accounts will be added up and recorded separately from debit balances in a sales ledger control account. Like a purchases ledger control account, a sales ledger control account can also show a debit and a credit balance at the same time.

▼ Balances on a sales ledger control account

Debit balance	Total amount owed to the business by credit customers (trade receivables)	Opening debit balance brought down is entered to the debit side
		Closing debit balance carried down is entered to the credit side to balance off the account
Credit balance	Total amount owed by the business to its credit customers (trade receivables)	Opening credit balance brought down is entered to the credit side
		Closing credit balance carried down is entered to the debit side to balance off the account

For example, during August last year Hedjo Plastics was overpaid $800 by one of its credit customers and was returned goods to the value of $700 that had already been paid for by another credit customer. Together there was a combined credit balance at the end of August of $1 500 on the trade receivable accounts of these two customers in the sales ledger of Hedjo Plastics. This is shown as the **credit trade receivable balances** in the following list of totals Hedley extracted from his books of prime entry for August:

Date	Monthly totals for August (accounting year 1)	$
Aug 1	Balance c/d from sales ledger control account for July	12 480 Dr
Aug 31	Totals for the month:	
	Sales from the sales journal	9 800
	Refunds issued to trade receivables	0
	Interest charged on overdue trade receivable accounts	0
	Dishonoured cheques	220
	Total sales returns from the sales returns journal	1 300
	Payments received from the cash book	10 200
	Discounts allowed from the cash book	200
	Irrecoverable debts written off from general journal	1 000
	Contra entries for transfers from the purchases ledger	500
	Credit trade receivable balances	1 500

From these totals Hedley prepared his sales ledger control account for August by first listing those amounts he would enter to the debit side of the account and those he would enter to the credit side of the account as follows:

Date	Debits	$	Credits	$
Aug 1	Debit balance b/d	12 480	Credit balance b/d	0
Aug 31	Sales	9 800	Sales returns	1 300
	Refunds issued	0	Payments received	10 200
	Interest charged	0	Discounts allowed	200
	Dishonoured cheques	200	Irrecoverable debts	1 000
	Credit trade receivable balances	1 500	Contra entries	500
	Total debits	24 000	Total credits	13 200

The difference between total debits and total credits to the sales ledger control account was a debit balance of $10 800 (total credits of $13 200 less total debits of $24 000).

2.42 A SALES LEDGER CONTROL ACCOUNT WITH CREDIT AND DEBIT BALANCES

Hedjo Plastics

Sales ledger control account

Dr						
Year 1		$		Year 1		$
Aug 1	Balance b/d	12 480		Aug 31	Sales returns	1 300
Aug 31	Sales	9 800			Bank	10 200
					Discounts allowed	200
					Irrecoverable debts	1 000
	Bank (dishonoured cheques)	220			Contra entries	500
	Balance c/d	1 500			Balance c/d	10 800
		24 000				24 000
Sept 1	Balance b/d	10 800		Sept 1	Balance b/d	1 500

The sales ledger control account records two closing balances at 31 August:

- total credit trade receivable balances of $1 500 for money owed by Hedley Johnson for overpayments or returns received from credit customers of his business during the month
- total debit trade receivable balances of $10 800 for money owed to Hedley Johnson by all other credit customers of his business.

ACTIVITY 2.17

The following information was taken from the books of a business for the month of March last year:

Opening balances on sales ledger, 1 March	$
Debit	90 000
Credit	5 000
Totals for March	
Sales	172 000
Sales returns	12 000
Payments received	163 200
Discounts allowed	4 000
Refunds issued	8 700
Interest charged	3 400
Irrecoverable debts written off	5 800
Contra entries transferred from trade payables	7 000
Dishonoured cheques	6 400
Closing balances on sales ledger, 31 March	
Debit	?
Credit	9 500

1. From the information prepare the sales ledger control account for March.
2. Calculate as necessary and show the credit and debit balances brought down in the control account on 1 April.
3. Explain why the control account has opening and closing balances on both sides.

280 Accounting procedures

QUICK TEST

1. State the purpose of (a) a purchases ledger control account; (b) a sales ledger control account.
2. State **three** advantages to a business of preparing control accounts for its purchases and sales ledgers.
3. From which book of prime entry will a business be able to find and calculate the following entries to its purchases ledger control account?
   - credit purchases
   - purchases returns
   - discounts received
   - refunds received
   - interest charged on overdue accounts
4. From which book of prime entry will a business be able to find and calculate the following entries to its sales ledger control account?
   - credit sales
   - sales returns
   - discounts allowed
   - refunds issued
   - interest charged on overdue accounts
   - irrecoverable debts written off
   - dishonoured cheques
5. Aran maintains a full set of books of prime (original) entry and prepares purchases ledger and sales ledger control accounts at the end of every month. On 1 January last year the balances brought down in his control accounts were:

Purchases ledger control account	$	Sales ledger control account	$
Credit	55 100	Credit	5 700
Debit	7 000	Debit	75 000

He also supplied the following information for the same month ending 31 January:

Totals for the month	$	Totals for the month	$
Purchases	66 000	Sales	140 000
Purchases returns	11 220	Sales returns	9 200
Payments to suppliers	43 000	Payments received from credit customers	130 000
Discounts received from suppliers	1 080	Cheque payments dishonoured by the bank	5 600
Refunds received from suppliers	6 900	Discounts allowed to credit customers	3 100
Contra entries *(transfers from sales ledger)*	2 500	Refunds issued to credit customers	5 000
		Interest charged on overdue accounts	1 400
		Irrecoverable debts written off	4 200
		Contra entries *(transfers from purchases ledger)*	2 500

Closing balances on Aran's control accounts at 31 January were:

Purchases ledger control account	$	Sales ledger control account	$
Credit	?	Credit	8 600
Debit	3 500	Debit	?

(a) From the information provided prepare the following control accounts for Aran for the month of January last year (i) the purchases ledger control account; and (ii) the sales ledger control account.

(b) Calculate as required and show the closing credit and debit balances on the two control accounts brought down on 31 January.

6 (a) State **two** reasons why it is possible to have a debit balance brought down on a purchases ledger control account; and (b) state **two** reasons why it is possible to have a credit balance brought down on a sales ledger control account.

7 Explain the meaning of a contra entry in control accounts and explain why it may be necessary.

Check your understanding with the Unit 2 revision summary and assessment activities.

3 Final statements

Content at a glance

3.1	Income statements
3.2	Statements of financial position

Unit 3.1 Income statements

AIMS

By the end of this unit you should be able to

- calculate the **gross profit** and **profit (or loss) for the year**, based on accounting principles
- recognise that profit (or loss) for the year is the increase (or decrease) in the **net assets** during a financial year
- prepare simple columnar **trading accounts** when dealing with a business that has two departments

3.1.1 Preparing financial statements

Business owners aim for profit and capital gain from their business investments

Making a profit is the main reason people invest their time, effort and money in businesses.

A successful business is a profitable one and any profit will increase the value of that business. This is because profit will increase the asset of cash held in the business bank account and the equity of the owner. ▶ **1.2**

▼ The two sections of an income statement

> **(1) Trading account**
>
> *What is it for?* To calculate **gross profit**
>
> *What does it show?* Profit from the purchase and sale of goods
>
> *Why is it important?* It tells the business how successful it has been at selling goods at a price greater than their cost

> **(2) Profit and loss account**
>
> *What is it for?* To calculate **profit for the year**
>
> *What does it show?* The profit remaining after all business expenses have been deducted from gross profit
>
> *Why is it important?* It tells the business how successful it has been at using its assets and controlling its expenses

For example, imagine a business owner had just invested $5 000 of his or her own money in a new business venture all of which was used to purchase goods for resale. The owner was then able earn a total of $7 000 from the sale of these goods to customers. In doing so the owner had turned $5 000 of owner's equity held in cash in the business bank account into $7 000. This increase or gain in owner's equity is **profit**.

Profit is the difference between the total revenue or income of a business and its total costs or expenses. It provides the business owners with additional equity they can withdraw for their own personal use or which they can use to expand their business and increase its future profitability.

Financial statements are prepared to calculate and record the profit and value of a business at the end of each accounting year

Given the importance of profit and capital gain to business owners it is vital that they are able to calculate and demonstrate the value and profitability of their businesses. This is done by preparing financial statements from their accounting records, usually at the end of each accounting year. ▶ 1.8

An **income statement** is used to calculate and report two measures of profit and consists of two parts.

A **statement of financial position** is used to calculate and report the value of the business assets, liabilities and capital. ▶ 3.2

In this unit we will look at the preparation of simple financial statements over a five-year period for a small trading business owned by a single person or **sole trader**.

The financial statements of larger businesses and organisations such as charities, clubs and societies may look a little different but they will all be prepared in much the same way. ▶ 4.1–4.6

3.1.2 Calculating gross profit from the sale of goods

A trial balance should be drawn up before financial statements are prepared

Jamila Khan started her small business five years ago with $5 000 of her own capital. The business is called Go Faster Sports and buys and sells fashionable sportswear.

At the end of her first accounting year ending 31 December she posted all the remaining entries from her journals for transactions made during December to complete and balance off her ledger accounts for the year.

3.1 SALES AND PURCHASES ACCOUNTS AT THE END OF ACCOUNTING YEAR 1

Sales ledger — Go Faster Sports

Sales account

Dr			Cr
Year 1	$	Year 1	$
		Dec 1 Balance b/d	70 000
		Dec 31 Bank	7 000
			77 000

Purchases ledger — Go Faster Sports

Purchases account

Dr			Cr
Year 1	$	Year 1	$
Dec 1 Balance b/d	54 300		
Dec 31 Bank	2 700		
Dec 31 Sports Mart plc	3 000		
	60 000		

The end of year balance on Jamila's sales account shown in illustration 3.1 was a credit balance of $77 000 for revenue earned during the year. The end of year balance on her purchases account also in illustration 3.1 was a debit balance of $60 000 for the amount Jamila had spent buying goods for resale in her shop. From these balances she was able to calculate her gross profit for the year very simply as:

	$
Sales	77 000
less Purchases	60 000
Gross profit	**17 000**

Jamila then balanced off all her expense accounts in her general ledger as shown in illustration 3.2. From these balances for her business expenses she was able to calculate her profit for the year as follows:

	$	$
Gross profit		17 000
less Total expenses:		
Rent	9 000	
Electricity	2 400	
Advertising	1 500	
Sundry expenses	1 100	
		14 000
Profit for the year		**3 000**

Income statements 285

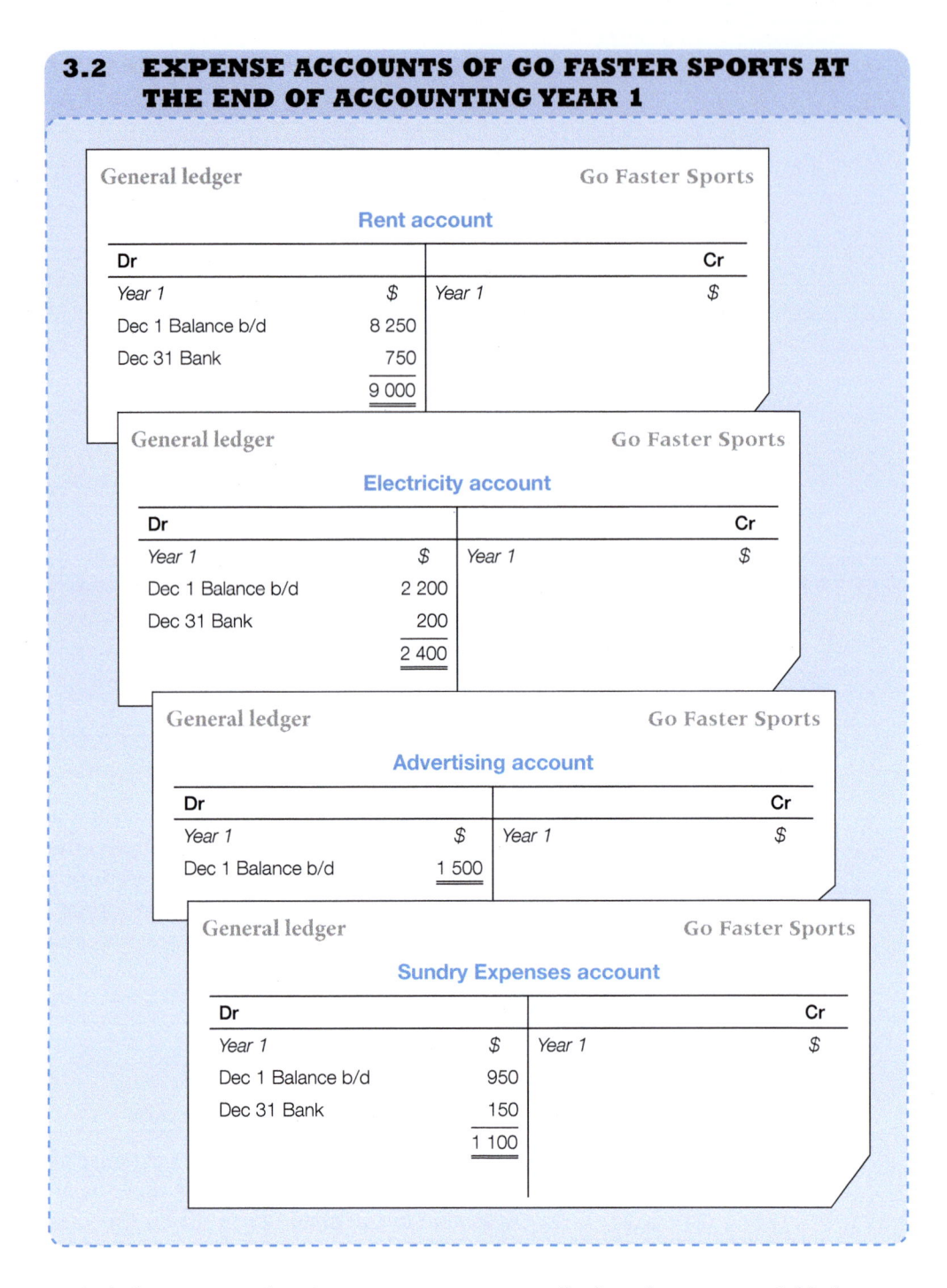

3.2 EXPENSE ACCOUNTS OF GO FASTER SPORTS AT THE END OF ACCOUNTING YEAR 1

General ledger   Go Faster Sports

Rent account

Dr			Cr
Year 1	$	Year 1	$
Dec 1 Balance b/d	8 250		
Dec 31 Bank	750		
	9 000		

General ledger   Go Faster Sports

Electricity account

Dr			Cr
Year 1	$	Year 1	$
Dec 1 Balance b/d	2 200		
Dec 31 Bank	200		
	2 400		

General ledger   Go Faster Sports

Advertising account

Dr			Cr
Year 1	$	Year 1	$
Dec 1 Balance b/d	1 500		

General ledger   Go Faster Sports

Sundry Expenses account

Dr			Cr
Year 1	$	Year 1	$
Dec 1 Balance b/d	950		
Dec 31 Bank	150		
	1 100		

To help her prepare her income statement Jamila first drew up a trial balance from all the balances on her ledger accounts including those for assets, liabilities and capital. In doing so she remembered the following:

- Accounts for assets, purchases, expenses and drawings all have debit balances.
- Accounts for liabilities, income, capital and sales all have credit balances.
- The total of debit balances must equal the total of credit balances. ➤ **1.8**

3.3 THE TRIAL BALANCE FOR GO FASTER SPORTS AT THE END OF ACCOUNTING YEAR 1

Go Faster Sports
Trial Balance For Year 1 As At 31 December

	Dr $	Cr $
Sales		77 000
Purchases	60 000	
Rent	9 000	
Electricity	2 400	
Advertising	1 500	
Sundry expenses	1 100	
Equipment	6 500	
Bank	4 500	
Sports Mart Ltd. (trade payable)		3 000
Opening capital (at the start of year 1)		5 000
	85 000	85 000

Her completed trial balance for her first accounting year is shown in illustration 3.3. Each balance in the trial balance can only be used once in the end of year financial statements:

- balances on sales, purchases, income and expenses accounts will be used to prepare the income statement

- balances for assets, liabilities and capital will be used to prepare the statement of financial position ➤ 3.2

Transfer these account balances to the statement of financial position

Transfer these account balances to the income statement

If revenue from sales exceeds the cost of the items sold a business will make a gross profit

It is important to match revenue recorded in an income statement only with those costs or expenses incurred earning it. This is called the matching principle in accounting. ➤ 1.9 & 5.2

- If revenue from sales exceeds the cost of the goods sold (the **cost of sales**) the business will have made a **gross profit.**

- If the cost of goods sold is greater than the revenue earned from their sale the business will have made a **gross loss**.

> Gross profit = Revenue − Cost of sales

GROSS PROFIT
REVENUE > COST OF SALES

GROSS LOSS

REVENUE < COST OF SALES

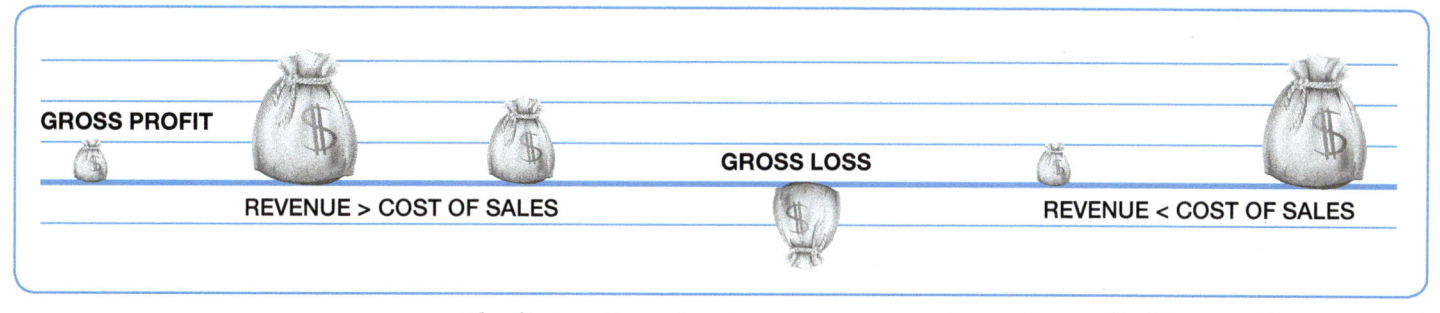

The first section of an income statement (sometimes called the **trading account**) is used to record:

- revenue from sales for the year

- the cost of the goods actually sold in the same year, called the **cost of sales**

- the gross profit or loss from the goods sold.

It shows how good the business is at selling goods at a price greater than their cost. ➤ 5.1

From her trial balance in illustration 3.3 Jamila knew she had spent $60 000 purchasing sportswear for resale during her first year of trading and had

Income statements 287

earned a total of $77 000 from the sale of the same items to her customers. This meant:

(1) her cost of purchases was her cost of sales because, since there were no unsold goods left over at the end of the accounting year, she had sold all the sportswear she had bought during the year

(2) she had made a gross profit of $17 000 from the sale of all the sportswear she had purchased during the year.

Jamila applied the rules of double-entry book-keeping to record her sales and purchases for the year in the first part of her income statement as follows:

- Debit the sales account with the closing balance and credit the income statement.
- Credit the purchases account with the closing balance and debit the income statement.

The double entries for the above transfers to the income statement are shown in the following illustration.

3.4 PREPARING THE FIRST PART OF THE INCOME STATEMENT FROM LEDGER ACCOUNT BALANCES

To calculate and record gross profit in the income statement

1 Debit the sales account with the final credit balance to "close" the account for the year.

Transfer this closing balance to the credit column of the income statement.

2 Credit the purchases account with the final debit balance to "close" the account for the year.

Transfer this closing balance to the debit column of the income statement.

3 Deduct the debit balance for purchases from the credit balance for sales to calculate gross profit.

4 Record gross profit as a debit entry to balance off the two sides of the income statement.

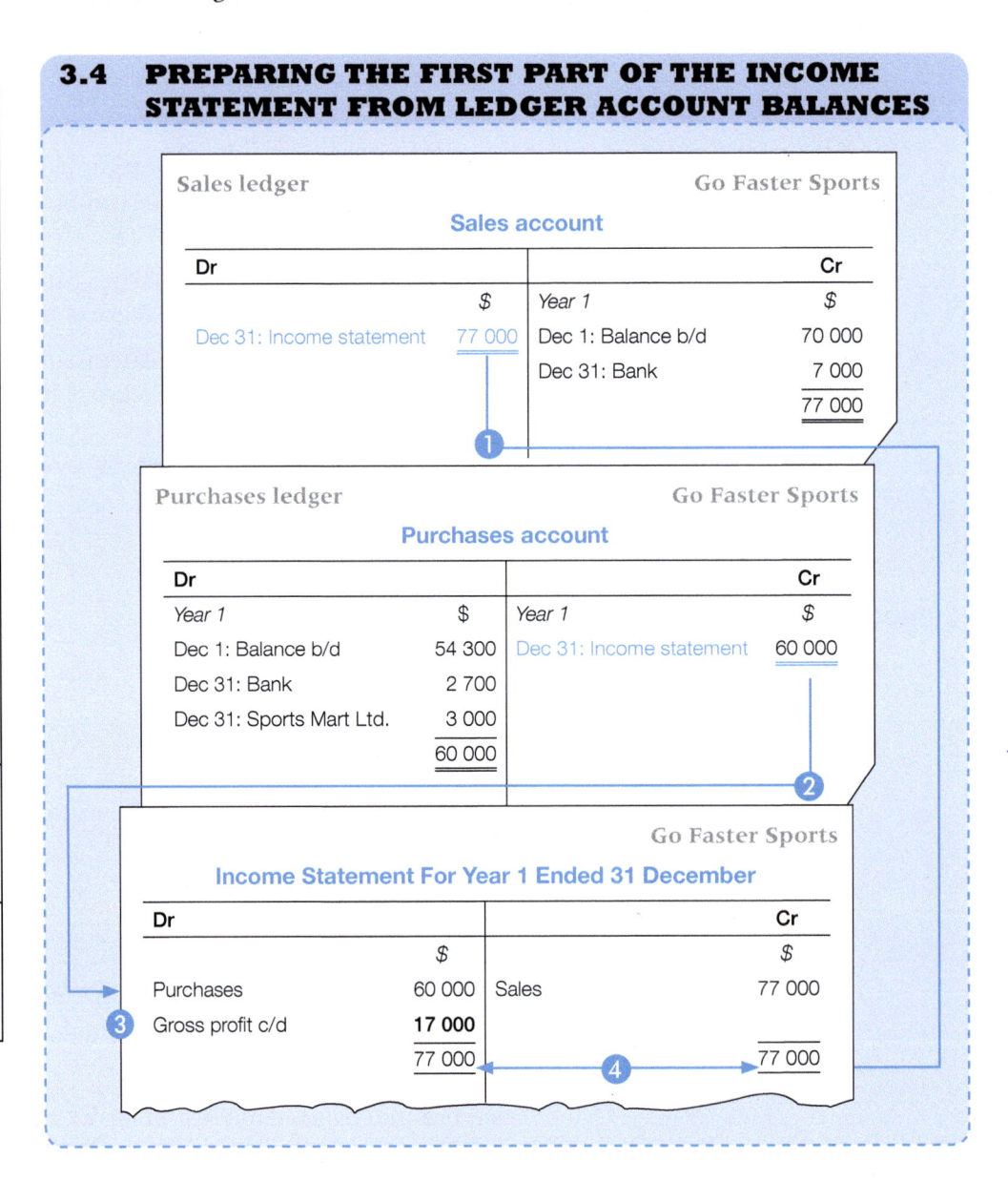

Sales ledger — Go Faster Sports

Sales account

Dr			Cr
	$	Year 1	$
Dec 31: Income statement	77 000	Dec 1: Balance b/d	70 000
		Dec 31: Bank	7 000
			77 000

Purchases ledger — Go Faster Sports

Purchases account

Dr			Cr
Year 1	$	Year 1	$
Dec 1: Balance b/d	54 300	Dec 31: Income statement	60 000
Dec 31: Bank	2 700		
Dec 31: Sports Mart Ltd.	3 000		
	60 000		

Go Faster Sports

Income Statement For Year 1 Ended 31 December

Dr			Cr
	$		$
Purchases	60 000	Sales	77 000
Gross profit c/d	17 000		
	77 000		77 000

288 Final statements

The income statement in illustration 3.4 is arranged in a **horizontal format** with two sides, one for debits and the other for credits.

The difference, $17 000, between the debit and credit sides of the first part of the statement was Jamila's gross profit for the year from the sale of sportswear. It was added to the debit side to balance off the two sides of the trading account in the income statement.

3.1.3 Calculating profit for the year

Profit for the year is what remains from gross profit after all business expenses incurred in the same year have been deducted

Like all other business organisations Jamila's business will incur many different expenses each day which must be paid for from its sales revenue and other incomes. These are called the running costs, **overheads** or **operating expenses** of the business and they will include:

- rental payments for business premises
- electricity and telephone charges
- advertising and marketing costs
- insurance premiums
- maintenance and repairs
- bank charges
- the wages and salaries of employees
- provisions for depreciation of non-current assets ➤ 2.2
- provisions for doubtful debts ➤ 1.9
- **sundry expenses**, for example the purchase of light bulbs, stationery and other miscellaneous items that are not recorded in individual ledger accounts because they are too small and too infrequent. ➤ 1.6

In addition, a business may also incur other expenses that are unrelated to its normal business operations such as interest charges on bank loans. These are **non-operating expenses** and will also include one-time or unusual costs such as fees for exchanging foreign currencies, expenditure required to reorganise the business and one-off legal costs.

To calculate the final profit or **profit for the year** from trading, all expenses incurred in the same accounting year by the business must be deducted from its gross profit. This is done in the second part of the income statement:

- If gross profit is greater than total expenses incurred in the same year the business will have made a **profit for the year**.
- If total expenses incurred exceed gross profit in the same year the business will have made a **loss for the year**.

> Profit for the year = Gross profit − Expenses

PROFIT FOR THE YEAR
GROSS PROFIT > TOTAL EXPENSES

LOSS FOR THE YEAR
GROSS PROFIT < TOTAL EXPENSES

The second part of an income statement, also known as the **profit and loss account**, therefore shows how good a business is at controlling its total costs. Profit for the year is also called **net profit** and can be increased by reducing business expenses.

To complete the second part of her income statement to calculate profit for the year Jamila applied the rules of double-entry book-keeping as follows:

- Bring down gross profit from the debit side from the first part of the income statement and credit it to the second part of the income statement.

- Credit each expense account (from illustration 3.2) with its closing balance and transfer them as debits to the second part of the income statement.

Jamila was then able to add up and deduct total expenses of $14 000 from the credit balance of $17 000 for gross profit to calculate a profit of $3 000 for the year to complete her income statement. This is shown in illustration 3.5.

To calculate and record profit for the year in the income statement
⑤ Bring down gross profit to the credit column of the income statement.
⑥ Credit each expense account with its final debit balance to "close" each account for the year. Transfer these closing balances to the debit column of the income statement.
⑦ Deduct the total of debit balances for expenses from the credit balance for gross profit to calculate profit for the year.
⑧ Record profit for the year as a debit entry to balance off the two sides of the income statement.

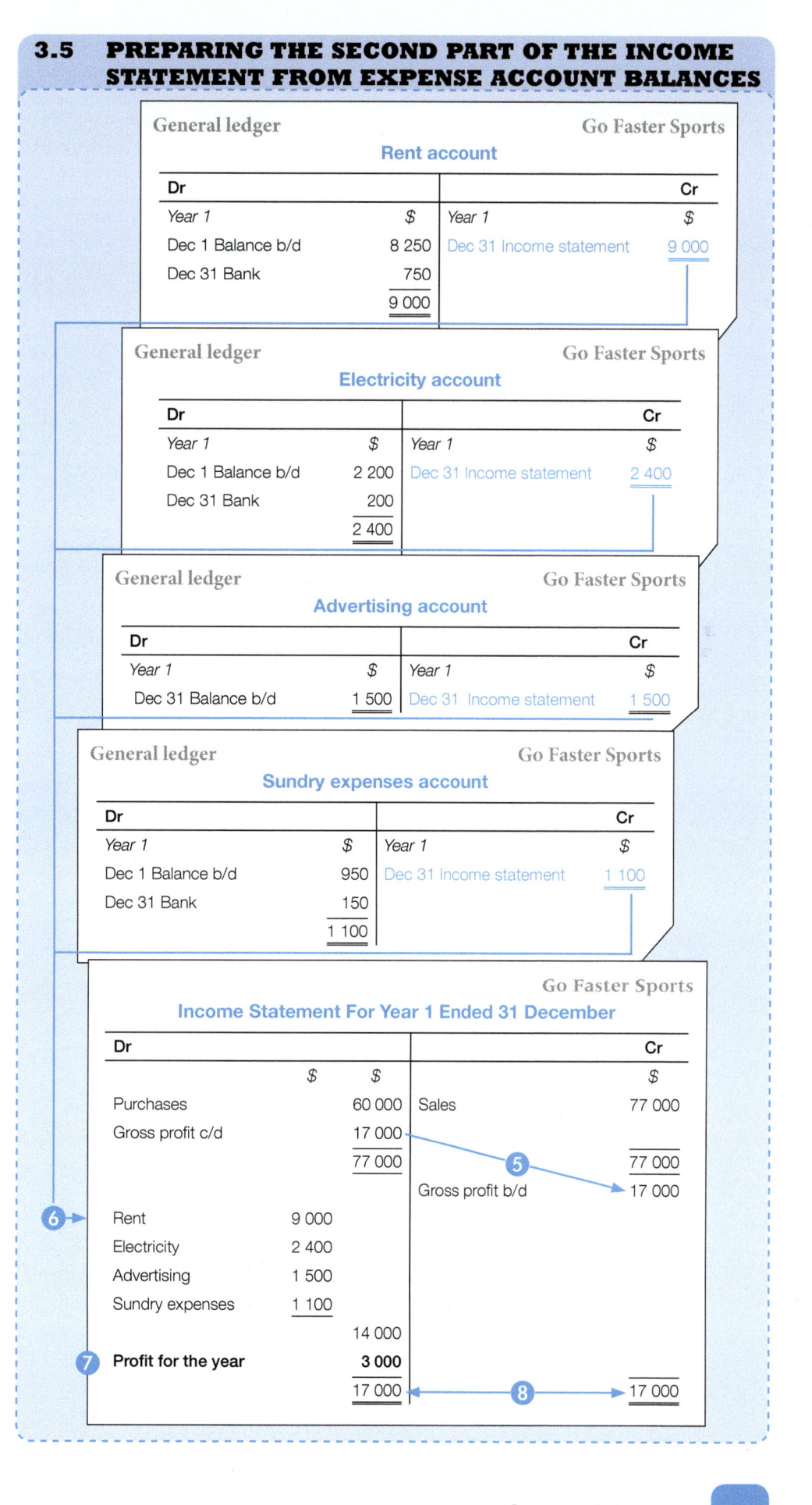

3.5 PREPARING THE SECOND PART OF THE INCOME STATEMENT FROM EXPENSE ACCOUNT BALANCES

General ledger — Go Faster Sports
Rent account

Dr			Cr	
Year 1		$	Year 1	$
Dec 1 Balance b/d		8 250	Dec 31 Income statement	9 000
Dec 31 Bank		750		
		9 000		

General ledger — Go Faster Sports
Electricity account

Dr			Cr	
Year 1		$	Year 1	$
Dec 1 Balance b/d		2 200	Dec 31 Income statement	2 400
Dec 31 Bank		200		
		2 400		

General ledger — Go Faster Sports
Advertising account

Dr			Cr	
Year 1		$	Year 1	$
Dec 31 Balance b/d		1 500	Dec 31 Income statement	1 500

General ledger — Go Faster Sports
Sundry expenses account

Dr			Cr	
Year 1		$	Year 1	$
Dec 1 Balance b/d		950	Dec 31 Income statement	1 100
Dec 31 Bank		150		
		1 100		

Go Faster Sports
Income Statement For Year 1 Ended 31 December

Dr		$	$	Cr	$
Purchases			60 000	Sales	77 000
Gross profit c/d			17 000		
			77 000		77 000
				Gross profit b/d	17 000
⑥ Rent			9 000		
Electricity			2 400		
Advertising			1 500		
Sundry expenses			1 100		
			14 000		
⑦ Profit for the year			3 000		
			17 000	⑧	17 000

Income statements 291

Profit for the year will increase the net assets and capital of the business

Profit is accumulated over time as goods are sold and revenue is received. This means that profit increases the current assets of cash held in the business bank account. ➤ 1.2

The accounting equation states that:

> **Assets = Capital + Liabilities**

Or put another way, the value of assets remaining after any liabilities have been paid in full will be equal to the value of the owner's equity invested in the business. That is:

> **Net assets = Assets − Liabilities = Capital**

The increase in cash in bank due to profit increases the net assets of the business and therefore the owner's equity.

It follows that once the income statement has been completed the capital account in the general ledger should be updated with profit for the year.

Illustration 3.6 shows Jamila's capital account at the start of her first accounting year when she set up Go Faster Sports with $5 000 of her own capital.

3.6 CAPITAL ACCOUNT SHOWING OPENING EQUITY AT THE START OF ACCOUNTING YEAR 1

General ledger — Go Faster Sports

Capital account

Dr			Cr
Year 1	$	Year 1	$
		Jan 1 Bank	5 000

At the end of her first accounting year Jamila updated her capital account as follows:

- Debit the income statement with $3 000 of profit for the year.
- Credit the capital account with $3 000 of profit for the year.

As a result, her equity increased from $5 000 at the start of the accounting year to $8 000 by the end of the year. Her **closing equity** of $8 000 at the year end is shown in illustration 3.7 as the balance carried down in her updated capital account.

▼ Uses of profit for the year

- Pay off business liabilities
- Withdraw it for personal use (drawings)
- Buy more goods for resale (inventory)
- Invest in new machinery or other non-current assets

3.7 CAPITAL ACCOUNT SHOWING CLOSING EQUITY AT THE END OF ACCOUNTING YEAR 1

General ledger — Go Faster Sports

Capital account

Dr			Cr
Year 1	$	Year 1	$
Dec 31 Balance c/d	8 000	Jan 1 Bank	5 000
		Dec 31 Income statement	3 000
	8 000		8 000
		Year 2	
		Jan 1 Balance b/d	8 000

Simply leaving profit in the business bank account as cash is not a very productive use of the money. It is better to use any profit to reduce business liabilities, buy more goods for resale to earn additional revenue or to expand the scale of the business through investments in new equipment or larger premises. This strategy can help the business to sell more goods and earn more profit in the future.

ACTIVITY 3.1

1. Complete the horizontal income statement below.
2. How much gross profit and profit for the year did the business make?

Serge Bashir

Income Statement For Year Ended 31 March 201X

Dr			Cr
	$		$
Cost of sales	124 300	Sales	255 000
Gross profit c/d			
			255 000
		Gross profit b/d	
Rent	14 700		
Electricity	6 600		
Insurance premium	2 100		
Telephone charges	3 200		
Wages and salaries	39 000		
Other operating expenses	18 900		
Net profit			
	120 700		

Don't forget sample answers for all activities can be found on the support website!

You have now covered everything you need to know to prepare a very simple income statement to show gross profit and profit for the year. In sections 3.1.2 to 3.1.6 we will follow Go Faster Sports as it expands. We will see how new items are introduced to its accounts and end-of-year income statements, and how they affect the calculation of its gross profit and profit for the year.

Income statements

3.1.4 The impact of sales and purchases returns on gross profit

Any goods returned by customers will reduce revenue from sales and any goods returned to suppliers by the business will reduce the cost of purchases

We now move on one year to look at how Jamila prepared the income statement for her business Go Faster Sports at the end of its second accounting year. To begin this process Jamila prepared the following trial balance from the accounts in her ledger at the end of the year. This is shown in illustration 3.8.

3.8 THE TRIAL BALANCE FOR GO FASTER SPORTS AT THE END OF ACCOUNTING YEAR 2

Go Faster Sports
Trial Balance For Year 2 At 31 December

	Dr $	Cr $
Sales		110 000
Sale returns	4 000	
Purchases	85 000	
Purchases returns		2 000
Rent	9 000	
Electricity	3 000	
Advertising	2 100	
Sundry expenses	1 400	
Equipment	8 800	
Bank	4 700	
Sports Mart Ltd. (trade payable)		3 000
Drawings	5 000	
Opening equity (at the start of year 2)		8 000
	123 000	123 000

Notice that Jamila's **opening equity** at the start of her second accounting year was her **closing equity** of $8 000 at the end of year 1 (the balance brought down in her capital account in illustration 3.7).

In addition, her trial balance for year 1 contained a number of new balances:

- a debit balance of $4 000 for **sales returns** from the sales returns account to record goods returned by credit customers during the year. Sales returns reduce revenue. ▶ 1.7

- a credit balance of $2 000 for **purchases returns** from the purchases returns account to record goods Jamila had returned to her supplier during the year. Purchases returns reduce the cost of goods sold. ▶ 1.7

- a debit balance of $5 000 for **drawings** of cash Jamila had made from the business bank account for her own personal use. Drawings reduce the owner's equity. ▶ 1.7

ACTIVITY 3.2

The table below lists balances taken from the books of small trader Paulo De Santos at the end of the accounting year ending 31 December. Note that all goods purchased during the year were sold in the same period.

	$
Sales	100 000
Purchases	75 000
Electricity charges	1 500
Telephone charges	4 000
Insurance premiums	1 000
Other expenses	3 500
Opening equity (1 Jan)	20 000

1. Use the information to prepare a trial balance for the year ending 31 December.

2. Prepare the first part (trading account) of the income statement for the year: transfer the balances for sales and purchases from the trial balance to the statement and then record gross profit on the debit side.

3. Now complete the second part (profit and loss account) of the income statement: bring down gross profit from the trading account to the credit side and then transfer balances for expenses to the debit side.

4. Finally, update the capital account for the business with profit for the year.

294 Final statements

In exactly the same way as for the previous year Jamila used her trial balance to prepare the first part of her income statement for her second accounting year as follows:

- Debit the sales account with the closing balance and credit the income statement.
- Credit the purchases account with the closing balance and debit the income statement.

However, unlike the previous year Jamila could not simply deduct purchases from sales to calculate her gross profit. This was because there had been returns for items sold and purchased during the year. She needed to adjust her income statement as follows:

- Sales returns had to be deducted from total sales to find her **net sales** (revenue) for the year: $106 000 ($110 000 *less* $4 000).
- Purchases returns had to be deducted from total purchases to find her **net purchases** for the year: $83 000 ($85 000 *less* $3 000).

Her gross profit, $23 000, was the difference between her revenue from net sales ($106 000) and the cost of those sales (net purchases of $83 000). To make these entries and calculations Jamila added a second column for figures to each side of her income statement as shown in illustration 3.9.

3.9 RECORDING RETURNS IN THE FIRST PART OF THE INCOME STATEMENT

Go Faster Sports

Income Statement For Year 2 Ended 31 December

Dr						Cr
	$	$			$	$
Purchases	85 000		Sales		110 000	
⑩ *less* Purchases returns	2 000		*less* Sales returns		4 000	⑨
Cost of sales		83 000				106 000
⑪ Gross profit c/d		23 000				
		106 000	⑫			106 000

To record returns and calculate gross profit in the income statement

Credit the sales returns account with the final debit balance to "close" the account for the year.

⑨ Deduct this closing balance from the credit balance for sales in the income statement to find net sales or revenue for the year.

Debit the purchases returns account with the final credit balance to "close" the account for the year.

⑩ Deduct this closing balance from the debit balance for purchases to find net purchases (the cost of sales if there are no unsold goods at the end of the year).

⑪ Deduct the debit balance for net purchases from the credit balance for revenue to calculate gross profit.

⑫ Record gross profit as a debit entry to balance off the two sides of the income statement.

As Jamila had once again been successful at selling all the goods she had purchased during the year net of any returns, her cost of sales was exactly equal to her net purchases. She was able to calculate her gross profit as follows:

Gross profit = Revenue − Cost of sales

where: revenue = sales − sales returns
cost of sales = net purchases
net purchases = purchases − purchases returns

After calculating and recording gross profit Jamila was able to complete the second part of her income statement by applying the same rules and procedures she followed the previous year:

- Bring down gross profit from the debit side of first part of the income statement to the credit side of the second part of the income statement.
- Credit each expense account in the general ledger with its closing balance and debit the income statement.

Jamila's completed income statement for her second accounting year is shown in illustration 3.10.

3.10 GO FASTER SPORTS INCOME STATEMENT FOR ACCOUNTING YEAR 2

Go Faster Sports

Income Statement For Year 2 Ended 31 December

Dr		$	$			$	Cr $
Purchases		85 000		Sales		110 000	
less Purchases returns		2 000		less Sales returns		4 000	
Cost of sales			83 000				106 000
Gross profit c/d			23 000				
			106 000				106 000
				Gross profit b/d			23 000
Rent		9 000					
Electricity		3 000					
Advertising		2 100					
Sundry expenses		1 400					
			15 500				
Profit for the year			7 500				
			23 000				23 000

With a gross profit from sales of $23 000 and total expenses of $15 500 Go Faster Sports recorded a healthy profit for the year of $7 500, up from $3 000 the previous year.

Personal drawings will reduce the net assets and owner's equity of the business

Following completion of the income statement for her second accounting year Jamila updated her capital account with her profit for the year. However, earlier that year on 12 December Jamila had withdrawn $5 000 in cash from the business bank account for her own personal use. This meant she had not kept or retained all of her profit for the year in her business.

ACTIVITY 3.3

Use the information in the table from the books of a small business to:

1. Calculate (a) gross profit; and
   (b) profit for the year.

2. Prepare (a) a trial balance; and
   (b) an income statement to show gross profit and profit for the year.

Balances for accounting year ended 30 September	$
Sales	355 000
Sales returns	17 000
Purchases	260 000
Purchases returns	15 600
Rent	18 000
Electricity	12 800
Insurance	4 500
Cleaning	6 700
Sundry expenses	10 000

Illustration 3.11 shows her ledger accounts for capital and drawings at the end year 2 before they were updated and balanced off at the end of accounting year 2.

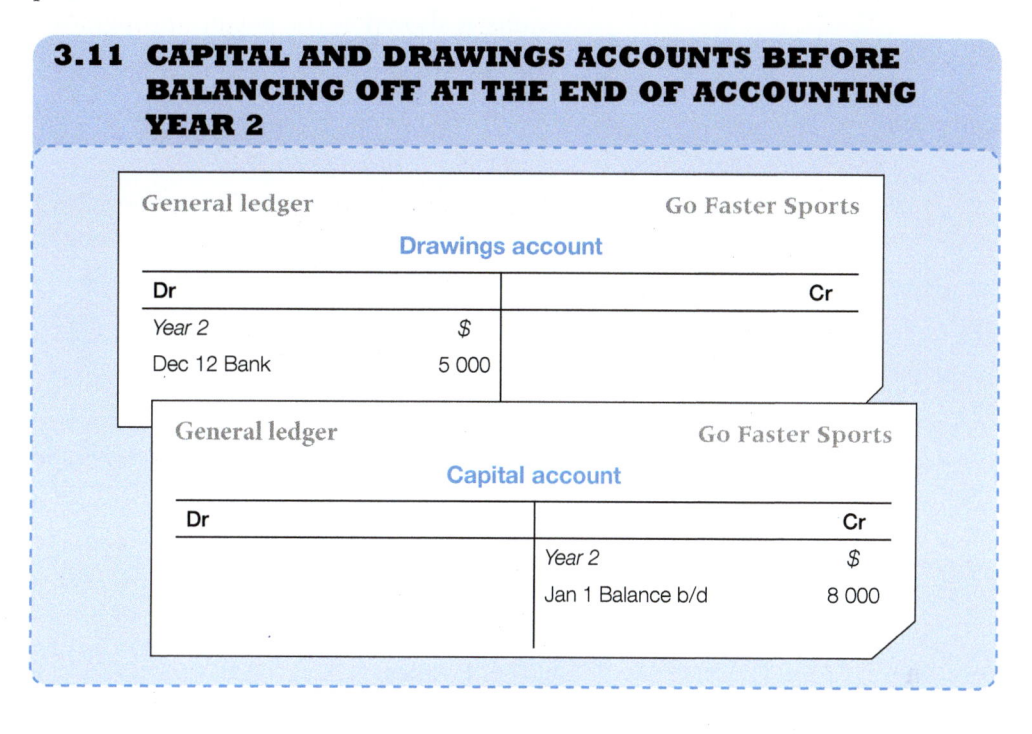

3.11 CAPITAL AND DRAWINGS ACCOUNTS BEFORE BALANCING OFF AT THE END OF ACCOUNTING YEAR 2

General ledger — Go Faster Sports

Drawings account

Dr			Cr
Year 2	$		
Dec 12 Bank	5 000		

General ledger — Go Faster Sports

Capital account

Dr			Cr
		Year 2	$
		Jan 1 Balance b/d	8 000

The capital account shows Jamila's opening equity of $8 000 (from illustration 3.7) at the start of year 2 while the drawings account records her debit of $5 000 in cash from the business bank account. To update the accounts Jamila made the following entries:

3.12 CAPITAL AND DRAWINGS ACCOUNTS AFTER BALANCING OFF AT THE END OF ACCOUNTING YEAR 2

13 • Credit the drawings account with $5 000 to balance off and close the account for the year.
 • Debit the capital account to record drawings from the owner's equity of $5 000

14 • Debit the income statement with $7 500 of profit for the year.
 • Credit the capital account with $7 500 of profit for the year to record the increase in owner's equity.

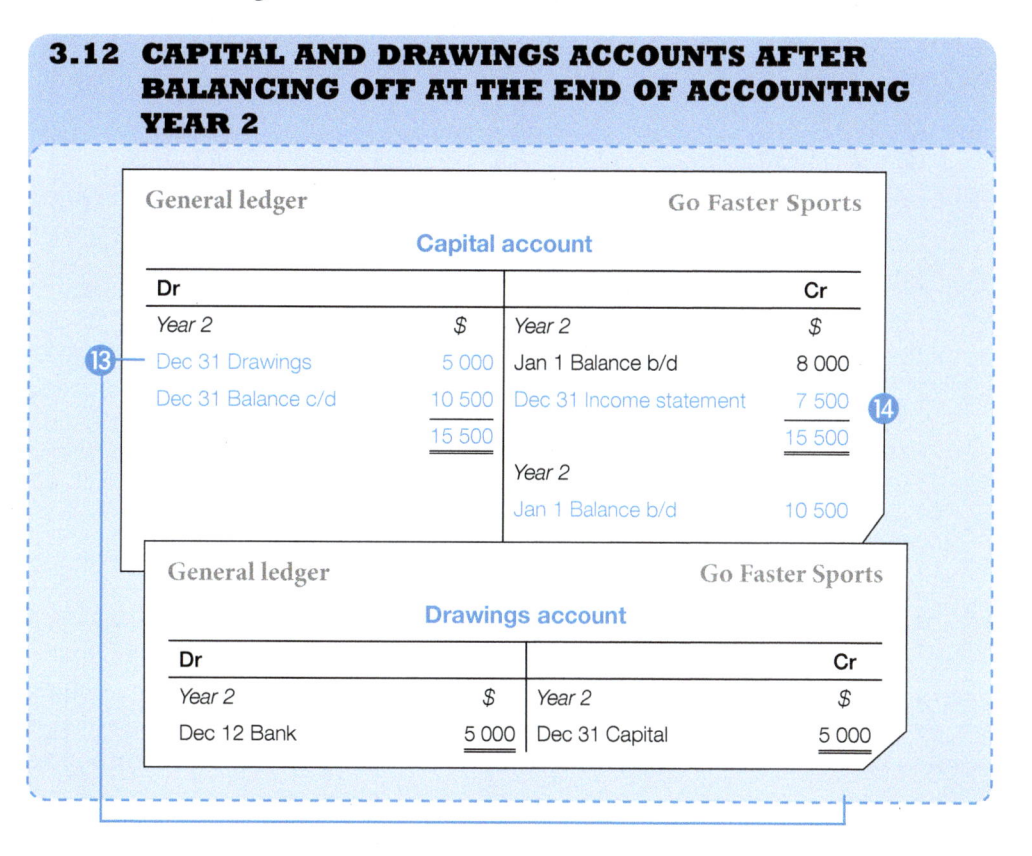

General ledger — Go Faster Sports

Capital account

Dr			Cr	
Year 2	$	Year 2	$	
Dec 31 Drawings	5 000	Jan 1 Balance b/d	8 000	
Dec 31 Balance c/d	10 500	Dec 31 Income statement	7 500	
	15 500		15 500	
		Year 2		
		Jan 1 Balance b/d	10 500	

General ledger — Go Faster Sports

Drawings account

Dr			Cr
Year 2	$	Year 2	$
Dec 12 Bank	5 000	Dec 31 Capital	5 000

Income statements 297

As the updated capital account in illustration 3.12 shows, Jamila's closing equity at the end of year 2 was $10 500 – up from $8 000 at the start of the year after adding profit for the year and deducting drawings. Her closing equity is shown as the balance brought down in her capital account.

This meant Jamila had kept or retained $2 500 of profit in her business (profit for the year of $7 500 less drawings of $5 000).

> Retained profit = Profit for the year – Drawings
> Closing capital = Opening capital + Retained profit

ACTIVITY 3.4

1. Complete the words and figures missing in the income statement below.

JP Drexwell
Income Statement For Year Ended 31 December 2013

Dr	$	$	Cr	$	$
Purchases	140 000		Sales	190 000	
less purchases returns	10 000		less	14 000	
Cost of sales					
		176 000			176 000
Rent	5 400		Gross profit b/d		
Electricity	2 000				
Wages	15 000				
Insurance	600				
Loan interest	500				
Profit for the year					

2. The debit balance on the drawings account at the end of the accounting year was $12 500. Use this information and profit for the year from the income statement to update and balance off the capital account of JP Drexwell below.

General ledger — **JP Drexwell**

Capital account

Dr		Cr
		$
	Jan 1 Balance b/d	25 000

3.1.5 The impact of unsold inventory on gross profit

Goods purchased but not sold during the accounting year will not contribute to the cost of sales and gross profit for that year

During her first two years in business Jamila was able to sell all the sportswear she purchased. This meant she had no unsold goods left over at the end of each year. She was able to calculate her gross profit very simply by deducting her net purchases from her revenue from sales, net of sales returns.

However, it is more usual for a business to have some unsold goods remaining at the end of its accounting year and this will affect the calculation of gross profit.

We will now examine the impact of unsold goods on the preparation of Jamila's income statement for Go Faster Sports at the end of its third accounting year. At the end of that year Jamila had unsold goods remaining in her business valued at $9 000. She made a note of this fact at the bottom of her trial balance for the year as shown in illustration 3.13.

3.13 THE TRIAL BALANCE FOR GO FASTER SPORTS AT THE END OF ACCOUNTING YEAR 3

Go Faster Sports
Trial Balance For Year 3 At 31 December

	Dr $	Cr $
Sales		120 000
Sale returns	6 000	
Purchases	96 000	
Purchases returns		5 000
Rent	9 000	
Electricity	3 200	
Advertising	2 500	
Sundry expenses	1 500	
Equipment	9 500	
Bank	5 300	
Sports Mart Ltd. (trade payable)		4 500
Drawings	7 000	
Opening equity (at the start of year 3)		10 500
	140 000	140 000

Note:
Closing inventory was valued at $9 000 at 31 December

The trial balance shows Jamila had net sales of $114 000 and net purchases of $91 000 during her third accounting year. It would appear that she had made a gross profit from sales of $23 000 (revenue of $114 000 less net purchases of $91 000).

However, the note Jamila made to her trial balance records unsold sportswear at the end of that year – a **closing inventory** – valued at $9 000. As these unsold goods had not contributed to her sales during the year their cost had to be excluded from the calculation of her gross profit from sales that year.

To calculate gross profit Jamila had to do the following:

- Deduct closing inventory from the debit balance for net purchases to find the cost of goods actually sold during the year (the cost of sales).

- Deduct the cost of sales from the credit balance for revenue from net sales.

Her calculation of gross profit for that year was as follows:

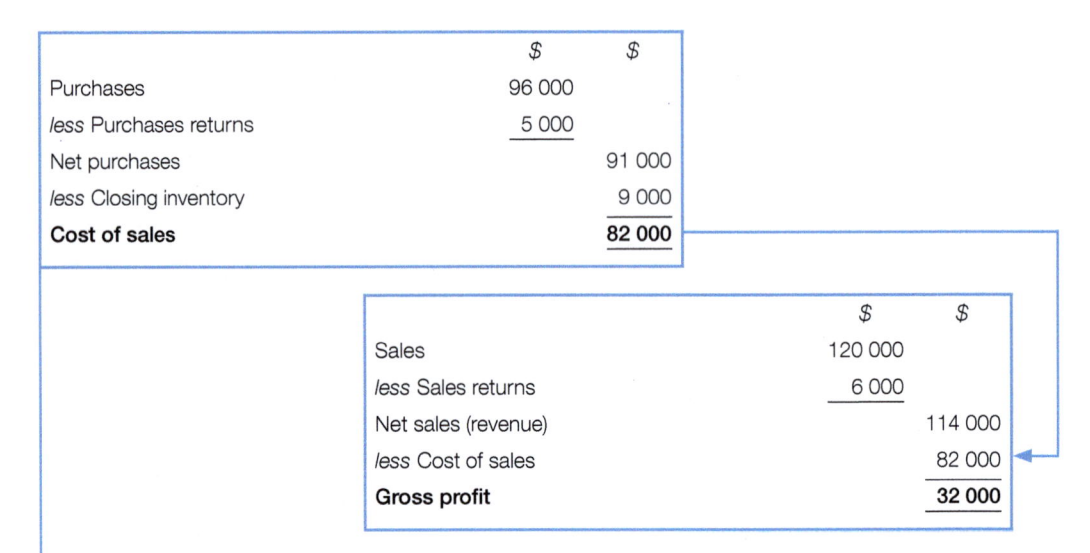

	$	$
Purchases		96 000
less Purchases returns		5 000
Net purchases		91 000
less Closing inventory		9 000
Cost of sales		**82 000**

	$	$
Sales		120 000
less Sales returns		6 000
Net sales (revenue)		114 000
less Cost of sales		82 000
Gross profit		**32 000**

These adjustments are shown in the first part of Jamila's income statement for year 3 in illustration 3.14.

3.14 RECORDING A CLOSING INVENTORY IN THE FIRST PART OF THE INCOME STATEMENT

Go Faster Sports

Income Statement For Year 2 Ended 31 December

Dr			Cr		
	$	$		$	$
Purchases	96 000		Sales	120 000	
less Purchases returns	5 000		less Sales returns	6 000	
	91 000				114 000
less Closing inventory	9 000				
Cost of sales		82 000			
Gross profit c/d		32 000			
		114 000			114 000

Unsold goods – or **closing inventory** – is a current asset because the goods can be sold to raise revenue in the next accounting year. As a result, it is necessary to record the asset in the general ledger of the business so it can be included in the statement of financial position. ▶ **3.2**

3.15 RECORDING A CLOSING INVENTORY IN THE GENERAL LEDGER

General ledger   Go Faster Sport

Inventory account

Dr		Cr
Year 3	$	
Dec 31 Income statement	9 000	

Illustration 3.15 shows how Jamila recorded her closing inventory as a debit balance in her ledger account for inventory at the end of her second accounting year.

You may remember from section 3.1.2 that when all goods purchased are sold during the same accounting year gross profit is calculated very simply as follows:

Gross profit = Revenue − Cost of sales

where: cost of sales = net purchases

But if there are unsold goods at the end of the accounting year then:

Gross profit = Revenue − Cost of sales

where: cost of sales = net purchases − closing inventory

3.16 GO FASTER SPORTS INCOME STATEMENT FOR ACCOUNTING YEAR 3

Go Faster Sports

Income Statement For Year 3 Ended 31 December

Dr				Cr	
	$	$		$	$
Purchases	96 000		Sales	120 000	
less Purchases returns	5 000		less Sales returns	6 000	
	91 000				114 000
less Closing inventory	9 000				
Cost of sales		82 000			
Gross profit c/d		32 000			
		114 000			114 000
			Gross profit b/d		32 000
Rent	9 000				
Electricity	3 200				
Advertising	2 500				
Sundry expenses	1 500				
		16 200			
Profit for the year		15 800			
		32 000			32 000

After calculating a gross profit of $32 000 Jamila completed the income statement for her third accounting year with the debit balances for expenses from the trial balance for year 3 in illustration 3.13.

With total expenses of $16 200 Jamila's profit for the year from Go Faster Sports was $15 800, more than doubling what she had earned from her business in year 2. Jamila's full income statement for her third accounting year in business is shown in illustration 3.16.

ACTIVITY 3.5

Use the jumbled information below taken from the books of a business to calculate:

(a) net sales or revenue;
(b) net purchases;
(c) cost of sales;
(d) gross profit;
(e) profit for the year;
(f) increase in owner's equity.

Balances at end of year ended 31 March 2013	
	$
Purchases returns	13 450
Sales	121 900
Closing inventory	12 600
Sales returns	18 300
Purchases	67 700
Total expenses	22 730
Drawings	25 000

During her third accounting year Jamila had withdrawn a total of $7 000 from the business bank account for her own personal use. This meant the profit retained in her business was $8 800 (profit of $15 800 less drawings of $7 000)

The retained profit increased her owner's equity in the business from $10 500 at the start of the year to $19 300 by the year end. This is shown as the balance carried down in the updated capital account in illustration 3.17.

3.17 CAPITAL AND DRAWINGS ACCOUNTS AFTER BALANCING OFF AT THE END OF ACCOUNTING YEAR 3

General ledger — Go Faster Sports

Capital account

Dr				Cr
Year 3	$	Year 3		$
Dec 31 Drawings	7 000	Jan 1 Balance b/d		10 500
Dec 31 Balance c/d	19 300	Dec 31 Income statement		15 800
	26 300			26 300
		Year 4		
		Jan 1 Balance b/d		19 300

General ledger — Go Faster Sports

Drawings account

Dr				Cr
Year 3		$	Year 3	$
Oct 27	Bank	3 000	Dec 31 Capital	7 000
Nov 29	Bank	4 000		
		7 000		

The closing inventory at the end of one accounting year will be the opening inventory available for sale from the start of the next year

Jamila's closing inventory of $9 000 of unsold sportswear items at the end of year 3 were available to sell for revenue during her fourth accounting year. Her closing inventory became her opening inventory in the following accounting year.

Opening inventory at the start of an accounting year will contribute to the cost of sales and gross profit for that year. It must be recorded in the income statement for the year. Jamila did this by crediting her inventory account with the closing inventory from year 3 and transferring it to the debit column of her income statement for year 4 as shown in illustration 3.18.

3.18 RECORDING AN OPENING INVENTORY IN THE GENERAL LEDGER

General ledger — Go Faster Sports

Inventory account

Dr			Cr
Year 3	$	Year 4	$
Dec 31 Income statement	9 000	Dec 31 Income statement	9 000

Closing inventory at the end of the previous year

Opening inventory at the start of the year

The inventory account in the general ledger is only ever used once at the end of each accounting year:

(1) to record the opening inventory and transfer it to the income statement;

(2) to record the closing inventory as a current asset available to sell in the next accounting year to show in the statement of financial position of the business. ➤ 3.2

It is important to record opening and closing inventory in this way because they will affect both the calculation of gross profit in the income statement and the calculation of current assets in the statement of financial position.

Jamila's trial balance for year 4 shown in illustration 3.19 records her opening inventory for the year in the debit column. The closing inventory of $12 000 of unsold goods that she ended the same year with was in turn recorded as a note to the trial balance.

3.19 THE TRIAL BALANCE FOR GO FASTER SPORTS AT THE END OF ACCOUNTING YEAR 4

Go Faster Sports

Trial Balance For Year 4 At 31 December

	Dr $	Cr $
Sales		135 000
Sale returns	8 000	
Purchases	98 000	
Purchases returns		5 400
Opening inventory (at the start of the year)	9 000	
	9 600	
Rent	3 300	
Electricity	2 800	
Advertising	1 700	
Sundry expenses	13 200	
Equipment	7 400	
Bank		5 300
Sports Mart Ltd. (trade payable)	12 000	
Drawings		19 300
Opening equity (at the start of year 4)	165 000	165 000

Note:
Closing inventory valued at $12 000 at 31 December

As Jamila was able to sell all the items in her opening inventory during year 4 they contributed to revenue for the year and it was necessary to include their cost in the calculation of the cost of sales and gross profit as follows:

- Credit the inventory account with $9 000 of opening inventory and debit the income statement.

- Add net purchases of $92 600 ($98 000 *less* purchases returns of $5 400) to the opening inventory to find the total cost of goods available to sell during the year, $101 600 ($9 000 *add* $92 600).

Income statements 303

- Deduct $12 000 of goods unsold at the end of the year (closing inventory) from the sum of opening inventory plus net purchases to find the cost of goods actually sold during the year: a cost of sales of $89 600 ($101 600 less $12 000).
- Finally, deduct the cost of goods sold, $89 600, from the credit balance for revenue, $127 000, to calculate gross profit of $37 400.

Jamila's calculation of gross profit for year 4 was as follows:

	$	$
Opening inventory		9 000
Purchases	98 000	
less Purchases returns	5 400	
Net purchases		92 600
Cost of goods available to sell		101 600
less Closing inventory (unsold goods)		12 000
Cost of sales		**89 600**

	$	$
Sales		135 000
less Sales returns		8 000
Net sales (revenue)		127 000
less Cost of sales		89 600
Gross profit		**37 400**

Jamila recorded revenue of $127 000, a cost of sales of $89 600 and a gross profit of $37 400 in the first part of her income statement for her fourth accounting year as shown in illustration 3.20.

ACTIVITY 3.6

1. Complete the second part of Jamila's income statement for Go Faster Sports in illustration 3.20. Bring down gross profit to the credit side and then use the debit balances for expenses recorded in her trial balance in illustration 3.19 to calculate and show:

   (a) total expenses;

   (b) profit for the year.

   Remember to balance off the two sides of the income statement.

2. Update Jamila's capital and drawings account at the end of year 3 from illustration 3.17 with her drawings and profit for year 4.

   (a) How much profit did she retain in the business?

   (b) How much was her closing equity at the end of accounting year 4?

3.20 RECORDING OPENING AND CLOSING INVENTORY IN THE FIRST PART OF THE INCOME STATEMENT

Go Faster Sports
Income Statement For Year 4 Ended 31 December

Dr	$	$	Cr	$	$
Opening inventory		9 000	Sales		135 000
Purchases	98 000		less Sales returns		8 000
less Purchases returns	5 400				127 000
		92 600			
		101 600			
less Closing inventory		12 000			
Cost of sales		89 600			
Gross profit c/d		**37 400**			
		127 000			127 000

When there are unsold goods both at the start and end of an accounting year gross profit is calculated in an income statement as follows:

> Gross profit = Revenue − Cost of sales
>
> where: cost of sales = opening inventory + net purchases − closing inventory

3.1.6 The impact of carriage charges on profit

Separate charges for the carriage or delivery of goods purchased and sold will affect the calculation of profit in the income statement

We now jump another year to the end of Jamila's fifth accounting year. The trial balance she produced at the end of the year from all the balances on the accounts in her ledger is shown in illustration 3.21.

3.21 THE TRIAL BALANCE FOR GO FASTER SPORTS AT THE END OF ACCOUNTING YEAR 5

Go Faster Sports

Trial Balance For Year 5 At 31 December

	Dr $	Cr $
Sales		159 000
Sale returns	4 000	
Purchases	115 000	
Purchases returns		900
Carriage inwards	3 900	
Carriage outwards	1 500	
Opening inventory (at the start of the year)	12 000	
Rent	9 600	
Electricity	3 400	
Advertising	2 800	
Sundry expenses	1 700	
Equipment	14 100	
Trade receivables	1 400	
Bank	5 600	
Fast Fashions plc (trade payable)		2 800
Drawings	15 000	
Opening equity (at the start of year 5)		27 300
	190 000	190 000

Note:
Closing inventory was valued at $16 000 at 31 December

In the trial balance you will see that closing inventory of $12 000 at the end of year 4 became the opening inventory for year 5.

You will also notice two new balances were recorded in the trial balance:

- A debit balance of $3 900 was recorded for **carriage inwards** from the carriage inwards account in the general ledger. Carriage inwards are delivery charges paid to a supplier. They are an additional cost of making purchases.

- A debit balance of $1 500 was recorded for **carriage outwards** from the carriage outwards account in the general ledger. Carriage outwards are charges incurred posting or delivering goods to customers. They are an additional operating expense and will increase the total expenses of the business.

The inclusion of carriage inwards and outwards in the trial balance will affect the calculation of gross profit and profit for the year in the income statement.

Carriage inwards will increase the cost of purchases and reduce gross profit

During her fifth accounting year Jamila changed her main supplier of sports wear from Sports Mart Ltd. to Fast Fashion Ltd. Unlike her previous supplier, Fast Fashion Ltd. charged separately to deliver items she had purchased. She recorded these charges as carriage inwards in a separate account in her ledger. However, carriage inwards was an additional cost she incurred making purchases.

To calculate the total cost of her purchases of goods for resale in her income statement Jamila had to add the debit balance for carriage inwards to the debit balance for purchases. Then to calculate the total cost of only those goods she sold during the year Jamila had to adjust for purchases returns and unsold items as follows:

	$	$
Opening inventory		12 000
Purchases	115 000	
add Carriage inwards	3 900	
less Purchases returns	900	
Net purchases		118 000
Cost of goods available to sell		130 000
less Closing inventory		16 000
Cost of sales		**114 000**

	$	$
Sales		159 000
less Sales returns		4 000
Net sales (revenue)		155 000
less Cost of sales		114 000
Gross profit		**41 000**

Carriage inwards charges of $3 900 over the year had increased her cost of purchases from $115 000 to $118 900. After deducting purchases returns of $900 during the year Jamila's net purchases for the year had cost her business $118 000.

3.22 RECORDING CARRIAGE INWARDS IN THE FIRST PART OF THE INCOME STATEMENT

Go Faster Sports

Income Statement For Year 5 Ended 31 December

Dr					Cr
	$	$		$	$
Opening inventory		12 000	Sales	159 000	
Purchases	115 000		less Sales returns	4 000	
add Carriage inwards	3 900				155 000
less Purchases returns	900				
		118 000			
		130 000			
less Closing inventory		16 000			
Cost of sales		114 000			
Gross profit c/d		**41 000**			
		155 000			155 000

To write up the first part of her income statement Jamila added her net purchases of $118 000 to her opening inventory at the start of the year of $9 000 and then deducted closing inventory of $16 000 at the end of the year. This sum gave her the cost of goods she actually sold during the year: $114 000.

Gross profit was $41 000 – the difference between revenue from net sales of $155 000 and a cost of sales of $114 000 – and is shown in illustration 3.22 in the first part of Jamila's income statement for year 5.

Charges for carriage inwards are included in the calculation of costs of sales and gross profit as follows:

> Gross profit = Revenue – Cost of sales
>
> where: cost of sales = opening inventory + net purchases – closing inventory
> net purchases = purchases + carriage inwards – purchases returns

Carriage outwards is a business expense and will reduce profit for the year

During year 5 Jamila began to advertise and sell her sportswear online. Although this enabled her to reach more customers and increase sales, it also meant she incurred additional costs from posting or arranging delivery of items to customers who had purchased them over the Internet.

Carriage outwards charges are incurred by a business when transporting or delivering goods to customers. They are an additional operating expense and will increase total expenses recorded in the second part of an income statement and reduce profit for the year.

Income statements

Jamila wrote up the second part of her income statement with carriage outwards expenses as follows:

- Credit the carriage outwards account with its final debit balance to close the account.
- Debit the income statement with the closing balance for carriage outwards

From her trial balance for her fifth accounting year in illustration 3.21 Jamila completed her income statement for the year as shown in illustration 3.23 below.

3.23 GO FASTER SPORTS INCOME STATEMENT FOR ACCOUNTING YEAR 5

Go Faster Sports

Income Statement For Year 5 Ended 31 December

Dr	$	$	Cr	$	$
Opening inventory		12 000	Sales	159 000	
Purchases	115 000		less Sales returns	4 000	
add Carriage inwards	3 900				155 000
less Purchases returns	900				
		118 000			
		130 000			
less Closing inventory		16 000			
Cost of sales		114 000			
Gross profit c/d		41 000			
		155 000			155 000
			Gross profit b/d		41 000
Rent	9 600				
Electricity	3 100				
Advertising	3 000				
Sundry expenses	1 800				
Carriage outwards	1 500				
		19 000			
Profit for the year		22 000			
		41 000			41 000

ACTIVITY 3.7

Rahul Sababady has provided some details about his business at the end of his second accounting year ending 30 June 2013.

(a) Use the information provided to write up Rahul's income statement for the year ended 30 June 2013 (i) first using a horizontal format then; (ii) using a vertical format.

(b) If Rahul's drawings during the year were $20 000 by how much had the value of his net assets changed by the end of his second year of trading?

(c) What was the value of Rahul's closing equity on 30 June?

	$
Sale	93 000
Sales returns	5 400
Purchases	47 800
Purchases returns	5 000
Carriage inwards	2 000
Carriage outwards	1 000
Rent	10 000
Electricity	3 000
Insurance	2 800
Cleaning and maintenance	2 100
Sundry expenses	900
Opening inventory (1/7/12)	12 900
Closing inventory (30/6/13)	16 900
Opening equity (1/7/12)	25 000

An income statement will usually be prepared using a vertical format

Most businesses now use a vertical format for their end-of-year financial statements. Vertical presentations are often easier to follow and involve simpler arithmetical calculations to derive gross profit and profit for the year.

Illustration 3.24 reproduces the income statement from 3.23 in a vertical format. Apart from their different layouts they are identical in every other way. The final column in the vertical income statement has been used to record the most important figures for revenue, cost of sales, gross profit, total expenses and profit for the year. The middle column shows how key figures were calculated.

3.24 GO FASTER SPORTS INCOME STATEMENT FOR ACCOUNTING YEAR 5 IN A VERTICAL FORMAT

Go Faster Sports
Income Statement For Year 5 Ended 31 December

	Dr $	Cr $
Sales		159 000
less Sales returns		4 000
		155 000
less Cost of sales:		
Opening inventory	12 000	
add Purchases	115 000	
add Carriage inwards	3 900	
less Purchases returns	900	
less Closing inventory	16 000	
		114 000
Gross profit		41 000
less expenses		
Rent	9 600	
Electricity	3 100	
Advertising	3 000	
Sundry expenses	1 800	
Carriage outwards	1 500	
		19 000
Profit for the year		**22 000**

> **Preparing a simple income statement: a checklist**
>
> ✓ First prepare a trial balance of all the debit and credit balances on ledger accounts at the end of the accounting year. Total debits must equal total credits. If they do not, check and correct your ledger accounts and then check the trial balance for any errors.
>
> ✓ Note the cost of any unsold goods at the year end – or **closing inventory** – below the trial balance.
>
> ✓ Transfer balances for sales, purchases, returns, carriage inwards, inventory and expenses to the first part of the income statement. Remember that each balance in the trial balance can only be used once in the financial statements.
>
> ✓ Calculate **gross profit (or loss)** from sales in the first part (trading account) of the income statement as **revenue – costs of sales**.
>
> ✓ If some sales were returned during the year then **revenue = sales – sales returns**.
>
> ✓ To calculate the **cost of sales**:
>
> | If all purchases were sold | If there were purchases returns | If there was a closing inventory | If there were opening and closing inventories | If there were also charges for carriage inwards |
> |---|---|---|---|---|
> | | | | Opening inventory | Opening inventory |
> | Purchases | Purchases | Purchases | add purchases | add purchases |
> | | | | | add carriage inwards |
> | | less purchases returns | less purchases returns | less purchases returns | less purchases returns |
> | | | less closing inventory | less closing inventory | less closing inventory |
>
> ✓ Calculate **profit (or loss) for the year** in the second part (profit and loss account) of the income statement as **gross profit – total expenses**.
>
> ✓ Remember to record profit for the year as a debit in a horizontal income statement to balance the two sides of the statement.

3.1.7 Recording a loss for the year

If total expenses exceed gross profit a business will record a loss for the year

Jamila's sportswear business, Go Faster Sports, operates at a profit. The profit she makes each year adds to the amount of net assets and capital available to her business. But what happens when a business operates at a loss?

Yash set up a small online business selling computer parts. The balances on his books at the end of his first year of trading are listed in illustration 3.25 and were used to write up the horizontal income statement in illustration 3.26.

3.25 YASH'S BALANCES AT THE END OF YEAR 1

Yash Computer Sales
Balances At The End Of The Year

	$
Sales	36 000
Purchases	27 000
Carriage outwards	3 500
Telephone	1 500
Other expenses	8 000
Equipment	3 400
Cash at bank	550
Equity (at the start of the year)	4 000

Note:
Closing inventory at the year end was valued at $3 000

Despite being able to sell his goods at a price greater than their cost to make a gross profit, Yash failed to control his business expenses and has been running his business at a **net loss** – or **loss for the year**.

That is, his total expenses for the year of $13 000 exceeded his gross profit from sales of $12 000 by $1 000. If Yash continues to operate at a loss he may be forced to close his business.

3.26 AN INCOME STATEMENT RECORDING A NET LOSS

Yash Computer Sales
Income Statement For Year Ended 31 December

Dr					Cr
	$	$			$
Purchases	27 000		Sales		36 000
less Closing inventory	3 000				
		24 000			
Gross profit c/d		12 000			
		36 000			36 000
			Gross profit b/d		12 000
Carriage outwards		3 500			
Telephone		1 500			
Other expenses		8 000	Loss for the year		1 000
		13 000			13 000

A net loss will reduce net assets and the owner's equity

Notice that the loss is recorded on the credit side of the income statement shown in illustration 3.26. This is because the debit balance for expenses exceeds the credit balance for gross profit brought down. Loss for the year must be entered as a credit to balance the two sides of the statement.

The double entry for a loss recorded as a credit in the income statement is a debit to the capital account, as shown in illustration 3.27.

Income statements   311

3.27 CAPITAL ACCOUNT SHOWING THE IMPACT OF A LOSS

General ledger — Yash Computer Sales

Capital account

Dr				Cr
Year 1	$	Year 1		$
Dec 31 Income statement	1 000	Jan 1 Bank		4 000
Dec 31 Balance c/d	3 000			
	4 000			4 000
		Year 2		
		Jan 1 Balance b/d		3 000

The debit to the capital account shows that the loss of $1 000 reduced the net assets of Yash's business and owner's equity from $4 000 to $3 000. This is because the asset of cash in the bank decreased as cash paid out for purchases and expense items over the year exceeded revenue received.

ACTIVITY 3.8

1 A retailer has provided the following information for the year ended 31 July. Calculate:

	$
Opening inventory	18 000
Purchases	370 000
Carriage inwards	25 000
Revenue	500 000
Closing inventory	23 000
Total expenses	120 000
Drawings	30 000

(a) the cost of sales;

(b) gross profit;

(c) profit or loss for the year;

(d) the change in the owner's equity.

2 Write up the income statement for Yash's Computer Sales shown in illustration 3.26 in a vertical format.

3 The trial balance opposite is for a small, loss-making business.

(a) Prepare the income statement of the business for the accounting year ended 31 March 2013.

(b) Draw up the capital account showing the balances for drawings, loss for the year and capital at 31 March 2013.

Trial balance as at 31 March 2013

	Dr $	Cr $
Sales		67 500
Sales returns	7 600	
Purchases	42 400	
Purchases returns		3 500
Opening inventory	7 980	
Expenses	32 950	
Fixtures and equipment		10 300
Trade receivables	830	
Trade payables		3 810
Bank		3 200
Opening equity		9 400
Drawings	5 950	
	97 710	97 710

Note:
Closing inventory at 31 March was valued at $15 800.

3.1.8 Departmental accounts

It is important to identify the contribution to profit or loss of each department in a business

Jamila's friend Fabrice owns and manages a combined art and book store. His shop made a total profit of $18 000 in his last accounting year ended 31 December. However, at that time Fabrice was unaware of the following contributions to his profit for the year:

Fabrice: profit for the year	$	
Book department	28 620	Profit
Art department	10 620	Loss
Combined profit	**18 000**	

His profit for the year was entirely due to buying and selling books. In contrast, the sale of papers, paints, brushes and other art materials and equipment resulted in a loss for the year of $8 620. If Fabrice had shut down his art department and only sold books he may have made a profit for the year of $28 620.

It is important for a business with two or more different departments to prepare **departmental accounts** showing how much profit or loss each department has made. This is because the losses made by one or more departments may be hidden by the profits made by others.

By preparing a separate account for each department a business can identify its best and worst performing departments so that it is able to:

- identify the contribution to profit (or loss) of each department
- identify and investigate poor performance
- reward managers and employees fairly in each department for good performance
- improve overall profitability by taking action to improve the performance of poor performing departments or by closing down loss making ones.

A departmental income statement should be prepared with a separate column to show the income, expenses and profit or loss of each department

Jamila had suggested to Fabrice that it was sensible for him start producing departmental accounts. This would require him to:

- record the purchases, purchases returns, sales and sales returns of each department separately in his journals using analysis columns
- value the inventory of each department separately at the start and end of the accounting year

Income statements

- prepare a departmental income statement with separate columns showing the gross profit and profit or loss for the year of each department (also known as **columnar trading and profit and loss accounts**).

With Jamila's help Fabrice was able to extract the following information from the books he maintained over his previous accounting year:

	Art Department $	Book Department $
Sales	40 000	73 000
Sales returns	10 000	3 000
Purchases	35 000	31 000
Purchases returns	5 700	3 400
Carriage inwards	2 100	1 500
Opening inventory at 1 January	12 700	5 800
Closing inventory at 31 December	17 000	5 200

From this information Fabrice was then able to prepare the following departmental trading account for his accounting year ended 31 December.

3.28 A DEPARTMENTAL TRADING ACCOUNT FOR A BUSINESS WITH TWO DEPARTMENTS

Fabrice

Departmental Trading Account For Year Ended 31 December

	Art Department $	$	Book Department $	$	Total $	$
Sales		40 000		73 000		113 000
less Sales returns		10 000		3 000		13 000
Revenue		30 000		70 000		100 000
less Cost of Sales:						
Opening inventory	12 700		5 800		18 500	
add Purchases	35 000		31 000		66 000	
add Carriage inwards	1 800		1 500		3 600	
	49 800		38 300		88 100	
less Purchases returns	5 700		3 400		9 100	
	44 100		34 900		79 000	
less Closing inventory	17 000		5 200		22 200	
		27 100		29 700		56 800
Gross profit		2 900		40 300		43 200

The trading account, being the first part of the income statement, records the gross profit of each department as well as their combined gross profit. It is clear from the account that the art department contributed just 30% of total revenue and that the margin for gross profit in revenue from sales of art equipment and materials was low. To improve this Fabrice could consider increasing his selling prices, although this might reduce sales, or finding cheaper suppliers of these products. ▶ **5.1**

Expenses will need to be shared between departments in proportion to their sales, the floor space they occupy or using other valid allocation methods

Business expenses including advertising, electricity, insurance, cleaning and office costs are difficult to identify and record separately for each department. Therefore, to complete his departmental income statement for the year Fabrice had to find a way to allocate a proportion of his business expenses to each department.

Where possible each type of expense should be charged to departments according to the benefit each department receives from each expense. So, for example, if Fabrice spent most of his advertising budget on the advertising of books then he should charge the largest proportion of total advertising expenses to his book department. Similarly, if the art department takes up more floor space in his shop than his book department then it may be appropriate to charge more cleaning expenses to his art department than to his book department.

There are several ways Fabrice can allocate the expenses of his business between its different departments. These include the following.

▼ Methods used to allocate expenses to different business departments

Type of expenses	Allocation method
Wages and salaries	Total wage or employment costs per department
Depreciation of non-current assets	By separately identifying the cost or book value of each type of equipment or other non-current asset or assets used in each department, or
	In proportion to the total cost or book value of the non-current assets employed in each department
Rent, electricity, insurance, cleaning, etc.	In proportion to the floor space occupied by each department
Advertising	In proportion to the sales of each department
Office expenses including stationery, postage, etc.	In proportion to the sales of each department, or
	In proportion to the number of employees in each department

Different businesses may adopt different methods or policies to determine how to allocate their expenses to their different departments. However, it is important that each expense is allocated to each department in the most appropriate way possible so that income statements provide fair and reasonable measures of the profits or losses of each department. ► 5.2

Fabrice extracted the following balances from his books at the end of his accounting year.

Expenses	$
Wages	10 000
Provision for depreciation of fixtures and fittings	4 000
Rent	6 000
Electricity	1 600
Insurance	1 000
Cleaning	600
Advertising	2 000

He also provided the following additional information about his business:

- 70% of total revenue was from book sales and 30% from art sales
- two part-time employees were employed, one in each department
- the art department occupies 60% of the total floor space of the shop and the book department occupies the remaining 40%
- the net book values of fixtures and fittings on 1 January were as follows:

    Art Department $12 000

    Book Department $8 000

- depreciation of fixtures and fittings is charged at 20% of their net book value at the start of each accounting year.

Using this information Fabrice allocated the expenses to the art and book departments of his business as shown:

▼ Allocation of expenses to departments in Fabrice's art and book store

Expenses $	Allocation method	Art Department Workings	$	Book Department Workings	$
Wages $10 000	Actual costs		5 000		5 000
Depreciation $4 000	Net book value of fixtures & fittings	20% of $12 000	2 400	20% of $8 000	1 600
Rent $6 000	Floor space	60% of $6 000	3 600	40% of $6 000	2 400
Electricity $1 600	Floor space	60% of $1 600	960	40% of $1 600	640
Insurance $1 000	Floor space	60% of $1 000	600	40% of $1 000	400
Cleaning $600	Floor space	60% of $600	360	40% of $600	240
Advertising $2 000	Sales	30% of $2 000	600	70% of $2 000	1 400

Once Fabrice had calculated the expenses to allocate to his two departments he was able to prepare the income statement shown in illustration 3.29. This he did in exactly the same way as he would any other income statement except that a departmental income statement contains separate statements of the profit or loss of each department side-by-side as well as a total column showing the total income, expenses and profit or loss for the entire business.

3.29 A DEPARTMENTAL INCOME STATEMENT FOR A BUSINESS WITH TWO DEPARTMENTS

Fabrice

Departmental Income Statement For Year Ended 31 December

	Art Department		Book Department		Total	
	$	$	$	$	$	$
Sales		40 000		73 000		113 000
less Sales returns		10 000		3 000		13 000
Revenue		30 000		70 000		100 000
less Cost of Sales:						
Opening inventory	12 700		5 800		18 500	
add Purchases	35 000		31 000		66 000	
add Carriage inwards	1 800		1 500		3 600	
	49 800		38 300		88 100	
less Purchases returns	5 700		3 400		9 100	
	44 100		34 900		79 000	
less Closing inventory	17 000		5 200		22 200	
		27 100		29 700		56 800
Gross profit		2 900		40 300		43 200
less Expenses:						
Wages	5 000		5 000		10 000	
Depreciation	2 400		1 600		4 000	
Rent	3 600		2 400		6 000	
Electricity	960		640		1 600	
Insurance	600		400		1 000	
Cleaning	360		240		600	
Advertising	600		1 400		2 000	
		13 520		11 680		25 200
Profit (or loss) for the year		(10 620)		28 620		18 020

A decision to close a poor performing department should be based on an analysis of the impact it could have on the whole business

The departmental income statement produced by Fabrice revealed that his art department was running at a loss. Overall profitability would have been higher without the art department. Fabrice must consider whether or not to close his art department, do something different or concentrate his business solely on the sale of books.

However, before Fabrice makes such a decision he should first investigate the causes of the poor performance of his art department and any improvements he could make to generate a profit. For example, is he selling the right materials and equipment? He could investigate which products are most in demand and focus on these. He could also try to increase their selling prices and source cheaper suppliers of the items to increase gross profit. Increased advertising might also help to boost sales.

Other factors Fabrice should consider will include:

- whether he has allocated his business expenses to the department in the most appropriate way. This will affect the calculation of the profit or loss for the year from the department. For example, if Fabrice had simply divided his rent, electricity, insurance and cleaning expenses equally between his two departments the loss made by his art department would have been $10 020 instead of $10 620.

- how closure of the department will affect the sales and profitability of other departments. Fabrice sells many art books to artists who visit his store to buy art materials and equipment. If he did not sell these he would attract fewer customers to his shop and sell fewer art books which would reduce the sales and profits of his book department.

- how else he can use the floor space freed up by closure of the art department. Should he expand his book department or find something else to sell or even sub-let (lease) the space to another business to use to earn rental income?

- how closure of the department will affect the expenses of the art department. Savings may be small. Many expenses, including rent, electricity and cleaning would remain unchanged unless Fabrice moved to smaller and cheaper premises. The costs of advertising his shop would also be unchanged. However, the cost of employing one part-time employee could be saved if Fabrice closed his art department and terminated (ended) the employment of one of his employees.

QUICK TEST

1. (i) What is gross profit and how is it calculated?
   (ii) What is profit for the year (or net profit) and how is it calculated?

2. A business purchases goods from suppliers to sell on to its customers. Explain why its cost of sales during an accounting year is unlikely to be the same as its total purchases of goods for resale over the same period.

3. Explain how a business that has made a gross profit from sales could record a net loss or loss for the year over the same period.

4. Explain how profit for the year increases the net assets of the business.

5. Why is profit for the year credited to the capital account at the end of an accounting year?

6. Amrita owns a flower shop. The following balances were taken from her books at the end of her last accounting year ending 31 October. Prepare a simple income statement for her business for the year ended 31 October using a horizontal format.

	$
Sales	465 000
Sales returns	14 000
Purchases	300 000
Purchases returns	6 000
Opening inventory	35 000
Closing inventory	47 000
Total expenses	52 000

7. The information below is available for two businesses. Both their accounting years ended 30 September last year. Prepare a simple horizontal income statement for each business.

Business A	$
Sales	76 000
Sales returns	1 000
Purchases	39 000
Purchases returns	2 500
Opening inventory	1 500
Closing inventory	3 000
Total expenses	12 000

Business B	$
Sales	45 000
Sales returns	3 000
Purchases	38 000
Purchases returns	1 300
Opening inventory	2 400
Closing inventory	1 800
Total expenses	8 000

8. The information below is from the books of two other businesses. Both their accounting years ended 31 July last year. Prepare a simple vertical income statement for each business.

Business C	$
Sales	333 000
Sales returns	13 000
Purchases	270 000
Carriage inwards	12 000
Purchases returns	16 000
Opening inventory	50 000
Closing inventory	23 000
Total expenses	53 000

Business D	$
Sales	750 000
Sales returns	60 000
Purchases	470 000
Carriage inwards	40 000
Purchases returns	18 900
Opening inventory	58 000
Closing inventory	44 100
Total expenses	75 000

Unit 3.2 Statements of financial position

AIMS

By the end of this unit you should be able to

- understand that statements of financial position record **assets** and **liabilities** on a specified date
- recognise and define the content of a statement of financial position: **non-current assets**, **intangible assets**, **current assets**, **current liabilities**, **non-current liabilities**, and **capital**; also **capital employed** and **capital owned**
- understand the inter-relationship of items in a statement of financial position
- relate **working capital** to the **liquidity** of a business
- understand the basis of valuation of assets as follows:
  - non-current assets at cost less accumulated **depreciation**
  - inventory at the lower of cost or **net realisable value**
  - **trade receivables** at expected collectible amount; that is, after deduction of provisions for doubtful debts
- distinguish between, and show understanding of, **equity** and **capital employed**
- prepare simple inventory valuation statements

3.2.1 Assets and liabilities

A statement of financial position reports the assets, liabilities and owner's equity of a business at a given point in time

A statement of financial position is one of the most important financial statements a business can produce because it reports the financial health of the business at a given point in time.

It does this by identifying everything of value that the business *owns* and the total amount of money it *owes* to other people and organisations on the same day. The difference between the two is the value of the **net assets** of the business at that time. A business that owes more than it owns is clearly one that is not in a very good financial position and may be at risk of closing down if it is unable to raise enough money to pay off its debts.

A statement of financial position records the following financial information about a business, usually on the last day of each accounting year:

Assets: items of value owned by the business

Capital: the amount of money invested in the business

Liabilities: the amount of money owed to external creditors

The financial position of a business will change from day to day with every transaction the business makes. This is because each transaction will affect the value of the assets or liabilities of the business and therefore the amount of owner's equity.

So, for example, when a business borrows money from a bank to buy new equipment its liabilities and assets will increase by the same amount. Similarly, if the owners withdraw cash from their business for their own personal use both the assets and therefore the owner's equity invested in the business will fall. ➤ 1.2

Business assets are things of value owned by a business that are used to generate profit

Business assets are needed to run a business. For example a business needs to hold cash, an inventory of goods for resale, computers, machinery and other equipment. Such assets have value because they enable a business to make sales and generate profit.

Business assets consist of **current assets** and **non-current assets**.

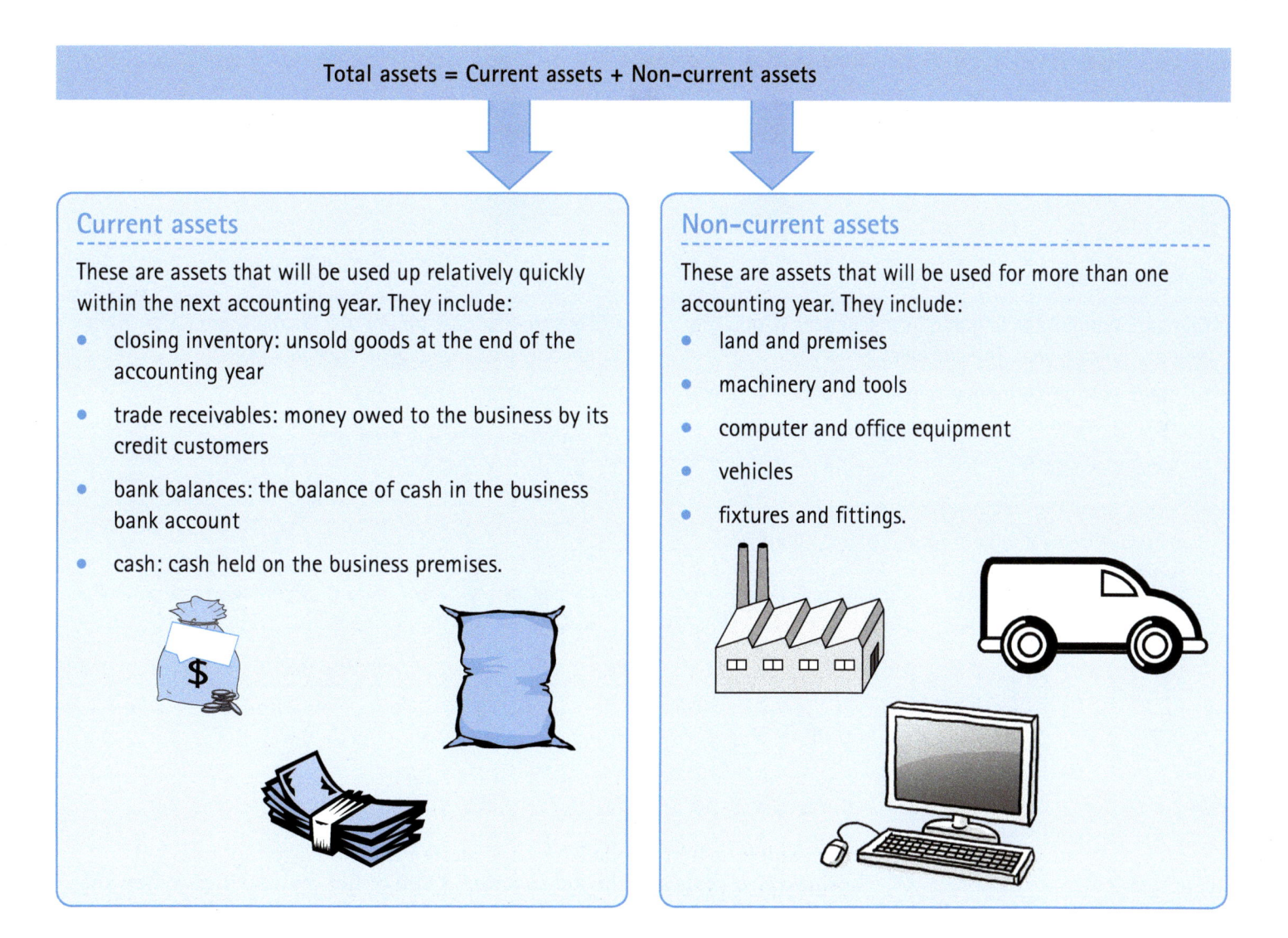

Total assets = Current assets + Non-current assets

Current assets

These are assets that will be used up relatively quickly within the next accounting year. They include:

- closing inventory: unsold goods at the end of the accounting year
- trade receivables: money owed to the business by its credit customers
- bank balances: the balance of cash in the business bank account
- cash: cash held on the business premises.

Non-current assets

These are assets that will be used for more than one accounting year. They include:

- land and premises
- machinery and tools
- computer and office equipment
- vehicles
- fixtures and fittings.

Statements of financial position | 321

Business assets are financed from the owner's equity and from liabilities

Money invested in business assets must be financed from either the owner's equity or from borrowing. That is:

> Total assets = Owner's equity + Total liabilities

or simply:

> Assets = Equity + Liabilities

This is the important **accounting equation** we learnt about in Unit 1.2.

Owner's equity is money invested in a business by the owner or owners of that business, for example from their own savings and retained profits. It is sometimes regarded as money owed by the business to its owners.

A **liability**, on the other hand, is money owed to another person or organisation, such as a bank or a supplier who has sold the business goods on credit. Liabilities can be long-term or short-term depending on how quickly they need to be paid off.

> Total liabilities = Current liabilities + Non-current liabilities

Current liabilities

These are amounts falling due for repayment within the next accounting year. They include:

- trade payables – money owed to suppliers for goods purchased on credit
- a bank overdraft
- other payables – money owed to organisations for expense items and non-current assets bought on credit.

Non-current liabilities

These are amounts falling due for repayment after more than one accounting year. They include:

- commercial bank loans
- mortgages to buy premises.

For example, when Jamila Khan first started her Go Faster Sports retail business five years ago she did so with $5 000 of her own savings. When she transferred this amount from her personal bank account to her business bank account she created an investment of $5 000 of owner's equity in business assets (cash in bank). At the end of the first day of trading Jamila's business had $5 000 of capital and owned $5 000 of current assets.

▼ Financial position at start-up

	Go Faster Sports
	Financial Position (Day 1)
	$
Assets: Cash in bank	5 000
Equity	5 000

The next day Jamila purchased inventory of $1 000 of sportswear to sell in her shop. Jamila bought the items on credit which meant that she did not have to pay for them immediately from cash in her business bank account. Her owner's equity was unchanged but the total assets of her business had increased by $1 000 to $6 000 by creating a business liability of $1 000 to the supplier (a trade payable). By the end of her second day of trading Jamila's business owned $6 000 of assets financed by $5 000 of owner's equity and $1 000 of liabilities.

▼ Financial position at end of next day

	Go Faster Sports	
	Financial Position (Day 2)	
		$
Assets:	Inventory	1 000
	Cash in bank	5 000
		6 000
Liabilities:	Trade payable	1 000
Equity		5 000
Equity + liabilities		6 000

ACTIVITY 3.9

1. From the article below identify the impact an investment in solar panels will have on (a) the non-current assets; and (b) the current assets of Walmart.

2. Suggest two ways Walmart could finance the investment in solar panels.

Walmart adds solar panels to 60 more stores

WALMART, the world's largest retailer, has announced that it will install solar panels on up to 60 additional stores in California by 2013.

Walmart's Vice President of Energy said in a statement: "Walmart has reduced energy expenses by more than a million dollars through our solar program, allowing us to pass these savings on to our customers in the form of everyday low prices."

Analysts said that the reduction in energy costs will also reduce the amount of cash that Walmart needs to keep available for everyday running costs. The company is now understood to be testing low-energy freezers for its large frozen food business, enabling it to expand its cold storage facilities and increase the quantity and range of products it holds in its retail stores.

The long-term capital employed in a business is financed from owner's equity and non-current liabilities

The amount of **capital employed** in a business refers to the amount of money it can continue to use over a number of years to finance investments in business assets. This means capital employed is made up of the owner's equity plus non-current liabilities such as bank loans and mortgages. Capital employed excludes finance from current liabilities because these must be repaid relatively quickly within the following 12-month period or accounting year.

> Capital employed = Total assets − Current liabilities

The amount of capital employed in a business can also be measured by:

- the amount of money invested in **non-current assets**
- the amount of money invested in **net current assets**, also called the **working capital** of the business.

> Capital employed = Non-current assets + Net current assets

Non-current assets

Non-current assets such as land, premises, machinery, vehicles and other equipment are used over a long period of time so they have to be financed from capital that will be available to the business for an equally long period of time: owner's equity and non-current liabilities.

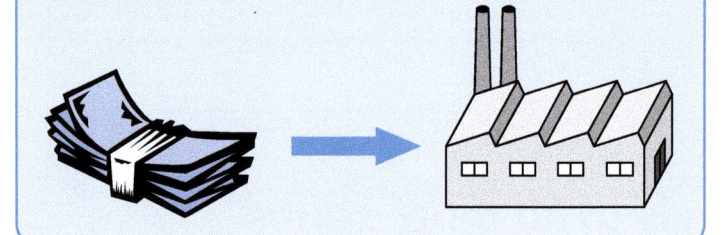

Net current assets

The money available to a business from its net current assets is called **working capital**. It is the money a business has available to fund its day-to-day running expenses after all its current liabilities have been met.

Working capital is money held as cash or invested in other current assets that can be converted reasonably quickly to cash.

Banks, suppliers and investors will use the statement of financial position to assess the credit worthiness and liquidity risk of the business

One of the most important reasons why people and organisations look at the statement of financial position of a business is to find out how much working capital it has.

This is because a business must have sufficient working capital to pay its day-to-day running expenses such as rent, electricity and wages. If a business cannot pay its expenses, suppliers will eventually stop providing it with the expense items and services it needs to keep running and earning revenue. ▶ 5.1

To pay its regular running expenses a business will need cash. A business can normally raise enough cash to pay these expenses reasonably quickly day to day from:

- cash in hand
- cash in bank
- revenue from the sale of goods held in inventory

- payments received from credit customers to settle their debts (trade receivables).

That is, the current assets of the business will provide it with cash to pay its running expenses. They are **liquid assets** because they can provide the business with cash relatively quickly and easily.

However, before running expenses can be paid for a business will need cash to pay off any current liabilities the business owes to other organisations. These will include payments to its bank to pay off a bank overdraft or to its trade payables to pay for purchases it made on credit.

The difference between current assets and current liabilities is the amount of **working capital** or **net current assets** a business has left to pay its future running expenses:

> **Net current assets = Current assets − Current liabilities**
> **(working capital)**

A business that has **positive working capital** has more cash tied up in current assets than it owes in current liabilities, with the following results:

(1) It is in a **good liquidity position** because it holds sufficient current assets that can be used to raise cash easily and quickly to pay its current liabilities as they fall due.

(2) Once it has paid off those liabilities it will still have money left over to pay its future running expenses.

For example, at the end of her first accounting year Jamila Khan's business Go Faster Sports had $4 500 of cash in the business bank account and owed only $3 000 to Sports Mart Ltd. for goods she had purchased on credit from them.

As the business had no other current assets or liabilities it had working capital of $1 500 to continue paying for rent, electricity and other running expenses.

▼ Positive working capital

Current assets > Current liabilities

Go Faster Sports	
Working Capital Position At 31 December Year 1	
	$
Current assets	4 500
less Current liabilities	3 000
Net current assets (working capital)	1 500

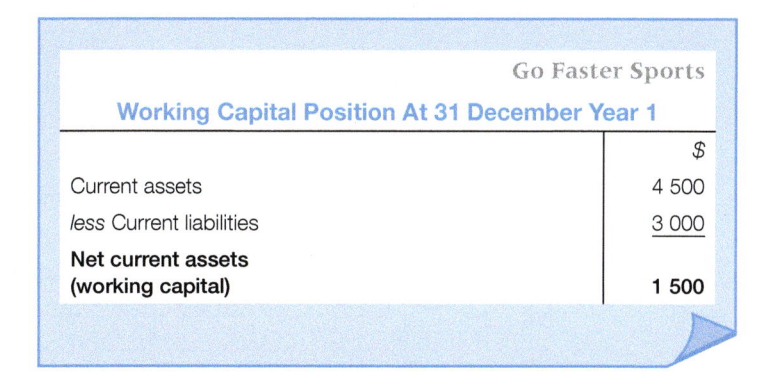

However, if the current liabilities of a business exceed its current assets then it will have **negative working capital**, with the following results:

(1) It may be unable to raise sufficient cash from its current assets to pay off its current liabilities in full when they fall due.

(2) It will have no cash left over to fund future running expenses.

Statements of financial position

For example, if a business had current assets in cash, inventory and trade receivables valued at $5 000 at the end of its accounting year but at the same time had current liabilities of $7 000 to pay it would have negative working capital of $2 000.

Risky Business
Working Capital Position At 31 December

	$
Current assets	5 000
less Current liabilities	7 000
Net current assets (working capital)	(2 000)

Having insufficient current assets to pay off current liabilities (i.e. negative working capital) is very risky. Suppliers may stop supplying goods or services on credit to the business if it is unable to find enough cash to pay off its debts to them when they are due. Moreover, unless the business can find other sources of cash, it may be unable to pay future expenses needed to keep it running.

If this happens the business will have to try to raise cash to pay its bills from alternative sources including:

- additional equity provided by the business owners
- a new bank overdraft or bank loan
- selling off unwanted equipment and other non-current assets.

However, it may take some time to raise cash in these ways. Banks may be reluctant to lend to the business because of its poor financial position. Buyers must be found for the unwanted equipment and other non-current assets. Owners may also have to sell off some of their own possessions to raise new capital for their business. If so, the business will be in a very **poor liquidity position**. That is, it will have few – if any – assets that it can convert to cash quickly and easily to meet its current liabilities.

The **liquidity** of a business is a key measure of how quickly and easily it can raise cash from its assets to pay off its current liabilities as they fall due. Current assets, especially cash, are the most liquid assets a business can hold, while non-current assets are the least liquid because they will often take time to sell off and this may involve selling them at a loss. The liquidity of a business is closely related to the amount of working capital the business has invested in current assets. ➤ **5.1**

ACTIVITY 3.10

The values of the current assets and current liabilities of two businesses at the end of the same day are given below.

Alpha Repairs

	$
Inventory	8 000
Trade receivables	0
Bank	5 800
Cash	1 200
Trade payables	6 500
Bank overdraft	7 000

Beta Supplies

	$
Inventory	15 000
Trade receivables	5 500
Bank	4 100
Cash	400
Trade payables	5 000
Bank overdraft	12 000

1. Calculate the working capital of each business.
2. Which business had the more favourable liquidity position? Explain your answer.

3.2.2 Preparing a statement of financial position

Values for assets, capital and liabilities recorded in the trial balance at the end of a trading period are used to prepare a statement of financial position for a business

The trial balance below, from illustration 3.3 in unit 3.1, was prepared by Jamila for her Go Faster Sports business at the end of its first accounting year. The balances for sales, purchases and expenses that she used to prepare her income statement for that year have been crossed through. This left her the account balances for assets, liabilities and opening capital she needed to prepare a statement of financial position for her business.

Turn back to page 287 to see how this balance was created

TRIAL BALANCE FOR GO FASTER SPORTS AT THE END OF ACCOUNTING YEAR 1 AFTER COMPLETION OF THE INCOME STATEMENT

Go Faster Sports
Trial Balance For Year 1 At 31 December

	Dr	Cr
~~Sales~~		~~77 000~~
~~Purchases~~	~~60 000~~	
~~Rent~~	~~9 000~~	
~~Electricity~~	~~2 400~~	
~~Advertising~~	~~1 500~~	
~~Sundry expenses~~	~~1 100~~	
Equipment	6 500	
Bank	4 500	
Sports Mart Ltd. (trade payables)		3 000
Opening equity (at the start of year 1)		5 000
	85 000	**85 000**

Transfer these account balances to the statement of financial position

However, to prepare a statement of financial position for her business on 31 December she also needed the balance for closing capital at the end of that day.

In her income statement Jamila had calculated profit for the year as $3 000. This profit had increased the net assets and the owner's equity she had invested in her business from $5 000 at the start of the accounting year to $8 000 at the year end.

Closing capital of $8 000 as at 31 December that year was recorded in the capital account of her business as shown in illustration 3.7 from Unit 3.1.

Turn back to page 293 to see how this balance was created

CAPITAL ACCOUNT SHOWING CLOSING EQUITY AT THE END OF ACCOUNTING YEAR 1

General ledger — Go Faster Sports

Capital Account

Dr			Cr
Year 1	$	Year 1	$
Dec 31: Balance c/d	8 000	Jan 1: Bank	5 000
		Dec 31: Income statement	3 000
	8 000		8 000
		Year 2	
		Jan 1: Balance b/d	8 000

Business assets are recorded on the left-hand side of a horizontal financial statement of position and how they are financed is recorded on the right

To prepare her first statement of financial position Jamila divided a sheet of paper into two sides:

- the left-hand side to record business assets
- the right-hand side to record the capital and liabilities used to finance those assets.

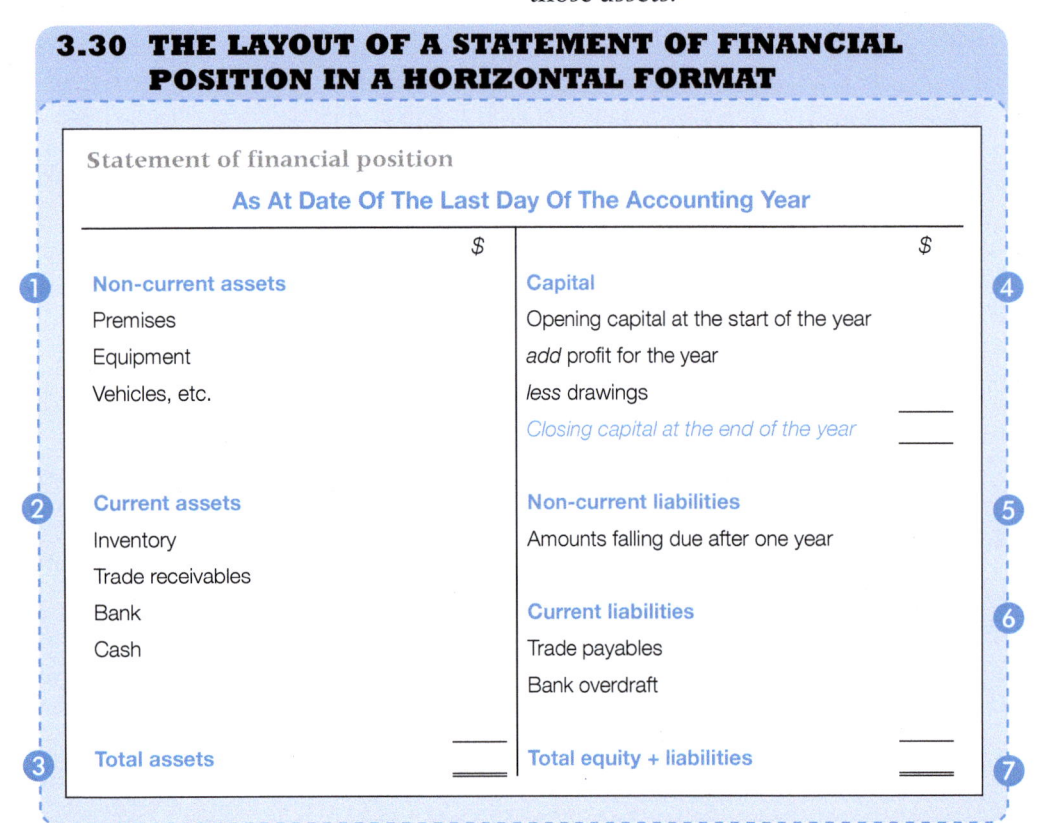

3.30 THE LAYOUT OF A STATEMENT OF FINANCIAL POSITION IN A HORIZONTAL FORMAT

She then divided each side into a top half and a bottom half and wrote down all the different types of assets and liabilities she would need to include as well as placeholders for opening and closing capital, profit for the year and personal drawings.

This provided her with a template to complete for a statement of financial position using a horizontal presentation.

Statement of financial position
As At Date Of The Last Day Of The Accounting Year

	$		$
① **Non-current assets**		**Capital**	④
Premises		Opening capital at the start of the year	
Equipment		*add* profit for the year	
Vehicles, etc.		*less* drawings	
		Closing capital at the end of the year	
② **Current assets**		**Non-current liabilities**	⑤
Inventory		Amounts falling due after one year	
Trade receivables			
Bank		**Current liabilities**	⑥
Cash		Trade payables	
		Bank overdraft	
③ **Total assets**		**Total equity + liabilities**	⑦

Final statements

On the left-hand side of a horizontal statement of financial position

① The values of any non-current assets owned by the business are listed in the top half of the left-hand column of the statement. Non-current assets that will remain useful for the longest period of time, such as premises, are listed before others that will depreciate more quickly, such as vehicles. ➤ **2.2**

② Current assets are listed below non-current assets in the following order:
- closing inventory
- trade receivables
- bank
- cash.

Current assets should be listed in increasing order of their liquidity. This shows how quickly and easily each type of current asset can be converted into cash to settle current liabilities as they fall due.

An inventory of unsold goods is the least liquid current asset and is listed first. This is because it may take some time to sell off those goods to raise cash.

Next in the list are trade receivables. This is because credit customers may take some time to pay off their debts to the business.

Cash is clearly the most easily and readily accessible source of money available to a business to make payments, especially cash in hand held on the business premises. Cash in bank and then cash in hand are always listed last.

③ The sum of entries to the left-hand side of a statement of financial position is the **total assets** of the business.

On the right-hand side of a horizontal statement of financial position

④ The value of owner's equity is recorded first, starting with the opening equity at the start of the accounting year. Profit for the year must be added to this.

Total drawings from equity during the year by the business owners are then deducted to find the closing equity invested in the business at the end of the accounting year. ➤ **3.1**

⑤ The liabilities of the business are listed in the bottom half of the left-hand side. Non-current liabilities are listed first. These include bank loans and any other amounts owed to other people or organisations that will be repaid over more than one accounting year.

⑥ Current liabilities, payable within the next year, are listed last, notably amounts payable to suppliers for goods purchased on credit or to a bank to pay off an overdrawn bank account. ➤ **1.5**

⑦ The sum of entries to the right-hand side of a statement of financial position is the **total capital and liabilities** of the business.

ACTIVITY 3.11

The information in the table is from the books of G Stannard.

Produce a horizontal statement of financial position at the end of the final day of his accounting year.

Use illustration 3.30 to help you and remember to list assets in increasing order of their liquidity.

Values on the final day of the accounting year	
	$
Trade payables	15 000
Bank	4 000
Computer equipment	12 000
Profit for the year	10 000
Premises	66 000
Opening equity at the start of the year	60 000
Trade receivables	3 000

A statement of financial position must always balance

At the end of its first accounting year Jamila's business had very few assets and liabilities so she was able to produce a simple statement of financial position from her trial balance and capital account.

3.31 FINANCIAL POSITION OF GO FASTER SPORTS ON 31 DECEMBER ACCOUNTING YEAR 1

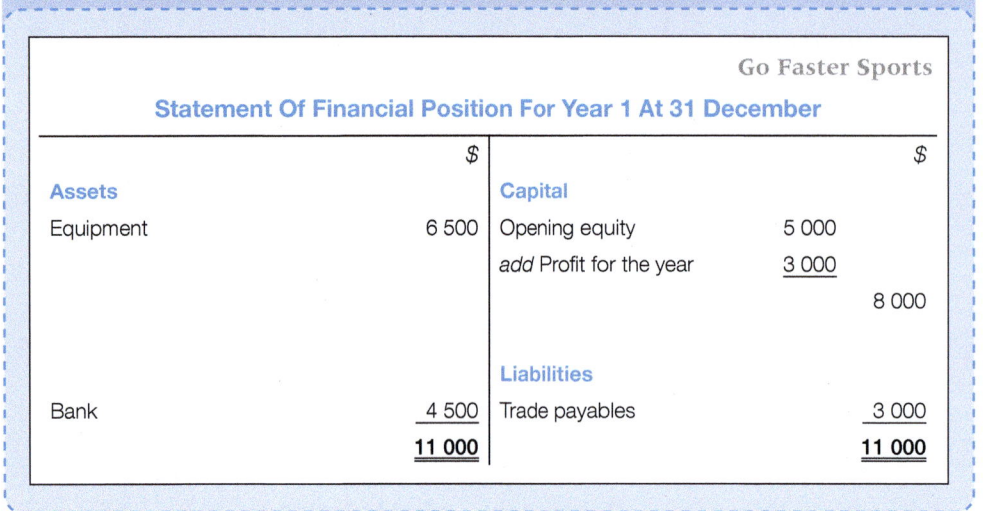

Go Faster Sports
Statement Of Financial Position For Year 1 At 31 December

Assets	$	Capital	$	$
Equipment	6 500	Opening equity	5 000	
		add Profit for the year	3 000	
				8 000
		Liabilities		
Bank	4 500	Trade payables		3 000
	11 000			**11 000**

From the statement of financial position we can calculate that the following applied on 31 December:

- The **net current assets** or **working capital** of the business was $1 500: current assets of $4 500 less current liabilities of $3 000.

- The **capital employed** in the business was $8 000: non-current assets of $6 500 plus net current assets of $1 500.

- The **owner's equity** was $8 000: opening capital of $5 000 plus profit for the year of $3 000.

You will also notice that the value of $11 000 for total assets that Jamila recorded in the statement of financial position for her business was exactly equal to the combined value of the capital and liabilities of her business.

This is because the value of business assets can never be more or less than the money invested in them from the owner's equity and liabilities of the business. This of course is the accounting equation:

> **Assets = Capital + Liabilities**

The accounting equation and a statement of financial position show that all of the money or capital invested in the assets of the business is owed to someone else, either to the business owners or to the other people or organisations that have provided it with items on credit or loans. ▶ **1.2**

It is important that the two sides of a statement of financial position are in balance. If they are not then an error has been made in its preparation.

Because of this the statement of financial position is also called the **balance sheet** in many countries.

Illustration 3.32 shows the statement of financial position prepared by Jamila Khan for Go Faster Sports on the final day of its third year of trading and the third accounting year of her business.

She prepared the statement from the balances for assets, liabilities and capital in the trial balance that she had written up prior to producing her income statement for the year. This recorded a profit for the year of $15 800 (see illustration 3.16 in Unit 3.1).

Turn back to page 299 to see how this balance was created

3.32 THE TRIAL BALANCE FOR GO FASTER SPORTS AT THE END OF ACCOUNTING YEAR 3

Go Faster Sports

Trial Balance For Year 3 As At 31 December

	Dr $	Cr $
Sales		120 000
Sale returns	6 000	
Purchases	96 000	
Purchases returns		5 000
Rent	9 000	
Electricity	3 200	
Advertising	2 500	
Sundry expenses	1 500	
Equipment	9 500	
Bank	5 300	
Sports Mart Ltd. (trade payables)		4 500
Drawings	7 000	
Opening equity (at the start of year 3)		10 500
	140 000	140 000

Note:
Closing inventory was valued at $9 000 as at 31 December

FINANCIAL POSITION OF GO FASTER SPORTS AT THE END OF ACCOUNTING YEAR 3

Go Faster Sports

Statement Of Financial Position For Year 3 At 31 December

Assets	$	Capital	$	$
Equipment	9 500	Opening equity	10 500	
		add Profit for the year	15 800	
		less Drawings	7 000	
				19 300
		Liabilities		
Inventory	9 000	Trade payables		4 500
Bank	5 300			
	23 800			**23 800**

Profit for the year is taken from the income statement

The left-hand side of the statement of financial position records the value of total assets owned by the business on the final day of its third accounting year as $23 800. To the right, the statement records capital of $19 300 and liabilities of $4 500 invested in these assets.

Statements of financial position

The two sides of the statement are in balance with the value of assets exactly equal to the amount of capital and liabilities used to finance them.

The trial balance below is the one from illustration 3.21 in unit 3.1 that Jamila Khan prepared at the end of the fifth accounting year of her business Go Faster Sports. This was used to write up an income statement that recorded a profit for the year of $22 000.

Turn back to page 305 to see how this balance was created

THE TRIAL BALANCE FOR GO FASTER SPORTS AT THE END OF ACCOUNTING YEAR 5

Go Faster Sports
Trial Balance For Year 5 At 31 December

	Dr $	Cr $
Sales		159 000
Sale returns	4 000	
Purchases	115 000	
Purchases returns		900
Carriage inwards	3 900	
Carriage outwards	1 500	
Opening inventory (at the start of the year)	12 000	
Rent	9 600	
Electricity	3 400	
Advertising	2 800	
Sundry expenses	1 700	
Equipment	14 100	
Trade receivables	1 400	
Bank	5 600	
Fast Fashions plc (trade payable)		2 800
Drawings	15 000	
Opening equity (at the start of year 5)		27 300
	190 000	190 000

Note:
Closing inventory was valued at $16 000 as at 31 December

ACTIVITY 3.12

The information in the table is from the books of A Mamoud.

Produce a horizontal statement of financial position as at the end of the final day of her accounting year.

Use illustration 3.30 to help you and remember to list assets in increasing order of their liquidity.

Also remember to list non-current liabilities before current liabilities.

Values on final day of accounting year	
	$
Machinery	26 700
Cash	1 200
Bank loan	38 000
Trade payables	7 800
Bank	3 450
Computer equipment	5 600
Profit for the year	55 800
Premises	145 000
Opening equity at start of year	190 000
Delivery vehicles	22 400
Drawings	45 000
Closing inventory	18 900
Trade receivables	12 450
Fixtures and fittings	10 900

Balances from the trial balance used to prepare the statement of financial position are highlighted. Jamila prepared two versions of her statement of financial position at 31 December that year: one in a horizontal format shown in illustration 3.33; the other in a vertical format as shown in illustration 3.34. Although their layout differs they both contain the same information.

3.33 FINANCIAL POSITION OF GO FASTER SPORTS AT THE END OF YEAR 5

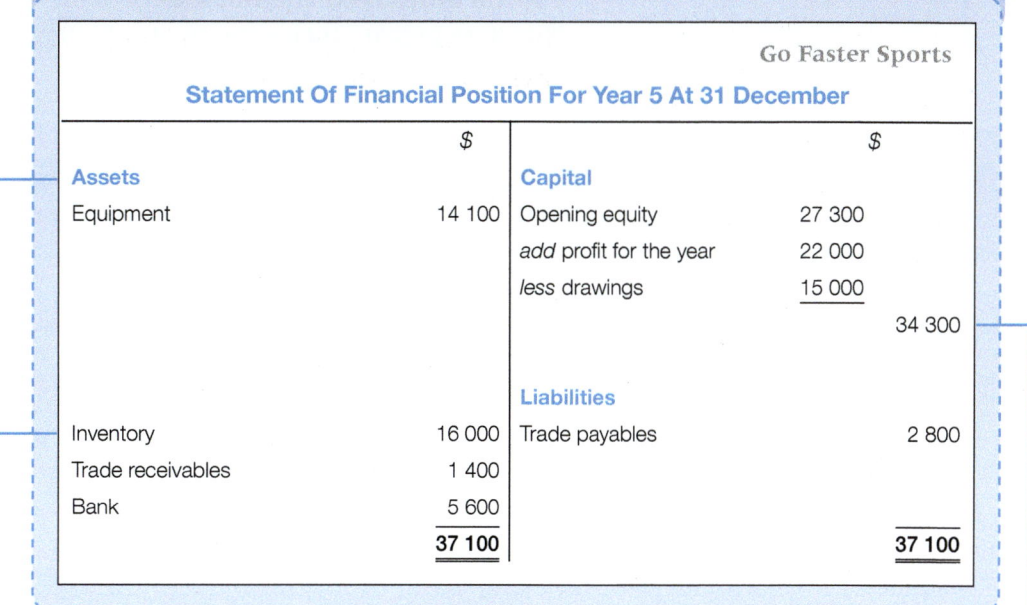

Go Faster Sports

Statement Of Financial Position For Year 5 At 31 December

Assets	$	Capital	$
Equipment	14 100	Opening equity	27 300
		add profit for the year	22 000
		less drawings	15 000
			34 300
		Liabilities	
Inventory	16 000	Trade payables	2 800
Trade receivables	1 400		
Bank	5 600		
	37 100		37 100

3.34 STATEMENT OF FINANCIAL POSITION IN A VERTICAL FORMAT

Go Faster Sports

Statement Of Financial Position For Year 5 At 31 December

			$	$	$
A	**Non-current assets**				
	Equipment		14 100		
					14 100
B	**Current assets**				
	Inventory			16 000	
	Trade receivables			1 400	
	Bank			5 600	
				23 000	
C	*less* **Current liabilities**				
	Trade payables			2 800	
				2 800	
D	**Net current assets (working capital)** [B – C]				20 200
E	**Total assets** *less* **current liabilities** [A + D]				34 300
F	*less* **Non-current liabilities**				
	Amounts falling due in more than one year				0
G	**Net assets** (E – F)				34 300
H	Financed by:				
	Capital at start of year				27 300
	add Profit for the year				22 000
					49 300
	less Drawings				15 000
					34 300

Statements of financial position

The great advantage of a statement of financial position in a vertical format is that it is easier to follow and shows more clearly the **working capital, capital employed** and **net assets** of the business. Most businesses today therefore prepare their statements of financial position using the vertical format.

▼ The sections of a vertical statement of financial position

		$	$	$
A	**Non-current assets** are listed first in a vertical statement of financial position in the same order as they would be in a horizontal statement, starting with the longest lived assets such as premises.	Value of each non-current asset at cost	Accumulated depreciation, if any, on each non-current asset	Total non-current assets (net of accumulated depreciation)
B	**Current assets** are listed in order of their liquidity: inventory, trade receivables, cash in bank, cash in hand.	Adjustments to account balances	Individual values and total current assets	
C	List **current liabilities**: trade payables and cash in bank if the business current account is overdrawn.		Individual values and total current liabilities	
D	Deduct current liabilities from current assets to find the **net current assets** or **working capital** of the business: **NET CURRENT ASSETS = CURRENT ASSETS − CURRENT LIABILITIES**			Net current assets (or working capital)
E	Add net current assets to the value of non-current assets to calculate the **capital employed** in the business: **CAPITAL EMPLOYED = NON-CURRENT ASSETS + NET CURRENT ASSETS** Capital employed is the sum of long-term funds available to the business to invest in assets used to generate revenue. Current liabilities are excluded because they must be repaid relatively quickly from the cash and the other current assets of the business.			Total assets less current liabilities (or capital employed)
F	List any **non-current liabilities** including long-term bank loans and mortgages.		Individual values	Total non-current liabilities
G	Deduct non-current liabilities from capital employed to find the **net assets** of the business: **NET ASSETS = CAPITAL EMPLOYED − NON-CURRENT LIABILITIES** This shows the value of assets that would remain in the business after all liabilities had been met.			Net assets
H	Add profit for the year to opening capital and then deduct drawings to find closing capital: the equity **owned** by the business owner(s). This will always be exactly equal to the value of net assets: **NET ASSETS = CAPITAL**			Individual values and total capital owned

Final statements

The vertical statement of financial position has a number of columns into which values can be recorded.

Column 1: The top of the column is used to list the cost price of the different non-current assets owned by the business.

Column 2: The top of the column is used to list any accumulated depreciation changes for each non-current asset (see section 3.2.3 below). It is then used to list the values of the current assets and current liabilities of the business and their totals.

Column 3: This is used to record the most important financial values of the business, including non-current assets after depreciation, its net current assets or working capital, capital employed, net assets and owner's equity. ➤ 5.1

For example, the final column in the statement for Go Faster Sports in illustration 3.34 clearly shows that for year 5 as at 31 December the business had the following:

- It had **positive working capital** or net current assets of $20 200: the sum of the sub-total of $23 000 for current assets less the sub-total of $2 800 for current liabilities recorded in the second column.

- It had **capital employed** in business assets of $34 300: the sum of non-current assets plus working capital recorded in the final column.

- It had **net assets** of $34 300: this is the accounting value or **book value** of the business on the day of the statement. It provides a measure of the amount of money that could remain available to the business after all its assets had been converted to cash and used to pay off its current and non-current liabilities in full.

- Owner's equity or **capital owned** by the business owner was $34 300. This sum is exactly equal to the net assets of the business. This is because if all the assets of Go Faster Sports were converted to cash and all business liabilities were paid off, the remaining cash would belong to Jamila.

ACTIVITY 3.13

John Fofana's accounting year runs from 1 April to 31 March.

The following balances were taken from his books on 31 March last year.

	$
Premises	100 000
Equipment	20 000
Inventory	19 000
Trade receivables	8 000
Cash	1 000
Trade payables	11 000
Bank (overdrawn amount)	(2 000)
Loan (repayable over 15 years)	40 000
Opening equity	80 000
Drawings	15 000

John Fofana's income statement for the accounting year showed a profit for the year of $30 000.

Use the information provided to complete the vertical statement of financial position for John Fofana opposite.

John Fofana
Statement Of Financial Position At 31 March 201X

	$	$	$
Non-current assets:			
_____			
_____		___	
Current assets:			
_____			
_____			
_____		___	
less **Current liabilities:**			
_____			
_____		___	
Net current assets (working capital)			___
Total assets *less* Current liabilities			
less **Non-current liabilities**			
_____			
			___
Net assets			
Capital			
Equity at start of year			
add Profit for the year			
less Drawings			___

3.2.3 Valuing assets in a statement of financial position

The values of assets presented in a statement of financial position should be fair and realistic

A number of rules or principles must be followed when recording the values of different assets in a statement of financial position. These are as follows:

- Each non-current asset must be recorded at its written down value or **net book value** (its cost price less **accumulated depreciation**). ➤ **2.2**

- Inventory must be recorded at its cost price or its **net realisable value** (the revenue it is likely to earn when sold less any selling costs), whichever is the lower of these two values. ➤ **5.2**

- The value of trade receivables should be equal to what the business expects to collect from those credit customers that owe it money and not the total amount owed. This means deducting any provisions for **doubtful debts**. ➤ **1.9**

Following these rules helps to ensure that the values presented in a financial statement by a business are realistic and not overstated.

Non-current assets should be valued at historic cost less accumulated depreciation

Non-current assets such as machinery, vehicles and equipment should be valued at what they cost to buy. This makes their values easy to check against amounts recorded in source documents including invoices and receipts. ➤ 1.3

However, non-current assets lose value over time as they are used by a business because they wear out or become out of date due to advances in technology. Their loss of value is an expense called **depreciation**. ➤ 2.2

Each year losses due to depreciation will accumulate. This means that each year the values of non-current assets will fall further. It is important to record non-current assets in a financial statement at their depreciated values rather than their historic cost prices. This means deducting the accumulated depreciation on each non-current asset from its original price.

For example, imagine Jamila Khan purchased a delivery van for her business two years ago at a cost of $5 000. She estimated it would have a useful life of five years over which its value would fall as it wore out through usage.

She assumed the value of the van would reduce by $1 000 each year over its useful life. This meant that at the end of each accounting year Jamila would reduce or "write down" the value of the van in the statement of financial position for her business by an additional $1 000.

So, after two years the written down value or **net book value** of the van will be $3 000 and recorded in her statement of financial position as follows:

▼ Recording the value of a non-current asset at cost less accumulated depreciation

	Cost $	less accumulated depreciation $	Net book value $
Non-current assets			
Delivery vehicle	5 000	2 000	3 000

It is prudent to value inventory at its net realisable value

An **inventory** of unsold goods is a current asset because it can be sold at a later date to raise cash for the business. Inventory will usually be valued by how much in total it cost to purchase the unsold goods even if they could be sold for much more.

However, it may sometimes be necessary to sell off goods held in inventory at a price lower than their cost for the following reasons:

- Customer demand for the goods has fallen as tastes or fashions have changed.
- The goods are out of date and new, better goods are available to buy.
- The goods are damaged or faulty in some way.

Statements of financial position

In these cases businesses will often sell old and damaged goods at substantially reduced prices so they can create room to buy in and store new products. For example, stocks of summer clothes are often sold off at heavily reduced prices at the end of summer so that new winter clothes can be bought in instead.

If a business expects to earn less revenue from the sale of goods held in inventory than they cost to purchase then it must value those goods accordingly. This means an inventory must be valued at the lower of its cost or **net realisable value**.

For example, when Jamila Khan was preparing a statement of financial position for Go Faster Sports she had to determine the value she would record for closing inventory. Included in the inventory were 10 pairs of sports training shoes that had cost $50 each to purchase and were slightly damaged with scuffmarks and missing shoelaces. Jamila estimated that she would only be able to sell off the training shoes at a much reduced price of $30 per pair and would need to spend $2 per pair on minor repairs and shoelaces before she could do so.

This meant there were three possible values for the damaged sports shoes:

▼ Valuation methods for inventory

	Quantity	Value per item $	Valuation $
At cost	10	Cost per item: $50	10 × $50 = **$500**
Realisable value	10	Expected selling price per item: $30	10 × $30 = **$300**
Net realisable value	10	Expected selling price per item: $30 *less* expected additional costs per sale: $2	10 × $28 = **$280**

It is important not to overstate asset values in a statement of financial position. This meant Jamila included the net realisable value of $280 in her valuation of inventory for the 10 pairs of unsold training shoes rather than their value at cost of $500.

Net realisable value is the term used to describe an item's estimated selling price less any additional costs that will be incurred before the sale can occur. These costs could include repairs (as with shoes), repackaging, additional advertising or promotion and transport and shipping. Items in an inventory should always be valued in a statement of financial position at their net realisable value when that value is less than their cost price.

It is prudent to record the expected collectible amount from trade receivables

Trade receivables arise from credit sales: the trade receivables amount is the amount of money owed to a business by customers who were allowed to buy goods from it on credit terms. **Trade receivables** in a statement of financial position are a current asset because they will bring cash into the business as they are repaid by credit customers over the coming accounting year. ▶ 1.4

As with other assets it is important not to overstate the value of trade receivables. This means recording a value in a statement of financial position that the business expects to collect from them. This may be less than the total amount owed by credit customers for the following reasons:

ACTIVITY 3.14

1. Jenny Capilli runs a gift shop. She bought computer equipment for $2 000 on the day she started her business. She decided to write down the value of the equipment by $500 per year over four years.

   At the end of her third year in business what was (a) the value of the equipment at cost; (b) the accumulated depreciation included in the accounts for the equipment; and (c) the net book value of the equipment recorded in her statement of financial position?

2. At the end of her third year in business Jenny had an inventory of 200 unsold decorative money boxes she had purchased for $5 each. She normally sells the items for $9 each but due to a slump in demand only expects to be able to sell them for $4 each in the next accounting year.

   Calculate (a) the value of her inventory at cost; (b) the value of her inventory under normal selling conditions; and (c) the net realisable value of the inventory. Explain which value Jenny should record in her statement of financial position for her inventory.

3. At the end of her third year in business Jenny had trade receivables of $900 but had created a provision for doubtful debts in her accounts equal to 10% of this amount. What value should Jenny include in her statement of financial position for trade receivables?

- Some credit customers may fail to pay off their debts in full.
- Some business customers may cease trading without first settling their accounts.

For example, Jamila's business Go Faster Sports only began to sell sportswear on credit to selected customers during its fifth accounting year. By the end of that year the total amount owed to her business by its credit customers was $1 600. However, one business customer was in financial trouble and Jamila was worried it would be unable to pay its debt of $200 when it fell due in the next year. The debt was doubtful so Jamila excluded it from the value of trade receivables she recorded in the statement of financial position as follows:

- create a provision for doubtful debts for $200 ➤ **1.9**
- (in column 1) deduct the provision from total trade receivables to derive the net value for trade receivables or **expected collectable amount** (in column 2)
- finally, add the adjusted or net value for trade receivables to the values of other current assets (listed in column 2) to calculate and record the total for all current assets.

▼ Adjusting trade receivables for doubtful debts

	$	$	$
Current assets			
Inventory		16 000	
Trade receivables	2 000		
less provision for doubtful debts	600		
		1 400	
Bank		5 600	
		20 300	

We will learn more about how to make and record adjustments to the values for assets in statements of financial position in Unit 4.1.

3.2.4 Goodwill and intangible assets

The price at which a business can be sold may be greater than the book value of its net assets because of goodwill and other intangible assets

Jamila had been thinking for some time about selling her business Go Faster Sports. The statement of financial position at the end of her fifth accounting year reported the book value of the net assets of her business as $34 300 – see illustration 3.34.

Go Faster Sports
Summarised Statement Of Financial Position For Year 5 At 31 December

	$
Total assets	37 100
less Total liabilities	2 800
Net assets	**34 300**

The owners of a sports gym called Fitness Mania offered to pay Jamila the book value of the net assets of Go Faster Sports plus an extra $5 700 for "goodwill". Jamila accepted the offer and sold her business to Fitness Mania on 31 December for $40 000.

For the purchase of Go Faster Sports
On 31 December Year 5

	$
Net assets	34 300
add Goodwill	5 700
Total price paid	**40 000**

Goodwill is a "premium" paid by the buyer of a business over and above the book value of its net assets:

> **Total price paid for a business = net assets + goodwill**

Fitness Mania was willing to pay a premium of $5 700 for Jamila's business because it was already an established business with a clear record of success:

- It was located in a prime location.
- It had developed a strong reputation.
- It had built up a large customer base over five years of trading.

Fitness Mania thought these advantages were worth paying extra for. The advantages had been developed by Go Faster Sports over time but were not valued in its statement of financial position because they were difficult to value accurately. The amount of goodwill paid for them by Fitness Mania provided a definite measure of their value.

Financial statements must only record and report items that have a definite monetary value. This means that the value of goodwill can only be included in a statement of financial position when it has been paid for – that is, when the business is sold. ▶ 2.2

Fitness Mania was able to draw up the following business purchase account in its ledger to record its purchase of Go Faster Sports. In the account it listed the values of all of the assets and liabilities it took over from Go Faster Sports from its statement of financial position in illustration 3.34 plus the value it paid for goodwill.

3.35 BUSINESS PURCHASE ACCOUNT OF FITNESS MANIA FOR THE PURCHASE OF GO FASTER SPORTS

General ledger   Fitness Mania

Business purchase account

Dr			Cr
Year	$	Year	$
Dec 31 Goodwil	5 700	Dec 31 Trade payables	2 800
Dec 31 Equipment	14 100	Dec 31 Go Faster Sports	40 000
Dec 31 Inventory	16 000		
Dec 31 Trade receivables	1 400		
Dec 31 Bank	5 600		
	42 800		42 800

From this, Fitness Mania was able to produce the statement of financial position shown in illustration 3.36 on the day it purchased Go Faster Sports.

The revised statement of financial position prepared for Go Faster Sports by Fitness Mania shows the following.

- Goodwill was recorded as a type of non-current asset.
- The value recorded for goodwill increased the net assets of the business from $34 300 to $40 000.
- The capital invested in Go Faster Sports by the owners of Fitness Mania was the sum of $40 000 they paid to Jamila to take over the assets and liabilities of her business.

Goodwill is a type of **intangible asset**. This means it is a non-physical, non-financial asset: it cannot be seen or touched and is difficult to value. In line with the monetary measurement principle (▶ 5.2), its value can only be included in a statement of financial position when it is paid for by another business because only this will establish a definite monetary value for the asset.

Statements of financial position

3.36 STATEMENT OF FINANCIAL POSITION FOR FITNESS MANIA – GO FASTER SPORTS DIVISION FOLLOWING ITS PURCHASE

Fitness Mania's Go Faster Sports
Statement of Financial Position At 31 December

	$	$	$
Non-current assets			
Goodwill		5 700	
Equipment		14 100	
			19 800
Current assets			
Inventory		16 000	
Trade receivables		1 400	
Bank		5 600	
		23 000	
less **Current liabilities**			
Trade payables		2 800	
		2 800	
Net current assets (working capital)			20 200
Total assets less current liabilities			40 000
less **Non-current liabilities**			
			0
Net assets			40 000
Capital			40 000

In addition to reputation and other advantages generally referred to as goodwill, a modern business may also have a number of other valuable intangible assets that give it a competitive advantage over rival organisations. These will include brands, trademarks, copyrights, publishing titles, patents and other intellectual property. While some of these may be fairly easy to identify separately, they are often very difficult to measure in monetary terms, and until paid for are therefore not recognised in statements of financial position.

3.2.5 Valuation of inventory

We have seen that the value of inventory is a significant factor in compiling both the income statement and the statement of financial position. But how do we go about establishing the value of that inventory?

How do we value inventory?

To calculate the value of closing inventory, we first need to know two things:

- The physical quantity of goods – how many items are left over?
- The price of these goods – what did we pay for each item?

If we multiply one by the other we will arrive at the cost of the goods in the closing inventory, and it is this amount that we will use to value our inventory. We call this **valuing inventory at cost**.

> Cost of inventory = number of items (quantity) x price per item (price)

How do we establish quantity?

It is normally not difficult to establish the quantity of goods in inventory. There are two main ways of doing this:

- Carry out a physical count of the inventory items on the year end date; this is often referred to as a **stock-take** or **stock check**. It is particularly suitable for small businesses or those holding very low levels of inventory.

- Maintain a stock book or register, either manual or computerised, in which a record is made of when inventory is purchased and sold. This then keeps a running balance of the items of inventory in stock at any time including the year end.

This is exactly what a supermarket retailer is doing when your shopping is checked out at the till; as well as calculating how much you have to pay, the system is identifying the goods from the bar-code and taking them off the physical inventory record.

As soon as the records show that the inventory has reduced to a certain level, an order will be sent to the distribution centre for more goods to be delivered to the store. The computer system will then add the incoming goods to the record when they arrive. This **point-of-sale** inventory recording enables the store management to review the sales of individual lines of merchandise on a daily basis and obtain information important to the business's marketing strategy and for other purposes.

It is usually good practice to double-check the amount shown in the inventory records by carrying out periodic stock checks and following up any differences between the actual goods included in the count and the quantities shown in the running inventory records. This may reveal useful information about the extent of staff or customer theft or shop-lifting, damaged or spoiled goods or other situations where the movement of goods in or out is being incorrectly entered in the inventory records.

How do we establish price?

Where the goods held in the inventory are large, easily distinguishable items or where the number of items held is small, it may be a simple and straightforward matter to identify the actual price paid for those specific items. For example, a small business selling garden machinery will normally have no problem in determining what was paid for the actual lawnmowers in inventory at the year end. It is then an easy exercise to multiply the number of items by the price paid to establish the cost of the inventory held.

The situation is different when the inventory is made up of a large number of indistinguishable items, quite possibly stored in common containers, and where the purchase prices have changed, maybe several times during the year. Take the example of Omar's Hardware Store which starts to sell size 10 steel screws, which it keeps in a large container and sells by weight. During the first month of selling the screws, it makes several purchases and books out several sales as shown by the following extract from its inventory records:

3.37 INVENTORY RECORDS

Omar's Hardware Store — **Size 10 steel screws**

Date	Purchase/(sale)	Quantity (kg)	Price ($/kg)	Purchase value ($)
1 October	Purchase	20	1.00	20
3 October	(Sales week 1)	(8)		
10 October	(Sales week 2)	(7)		
15 October	Purchase	20	2.00	40
17 October	(Sales week 3)	(10)		
22 October	Purchase	20	1.50	30
24 October	(Sales week 4)	(10)		
25 October	Purchase	20	2.50	50
31 October	(Sales week 5)	(20)		
		80 (55)		140

By netting off the in and out transactions, we can see that at the end of the month there are 25kg of size 10 screws still in inventory. But which ones are they? What was their purchase price? Is it the last batch purchased (plus some others) which are left? Or perhaps the first ones? In fact they are all in the container and it is impossible to distinguish between them.

In situations where it is impossible or impractical to assign an actual price to specific items of inventory, there are three conventions which can be adopted to deal with this:

- Assume all items left in inventory are the latest ones to be purchased, and it is the earliest ones which have been used or sold. This is known as **"first in first out" or FIFO**. The price of the latest batches purchased are therefore used to value the inventory

- Assume all items left in inventory are the earliest ones to be purchased, and it is the latest ones which have been used or sold. This is known as **"last in first out" or LIFO**. In this case it is the price of the earliest batches purchased which is used to value the inventory
- Another approach might be to take the average price across all the purchases made and value the inventory using this average price. This is known as **average cost or AVCO**.

We can now prepare the valuation statement for Omar's inventory of size 10 steel screws at 31 October using the three different methods, as follows:

3.38 VALUATION STATEMENT

Omar's Hardware Store

Size 10 steel screws – inventory valuation 31 October

Method	kg	price	value
FIFO (counting backwards from last purchases)	20	2.50	50.00
	5	1.50	7.50
			57.50
LIFO (counting forward from first purchases)	20	1.00	20.00
	5	2.00	10.00
			30.00
AVCO (average price across ALL purchases)	25	80 kg bought for $140. Average price = 140/80 = 1.75/kg	43.75

We can see that all three methods produce a different result. Generally, when prices are rising, FIFO will give the highest valuation, LIFO the lowest, with AVCO coming somewhere in between. Different valuations will affect the profits, assets and equity differently.

	Higher inventory valuation	Lower inventory valuation
Cost of sales	Lower	Higher
Gross profit	Higher	Lower
Profit for year	Higher	Lower
Current assets	Higher	Lower
Total assets	Higher	Lower
Equity	Higher	Lower

US Accounting Standards (US GAAP) allow the use of all three methods; International Accounting Standards (IFRS) allow FIFO and AVCO, but not LIFO when valuing inventory for inclusion in financial statements.

Statements of financial position

ACTIVITY 3.15

Omar's store also started to sell 2kg bags of easy-mix cement. The cement mix is delivered in bulk and put into 2kg bags when required by customers. Over the first three months of selling, the purchases and sales have been as follows:

Omar's Hardware Store			Easy-mix cement
Date	Purchase/sale	Quantity	Price – $/kg
1 August	Purchase	10 kg	1.00
1 September	Purchase	15 kg	1.50
1 October	Purchase	20 kg	2.00
15 September	Sales	10 bags	
15 October	Sales	8 bags	

Prepare an inventory valuation statement at 31 October using FIFO, LIFO and AVCO.

QUICK TEST

1. Explain the purpose of a statement of financial position?

2. Explain the difference between (a) a current asset and a non-current asset; and (b) a current liability and a non-current liability? Give examples of each.

3. In which order are current assets listed in a statement of financial position and why?

4. Explain why a statement of financial position must always balance.

5. Explain the following terms:
   - positive working capital
   - negative working capital
   - capital employed
   - net assets
   - intangible assets
   - net realisable value
   - liquid assets
   - goodwill

6. A business has current assets of $83 000 and current liabilities of $57 000. How much working capital does it have?

7. A business has current assets of $120 000 and current liabilities of $156 000. (a) How much working capital does it have?; (b) Explain **two** problems this will cause the business.

8. A business has total assets of $290 000, non-current liabilities of $88 000 and current liabilities of $50 000. What is the value of its capital employed?

9. QWE Ltd. purchased Arkness on 30 September for $30 000. The total assets and liabilities of Arkness were valued at $28 000 and $3 000 respectively on that day. How much goodwill did QWE Ltd. include in the price it paid to take over Arkness?

10. A business had the following assets and liabilities on 30 June. The values of all non-current assets are shown net of accumulated depreciation.

	$
Premises	100 000
Machinery	50 000
Vehicles	25 000
Inventory (at net realisable value)	26 000
Trade receivables (net of provision for doubtful debts)	14 000
Bank	5 000
Trade payables	20 000
Bank loan repayable over 15 years	60 000

(a) calculate the (i) working capital (ii) capital employed (iii) net assets (iv) capital owned.

(b) prepare a statement of financial position for the business as at 30 June in (i) a horizontal format (ii) a vertical format.

11 Why do we need to carry out valuation of inventory?

12 Describe the **three** methods of valuing inventory

13 In times of rising purchse prices, which method of valuation results in higher profits – and why?

14 The rule for valuing inventories is that they should be valued at the lower of their cost or net realisable value. This rule is a practical application of which accounting principle?

15 Temilah Adiwole operates a small music store. Over a number of years he has accumulated an inventory of CDs. These have cost an average of $6.00 to purchase. Due to the increasing popularity of digital downloading of music, it has become more difficult to sell these CDs and a decision has been taken to have an immediate "clear out" sale at a price of $4.00 for every disc following the accounting year end. An additional $0.50 will be spent on repackaging. At what price should these CDs be valued at the year end?

16 Suburban Services Ltd. have just started up in business supplying cordless vacuum cleaners. During the first three months trading they have been buying from various suppliers at different prices to establish where they can get the best deals.

Suburban Services Ltd.			Turbocleaners	
Date	Purchase/(sale)	Quantity	Price ($)	Purchase value ($)
1 October	Purchase	50	100	5 000
31 October	(Sales month 1)	(32)		
1 November	Purchase	30	125	3 750
15 November	Purchase	15	100	1 500
30 November	(Sales month 2)	(28)		
15 December	Purchase	50	140	7 000
31 December	Purchase	20	115	2 300
31 December	(Sales month 3)	(50)		

(a) Prepare a valuation statement for Suburban Services at 31 December using FIFO, LIFO and AVCO.

(b) Which method will result in a) the largest gross profit; and b) the largest cost of sales?

Recap what you've learnt by working through the revision summary for Unit 3. Then test yourself with the Unit 3 assessment activities.

4 Preparation of financial statements

Content at a glance

4.1	Sole traders
4.2	Partnerships
4.3	Clubs and societies
4.4	Incomplete records
4.5	Limited companies
4.6	Manufacturing accounts

Unit 4.1 Sole traders

AIMS

By the end of this unit you should be able to

- explain the advantages and disadvantages of working as a sole trader
- explain the importance of preparing income statements and statements of financial position
- explain the difference between a **trading business** and a **service business**
- prepare **income statements** for trading businesses and for service businesses
- prepare statements of financial position for trading businesses and service businesses
- make adjustments for **provision for depreciation** using the straight-line, reducing balance and revaluation methods
- make adjustments for **accrued** and **prepaid expenses** and **outstanding** and **prepaid income**
- make adjustments for irrecoverable debts and provisions for doubtful debts
- make adjustments for goods taken by business owners for their own use

4.1.1 Different types of business organisation

Businesses can be owned, organised and financed in different ways.

There are many different types of business organisation, ranging from small sole traders and partnerships to large, national and multinational companies. Most are run in order to make a profit for their owners, but some organisations, such as clubs and charities, are not run for profit. ➤ 4.4

Some businesses provide services, such as vehicle servicing and repair or accounting and legal services. Others are involved in manufacturing – turning raw and semi-finished materials into finished products. Some manufacturers produce machinery for other businesses and others produce the goods other businesses use for their own purposes or, in the case of retailers, buy to sell on to consumers. We will look further at the special accounting requirements of manufacturers later in this chapter. ➤ 4.5

As all these organisations are owned and financed in different ways they produce their financial statements in different ways.

Operating as a "sole trader" is the simplest way to be in business. There are both advantages and disadvantages of trading in this way

Trading as a "sole trader" has a number of advantages:

It is very easy to set up

There are very few legal requirements involved in setting up in business as a sole trader. When communicating with third parties, an individual need only indicate that any trading name relates to them personally; "Hedley Johnson trading as Hedjo Plastics" or "Hedjo Plastics is a trading name of Hedley Johnson".

External regulation is light

All businesses must comply with certain regulations and legal restrictions. These will include local health and safety requirements, planning permissions, employment and taxation obligations and general compliance with the law.

Many sole traders run very small businesses with few, if any, employees and with relatively low amounts of revenue and expense. Until they reach specified levels of employment, income, expense or value of assets, these smaller businesses are often exempt, either wholly or in part, from compliance with certain regulations and operation of taxes such as VAT.

The business is answerable only to the owner

There are no other business partners or shareholders whose interests must be considered when making business decisions. Many business people like the idea that the benefit of their good ideas and hard work will belong to them, and them alone.

The business's finances are kept private

Although financial statements will need to be shared with the tax authorities and sometimes with the bank (and others who lend money to the business),

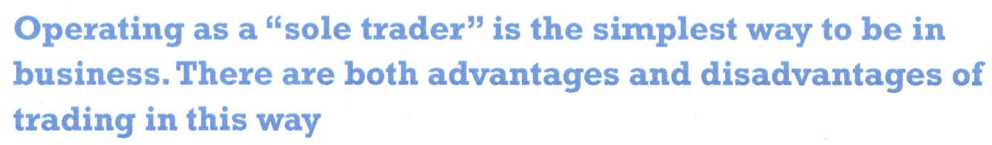

▲ Some businesses sell goods, others sell services

there is no obligation to publish the financial results for public view. The privileges of privacy also extend to partnerships. ➤ 4.2

However, acting as a sole trader can also have several disadvantages.

The owner may have limited resources

In many cases the sole owner of a business may not have the necessary skills or financial resources successfully to develop the business beyond a very basic and limited level. Bringing in other people as partners or shareholders may be the answer to this problem, since they will be able to contribute both funds and skills or experience to satisfy the business needs.

Being a sole trader can sometimes be a lonely business

A sole trader may have no one with whom to discuss and share business problems. They may feel very much on their own – especially when the business encounters hard times. Having partners or other shareholders who can share these burdens may be valuable.

Liability for business obligations is unlimited

Probably the principal drawback of operating as a sole trader is that, because there is no legal separation between the owner and his or her business, the owner is personally responsible (liable) for any legal or financial obligation which arises from the business activities. This will cover such things as financial failure of the business, liability to third parties for shortcomings in the products or services supplied and any non-payment of taxation or other legally required payments. We discuss in a later unit the process of "incorporation" which can limit the business liabilities of owners. ➤ 4.3

Whatever the legal requirements, it is essential for the proper running of a business to keep adequate books of account and prepare regular financial statements to monitor the progress of the business.

4.1.2 Preparing financial statements for trading and service businesses

Trading businesses buy goods for resale to customers while service providers sell their services in return for fees

Trading businesses buy goods that will be resold to customers. Trading businesses usually hold inventories of goods to be resold. Service businesses do not. They earn revenue from the provision of services to other businesses or private individuals. For example, a vehicle repair workshop provides a service in repairing vehicles and will only hold inventory of spare parts and consumables used in that activity, which are not separately for sale to customers.

Trading businesses and service providers prepare financial statements in the same way but only trading businesses calculate gross profit from their sales

Service providers earn revenues from fees or charges made to customers; they need only a basic income statement to calculate the difference between total revenue from services and total operating expenses, which is their net income or profit for the year. They do not need any further information to measure and assess their results.

By contrast, trading businesses earn income by buying and selling goods. The process of buying and selling goods requires additional accounts and concepts – and therefore additional items in the income statement. For example, these businesses will wish to calculate gross profit from sales as well as profit after all expenses have been paid. Gross profit is the "margin" between the cost of the goods or merchandise sold and the sales value charged to customers and is an important indicator in assessing how well a trading business has performed in the year. ➤ **3.1**

However, both types of business will prepare a statement of financial position in the same way; both will have non-current and current assets and liabilities as well as owners' equity.

A **sole trader**, or sole proprietorship, is a business owned by one person. Tariq and Amrita are both sole traders with accounting years that end on 31 December. For several years, Tariq has been operating a small corner shop, while Amrita has just started a small computer services business, offering web design services and computer repairs and tuition. At the close of the year they both produce trial balances, and from these they produce their income statements and statements of financial position.

Tariq Stores – trading business
Trial Balance At 31 December 2012

	Dr ($)	Cr ($)
Revenue		213 000
Sales returns	10 000	
Purchases	171 000	
Purchases returns		5 000
Opening inventory	15 000	
Expenses	24 000	
Fixtures and equipment	250 000	
Trade receivables	1 500	
Trade payables		8 000
Bank	3 500	
Opening equity		261 000
Drawings	12 000	
	487 000	487 000

Note: Closing inventory was valued at $16 000.

Amrita.com – service business
Trial Balance At 31 December 2012

	Dr ($)	Cr ($)
Revenue		75 000
Sales returns	1 500	
Expenses	47 500	
Fixtures and equipment	15 000	
Trade receivables	2 000	
Trade payables		5 000
Bank	9 000	
Opening equity		7 000
Drawings	12 000	
	87 000	87 000

Tariq Stores
Income Statement For The Year Ended 31 December 2012

	$	$
Revenue		213 000
less returns		(10 000)
Net sales		203 000
Opening inventory (at 1 Jan 2012)	15 000	
Purchases	171 000	
less returns	(5 000)	
	181 000	
less closing inventory (at 31 Dec 2012)	(16 000)	
Cost of sales		165 000
Gross profit		38 000
Expenses		24 000
Profit for the year		14 000

Preparation of financial statements

Amrita.com
Income Statement For The Year Ended 31 December 2012

	$	$
Revenue		75 000
less returns		(1 500)
Net sales		73 500
Expenses		48 500
Profit for the year		25 000

Tariq Stores
Statement Of Financial Position At 31 December 2012

	$
Non-current assets	
Fixtures and equipment	250 000
Current assets	
Inventory	16 000
Trade receivables	1 500
Cash	3 500
	21 000
Total assets	271 000
Current liabilities	
Trade payables	8 000
Owner's equity	
Capital at 1 Jan 2012	261 000
Profit for the year	14 000
less drawings	(12 000)
Capital at 31 Dec 2012	263 000
Total liabilities and capital	271 000

Amrita.com
Statement Of Financial Position At 31 December 2012

	$
Non-current assets	
Fixtures and equipment	15 000
Current assets	
Trade receivables	2 000
Cash	9 000
	11 000
Total assets	26 000
Current liabilities	
Trade payables	5 000
Owner's equity	
Capital at 1 Jan 2012	7 000
Profit for the year	25 000
less drawings	(12 000)
Capital at 31 Dec 2012	21 000
Total liabilities and capital	26 000

The statements are prepared and presented in the same way, but you will notice the following differences:

- Inventory appears in the financial statement for the trading business but not in the service business.
- In the income statement, Tariq Stores has an opening section where the gross profit is calculated; Amrita.com has no such section.
- In the income statement, Tariq Stores uses purchases and opening and closing inventories to calculate the cost of sales (cost of goods sold); Amrita.com does not do this.

The following table summarises the differences in content between a trading and service business.

Sole traders

▼ Summary of content for income statement

	Trading business	Service business
Revenue	✓	✓
Sales returns	✓	✗
Opening inventory	✓	✗
Purchases	✓	✗
Carriage inwards	✓	✗
Purchases returns	✓	✗
Closing inventory	✓	✗
Gross profit	✓	✗
Discounts received	✓	✗
Other incomes	✓	✓
Expenses	✓	✓
Discounts allowed	✓	✓
Profit for the year	✓	✓

There are no differences in preparation and format of statements of financial position – both contain non-current and current assets. For example, a cleaning business will need a van, machinery and an inventory of detergents – the difference from a trading business is that these inventories are not for resale and so when they are used they are not included as cost of sales in the income statement.

ACTIVITY 4.1

Pravind Bachoo buys and sells shirts and jackets. Maxine Lesage owns a small business providing cleaning services. They have both completed their first year in business and have prepared the trial balances below.

From their trial balances prepare an income statement for the year ending 31 December for each business.

Pravind Bachoo
Trial Balance At 31 December 2011

	Dr $	Cr $
Revenue		320 000
Sales returns	15 000	
Purchases	255 000	
Purchases returns		20 000
Opening inventory	15 000	
Expenses	35 000	
Fixtures and equipment	250 000	
Trade receivables	10 000	
Trade payables		15 000
Bank	15 000	
Opening equity		265 000
Drawings	25 000	
	620 000	620 000

Note: Closing inventory was valued at $20 000.

Maxine Lesage
Trial Balance At 31 December 2011

	Dr $	Cr $
Revenue		142 000
Sales returns		
Purchases		
Purchases returns		
Opening inventory		
Expenses	96 000	
Fixtures and equipment	30 000	
Trade receivables	6 000	
Trade payables		5 500
Bank	12 000	
Opening equity		12 500
Drawings	16 000	
	160 000	160 000

4.1.3 Making adjustments to financial statements

Both types of business will need to make adjustments to their financial statements for depreciation, irrecoverable and doubtful debts and accrued and prepaid expenses and incomes

These adjustments will include the following:

- **Depreciation** – this recognises the systematic using up of non-current assets over several accounting years and can be calculated using a number of different methods. ➤ **2.2**

- **Irrecoverable and doubtful debts** – this allows for any money which will not be collected from credit customers. The business should regularly estimate how much should prudently be allowed for this. ➤ **1.9**

- **Accrued expenses** – these are the costs incurred for goods or services supplied and used during an accounting year but which have not yet been entered into the books of account. These costs need to be recognised as part of the operating costs for the year along with the corresponding liability to pay for them. ➤ **1.9**

- **Prepaid expenses** – these are expenses that have been entered into the books, but where all or part of the expenditure relates to the next accounting year. These future costs need to be eliminated from the current expenses and carried forward as a current asset – prepayments, within "other receivables" – until such time as the benefit occurs. ➤ **1.9**

- **Accrued or outstanding income** – where income builds up over time, for example under a rental agreement or as interest on a loan is incurred day by day. Proper matching requires that it is brought to account in the year in which it has been earned, even though the actual receipt may not happen until sometime after the end of the accounting year. ➤ **1.9**

- **Prepaid income** – where a payment has been received in advance of the provision of the related goods or services. Recognition of this income must be deferred (put off) until the eventual performance of the service or delivery of the goods. For example, a deposit is usually paid when a holiday is booked, perhaps several months before the trip actually occurs and until then recognition of the revenue represented by the deposit is held back. ➤ **1.9**

- **Goods for own use** – from time to time an owner may take goods for their own use. This is not a business expense; it represents the drawing out of equity by the owner and should be accounted for accordingly. In a service business, an owner may draw from other inventories such as stationery or other consumable items and this will reduce equity in the same way. ➤ **1.7**

These adjustments are applicable to both types of business – trading and service. The following table summarises the impact they will have on the financial statements.

▼ Adjustments and their impact on the statements for income and financial position

Adjustment required	Impact on income statement	Impact on financial position
Provision for depreciation	Increase in expenses and a decrease in profit for the year	Decrease in non-current assets
Irrecoverable debts written off	Increase in expenses and a decrease in profit for the year	Decrease in trade receivables
Provision for doubtful debts	Increase in expenses and a decrease in profit for the year	Decrease in trade receivables
Accrued expenses	Increase in expenses and a decrease in profit for the year	Increase in current liabilities
Prepaid expenses	Decrease in expenses and an increase in profit for the year	Increase in current assets
Accrued income	Increase in income and increase in profit for the year	Increase in current assets
Prepaid income	Decrease in income and decrease in profit for the year	Increase in current liabilities
Goods for own use	Reduction in cost of sales (trading business only) or other relevant expense (trading and service businesses)	Increase in drawings and a reduction in owner's equity

We now look at how Pravind Bachoo makes these adjustments in his financial statements.

Adjustments required in financial statements will be listed at the end of the trial balance

It is the end of the second year after Pravind started business and he has drawn up the following trial balance from his books.

4.1 TRIAL BALANCE

Pravind Bachoo Shirts and Jackets

Trial Balance At 31 December 2012

	Dr $	Cr $
Revenue		394 000
Sales returns	18 000	
Purchases	296 000	
Purchases returns		24 000
Opening inventory	20 000	
Salaries and wages	18 000	
Heating and lighting	9 000	
Telephone and communications	6 000	
Cleaning and maintenance	3 000	
Repairs and renewals	4 000	
Insurance	5 000	
Advertising and promotion	4 000	
Office supplies	2 000	
Bank interest receivable		1 000
Fixtures and equipment	250 000	
Trade receivables	12 000	
Trade payables		18 000
Bank	46 000	
Opening capital		280 000
Drawings	24 000	
	717 000	717 000

Additional information at 31 December 2012:
1. Depreciate equipment by $25 000.
2. Write off $1 000 of irrecoverable debt.
3. Create provision of 5% for doubtful debts for $550 on remaining debts.
4. Insurance expenses of $1 000 were prepaid.
5. Telephone expenses of $500 were accrued.
6. Bank interest income of $500 was accrued.
7. Goods taken for own use during the year were $250.
8. Closing inventory was valued at $25 000 at 31 December.

The additional information supplied requires adjustments in the following ledger accounts, as shown in illustration 4.2.

4.2 ADJUSTMENTS TO THE LEDGER ACCOUNTS

General Ledger — Pravind Bachoo

Provision for depreciation account

Dr			Cr
	$		$
Dec 31 Balance c/d	25 000	Dec 31 Income statement	25 000
		Jan 1 Balance b/d	25 000

❶

General Ledger — Pravind Bachoo

Irrecoverable debts account

Dr			Cr
	$		$
Dec 31 Trade receivables	1 000	Dec 31 Income statement	1 000

❷

General Ledger — Pravind Bachoo

Provision for doubtful debts account

Dr			Cr
	$		$
Dec 31 Balance c/d	550	Dec 31 Income statement	550
		Jan 1 Balance b/d	550

❸

General Ledger — Pravind Bachoo

Insurance account

Dr			Cr
	$		$
Jan 1 Balance c/d	1 000	Dec 31 Income statement	4 000
Oct 1 Bank	4 000	Dec 31 Prepayment c/d	1 000
	5 000		5 000
Jan 1 Balance b/d	1 000		

❹

General Ledger — Pravind Bachoo

Telephone and communications account

Dr			Cr
	$		$
Dec 31 Income statement	5 500	Jan 1 Balance b/d	1 000
Dec 31 Accrual c/d	500	Bank	5 000
	6 000		6 000
		Jan 1 Balance b/d	500

❺

Sole traders 357

```
General Ledger                                              Pravind Bachoo
                    Interest receivable account
Dr                                                                       Cr
                              $                                           $
Dec 31  Income statement   1 500    Oct 1   Bank                      1 000
                                    Dec 31  Interest receivable c/d     500
                           1 500                                      1 500
Jan 1   Balance b/d          500
```

```
General Ledger                                              Pravind Bachoo
                        Drawings account
Dr                                                                       Cr
                                 $                                        $
Nov 30  Bank                30 000
Dec 31  Goods for personal use 250  Dec 31  Capital account          30 250
                            30 250                                   30 250
```

Next, Pravind must prepare financial statements. The impact of the adjustments on the balances in the trial balance are summarised in the table below.

▼ **Impact of adjustments on financial statements**

Balance in the trial balance	Amount	Adjustment required	Adjusted value to record in the income statement	Adjusted value to record in the statement of financial position
Equipment	$250 000	① Depreciation of $25 000	Depreciation expense $25 000	Equipment $225 000
Trade receivables	$12 000	② Irrecoverable debt	Irrecoverable debt expense $1 000	Trade receivables $11 000
Trade receivables	$12 000	③ Provision of 5% against remaining receivables	Irrecoverable debt expense $550	Trade receivables $10 450
Insurance	$5 000	④ Prepayment of three months of annual premium of $4 000	Insurance expense reduced to $4 000	Prepayment of $1 000 (add to other receivables)

Preparation of financial statements

Balance in the trial balance	Amount	Adjustment required	Adjusted value to record in the income statement	Adjusted value to record in the statement of financial position
Telephone and communications	$6 000	⑤ Unbilled usage of $500	Increase telephone and communications to $6 500	Accrued liability of $500 (add to other payables)
Bank interest receivable	$1 000	⑥ Interest of $500 accumulated since last receipt from bank	Increase bank interest receivable to $1 500	Other receivables in current assets $500
Purchases	$296 000	⑦ Goods to value of $250 taken by owner	Decrease purchases to $295 750	Drawings increase to $24 250
		⑧ Closing inventory of $25 000	Reduce costs of sales by $25 000	Inventory $25 000

4.3 INCOME STATEMENT

Adjustments for income and expenses will be made in the income statement to ensure a true and fair calculation of the profit or loss for the year

From the trial balance and adjustments, the business produced the income statement shown in illustration 4.3.

Note how the information listed on the trial balance in illustration 4.1 and adjusted in illustration 4.2 have been made in the statement.

Pravind Bachoo

Income Statement For The Year Ended 31 December 2012

	$	$
Revenue		394 000
less returns		(18 000)
Net sales		376 000
Opening inventory (at 1 Jan 2012)	20 000	
⑦ Purchases	295 750	
less returns	(24 000)	
	291 750	
⑧ less closing inventory (at 31 Dec 2012)	(25 000)	266 750
Cost of sales		109 250
Gross profit		
Add: Other income:		1 500 ⑥
Bank interest receivable		110 750
Less: Expenses:		
Salaries and wages	18 000	
Heating, light and rates	9 000	
⑤ Telephone and communications	6 500	
Cleaning and maintenance	3 000	
Repairs and renewals	4 000	
④ Insurance	4 000	
Advertising and promotion	4 000	
Office supplies and sundries	2 000	
① Depreciation expense	25 000	
③② Irrecoverable debts expense	1 550	
		77 050
Profit for the year		33 700

Sole traders 359

Adjustments for assets and liabilities at the end of the accounting year will be made in the statement of financial position

From the trial balance and adjustments Pravind Bachoo produced the following statement of financial position.

4.4 STATEMENT OF FINANCIAL POSITION

Pravind Bachoo
Statement Of Financial Position
At 31 December 2012

	$	$
Fixtures and equipment		
① Cost	250 000	
less accumulated depreciation	25 000	
		225 000
⑧ Current assets		
Inventory	25 000	
③② Trade receivables	10 450	
Other receivables	1 500	
⑥④ Cash	46 000	
		82 950
Total assets		307 950
Current liabilities		
Trade payables	18 000	
⑤ Other payables	500	
		18 500
Owner's equity		
Capital at 1 Jan 2012		280 000
Profit for the year		33 700
less drawings		(24 250)
⑦ Capital at 31 Dec 2012		289 450
Total liabilities and capital		307 950

Now we'll look at how each of these adjustments are calculated and made.

Adjusting for the provision of depreciation

Depreciation is needed each year to reflect the "using up" of non-current assets over time.

As each year's depreciation is entered in the books and shown as an expense for that year, the total depreciation on the assets increases. This increasing figure is known as **accumulated depreciation**. The net book value of the non-current assets to be shown in the statement of financial position is calculated as the cost of the assets less the accumulated depreciation to date. ➤ **2.2**

Only in the first year of depreciation will the amount of the year's expense and the accumulated depreciation be the same. After that, the accumulated amount will increase every year.

Pravind has acquired premises and equipment for $250 000 on a 10-year lease. The depreciation on this non-current asset is 10% of the cost each year until the lease expires.

Cost of $250 000 at 10% = $25 000. This is the annual depreciation expense and in the first year of application it will also be the accumulated depreciation.

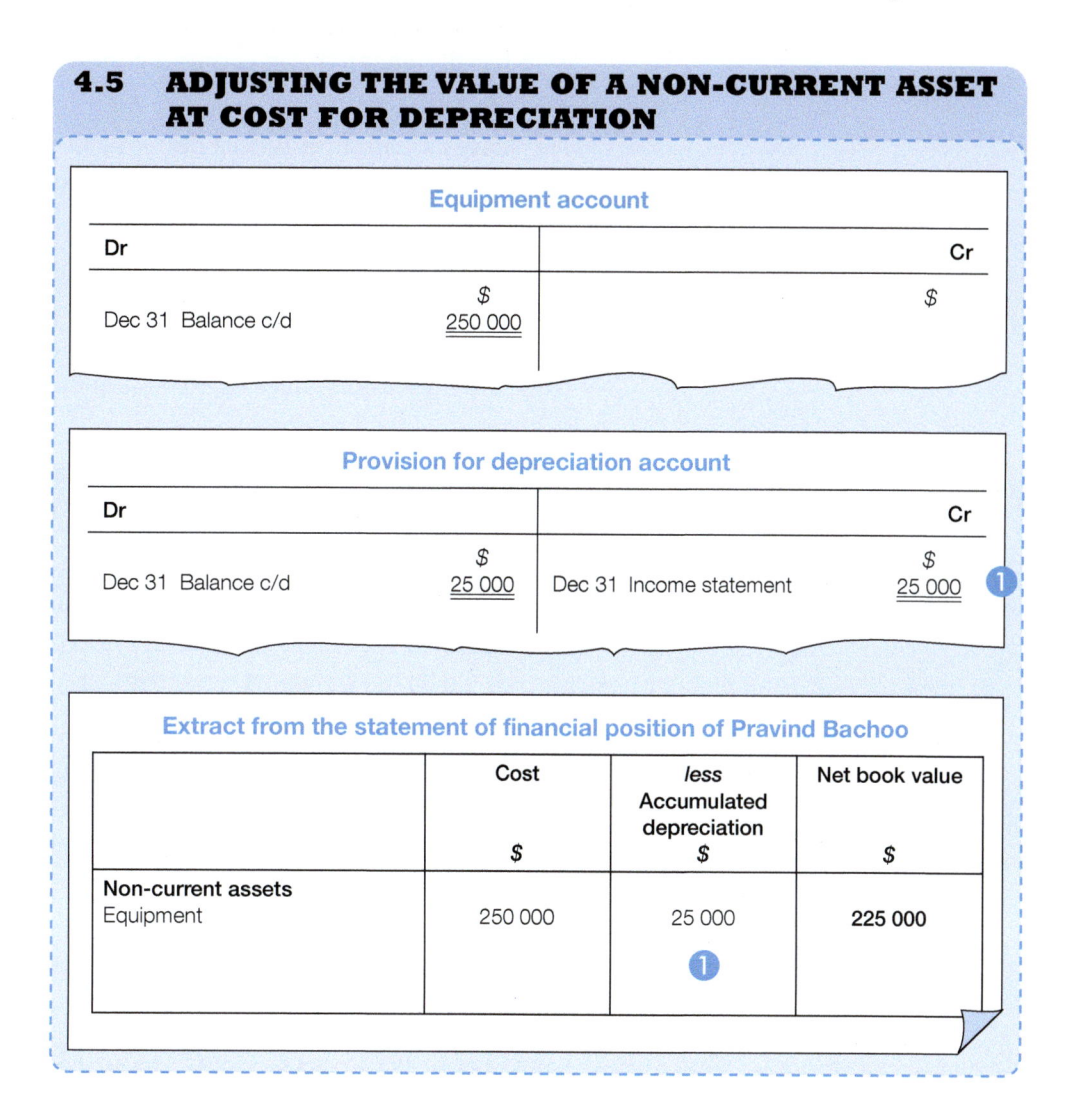

4.5 ADJUSTING THE VALUE OF A NON-CURRENT ASSET AT COST FOR DEPRECIATION

Equipment account

Dr			Cr
	$		$
Dec 31 Balance c/d	250 000		

Provision for depreciation account

Dr			Cr
	$		$
Dec 31 Balance c/d	25 000	Dec 31 Income statement	25 000

Extract from the statement of financial position of Pravind Bachoo

	Cost	less Accumulated depreciation	Net book value
	$	$	$
Non-current assets Equipment	250 000	25 000	225 000

Adjusting for irrecoverable debts and a provision for doubtful debts

Making adjustments to write off irrecoverable debts or making an allowance (provision) for doubtful debts is an application of the prudence concept. This ensures that a business is not putting assets (in this case trade receivables) into its statement of financial position at more than their recoverable amount; that is, at more than the business will actually collect.

A business can make this adjustment in respect of specific customers who cannot or will not pay; in Pravind's case a customer owes $1 000 which will never be recovered. A general provision can also be made to allow for any other customers who may default on payment in the future. Businesses can make an estimate of the proportion or percentage of the total receivable amount which will never be collected. Pravind's estimate is that this percentage may amount to 5% of all trade receivables, after making adjustment for those specific customers where we are aware of default.

Pravind's total trade receivables at 31 December 2012 amounted to $12 000.

The first adjustment is to write off in full the amount owed by his customer who has disappeared and cannot be found. This is an irrecoverable debt of $1 000.

This leaves an amount of $12 000 – $1 000 = $11 000 and Pravind's estimate is that a possible 5% of this total will never be collected. The provision for doubtful debts can now be calculated as:

5% × $11 000 = $550

The total irrecoverable and doubtful debt expense is therefore $1 000 + $550 = $1 550. This is shown as an expense in the income statement and deducted from the trade receivables in the statement of financial position.

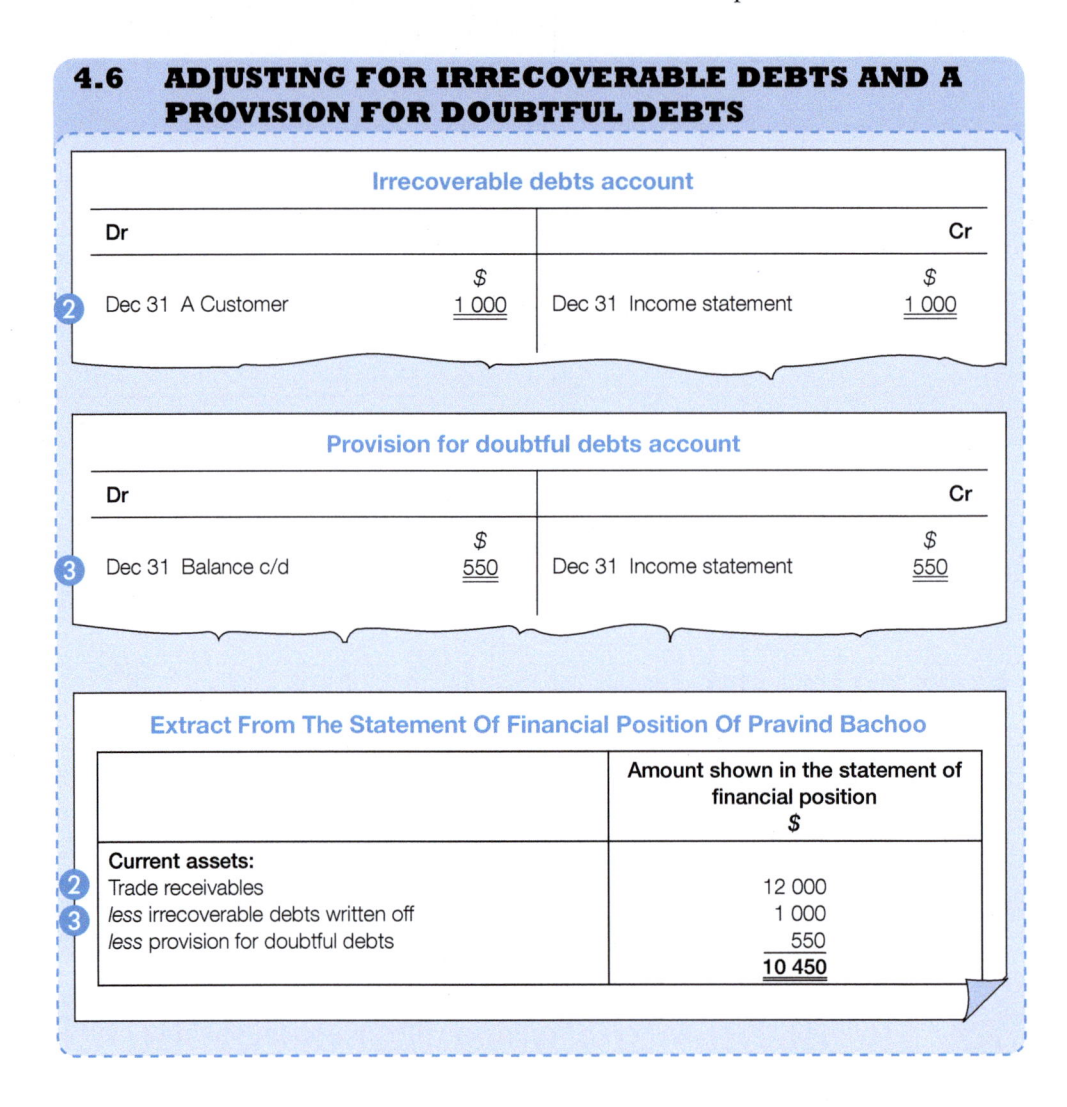

4.6 ADJUSTING FOR IRRECOVERABLE DEBTS AND A PROVISION FOR DOUBTFUL DEBTS

Irrecoverable debts account

Dr				Cr
		$		$
Dec 31 A Customer		1 000	Dec 31 Income statement	1 000

Provision for doubtful debts account

Dr				Cr
		$		$
Dec 31 Balance c/d		550	Dec 31 Income statement	550

Extract From The Statement Of Financial Position Of Pravind Bachoo

	Amount shown in the statement of financial position $
Current assets:	
Trade receivables	12 000
less irrecoverable debts written off	1 000
less provision for doubtful debts	550
	10 450

Adjusting for accruals and prepayments

Adjustment for accrued and prepaid expenses and income is an application of the matching principle to ensure that all, but only, the expenses and income applicable to the accounting period are brought into account.

Accrual of expense and elimination of prepaid income results in an increase in expense or a reduction in income shown in the income statement and a corresponding increase in current liabilities in the statement of financial position.

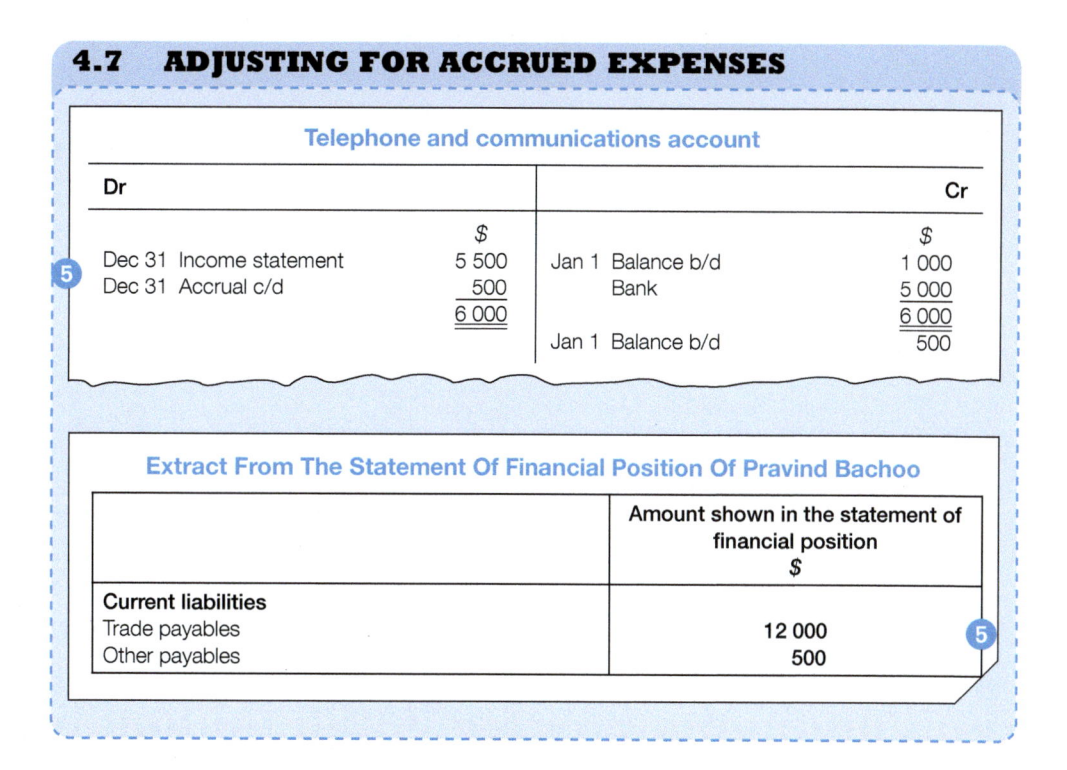

4.7 ADJUSTING FOR ACCRUED EXPENSES

Telephone and communications account

Dr					Cr
		$			$
Dec 31 Income statement		5 500	Jan 1 Balance b/d		1 000
Dec 31 Accrual c/d		500	Bank		5 000
		6 000			6 000
			Jan 1 Balance b/d		500

Extract From The Statement Of Financial Position Of Pravind Bachoo

	Amount shown in the statement of financial position $
Current liabilities	
Trade payables	12 000
Other payables	500

Prepayment of expense and accrual of income results in reduction of expense or increase of income in the income statement and a corresponding increase in current assets in the statement of financial position.

Sole traders 363

4.8 ADJUSTING FOR PREPAYMENTS AND ACCRUED INCOME

Insurance account

Dr				Cr	
		$			$
Jan 1	Balance b/d	1 000	Dec 31	Income statement	4 000
Oct 1	Bank	4 000	Dec 31	Prepayment c/d	1 000
		5 000			5 000
Jan 1	Balance b/d	1 000			

Interest receivable account

Dr				Cr	
		$			$
Dec 31	Income statement	1 500	Oct 1	Bank	1 000
			Dec 31	Interest receivable c/d	500
		1 500			1 500
Jan 1	Interest receivable b/d	500			

Extract From The Statement Of Financial Position Of Pravind Bachoo

	Owed by customers $	Amount shown in the statement of financial position $
Current assets		
Trade receivables (after bad debts)	10 450	10 450
Other receivables:		
Prepaid insurance		
Bank interest receivable		1 500

Adjusting for goods taken for own use

When the owner of a business takes goods, or receives services, from the business for his or her own use, this is clearly not a business expense and the items concerned should be dealt with as drawings in the same way as cash taken out of the business. This will reduce the owner's equity when the balance on the drawings account is deducted from equity in the statement of financial position.

Pravind Bachoo has taken shirts and jackets for his own use. The cost of these items, included in the business's purchases, is $250. This amount must be added to the debit of the drawings account alongside the cash withdrawn. At the end of the year, the balance on the drawings account is transferred as a deduction from the equity in the statement of financial position.

4.9 ADJUSTING FOR GOODS TAKEN FOR OWN USE

Drawings account

Dr		$			Cr $
Dec 1	Bank	24 000	Dec 31	Capital	24 250
	Purchases	250			
		24 250			
					24 250

Extract From The Statement Of Financial Position Of Pravind Bachoo

	Amount shown in the statement of financial position $
Opening capital	280 000
Profit for the year	33 700
Drawings	(24 250)
	289 450

ACTIVITY 4.2

The following trial balance for the accounting year ending 31 December 2012 was extracted from the books of Lorenzo who started a business as a painter and decorator on 1 January 2012. He also rents out his van for small house removals.

	Dr $	Cr $
Sales		125 000
Purchases of paint	50 000	
Purchases of other consumables	15 000	
Inventory of paint at start of year	4 000	
Salaries and wages	5 000	
Van running costs	6 000	
Telephone and communications	1 000	
Small tool replacement	5 000	
Insurance	2 400	
Advertising and promotion	600	
Office and computer supplies	1 500	
Van rental income		4 000
Bank interest payable	500	
Van and equipment	20 000	
Trade receivables	2 000	
Trade payables		3 000
Bank overdraft		6 000
Opening equity		5 000
Drawings	30 000	
	139 000	139 000

At 31 December 2012:
1. An insurance premium was prepaid by $600
2. There was uninvoiced van rental receivable of $500
3. Depreciation on the van and equipment needed to be provided at 20% of cost
4. An irrecoverable debt had been incurred of $500
5. Additional provision for doubtful debts was estimated at $150

In addition, Lorenzo recorded a number of adjustments to the trial balance. He also had an inventory of paint at the end of the year amounting to $4 000.

1. Draw up ledger accounts to record the adjustments.
2. Prepare Lorenzo's income statement for his first year ended 31 December 2012.
3. Prepare a statement of financial position at 31 December 2012.

4.1.4 Adjusting for accumulated depreciation

Now we'll look at the accounting process for dealing with accumulated depreciation on a year-by-year basis. The accumulated depreciation account continues to increase as each year's depreciation is debited as an expense in the income statement and added as a credit to the growing balance on the accumulated depreciation account.

In Pravind Bachoo's case, in his next year the accounts would look as shown in illustration 4.10.

4.10 ADJUSTING THE VALUE OF A NON-CURRENT ASSET AT COST FOR DEPRECIATION

Equipment account

Dr			Cr
	$		$
Dec 31 Balance c/d	250 000		

Depreciation expense account

Dr			Cr
	$		$
Dec 1 Accumulated depreciation	25 000	Dec 31 Income statement	25 000

Accumulated depreciation account

Dr			Cr
	$		$
		Jan 1 Balance b/d	25 000
Dec 31 Balance c/d	50 000	Dec 31 Depreciation expense for 2013	25 000
	50 000		50 000
		Jan 1 Balance b/d	50 000

Extract From The Statement Of Financial Position Of Pravind Bachoo

	Cost	less Accumulated depreciation	Net book value
	$	$	$
Non-current assets Equipment	250 000	50 000	200 000

In summary, the year's depreciation of $25 000 for 2013 has been charged as an expense in the income statement; it has increased the accumulated depreciation account by $25 000 from $25 000 to $50 000 and decreased the net book value of the non-current assets in the statement of financial position by $25 000 from $225 000 at the end of 2012 to $200 000 at the end of 2013.

> **ACTIVITY 4.3**
>
> Henry Cheung runs a plumbing business based in his home. He has extracted the following trial balance at his year end – 31 March 2012. The only adjustments not yet made involve the closing inventory of plumbing spares and supplies amounting to $5 000 and the depreciation of his van and equipment which is depreciated at 25% of the net book value.
>
> | | Dr | Cr |
> |---|---|---|
> | | $ | $ |
> | Sales | | 82 000 |
> | Purchases | 30 000 | |
> | Purchases returns | | 2 000 |
> | Opening inventory of plumbing supplies | 3 000 | |
> | Telephone and communications | 500 | |
> | Van running costs | 1 500 | |
> | Insurance | 1 000 | |
> | Advertising and promotion | 750 | |
> | Office supplies | 750 | |
> | Home office expenses | 1 000 | |
> | Van and equipment at cost | 30 000 | |
> | Accumulated depreciation | | 14 000 |
> | Trade payables | | 1 000 |
> | Bank | 12 500 | |
> | Opening equity | | 18 000 |
> | Drawings | 36 000 | |
> | | 117 000 | 117 000 |
>
> 1 Calculate the depreciation expense for the year.
>
> 2 Prepare an income statement for the year ended 31 March 2012.
>
> 3 Prepare a statement of financial position at 31 March 2012.

4.1.5 Adjusting the provision for doubtful debts

The level of provision needed to cover the possibility of doubtful debts is likely to fluctuate over time for various reasons:

- Economic conditions might make it more or less likely that customers will be unable to pay.
- The number of trade receivables will vary.
- The business may take on more (or fewer) credit-worthy customers.

We have seen that an established provision remains as a continuing deduction from receivables in the statement of financial position, but with no additional impact on the income statement, until such time as it is adjusted. If a higher level of provision needed, an additional expense is charged to the income statement to top up the existing provision. If the provision is no longer required at the former level, the reduction is made by crediting the income statement and reducing the provision to be deducted from trade receivables in the statement of financial position.

For Pravind Bachoo the situation has changed in the current year; he has experienced no more irrecoverable debts; but his trade receivables have gone up to $20 000. However, he is confident that he only needs to make provision at 3% of the total. The amount now needed is 3% × 20 000 = $600 and a further

$50 is needed to top up the existing $550 to the new level of $600. This will be treated as an irrecoverable debt expense of $50 in the income statement.

Pravind's provision for doubtful debts account now looks as follows:

4.11 ADJUSTING THE PROVISION FOR DOUBTFUL DEBTS

Provision for doubtful debts account

Dr			Cr
Last year	$	*Last year*	$
Dec 31 Balance c/d	550	Dec 31 Income statement	550
This year		*This year*	
Dec 31 Balance c/d	600	Jan 1 Balance b/d	550
		Dec 31 Income statement	50
	600		600
		Jan 1 Balance b/d	600

ACTIVITY 4.4

Sharwaz Hussain buys and sells packaging materials. His customers vary in their credit-worthiness and he estimates that a 10% provision is required against total trade receivables to cover the possibility of bad debts.

His trial balance at 30 September 2014 is given below.

Sharwaz Hussain

Trial Balance At 30 September 2014

	Dr	Cr
	$	$
Sales		157 000
Sales returns	5 000	
Purchases	77 000	
Purchases returns		3 000
Opening inventory at 1 Oct 2013	7 000	
General operating expenses	35 000	
Bad debt expense	700	
Depreciation for year	5 000	
Fixtures and equipment at cost	25 000	
Accumulated depreciation at 30 Sep 2014		15 000
Trade receivables (after irrecoverable debt written off $700)	25 000	
Provision for doubtful debts at 1 Oct 2013		1 700
Trade payables		18 000
Bank	11 000	
Opening equity		26 000
Drawings	30 000	
	220 700	220 700

Note: Closing inventory is valued at $11 000.

1 Calculate the revised level of provision required against doubtful debts.

2 Prepare an income statement for the year ended 30 September 2014.

3 Prepare a statement of financial position at 30 September 2014.

QUICK TEST

1. Explain the differences between a trading and a service business.

2. Which accounting principles are being used in making the following accounting adjustments (there may be more than one for each item)?
   - Provision of an annual charge for depreciation expense
   - Establishment of a provision for irrecoverable and doubtful debts
   - Calculation of prepaid and accrued expenses
   - Adjustments made for goods taken for an owner's own use

3. Joseph Layiwola maintains a provision for doubtful debts. On 1 February 2012 there was a credit balance of $920 on the provision for doubtful debts account.

   At 31 January 2013 Joseph Layiwola's trade receivables amounted to $28 600 and he decided to maintain the provision for doubtful debts at 3% of the trade receivables.

   Write up the provision for doubtful debts account as it would appear in Joseph Layiwola's ledger for the year ended 31 January 2013.

4. Gulrez has bought a machine costing $7 200 for use in his business. He estimates the machine will have a useful life of three years and will have a scrap value of $900 after that time. Gulrez decides he will depreciate the machine on the straight line method.

   Calculate the depreciation to be charged on the machine in Gulrez's income statement for each of the three years of its useful life. Show your workings.

5. Gulrez is preparing his financial statements for the year ended 30 September 2013 and has extracted the following items from his books of account at that date.

	$
Revenue (sales)	145 000
Rent receivable	13 000
Sales returns	1 600
Inventory at 1 October 2012	12 000
Raw materials (purchases)	97 600
Distribution expenses	5 160
Administrative expenses	16 450
Other operating expenses	3 200
Finance costs	2 760
Drawings	24 000

No entry has yet been made for depreciation on the machine shown in question 4.

The following additional information is available.

1. Gulrez has valued his inventory at 30 September 2013 at $15 200.
2. Rent receivable includes $2 600 received in advance.
3. Additional administrative expenses of $750 are to be accrued.
4. Depreciation (as calculated in question 4 above) is to be included.

Prepare Gulrez's income statement (showing the trading account) for the year ended 30 September 2013.

6 Josephine rents a photocopying machine for her business. The annual rental is a total of $1 800, half of which is paid in advance every six months on 1 October and 1 April. The last six-monthly payment was on 1 October 2012. There is also a charge of $0.01 per copy, which is billed and settled at the same time as the rental. Josephine's year end is 31 December. At 31 December 2012, the meter on the machine showed that 25 000 copies had been made since the last billing.

Calculate the prepayment and accrued expense for renting and using the photocopier which will require adjustment in Josephine's financial statements at 31 December 2012.

Unit 4.2 Partnerships

AIMS

By the end of this unit you should be able to

- explain the advantages and disadvantages of forming a **partnership**
- outline the importance and contents of a **partnership agreement**
- explain the purpose of an **appropriation account**
- prepare income statements, appropriation accounts and statements of financial position
- record **interest on partners' loans, interest on capital, interest on drawings, partner's salaries,** and the **division of the balance of profit or loss**
- make adjustments to financial statements as detailed in 4.1 (sole traders)
- explain the uses of and differences between capital and current accounts
- draw up partners' current and capital accounts in ledger account form and as part of a statement of financial position
- make simple entries for the formation of a partnership via capital contribution by each partner in cash and/or non-cash assets and amalgamation of two

4.2.1 Forming a partnership

A partnership has at least two owners who agree to share the profits and losses of their business

A **partnership** is a legal agreement between two or more people, usually no more than 20, to own, finance and jointly run a business. The partners also agree to share any profits or losses.

Most partnerships are small businesses run by professionals including solicitors, doctors and accountants.

Most partners are **general partners** who share **unlimited liability**. This is often expressed as being jointly and severally liable for the debts of the partnership. This means that each partner is fully liable for the entire debts of and claims against the business – not limited to the amount of capital that partner has already put in and not limited to just the partner's proportionate stake in the business. This could lead to partners, or indeed one partner, having to pay from their personal resources, even to the extent of bankruptcy and personal financial ruin. Each partner is therefore in much the same position as a sole trader. ▶ 4.1

However, it is possible for a partnership to have some **limited partners** with **limited liability**. This means that they are liable only to the extent of the capital they have put in to the business and that limits the amount they can lose. To obtain this benefit of limited liability, the partnership must be registered as a limited partnership, and limited partners are allowed no formal say in how the business is run.

In addition, a partnership may have a number of silent partners or **sleeping partners.** They will provide money to the partnership in return for a share of the profits, but, again, will not be involved in the management and decision making of the business.

Forming a partnership can bring new capital and skills into a small business, but disagreements between partners may cause problems

A partnership has a number of advantages:

It is relatively easy to set up.

There are few legal requirements involved in drawing up a partnership agreement or deed of partnership. Most partnerships are not required by law to publish annual financial accounts, though statements will be required for the partners themselves and, usually, by the local tax authorities.

Partners can bring new skills and ideas to a business.

New partners can be brought in when they have skills that the business needs – for example manufacturing experience, financial knowledge or marketing and communications abilities.

Partners share the tasks of management.

Partners take their part in sharing the burdens of managing the business by participating in decision making and taking on administrative roles in running the business from day to day. They can also participate in decision making and managing the business from day to day.

Partners will invest new capital into the business to finance expansion.

New partners will often bring their own capital to invest in the business. New partners provide capital that can be used to finance business expansion in return for a share of the profits. Partners are motivated to work hard because they share the profits of their business.

However, a partnership can also have several disadvantages.

Decision making can be difficult.

Discussions between partners can slow down decision making and the more partners there are, the more likely they are to disagree. If they cannot agree on important decisions affecting the running of the partnership, the business may suffer.

Problems can also arise if one or more partners are lazy, inefficient or even dishonest. For a partnership to succeed there must be good working relationships and mutual trust between partners.

General partners are jointly responsible for the debts of the business.

As with a sole trader, general partners could lose all their possessions of value if the partnership fails or is negligent and causes injury to a third party. In addition, each partner can be held responsible for the actions of other partners. Limited partners have limited liability.

Partnerships lack capital.

Raising additional capital to finance further business expansion can be difficult because many countries place a legal limit on the number of partners allowed in a partnership.

Partnerships may have to be wound up if a partner leaves or dies.

Unless specifically overridden by a formal partnership agreement, a partnership is considered to be dissolved on the death or departure of any of the general partners. This can cause unforeseen and unwelcome consequences for the personal taxation of the partners, and also for relationships with other people with whom the partnership may have legal agreements. The arrival of new partners can also be regarded as the creation of a "new" partnership alongside the dissolving of the former one.

Partners will formalise how they will share the finance, running and profits of their business in a partnership agreement or deed of partnership

It is normally regarded as essential for the affairs of a partnership to be governed by a formal partnership agreement or deed of partnership because of:

- the potential for disagreement
- the unlimited nature of the partners' liabilities
- the likely differences in remuneration between partners
- the way in which new partners may be asked to contribute capital
- the significance of potential termination following the death or departure of partners.

The table below shows the key issues addressed in such a partnership agreement.

▼ Content of a partnership agreement

Key contents	
Continuation of partnership	There will often be provision made for the continuation of the partnership on the death, departure or arrival of partners.
Management and regulation of partnership activities	This will deal, for example, with the holding of meetings, the notice that must be given to partners of any proposed changes in their arrangements and the way in which disputes may be resolved.
Partners' capital	This refers to the amount that new partners are expected to contribute and pay in to the partnership to be admitted. This may, or may not, include a payment in respect of the "goodwill" built up by existing partners.
	Arrangements should be made for the withdrawal of capital on the death or departure of partners – whether or not capital may be drawn out by continuing partners; and, if so, how this should be limited.
	Partners' capital contributions need not be equal. Any difference can be compensated for by allowing for interest on capital.
Partner's responsibilities	Specific responsibilities for performance of business activity and for management of the partnership affairs can be identified and allocated among the partners.
Interest on capital	There should be an agreed rate at which interest should be credited on partners' capital.
	This interest is not a business expense to be deducted in arriving at the business's profit but is an apportionment of part of the profit to compensate for differences in capital contributions.
Partner's salaries	This is a further apportionment of part of the business profits to reward individual partners for specific operational or management tasks they are asked to undertake.

How profits or losses are shared	Provision is made here for the way in which the residual profit will be divided between partners once interest on capital and specific salaries have been allocated.
This profit share does not need to be equal, and may, for example, reflect seniority or a particular level of responsibility not rewarded by the allocation of salary.
Partner's drawings	It is usual for partners to draw money from the business ahead of the profit share they will be allocated. They might not withdraw equal amounts and there is also a risk that they may draw more than the profits they are entitled to, possibly at a level that may harm the business. An agreement will usually set a limit on how much may be drawn out in cash and may also provide for interest to be charged on the drawings, in a similar way to interest allowed on capital, to compensate for partners drawing unequal amounts. Again, this is a readjustment of profits between the partners rather than representing any sort of income for the partnership business.
Partner's loans	Sometimes partners may wish to provide funds to the business by way of loans, rather than by contributing equity capital. Repayment of equity capital is likely to be restricted, whereas with a loan they would get full repayment at the agreed time. Interest on the loan will be agreed, and this time it is a proper expense of the business and should be shown in the income statement as part of the calculation of the partnership profits.

When Robin and Marion agreed to form a partnership they decided that:

1. Robin would contribute $50 000 as fixed capital and Marion would contribute $100 000.
2. Interest on capital would run at 5% per annum.
3. Since he would have the main responsibility for the business activities, Robin would have a salary of $10 000.
4. Residual profit was to be shared out equally between them.
5. Neither of them would draw anything out of the business until their profit shares had been calculated.
6. In the first year, they expect to make a business profit of $85 000.

The effect of this arrangement is shown in illustration 4.12.

4.12 PARTNERSHIP ARRANGEMENT – PROFIT AND INTEREST ON CAPITAL

	$	$
Profit for the year		85 000
Interest on capital		
Robin: $50 000 × 5%	2 500	
Marion: $100 000 × 5%	5 000	
		(7 500)
Salary		
Robin		(10 000)
		67 500
Share of profit		
Robin	33 750	
Marion	33 750	
		(67 500)

Marion has been compensated for contributing a higher capital than Robin; while Robin has been compensated for his greater responsibilities. After these rewards they have shared equally in the residual profits.

4.2.2 Preparing accounting records

The ledger will record the capital contributions, drawings, salaries and profit share of each individual partner

Each partner will keep separate records of his or her capital contributions, drawings, salaries and profit share. These will be recorded in the following ledger accounts and the balances on these accounts will appear in the capital section of the statement of financial position.

▼ Ledger accounts for partners

Ledger account	
Capital account	This will record the capital contributions of partners. They will be credited with the contributions they make on joining the partnership and with any further contributions they may make from time to time. They will be debited with any withdrawal of capital. The balances on this account will probably change only infrequently.
Drawings account	This will be debited with any cash drawings made during the year and with any goods taken for a partner's own use, if this applies. At the end of the year the account is balanced off and the balance transferred to the current account.
Current account	This will be credited with any interest on capital and any salary. It will be debited with any interest on drawings. At the end of the year it will be debited with the total drawings transferred from the drawings account; and credited with the shares of residual profit once these have been calculated in the appropriation account.

4.13 PARTNERSHIP ARRANGEMENT – CAPITAL AND DRAWINGS

Stanley, with capital of $50 000, and Oliver, with capital of $30 000, are in partnership.

The terms of their partnership agreement state that:

1. Interest is to be charged on drawings at 10% per annum on the balances in the drawings accounts at the end of the financial year.
2. Interest is to be allowed on capital at 10% per annum on the balances in the capital accounts at the end of the financial year.
3. In recognition of Stanley's special expertise he will receive a salary of $10 000.
4. Residual profit will then be shared with Oliver as senior partner taking 60% and Stanley 40%.

During their first year the business recorded the following in the ledger accounts.

Partners' capital accounts

Dr ($)	Stanley	Oliver	Cr ($)	Stanley	Oliver
Dec 31 Balances c/d	50 000	30 000	Jan 1 Bank	50 000	30 000
			Jan 1 Balances b/d	50 000	30 000

Partnerships 375

The capital accounts are credited with the capital introduced by each partner. A columnar format is adopted rather than setting up a separate account for each partner.

Partners' drawings accounts

Dr ($)	Stanley	Oliver	Cr ($)	Stanley	Oliver
Jun 30 Cash	25 000	8 000	Dec 31 Transfer to current accounts	50 000	25 000
Sep 30 Cash	25 000	17 000		50 000	25 000
	50 000	25 000			

The drawings accounts are debited with the cash drawings as they arise during the year. Again, a columnar format is used. At the end of the year the balances are transferred to the current accounts and any applicable interest is calculated.

Partners' current accounts

Dr ($)	Stanley	Oliver	Cr ($)	Stanley	Oliver
Drawings	50 000	25 000	Interest on capital	5 000	3 000
Interest on drawings	5 000	2 500	Salary	10 000	

The current accounts are debited with the drawings transferred from the drawings account and with the interest on those drawings. The partnership agreement allows for interest at 10% on the closing balance of drawings:

Stanley: $50 000 × 10% = $5 000; Oliver: $25 000 × 10% = $2 500.

The current accounts are then credited with the interest on capital. Once again, the partnership agreement allows for this at 10% of the closing balances on the capital account:

Stanley: $50 000 × 10% = $5 000; Oliver: $30 000 × 10% = $3 000.

Next, Stanley is credited with the salary allowed to him in accordance with the partnership agreement: $10 000.

The current accounts will be closed off and carried down once the transfers of the residual profit shares have been made from the appropriation account.

In addition to an income statement a partnership will prepare an appropriation account at the end of each accounting year to show the distribution of profits

The current accounts of each partner can only be completed with profit shares once the income statement and appropriation account have been prepared. The income statement follows exactly the same format and principles as for a sole trader; the appropriation account section follows the same format as shown in 4.14.

4.14 PARTNERSHIP INCOME STATEMENT AND APPROPRIATION ACCOUNT

After the first year's trading, Stanley and Oliver have extracted the following information from their accounting records as at 31 December.

	$
Revenue	350 000
Purchases of goods	120 000
Closing inventory of goods	20 000
Wages and salaries	24 500
Other operating costs	115 000
Fixtures and equipment at cost	75 000
Trade receivables	30 000

Additional information at 31 December:

Depreciation of fixtures and equipment is to be charged at 10% per annum on cost

A provision for doubtful debts is required of 5% of trade receivables

Wages of $2 000 were accrued

Prepaid operating costs were $1 000

The income statement, drawn up in exactly the same way as for a sole trader will be as shown, and is immediately followed by the appropriation account.

Stanley and Oliver

Income Statement For The Year Ended 31 December

	$	$
Revenue		350 000
Purchases of goods	120 000	
less closing inventory of goods	20 000	
Cost of sales		100 000
Gross profit		250 000
Less: expenses		
Wages and salaries $24 500 + $2 000 accrued	26 500	
Other operating costs $115 000 − $1 000 prepaid	114 000	
Depreciation of fixtures and equipment $75 000 × 10%	7 500	
Irrecoverable debt provision 5% of trade receivables $30 000 × 5%	1 500	
		149 500
Profit for year		100 500

The appropriation account can now be drawn up – once again in columnar form.

Stanley and Oliver

Appropriation Account For The Year Ended 31 December

	Stanley $	Oliver $	Total $
Profit from income statement			100 500
add interest on drawings	(5 000)	(2 500)	7 500
			108 000
less interest on capital	5 000	3 000	(8 000)
			100 000
less salary	10 000		(10 000)
Residual profit to share			90 000
Oliver: 60% × $90 000		54 000	54 000
Stanley: 40% × $90 000	36 000		36 000
			90 000
	46 000	54 500	100 500

The residual profit shares can now be transferred to the current accounts, which can then be balanced off and carried down to next year as follows.

Partners' current accounts

Dr	Stanley $	Oliver $	Cr	Stanley $	Oliver $
Drawings	50 000	25 000	Interest on capital	5 000	3 000
Interest on drawings	5 000	2 500	Salary	10 000	
			Share of residual profit	36 000	54 000
Balance c/d		29 500	Balance c/d	4 000	
	55 000	57 000		55 000	57 000
Jan 1 Balance b/d		4 000	Jan 1 Balance b/d		29 500

You will notice that Stanley has a debit balance on his account. This means that he owes the partnership this amount on his current account. This has arisen because of the substantial amount he has drawn during the year – more than can be compensated for by his salary and residual profit share together.

ACTIVITY 4.5

Vladimir and Igor are in partnership. The following information was extracted from their business records on 31 December 2012.

	$
Capital accounts at 1 Jan and 31 Dec 2012	
Vladimir	70 000
Igor	50 000
Current accounts at 1 Jan 2012:	
Vladimir in credit	8 000
Igor in credit	12 000
Profit for the year ended 31 Dec 2012 per income statement	225 000
Drawings balance on accounts at 31 Dec 2012	
Vladimir	120 000
Igor	40 000
Interest on capital – per annum	5%
Interest on drawings – per annum	4%
Salary	
Igor	12 000
Share in residual profit	
Vladimir	75%
Igor	25%

Draw up the partners' current accounts including their respective profit shares.

The statement of financial position of a partnership will show the capital and current accounts of each partner in the equity section

A partnership's statement of financial position will look exactly the same as for a sole trader, except that the equity section will give details of the partners' capital and current accounts.

4.15 STATEMENT OF FINANCIAL POSITION

Stanley and Oliver had the following assets and liabilities on 31 December at the end of their first accounting year. The provision for doubtful debts – $1 500 – and the accumulated depreciation arising from the first year's depreciation – $7 500 – have been created as shown in the previous detailed income statement.

	$
Fixtures and equipment at cost	75 000
Accumulated depreciation at 31 Dec	7 500
Closing inventory of goods	20 000
Trade receivables	30 000
Provision for doubtful debts at 31 Dec	1 500
Wages outstanding at 31 Dec	2 000
Operating costs prepaid at 31 Dec	1 000
Trade payables	10 000
Cash at bank	500

Partnerships

Stanley and Oliver's statement of financial position will look like this.

Stanley and Oliver

Statement Of Financial Position At 31 December

	$	$	$
Non-current assets			
Fixtures and equipment – cost			75 000
less accumulated depreciation			7 500
			67 500
Current assets			
Inventory		20 000	
Trade receivables	30 000		
Less provision for doubtful debts	1 500		
		28 500	
Other receivables		1 000	
Cash at bank		500	
			50 000
Total assets			117 500
Current liabilities			
Trade payables		10 000	
Other payables		2 000	
			12 000
Capital accounts at 31 Dec			
Stanley	50 000		
Oliver	30 000		
		80 000	
Current accounts at 31 Dec			
Stanley	(4 000)		
Oliver	29 500		
		25 500	
			105 500
Total liabilities and capital			117 500

ACTIVITY 4.6

A list of balances extracted at the year ending 31 December from the books of the partnership between Pedro and Louisa is given below.

		$
Fixtures and equipment at cost		90 000
Accumulated depreciation at 31 Dec		27 000
Closing inventory of goods		40 000
Trade receivables		65 000
Provision for doubtful debts at 31 Dec		3 500
Other receivables		8 000
Trade payables		46 000
Other payables		10 000
Cash at bank		14 000
Capital (interest at 10%) Pedro		50 000
Louisa		40 000
Current accounts at 1 Jan Pedro		8 000
Louisa		9 000
Drawings (interest at 10%) Pedro		50 000
Louisa		30 000

Profit for the year was $103 500 and the profit share was Pedro: 55%; Louisa: 45%.

Prepare:

- an appropriation account
- partners' current accounts
- a statement of financial position.

4.2.3 Expanding a partnership

To expand their business partners may increase their capital contributions, provide loans or even take on additional partners

In each example below, the necessary procedures may already be addressed in the partnership agreement but if they are not, the partners will need to change the agreement.

- Increasing capital contributions is a relatively straightforward process. As with a sole trader, the partner or partners simply pay cash into the partnership bank account and the increase in their contribution will be recorded by an equivalent addition to their capital accounts.

- A partner may be willing to provide additional resources to the business by way of a loan rather than an increase in equity. As with loans from other sources, the amount borrowed will be entered in the statement of financial position. Interest will be charged as agreed between the partner and the business, and will be shown as an expense in the income statement. The interest will be credited to the current account of the partner concerned.

- New partners may also bring in new capital. Usually, they will be expected to buy their way into the business by making a capital contribution. This would normally represent an appropriate proportion of the business's net assets (possibly including goodwill and other intangible assets) at the date of admission. This will certainly require amendment of the partnership agreement to reflect the amount of contribution made, and salary that is to be allowed and the adjusted profit shares of the increased number of continuing partners.

We will now look in more detail at the second of these approaches; we do not deal with the admission of a new partner.

A partner may loan the business a sum of money over and above his or her capital contribution

---

4.16 LENDING TO A PARTNERSHIP

Stanley and Oliver needed some more funds for the business. On 1 January Stanley agreed to lend the partnership $50 000 for five years, at which time he will need repayment of the money. The partners have agreed to allow interest on this loan at 12% per annum.

The loan has not yet been brought into the partnership books and neither has any interest been paid or accrued.

When a partner lends the partnership money

Loan account	Bank account
Impact: liabilities are increased – credit partner's loan account	Impact: cash in bank is increased – debit bank account

> **ACTIVITY 4.7**
>
> To reflect the adjustments needed to record the loan and its interest, prepare these revised end of year statements for Stanley and Oliver:
>
> ▸ an income statement
>
> ▸ an appropriation account and partners' current accounts for Stanley and Oliver
>
> ▸ a statement of financial position.

When the partner receives interest

Partner's current account	Income statement
Impact: the partner receives the benefit as a credit to his or her current account	Impact: expenses are increased – debit loan interest account – and profit is reduced

The entries in the relevant loan and interest accounts will appear as follows.

Partner's loan account – Stanley

Dr			Cr
	$		$
		Jan 1 Bank	50 000

Loan interest account

Dr			Cr
	$		$
Dec 31 Stanley current account	6 000	Dec 31 Income statement	6 000

4.2.4 Forming a partnership from existing businesses

Two or more sole traders may agree to amalgamate their businesses to form a partnership

Unlike Stanley and Oliver, who did not have existing businesses before they went into partnership, sole traders planning a partnership will need to agree values for the assets and liabilities they will bring into the partnership. This may include the values of their intangible assets, including goodwill.

The opening capital for each partner will be the net assets (assets less liabilities) of their respective businesses.

4.17 SOLE TRADERS FORMING A PARTNERSHIP

Francis and Justinia are sole traders. They have decided to combine their businesses to form a partnership which they will call Francis and Justinia Enterprises. Here are their statements of financial position:

Francis Industries
Statement Of Financial Position
At 31 December 2012

	$	$
Non-current assets		
Property		45 000
Fixtures and equipment		455 000
		500 000
Current assets		
Inventory	32 000	
Trade receivables	3 000	
Cash	7 000	
		42 000
Total assets		542 000
Current liabilities		
Trade payables		16 000
Capital at 31 Dec 2012		526 000
Total liabilities and capital		542 000

Justinia Services
Statement Of Financial Position
At 31 December 2012

	$	$
Non-current assets		
Fixtures and equipment		300 000
Current assets		
Trade receivables	40 000	
Cash	180 000	
		220 000
Total assets		520 000
Current liabilities		
Trade payables		100 000
Capital at 31 Dec 2012		420 000
Total liabilities and capital		520 000

Following negotiation they agreed that the partnership would take over the assets and liabilities of their existing businesses after the following adjustments:

- Francis would revalue his property to $100 000.
- Justinia would write off $10 000 of irrecoverable debts.
- Goodwill would be valued at $50 000 for Francis and $35 000 for Justinia.

All other values were agreed by the prospective partners as acceptable. From these they prepared the opening capital account for each partner and the opening statement of financial position for Francis and Justinia Enterprises at the start of its first day of trading.

Partners' capital accounts

Dr	Francis	Justinia	Cr	Francis	Justinia
	$	$		$	$
Jan 1 Trade receivables		10 000	Jan 1 Balance	526 000	420 000
			Property revaluation	55 000	
	631 000	445 000	Goodwill	50 000	35 000
Balance c/d	631 000	455 000		631 000	455 000
			Jan 1 Balance b/d	631 000	445 000

Francis and Justinia Enterprises
Statement Of Financial Position At 1 January 2013

	$	$
Non-current assets		
Property		100 000
Fixtures and equipment		755 000
Intangible asset – goodwill		85 000
		940 000
Current assets		
Inventory	32 000	
Trade receivables	33 000	
Cash	187 000	
		252 000
Total assets		1 192 000
Current liabilities		
Trade payables		116 000
Capital at 1 January 2013		
Francis		631 000
Justinia		445 000
		1 076 000
Total liabilities and capital		1 192 000

You will note that the intangible asset of goodwill continues to be shown under non-current assets in the statement of financial position as the combined amount assessed for the goodwill of each of the separate businesses.

If the goodwill is written off it should be debited to the partners' capital accounts in the proportion that they will share profits in the new partnership.

ACTIVITY 4.8

Sole traders Brett and Daley have agreed to amalgamate their businesses. Here are their most recent year end statements of financial position.

Brett
Statement Of Financial Position
At 31 December 2012

	$	$
Non-current assets		
Fixtures and equipment		125 000
Current assets		
Inventory	10 000	
Trade receivables	5 000	
Cash	7 500	
		22 500
Total assets		147 500
Current liabilities		
Trade payables		7 500
Capital at 31 Dec 2012		140 000
Total liabilities and capital		147 500

Daley
Statement Of Financial Position
At 31 December 2012

	$	$
Non-current assets		
Fixtures and equipment		15 000
Current assets		
Trade receivables	3 000	
Cash	6 000	
		9 000
Total assets		24 000
Current liabilities		
Trade payables		2 500
Capital at 31 Dec 2012		21 500
Total liabilities and capital		24 000

They agree the following adjustments to the statements before the amalgamation.

- There will be additional depreciation of $15 000 on Brett's fixtures and equipment.
- Provision will be made for an outstanding legal claim of $2 000 against Daley.
- Brett will write off obsolete inventory of $3 000.
- They agree that no goodwill should be recognised.

Prepare capital accounts for the new partners and a statement of financial position on the first day of the new combined business – Dalbrett Services.

QUICK TEST

1. Outline **four** advantages and **four** disadvantages of trading as a partnership.
2. Explain what is meant by the "unlimited liability" of partners (and sole traders) in connection with their business activity.
3. Define what is meant by the terms (a) limited partner; and (b) sleeping partner.
4. Arne, Boris and Carl are planning to go into partnership. Three profit-sharing schemes are being considered, and they expect a profit of $96 000 in the first year. The schemes are:
   - equal shares
   - 4:2:2 respectively
   - 5:4:3 respectively.

   Calculate the partners' profit shares for each of these schemes.

5 Mick, Nick and Oscar are in partnership sharing profits and losses 3:2:1 respectively. The partnership agreement specifies:

   1. Interest is allowed on capital at 6% per annum.
   2. Oscar is to receive a salary of $12 000
   3. Residual profits or losses are to be shared Mick 3:Nick 2:Oscar 1.

   The partnership made a profit last year of $225 000. Partners' capital is:

   Mick $250 000
   Nick $400 000
   Oscar $320 000.

   Calculate the partners' profit shares.

6 Peggy and Ruth are in partnership. The partnership agreement specifies:

   1. Interest is chargeable on drawings at 10% per annum.
   2. Residual profits or losses are to be shared Peggy 60%: Ruth 40%.

   The partnership made a profit last year of $85 000. Partners' drawings were:

   Peggy $25 000
   Ruth $15 000.

   Calculate the partners' profit shares.

7 Ashok and Zafira are in partnership. The partnership agreement specifies:

   1. Interest is chargeable on drawings at 10% per annum.
   2. Interest on capital is allowed at 8% per annum.
   3. Zafira will get a salary of $12 000.
   4. Residual profits or losses will be shared Ashok 4: Zafira 2.

   The partnership made a profit last year of $196 000. Partners' drawings and capital were:

	Drawings	Capital
Ashok	$25 000	$60 000
Zafira	$15 000	$40 000

   Prepare:
   - partners' capital accounts
   - an appropriation account for the last year
   - partners' current accounts.

8 Twin brothers Malik and Tariq are in a partnership as M&T Traders. The partnership agreement specifies the following:
   - Malik is entitled to interest of 9% per annum on the loan he has made to the business.
   - Interest on total drawings is to be charged at 10% per annum.
   - Interest on capital is allowed at 8% per annum.
   - Tariq is awarded a partnership salary of $42 000 per annum.

The trial balance at 31 December 2012 is as follows:

	Dr $	Cr $
Capital accounts		
Malik		375 000
Tariq		450 000
Current accounts		
Malik	9 000	
Tariq		12 000
Drawings		
Malik	60 000	
Tariq	90 000	
Loan from Malik – repayable 31 Dec 2020		30 000
Bank overdraft		10 500
Trade payables		27 000
Property at cost	540 000	
Furniture and equipment at cost	330 000	
Accumulated depreciation on furniture and equipment at 1 Jan 2012		99 000
Inventory at 31 Dec 2012	102 000	
Trade receivables	60 000	
Provision for doubtful debts 1 Jan 2012		9 000
Gross profit		436 500
Discounts received		22 500
Discounts allowed	16 500	
Wages and salaries	195 000	
Insurance	40 500	
General expenses	28 500	
	1 471 500	1 471 500

Additional information:

▸ Insurance of $4 500 was prepaid at 31 December 2012.

▸ Wages and salaries of $18 000 were outstanding and unpaid at 1 December 2012.

▸ Straight-line depreciation at 15% on cost will be provided on furniture and equipment.

▸ Provision for doubtful debts should be calculated at 4% of trade receivables.

Prepare:

▸ an income statement and appropriation account for M&T Traders for the year ended 31 December 2012

▸ an appropriation account for the year ended 31 December 2012

▸ partners' current accounts

▸ a statement of financial position for M&T Traders at 32 December 2012.

Unit 4.3 Clubs and societies

AIMS

By the end of this unit you should be able to
- distinguish between **receipts and payments accounts** and **income and expenditure accounts**
- prepare receipts and accounts
- prepare accounts for revenue-generating activities, e.g. refreshments and subscriptions
- prepare income and expenditure accounts and statements of financial position
- make adjustments to financial statements as detailed in 4.1 (sole traders)
- define and calculate the accumulated fund

4.3.1 Running a club or society

Clubs and societies are run for their members and do not aim to make a profit

Clubs and societies are run locally, nationally or internationally for the benefit of society. For example, a local soccer club or choir might be run for the benefit of members, while organisations such as the Royal Society for the Protection of Birds (RSPB) and the World Wide Fund for Nature (WWF) are run for the benefit of society.

The larger national and international societies are often very complex organisations and operate in a similar manner to big businesses. They often seek to influence the policies of governments and legislators on a national and international scale.

Alternatively, the objectives of smaller clubs and societies are to provide facilities and services for members to use and benefit from. They do not exist to deliver a profit to an owner, and it is these clubs and societies that this unit will cover.

As most of these societies are relatively small and not for profit they are organised and financed differently from businesses and produce more limited accounts. The vast majority do not sell goods, and get their income mainly from monthly or annual subscriptions or membership fees and additional fund-raising activities.

However, they still need to manage their finances, control costs sensibly and account for how they have spent their members' subscriptions. They need also to report any surplus or deficit that has been generated, and the state of affairs, especially the amount of cash held in the bank and any current or non-current assets they own. Where they do raise funds by, for example, selling goods or providing refreshments they may very well hold inventory and will need to account for these trading activities.

Clubs and societies will normally appoint a treasurer who should keep an up-to-date cash book and periodically (at least once a year) prepare:

- a **receipts and payments account** reflecting the cash transactions and balances
- a **subscription account** to record the collection of money from the members
- an **income and expenditure account**, which will show what surplus or deficit has been made as a result of the period's activities
- a **statement of financial position** including assets, liabilities and the accumulated fund.

The treasurer will report to the society or club committee and any general meetings held for all the members. There will be provision for an **annual general meeting (AGM)** at which the year's statements will be presented and discussed. The constitution may also make provision for the financial statements to be independently examined by someone to ensure that they have been drawn up properly to reflect the society's activities and state of affairs.

There is some difference in terminology between the profit-making business and the not-for-profit society or club.

Terminology in business includes:	The equivalent terminology for clubs and societies is:
income statement	income and expenditure account
profit for the year	surplus
loss for the year	deficit
capital	accumulated fund

Transactions are recorded in a receipts and payments account

Clubs and societies receive money from a variety of sources:

- members' fees or subscriptions
- fund-raising activities – which can earn profit, which goes to increase the total surplus of the club or society
- donations
- legacies
- other gifts
- loans can be taken out if the organisation is permitted to do so by its constitution.

From all the cash raised the organisation will need to pay for things including:

- the day-to-day running costs, which, depending on its nature and size, may range from small to substantial
- one-off events, run for the benefit of members (for example day trips), or in order to raise funds (for example the purchase of prizes for a raffle or competition)

- some non-current assets, for example sporting equipment or a library of reference books
- bank charges and financing costs of any loans – as well as repayment of loans in due course.

The treasurer will keep a detailed record in a receipts and payments account – essentially the same as a cash book.

The receipts and payments account records:

- opening balances for cash in hand and in bank at start of year
- closing balances at end of year
- a summary of all receipts and payments during year, including purchase of non-current assets and the receipt of a loan.

It will show why and how cash in hand or in bank has increased or decreased over the course of the year; and whether the society is solvent in terms of the available cash balances.

For many small clubs and societies this level of information is sufficient. Members and their elected committee can see the state of the bank balances and whether the year has resulted in a net inflow or outflow of cash, and, when compared with previous periods, if this represents a healthy or problematic trend. Action can then be taken by the committee to reverse an adverse trend by, for example, increasing the annual subscription, or making savings in the administration expenses.

▼ Managing finances is key to a club's success – whatever its size or purpose

4.18 THE RIGTON NATURE SOCIETY

The Rigton Nature Society was formed 25 years ago to encourage local interest in the wildlife of the area surrounding the town of Rigton.

Duncan Enderby, the treasurer, drew up the following receipts and payments account at the end of last year.

The Rigton Nature Society

Receipts And Payments Account For The Year Ended 30 June 2012

Receipts	$	Payments	$
Opening balance at bank – 1 Jul 2011	7 500	Hire of a hall for meetings	60
Subscriptions	5 000	Hire of hall for winter sale	150
Donations	500	Food and drink – coffee mornings	75
Loan from the Northern Region Naturalists Federation (NRNF)	10 000	Goods for a winter sale	200
		Wages for winter sale	50
Fund-raising receipts:		Hire of a tent for the open day	125
Open day	875	Hire of a minibus for excursions	190
Winter sale	900	Fee for the speaker at the AGM	30
Coffee mornings	375	Interest on loan	500
Grant from local council	1 500	NRNF affiliation fee	750
Lottery grant	5 000	Purchase of binoculars and telescope	6 000
		Fencing at Sandy Bank nature reserve	12 500
		Administration expenses	1 650
		Closing balances at bank – 30 Jun 2012	9 370
	31 650		31 650

390 Preparation of financial statements

ACTIVITY 4.9

On 1 April 2012, The Jaipur Trainspotters Club had an opening balance at the bank of $15 000.

During the year ended 31 March 2013, receipts and payments recorded by the treasurer were:

Receipts	$	Payments	$
Subscriptions	5 500	Speakers and meetings	2 500
Donations	550	Publicity	1 250
Fund-raising activities – receipts	5 000	Administration	1 500
Heritage Fund grant	1 500	Excursions	2 500
		Conservation work	3 500
		Fund-raising activities – payments	2 000

Prepare a receipts and payments account for year ended 31 March 2013.

- Add the opening balance to the left-hand, receipts column.
- The closing bank balance to carry down will be the amount needed on the right-hand, payments, side to balance the account.

4.3.2 Preparing an income and expenditure account

An income and expenditure account will record the surplus or deficit of the club or society at the end of the year

As with any organisation, a club or society must generate enough income to cover expenditure. The **income and expenditure account** is drawn up to give this information to members, and to tell them whether the society is generating a surplus or a deficit.

This statement is the not-for-profit organisation's equivalent to the income statement and is drawn up in much the same way as a sole trader would prepare an income statement. In particular it complies with the matching principle.

In complying with the matching principle, the familiar adjustments will be made to include:

- inclusion of accrued expenses
- exclusion of prepaid amounts
- provision for depreciation
- carry forward of any inventory of food, drink, cleaning materials etc.
- write off as irrecoverable any uncollectable subscriptions

Where income exceeds expenditure, the result is described as 'surplus for the year' (rather than 'profit'); where expenditure exceeds income, the result is a 'deficit for the year' (rather than a 'loss').

Illustration 4.19 shows the income and expenditure account produced by Rigton Nature Society from the receipts and payments account in illustration 4.18 and the following additional information:

- The affiliation fee is prepaid by $250.
- The administration costs require the addition of accrued costs amounting to $300.
- Some members still owe their subscriptions totalling $450.
- Half the goods purchased for the winter sale, which cost $100, remained and will be used in future fund-raising activities.
- Depreciation on a straight-line basis is required on the new fencing, expected to last for 25 years, and the binoculars and telescope, which have a life of 10 years.

You will note that the account records:

- only revenue receipts and expenditures – no assets are included, including purchase of the non-current assets of fencing and binoculars and telescope; the current asset balances of cash at the bank are also not included
- in this case, the net income from each fund-raising activity is shown – we deal below with drawing up accounts for the individual fund-raising activities
- overall surplus or deficit.

4.19 INCOME AND EXPENDITURE ACCOUNT

Rigton Nature Society
Income And Expenditure Account For The Year Ended 30 June 2012

	$	$
Income		
Subscriptions ($5 000 + $450)	5 450	
Donations	500	
Coffee mornings	300	
Summer open day	750	
Winter sale	600	
Grant from Rigton local council	1 500	
Lottery grant	5 000	
		14 100
Expenditure		
Hire of a hall for meetings	60	
Hire of a minibus for excursions	190	
Fee for the speaker at the AGM	30	
Interest on the NRNF loan	500	
NRNF affiliation fee ($750 – $250)	500	
Depreciation of binoculars and telescope ($6 000/10)	600	
Depreciation of fencing ($12 500/25)	500	
Administration expenses ($1 650 + $300)	1 950	
		4 330
Surplus for the year		9 770

Members can use the account to examine whether the club was able to make enough income to cover its expenditure, and how much surplus it could carry over into the next year so they can plan future activities or events. If deficits are incurred, there may be clear signals from the account as to what actions can be taken to recover the situation.

Separate accounts can usefully be prepared to show the profit or loss from individual fund-raising activities

The income and expenditure account in illustration 4.19 shows only profit or loss from fund-raising activities in total. Members of Rigton Nature Society might find it useful to see how much each activity made or lost. It would help the committee to decide whether to continue with the same activities in future years, how the surplus from the separate activities might be increased or whether to try something completely new.

The society ran two events during year – the winter sale and the summer open day. One event was more successful than the other – accounts for each are shown in illustration 4.20.

ACTIVITY 4.10

Blackfoot Swimming Club had cash and bank balances at 1 May 2012 of $15 000.

During the year ended 30 April 2013, the treasurer recorded the following receipts and payments.

Blackfoot Swimming Club
Receipts And Payments Account For The Year Ended 30 April 2013

Receipts	$	Payments	$
Bank balance b/d	15 000		
Subscriptions	20 000	Hire of a pool for training	7 500
Donations	1 500	Hire of a pool for a gala	250
Swimming gala refreshments	2 000	Cost of the gala refreshments	750
Grant from Health in the Community	4 000	New minibus	15 000
Insurance claim for damaged trophy	550	National Federation affiliation fee	500
Fund-raising raffle tickets	4 000	Insurance	3 000
		Repairing a damaged trophy	650
		Coaching staff	5 000
		Competition fees	1 500
		Prizes for a raffle	1 000
		Competition medals	200
		Minibus running costs	2 000
		Secretary's and administration expense	2 500
		Bank balance c/d	7 200
	47 050		47 050
Bank balance b/d	7 200		

Members can clearly see the drain on the club's cash resources from the purchase of the new minibus.

In addition the following information was made available by the treasurer:

- $500 was prepaid on the pool hire for training.
- $200 was outstanding payable to coaching staff.
- A depreciation charge of $3 750 was required on the new minibus.
- The club owns equipment with a net book value of $2 500; depreciation of $500 on this is required for the current year.
- There were outstanding subscriptions receivable of $500.
- Food and drink amounting to $150 were left after the gala and would be used on a future occasion.

Prepare an income and expenditure account for the year ended 30 April 2013.

4.20 FUND-RAISING ACCOUNTS

Rigton Nature Society
Fund-raising accounts

Summer open day	$
Receipts	875
less hire of a tent	125
Profit from event	750

Winter sale		$
Receipts		900
less goods purchased	200	
inventory remaining	100	
Cost of sales		100
Gross profit		800
less expenses		
Hire of hall	150	
Caretaker's wages	50	
		200
Profit from event		600

In this case the profits from these activities have been shown separately in the income and expenditure account. The combined profit from the fund-raising events – including the profit of $300 on the coffee mornings held throughout the year in members' houses – contributed $1 650 to the overall surplus of the club that year.

The separate accounts show that running the summer open day generated more funds for the society than the winter sale. The committee may wish to consider the time and effort spent on each event, the effectiveness of any publicity, the extent to which the events are social occasions as well as fund-raisers, and other issues, before deciding whether or not to run the same events next year.

Annual subscriptions paid or falling due during the year must be adjusted for accruals and prepayments to calculate subscription income for the year

The income and expenditure account must show subscription income earned during the year – not just income that has been received.

- Some receipts in respect of next year's subscriptions may come in during the year and be prepaid.
- Some subscriptions may not have been paid on time by the end of the year.
- Some of this year's receipts may represent settlement of last year's outstanding amounts.
- Cash may already have been received last year in relation to some of this year's subscriptions.
- Complications may also arise when subscription levels vary from year to year.

For these reasons it is helpful to prepare a separate **subscriptions account** to record receipts as well as prepaid and accrued amounts, to reconcile these with the membership records and to calculate the true subscription income belonging to the year in compliance with the matching principle.

4.21 THE HONG KONG OYSTERS

The Hong Kong Oysters, a seafood dining club, has 50 members and the subscription for the year ended 31 July 2011 was $40 per member. The following year the subscription increased to $50 per member and will stay at that level for the next three years.

At 31 July 2011 10 members' subscriptions were outstanding and unpaid, while a further 10 members had paid the subscription for the year ended 31 July 2012 in advance; at 31 July 2012 the same people had paid in advance for the next year.

By the end of the year ended 31 July 2012, all the previous year's outstanding amounts had been settled, but five subscriptions remained unpaid and outstanding in respect of the current year.

The treasurer has recorded subscription receipts into the bank of $2 650 during the year ended 31 July 2012. The subscriptions are reconciled with the membership and the subscription account for the year ended 31 July 2012 is prepared as follows:

Subscriptions account

Dr		$			$
Aug 1	Balance b/d	400	Aug 1	Balance b/d	500
Jul 31	Income and expenditure	2 500		Cash	2 650
Jul 31	Balance carried down	500	Jul 31	Balance c/d	250
		3 400			3 400
Aug 1	Balance b/d	250	Aug 1	Balance b/d	500

The account shows:

▸ credit for cash received during the year

▸ debit for income earned to the income and expenditure account

▸ subscriptions due – a debit balance brought and carried down – a current asset

▸ subscriptions prepaid – a credit balance brought and carried down – a current liability.

During the following year the treasurer recorded $2 050 received for subscriptions, and at 31 July 2013 there remained eight outstanding subscriptions and five members had prepaid their 2014 subscriptions.

The subscriptions account for the year ended 31 July 2013 would look like this:

Subscriptions account

Dr		$			$
Aug 1	Balance b/d	250	Aug 1	Balance b/d	500
Jul 31	Income and expenditure	2 500		Cash	2 050
Jul 31	Balance carried down	250	Jul 31	Balance c/d	400
		2 950			2 950
Aug 1	Balance b/d	400	Aug 1	Balance b/d	250

> **ACTIVITY 4.11**
>
> 1 The following information is available on a fund-raising event of the Hightown Drama Society.
>
> | **Quiz night** |
> |---|
> | 150 persons attending |
> | Ticket price, including food, $12 each |
> | Hall hire $150 |
> | Microphone and equipment hire $50 |
> | Catering $5 per attendee |
>
> Prepare the profit or loss account for this event.
>
> - The society charges an annual subscription of $20 per year.
> - At the start of the year there was a balance brought down for subscriptions prepaid $400.
> - At the start of the year there was a balance brought down for subscriptions due $200.
> - During the year $4 740 was received in respect of subscriptions.
> - At the end of the year $260 was outstanding on unpaid subscriptions.
> - At the end of the year, $200 had been paid in advance for the following year's subscriptions.
>
> 2 Prepare the subscriptions account that records these transactions.

4.3.3 Preparing a statement of financial position

The accumulated surpluses of a club or society are recorded in the statement of financial position

The statement of financial position will be prepared in the same way as for any commercial organisation – a club or society can own assets and have liabilities. However, unlike business owners, members do not invest their own funds and cannot withdraw cash or goods for their own use.

Any surplus will accumulate until spent to benefit all members. The constitution will provide that in the event that the society or club is dissolved, any remaining funds must be transferred to an organisation with similar aims and objectives. This is a mandatory feature of any organisation with charitable status. This fund, built up over time, is called the accumulated fund, and is the equivalent of the capital shown in the statement of financial position of commercial undertakings.

The statement of financial position is used to show values of assets and liabilities and the accumulated fund – measured as the difference between total assets and liabilities = net assets = accumulated fund – an application of the accounting equation. ➤ 3.2

For example, at 30 June 2013, the Rigton Nature Society had the following assets and liabilities – its accumulated fund was $17 220. Duncan Enderby, the treasurer, prepared the statement of financial position shown in illustration 4.22.

4.22 STATEMENT OF FINANCIAL POSITION AT 30 JUNE 2012

Rigton Nature Society
Statement Of Financial Position At 30 June 2012

	$
Binoculars and telescope	6 000
Accumulated depreciation	600
Fencing at Sandy Bank	12 500
Accumulated depreciation	500
Subscriptions receivable	450
Inventory of goods	100
Prepaid affiliation fee	250
Accrued administration expenses	300
Loan from the NRNF	10 000
Bank deposit	7 000
Bank current account	2 320

	$
Non-current assets	
Binoculars and telescope	6 000
less accumulated depreciation	(600)
	5 400
Fencing at Sandy Bank reserve	12 500
less accumulated depreciation	(500)
	12 000
	17 400
Current assets	
Inventory of goods	100
Outstanding subscriptions	450
Other receivables	250
Bank deposit	7 000
Bank current account	2 320
	10 120
Total assets	27 520
Current liabilities	
Other payables	300
Non-current liabilities	
Loan from the NRNF	10 000
Total liabilities	10 300
Accumulated fund at 30 Jun 2011	7 450
Surplus for the year	9 770
Accumulated fund at 30 Jun 2012	17 220
Total liabilities and accumulated fund	27 520

By 30 June 2013 its assets and liabilities had changed, as shown in illustration 4.23.

Clubs and societies

4.23 STATEMENT OF FINANCIAL POSITION AT 30 JUNE 2013

Rigton Nature Society

Statement Of Financial Position At 30 June 2013

	$
Binoculars and telescope	6 000
Accumulated depreciation	1 200
Fencing at Sandy Bank	12 500
Accumulated depreciation	1 000
Subscriptions receivable	600
Inventory of goods	75
Prepaid fee	250
Accrued administration expenses	250
Loan from the NRNF	10 000
Bank deposit	7 000
Bank current account	1 520

		$
Non-current assets		
Binoculars and telescope		6 000
less accumulated depreciation		(1 200)
		4 800
Fencing at Sandy Bank reserve		12 500
less accumulated depreciation		(1 000)
		11 500
		16 300
Current assets		
Inventory of goods	75	
Outstanding subscriptions	600	
Other receivables	250	
Bank deposit	7 000	
Bank current account	1 520	9 445
Total assets		25 745
Current liabilities		
Other payables		250
Non-current liabilities		
Loan from the NRNF		10 000
Total liabilities		10 250
Accumulated fund at 30 Jun 2012		17 220
Deficit for the year		(1 725)
Accumulated fund at 30 Jun 2013		15 495
Total liabilities and accumulated fund		25 745

ACTIVITY 4.12

Agromin Farm Co-operative had the following assets and liabilities at 31 October 2012. The income and expenditure account showed a deficit of $7 560 for the year ended 31 October 2012.

	$
Society office	30 000
Accumulated depreciation	7 500
Farm machinery	20 500
Accumulated depreciation	7 500
Subscriptions receivable	1 600
Inventory of consumables	5 000
Prepaid advertising	1 250
Accrued admin expense	2 350
Loan from the NFU	15 000
Bank deposit	12 000
Bank overdraft	3 230

Prepare a statement of financial position at 31 October 2012.

Note that the closing balance on the accumulated fund must be the same as the net assets (total assets less total liabilities) and given the deficit for the year the opening balance on the fund at 31 October 2011 can be calculated.

QUICK TEST

1. Identify and explain **three** features that distinguish a receipts and payments account from an income and expenditure account.

2. Describe and explain how the members of a club or society differ from the members of a commercial business.

3. Explain the purpose of a subscriptions account.

4. What are the **three** principal statements adopted by clubs and societies to report their financial affairs? What information is intended to be given by these statements?

5. The treasurer of the Singapore Singers extracted the following information for the year's subscriptions. Prepare a subscriptions account for the year ended 31 October 2012, indicating clearly the amount to transfer to the income and expenditure account.

	$
Subscriptions paid in cash during the year	10 080
Subscriptions received in advance at 1 Nov 2011	445
Subscriptions received in advance at 31 Oct 2012	625
Outstanding subscriptions in arrears at 1 Nov 2011	350
Outstanding subscriptions in arrears at 31 Oct 2012	500

6. The Munro Mountaineering Club has extracted the following information; the treasurer has reported a surplus for the year ended 31 January 2013 of $4 400. Prepare the club's statement of financial position at 31 January 2013.

	$
Accumulated fund – 1 Feb 2012	59 475
Loans from the Scottish Mountaineering Federation – repayable 1 Feb 2020	5 200
Climbing equipment at net book value	68 000
Secretary's expenses accrued	140
Cash at bank	1 440
Outstanding subscriptions due	1 000
Subscriptions paid in advance	1 800
Prepaid rent on the club's mountain hut	575

7   The Friday the 13th Walking Club started the year with $2 500 in the bank account at 1 January 2012 and has had the following money paid in to and out of the club's account during the year to 31 December 2012. Prepare a receipts and payments account for the year ended 31 December 2012.

	$
Members' subscriptions received	1 000
Bank interest received	5
Purchase of equipment	350
Hire of a minibus	150
Subscriptions to walkers' magazines	100
Postage and stationery expense	100
Donation to the mountain rescue team	250
Retirement presentation to the outgoing secretary	145

8   From the following additional information at 31 December 2012, and the receipts and payments account from question 7 above, draw up an income and expenditure account for the Friday the 13th Walking Club for the year ended 31 December 2012.

- The only equipment the club owns is that purchased this year; depreciation of that equipment amounting to $175 is required.
- $25 of the magazine subscriptions is prepaid.
- An accrual of $35 is needed for postage.
- Subscriptions of $75 are owed to the club.

Unit 4.4 Incomplete records

AIMS

By the end of this unit you should be able to

- prepare opening and closing **statements of affairs**
- calculate profit or loss for the year from the changes in capital over time
- calculate sales, purchases, gross profit, trade receivables and trade payables from **incomplete information**
- prepare **income statements** and **statements of financial position** from incomplete records
- make adjustments to financial statements as detailed in 4.1 (sole traders)
- apply the techniques of mark-up, margin and inventory turnover to arrive at missing figures

4.4.1 Preparing a statement of affairs from limited accounting records

If only the assets and liabilities are known at the start and end of a year a business can prepare an opening and closing statement of affairs

So far we have assumed that all the businesses considered maintain a full set of accounting books and records. However, many small businesses, particularly sole traders, do not keep detailed double-entry accounts, and there is no legal requirement for sole traders or partnerships to do so. There can be a number of reasons for this including:

- Lower volumes of transactions mean that simple records are enough to control the business.
- The owner may not have the inclination or time to spend on the task of book-keeping.
- The business may not have enough staff with adequate accounting skills or time to carry out these tasks.
- The expense of paying an accountant to do the job on a day-to-day basis may seem excessive for a small business.

This means that many small businesses keep less detailed records. The disadvantages of this are:

- The owner has significantly less information about financial performance to use in decision making.
- Incompleteness makes preparation more difficult when financial statements are needed for legal or other purposes.

It is important for a business to be able to produce and use information on profitability and financial position because only then can the following occur:

- Proper control can be exercised over the business activity – in particular, when things begin to go wrong, problems can be identified, the reasons for them diagnosed, and the appropriate actions and corrections taken.
- Informed decisions can be made about which products or services are most profitable and valuable to the business.
- Adequate historical information can be used as a guide to possible future developments.
- Proper comparisons can be made with other businesses and the outside world.
- When an overdraft or loan is required proper information can be made available to the bank or other lenders.

Despite lack of full records, there are several ways a business can prepare financial statements from missing or incomplete records.

If a business has information on its assets and liabilities at the start and end of each year then it can prepare statements of affairs and in turn use these to discover equity and total profit or loss for year.

For example, Saleem owns a small business. He hasn't kept detailed records of income and expenses but was able to provide the following information on his business assets and liabilities:

▼ Saleem Trading – list of assets and liabilities

31 December 2011	$
Property	20 000
Plant and equipment	8 600
Trade receivables	1 500
Other receivables	750
Trade payables	2 000
Other payables	1 000
Cash in bank	3 750
Inventory	5 000
Loan from cousin	10 000

31 December 2012	$
Property	20 000
Plant and equipment	8 000
Trade receivables	1 600
Other receivables	1 000
Trade payables	1 800
Other payables	1 250
Cash in bank	5 200
Inventory	5 750
Loan from cousin	10 000

From this information Saleem was able to produce an opening statement of affairs and a closing statement at the end of the year as shown in illustration 4.24.

Equity and profit or loss for the year can be calculated from the opening and closing balances for assets and liabilities in statements of affairs

If a business has opening and closing balances for its assets and liabilities it will be able to calculate owner's equity and profit or loss for that year.

The total assets are financed from owner's equity or liabilities; owner's equity = net assets. ➤ 3.2

4.24 STATEMENTS OF AFFAIRS

Saleem Trading
Statement Of Affairs
At 31 December 2011

Assets	
Property	20 000
Fixtures and equipment	8 600
Trade receivables	1 500
Other receivables	750
Cash in bank	3 750
Inventory of goods	5 000
Total assets	**39 600**
Liabilities	
Trade payables	2 000
Other payables	1 000
Loan from cousin	10 000
Total liabilities	**13 000**
Capital	**26 600**

Saleem Trading
Statement Of Affairs
At 31 December 2012

Assets	
Property	20 000
Fixtures and equipment	8 000
Trade receivables	1 600
Other receivables	1 000
Cash in bank	5 200
Inventory of goods	5 750
Total assets	**41 550**
Liabilities	
Trade payables	1 800
Other payables	1 250
Loan from cousin	10 000
Total liabilities	**13 050**
Capital	**28 500**

From his statements of affairs in illustration 4.24 Saleem is now able to calculate the change in total assets and liabilities, and therefore equity during year.

Owner's equity can only increase in two ways:

- introduction of new capital
- earning and retention of profit.

In Saleem's case, as there was no additional capital introduced, the increase in equity can only be due to profit.

Equity, however, can be reduced by drawings, and Saleem had withdrawn $5 000 in cash during the year for his own use.

> **Profit (or loss) for the year = closing equity − opening equity + drawings**

Profit or loss for the year (profit in this case) is calculated as follows: $28 500 − $26 600 + $5 000 = $6 900

From this information Saleem is able to prepare a capital account as follows:

4.25 CAPITAL ACCOUNT

Saleem Trading

Capital account

Dr		$				Cr $
Bank drawings		5 000	Jan 1	Balance b/d		26 600
Dec 31 Balance c/d		28 500	Dec 31	Profit for year		6 900
		33 750				33 750
			Jan 1	Balance b/d		28 500

ACTIVITY 4.13

Consuela recently started her own hairdressing salon – and while she did not keep a full set of accounting books, she was able to supply the following information regarding the business assets and liabilities at the start and end of her first year.

	1 June 2012 $	31 May 2013 $
Fittings and equipment	12 250	10 000
Computer		1 800
Trade receivables		1 650
Trade payables		3 000
Cash in bank	4 000	
Bank overdraft		1 150
Inventory of salon supplies	5 000	6 200
Loan from sister	8 000	8 000

During the year she had withdrawn $12 000 for her own use.

1. Prepare an opening statement of affairs as at 1 June 2012.
2. Prepare a closing statement of affairs for year ended 31 May 2013.
3. Calculate profit or loss for the year. Show your workings in full.

Preparation of financial statements

4.4.2 Finding values for missing items to complete financial statements

If assets, liabilities and all cash and bank transactions are known then a business can discover values it needs to complete statements of income and financial position

Even if a business has kept only limited accounting records it is still possible to prepare its end of year financial statements so long as it has kept details of:

- the value of its assets and liabilities at the start and end of the year
- all its cash and bank transactions, recorded in a simple cash book.

From these records the business will be able to calculate annual values for:

- cash and credit sales
- cash and credit purchases
- total cost of goods sold
- gross profit
- expenses.

To prepare an income statement the business will have to calculate the total sales and purchases for the year

To prepare an income statement we will need information about sales and purchases. This is relatively easy where a business has only cash sales and purchases – the summarised cash book can be used to extract this information.

However, where there are also credit sales, the actual sales will not be fully represented by the cash received from credit customers. Adoption of the matching principle means that there will be amounts owing by customers at the beginning and end of the year for uncollected sales income. These are the trade receivables.

To complete this process we will need information on the value of trade receivables at the start and end of the year as well as the receipts from credit customers during the year. We will also need to know about any discounts allowed.

The same considerations will apply to purchases on credit. We will need information about trade payables at the start and end of the year, payments to suppliers of goods on credit and details of any discounts taken.

▼ Steps to calculate credit sales and purchases

To calculate credit sales	To calculate credit purchases
Total receipts from credit customers	Total payments to suppliers
add discounts allowed	*add* discounts allowed
less opening balance for trade receivables	*less* opening balance for trade payables
add closing balance for trade receivables	*add* closing balance for trade payables
= credit sales income for the year	= credit purchases for the year

For example, illustration 4.24 shows that Saleem has only limited accounting records.

However, as well as the figures extracted for his statements of affairs, he was also able to provide the following information:

▼ Information about customers

Listed trade receivables:	
1 January 2012	1 700
31 December 2012	1 850
Irrecoverable debts in year	250
Provision for doubtful debts:	
1 January 2012	200
31 December 2012	250
Cash book receipts from customers	
Cash sales	60 100
Credit sales	20 000

▼ Information about suppliers

Listed trade payables:	
1 January 2012	2 000
31 December 2012	1 800
Cash book payments to suppliers	59 060

Saleem pays very promptly, so he receives cash settlement discount of 2.5% from suppliers.

From the information he was able to calculate credit sales and purchases as follows:

▼ Saleem Trading – calculation of credit sales and purchases

Credit sales	$	Credit purchases	$
Closing trade receivables	1 850	Closing trade payables	1 800
Cash received	20 000	Cash paid	59 060
Irrecoverable debts	250	Discounts taken	1 515
less opening trade receivables	(1 700)	*less* opening trade payables	(2 000)
Credit sales for year	20 400	Credit purchases for year	60 375

Preferably, Saleem could prepare ledger accounts for total trade receivables and payables to calculate missing figures for credit sales and purchases. Effectively, these total accounts are the same as control accounts.

4.26 TOTAL TRADE RECEIVABLES ACCOUNT

Total trade receivables account					
Dr					Cr
		$			$
Jan 1	Balance b/d	1 700	Dec 31	Cash	20 000
Dec 31	**Credit sales for year**	**20 400**	Dec 31	Irrecoverable debts	250
			Dec 31	Balance c/d	1 850
		22 100			22 100
Jan 1	Balance b/d	1 850			

1. The opening trade receivables are entered as a debit item brought down.
2. The cash received and the irrecoverable debts are both entered as credits to the account.
3. The closing trade receivables are entered in the credit side and carried down.
4. The debit entry to balance the account then represents the total credit sales made in the year and will be credited to the income statement when that is prepared.

The procedure for the total payables account is a mirror image of that for the receivables.

4.27 TOTAL TRADE PAYABLES ACCOUNT

Total trade payables account					
Dr					Cr
		$			$
Dec 31	Cash	59 060	Jan 1	Balance b/d	2 000
Dec 31	Discounts taken	1 515	Dec 31	**Credit purchases for year**	**60 375**
Dec 31	Balance c/d	1 800			
		62 375			62 375
			Jan 1	Balance b/d	1 800

1. The opening trade payables are entered as a credit item brought down.
2. The cash paid and the discounts taken are both entered as debits to the account.
3. The closing trade payables are entered in the debit side and carried down.
4. The credit entry to balance the account then represents the total credit purchases made in the year and will be debited to the income statement when that is prepared.

Incomplete records

Saleem has also prepared the following summary of his cash transactions:

	Dr $	Cr $
Opening balance at 1 Jan 2012	3 750	
Receipts from cash sales	60 100	
Receipts from credit customers	20 000	
Payments to suppliers		59 060
Wages		9 465
Utilities		2 000
Publicity		250
Office and sundry costs		2 375
Interest on loan		500
Drawings		5 000
Closing balance at 31 Dec 2012		5 200
	83 850	83 850

In addition Saleem has this information:

- There were wages outstanding at 1 January 2012 of $500 and 31 December 2012 of $750.
- Utilities were prepaid at 1 January 2012 by $750 and at 31 December 2012 by $1 000.
- Accrued office costs at 1 January 2012 were $500 and at 31 December 2012 were $500.
- Fixtures and equipment have been valued at $8 000 on 31 December 2012.

Once the values for total cash and credit sales and purchases had been calculated and using details from the statements of affairs, summarised cash book and additional information, Saleem was able to prepare the following income statement and statement of financial position, in the normal way as for any business.

4.28 INCOME STATEMENT

Saleem Trading

Income Statement Prepared From Incomplete Records

	$	$
Revenue		
Cash sales		60 100
Credit sales		20 400
		80 500
Opening inventory	5 000	
Purchase of merchandise	60 375	
less closing inventory	(5 750)	
Cost of sales		59 625
Gross profit		20 875
Wages	9 715	
Utilities	1 750	
Publicity	250	
Office and sundry costs	2 375	
Irrecoverable and doubtful debts	300	
Depreciation	600	
Interest on loan	500	
Discounts taken	(1 515)	
		13 975
Profit for the year		6 900

4.29 STATEMENT OF FINANCIAL POSITION

Saleem Trading
Statement Of Financial Position Prepared From Incomplete Records

	$	$
Non-current assets		
Property at cost		20 000
Fixtures and equipment at valuation		8 000
		28 000
Current assets		
Inventory	5 750	
Trade receivables	1 600	
Other receivables	1 000	
Cash at the bank	5 200	
		13 550
Total assets		41 550
Current liabilities		
Trade payables	1 800	
Other payables	1 250	
		3 050
Non-current liabilities		
Loan from cousin		10 000
Net assets		13 050
Equity		
At 1 Jan 2012	26 600	
Profit for the year	6 900	
less drawings	(5 000)	
At 31 Dec 2012		28 500
Total equity		41 550

ACTIVITY 4.14

Zafira Khan runs a company trading in office supplies. She does not keep a full set of books and ledgers, but has produced the following information about the opening and closing assets and liabilities, a summary of the cash transactions during the year and some additional information.

31 December 2011

	$
Property	50 000
Plant and equipment	12 800
Trade receivables	5 000
Other receivables	1 750
Trade payables	15 000
Other receivables	1 000
Cash in bank	8 120
Inventory	10 300
Loan from bank	10 000

31 December 2012

	$
Property	50 000
Plant and equipment	10 000
Trade receivables	6 300
Other receivables	2 250
Trade payables	13 750
Other receivables	1 750
Cash in bank	10 145
Inventory of goods	11 100
Loan from bank	10 000

	Dr $	Cr $
Opening balance at 1 January 2012	8 120	
Receipts from credit customers	125 000	
Payments to suppliers		82 600
Wages		13 100
Utilities		3 500
Selling costs		5 400
Office and sundry costs		2 375
Interest on the bank loan		1 000
Drawings		15 000
Closing balance		10 145
	$133 120	$133 120

Incomplete records

- Utilities were prepaid at 1 January 2012 by $1 750 and at 31 December 2012 by $2 250.
- Accrued selling costs were $1 000 at 1 January 2012 and $1 250 at 31 December 2012.
- Fixtures and equipment were valued at $10 000 on 31 December 2012.

1 Calculate:
  (a) equity as at 1 January and 31 December 2012;
  (b) revenue and purchases for the year;
  (c) total expenses to be charged to the income statement.

2 Prepare an income statement for year ended 31 December 2012.

3 Prepare a statement of financial position as at 31 December 2012.

4.4.3 Using financial ratios to find the value of missing items

Using the rate of inventory turnover, it is possible to calculate the cost of sales and total purchases for the year

Inventory turnover is the measure of how quickly a business uses its inventory and replaces it in the ordinary day-to-day operating activity. It is expressed in terms of how many times average inventory goes to make up the total cost of sales for the year.

A business with cost of sales of $24 000 and average inventory of $2 000 has an inventory turnover of 24 000/2 000 = 12. It keeps in hand one-twelfth of its annual requirement.

Looked at another way, it keeps its inventory, on average, for one-twelfth of a year – a month or approximately 30 days. ▶ 5.1

If we know what to expect for this inventory turnover relationship we can use it to calculate cost of goods sold and purchases for the year. To do this, we need to know the opening and closing inventory levels and the rate of inventory turnover.

For example, Lily Zhu, who runs a small cosmetics and beauty products shop, had the following information about her inventory of goods for resale at the start and end of the year:

▼ Lily Zhu – Beautiful You

	$
Opening inventory	10 000
Closing inventory	12 000
Rate of inventory turnover	8.5 times

The first step is to calculate average inventory.

Average inventory = (opening inventory + closing inventory)/2

($10 000 + $12 000)/2 = $22 000/2 = $11 000.

So, **average inventory was $11 000**.

The second step is to calculate the cost of sales; this is the cost of goods she sold during the year. Lily did this as follows.

Cost of sales/average inventory = rate of inventory turnover

Cost of sales/$11 000 = 8.5 times

Cost of sales = 8.5 times × $11 000 = $93 500.

So, **cost of sales was $93 500**.

The final step is for Lily to calculate her total purchases during the year as follows:

	$
Cost of sales	93 500
add closing inventory	12 000
	105 500
less opening inventory	(10 000)
Purchases	95 500

Purchases = cost of sales − opening inventory + closing inventory

Purchases = $93 500 − $10 000 + $12 000 = $95 500.

So, the missing value for **purchases is $95 500**.

Using the cost of sales and the mark-up added for profit it is possible to calculate the total revenue and gross profit for the year

Having calculated the cost of sales, and if we know the mark-up added on by the trader to arrive at the selling price, we can move on to calculate the sales revenue and gross profit.

Lily Zhu always applies a mark-up of 50% for profit on the purchase price of goods when pricing them for sale to customers. This means that if merchandise costs $10 for her to buy, Lily will price it for sale at $15.

Now that Lily has been able to calculate her cost of sales for the year she is also able to calculate total revenue and gross profit from the sale of those goods.

The first step is to apply the mark-up percentage to the cost of sales to calculate the sales value of those goods. This will be the sales revenue for the year.

The mark-up is 50% of the cost. Therefore the sales value will be 150% of the cost.

$93 500 × 150% = **$140 250**.

The second step is to calculate the gross profit.

> **Gross profit = sales revenue − cost of sales**

▼ Lily Zhu – Beautiful You

	$
Sales revenue	140 250
less cost of sales	93 500
Gross profit	46 750

Gross profit = $140 250 − $93 500 = $46 750.

You will notice that the gross profit amounts to half (50%) of the cost of sales. This must be the case since we know that the mark-up profit added to the cost is 50%.

So we can also think of the gross profit in this way:

> **Gross profit = cost of sales × percentage mark-up for profit**

Gross profit = $93 500 × 50% = $46 750.

> **Revenue = cost of sales + gross profit**

Revenue = $93 500 + $46 750 = $140 250.

By combining these values Lily was able to produce the first part of her income statement for the year in the normal way as shown in illustration 4.30.

Mark-up is the percentage applied to the **cost** of goods or services to arrive at the selling price. The amount calculated represents the gross profit. For example: goods cost $2 000 and a mark-up of 25% is applied, which amounts to $500. The gross profit is therefore $500 and the selling price will be $2 000 (cost) + $500 (the mark-up) which gives $2 500.

The **margin (or gross profit margin)** is the gross profit expressed as a percentage of the **sales value**. It is the proportion of the sales value that represents profit rather than the recovery of the cost of the goods or services sold. Goods sold for $2 500 which cost $2 000 generate a gross profit of $500 which represents one fifth – 20% – of the sales value.

Goods costing $2 000 sold for $2 500 therefore represent a **mark-up** of 25% and a **margin** of 20%.

4.30 INCOME STATEMENT

Lily Zhu – Beautiful You
Income Statement (Extract) Prepared Using Financial Ratios

	$	$
Revenue		140 250
Opening inventory	10 000	
Purchases	95 500	
	105 500	
less closing inventory	12 000	
Cost of sales		93 500
Gross profit		**46 750**

It is also possible to calculate the total revenue and gross profit for the year using the cost of sales and the gross profit margin.

Joe Frazer runs Promostyle. He sells many different products with different mark-ups and seasonal variations. Joe aims to achieve an overall consistent gross profit margin of 25% on his total sales, which he has managed to do for a number of years.

This means that if he knows the cost of sales for the year he can calculate the sales revenue figure and gross profit. The cost of sales for the current period is $900 000 and his opening and closing inventory are $90 000 and $86 000 respectively.

If gross profit amounts to 25% of the sales revenue, then cost of sales must amount to 75% of the sales revenue.

Sales revenue × 75% = cost of sales

Sales revenue = cost of sales/75%

Sales revenue = $900 000/0.75 = $1 200 000.

Now we have the sales revenue figure, the next step is to calculate the purchases for the year.

> **Purchases = cost of sales − opening inventory + closing inventory**

Purchases = $900 000 − $90 000 + $86 000 = $896 000.

We are now in a position to prepare the first section of the income statement.

Incomplete records

4.31 INCOME STATEMENT

Joe Frazer – Promostyle

Income Statement (Extract) Prepared Using Financial Ratios

	$	$
Revenue		1 200 000
Opening inventory	90 000	
Purchases	896 000	
	986 000	
less closing inventory	86 000	
Cost of sales		900 000
Gross profit		**300 000**

ACTIVITY 4.15

LabFab buys and sells laboratory equipment. The following information is available from the business.

1. Calculate:
   (a) costs of goods sold;
   (b) total purchases;
   (c) gross profit;
   (d) revenue.
2. Prepare an income statement for LabFab.

	$
Opening inventory	200 000
Closing inventory	220 000
Average mark-up for profit	33.33%
Inventory turnover	6 times
Wages	88 000
Other operating costs	222 000
Depreciation	8 000
Accrued wages	8 000
Operating costs prepaid	12 000

QUICK TEST

1. Explain the difference between mark-up and margin.

2. Brenda has provided the following information from her incomplete accounting records:

	$
Trade receivables at 1 Apr 2012	14 365
Trade receivables at 31 Mar 2013	17 145
Trade payables at 1 Apr 2012	10 740
Trade payables at 31 Mar 2013	8 975
During the year ended 31 Mar 2013:	
Cash received from customers	77 865
Cash paid to suppliers	64 050

   From this, using total accounts, calculate the total credit sales and purchases for the year ended 31 March 2013.

3. Isaac does not keep full accounting records. He has produced the following information about his assets and liabilities on 1 August 2012 and 31 July 2013.

   During the year he has taken drawings of $14 700 and he has put into the business a legacy of $7 500 received from his aunt when she died.

   Prepare statements of affairs at 1 August 2012 and 31 July 2013 calculating the capital.

   Calculate the business's profit or loss for the year ended 31 July 2013.

	1 Aug 2012 $	31 Jul 2013 $
Trade receivables	2 350	1 955
Trade payables	2 945	3 485
Inventories	7 000	8 340
Cash at bank	3 930	
Bank overdraft		3 235
Legacy from aunt		7 500
Equipment	10 815	9 315
Outstanding wages		330
Prepaid insurance	465	

Incomplete records

4 Cindy Draper runs a company trading in silk fabrics. She does not keep a full set of books and ledgers, but has produced the following information about the opening and closing assets and liabilities, a summary of the cash transactions during the year and some additional information.

31 December 2011	$
Property	70 000
Plant and equipment	17 920
Trade receivables	7 000
Other receivables	2 450
Trade payables	21 000
Other payables	1 400
Cash in bank	11 368
Inventory	14 420
Loan from the bank	14 000

31 December 2012	$
Property	70 000
Plant and equipment	14 000
Trade receivables	8 820
Other receivables	3 150
Trade payables	19 250
Other payables	2 450
Cash in bank	14 203
Inventory	15 540
Loan from the bank	14 000

	Dr $	Cr $
Opening balance at 1 Jan 2012	11 368	
Receipts from credit customers	175 000	
Payments to suppliers		115 640
Wages		18 340
Utilities		4 900
Selling costs		7 560
Office and sundry costs		3 325
Interest on the bank loan		1 400
Drawings		21 000
Closing balance at 31 Dec 2012		14 203
	186 368	186 368

Additional information:
- All sales are on credit.
- Selling costs were prepaid at 1 January 2012 by $2 450 and at 31 December 2012 by $3 150.
- Accrued office costs were $1 400 at 1 January 2012 and $2 450 at 31 December 2012.
- Fixtures and equipment were valued at $14 000 on 31 December 2012.

(a) Calculate:

(i) capital as at 1 January;

(ii) revenue and purchases for the year;

(iii) expenses to be charged to income statement.

(b) Prepare an income statement for the year ended 31 December 2012.

(c) Prepare a statement of financial position at 31 December 2012.

Unit 4.5 Limited companies

AIMS

By the end of this unit you should be able to
- explain the advantages and disadvantages of operating as a limited company
- understand the meaning of the term **limited liability**
- understand the meaning of the term **equity**
- explain the **capital structure** of a limited company comprising preference share capital, ordinary share capital, general reserve and retained earnings
- understand and distinguish between **issued, called-up** and **paid-up share capital**
- understand and distinguish between share capital (preference shares and ordinary shares) and loan capital (debentures)
- prepare income statements, statements of changes in equity and statements of financial position
- make adjustments to financial statements as detailed in 4.1 (sole traders)

4.5.1 Limited companies

The owners of private and public limited companies are called shareholders

In this section we look at a frequently used arrangement for running a business – as a limited liability company, more frequently known as a **limited company**.

We have seen that one of the drawbacks of operating as a sole trader or in partnership is that the owners have an unlimited liability personally to settle all the debts and claims against the business when there are insufficient business assets available to cover these obligations.

Protection against this risk can be obtained by "incorporating" the business as a limited company, which creates a separate legal business entity.

A limited company will have a formally registered Memorandum and Articles of Association

The **Memorandum and Articles of Association** will:

1. outline the aims and objectives of the company
2. specify the number of authorised shares
3. describe how shares may be transferred between people
4. specify how the company will be regulated and run.

Once this has been done the owners are no longer personally liable for business obligations to any extent beyond the capital that shows to their credit in the business accounts. Unlike sole traders or partnerships they cannot be asked to pay for any liabilities or claims in excess of the business assets from their own personal assets.

> If you go to the Spicy Bites Snack Bar and get food poisoning, you may well decide to sue for compensation. If the snack bar is simply owned by Saleem Saddiqi and run as a sole trader, or if it is owned by Saleem and his brother Sohal in partnership, then it is Saleem or the Saddiqi brothers, personally, that you will claim against. If the cost of any damages you may be awarded exceeds the business's ability to pay you from the business assets, then the Saddiqis are obliged to settle any excess with you out of their private resources.
>
> On the other hand, if the business trades as Spicy Bites Snack Bar Ltd. (the shareholders and directors of which are the Saddiqi brothers and possibly their families) it is an incorporated company with its own separate legal existence. You will find yourself suing the company; and if the company is unable to pay you the compensation awarded, while the company may be forced into bankruptcy, the Saddiqis will not have to pay you out of their private resources to meet any shortfall.

This protection is a most important one for traders and to compensate for it they have to comply with more restrictive rules and regulations in running their companies than they would if they traded as unincorporated sole traders or partnerships.

The capital of a limited company is divided into shares and the owners of the shares (or "members" of the company) are known as shareholders. They participate in the **equity** of the company in proportion to their shareholdings.

Limited companies range in size from the very small, for example a car repair workshop, to very large, for example global corporations such as Microsoft, Vodafone, Tata, Mitsubishi or Exxon Mobil.

These largest multi-national businesses have grown into huge economic entities and some of them have operations and assets larger than the whole economies of some smaller countries.

Smaller businesses will be incorporated as **private limited companies**, using the word "Limited" or "Ltd." in their title, with the shareholdings restricted to a few people. The Articles of Association will specify how those shares can be transferred, and the exchange of shares will normally require the agreement of all the shareholders. By contrast, once a company exceeds a certain number of shareholders it is described as a **public limited company**, which is shortened to PLC. The shares of these companies can be freely traded on the Stock Exchanges where they are listed.

	Private company	Public company
Shareholders	Few	Many
Size of company	Smaller	Larger
Designation	Ltd.	PLC
Management	Owner-managed	Run by directors on behalf of shareholders
Reporting	To shareholders annually	To shareholders annually and halfway through the year
Share types	Ordinary and preference	Ordinary and preference
Issue of shares	Privately arranged between shareholders.	Publicly offered on Stock Exchange
	Cash raised paid in to company	Cash raised paid in to company
Transfer of shares	Difficult – restricted by company's constitution	Easy – openly traded on Stock Exchange
	No effect on company's statements	No effect on company's statements
Approval of transfer	By shareholders	None needed
Price of shares	Difficult to establish because there is no free market for the shares	Easy to establish because there is a free market for the shares and the prices are quoted on the Stock Exchange
Borrowing types	Loans and debentures	Loans and debentures plus bonds and other borrowings

In all trading companies the profits earned by the business increase the equity of the owners – after deducting any amount that has been distributed to them.

In earlier sections we have looked at how profit is distributed in sole traders and partnerships. ➤ **4.1, 4.2** (See also the table summarising characteristics of trading businesses on the next page.)

In a limited company, the directors will make a recommendation as to how much profit should be distributed as a **dividend** and the shareholders will be invited to agree to this at the Annual General Meeting (AGM). The remaining profits accumulate as retained earnings (reserves) and are added to the total equity attributable to the shareholders.

In the case of smaller companies, the owners are very likely to be actively involved in the management of the business and will be the directors of the company; in many cases *all* the shareholders will also be directors.

As a company gets bigger and the number of shareholders increases, it becomes impossible for all the shareholders to participate in the management of the business. The shareholders appoint directors to run the business on their behalf. Directors are regularly elected or re-elected at the AGMs.

Directors have a wide range of legal duties and responsibilities. The following are among the more important ones from a financial point of view. Directors must:

- always act in the best interests of the shareholders, even when this conflicts with their own personal interests
- take steps to ensure that the company is able to trade as a going concern
- not allow the company to trade when they know that it is insolvent
- report to the shareholders annually on the company's performance and position – larger companies may be required to report more frequently
- prepare annual statements to include a statement of financial position and income statement – larger companies are also required to prepare a statement of cash flows and a statement of changes in equity, which shows how new equity has been raised and how profits have been distributed
- ensure that these statements give a true and fair view of the company's financial position and results
- comply with all applicable Accounting Standards. ➤ **5.2**

Limited companies

The following table summarises and compares some of the features of unincorporated and limited company businesses.

▼ **Characteristics of trading businesses**

	Sole trader	Partnership	Limited company
Legal status	Legal status is indivisible from the owner.	Legal status is indivisible from the partners.	The company exists as a separate legal entity.
Management	The organisation is run by the owner.	The organisation is run by the partners.	The organisation is run by directors appointed by the owners to act on their behalf.
Liability to settle claims	There is unlimited liability.	There is unlimited liability.	Liability is limited to the amount of equity capital invested.
Profits	Profits belong entirely to the owner and may be drawn out as and when desired.	Profits belong to the partners in the proportions agreed between them and may be drawn out as and when desired, subject to any restrictions in the partnership agreement.	Profits belong to the company – they are held on behalf of the shareholders. They may be distributed as dividends on the recommendation of the directors and with the agreement of shareholders.
Capital	Capital comprises the single amount of owner's equity.	Capital comprises the total of the individual partners' capital and current accounts.	Equity is represented by the issued share capital and reserves of the company.
Size	Sole traders are usually small.	Partnerships are usually small. Historically they have been limited to a maximum of 20 partners. Some partnerships of professional persons – accountants, lawyers, architects etc. – have become very large in size.	Limited companies range from very small to very large.
Publication of financial statements	Financial statements are "private" to the owners, and there is no legal requirement to produce "public" statements. A simple income statement and a statement of financial position may be requested by tax authorities, banks and other interested persons.	Financial statements are "private" to the partners, and there is no legal requirement to produce "public" statements. An income statement and a statement of financial position may be requested by tax authorities, banks and other interested persons. Partners will want to see an appropriation account and details of their capital and current accounts.	Financial statements are legally required to be prepared by directors and provided to shareholders. After shareholder approval, they are placed on public record in a company registry, where they can be inspected by anyone.
Audit (checking) of financial statements	This is not legally required.	This is not legally required, although the partnership agreement may specify that an audit should be carried out.	Large companies must have their financial statements audited by an independent, professionally qualified, person. Smaller companies may be exempt from this requirement.

Limited companies are financed with share capital and loan capital

Issuing of share capital

Limited companies raise money by issuing shares to shareholders for cash. This cash is debited to the company's bank account and credited to "share capital" in the equity section of the statement of financial position. It is *not* regarded as revenue or income of the company.

Once this money has been paid to the company it forms permanent capital. It is not possible for the shareholder to ask for repayment from the company or in any way to draw out capital.

The reason for this is to protect other people who are owed money by the company – the creditors. Remember that the liability of the shareholders to ensure that the company can pay those creditors has been limited, by incorporating the business as a company, to the amount of capital paid in by the shareholders. It is important for the creditors to be confident that the money paid in cannot be removed whenever the shareholders feel like it.

The only way shareholders can get their capital investment back is to get someone else to buy their shares. Occasionally, a company may seek permission from the courts to repay or buy back some shares from shareholders. This process is very carefully controlled by the courts.

When the company is formed, an assessment is made of how much cash the company may need to raise in the foreseeable future. The share capital is set up and entered into the Memorandum and Articles of Association, which form the company's constitution.

Authorised share capital – is the total number of shares a company is allowed to issue under its constitution.

This amount can be increased later, if necessary, with the agreement of the shareholders.

Issued share capital – is the actual number of shares issued to members for cash.

The authorised capital does not all need to be raised immediately or all at once, and shares may be issued over a period of time.

Called-up share capital – is the total amount of the issued share capital for which payment has been demanded.

The issued share capital may be paid for in instalments, in which case the amount asked for is designated as "called-up".

Paid-up share capital – is the total amount of the called-up share capital for which the cash has actually been received.

Issued, called-up, shares on which cash is still outstanding are called "partly paid".

Once the total amount demanded on the shares has been received they are designated as "issued and fully paid".

A company can issue different types of share – distinguished by degree of risk, voting rights and dividends.

▼ Types of shares

Ordinary shares (These are equity shares)	• These shares have a face or nominal value – typically $1.50, 25 cents etc. • They may be issued for a price above the face value – the extra amount paid is called "share premium". • These shares have voting rights. • These shares qualify for an "ordinary dividend", paid **after** the preference shareholders have received their dividends. • The amount of ordinary dividend recommended by the directors for payment to the ordinary shareholders may vary from year to year, and in some years an ordinary dividend may not be paid at all. • The dividend is expressed in cents per share.
Preference shares (These are not equity shares)	• These shares have a face or nominal value – typically $1.50, 25 cents, etc. • These shares do not have voting rights. • Dividends are paid at a fixed % of the face value and are paid **before** the dividend to ordinary shareholders. • These dividends do not have to be paid if the directors decide not to do so. • Preference shares may be **cumulative**, when any past arrears of dividend must be paid before the ordinary shareholders can receive a dividend, or **non-cumulative** where past unpaid dividends are not accumulated. • Preference shares may be redeemable, which means that, under certain circumstances, they can be repaid in the future. • It may also be agreed that, under certain circumstances, preference shares may be **convertible** into ordinary shares. • Should the company be wound up, either voluntarily or compulsorily, the preference shareholders will receive their investment back **before** the ordinary shareholders.

Because preference shares receive this preferential treatment over the ordinary shares in respect of both the fixed rate dividend payment and repayment in a winding-up, they are less risky for investors than the ordinary shares.

As a result, preference shares are therefore seen as very similar to loan capital and are therefore not included in equity. It is the ordinary shareholders who take the ultimate risk in the company and they are the ones designated as equity.

When these preference shares are not classified as equity:

1. The preference share dividends are shown in the income statement, together with interest, among the finance expenses.
2. The amount of preference share capital is shown in the Statement of Financial Position as a non-current liability, alongside debentures and other long-term borrowings

Issuing of loan capital

To raise long-term finance, a company may also borrow money on a long-term basis.

It can do this with a bank or other financial institution, but public companies will often do so by issuing long-term loan capital in the market by inviting the public to lend money to the company.

The terms "debenture", "mortgage", "loan stock" or "bond" are used to describe various types of borrowing. Although these may differ in some of their characteristics they all share features in common. They form part of the company's liabilities – the non-current liabilities – and are not part of equity. Loan stock and bonds are only applicable to public companies.

▼ Company loan capital

Debentures, mortgages, loan stock, bonds

- They are for the long term – often repayable over several accounting years. The loan agreements will specify when and how repayments will be made.
- The loan agreements will specify at what % rate, and how frequently, interest should be paid.
- "10% debenture 2025–2030" is a loan repayable between 2025 and 2030 on which interest will be paid at an annual rate of 10% of the loan's face value.
- The loan agreement will specify any arrangements made to guarantee the loan repayment or otherwise protect the lender from the risk of non-payment. Loans are often 'secured' by using non-current assets as collateral. If the company is unable to pay interest or make repayment of the loan, the lender is entitled to take possession of the specified asset and sell it in order to recover the amounts owed.
- Interest is paid before any dividends are distributed either to preference or ordinary shareholders.
- Interest is an expense which is charged to the income statement. It must be paid irrespective of the profits made by the company.
- In the event of company failure or other winding up of the company, the lenders will be repaid before any money is recovered by preference or ordinary shareholders.

The uses or distribution of company profit is recorded in a statement of changes in equity

4.32 CAPITAL STRUCTURE

Centurion Products Ltd. was formed on 1 January 2011 with authorised capital of 200 000, 8% preference shares of $1 each and 1 800 000 ordinary shares of $1 each. Initially, all the preference shares were issued, along with 800 000 ordinary shares.

The preference shares were payable in full, and by 30 June 2011 all the cash had been received.

On 1 January 2011, 50 cents per share was called-up on the issued ordinary shares and by 30 June 2011 all the cash had been received. On July 1 2011, the second instalment of 50 cents was called up, and by 31 December 2011, 80% of the cash had been received.

On 31 December 2011, at the end of the first year, the company's capital structure was as follows:

▼ Capital structure of Centurion Products Ltd.

Capital	Preference shares – $1 each		Ordinary shares – $1 each		Total
	Number	$	Number	$	$
Authorised	200 000	200 000	1 800 000	1 800 000	2 000 000
Issued	200 000	200 000	800 000	800 000	1 000 000
Called-up		200 000		800 000	1 000 000
Paid-up		200 000		720 000	920 000

The company made a modest profit of $8 000 in the first year ended 31 December 2011. The directors did not consider it appropriate at that stage to recommend a dividend on the ordinary shares or even to declare a dividend on the preference shares.

On 1 January 2012, the company issued a 10% debenture of $500 000 repayable in 25 years' time. During the year ended 31 December 2012, the remainder of the called-up ordinary shares were paid.

For the year ended 31 December 2012, Centurion Products Ltd.'s income statement showed it had made a profit – after payment of debenture interest and directors salaries – of $103 000. Centurion Ltd.'s directors had to decide how the profit was to be used. The choices before them were:

- distribute some or all the profit to shareholders – will there be sufficient cash to do this?
- retain some or all of the profit for reinvestment – it could be transferred to general reserve to signal the directors' intention not to use these earnings to pay dividends.

They chose to:

- retain $55 000, transferring $50 000 to general reserve
- distribute the remainder of $48 000 to shareholders.

▼ Calculating dividends

	8% preference shares	Ordinary shares
Number of shares issued	200 000	800 000
Share capital ($)	200 000	800 000
Total dividend ($)	16 000	32 000
Expressed as	8.00 cents/share ($16 000/$200 000)	4.00 cents/share ($32 000/$800 000) or 4.0% (of the value of issued ordinary share capital) ($32 000/$800 000 × 100)

This meant preference shareholders were paid $16 000 in total (8% of $200 000) and 8.00 cents per share.

What was left was distributed to ordinary shareholders. This meant that they were paid a total dividend of $32 000 ($103 000 – $55 000 – $16 000 = $32 000 – usually expressed as 4.00 cents per share – sometimes expressed as 4.0% ($32 000/$800 000 × 100).

Directors' decisions about payment of ordinary dividends are shown in the Statement of Changes in Equity.

4.33 STATEMENT OF CHANGES IN EQUITY

Centurion Products Ltd.

Statement Of Changes In Equity For The Year Ended 31 December 2012

	Ordinary share capital	General reserve	Retained earnings	Total equity
	$	$	$	$
Balances at 1 Jan 2012	720 000		8 000	728 000
Ordinary share capital paid in	80 000			80 000
Profit for the year			87 000	87 000
Ordinary dividend paid			(32 000)	(32 000)
Transfer to general reserve		50 000	(50 000)	
	800 000	50 000	13 000	863 000

You will see that the profit after debenture interest of $103 000 has been reduced by the preference dividend of $16 000, which is treated in the income statement as a finance expense, to give the $87 000 taken as profit into the statement of changes in equity.

Now check your answer against the sample on the website.

ACTIVITY 4.16

Two friends, Mark and Carrie, agreed to form a private limited company – Skywalker Ltd. – on 1 April 2011 with authorised share capital as follows:

Table 1

10% Preference shares of $1	500 000
Ordinary shares of $5	500 000

They agreed the following issue and distribution of shares:

Table 2

10% Preference shares of $1	500 000	Ordinary shares of $5	100 000
Mark	250 000	Mark	60 000
Carrie	250 000	Carrie	40 000

They agreed shares should be paid for at face value as follows:

Table 3

Preference shares of $1	immediately
Ordinary shares of $5	$2.50 immediately; $2.50 on 1 Mar 2012

By 31 March 2012 all cash due on the called-up share capital had been received.

At end of the first accounting year on 31 March 2012, the company profit for the year after all expenses was $150 000. Mark and Carrie agreed to retain $50 000 and distribute $100 000.

1. Calculate:
   (a) the total dividend payments received by (i) Mark; and (ii) Carrie;
   (b) the dividend paid per (i) preference share; (ii) ordinary share.

2. Prepare a statement of changes of equity for the year ended 31 March 2012.

Limited companies 425

4.5.2 Preparing company financial statements

The income statement will include debenture interest, preference dividends and directors' salaries and reported profit before and after finance costs

Additional expenses which appear in company financial statements are directors' salaries or fees, debenture interest and preference dividends.

4.34 CENTURION PRODUCTS LTD. – YEAR 2 BALANCES

At 31 December 2012 – the end of the company's second year of trading – the following balances were extracted from the books. These included salaries paid to company directors over the year of $125 000; because the company had also issued $500 000 of 10% debentures it had also paid out $50 000 in debenture interest.

▼ Centurion Products Ltd. – balances at 31 December 2012

	Dr	Cr
	$	$
Revenue		2 550 000
Purchases	1 883 500	
Inventory at 1 January 2012	80 000	
Salaries and wages	124 000	
Other operating costs	130 500	
Directors' salaries	125 000	
Debenture interest	50 000	
Property at cost	1 000 000	
Fixtures and equipment at cost	1 000 000	
Accumulated depreciation on furniture and equipment 1 January 2012		200 000
Trade receivables	212 500	
Provision for doubtful debts		11 500
Other receivables	20 000	
Trade payables		365 000
Other payables		80 000
Cash in bank	41 000	
10% debenture 2025–2030		500 000
Preference share capital		200 000
Ordinary share capital		800 000
Retained earnings at 1 January 2012		8 000
Preference dividend paid	16 000	
Ordinary dividend paid	32 000	
	4 714 500	4 714 500

At 31 December 2012

1. Depreciation is required at 20% of cost on the fixtures and equipment.
2. Additional directors' salaries totalling $25 000 are to be provided.
3. Other operating costs of $30 000 are prepaid.
4. Inventory amounts to $141 000.

The income statement for the year ended 31 December 2012, prepared in the usual way, will appear as follows:

▼ Centurion Products Ltd. – income statement for the year ended 31 December 2012

	Dr	Cr
	$	$
Revenue		2 550 000
Inventory at 1 January 2012	80 000	
Purchases	1 883 500	
Inventory at 31 December 2012	(141 000)	
Cost of sales		1 822 500
Gross profit		727 500
Less: Expenses		
Salaries and wages	124 000	
Other operating costs ($130 500 – $30 000)	100 500	
Directors' salaries ($125 000 + $25 000)	150 000	
Depreciation ($1 000 000 × 20%)	200 000	
		574 500
Operating profit		153 000
Finance costs:		
Debenture interest	50 000	
Preference dividend	16 000	
		66 000
Profit for the year		87 000

You will notice that the format of the statement differs slightly from those for a sole trader or partnership in that a figure for operating profit is shown before deducting the finance costs. In this case these finance costs comprise the debenture interest and preference dividend ➤ **4.5.1**; in other cases it might include bank overdraft or other loan interest. This treatment complies with international accounting standards. The statement of changes in equity can be seen in illustration 4.33 and includes the profit for the year of $87 000.

The statement of financial position will report details of issued share capital, the general reserve and retained earnings

The statement of financial position for a limited company is prepared in the same way as for sole traders and partnerships, although there are some differences:

- Debentures, mortgages, loan stock and bonds – all long-term loans – are included under non-current liabilities.
- The capital section is headed "Equity" and records details of issued share capital, the retained earnings and the general reserve.
- The authorised capital of the company is added as a note to the statement.

From the assets and liabilities shown in the trial balance in illustration 4.34, and the additional information given below the trial balance and the statement of changes in equity in illustration 4.33, the following statement of financial position can be prepared.

4.35 STATEMENT OF FINANCIAL POSITION – YEAR 2

Centurion Products Ltd.

Statement Of Financial Position At 31 December 2012

	$	$
Non-current assets		
Property		1 000 000
Fixtures and equipment		
Cost	1 000 000	
Less: accumulated depreciation	400 000	
		600 000
		1 600 000
Current assets		
Inventory	141 000	
Trade receivables	212 500	
Less: provision for doubtful debts	(11 500)	
	201 000	
Other receivables ($20 000 + $30 000)	50 000	
Cash in bank	41 000	
		433 000
Total assets		2 033 000
Current liabilities		
Trade payables	365 000	
Other payables ($80 000 + $25 000)	105 000	
		470 000
Non-current liabilities		
10% debenture 2025–2030	500 000	
8% preference shares – authorised, issued and fully paid	200 000	
		700 000
Equity		
Ordinary share capital		
Authorised – 1 800 000 shares of $1 each – $1 800 000		
Issued and fully paid – 800 000 shares of $1 each	800 000	
General reserve	50 000	
Retained earnings	13 000	
Total equity		863 000
Total liabilities and equity		2 033 000

It shows:

▶ the 10% debenture under non-current liabilities

▶ the preference shares under non-current liabilities

▶ a note of the authorised ordinary share capital.

Preparation of financial statements

ACTIVITY 4.17

Trendsetter Ltd. has an authorised share capital of 10 000 6% preference shares of $10 each and 50 000 ordinary shares of $5 each. Of these, 5 000 preference shares and 30 000 ordinary shares were issued and fully paid.

The following information was taken from the company books at the end of its accounting year ended 30 June 2012.

	$
Revenue	800 000
Purchases	520 000
Inventory at 1 July 2011	30 000
Wages and salaries	36 000
Directors' salaries	50 000
Other operating costs	140 000
Property at cost	250 000
Fixtures and equipment at cost	75 000
Accumulated depreciation of fixtures and equipment	22 500
Trade receivables	68 000
Provision for doubtful debts	2 000
Cash in bank	10 000
Trade payables	40 000
8% debenture – 2020	50 000
Retained earnings	39 500
General reserve	25 000

Additional information at 30 June 2012:

- Operating costs prepaid were $10 000.
- Depreciation is required at 10% straight line on the cost of fixtures and equipment.
- Debenture interest for the year is outstanding.
- Inventory was $40 000.
- Additional directors' salaries of $25 000 should be provided.
- The required provision for doubtful debts is 5% of trade receivables.

The company directors agreed to the following distribution:

- Preference dividend would be paid on 30 June 2012.
- Ordinary dividend of 10 cents per share would be paid on 30 June 2012.
- $10 000 would be transferred to general reserve.

1. Prepare an income statement for the year ended 30 June 2012. If prepared correctly this will show a profit for the year of $33 100.
2. Prepare a statement of changes in equity for the year ended 30 June 2012.
3. Prepare a statement of financial position at 30 June 2012.

Limited companies

QUICK TEST

1. Identify and explain the differences between preference shares and ordinary shares.
2. What are the principal differences between trading as a sole trader or partnership and trading as a limited liability company?
3. Describe what is meant by the phrase "limited liability".
4. Gadgetrix was formed on 1 October 2012 with a maximum capital specified in the Memorandum and Articles of Association of 200 000 8% preference shares of $5 each and 2 000 000 ordinary shares of $0.50 each.

   On 2 October 2012, 100 000 of the preference shares and 1 600 000 of the ordinary shares were issued at their face value.

   The company required immediate payment for the full amount of the preference shares and this was received by 15 October.

   Ordinary shareholders were asked immediately for $0.25 per share with a further $0.25 per share being payable on 1 April 2013.

   By 30 September 2013, all money due on the called-up capital had been received.

   Gadgetrix had made a profit after all expenses and costs but before dividends of $150 000. The directors have decided to retain $30 000, to transfer $20 000 of this to general reserve, to pay the preference dividend on 30 September 2013 and to pay the balance of the profit as an ordinary dividend also on 30 September 2013.

   Calculate the total dividends to be paid and calculate the dividend per share payable to ordinary shareholders.

5. From the information given and calculated in 5 above, prepare a statement of changes in equity for Gadgetrix for the year ended 30 September 2013.

6. Following is a list of balances and other information extracted from Gadgetrix Ltd.'s records at 30 September 2013.

	$
Purchases	417 000
Purchase returns	14 000
Carriage inwards	24 500
Revenue	795 000
Office expenses	80 000
Office salaries	88 000
Property at cost	1 075 000
Computer equipment (cost)	120 000
Office fixtures and fittings (cost)	60 000
Other operating expenses	14 500
Advertising and marketing costs	36 000
Debenture interest paid	10 000
1 600 000 $0.50 ordinary shares	800 000
100 000 $5.00 8% preference shares	500 000
10% debentures repayable 31 December 2025	100 000
Trade receivables	64 000
Trade payables	53 500
Cash in hand and in bank	153 500
Preference dividend paid	40 000
Ordinary dividend paid	80 000

Additional information at 30 September:

- Inventory was $57 000.
  - Office expenses, $4 200, were prepaid.
  - Office salaries, $5 000, were accrued.
- Depreciation is to be charged on:
  - computer equipment at 25% per annum using the diminishing (reducing balance) method
  - office fixtures and fittings using the straight-line method at 20% on cost.
- A provision for doubtful debts is to be set up at 5% of trade receivables.

Prepare an income statement for the year ended 30 September 2013 and a statement of financial position at that date for Gadgetrix Ltd.

Unit 4.6　Manufacturing accounts

AIMS

By the end of this unit you should be able to
- distinguish between **direct and indirect costs**
- understand **direct material, direct labour, prime cost** and **factory overheads**
- understand and make adjustments for **work in progress**
- calculate **factory cost of production**
- prepare **manufacturing accounts, income statements** and **statements of financial position**
- make adjustments to financial statements as detailed in 4.1 (sole traders)

4.6.1　The process and costs of manufacturing

The process of manufacturing involves converting raw materials, components and other unfinished products into finished goods for sale

Until now we have only considered the accounts of businesses that sell services or finished goods they have bought from other organisations. Businesses that make the goods they sell are manufacturing organisations.

Manufacturing involves buying raw materials, or sometimes components and converting them into the finished goods that are then sold on to other businesses.

A cloth manufacturer buys wool, spins it into yarn, dyes it and weaves it into lengths of fabric. The fabric is sold to a garment manufacturer, who cuts and sews it into garments. The garments are then sold to a fashion store, which sells them to the public. Once the customer has bought and worn the clothing, it may require occasional cleaning at a dry cleaner.

The first two businesses, making the cloth and garments, are manufacturers; the third, selling to the public, is a trading business; the dry cleaner is a service business.

The book-keeping system for a manufacturing business will be similar to that of other organisations, keeping books of prime entry and ledger accounts to record the different types of revenue and expenditure and assets and liabilities.

At end of the accounting year the records will be used to prepare an income statement and statement of financial position using the procedures already discussed.

However, unlike trading businesses that simply buy goods for resale, manufacturers record and monitor the cost of making or producing goods, not just the cost of their purchase.

▲ Manufacturing processes

A manufacturing business will record the direct costs of producing items in addition to the indirect costs of running the organisation

A manufacturing business will need to keep accurate and up-to-date records of its total income and total costs. For example, the following costs will be incurred on a regular basis by a manufacturer of washing machines:

- the cost of raw materials and components, including steel, plastic, rubber, copper wire, springs, bolts and washers
- sub-assemblies such as switches, circuit boards, pumps and motors
- the wages and salaries of employees
- energy costs of the production processes
- the cost of tools, equipment, machinery and other non-current assets, including repair and maintenance, consumable materials as well as the depreciation of the factory buildings and machinery
- various other expenses including rent, electricity, insurance, advertising, depreciation of office equipment and vehicles and any loan interest.

However, not all of these costs will be directly related to the production process. Some will be incurred running the office and other functions of the organisation. It is therefore necessary for a manufacturing business to group together different costs.

Factory costs of production are costs incurred running a production line or production department.

Direct costs are those that can be specifically identified with the goods being made. They will include the raw materials and the other costs incurred in converting them into the finished product.

Indirect costs are items such as factory rent and insurance, heating and lighting of the premises, cleaning the factory and running the factory canteen. These are referred to as factory overheads.

Non-factory costs are incurred on running the business, and will include advertising and promotion, selling and distribution, staff training, the accountancy and legal departments, payroll and personnel activity as well as overall management of the business. These are often referred to as the office overheads.

Manufacturing accounts

▼ Different types of production costs

Direct costs	Indirect costs
Direct materials include: - physical commodities – steel, aluminium, wood, rubber, plastic, etc. - chemicals - edible ingredients for foodstuffs and drinks – sugar, flour, cereals, meat, fish, eggs and dairy products - sub-assemblies – switches, pumps, motors, etc. - components – nuts, bolts, screws, washers, springs, tubes, hoses, etc. *All these can be directly identified with and traced to the actual goods being made.* **Direct labour** is the labour cost – wages or salary, social security, pension, etc. – of operatives engaged in "hands-on" productive activity. These people include: - machine operatives - technicians initiating and monitoring processes - assembly line workers. *All these are directly involved in the conversion of raw materials into finished goods.* **Direct expenses** may include: - power - lubrication of machinery - packaging – milk bottles, soft drinks cans, cartons and boxes.	**Indirect labour** may include: - cleaning staff - security - Health and Safety supervisors - canteen staff - staff running the nursery or medical centre - the factory manager - production supervisors - the factory accountant. *All these are employed to run the production facility rather than being engaged in direct productive activity. However, the costs would not be incurred in the absence of the factory, hence they are part of the overall cost of production.* **Indirect expenses** will include: - cleaning materials - factory and office supplies - telephone - heat and light for the factory (as opposed to process energy) - property taxes - building repairs and depreciation - insurance - materials handling and stores. *These costs are all incurred as a result of occupying and running the factory and are therefore part of the overall cost of production.*

A manufacturer will prepare a separate manufacturing account to calculate how much it has cost to make the volume of goods produced during the accounting year

In addition to other financial statements a manufacturing business will prepare a manufacturing account at the end of each accounting year.

This is important so the business can establish the full product cost of the goods sold and calculate its gross profit. The information is also useful in comparing the product costs and profitability of different products in a multi-product business, and in comparing the relative costs of in-house production or outsourcing of various goods.

For example, Ready Registers manufactures cash tills for sale to other businesses.

The following information about production costs was taken from the books of the business for the year ended 31 December 2014.

▼ Ready Registers – manufacturing data

	$	Used to calculate
Opening inventory of raw materials – 1 Jan 2014	39 000	Raw material cost
Closing inventory of raw materials – 31 Dec 2014	46 500	Raw material cost
Raw materials purchased	260 000	Raw material cost
Carriage inwards of raw materials	5 000	Raw material cost
Factory wages	330 000	Prime cost
Power for machines	25 000	Prime cost
Machine hire	5 000	Prime cost
Machine repairs	3 500	Production cost
Machine depreciation	70 000	Production cost
Factory rent and property taxes	45 000	Production cost
Insurance	7 500	Production cost
Heat and light	15 000	Production cost
Indirect wages and salaries	95 000	Production cost

In addition, the final week's factory wages amounting to $6 500 remained unpaid; and machine hire paid in advance at the year end amounted to $1 000.

From this information Ready Registers produced the following manufacturing account.

4.36 MANUFACTURING ACCOUNT

Ready Registers
Manufacturing account for the year ending 31 December 2014

	$	$
Opening inventory	39 000	
add purchases	260 000	
add carriage inwards	5 000	
less closing inventory	(46 500)	
Cost of raw materials consumed		257 500 ❶
Factory wages	❷	336 500
Power for machines		25 000 ❷
Machine hire		4 000
Prime cost		623 000 ❸
Machine repairs	3 500	
Machine depreciation	70 000	
Factory rent and property taxes	45 000	
Insurance	7 500	
Heat and light	15 000	
Indirect factory wages and salaries	95 000	
Total indirect cost		236 000 ❹
Cost of production		**859 000**

You will notice that in drawing up this statement, the matching principle has been applied – only the cost of materials, labour and expenses actually used to produce the goods during the accounting year have been included.

Let's look at some of the specific areas where this applies, using the example of Ready Registers.

❶ The first step is to calculate cost of materials and components actually used. This takes in the various costs incurred in obtaining the materials and also takes into account the opening and closing inventory of materials, leaving only the cost relating to the materials used.

Manufacturing accounts

2 Matching next requires us to see whether there are any accruals or prepayments to apply to the direct or indirect production costs. In our example, there are some factory wages left unpaid, although earned by the year end; these require an accrual adding to the direct wages. There is also an amount prepaid relating to the machine hire, which is also a direct production cost; this requires a reduction in the recorded amount.

	$
Factory wages	330 000
add unpaid wages accrued	6 500
Factory wages for manufacturing account	336 500
Machine hire	5 000
less hire prepaid	(1 000)
Machine hire for manufacturing account	4 000

3 **Prime cost** is the term used to describe the total of all the **direct costs** of production. We calculate prime cost as follows:

> Prime cost = direct materials + direct labour + direct expenses

4 Now we can calculate **total costs**. Adding the indirect, factory overhead costs to the prime costs gives us the total cost of production.

> Factory (total) cost of production = prime cost + factory overheads

Work in progress

However, this is only the case where there is no **work in progress** – semi-finished items not yet completed and ready for sale. At any point in time, most manufacturing businesses will have some level of work in progress. This is the case even where they only order raw materials when needed and hold no inventory of raw materials; and even where they make to order and do not hold any finished goods. In these cases the only inventory they hold will be the work in progress passing through the factory at any point in time. An adjustment for this must be made in order to establish the cost of production for only those items finished during the period and ready for sale.

5 An adjustment is made for opening and closing work in progress to calculate the total cost of production of finished goods.

Ready Registers has an inventory of work in progress:

| work in progress at 1 January 2014 | 6 300 |
| work in progress at 31 December 2014 | 7 800 |

	$	$
Opening inventory	39 000	
add purchases	260 000	
add carriage inwards	5 000	
less closing inventory	(46 500)	
Cost of raw materials consumed		257 500 ①
Factory wages	②	336 500
Power for machines		25 000
Machine hire		4 000 ②
Prime cost		623 000 ③
Machine repairs	3 500	
Machine depreciation	70 000	
Factory rent and property taxes	45 000	
Insurance	7 500	
Heat and light	15 000	
Indirect factory wages and salaries	95 000	
Total indirect cost		236 000 ④
Cost of production		859 000
add opening inventory of work in progress		6 300
less closing inventory of work in progress		(7 800) ⑤
Factory cost of production of finished goods		**857 500**

ACTIVITY 4.18

Potluck manufactures ceramic flower pots. The following information was available about the business's accounting year ended 30 June 2013:

	$	Used to calculate
Opening inventory of raw materials – 1 Jul 2012	70 000	Raw material cost
Closing inventory of raw materials – 30 Jun 2013	90 000	Raw material cost
Raw materials purchased	550 000	Raw material cost
Carriage inwards of raw materials	15 000	Raw material cost
Factory wages	320 000	Prime cost
Power for machines	75 000	Prime cost
Machine repairs	13 500	Production cost
Machine depreciation	150 000	Production cost
Opening inventory of work in progress – 1 Jul 2012	12 000	Production cost
Closing inventory of work in progress – 30 Jun 2013	10 000	Production cost
Factory rent and property taxes	60 000	Production cost
Insurance	10 000	Production cost
Heat and light	30 000	Production cost
Indirect wages and salaries	120 500	Production cost

At 30 June 2013:
- Insurance had been prepaid, $2 000.
- Power accrued was $5 000.

Prepare a manufacturing account. Remember to adjust for work in progress to calculate and record the total cost of production of all finished items produced during the year.

Manufacturing accounts

4.6.2 Preparing the financial statements of a manufacturing business

The first part of the income statement of a manufacturing business will record production costs and revenues only

The income statement of a manufacturing business will adopt normal accounting procedures in a similar way to a trading business. However, in calculating the gross profit, the first part of the statement will now show the cost of production for the year instead of the purchase cost of the goods that a trading business would show.

To calculate the cost of sales, the usual adjustment for inventory of finished goods will be required.

Ready Registers produced the following information about its revenue, general non-factory costs and inventory of finished goods.

▼ Ready Registers – general overheads and finished goods inventory

	$
Revenue	1 520 000
Opening inventory of finished goods – 1 Jan 2014	125 000
Closing inventory of finished goods – 31 Dec 2014	135 000
Telephone and communications	15 000
Office salaries	60 000
Advertising and promotion	80 000
Selling costs	55 500
Transport and distribution	160 000
Office rent	52 000
General insurance	12 000
Office supplies	15 000
Depreciation of office equipment and computers	40 000
Heat and light	14 000
Office repairs and maintenance	10 500
Interest payable	12 500

Additional information:

- Office rent is prepaid by one month: $4 000.
- All other prepayments and accrued expenses have been taken into account

Ready Registers has produced the income statement shown in illustration 4.37.

4.37 INCOME STATEMENT

Ready Registers
Income Statement for the year ending 31 December 2014

	$	$
Revenue		1 520 000
Opening inventory of finished goods – 1 January 2014	125 000	
Cost of production for year	857 500	
less closing inventory of finished goods – 31 December 2014	(135 000)	
Cost of sales		847 500
Gross profit		672 500
less: expenses:		
Office salaries	60 000	
Advertising and promotion	80 000	
Selling costs	55 500	
Transport and distribution	160 000	
Office rent	48 000	
General insurance	12 000	
Heat and light	14 000	
Office repairs and maintenance	10 500	
Telephone and communications	15 000	
Office supplies	15 000	
Depreciation of office equipment and computers	40 000	
		510 000
Operating profit		162 500
Interest payable		12 500
Profit for year		**150 000**

A statement of the financial position of a manufacturer will include inventories for materials, work in progress and finished goods

The manufacturer's statement of financial position will have the same entries as for any other business but with one important difference; there will now be three inventory figures; raw materials, work in progress and finished goods.

Ready Registers general ledger reveals the following information additional to that already given or calculated.

▼ **Ready Registers – extract from general ledger balances**

	$
Factory machinery at cost	1 500 000
Accumulated depreciation on factory machinery – 31 December 2014	650 000
Office equipment and computers at cost	160 000
Accumulated depreciation on office equipment – 31 December 2014	80 000
Trade receivables	253 000
Trade payables	136 000
Other payables	25 000
Other receivables	10 000
Cash in hand	5 000
Bank overdraft	95 000
Capital – 1 January 2014	981 300

4.38 STATEMENT OF FINANCIAL POSITION

Ready Registers

Statement Of Financial Position At 31 December 2014

	$	$
Non-current assets		
Factory machinery at cost	1 500 000	
Accumulated depreciation on factory machinery	650 000	
		850 000
Office equipment and computers at cost	160 000	
Accumulated depreciation on office equipment	80 000	
		80 000
		930 000
Current assets		
Inventory:		
Raw materials	46 500	
Work in progress	7 800	
Finished goods	135 000	
	189 300	
Trade receivables	253 000	
Other receivables	10 000	
Cash in hand	5 000	
		457 300
Total assets		1 387 300
Current liabilities		
Trade payables	136 000	
Other payables	25 000	
Bank overdraft	95 000	
Total liabilities		256 000
Capital at 1 January 2014		981 300
add profit for the year		150 000
Capital at 31 December 2014		1 131 300
Total liabilities and capital		1 387 300

QUICK TEST

1. Explain how a manufacturing business differs from other types of business.
2. What additional accounting report is needed in a manufacturing business and what is its purpose?
3. Identify and describe the **three** types of inventory found in a manufacturing business.
4. Explain the difference between direct and indirect costs, giving examples of each; describe how these costs are dealt with in the financial statements of a manufacturing business.

5 Abishek manufactures plastic jewellery boxes. The following information is available for the year ended 31 July 2013.

	$
Inventory of raw materials – 1 Aug 2012	46 900
Inventory of raw materials – 31 Jul 2013	42 800
Purchases of raw materials	275 400
Direct wages	308 600
Depreciation of machinery	60 900
Factory rent	48 000
Factory light and heat	25 500
Factory insurance	6 000
Factory maintenance	3 700
Factory manager's salary	48 000

Prepare a manufacturing account for the year ended 31 July 2013. Show the cost of materials consumed, prime cost, factory overhead and the total cost of production.

6 Lawrence manufactures bedroom furniture. The following information is available for the year ended 31 March 2013.

	$
Inventory of raw materials at 1 Apr 2012	49 500
Inventory of raw materials at 31 Mar 2013	47 000
Inventory of work in progress at 1 Apr 2012	8 010
Inventory of work in progress at 31 Mar 2013	9 000
Purchases of raw materials	380 500
Direct wages	339 750
Rent	27 800
Factory utilities	16 500
Supervisors' salaries	58 250

The final week's wages $6 750 must be accrued.

Depreciation of machinery $22 000 must be provided.

Rent of $2 800 is prepaid.

Rent should be divided as factory 4/5 and office 1/5.

Prepare a manufacturing account for the year ended 31 March 2013. Show the cost of materials consumed, prime cost, factory overhead and the total cost of production.

Now you're ready to try the Unit 4 assessment activities.

5 Advanced principles

Content at a glance

5.1	Financial relationships (ratio analysis)
5.2	Accounting principles

Unit 5.1 Financial relationships (ratio analysis)

AIMS

By the end of this unit you should be able to

- calculate and understand the following accounting ratios:
  - gross margin
  - profit margin
  - return on capital employed (ROCE)
  - current ratio
  - liquid (acid test) ratio
  - rate of inventory turnover (times)
  - trade receivables turnover (days)
  - trade payables turnover (days)
- prepare and comment on simple statements showing comparison of results for different years
- make recommendations and suggestions for improving profitability and working capital
- understand the significance of the difference between the gross margin and the profit margin as an indicator of a business's efficiency
- explain the relationship of **gross profit** and **profit for the year** to the **valuation of inventory, rate of inventory turnover, revenue, expenses**, and **equity**
- understand the problems of inter-firm comparison

- apply accounting ratios to inter-firm comparisons
- recognise the importance of **valuation of inventory** and the effect of an incorrect valuation of inventory on gross profit, profit for the year, equity and asset valuation
- discuss the uses of accounting statements by the following interested parties:
  - owners
  - managers
  - suppliers
  - banks
  - investors
  - club members
  - other interested parties such as governments, tax authorities, etc.
- recognise the limitations of accounting statements due to such factors as historic cost, difficulties of definition and non-financial aspects

5.1.1 Analysing and interpreting accounts

Accounting data will be used to calculate financial ratios to analyse the financial health and performance of a business

Imagine you are an investor. You have a sizeable sum of money you want to invest in a business enterprise through the purchase of some shares. Your goal is to make a return each year on your investment that is greater than the return you would get by saving the same amount in a bank, and also a return that exceeds returns you could make from other business investments. So, how do you decide which business to invest in?

The answer is you can look at and compare the financial information contained in statements of income and financial position produced by different businesses to identify those that have been the most successful in the past and have sensible plans for the future.

However, simply comparing the profits, assets, liabilities and capital of different businesses will not tell you very much about their financial strength and performance over time.

Consider the financial information from the accounts of two supermarket chains on the left. Which one do you think has been more successful?

Better Buy plc made a gross profit which was three times bigger than the gross profit made by Smart Buy plc. However, after expenses were deducted, the profit for the year for Better Buy was only twice that of Smart Buy. So it appears that Smart Buy was better at controlling its costs than its business rival.

Better Buy plc
Year ended 30 June

	$m
Gross profit	9
Expenses	6
Profit for the year	2
Closing capital	10

Smart Buy plc
Year ended 30 June

	$m
Gross profit	3
Expenses	2
Profit for the year	1
Closing capital	4

Profit is a reward for risking capital invested in business assets. It is useful to compare the amount of profit made by each company with the amount of **capital employed** in each one. ➤ 3.2

Better Buy had closing capital at the end of its accounting year on 30 June of $10 million and made a profit for the year of $2 million on this investment. This means it had achieved a return of 20% on its capital employed.

In contrast, although Smart Buy had a smaller profit of just $1 million, this was returned on an investment in assets of just $4 million. Smart Buy therefore achieved a higher return of 25% on its capital employed.

Picking just one figure from the financial statements of a business to judge its performance can be misleading. Analysing financial information by comparing two or more figures in them provides a much better picture of performance and is called **ratio analysis**.

Accounting ratios are used to monitor and compare the financial performance of different businesses over time in terms of their profitability and liquidity

An **accounting ratio** or **financial ratio** is simply a comparison of two figures in the financial statements of a business. A ratio is produced by dividing one key figure by another and producing a value. This value could be presented as a percentage (20%), a ratio (2:10) or a multiple (five times as much). All ratios will require a descriptor such as these.

Financial ratios are a good way to see how the performance of a business has changed over time and how it compares to other businesses using the same measures.

Many different accounting ratios can be calculated. These are the main ones used to analyse business accounting information:

- **Profitability ratios.** Making a profit is the primary objective of privately owned businesses. The ability to make a profit from investments in business assets is called profitability. Profitability ratios measure the success or otherwise a business has in making a profit.

- **Liquidity ratios.** Having enough cash available to pay day-to-day expenses and liabilities as they fall due is critical to the survival of a business. This is called **liquidity**. Liquidity ratios measure the ability of a business to pay its trade and other payables. ➤ 3.2

However, comparing financial ratios will not tell us why performance varies. For example, financial ratios will not tell us why one business was able to earn more profit per item sold compared to another business of a similar size selling exactly the same products or why it was able to increase its profitability over time.

To understand why performance and why financial ratios differ requires additional investigation and the interpretation of results.

Illustration 5.1 summarises key results from the financial statements for Electra Ltd., a retailer selling electrical products from large out-of-town retail outlets.

5.1 KEY FINANCIAL DATA FOR ELECTRA LTD.

Electra Ltd.
Income statement for the year ended 31 December

	$ million	
	Year 1	Year 2
Revenue (sales)	20.0	25.0
less Cost of sales:		
Opening inventory at 1 Jan	2.2	1.8
add Purchases (all on credit)	12.0	16.0
less Closing inventory at 31 Dec	1.8	1.2
	16.0	19.0
Gross profit	4.0	6.0
less Operating expenses	2.5	3.0
Profit for the year	1.5	3.0

Electra Ltd.
Statement of financial position at 31 December

	$ million	
	End year 1	End year 2
Non-current assets	5.4	6.2
Cash	0.4	0.8
Inventory	1.8	1.2
Trade receivables	1.4	1.8
Current assets	3.6	3.8
less Current liabilities (trade payables only)	3.0	2.0
Net current assets	0.6	1.8
Total assets less Current liabilities	6.0	8.0
less Non-current liabilities	3.0	2.5
Net assets	3.0	5.5

The retailer opened a number of mega-stores two years ago and business managers at Electra Ltd. are confident that performance has improved over time. This follows an expansion in year 2 that increased its retail floorspace and product range further.

We will use the information from its financial statements to calculate and compare a number of key profitability and liquidity ratios for the company. ▶ 3.1

5.1.2 Profitability ratios

Profitability ratios measure how successful a business has been at selling and using assets to generate profit

Three key ratios are used to determine and compare the ability of businesses to generate profits:

- the **gross profit margin** is calculated as the **percentage of gross profit to revenue**: it measures the amount of gross profit earned as a proportion of its revenue from sales.

- the **profit margin** is calculated as the **percentage of profit for the year to revenue**: it measures the amount of profit for the year earned as a proportion of its revenue from sales.

- the **return on capital employed (ROCE)** is calculated as **profit for the year/capital employed**: it measures profit for the year as a percentage of the total amount of capital invested in business assets. It is the most important measure of the return on business investment.

Factors that will increase the gross profit margin

- an increase in revenue from sales greater than an increase in the cost of those sales
- increasing the selling price of each item, for example because demand is rising and there are few other businesses to compete with for customers
- cutting rates of trade discounts allowed to credit customers
- a reduction in the cost of each item sold including, for example, by buying more in bulk and paying invoices quickly to increase trade and cash discounts received

Factors that will reduce the gross profit margin

- an increase in the cost of sales that exceeds the growth in revenue from sales
- by reducing the selling price of each item, for example because competing businesses have cut their prices
- by offering more generous trade discounts allowed to attract more customers and increase sales
- from an increase in the cost of each item sold, for example because suppliers have increased their prices and/or cut the trade and cash discounts they allow to cover their increased costs

The margin in sales revenue for gross profit shows how successful a business is at selling items at a price greater than their cost

The **percentage of gross profit to revenue** is a measure of how much gross profit is made as a percentage of revenue sales. It is calculated as follows:

$$\text{Percentage of gross profit to revenue (\%)} = \frac{\text{gross profit}}{\text{revenue}} \times 100$$

where

gross profit = revenue − cost of sales

Using the information on gross profit and revenue from the income statements of Electra Ltd. on the previous page we can calculate and compare the percentage of gross profit achieved in sales by the company during its first two years of trading:

$$\frac{\text{Gross profit}}{\text{Sales}} \quad \begin{array}{c} \text{Year 1} \\ \frac{\$4m}{\$20m} \times 100 = 20\% \end{array} \quad \begin{array}{c} \text{Year 2} \\ \frac{\$6m}{\$25m} \times 100 = 24\% \end{array}$$

These ratios show that Electra Ltd. made a gross profit of $2 from every $10 of revenue raised from the sale of electrical products in year 1. The business improved on this margin in year 2 to $2.40 of gross profit per $10 of revenue: a good result.

Electra Ltd. was able to increase its gross profit as a percentage of revenue in year 2 in a number of ways:

- it increased its revenue from sales faster than its cost of sales increased. Through increased advertising it had attracted more customers to its store and website
- in turn this enabled the retailer to raise the average price of each product it sold
- it had also cut rates of trade discounts it allowed its credit customers, and
- it had reduced the cost of each item it sold by purchasing from cheaper suppliers and buying in bulk to take advantage of more generous trade discounts on offer for bulk purchases.

The percentage of profit for the year in revenue shows the ability of a business to control its expenses

The **percentage of profit for the year in revenue**, or profit margin, is calculated from accounting data as follows:

$$\text{Percentage of profit for the year to revenue (\%)} = \frac{\text{profit for the year}}{\text{revenue}} \times 100$$

where profit for the year = gross profit − total expenses

The difference between gross profit and profit for the year indicates the ability of the business to control its expenses. The more the revenue of a business exceeds its expenses, the higher its margin for profit in revenue. ▶ 3.1

Factors that will increase the profit margin

- an increase in gross profit
- an increase in other incomes earned by the business, including sales commission and interest on savings
- a reduction in expenses

Factors that will reduce the profit margin

- a fall in gross profit
- a fall in other income
- an increase in expenses

Profit margins provide a useful means of judging business performance when comparing performance across two or more years. For example, if the gross profit margin stays the same but profit margins decrease it means that expenses must have increased over time. This suggests the business has not been effective at controlling its expenses. The owners and managers will have to introduce tougher measures to control costs and improve profit margins.

The profit margins of Electra Ltd. were:

$$\frac{\text{Profit for the year}}{\text{Revenue}} \quad \begin{array}{|c|}\hline \text{Year 1} \\ \frac{\$1.5m}{\$20m} \times 100 = 7.5\% \\ \hline\end{array} \quad \begin{array}{|c|}\hline \text{Year 2} \\ \frac{\$3m}{\$25m} \times 100 = 12\% \\ \hline\end{array}$$

These profit margins were a good outcome for Electra Ltd. They show that even after it had paid all its expenses the business was still making a profit of $0.75 from every $10 of revenue in its first year of trading. In year 2 the profit margin had improved to 12% or $1.20 for every $10 of revenue.

Electra Ltd. could try to improve its profit margin yet further over time by:

- earning additional revenue, for example by selling more electrical items and/or by raising their selling prices but not by so much that customer demand falls
- cutting expenses, for example by reducing staff numbers and switching to cheaper suppliers of electricity, insurance and office stationery.

The return on capital employed shows how successful a business has been at using its assets to generate profit

The **capital employed** in the assets of a business is funded by owner's equity and any loan capital from non-current liabilities. Capital employed is equal to the value of its total assets less any current liabilities as reported in its statement of financial position. ▶ 3.2

The **return on capital employed (ROCE)** expresses the profit for the year of a business as a percentage of the value of its capital employed:

$$\text{Return on capital employed (ROCE \%)} = \frac{\text{profit for the year}}{\text{capital employed}} \times 100$$

where
capital employed = total assets − current liabilities

The higher the rate of return on capital, the more efficiently it is being used in the business to generate profit. Ideally the return should be more than the rate of interest investors could earn by saving the same amount of capital in a bank account. This is because business investors are taking more risk with their money than savers. If their ROCE is lower than the return on savings, the business investors would be better off selling their assets for cash and putting this money into an interest-earning savings account.

Rates of ROCE in Electra Ltd. are calculated from financial data on profit for the year from its income statements and its total assets less current liabilities from its statements of financial position.

Financial relationships (ratio analysis)

	Factors that will increase ROCE
•	an increase in profit for the year
•	a reduction in capital employed
•	capital employed is unchanged but is used more efficiently

	Factors that will reduce ROCE
•	a fall in profit for the year
•	an increase in capital employed
•	capital employed is unchanged but is used less efficiently

$$\frac{\text{Profit for the year}}{\text{Capital employed}} \quad \text{Year 1: } \frac{\$1.5m}{\$6m} \times 100 = 25\% \quad \text{Year 2: } \frac{\$3m}{\$8m} \times 100 = 37.5\%$$

The ROCE in year 1 was 25% – clearly a very good result for the company.

The new investment in additional floorspace and an expanded product range in year 2 had clearly also been successful in raising the ROCE to a very attractive 37.5%. This meant that the company had generated a profit of $3.75 for every $10 of its capital employed.

This return was far higher than the same amount of capital would have earned in interest in a savings account. This high rate of return was the reward to the owners of the company for risking their capital in the company. But was it enough? The owners of Electra Ltd. were keen to know how it compared to other firms in the retailing sector. This required making industry and inter-firm comparisons.

It is useful to compare how well a business is performing compared to rival businesses and the industry average

A **firm** is simply another term for a business organisation, one often used by economists. Inter-firm comparisons involve comparing the financial performance of different businesses, usually those selling similar goods or services.

An **industry** consists of all those firms engaged in similar activities, for example, car manufacturing, hospitality or banking. Electra Ltd. is part of the retail industry. This is how its year 2 results compared to the average performance of all other firms retailing over the same period:

▼ Company financial performance compared to industry averages

	Industry average	Electra Ltd.
Gross profit margin	15%	24%
Profit margin	8%	12%
Return on capital employed	35%	37.5%

These results show that Electra Ltd. outperformed the rest of the retailing industry in terms of profitability and return on capital. However, this was not surprising. The retail industry is very broad and diverse, from shops selling food to clothes shops and pharmacists. The margins on many of these products tend to be much lower than those achieved on the sale of high-value electrical products sold from lower-cost locations outside town centres.

The owners of Electra Ltd. wanted to compare the financial performance of their company with a close rival called Electric Discount Plus, or EDP Ltd.

EDP Ltd. is a larger company with a greater number of retail stores than Electra and a successful online business. Electra's ability to compete for sales with EDP Ltd. in the future will depend on its relative financial strength. If its financial performance is poor in comparison Electra could fail to attract new capital to finance business expansion and may not be able to afford the best staff and equipment or to pay for the best advertising.

▼ An inter-firm comparison of key financial data and profitability ratios

Electra Ltd.
Financial summary for Year 2 ended 30 June

	$m
Revenue	25.0
Gross profit	6.0
Operating expenses	3.0
Profit for the year	3.0
Closing capital	8.0

EDP Ltd.
Financial summary for the year ended 30 June

	$m
Revenue	30.0
Gross profit	7.5
Operating expenses	2.7
Profit for the year	4.8
Closing capital	12.0

	Electra Ltd.	EDP Ltd.
Gross profit margin	$\dfrac{\text{Gross profit}}{\text{Revenue}} = \dfrac{\$6m}{\$25m} \times 100 = 24\%$	$\dfrac{\text{Gross profit}}{\text{Revenue}} = \dfrac{\$7.5m}{\$30m} \times 100 = 25\%$
Profit margin	$\dfrac{\text{Profit for the year}}{\text{Revenue}} = \dfrac{\$3m}{\$25m} \times 100 = 12\%$	$\dfrac{\text{Profit for the year}}{\text{Revenue}} = \dfrac{\$4.8m}{\$30m} \times 100 = 16\%$
Return on capital employed	$\dfrac{\text{Profit for the year}}{\text{Capital employed}} = \dfrac{\$3m}{\$8m} \times 100 = 37.5\%$	$\dfrac{\text{Profit for the year}}{\text{Capital employed}} = \dfrac{\$4.8m}{\$12m} \times 100 = 40\%$

Key financial data and profitability ratios for Electra Ltd. from its second accounting year are reproduced in the tables above alongside those of EDP Ltd. from its most recent 12-month accounting period. They show that EDP Ltd. performed better than Electra Ltd. on all the main profitability measures.

At 25% the gross profit margin of EDP Ltd. is only marginally higher than that of Electra Ltd. The higher margin suggests that EDP Ltd. has been able to sell electrical products at a higher price or purchase them at a lower cost than Electra Ltd.

At 16% the margin for profit in revenue earned by EDP Ltd. is significantly better than the 12% achieved by Electra Ltd. This indicates that EDP Ltd. has been more successful at controlling its expenses than Electra. Indeed, despite its larger size the total expenses of EDP Ltd. were $300 000 less than Electra Ltd's. Because EDP Ltd. had increased sales of its products over the Internet it was able to make significant cuts in staff and administration costs.

EDP Ltd. also employs more capital but as a result of generating more profit for the year, it achieved a higher ROCE than Electra Ltd. For every $10 of capital employed in EDP Ltd. it earned $4 compared to Electra's return of $3.75 on every $10 of its capital employed. Both are very good results but the difference may indicate that EDP Ltd. is using its capital more efficiently than Electra.

While the owners of Electra Ltd. were disappointed that the financial performance of their company was not quite as good as their close competitor they were still optimistic they could improve their margins and returns over the next accounting year by:

- growing their customer base
- increasing online sales, which should enable the company to cut its expenses.

Financial relationships (ratio analysis)

> **ACTIVITY 5.1**
>
> Key financial data from the financial statements of a small business that makes and sells wooden furniture are reproduced in the table below:
>
> | | Year 1 ($) | Year 2 ($) | Year 3 ($) |
> |---|---|---|---|
> | Revenue | 250 000 | 280 000 | 310 000 |
> | Cost of sales | 200 000 | 238 000 | 269 700 |
> | Operating expenses | 30 000 | 28 000 | 27 900 |
> | Capital employed | 125 000 | 125 000 | 124 000 |
>
> 1. For each year calculate the percentage of gross profit and profit for the year to revenue and the ROCE achieved by the business.
>
> 2. (a) Suggest **three** factors that might explain the changes over time you have observed in the profit margins and ROCE achieved by the business; and (b) for each financial ratio describe **three** ways the business could try to reverse the trend.

5.1.3 Liquidity ratios

Liquidity ratios measure the ability of a business to meet its current liabilities

A business that runs out of cash will be unable to pay its current liabilities, unless it is able to raise enough cash quickly and cheaply. A business that is able to do so will be in a good liquidity position. In contrast, a business that is unable to raise enough cash to pay its debts will become **insolvent**. ➤ **1.5**

The **liquidity** of a business is measured by how quickly and easily it can raise cash to pay its immediate and short-term debts. This is done by comparing the value of business assets that can be turned into cash quickly (its current assets) with the value of liabilities that will have to be settled within the next 12 months (its current liabilities).

The difference between current assets and current liabilities is the amount of **working capital** (or **net current assets**) a business has left to continue paying expenses that will keep it running. ➤ **3.2**

If a business has many current assets it can convert easily to cash to pay its current liabilities, it is said to be liquid. A business with plenty of cash, an inventory of goods it can sell easily or trade receivables it can collect payment from quickly, will be in a good liquidity position. In contrast, a business that has little cash, inventories of goods customers no longer want and too many irrecoverable or doubtful debts will have very low liquidity.

A business with poor liquidity may have to raise cash by taking out an expensive bank loan or selling off important non-current assets, such as its machinery and vehicles. The loss of non-current assets could in turn reduce the amount of goods the business is able to sell and its revenue.

Liquidity ratios are important indicators of the financial health of a business. They can provide an early warning of financial problems that might occur if there is an unexpected bill to pay and a sudden need for extra cash in a business.

We will look at five key liquidity measures:

- **current ratio**: this measure is also known as the **working capital ratio**. It compares the current assets of a business, those in the form of cash and those which can be relatively quickly and easily converted into cash within the next 12 months, with its current liabilities. It is a key measure of the ability of a business to meet its current liabilities as they fall due.

- **quick ratio**: this measure is very similar to the current ratio but excludes inventory from the calculation of assets that can easily be converted into cash. This is because an inventory of finished goods or work in progress can be difficult to sell off especially if they are old or unwanted items. Inventory can also lose its value quickly if it is perishable or becomes unfashionable. The quick ratio – also known as the **acid test** or **liquid ratio** – measures the immediate ability of a business to pay its current liabilities entirely from its cash and trade receivables (a total sometimes referred to as "cash and near-cash").

- **rate of inventory turnover**: this measures how many times a year a business is able to sell off and replace the goods it holds in inventory for resale. ➤ 1.7

- **accounts receivable turnover**, also known as the collection period, and often referred to as "debtor days". This measures, on average, how quickly the business gets the cash from customers buying on credit.

- **accounts payable turnover**, also known as the payment period. This measures, on average, how quickly the business pays cash to suppliers from whom it has bought on credit.

The working capital ratio (or current ratio) measures the ability of a business to pay its current liabilities from its current assets

One of the most important reasons why people and other organisations, especially banks and suppliers, look at the statement of financial position of a business is to find out whether it will be able to meet its liabilities to them as they fall due.

The working capital ratio (or current ratio) measures the ability of a business to pay its short-term debts by comparing the value of its current assets with the value of its current liabilities:

$$\text{Working capital ratio (or current ratio)} = \frac{\text{current assets}}{\text{current liabilities}}$$

A business that has a current ratio of less than 1:1 could have problems because the combined value of all its cash, inventories and trade receivables is not sufficient to pay off its current liabilities.

Thankfully for the owners of Electra Ltd. this was not the case for their business. Using information from its statements of financial position in illustration 5.1 (page 445) we can calculate the current ratios for Electra Ltd. at the end of each of its first two years of trading as follows:

	Year 1	Year 2
$\dfrac{\text{Current assets}}{\text{Current liabilities}}$	$\dfrac{\$3.6m}{\$3m} = 1.2:1$	$\dfrac{\$3.8m}{\$2m} = 1.9:1$

Financial relationships (ratio analysis)

The current ratio for Electra Ltd. in year 1 was higher than 1:1 but still rather low with just $1.20 of current assets for every $1 of current liabilities the business had. If the business had received a large and unexpected bill during that year, for example a repair bill for some broken equipment, it may not have been able to raise enough cash to pay it off.

The owners and managers were worried about this low level of liquidity and so in year 2 they took the following actions to improve liquidity in Electra Ltd.:

- increasing cash sales
- increasing the amount of cash held by the business
- reducing current liabilities
- issuing new shares to raise additional owner's equity.

Together these actions improved Electra Ltd.'s current ratio from 1.2:1 to 1.9:1.

Ideally, the value of the current assets of a business should be around double its current liabilities to give a current ratio at or near of 2:1. Any lower and a business could be in danger of running out of cash and other liquid assets if unexpected costs arise.

The quick ratio (acid test or liquid ratio) measures the ability of a business to pay its immediate and short-term debts without having to sell off inventory

The **quick ratio** – or **acid test** – is a much stronger test of the ability of a business to meet its short-term debts from cash and trade receivables only. Inventories of goods are excluded from the measure because they can sometimes be difficult to sell off quickly to raise cash, especially if there has been a fall in customer demand for the products held.

$$\text{Quick ratio (acid test)} = \frac{\text{current assets} - \text{inventory}}{\text{current liabilities}}$$

Quick ratios for Electra Ltd. at the end of its first two years of trading were as follows:

$$\frac{\text{Current assets} - \text{inventory}}{\text{Current liabilities}} \quad \begin{array}{c}\text{Year 1}\\ \dfrac{\$3.6m - \$1.8m}{\$3m} = 0.6:1\end{array} \quad \begin{array}{c}\text{Year 2}\\ \dfrac{\$3.8m - \$1.2m}{\$2m} = 1.3:1\end{array}$$

On this measure, liquidity in Electra Ltd. in year 1 was low at just 0.6 : 1. That is, for every $1 owed by the business in current liabilities it had just $0.60 in cash and trade receivables.

The business would have had a big problem if all of its trade payables suddenly demanded to be paid in full all at the same time or if a significant and unexpected bill arrived. It would not have had sufficient cash to meet these debts without selling off its inventory of electrical products. To do so quickly it may have had to sell its goods at much lower prices and potentially at a loss to the business.

If the business was still short of cash it would have been forced to increase its borrowing, sell off some of its non-current assets or even close down.

Recognising these dangers the owners and managers of Electra Ltd. subsequently cut back the amount of inventory the business held day to day and increased the amount of cash it held instead. By the end of year 2 this strategy had helped to improve its quick ratio to 1.3:1.

As a general rule, a quick ratio of 1:1 is considered reasonably safe for a business because it will allow current liabilities to be met without having to sell off any inventory.

Factors that will cause the working capital and quick ratios to improve	Factors that will cause the working capital and quick ratios to deteriorate
• increasing the amount of cash in hand or in bank in the business, for example by increasing cash sales • paying off current liabilities with a long-term loan or from an increase in owner's equity, for example by issuing more share capital • cutting wages, expenses and other revenue expenditures so more cash is kept in the business • delaying spending on new machinery and other non-current assets to keep cash in the business for longer • holding less inventory because it reduces the amount of working capital tied up in raw materials, work in progress and finished goods and will improve the quick ratio • ensuring that sole traders and partners reduce drawings of cash or goods for personal use from their businesses • reducing cash dividend payouts to company shareholders from profits	• a fall in cash balances held on the business premises or in the bank, for example due to falling cash sales • an increase in current liabilities, for example by increasing purchases of goods and expense items on credit • a failure to control costs in the business so more cash is used up paying higher wages and other expenses • an increase in capital expenditure from cash on non-current assets • an increase in the amount of inventory held • an increase in sole traders' and partners' drawings of cash or goods for personal use from their businesses • an increase in cash dividend payouts to company shareholders from profits

The rate of inventory turnover measures how successful a business is at selling off its inventory to keep the amount of working capital invested in inventory as low as possible

Cash is used up when a business purchases goods which will not bring cash back into the business until they are sold and paid for. Unsold goods held as inventory reduces the cash and working capital that is immediately available to a business.

Holding more goods in inventory than is necessary to meet customer demand therefore has the following disadvantages:

Too much inventory – too little cash

Less inventory – more cash

▲ Reducing inventory releases cash and improves liquidity

- more working capital than necessary, notably cash, is used up purchasing inventory. This leaves less working capital available to pay other commitments
- more space must be used or rented than would otherwise be necessary to store the excess inventory. Stored inventory may need to be insured against disasters of various sorts – for example, fire, flood or theft. This will increase business expenses
- goods held in storage for a long time may lose value if they perish or go out of fashion. They may even have to be sold off at a loss or thrown away and written off.

It makes good business sense to keep inventory as low as possible as long as it doesn't affect the ability of a business to satisfy customer demand and generate profit.

The **rate of inventory turnover** is a useful indicator of how successful a business is at selling its products and keeping its inventory low. It measures how frequently inventory is sold off and replaced during an accounting year. It is calculated as follows:

$$\text{Rate of inventory turnover} = \frac{\text{cost of sales}}{\text{average inventory}} = \text{Number of times inventory is replaced in accounting year}$$

where average inventory = (opening inventory + closing inventory)/2

Inventory turnover will vary by day and by product, for example:

- the amount of inventory held each day in a business will vary with changes in customer demand over time. Sales of electrical products at Electra, and its inventory turnover, tend to fall during the summer months as more people spend their money on holidays instead.
- inventory turnover tends to be lower for more expensive and durable items. For example, large 3D flat-screen televisions tend to sell more slowly than smaller, cheaper televisions.

To take account of these variations a measure of the average value of inventory held is used to calculate the rate of inventory turnover.

The average value of inventory held can be calculated by adding together the opening inventory at the start of an accounting year and the closing inventory at the end of that year, and then dividing by two. So, using information from Electra's financial statements in illustration 5.1 we can calculate its average inventory for years 1 and 2 as follows:

	Year 1	Year 2
Opening inventory	$2.2m	$1.8m
Closing inventory	$1.8m	$1.2m
	$4.0m	$3.0m
Average inventory	$4m/2 = $2.0m	$3m/2 = $1.5m

We can now calculate the rate of inventory turnover achieved by Electra Ltd. and examine how it changed over time:

	Year 1		Year 2	
$\dfrac{\text{Cost of sales}}{\text{Average inventory}}$	$\dfrac{\$16m}{\$2m}$	= 8 times	$\dfrac{\$19m}{\$1.5m}$	= 12.7 times

In year 1 the **rate of inventory turnover** was 8. This meant that during the year the inventory of items it held was replaced 8 times. Put another way, the inventory held by Electra was sold off and replaced on average every 46 days or so (365 days divided by 8). This period is often known as the **stockholding period**.

We can calculate the stockholding period or number of days it took on average to sell and replace its inventory by rearranging the equation above as follows:

$$\text{Average time period taken to turnover inventory} = \dfrac{\text{average inventory}}{\text{cost of sales}} \times 365 \text{ days}$$

where average inventory = (opening inventory + closing inventory)/2

During year 2 the rate of turnover of inventory had risen to almost 13 times, meaning that the stockholding period had come down to 28 days (365 days divided by 12.7). The increase in the rate of inventory turnover was achieved through:

- increased sales
- holding less inventory and only replacing it as and when sales required.

The improvement in the rate of turnover of its inventory was good news for the company. Its liquidity position improved because less working capital was tied up in inventory leaving more cash in the company. Also, the faster inventory was sold by the company the quicker it earned revenue and made profits.

In contrast, the following factors will tend to reduce inventory turnover and profit generation in a business:

- reduced sales
- increasing selling prices resulting in a fall in customer demand and sales
- holding too much stock.

Factors that will increase the rate of inventory turnover

- increased sales. These may be encouraged through reductions in selling prices and/or increased spending on advertising. However, these actions may harm profits
- a reduction in the average inventory held by the business.

Factors that will reduce the rate of inventory turnover

- reduced sales. This may occur if selling prices are raised and/or spending on advertising is cut. If the reduction in sales is significant this will also harm profitability
- an increase in the average inventory held by the business.

ACTIVITY 5.2

Chemtura Corporation is an established global manufacturer of speciality chemicals, crop protection products and pool, spa and home care products. The following information was taken from its financial statements over a three-year period:

All figures $ million for years ending 31 December:	Year 1	Year 2	Year 3
Sales	3 154	2 511	2 760
Cost of sales	2 437	1 947	2 103
Total expenses	1 690	856	1 243
Current assets	1 255	1 479	1 421
of which inventory:	611	540	528
Current liabilities	1 813	569	489

Financial relationships (ratio analysis)

1. (a) From the data calculate the gross and net profit margins and the current and quick ratios Chemtura achieved in each year;
   (b) Describe what happened to profitability and liquidity at the company over this period.

2. The article discusses issues arising at Chemtura during year 1 in the table above.

According to the article:

(a) what was the main cause of Chemtura's liquidity problems?;

(b) what actions did the company take to improve its liquidity position?

Don't forget to check your answer.

Chemtura discusses actions to improve liquidity

Chemtura Corp. today summarized recent actions it has taken to improve its liquidity.

The President of the company said: "Last year (year 1) Chemtura, like many companies, experienced a sharp drop in demand from customers. As a result Chemtura's overall financial performance and outlook deteriorated and we will therefore be taking firm measures to manage our liquidity".

These measures include taking out a long-term bank loan to pay off immediate debts, reducing operating expenses by $50 million, notably by cutting management, substantially reducing inventories and suspending payments from profits to shareholders.

The President said that one of the company's key objectives for the first half of this year (2) is to secure enough liquidity to meet its liabilities as they fall due on 15 July.

"Our preferred way to obtain this liquidity is the sale of non-current assets," he said, "and we are discussing this with a number of potential buyers".

The profitability, liquidity and financial position of a business will be misleading if the value of its inventory is incorrect

Electra Ltd. takes great care to count and value its inventory of products at cost. This is consistent with the rule that inventory should be valued at the lower of its cost or net realisable value. ➤ 3.1

However, at the end of its first year it made a minor mistake in the number of in-car satellite navigators ("satnavs") it had in store.

The satnavs had originally cost $200 each to purchase. However, instead of counting 1 000 (a total cost of $200 000) only 100 were recorded as inventory remaining at the end of the year. It appeared as if 900 had already been sold off during the year: a cost of goods sold of $180 000 (900 × $200).

As the company believed it had sold 900 more satnavs during the year than it actually had, the cost of goods charged to profit that year was overstated by $180 000. This had the following impacts on the company's profitability and financial position:

Closing inventory for satnavs: Year 1

Correct closing value:
1 000 × $200 = $200 000

Incorrect closing value:
100 × $200 = $20 000

Inventory understated by:
900 × $200 = $180 000

Cost of sales overstated by:
900 × $200 = $180 000

▼ If closing inventory is understated by $180 000

Income statement for year 1	
Cost of goods sold	Overstated by $180 000
Gross profit	Understated by $180 000
Profit for the year	Understated by $180 000

Statement of financial position end of year 1	
Current assets	Understated by $180 000
Liabilities	No effect
Working capital	Understated by $180 000
Owner's capital	Understated by $180 000

The understated closing inventory of satnavs caused the profits, assets and capital of the company to appear less than they actually were.

As the closing inventory at the end of year 1 was understated (and cost of goods overstated) by $180 000, the opening inventory for year 2 was overstated (and the cost goods understated) by the same amount. That is, the errors were reversed as they were carried down to year 2:

▼ If closing inventory is understated by $180 000

Income statement for year 2	
Cost of goods sold	Understated by $180 000
Gross profit	Overstated by $180 000
Profit for the year	Overstated by $180 000

In reality the company had 1 000 satnavs it could sell in year 2 that had cost $200 000 to buy. However, as its financial statements had recorded an opening inventory of just 100 units at a cost of $20 000 the total cost of the satnavs was understated by $180 000. This meant profit from the sale of satnavs in year 2 was overstated by the same amount.

However, once the inventory of satnavs had been sold off in year 2 the error in the valuation of the inventory no longer affected its financial position.

An inventory that is overstated will have the opposite impacts on profitability, assets and capital. For example, imagine instead that Electra Ltd. had overestimated the number of satnavs it held in inventory at the end of its first year by 500 units which had in fact been sold earlier in the year. This would result in the following errors:

Error in closing inventory for satnavs: Year 1
Inventory overstated by: 500 × $200 = $100 000
Cost of sales understated by: 500 × $200 = $100 000

Financial relationships (ratio analysis)

Overstating its closing inventory of satnavs would have had the following impacts on the company's profitability and financial position:

▼ If closing inventory is overstated by $100 000

Income statement for year 1	
Cost of goods sold	Understated by $100 000
Gross profit	Overstated by $100 000
Profit for the year	Overstated by $100 000

Statement of financial position end of year 1	
Current assets	Overstated by $100 000
Liabilities	No effect
Working capital	Overstated by $100 000
Owner's capital	Overstated by $100 000

An overstated closing inventory will cause profits, assets and capital to appear more than they actually were.

Unless corrected the incorrect closing inventory at the end of year 1 would then be carried down as the opening inventory for year 2.

▼ If opening inventory is overstated by $100 000

Income statement for year 2	
Cost of goods sold	Overstated by $100 000
Gross profit	Understated by $100 000
Profit for the year	Understated by $100 000

As opening inventory for year 2 contains 500 satnavs that were sold the previous year the cost of that inventory will be $100 000 more than it cost to purchase. As a result gross profit and profit for the year will be understated by the same amount.

Electra Ltd. has a turnover of over $20 million. For a large company, the above errors are therefore relatively small, and we would describe them as insignificant or **"immaterial"**. ▶ **5.2**

However, they show what can happen if inventory is not counted or valued correctly.

Inventory is often the largest amount included in the current assets in many trading organisations. An incorrect valuation for closing and opening inventory can cause significant errors in the calculation of cost of goods sold and, in turn, gross profit and profit for the year. Values for assets and equity in the statement of financial position will also be incorrect. These incorrect values for inventory can therefore lead to distortions in profitability and liquidity ratios.

Since users of financial statements depend upon accurate statements, great care must be taken to ensure that inventory at the end of each accounting year is counted and valued correctly.

The efficient management of inventory, credit and cash will improve liquidity and the working capital position of a business

Working capital is money "put to work" in a business to pay its day-to-day expenses. Working capital is what remains in current assets after current liabilities have been met.

The most liquid current asset a business can hold is cash. Holding too little could result in a business running out of cash and being unable to pay its bills.

This risk will be greatest in a business which has significant liabilities, a high proportion of which are short term, that ties up too much of its working capital in unnecessary inventory, sells most of its goods on credit and has too many unreliable trade receivables.

A business with many unreliable trade receivables may find it difficult to call in its debts to raise cash when it needs to. ➤ 1.9

▼ What determines the working capital position of a business and how can it be improved?

A business with a poor working capital position will have:	A business with a good working capital position will have:
✗ a high proportion of short-term total liabilities	✓ few short-term debts
✗ too little held in cash balances	✓ substantial cash balances
✗ too much old inventory	✓ efficient management of inventory levels
✗ a high proportion of total sales on credit	✓ a high proportion of total sales in cash
✗ poor credit control	✓ good credit control

Improve working capital by:

- ✓ introducing new owner's equity or taking out a long-term loan to pay off short-term debts
- ✓ encouraging more cash sales, for example, by offering more discounts for immediate payment
- ✓ holding less inventory and managing inventory more efficiently
- ✓ retaining more profit in the business and reducing owner's drawings of cash and goods for own use from inventory
- ✓ holding more cash
- ✓ improving credit control, for example by:
  - ▸ delaying payments to trade payables until required
  - ▸ limiting sales on credit only to the most financially stable and reliable customers
  - ▸ chasing up late payments
  - ▸ offering customers more generous cash discounts to encourage early repayments.

Impact on profitability:

- ▸ loan interest charges and repayments will reduce profits in the longer term
- ▸ cash discounts will reduce gross profit margins but may boost overall sales
- ▸ profit may increase if warehouse staff and storage costs can be reduced
- ▸ retained profit can be held as cash; interest from saving surplus cash in a bank deposit account will increase earnings and boost profits
- ▸ delaying payments to trade payables could reduce cash discounts received and therefore reduce profit
- ▸ more generous cash discounts allowed will reduce profit margins
- ▸ but total net profit will increase if there are fewer irrecoverable debts to be written off.

Financial relationships (ratio analysis)

However, holding too much cash can also be bad for a business. This is because cash is not a very productive asset. While cash can be saved in a bank deposit account and will earn some income in the form of interest it could be invested in more efficient equipment and machinery instead. This will help reduce expenses and expand the business so it is able to earn even more revenue in the future.

Similarly, restricting sales on credit to avoid the risk of irrecoverable debts may result in much lower sales. This will reduce the profitability of the business.

Maintaining a sufficient level of working capital in a business requires:

- keeping current liabilities as low as possible
- holding sensible levels of cash and other liquid assets that can be easily converted into cash.

During its second accounting year Electra Ltd. took a number of actions to improve its liquidity position and profitability including:

Actions taken to improve liquidity	Impact on working capital	Impact on profit for the year
Introduced new equity to pay off $700 000 of current liabilities	Increased by $700 000 by reducing current liabilities	No effect
Increased cash sales over the year from $10 million to $15 million without a reduction in credit sales	Increased by $5 million by increasing cash in bank	Increased by $5 million less the cost of the goods sold
Reduced cash discounts allowed by $225 000	Increased by $225 000 by increasing cash in bank	Increased by $225 000
Changing to cheaper suppliers saved the company $300 000. The saving was used to pay off its bank overdraft	Increased by $300 000 by reducing current liabilities	Increased by $300 000. Increased by the saving in overdraft interest
Increased retained profit held as cash in the business by $250 000	Increased by $250 000 by increasing cash in bank	Increased by any interest earned on the cash in bank
Provision for doubtful debts reduced by $350 000 by improving credit control	Increased by $350 000 by increasing trade receivables	Increased by $350 000
Sold off surplus office furniture at its net book value for $13 000	Increased by $13 000 by increasing cash in bank	No effect

Unfortunately, a few things also happened during the same year that had a negative impact on its working capital position and in some cases its profitability:

Items arising that reduced liquidity	Impact on working capital	Impact on profit for the year
$20 000 of damaged goods were written off	Decreased by $20 000 by reducing inventory	Decreased by $20 000
$15 000 of additional office equipment was purchased from cash	Decreased by $15 000 by reducing cash in bank	No effect
A cheque for $4 000 issued to a supplier was not recorded in the cash book	Overstated by $4 000: the payment will have reduced cash in bank by $4 000	No effect
A major customer unexpectedly failed leaving an irrecoverable debt of $30 000	Decreased by $30 000 by reducing trade receivables	Decreased by $30 000

However, the above problems were relatively minor and overall liquidity and profitability improved significantly at Electra Ltd. due to the sensible actions it took during the year.

ACTIVITY 5.3

State the likely impact of the following items on either the working capital, profit for the year or both of a sole trader.

Item	Impact on working capital	Impact on profit for the year
Out-of-date inventory valued at $400 is to be written off		
Took out a bank loan for $3 000 repayable over three years with interest		
The depreciation charge for equipment is to be increased by $600		
The owner of the business increases his drawings by $1 000		
The provision for doubtful debts is to be increased by $500		

Good credit control can improve the liquidity and profitability of a business

We shall now turn our attention to the last two of our important liquidity ratios: the accounts payable and accounts receivable turnover ratios. Good credit control is crucial in businesses that buy and sell a significant amount of products on credit terms. It involves the effective management of working capital in a business to ensure that its trade payables are paid on time and to improve cash flow from trade receivables. ➤ 1.9

Delaying payment to a supplier of goods on credit until the last minute can be a useful way of holding on to more cash for longer in a business. However, delaying payment may mean the loss of any cash discounts offered by the supplier for prompt payment of debts.

Financial relationships (ratio analysis) **461**

> **Is an increase in the trade payables payment period good or bad for business?**
>
> Good if:
> - the business previously paid its suppliers too quickly: by delaying payment it helps keep cash in the business for longer.
>
> Bad if:
> - taking longer to pay suppliers means the business loses cash discounts for prompt payments. This will reduce profits
> - late payments result in suppliers refusing further sales on credit to the business.
>
> **Is a reduction in the trade payables payment period good or bad for business?**
>
> Good if:
> - the business was previously taking too long to pay its suppliers. The business may receive cash discounts for paying promptly. This will increase its profits
> - settling accounts with suppliers promptly enables the business to purchase more on credit terms which helps keep cash in the business for longer.
>
> Bad if:
> - the business pays suppliers earlier than necessary and therefore uses up cash faster than required.

It is clearly not sensible to delay payment beyond the agreed credit period because:

- the supplier may refuse to sell goods on credit to the business again
- the supplier may charge the business a high rate of interest for late payment.

To make sure its trade payables are paid on time the management of Electra Ltd. keep an up-to-date **aged trade payables schedule**. This lists:

- the suppliers it owes money to for goods purchased on credit
- how much it owes to each one
- when payment is due
- how old each debt is.

The schedule helps the business to identify and plan its future working capital needs to meet its commitments to trade payables on time.

The schedule also allows the business to calculate the average time it takes to pay off its trade payables for its purchases of goods on credit. This is known as the **trade payables turnover** or payment period and it is calculated as follows:

> Trade payables turnover = $\dfrac{\text{trade payables at end of year}}{\text{credit purchases for the year}} \times 365$ days
> (average no. of days taken to make payment)

We can calculate the trade payables turnover for Electra Ltd. from the financial data in illustration 5.1:

Year 1: $\dfrac{\text{Trade payables at end of year}}{\text{Credit purchases for the year}} = \dfrac{\$3m}{\$12m} \times 365 = 91.3$ days

Year 2: $\dfrac{\$2m}{\$16m} \times 365 = 45.6$ days

Cash reserves at Electra Ltd. were low following start-up and so during its first year of trading the business delayed paying its trade payables right up until their final due date. Most of its suppliers had allowed the company up to 90 days to settle invoices or statements of accounts in full. It is not surprising that the company maintained a payment period at or around 90 days during year 1. In fact due to a small number of its payments being late and exceeding agreed credit terms the average payment period achieved by the company was just over 91 days.

However, by the end of year 2 Electra Ltd. had reduced the average time it took to pay off its trade payable accounts to just under 46 days. It was able to do this by:

- making prompt payment so that it could benefit from cash discounts offered by its trade payables – increasing its profit for the year
- keeping more cash in the business
- improved credit control which reduced the average length of time its trade receivables took to settle their accounts. This meant cash was received by the company earlier allowing it pay off its own debts more promptly.

The owners of Electra Ltd. also keep an up-to-date **aged trade receivables schedule.** This lists:

- customers who owe the business money for goods sold to them on credit
- how much is owed by each one
- when payment is due
- how old each debt is.

Below is an example of a simple schedule of aged trade receivables.

5.2 AN EXAMPLE OF AN AGED TRADE RECEIVABLES SCHEDULE

Aged trade receivables ($)					Day 97
Customer	1–30 days	31–60 days	61–90 days	Older	Total
AJS Audio Ltd.				3 000	3 000
J Bootle and sons	6 500	2 300			8 800
Screen Kings Ltd.		13 400	12 800		26 200
XTC Vision Ltd.		2 400	1 600		5 000
Total	6 500	18 100	14 400	3 000	42 000

The schedule shows that as at day 97 in its accounting year the business was due to receive $6 500 from its trade receivables within the next 30 days; a total of $18 100 within the next 31–60 days; and $17 400 thereafter. However, $3 000 of this amount had been outstanding for more than 90 days. There is probably good reason to consider the debt of AJS Audio Ltd. as doubtful. ▶ 1.9

Maintaining a schedule of aged trade receivables helps Electra Ltd. to

- estimate the provision it may need to make for any doubtful debts
- compare when it expects to receive cash from its trade receivables with when it has to pay cash to its trade payables.

It is sensible for the business to make sure it has enough cash coming in from its trade receivables at regular intervals to cover cash being paid out to its trade payables. That is, it is sensible for the business to maintain a trade receivables collection period that is shorter than its trade payables payment period.

The **trade receivables turnover** (or collection period) measures the average time taken by credit customers to settle their debts:

$$\text{Collection period} = \frac{\text{trade receivables at end of year}}{\text{credit sales for the year}} \times 365 \text{ days}$$

(average no. of days taken to receive payment)

Using the financial data from illustration 5.1 the trade receivables collection periods for Electra Ltd. were:

Financial relationships (ratio analysis)

	Year 1	Year 2
$\dfrac{\text{Trade receivables at end of year}}{\text{Credit sales for the year}}$	$\dfrac{\$1.4\text{m}}{\$10\text{m}} \times 365 = 51.1$ days	$\dfrac{\$1.8\text{m}}{\$14\text{m}} \times 365 = 43.8$ days

On average in year 1 each trade receivable settled its debt to Electra Ltd. for goods supplied on credit 51.1 days after the receipt of an invoice or statement of account. During year 2 this had improved to just under 44 days. This compared to a trade payables payment period of 45.6 days maintained by the company in year 2.

Electra Ltd. was able to reduce its collection period by:

- sending out regular statements and payment due reminders to its trade receivables
- offering them more generous cash discounts for early payment
- charging high rates of interest on late payments
- refusing to supply any more items to a customer with a debt that was overdue until it had been paid off in full
- when necessary, threatening a customer with legal action to recover an unpaid debt.

Not only did these actions encourage more customers to settle their debts earlier, it also reduced the number of irrecoverable debts. This is because the longer it takes for a customer to pay up the greater the risk of its debt becoming irrecoverable. ▶ **1.9**

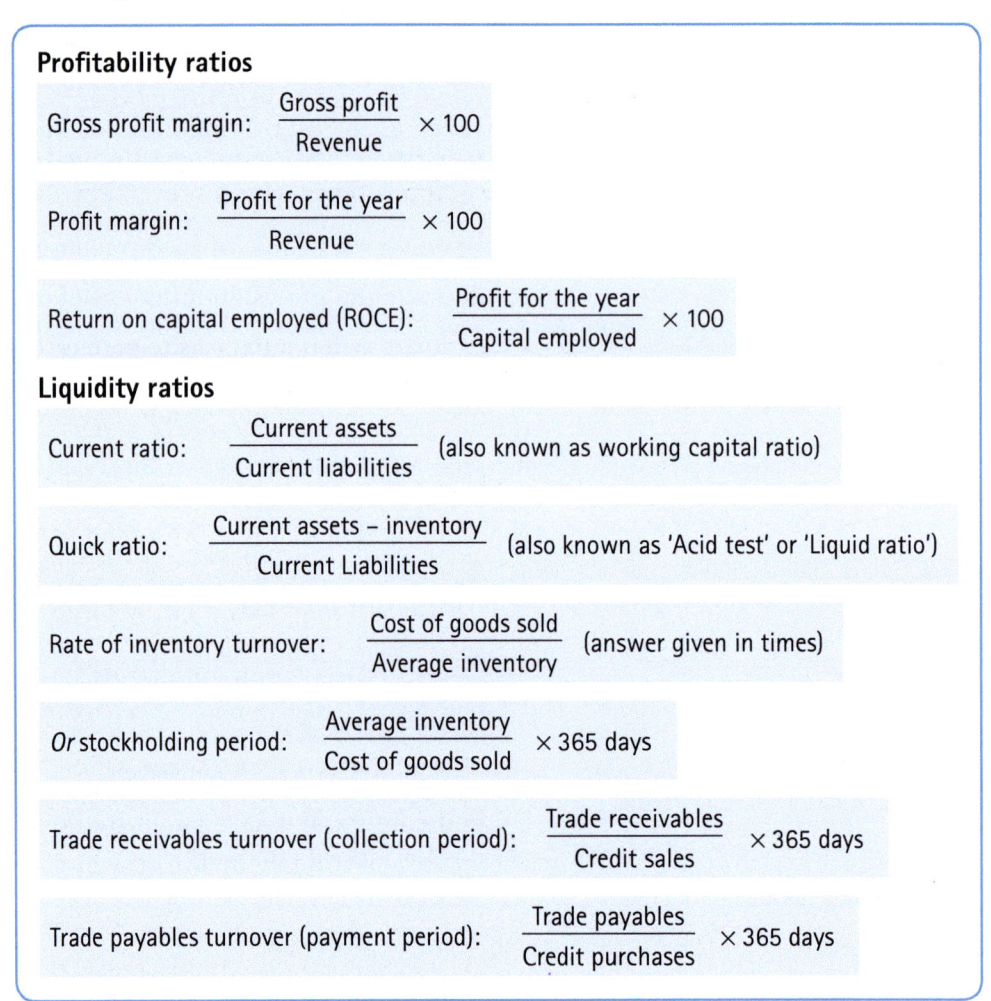

Is an increase in the trade receivables collection period good or bad for business?

Good if:
- the collection period was previously too short due to credit control being too tight which in turn had deterred customers and reduced sales.

Bad if:
- the collection period has now become too long due to poor credit control resulting in an increase in irrecoverable debts.

Is a reduction in the trade receivables collection period good or bad for business?

Good if:
- the collection period was previously too long and if improved credit control helps to reduce late payments and irrecoverable debts.

Bad if:
- the collection period was previously good and credit control has since become too tight leading to a reduction in customers and sales.

Profitability ratios

Gross profit margin: $\dfrac{\text{Gross profit}}{\text{Revenue}} \times 100$

Profit margin: $\dfrac{\text{Profit for the year}}{\text{Revenue}} \times 100$

Return on capital employed (ROCE): $\dfrac{\text{Profit for the year}}{\text{Capital employed}} \times 100$

Liquidity ratios

Current ratio: $\dfrac{\text{Current assets}}{\text{Current liabilities}}$ (also known as working capital ratio)

Quick ratio: $\dfrac{\text{Current assets} - \text{inventory}}{\text{Current Liabilities}}$ (also known as 'Acid test' or 'Liquid ratio')

Rate of inventory turnover: $\dfrac{\text{Cost of goods sold}}{\text{Average inventory}}$ (answer given in times)

Or stockholding period: $\dfrac{\text{Average inventory}}{\text{Cost of goods sold}} \times 365$ days

Trade receivables turnover (collection period): $\dfrac{\text{Trade receivables}}{\text{Credit sales}} \times 365$ days

Trade payables turnover (payment period): $\dfrac{\text{Trade payables}}{\text{Credit purchases}} \times 365$ days

▲ Summary of commonly used ratios

5.1.4 Limitations of accounting statements and ratio analysis

Many different stakeholders will use financial statements and ratios to analyse business performance

Business stakeholders are individuals, organised groups and other organisations with an interest in the activities and performance of a business. They will use the financial statements of a business to produce profitability and liquidity ratios to analyse its financial performance and prospects.

- The business owners will be especially interested in using ratio analysis to examine how profitable their business has been and to consider if their continued investment is worthwhile compared to other, possibly more profitable uses of their capital.

- Would-be business investors will also use ratio analysis to compare the financial performance of different businesses in an attempt to identify those new and existing business opportunities with the potential to provide the best return on their investments in future.

- Business managers will share similar concerns. Their jobs and salaries will depend on running businesses efficiently and profitability on behalf of business owners.

- In turn, employees and their representatives will be interested in whether their employers are making significantly more profit than they did in the past. If so, they may feel justified in asking for more generous wages and salaries.

- Services will be especially interested in the ability of a business to pay for its purchases on credit from them. Suppliers selling goods on credit terms will look closely at the liquidity of their customers.

- Similarly, a bank that has provided a business with an overdraft facility or long-term loan will review indicators of its liquidity and profitability to consider its potential to generate future revenues sufficient to meet repayments and any interest charges. A bank will also examine the financial position of a business before it lends it money to make sure it has assets of sufficient value, such as premises, that could be sold off to repay a loan if the business runs into financial difficulty. The loan can then be secured against those assets by the bank so that in the event the business defaults on loan repayments the bank can sell them off to recover the debt.

- The government may want to know how well all businesses are performing because this provides a useful indicator of the health of the economy. A government that collects taxes from the profits or revenues of businesses will also wish to calculate how much tax it is due from different firms.

- Members of not-for-profit organisations such as clubs, societies and charities will also wish to check that they are being well managed financially, notably their ability to generate enough income to cover total expenses and debts as they fall due. If they are not then the organisations will be unable to continue and the benefit of the services they provide to their members or to those in need will be lost.

However, making meaningful comparisons of the performance of different businesses and over time can sometimes be difficult. Each business or organisation is different. They can be at different stages of their development, have different capital requirements and use different accounting policies, and these can also change over time. Accounting data and ratios therefore have a number of limitations.

Financial statements may be compiled in different ways: accounting ratios may not be comparable or provide useful indicators of future business performance

Although financial statements and the financial ratios derived from them are used to monitor and compare business performance over time, there are some important limitations to be aware of:

- **Past performance may be a poor indicator of future performance**

    Financial statements and ratios are backward looking. This means they are based on historic information from previous accounting years.

    Many things can change over time and just because a business has performed well in the past does not mean it will continue to do so.

    The opposite may also be true. For example, a business seeking to develop new products, increase its market share or enter new markets overseas may have to spend significant amounts of money doing so which will reduce its current profitability and return on capital employed (ROCE) but which could help boost its profitability in the future.

- **Historic costs used to compile accounts can differ**

    Transactions are recorded in the books of a business as they occur and at the price paid or received. That is, accounting data reflects historic costs. Prices can change over time due to changes in inflation and technology. This makes comparisons over time difficult to interpret.

    For example, a business may record year-on-year increases in revenues simply due to increased selling prices each year. The business may not be selling any more goods year on year or making any additional profit if its costs have also been rising at the same rate as prices.

    Now imagine two businesses employ the same machines but one purchased them several years ago when their prices were much higher. Advances in technology have since reduced the price of the machines. The business that bought its machines several years ago will appear to have a higher capital employed simply because their historic cost was higher than the business that bought its machinery more recently and more cheaply.

    There is also a further complication. Despite owning the same machinery the two businesses may use different accounting policies to depreciate the value of their machinery over time. ▶ 2.2

- **Accounting years and policies differ**

    If different businesses adopt different accounting years and policies this makes it difficult for inter-firm comparisons of performance to be done on a like-for-like basis.

Accounting policies are the specific policies and procedures that are used by a business to prepare its financial statements. These will include valuation methods, measurement systems and procedures for presenting information in financial statements. ➤ 5.2

For example, some businesses may depreciate the value of their non-current assets using the straight-line method while others may use the reducing balance method. This in turn will affect the net values of their assets used to calculate their ROCE. ➤ 2.2

- **Definitions and the calculation of key financial results can differ**

If businesses refer to the same names for key financial figures but use slightly different definitions and calculations to derive them then inter-firm comparisons of accounting data and financial ratios will not be on a like-for-like basis.

For example, what exactly is profit for the year? Not all businesses or accountants use the same definition.

Some financial statements show profits for the year before and after interest payable on loans has been deducted. Some instead refer to these profits as operating profit (or earnings before interest) and net profit (gross profit less total expenses). ➤ 3.1

In turn, calculations of the profit margin and ROCE from different financial statements will vary and may not be strictly comparable.

- **Financial data and ratios alone will not reveal why performance differs**

There are many factors that affect the performance of a business which cannot be easily measured and will not appear in financial statements. For example, its financial performance may depend on the age and condition of its non-current assets, its level of customer loyalty and the quality and skills of its manager and workforce including their ability to adapt to changing technology and economic conditions. For example, if workforce skills are good but fail to keep pace with new developments in technology then future business performance may be at risk.

- **Not all indicators of business performance are financial**

Many businesses have non-financial objectives that represent important targets.

For example, many businesses are now far more aware of environmental issues and their owners and managers have set them targets to clean up their production processes, reduce waste and repair environmental damage caused by their past activities. These actions may reduce profits in the short term but businesses that fail to improve their environmental performance over time may eventually lose sales and revenue to those who do.

Company wins green award for water conservation project

DHL wins 'best place to work' award

Bus company helps local cancer charity

▲ Non-financial performance is also important in business

Financial relationships (ratio analysis)

QUICK TEST

The following accounting data has been provided for two business organisations:

	Business A $	Business B $
From income statements for year ending 31 December:		
Revenue (sales)	1 000 000	800 000
Cost of sales	700 000	500 000
Expenses	220 000	200 000
From the statement of financial position at 31 December:		
Non-current assets	700 000	480 000
Current assets	200 000	160 000
Current liabilities	200 000	80 000

1. Which business had the higher percentage of gross profit to revenue?
2. Suggest **two** ways each business could try to increase its gross profit margin.
3. Which business had the higher percentage of profit for the year to revenue?
4. Which business achieved the better return on its capital employed?
5. Describe how business owners and investors might use the return on capital employed to make decisions.
6. How is capital employed calculated?
7. (i) What is liquidity?; (ii) Which business was the more liquid?
8. What is the difference between the working capital ratio and the quick ratio?
9. (i) What is working capital?; (ii) How is working capital calculated?
10. Suggest **four** ways a business could try to increase its working capital.
11. Suggest **three** reasons why the rate of inventory turnover in a business may fall.
12. A business allows its customers 60 days to pay for items bought on credit but has an average trade receivables collection period of 85 days. (i) Why will this cause problems for the business?; (ii) Suggest three ways the business could improve its average collection period.
13. The same business is allowed 60 days credit by its suppliers but takes 70 days on average to pay them. (i) How is the trade payables payment period calculated?; (ii) What are the possible advantages and disadvantages to the business of delaying payment to its suppliers to 70 days on average?
14. State **three** limitations of using information in financial statements and financial ratios to compare the financial performance of different businesses.

Unit 5.2 Accounting principles

AIMS

By the end of this unit you should be able to

- explain and recognise the application of the following **accounting principles**
  - going concern
  - historic cost
  - business entity
  - money measurement
  - matching
  - prudence
  - materiality
  - consistency
  - duality
- recognise the influence of **international accounting standards** and understand the following objectives in selecting accounting policies:
  - comparability
  - reliability
  - understandability

5.2.1 The rules of accounting

For financial statements and information to be meaningful and comparable it is important to follow generally accepted accounting concepts and conventions

Imagine if every business owner, manager or accountant compiled financial accounts and statements in very different ways. It would be impossible to compare the performance of different businesses or judge how well each one was being managed financially. Banks would be reluctant to lend money to businesses, suppliers would be reluctant to sell them goods on credit and investors may prefer to save their money safely in a bank rather than risk it in business ventures.

It is important for all business owners, managers and accountants to follow the same generally accepted conventions, procedures or rules when preparing and presenting financial statements.

Accounting concepts

Rules that describe how financial information should be recorded and statements prepared

Accounting conventions

Generally acceptable methods for valuing income, expenses, assets, liabilities and capital

Each country has its own national standards-setting organisation in the accounting profession to determine what procedures or rules are acceptable to apply in book-keeping and accounting. These rules are known as **accounting principles** and together they have made the financial statements of different organisations and the information they contain, more reliable and easier to understand, check and compare.

Accounting principles combine a number of **accounting concepts** and **accounting conventions**. Many of these have evolved over time as the number of businesses and volume of financial information have grown and become more complex.

We have already encountered some of the most important accounting principles throughout this book including the prudence principle, matching principle and duality. We will now look at these and others in more detail.

Going concern principle:

"Assume that the business will continue to operate into the foreseeable future"

A business is a **going concern** if it is able to continue trading or providing a service to earn revenue well into the future.

Financial statements should be prepared on the assumption that the business will continue trading for many years to come and that the owners have no intention to close it down. This means that the assets of the business can be valued at their cost less accumulated depreciation.

Application of the going concern principle

The electrical products retailer, Electra Ltd., purchased a fleet of delivery vehicles two years ago at a cost of $200 000. Because the company is a going concern it valued its fleet at cost less a provision of $40 000 for depreciation in its most recent statement of financial position at 31 December.

If the company ever ceased trading it would have to value its assets at their realisable value. The company owners have estimated it would raise only around $100 000 from the sale of its vehicles if it had to sell them off quickly. Part of the reason is that the vehicles would need to be repainted by the new owner to cover up the company logo painted on the sides, bonnet and doors of each vehicle.

If there is any reason to believe the business cannot continue trading then it must be disclosed in its financial statements and its assets will need to be recorded at their **realisable values**. These are the values they could achieve if sold. These are likely to be much lower than their values had the business remained a going concern.

When a business is no longer a going concern and has to close there will be pressure to sell its assets as quickly as possible to raise cash and this often means selling them off cheaply.

There may also be obligations created when ceasing to trade which will create liabilities, e.g. for redundancy of the employees or compensation for others whose contracts may have to be broken – landlords, for example, who will want compensation for the rent they may lose from their tenants.

Advanced principles

Historic cost principle:

"The actual price paid for assets and expenses should be recorded in the accounts"

The principle requires that all assets and expenses are recorded in the ledger accounts at their **historic cost**.

The advantage of using the historic cost to value assets and expenses is that their values can be checked easily against the amounts recorded for the price paid on source documents including invoices and receipts. ▶ **1.3**

However, the values some assets could achieve on sale could be very different from their historic cost. For example, the market values of land and business premises may go up or down significantly over time. For this reason it is acceptable under international reporting standards to revise the values of property to "fair value" (the value it could realise if sold) on a regular basis.

Business entity principle

"The transactions of a business should be kept completely separate from the personal transactions of its owners"

This is known as the **business entity principle**. It means the transactions of a business should be accounted for separately from those of its owner or owners. That is, the business is considered to be a separate body or entity from its owners and only the activities of the business should be recorded and reported in its financial statements.

The only time that the personal resources of the owners should be recorded in the accounts of their business is when they introduce new capital to it from their own funds.

Accounting year principle:

"The lifetime of a business should be divided up into successive accounting years in order to produce financial statements at regular intervals"

The going concern principle assumes a business will continue to trade or provide a service well into the future. However, it is clearly not sensible to wait until it stops trading or is sold on to other owners to produce statements of its income and financial position.

The accounting year principle states that financial statements should be produced at regular intervals during the lifetime of a business. As a minimum they should be produced at least once each year at the end of the accounting year. ▶ **1.1**

Without regular annual statements it would be impossible to examine how the profitability and value of a business compared to those of other firms and have changed over time and why.

This intuitive principle is a legal requirement for any business trading as a limited company.

Application of the historic cost principle

At the end of its second accounting year the electrical products retailer, Electra Ltd., had non-current assets of $6.2 million mostly in land and property. The value reflects the price the company had paid for the land and the total cost of building and fitting out its retail outlets.

Application of the business entity principle

The owners of Electra Ltd. have recently purchased new cars for their family members.

Their accountant explained that the amount they spent would have to be treated as their own personal expenditure and the cars they purchased as their own personal assets. They could not be recorded in Electra's accounts.

Money measurement principle:

"All transactions must be expressed in monetary terms"

While it might be useful to list the number of items bought or sold by a business over time, the number of vehicles it owns and the number of staff it employs, these figures will not tell us how much the business is worth or how profitable it is.

Financial statements must therefore record and report items that have a definite **monetary value**. That is, incomes, expenses, assets, liabilities and capital should all be expressed in terms of their monetary values.

Money is generally accepted in payment for goods and services and is a widely recognised and accepted measure of their value.

Using monetary values also makes it easy to compare the performance of different businesses over time and to check valuations reported in their financial statements against records in source documents.

Other aspects of business performance, such as having a highly skilled and motivated workforce, loyal customers and a prime location, are difficult to measure and will not have a definite monetary value. The money measurement principle means these aspects should not be recorded in financial statements.

Matching principle:

"Costs must be matched against related income"

Business transactions occur at different times and in different accounting years. For example, a business may have supplied goods to a customer but will not receive payment for them until well into its next accounting year. It has nevertheless earned this income and this should be reflected in its profit for the year.

Similarly, a business may pay some of its expenses, such as rent and insurance, in advance but not use them until well into its next accounting year. Although the expenses have been paid for they will not contribute to the operation and the profit of the business until they are used up or incurred.

The matching principle requires that the profit or loss of the business for a given accounting year includes only those incomes earned and expenses incurred in that year regardless of whether they have been paid or not. This means including accrued income and expenses in the calculation of profit or loss for the year but excluding any income and expenses that have been prepaid. ➤ 1.9

In accounting, income is only earned by a business when it supplies goods or services to a customer. Similarly, an expense is only incurred by a business when resources are consumed in the day-to-day running of the business to supply goods or services to customers to earn income. This means that to calculate profit or loss for a year, incomes earned must be matched with the expenses incurred in that same accounting year. You may see the matching principle sometimes referred to as the accruals principle.

Application of the money measurement principle

Electra Ltd. has developed a strong reputation for being well managed and as a good company to work for and buy from.

Customer surveys about levels of service, the product range and the value for money offered at its retail outlets are very favourable. These factors clearly contribute to the sales success of the company and its profitability. However, the additional value created by customer satisfaction and loyalty are difficult to measure and different people may have very different views of their value to the business. As such they cannot and should not be valued in the company accounts.

Prudence principle:

"Profit should not be overstated by ignoring foreseeable losses and income should not be anticipated before it is earned"

Application of the prudence principle

At the end of its second accounting year Electra Ltd. valued its inventory of electrical products for resale at $1.2 million.

Most of the products it held will sell for more than they cost so to be prudent they were valued at their cost price rather than their selling price.

However, the store room manager noticed that 20 washing machines held in inventory had some minor scratches and dents and would need to be marked down for sale.

The washing machines had originally cost $150 each to purchase: a total historical cost of $3 000. However, they will now be placed on sale for $100 each: an estimated realisable value of $2 000.

With delivery costs of $10 each the net realisable value of each washing machine will be $90: a total net realisable value of $1 800.

To be prudent, a value of $1 800, being the lowest possible value for the washing machines, was selected to include in the statement of financial position for the company.

Financial statements should always provide a true and fair value of the profits, losses, assets, liabilities and capital of a business.

This means accountants must ensure that any values presented in financial statements are reasonable and do not mislead users into thinking the business may be performing better than it actually is.

This is because the values of many items included in financial statements are estimates. Their actual values are uncertain and judgments must be made about their most likely realisable values.

Where there is some doubt it is sensible to provide cautious or prudent valuations. This means valuing assets at their cost price unless their realisable values will clearly be lower, for example, in the case of goods held as inventory which are no longer fashionable or are defective in some way. ▶ 3.2

Similarly, it is prudent to include a provision for doubtful debts in the accounts in case some trade receivables cannot be collected. Any losses from debts becoming irrecoverable should also be written off in the accounts as soon as they are recognised so that profit is not overstated. ▶ 1.9

Materiality principle:

"Individual items which will not materially affect the profit or value of the business do not need to be recorded separately"

Imagine if Electra Ltd. had to record double entries for every taxi fare, newspaper, jar of coffee or other small expense items it purchased in separate expense accounts. The time and cost involved recording each item would be significant, especially if the company had to employ more staff to do so.

It is far more sensible simply to list small expense items and record their total in a single sundry expense or general expense account.

> **ACTIVITY 5.4**
>
> Liam trades over the Internet selling toys. He has 100 battery powered hamster toys in his inventory. They originally cost him $3 each.
>
> The toys sold last year for $10 each but they are no longer popular and Liam thinks he may now only be able to sell them at $4 each. Posting and packaging costs will be $1 each.
>
> 1. Calculate the value of Liam's inventory:
>   (a) at cost;
>   (b) at their usual selling price;
>   (c) at their realisable value;
>   (d) at their net realisable value.
> 2. Which value will you include in the statement of financial position and why?

The same principle can also be applied to items such as waste paper baskets, desk lamps, screwdrivers, staplers and pocket calculators. Such items may be used over many years: they are strictly non-current assets that should be depreciated in value over their useful lives. However, they are such low value items that to do so would probably cost far more than the items themselves. It is therefore permissible to ignore other accounting principles and instead record their purchases as revenue expenditures rather than capital expenditures. This means they can be recorded as expense items in their year of purchase rather than as depreciable non-current assets.

> ### Application of the materiality principle
>
> *There was a very hot summer during the second accounting year of Electra Ltd. To help keep the company office cool the head of accounts bought some desk cooling fans at a total cost of $70. Although the fans might be expected to last for around five years he simply recorded their purchase as a general expense to charge to profit for the year.*
>
> *'It's simply not worth the time or effort recording them as a non-current asset and then year after year having to create a provision for their depreciation,' he explained. 'We are a $20 million plus turnover business with net assets of over $5 million. Desk fans costing $70 will not make any material difference to our profit or value'.*

The principle of materiality applies when the value of an item is relatively low or insignificant and is not worth the time, cost or effort of recording separately. Only if items of expenditure are large or material enough to have an impact on the profit or value of the business should they be recorded separately in the accounts.

What makes an item significant or material is a matter of professional judgment. What is material to one business may not be material to another. So, for example, a very large company may adopt an accounting policy that any expenditure less than $500 is to be regarded as a sundry expense. Even items of expenditure such as computer laptops and mobile phone equipment may be treated as in-year expenses under this policy. However, for very small businesses these and other items of $500 or below could be material and should be recorded separately.

Consistency principle:

"The same accounting treatment should be applied to similar items each accounting year"

We know that the values of many items included in financial statements are estimates. Actual values are often uncertain and therefore judgments have to be made. This includes choosing between different valuation or accounting methods. For example, there are several different ways to calculate the depreciation of a non-current asset. The chosen method should be the one that results in the most realistic value. ➤ 2.2

Application of the consistency principle

Electra Ltd. uses the straight-line method to depreciate its non-current assets. For example, it bought its fleet of delivery vehicles two years ago at a cost of $200 000 and has since depreciated their value by 10% or $20 000 each year. At the end of its second accounting year the vehicle fleet will have a net book value of $160 000 and by the end of next year it will have a new book value of $140 000.

However, the business owners have suggested allowing for just 5% depreciation in the fourth year. The net book value of the vehicles would reduce to $130 000 instead of $120 000. Profit would appear to be $10 000 more.

The company accountant has advised against this because it would be inconsistent. If no other changes occur it might look as if the business had: (i) aquired another vehicle; and (ii) increased its profitability. Both would be misleading.

Once a business has chosen a particular accounting method to value a non-current asset it should then apply it to other similar assets and continue to use the same method in future accounting years. If not it will be impossible to compare financial results on a like-for-like basis from one year to the next.

For example, it would not be sensible to change from using the straight line method of depreciation one year to the reducing balance method the next. This would make it very difficult for users of financial statements to understand what had caused the value of the assets of the business to change over time. For example, if its assets had increased in value was this due to the change in the valuation method or because the business had expanded and acquired more assets, or a combination of both factors?

A business should only really change its accounting methods if the new methods would give more appropriate financial results. If a change is made then it must be explained and its effect on financial results and values fully documented in its statements.

Duality principle:

"Every transaction has two aspects and both aspects should be recorded in the double-entry accounts of the business"

The **duality** principle is the basis of all double-entry book-keeping and the accounting equation. ➤ 1.2

It means each business transaction has two aspects and both aspects must be captured in two double-entry accounts, one to the credit side of an account and the other to the debit side of another. This is because:

- each transaction will affect the assets of the business, and
- each transaction will affect the capital or liabilities of the business.

Application of the duality principle

During its second accounting year Electra Ltd. made many thousands of transactions. For example over the course of the year it:

Sold $12 million goods on credit

Aspect 1	Aspect 2
Assets (trade receivables) increased	Assets (inventory) decreased

Paid $5 million in expenses

Aspect 1	Aspect 2
Assets (cash in bank) decreased	Expenses increased

Borrowed $500 000 from a bank

Aspect 1	Aspect 2
Assets (cash in bank) increased	Liabilities increased

Accounting principles 475

So, for example, the purchase of a new machine will increase the non-current assets of a business but at the same time reduce cash or increase its liabilities if it is purchased on credit. The two aspects of a transaction will always be equal to each other. ➤ 1.9

Realisation principle:

"Revenue is recognised as being earned when legal liability to pay is incurred by the customer (this is when the risks and rewards of ownership of goods passes to the customer)"

When should a business record that a sale has taken place and revenue has been earned? We know from the matching principle that income is earned when goods and services are supplied regardless of when payment for them is received.

The realisation principle similarly states that a sale takes place when goods or a service are supplied to a customer whether payment is immediate (a cash sale) or deferred until later (a credit sale). A cash sale will be recorded when cash is received and a credit sale can be recognised when an invoice has been issued. The invoice issued when goods or services have been supplied on credit is notice of a legally binding agreement to pay and can be used as evidence of an incurred debt.

5.2.2 Meeting international accounting standards

Accounting practices and standards of financial reporting continue to differ around the world

Each country will have its own national standards-setting organisation to determine what accounting practices are acceptable and the technical and other skills accountants need to have. However, as business and finance becomes more complex all over the world and as technology advances, demands on accountants are increasing. Skills and standards of practice need to be constantly reviewed and updated.

Despite the accounting principles discussed in the previous section being generally accepted by accountants around the world, accounting conventions and reporting standards, as published by their national standards-setting bodies can be very different between different countries.

These national differences in the way accountants value expenses, assets and liabilities and calculate profits and net worth have at times resulted in some major accounting scandals. Some examples are shown on page 478.

ACTIVITY 5.5

Which accounting principles are being followed in the examples below and why?

1. The payment of a debt by a customer for goods it purchased on credit is long overdue. There is still some chance the debt will be paid but the business writes it off in its accounts as an irrecoverable debt.

2. A business partner has just bought a new computer for his family but has not included it in the accounts of his partnership.

3. A business has accounting periods ending on 31 July each year. On 24 August this year it received notice from its electricity supplier to pay charges of $670 for electricity supplied between 1 April and 30 June. The business paid the charges on 12 September but included the expense in its statement of income in its accounting year ended 31 July that year.

4. A business owner has just purchased a new clock for her office for $15. Although it is a non-current asset that could be used over many years she records it as an expense item in her accounts.

5. A marketing company has spent $150 000 on training its workforce to use the latest web design software. The company managers believe the quality of the workforce will make the company a market leader and could increase profitability by well over $500 000 per year. However, the company accountant will only reflect the cost of their training in its financial statements.

6. A business bought some land at a cost of $800 000 three years ago. The price of similar land in the area has since fallen to around $500 000. The accountant for the business reduces the value of non-current assets by $300 000 in its statement of financial position.

7. Jessica has just bought a new computer for her home business. To record its purchase she debits her equipment account and credits her bank account with the cash paid out.

8. The owners of a road haulage company own 20 large trucks and vans which they bought five years ago. Each year since the historic cost of the fleet has been depreciated by a fixed amount based on the assumption it will have a useful life of 10 years. The business owners now want to extend the period of depreciation to 20 years and use a reducing balance method. The company accountant has advised against this change.

> **LEHMAN BROTHERS COLLAPSE**
> An examiner's report released in 2008 revealed that Lehman Brothers hid more than $50 billion in loans by classifying them as sales.

> **Enron Shareholders Lose $74 Billion**
> ENRON, once America's seventh largest company, collapsed in 2001 after it failed to disclose huge debts in its statement of financial position.

> **Satyam – $1 billion fraud**
> In just one quarter, executives at the Indian outsourcing firm Satyam magically boosted revenues by 20 percent – or $1.04 billion – by falsifying company loans, the *New York Times* reported in 2009.

To overcome problems caused by differences in accounting practices between countries many national standards-setting bodies have come together to agree and adopt a set of **International Financial Reporting Standards (IFRS)**. These are developed and issued by the International Accounting Standards Board (IASB). The goal of the IASB is to create a single set of global standards in accounting and financial reporting that are clear, easy to understand and enforce, and of high quality.

International standards for accounting and financial reporting seek to improve the comparability, reliability and understandability of financial statements

It is important that investors and other users of accounting information are able to compare the financial performance of different businesses using the same metrics. Similarly, it is important for businesses operating in many different countries to be able to create financial statements that are understandable in all of the countries in which they operate. Having the same accounting requirements in every country should also reduce the time and cost to global businesses of preparing their financial statements.

International standards for accounting and financial reporting aim to:

Narrow areas of difference and variety of accounting practices

If the accounting methods or conventions used by businesses change each year or differ markedly between different businesses and in different countries it will be impossible to make meaningful comparisons of their financial performance or prospects.

The principle of consistency means that financial information should be gathered and presented in the same way across all periods. For example, a business should not be able to change the way it accounts for inventory from one accounting year to another without noting it in the financial statements, measuring the impact of the change on the financial statements and having a valid reason for the change.

Similarly, if all businesses adopt the same method of valuing inventory and other assets then it will be easier to compare their financial positions and liquidity.

Setting and enforcing international standards that will reduce differences in accounting practices will help to improve the ease with which financial information reported by different organisations can be understood and compared – with each other and over time.

Improve the comparability of financial data and statements

It is useful to examine how the financial performance of a business has changed over time and how well or badly it compares to its business rivals. However, differences in accounting methods and definitions used to prepare their financial statements make this difficult.

Users of accounting information must be able to identify similarities or differences between information reported in different financial statements. For example, international standards require income statements to show and use common definitions for both profit or loss of the business before and after any interest payable has been deducted.

Setting international standards to narrow the variety of accounting methods used will help to improve the comparability of financial statements.

Improve the reliability of accounting information

The information presented in financial statements will only be reliable if it provides a true picture of the transactions of a business and its past and current financial position and profitability. Financial information must be free from any significant errors and bias.

If accounting information is not reliable then fewer people will risk their money buying shares in companies or investing directly in sole traders and partnerships. This could mean fewer businesses being formed, fewer jobs and fewer goods and services being produced.

Increase the understandability of accounting information

It is important that the financial information reported by different organisations is comparable and reliable. However, it will not be of much use if it is too complicated to understand or use.

This of course does not mean everyone should be able to understand financial statements. It is reasonable to expect users of financial statements to have a good knowledge of finance and of accounting methods and terminology. However, the information reported in financial statements should still be clear, well presented and explained so it is meaningful to people already involved in business, finance or accounting professions and also to those studying to join these professions. "Economically aware" is a phrase sometimes used to describe these people.

5.2.3 Professional ethics in accounting

How accountants behave is as important as their skills and knowledge

Is it acceptable for an accountant to exaggerate the revenue of a business to make it more attractive to investors? Is it acceptable for an accountant to reveal confidential information about one of its clients to another or to the national press? The answer to both these questions is no. An accountant who behaved in these ways would not be acting professionally or ethically.

Professional accountants are expected to be thorough and trustworthy in their work, to act with honesty and to prevent fraud and corruption.

Being a good accountant is not just about having the right expertise and skills to analyse financial information and to prepare financial statements. It is also about accountants knowing how to behave and conduct themselves when carrying out these tasks.

Accountants are expected to comply with professional codes of ethics

Ethics are the beliefs or principles we have that govern our behaviours and the standards by which we and others judge our actions to be acceptable or not. For example, in most societies it is not acceptable for someone to swear loudly in public or to lie to or steal from other people.

Knowing what is and what is not acceptable behaviour and practice is also important in business. In the accounting profession many accountants and accounting organisations have adopted the Code of Ethics for Professional Accountants issued by the **International Federation of Accountants (IFAC)**. These require accountants to demonstrate five fundamental principles in their work and the way they behave:

Integrity: A professional accountant should be honest and trustworthy.

Objectivity: A professional accountant should not allow bias, personal interests or the views of others to exert unjustifiable influence on their judgment and business relationships.

Professional competence and due care: A professional accountant must keep their knowledge and skills in accounting at a high level and up-to-date with the latest developments so that they can provide an expert service to a client or employer. Their work should be thorough and meet all applicable technical and professional standards.

Confidentiality: A professional accountant should respect the privacy of information provided by a client and should not disclose any such information to others without the client's agreement or unless there is a legal or professional reason to do so, for example if their client has acted unlawfully.

Professional behaviour: A professional accountant should always comply with relevant laws and regulations and should avoid any action that discredits the accounting profession.

Most professional accounting firms will require their accountants to comply with these principles. Some large firms may even have their own very similar or even additional professional codes of conduct. The work and behaviour of their accountants will be regularly monitored and assessed against them. Trainee or experienced accountants who fail to reach the desired standards could lose their jobs.

In addition, many national and international professional associations regulate and provide oversight of individuals and firms operating in today's accountancy sector. Any accountant or accountancy firm that is found not to have been compliant with agreed codes of ethics could be guilty of professional misconduct and may lose their certificate or licence to practise. Some may even face fines or imprisonment if they have acted unlawfully.

▼ Professional misconduct in accounting can have serious consequences

Accountant with lavish lifestyle charged with stealing from clients

William Murray, a prominent accountant in the Sacramento area and partner in the Murray & Young accounting firm, has been accused of stealing more than $13.3 million from his clients, according to reports.

Accountant fined for submitting returns without consent

An accountant who disclosed the accounts of a former client without permission has been fined £10,000 by the Institute of Chartered Accountants in England and Wales and severely reprimanded.

Dell Reports It Has Found 'Misconduct'

Bosses at computer technology giant Dell Inc. have reported that an internal investigation at the company had uncovered "accounting errors, evidence of misconduct and deficiencies in financial management".

Dell did not say whether the misconduct involved criminal activity or a violation of company ethical standards. However, the company is facing investigations into its accounting practices by the US Securities and Exchange Commission and the United States attorney for the southern District of New York.

An accountant who is employed by or owns part of a large accountancy firm and is found guilty of professional misconduct could severely damage the reputation of his or her firm. That firm could lose its clients and therefore its source of revenue.

Similarly, if the accountant is employed directly in the accounts or finance department of another business then it could harm the reputation of that organisation with its investors, bankers, employees, suppliers and customers.

QUICK TEST

1. Which accounting principles do the following statements describe?
   (a) Accounting methods once adopted must be applied consistently in future and to similar items.
   (b) If there is uncertainty, profits should never be overstated or losses and liabilities understated.
   (c) Only the financial transactions of the business must be recorded in its books.
   (d) Accounts should contain only those transactions with definite monetary values.

2. Explain the following accounting principles:
   (a) matching
   (b) going concern
   (c) materiality
   (d) accounting year.

3. The rule for valuing inventories is that they should be valued at their cost or net realisable value, whichever is the lowest value. The rule is a practical application of which accounting principle?

4. Explain **three** ways international accounting standards can improve the quality and usefulness of information presented in financial statements.

5. Give **two** reasons why professional ethics in accounting will be important for the clients of a practising accountant.

6. The multinational company Flexem SA is an important client of your accountancy practice. The current owners are in the process of selling the company to a rival business and have asked you to add 30% to the values of non-current assets in its latest statement of financial position. What should you do?

7. The sales director of Django Ltd has made the following proposals to increase the profit of the company:
   (a) To include in the accounts $35 000 for the increased skill of the workforce.
   (b) To change the depreciation method on non-current assets from reducing balance to straight line.

   State the accounting principles that should prevent the company from adopting these proposals. Give reasons for your answer.

You can find a full revision summary for the whole of Unit 5 on the website.

Once you're feeling ready, try the Unit 5 assessment activities.

accounting 7
    difference between book-keeping and accounting 4–5
    meeting international accounting standards 476–79
    professional ethics 479–81
    purpose of accounting 5
    rules of accounting 469–76
accounting concepts 470
accounting conventions 470
accounting equation 9, 16–17, 29
    cash payment to acquire non-current asset 11
    collection of trade receivable 15
    creation of a non-current liability to acquire noncurrent asset 11–12
    creation of non-current liability 10–11
    double-entry book-keeping 23
    importance of accounting equation 9–10
    introduction of capital 10
    purchase of current asset on credit 12–13
    reduction in liability 14
    sale of current asset for immediate payment 13
    sale of current asset on credit terms and creation of another current asset 13–14
    transactions and balance 15–16
accounting principles 470–76, 481
accounting ratios 444–45
    limitations as indicators of performance 465–66
accounting year 5
    accounting year principle 471
accounts payable turnover 451
accrued expenses 156–58, 161–65
    sole traders 355, 363
accrued income 157, 159, 169–72
    sole traders 349, 363
accumulated fund 388, 396–97
acid test 451–53
adjustments to ledger accounts 189
    adjusting for accrued expenses 161–65
    adjusting for accrued income 159, 169
    adjusting for irrecoverable debt 160, 177, 179, 185
    adjusting for prepaid expenses 159, 165–69
    adjusting for prepaid income 159–60, 173
    calculating profits 157
    end of year adjustments 157
    income statements 160–61
    making provision for doubtful debt 160, 179–85
analysing accounts 444
    accounting ratios 444–45
    limitations of accounting statements and ratio analysis 465–67

    liquidity ratios 450–64
    profitability ratios 445–50
appropriation accounts 371, 377–79
assets 2, 8, 102–3, 320–21
    accounting equation 9–10
    asset acquired on credit payment terms 22
    current assets 8, 12–14, 321
    drawings 130–31, 296–98
    financed from capital and from liabilities 322–23
    intangible assets 342
    liquid assets 325
    net assets 320, 334–35
    net assets and capital 292–93, 311–12
    net current assets 324–25, 330, 450
    non-current assets 8, 11–12, 321, 324
    realisable values 470
    receipt of assets in full settlement of trade receivable account 100
    total assets 8–9, 329

balances b/d (balances brought down) 65, 135
balance sheets 330
balancing off 134
    balance on account 137
    closing balances 137
    ledger account with credit balance 136, 139
    ledger account with debit balance 135, 139
    ledger account with single entry 134–35
    opening balances 137
    trade payable account 139
    trade receivable account 138
    trade receivable account with debit and credit entries 137
bank charges 60, 86
bank current accounts 62–64, 74–75
    bank transfers 63
    overdrafts 79
    overdrawn accounts 76, 78–79
bank debit cards 63
bank deposit accounts 62–63
    cash paid into bank deposit or savings account 69–70
bank interest paid and received 60
bank loans 10–11
    commercial bank loans 72
bank reconciliation 87
    preparing a bank reconciliation statement: method 1 88–89
    method 2 89–90
    updating the cash book 87–88

banks 6–7, 324
bank statements 60, 83–84
    differences in bank statement and cash book 84–90
    timing differences and delays in processing 84, 86
behaviour 480–81
book-keeping 7
    difference between book-keeping and accounting 4–5
books of prime entry 4, 18, 44–46, 58–59
    posting entries to ledgers 18, 44, 112
    purchases journals 46–48
    purchases returns journals 48–50
    sales journals 50–52
    sales returns journals 53–54
business 2–4
    analysing business performance 465–67
business documents 30
    recording financial transactions 30–32
business entity and ownership principle 471
business performance comparison 448–50
business stakeholders 465
business transactions 4–5
    different types of business organisation 350
    purpose of accounting 5–6

capital 9, 320
    accounting equation 9–10
    capital employed 203, 320, 323–24, 330, 334–35, 444–45, 447–48
    capital owned 320, 335
    capital structure 417, 423–24
    capital was received 21
    closing capital 294
    drawings 130–31, 296–98
    loan capital 200, 203, 422–23
    net assets and capital 292–93, 311–12
    opening capital 294
    owner's capital 8, 102, 113, 322–23, 330
    partnerships 371, 375–76
    share capital 421
    total capital 329
    working capital 324–25, 330, 334, 450
capital accounts 19, 371, 375–76
capital expenditure 192, 194, 197, 207–8
    incorrect recording 198, 200
    non-current assets 192–93, 195–96
    recording as debit 196
capital gain 283
capital receipts 191, 200–201
    incorrect recording 205–6
    recording capital receipts 202–4
carriage charges 305–6
    carriage inwards 30, 306–7

carriage outwards 30, 306–8
cash books 18, 40, 44, 95–98
    accounting for cash 60–62
    analysed cash books 94
    balances b/d (balances brought down) 65
    balancing cash books 76–78
    bank loans 72–73
    cash expense 66
    cash paid into bank deposit or savings account 69–70
    cash purchase of goods for resale 65–66
    cash received and banked same day 68–69
    cash received from trade receivable and banked same day 69
    cash received that is banked at later date 67–68
    cash sale 67
    cash withdrawn from bank account 70
    cheque drawn from bank account to pay expense 73
    cheque or bank transfer received from trade receivable 71
    credit transfer from bank current account for purchase of asset 73
    current liability 75
    debit and credit 61–62
    differences in bank statement and cash book 84–90
    direct debit from bank current account to pay for
    errors and omissions in cash books 84, 86
    imprest system of petty cash 60, 90–96
    overdrawn bank account 78–79
    recurring expense 75
    standing order from bank current account to pay for
    three-column cash books 80
    using cash books 64–75
cash discounts 34, 60, 80
    discount allowed 80
    discount received 80
    income received 80–81
    trade receivables 80–81
cash float 91
cash in bank 60, 62
cash in hand 60, 62
cheques 40–42
    dishonoured cheques 256, 265, 269–70
    unpresented cheques 86
closing balances 137, 256, 276
closing capital 294
clubs and societies 388–89, 399–400
    annual subscriptions 394–96
    fund-raising activities 392–94
    income and expenditure account 391–92
    receipts and payments accounts 389–91
    statement of financial position 396–98
commission 129
competence 480

confidentiality 480
consistency principle 474–75
control accounts 256, 281–82
    contra entries 68, 70, 256, 268–69, 274
    dishonoured cheques 265, 269–70
    identifying errors and preventing fraud 256, 264–65
    interest on overdue accounts 265, 267
    inter-ledger transfers 265, 267–68, 273
    purchases ledgers 259–64, 275–78
    refunds 265–66, 272
    sales ledgers 256–59, 270–71, 275, 278–80
correction of errors 84, 86, 255
    correcting errors not revealed by trial balances 237
    draft and revised financial statements 247–53
    general journals 99–101
    trial balances 231–36
cost of sales 287, 411–14
costs 432
    direct and indirect costs 433–34, 436
    factory costs of production 433, 436
    non-factory costs 433
    prime cost 436
    total costs 156
credit control 184, 461–64
    aged trade receivables schedules 184, 462–63
    credit checks 184
    credit limits 184
    legal action 184
    penalties 184
    rewards 184
credit notes 32, 36–37
credit purchases 117–20
credits 20–23, 27–28, 113
    asset acquired on credit payment terms 22
    credit balance 136–37, 139
    credit trade receivable balances 278–79
    current assets 12–14
    goods sold on credit payment terms 22–23
    non-current assets 11–12
    trial balances 144–48
credit sales 123–24, 256
    credit sales returns 124–26
credit transfers 86
    credit transfer from bank current account for purchase of asset 74
credit worthiness 324
current accounts 371, 375–76
current assets 8, 12–14, 321
    net current assets 324–25, 330, 450
current ratio 452
customers 3

debits 20–23, 27–28, 113
    debit balance 135, 137, 139
    debit notes 32, 35–36
    debit trade payable balances 276–77
    trial balances 144–48
debtor days 451
decision making 372
defaulting 181
delivery notes 32
departmental accounts 313
    decision to close departments 317–18
    preparing departmental income statement 313–14, 317
    sharing expenses between departments 315–16
depreciation 209, 228–30, 320
    accumulated depreciation 212
    depreciation as expense 215
    disposal of non-current assets 221–27
    estimating increase of value in non-current assets 215
    estimating loss of value in non-current assets 210–12
    estimating useful life of non-current assets 213
    non-current assets 210, 213–15
    recording depreciation 216–20
    revaluation method 209, 214, 219–20
    sole traders 355, 361, 367
    straight-line (equal instalment) method 209, 212–13
    valuing non-current assets at historical cost less accumulated depreciation 337
direct debits 86
    direct debit from bank current account to pay for current liability 75
discounts
    cash discounts 34, 60, 80–81
    trade discounts 33, 55–57
disposal accounts 221–22
    closing accounts upon disposal of asset 223–25
    proceeds from disposal of asset 225
    recording loss on disposal of asset 226
    recording profit on disposal of asset 227
dividends 86
documentary records 43
    purchases and sales documents 33–39
    receipt documents 39
    recording financial transactions 30
double-entry book-keeping 8, 17, 20–21, 29
    accounting equation 23
    asset was acquired on credit payment terms 22
    capital was received 21
    cash payment of expense 26
    debit and credit entries 27
    goods were sold on credit payment terms 22–23
    ledger accounts 18–20
    writing up the books 18

doubtful debts 156, 158, 177
    making decreased provision for doubtful debts 183–84
    making increased provision for doubtful debts 181–82
    making provision for doubtful debts 160, 179–81, 185
    sole traders 361, 367
drawings 127, 130–33, 294, 296–98
    partnerships 375–76
dual aspect principle 476
due care 480

employees 3, 7
entrepreneurs 2, 6
equipment 11
equity 8, 320, 323, 330, 418
errors 101, 149–50, 237, 246, 264–65
    compensating errors 150, 243
    errors of commission 150, 237
    errors of complete reversal 150, 243–45
    errors of omission 150, 235, 239
    errors of original entry 150, 241–42
    errors of principle 150, 241
ethics 479–81
expenses 2, 34, 128–29
    cash payment of expense 26, 66
    cheque drawn from bank account to pay expense 73–74
    depreciation as expense 215
    non-operating expenses 289
    operating expenses 289
    recurring expense 75
    revenue expenditure 193, 195–97
    standing order from bank current account to pay for sundry expenses 93, 289
    undercast expenses 233

financial ratios 444–45
financial statements 6, 144
    analysing business performance 465–67
    draft and revised financial statements 247–53
    drawing up trial balance 284–87
    preparing financial statements 283–84
financial summaries 4–6
firms 448
fraud 264–65

general journals 18, 44, 99, 111
    correction of errors 99–101
    irregular transactions 99–100
    narrative 99–100
    opening entries 101–3
    purchase of non-current assets 104
    reducing risk of error and fraud 101

    sale of non-current assets 105
    transfers from ledger accounts to income statement 107–9
    writing off irrecoverable debts 106
general ledgers 20, 127
    expenses 128–29
    other income 129–30
    personal drawings 130–33
going concern principle 470
goods for own use 127, 131–32
    sole traders 258, 355
goods for resale 65–66, 114, 193
goodwill 340–42
gross profit 283, 319
    calculating and recording gross profit in income
    gross profit margin 412–13, 445–46
    revenue from sales 287–89, 411–12
    sales and purchases returns 294–96
    statement 288, 295
    unsold inventory 299–305

historic cost 469, 471

imprest system of petty cash 60, 90–96
income 157
    incomes received 129–30
    total income 156
    unearned income 173
income and expenditure accounts 391–92
income statements 5, 196–97, 284, 417
    calculating profit for the year 289–91
    carriage charges 305–8
    checklist 310
    cost of purchases 108
    departmental accounts 313–18
    expenses incurred 108
    horizontal format 289
    incomplete records 408
    limited companies 426–27
    net assets and capital 292–93
    partnerships 377–79
    personal drawings 296–98
    profit and loss account 284, 290
    profit or loss for the year 160–61
    recording loss for the year 310–12
    revenue earned 108
    revenue from sales 287–89
    sales and purchases returns 294–96
    summary income statements 109
    trading account 284, 287
    transfers from ledger accounts to income statement 107–9

unsold inventory 299
vertical format 309
incomplete records 416
    finding values for missing items 405, 410
    statements of affairs 404
industry 448
information and communication technology. *See* ICT
insolvency 61, 450
integrity 480
interest on overdue accounts 256, 266–67, 272
international accounting standards 476–79
International Federation of Accountants (IFAC) 480
International Financial Reporting Standards (IFRS) 478
inventory 12–14
    closing inventory 300–302
    drawings 131–32
    goods purchased but not sold 299–300
    goods purchased for resale 114
    inventory turnover 410–11
    opening inventory 302
    purchases returns 116
    rate of inventory turnover 451, 453–56
    Ready Registers 438
    sales 120
    sales returns 122
    valuing inventory 337–38, 456–58
investors 324
invoices 33–34
    allowing for errors and omissions (E & OE) 34
    purchase invoices 33
    purchases journals 46–47
    sales invoices 32–33
irrecoverable debt 177, 459
    improving credit control 184
    sole traders 355
    writing off irrecoverable debts 106, 177
irrecoverable debts account 106

ledger accounts 4, 18–20, 44, 60, 141–42
    "balancing off" accounts 134
    credit purchases 117–20
    debits and credits 20–23, 27–28, 113
    general ledgers 127–33
    nominal accounts 19–20
    partnerships 375
    personal accounts 19
    preparing ledger accounts 112
    real accounts 19
    recording purchases 114–20
    recording sales 120–26
    'T' account format 113
    transfers from ledger accounts to income statement 107–9
liabilities 2, 8–9, 102–3, 320–23
    accounting equation 9–10
    bank loans 72–73
    current liabilities 8–9, 320, 322
    current liability 75
    direct debit from bank current account to pay for
    limited liability 371, 417
    non-current liabilities 8, 10–12, 320, 322
    reduction in liability 14
    total liabilities 329
    unlimited liability 371
limited companies 417, 430
    capital structure 423–24
    income statement 426–27
    issuing of loan capital 422–23
    issuing of share capital 421
    Memorandum and Articles of Association 417–19
    statement of changes in equity 425
    statement of financial position 427–29
liquidity 320, 324–26
liquidity ratios 444, 450, 464
    accurate valuing of inventory 456–58
    credit control 461–64
    liquid ratio 451–53
    quick ratio 451–53
    rate of inventory turnover 451, 453–56
    working capital 458–61
    working capital ratio 452
loan capital 200, 203, 422–23
loss 2, 5–7
    draft statements 247–49
    gross loss 287
    revised statements 249–53
loss for the year 156–57, 160–61, 289
    recording loss for the year 310–12

management 373
manufacturing 432, 440–41
    direct and indirect costs 433–34
    income statement 438–39
    manufacturing account 434–36
    Ready Registers 438–39
    statement of financial position 440
margin 412–13
mark-up 412
matching principle 156
materiality principle 473–74
monetary value 472
money measurement principle 472

negative working capital 325–26
net assets 320, 334–35
    net assets and capital 292–93, 311–12
net current assets 324–25, 330, 450
net price 55
net profit 290
nominal accounts 19–20, 27
nominal ledgers 20, 127
non-current assets 8, 11–12, 321, 324
    capital expenditure 192–93, 195–96
    depreciation 209–10
    disposal of non-current assets 221–27
    estimating increase of value in non-current assets 215
    estimating loss of value in non-current assets 210–12
    estimating useful life of non-current assets 213–14
    purchase of non-current assets 104
    recording depreciation 216–20
    sale of non-current assets 105
    valuing non-current assets at historical cost less accumulated depreciation 337

objectivity 480
opening balances 137, 256, 276
opening capital 294
order confirmations 32
outstanding income 169–72
    sole traders 355, 363
overdrafts 79
overheads 289
    Ready Registers 438
owner's capital 8, 102, 113, 322–23, 330
owner's equity 102

partnerships 371, 385, 387
    capital 371–72
    capital and drawings 375–76
    debts 372
    expanding a partnership 381–82
    formal partnership agreements 373–74
    general partners 371–72
    income statement and appropriation account 377–79
    ledger accounts 375
    lending to a partnership 381
    limited liability 371, 417
    limited partners 371
    sleeping partners 372
    sole traders forming partnership 383–85
    statement of financial position 379–80
    unlimited liability 371
payees 40
payment documents 32
payments 256

receipts and payments accounts 389–91
    unforeseen or overlooked payments 86
personal accounts 19, 27
    trade payables 19
    trade receivables 19
petty cash 90
    cash withdrawn from bank account for imprest 93
    imprest system 91–93, 95
    petty cash book 92–93
    petty cash vouchers 90–91
    use of analysis columns 93–94
positive working capital 325, 335
posting entries to ledgers 18, 44, 112
    cash purchases returns 116
    cash purchases to the purchases account 115
    cash sales 122
    correcting misposting 233, 235
    credit sales 124
    drawings from cash 131
    drawings from stock 132
    expenses 129
    incomes received 130
    payment received from trade receivable 125
    payment to trade payable account 119
    posting credit purchases returns to the ledger 119
    posting credit purchases to the ledger 118
    purchases journals 47–48
    purchases ledgers 262
    purchases returns journals 49
    sales journals 51–52
    sales ledgers 258–59
    sales returns journals 54, 123, 125
prepaid expenses 156, 158–59, 165–69
    sole traders 349, 363
prepaid income 158–60, 173–76
    sole traders 355, 363
prepayment 165
professional ethics 479–81
profit 2, 5–7, 283–84
    carriage charges 305–8
    draft statements 247–49
    profit margin 447
    revised statements 249–53
profitability ratios 444–45, 464
    business performance comparison 448–50
    percentage of gross profit to revenue 445
    percentage of profit for the year to revenue 445–47
    profit for the year/capital employed 445, 447–48
profit for the year 161–2, 165–6, 288, 294–5, 461
    calculating and recording in the income statement 291
    net assets and capital 292–93

prudence principle 473
purchase orders 32
purchases 34, 46, 114
    cash only purchases 115
    cash purchases by cheque or bank transfer 115
    goods purchased for resale 114
    incomplete records 406
    net purchases 295
    posting cash purchases to the purchases account 115
    purchases on credit 117–20
purchases day books 46
purchases journals 18, 44, 46–48
purchases ledgers 8, 20
    control accounts 256, 259–64, 276–78
purchases returns 37, 294
    credit purchases returned 118–19
    posting cash purchases returns 116
purchases returns accounts 116
purchases returns journals 18, 44, 48–50
purpose/role of accounting 5–6

quick ratio 451–53

rate of inventory turnover 451, 453–56
ratio analysis 444, 468
    analysing business performance 465–66
    limitations as indicators of performance 465–66
real accounts 19, 27
    accounts for non-current assets 19
    capital accounts 19
    cash and bank accounts 19
    other payables 19
    other receivables 19
realisation principle 476
receipts 32, 39–40, 256
    receipts and payments accounts 389–91
    unforeseen or overlooked receipts 86
refunds 256, 265–66, 272
return on capital employed (ROCE) 445, 447–48
returns, returns outward 116
revenue 2, 120
    revenue from sales 287–89, 411–12
revenue expenditure 191–96, 207–8
    incorrect recording 199
    recording as debit 196–97
revenue receipts 191, 201
    incorrect recording 205–6
    recording revenue receipts 203–4

sales 120–21
    goods sold for cash or for payment by cheque 121–22
    incomplete records 406

net sales 295
    sales on credit 123–24
sales day books 50
sales journals 18, 44, 50–52
sales ledgers 8, 20
    control accounts 256–59, 270–71, 278–80
sales returns 37, 122–23, 294
    credit sales returns 124–26
sales returns accounts 122
sales returns journals 18, 44, 53–54
service businesses 351–52
share capital 421
shareholders 417
societies
sole traders 101, 284, 369
    accrued expenses 355, 363
    accrued or outstanding income 355, 363
    depreciation 355, 361, 366–67
    goods for own use 258, 355
    irrecoverable and doubtful debts 361, 367
    making adjustments to financial statements 355
    prepaid expenses 349, 363
    prepaid income 355, 363
    sole traders forming partnership 383–85
standing orders 63
    recurring expense 75
    standing order from bank current account to pay for
statements of account 30, 32, 37–39
statements of affairs 401–4
statements of changes in equity 417, 425
statements of financial position 5, 196, 231, 284, 320, 417
    assets and liabilities 320–26
    clubs and societies 396
    correction of errors 247–53
    goodwill and intangible assets 340
    horizontal format 328
    incomplete records 409
    limited companies 427–29
    partnerships 379–80
    preparing 327
    valuing assets 336–39
    vertical format 333
statements of revised profit or loss 231, 247–53
stockholding period 455
suppliers 3, 6, 324
suspense accounts 231–33

tax authorities 7
total assets 8–9, 329
total capital 329
total costs 156
total income 156

trade discounts 33, 55–57
trade payables 12, 19–20
    cash discounts 80–81
    debit trade payable balances 276–77
    posting payment to trade payable account 119
    total trade payables account 407–8
    trade payable account 139
    trade payable account in purchases ledger 261
trade receivables 13–14, 19–20, 320
    aged trade receivables schedules 184, 462–63
    cash discounts 80–81
    cash received from trade receivable and banked same day 69
    cheque or bank transfer received from trade receivable 71
    collection of trade receivable 15
    credit trade receivable balances 278–79
    expected collectable amount 339
    payment received from trade receivable 125
    receipt of assets in full settlement of trade receivable account 100
    total trade receivables account 407
    trade receivable account 138
    trade receivable account in sales ledger 257–58
    trade receivable account with debit and credit entries 137
    trade receivables collection period 463–64
    valuing assets 338–39
trading businesses 351–52
trial balances 143–44, 154–55, 231–32, 236
    checklist 153
    correcting misposting 233, 235
    correcting omitted entry 234–35
    correcting undercast expenses 233
    drawing up trial balance 284–87
    preparing 144–48
    sources of error 149–52
    suspense accounts 232–33

uncredited deposits 86
unrecoverable loan 177, 471

valuing assets 336–37
    estimating increase of value in non-current assets 215
    estimating loss of value in non-current assets 210–12
    finding values for missing items 405–14
    net book value 211–12, 220, 337–38
    net realisable value 320, 470
    residual value 211
    trade receivables 338–39
    valuing inventory 337–38
    valuing non-current assets at historical cost less accumulated depreciation 337

working capital 324–25, 330, 334, 450
    liquidity ratios 458–61
    working capital ratio 452
work in progress 436–37